HUMAN RECORD

The

HUMAN
RECORD

SOURCES OF GLOBAL HISTORY

SECOND EDITION / Volume I: To 1700

Alfred J. Andrea
University of Vermont

James H. Overfield
University of Vermont

HOUGHTON MIFFLIN COMPANY   BOSTON   TORONTO

GENEVA, ILLINOIS   PALO ALTO   PRINCETON, NEW JERSEY

Sponsoring editor: Sean Wakely
Senior development editor: Elizabeth Welch
Senior project editor: Rosemary Winfield
Production/design coordinator: Caroline Ryan
Senior manufacturing coordinator: Marie Barnes
Marketing manager: Rebecca Dudley

Cover design: Harold Burch, Harold Burch Design, New York City; cover image: courtesy of the John Carter Brown Library at Brown University.

Source credits appear on page 451.

Printed in the U.S.A.

Library of Congress Catalog Card Number: 93-78666

ISBN: 0-395-66872-7

9-DH-00 99 98 97

Contents

Geographic Contents

Topical
Contents

Society and Social Groups

City Life

Common People

Court Life and Ceremony

"Fringe People"

Marriage and the Family

Preface

Many goals and principles have guided our work on *The Human Record*. Foremost is our commitment to the proposition that all students of history must meet the challenge of analyzing primary sources, thereby becoming active inquirers into the past rather than passive recipients of historical facts. Involvement with primary-source evidence enables students to see that historical scholarship is principally the intellectual process of drawing inferences and perceiving patterns from clues yielded by the past, not of memorizing someone else's conclusions. Moreover, such analysis motivates students to learn by stimulating curiosity and imagination, and it helps them develop into critical thinkers who are comfortable with complex challenges.

Not only does primary-source evidence permit the student of history to discover what people in the past thought and did, it also allows the researcher to detect significant changes, as well as lines of continuity, in the institutions and ways of thought of a culture or cluster of cultures. This in turn allows the historian to divide the past into meaningful periods that highlight the historical turning points, as well as constancies, that constitute the human story. In short, primary-source analysis is the essence of the historian's craft and the basis for all historical understanding.

THEMES AND STRUCTURE

We have compiled a source collection that traces the long and intricate course of human history. Volume I follows the evolution of the cultures that most significantly influenced the history of the world from around 3500 B.C. to A.D. 1700, with emphasis on the development of the major religious, social, intellectual, and political traditions of that supercontinent of interconnected societies known as the "Afro-Eurasian ecumene." Although our primary focus in Volume I is on the eastern hemisphere, we do not neglect the Americas. This first volume concurrently develops the theme of the growing links and increasingly important exchanges among the world's cultures down to the early modern era. Volume II picks up this theme of growing human interconnectedness by tracing the gradual establishment of Western global hegemony, the simultaneous historical developments in other civilizations and societies around the world, the anti-Western, anticolonial movements of the twentieth century, and the emergence of today's still often bitterly divided but integrated "one world."

In order to address these themes in depth, we have chosen and arranged selections to present an overview of global history in mosaic form, in which each source contributes to a single large composition. We have been careful to avoid isolated sources that provide a "taste" of some culture or age but, by their dissociation, shed no light on patterns of cultural creation, continuity, change, and interchange — the essential components of world history.

In selecting and placing the various pieces of our mosaic, we sought to create a balanced picture of human history and to craft a book that reveals the contributions of all of the world's major societies. We also have attempted to give our readers a collection of sources representing a wide variety of perspectives and experiences. Believing that the study of history properly concerns every aspect of past human activity and thought, we sought sources that mirror the practices and concerns of a wide variety of representative persons and groups.

Our quest for historical balance has also led us into the arena of unwritten evidence. Although most historians center their research on documents, the discipline requires us to consider all the clues surrendered by the past, and these include its artifacts. Moreover, we have discovered that students enjoy analyzing artifacts and seem to remember vividly the conclusions they draw from them. For these reasons, we have included a number of illustrations of works of art and other artifacts that users of this book can analyze as historical sources.

LEARNING AIDS

Source analysis can be a daunting exercise for students. Therefore, to make these selections as accessible as possible, we have provided our readers with a variety of aids. First there is the Prologue, in which we explain, initially in a theoretical manner and then through concrete examples, how a student of history goes about the task of interpreting written and artifactual sources. Next we offer part, chapter, subchapter, and individual source introductions, all to help the reader place each selection into a meaningful context and understand each source's historical significance. Because we consider *The Human Record* to be an interpretive overview of global history and, therefore, a survey of the major patterns of global history, our introductions are significantly fuller than those one normally encounters in a book of sources.

Suggested questions for analysis also precede each source; their purpose is to help the student make sense of each piece of evidence and wrest from it as much insight as possible. The questions are presented in a three-tiered format designed to resemble the historian's approach to source analysis and to help students make historical comparisons on a global scale. The first several questions are specific and ask the reader to pick out important pieces of information. These initial questions require the student to address the issues: what does this document or artifact say, and what meaningful facts can I garner from it? Addressing concrete questions of this sort prepares the student researcher for the next, more significant level of critical thinking and analysis — drawing inferences. Questions that demand inferential conclusions follow the fact-oriented questions. Finally, whenever possible, we offer a third tier of questions that challenge the student to compare the individual or society that produced a particular source with an individual, group, or culture encountered earlier in the volume. We believe such comparisons help students fix more firmly in their minds the distinguishing cultural characteristics of the various societies they encounter in their brief survey of world history. Beyond that, we believe that global history is, by its very nature, comparative history.

Another form of help we offer is to gloss the sources, explaining fully words and allusions that college students cannot reasonably be expected to know. To facilitate reading and to encourage reference, the notes appear at the bottom of the page on which they are cited. Some documents also contain interlinear notes that serve as transitions or provide needed information.

Some instructors might use *The Human Record* as their sole textbook. Most, however, will probably use it as a supplement to a standard narrative textbook, and many of these professors might decide not to require their students to analyze every entry. To assist instructors (and students) in selecting sources that best suit their interests and needs, we have prepared two analytical tables of contents for each volume. The first lists readings and artifacts by geographic and cultural area; the second, by topic. The two tables suggest to professor and student alike the rich variety of material available within these pages, particularly for essays in comparative history.

NEW TO THIS EDITION

A major goal in crafting *The Human Record* has been to do everything in our power to set the student-reader up for success — success being defined as comfort with historical analysis, proficiency in critical thinking, and learning to view history on a global scale. To continue to meet these objectives, we have made a number of changes. Moreover, because the study of history is an ongoing dialogue between the present and the past, recent events, such as the collapse of Soviet Communism, the eruption of bitter ethnic rivalries in many parts of the world, and the growing appeal of militant religious fundamentalism, have made revision of some portions of our book desirable. In addition, recent scholarly discoveries, such as archeological evidence that strongly points to the historical reality of China's Xia Dynasty, have made revision not just desirable, but necessary.

Users of the first edition will discover that about one-third of the documents and artifacts are new to the second edition. Volume I, for example, has an entirely new chapter, Chapter 11, devoted to Africa and the Americas in the age preceding any significant contact with Europeans. The sources selected for this chapter illustrate the social, religious, and political structures of a number of significant African and American civilizations. Additionally, some of the new sources appearing in Volume I, such as the signature seals of ancient Mesopotamia, India, and Crete (source 9), Apuleius's *Metamorphoses* (source 41), and al-Bakri's account of ancient Ghana (source 85) were chosen because they reveal the important process of cultural syncretism, whereby elements from two or more cultures merge to form a new cultural complex, obviously an essential aspect of global history.

Likewise, we expanded Volume II's coverage of a number of new areas and topics. For example, sources 60 and 61 deal with developments in the South Pacific, specifically New Zealand and Tasmania, after the beginning of European settlement. Writings by Mazzini and Treitschke (sources 69 and 70) increase our coverage of nationalism. Readers will also find that sources 64, 126, and 127 deal with humanity's relationship with the environment. In the area of global politics, Mikhail Gorbachev's speech to the United Nations (source 113) illustrates the recent dramatic end of the Cold War, while Václav Havel's "New Year's Address to the Nation" of 1990 (source 124) underscores the equally amazing retreat of world communism in the past several years.

Other new sources reflect our ongoing commitment to social-cultural history. In this vein we added a number of documentary and artifactual sources that reflect everyday life and gender issues — topics emphasized in the first edition but important enough to justify expanded coverage. In Volume I these include *The Satire on the Trades* (source 5) from ancient Egypt, a rock painting of women gathering wild grains in the central Sahara (source 8), an account of the origins of Buddhist female monasticism (source 21), a source reflecting the role of female saints in the early Christian Church (source 56), a statue depicting the powerful role played by female leaders in the Yoruba culture of West Africa (source 87), and a number of other new sources. In Volume II they include two documents that reflect the impact on Amerindian peoples of Spanish policies of enforced labor (sources 19 and 20), an eyewitness account of eighteenth-century slavery in interior Africa (source 47), a description of the plight of Japanese peasants under the late Tokugawa Shogunate (source 59), Cao Ming's *A Native of Yan'an,* which illustrates the Maoist ideal of a heroic peasant woman (source 108), as well as other new sources.

Some new choices are simply new translations of documents that appeared in the previous edition. The main reason in those cases is to provide selections that are written in clear and idiomatic modern English. All translations from Chinese have been rendered into the *Pinyin* style of transliteration adopted by the People's Republic of China.

Although the book largely follows the format of the first edition, we made several structural changes to enhance its clarity and usefulness. Every source is now numbered, for easier reference. Moreover, each selection now has a descriptive title as a way of helping readers identify those sources that address their particular needs and interests. We have also reorganized along geographic lines Parts I and II of Volume II, which cover the period 1500–1850. We believe this new geographic-chronological structure will equally satisfy students, who will find it clear and straightforward, and instructors, who now will have greater flexibility in using these sources.

To reflect our rethinking and restructuring of many source selections, we also thoroughly revised many of the book's introductions and explanatory notes, occasionally expanding them in order to provide even greater help to the student-reader.

INSTRUCTOR'S RESOURCE MANUAL

Specific suggestions for assignments and classroom activities appear in the Instructor's Resource Manual that accompanies *The Human Record.* In this manual, prepared by the editor-authors, we explain why we have chosen the sources that appear in these volumes and what insights we believe students should be capable of drawing from them. Furthermore, we describe classroom tactics for eliciting thought and discussion on the various sources and offer bibliographic suggestions. The advice we present is the fruit of our own use of these sources in the classroom.

ACKNOWLEDGMENTS

We must not forget the many professionals who offered their expert advice and assistance during the preparation of both editions of this book. Scholars and friends at the University of Vermont who generously shared their expertise with us include Doris Bergen, Robert V. Daniels, Shirley Gedeon, Kristin M. Peterson-Ishaq, Abubaker Saad, Wolfe W. Schmokel, Peter Seybolt, John S. Seyller, Marshall True, Diane Villemaire, and Denise Youngblood. We wish to thank especially Peter D. Andrea, who drew the prototype for map 2 in Volume I.

We wish also to acknowledge the following instructors who read and commented on all or portions of the first and second editions in their various stages of preparation. Their comments and suggestions helped us to see more clearly what we were doing and where we were headed. They forced us to rethink a number of our conclusions and general statements, and in several instances we deleted or added a particular text in response to excellent advice. Even on those occasions when we disagreed with their interpretations and suggestions, we benefited from the exchange of ideas.

Donald R. Abbott, San Diego Mesa College
Jerry Bentley, University of Hawaii, Manoa
Dan Binkley, Hawaii Pacific College
Robert Carlisle, St. Lawrence University
James Casada, Winthrop College
Allen Cronenberg, Auburn University
Stephen Englehart, California Polytechnic State University, Pomona
Charles Frazee, California State–Fullerton
Lorraine Gesick, University of Nebraska at Omaha
Marc Gilbert, North Georgia College
Robert Gowen, East Carolina University
William Hamblin, University of Southern Mississippi
Janine Hartman, University of Cincinnati
Karen Jolly, University of Hawaii at Manoa
Marilynn Kokoszka, Oakland Community College
Craig Lockard, University of Wisconsin–Green Bay
Peter Mellini, Sonoma State University
Bruce Mouser, University of Wisconsin—La Crosse
Richard Porterfield, Glassboro State College
Roger Schlesinger, Washington State University
Kerry Spiers, University of Louisville

Special thanks are owed to the editors and staff of Houghton Mifflin. It is always a pleasure to work with a publishing firm that takes such pride in its professionalism.

Finally, our debt to our spouses is beyond payment, but the dedication of this book to them reflects in some small way how deeply we appreciate their support.

A. J. A.
J. H. O.

The
HUMAN
RECORD

Prologue: How to Read the Evidence

What Is History?

Many students believe that the study of history involves simply memorizing dates, names, battles, treaties, and endless numbers of similar facts. After all, so the argument goes, the past is over and done with. Historians know what has happened, and all that is left for students to do is to absorb this body of knowledge. But this notion is wrong. History, as is true of all branches of human understanding, involves discovery and interpretation. Historians are continually learning more about the past and shedding new light on its meaning. So our understanding of history is constantly changing. Just as significant, each person who studies the past brings to it a perspective and questions that are unique to that individual. Although there is certainly an objective past that we all must endeavor to discover and understand, each of us must personally explore a past that has meaning to us in order to find in it insights and truths relevant to our own needs and concerns. We trust that as you become involved in interpreting historical evidence, you will come to understand and appreciate the creative process that takes place as each individual investigates the past.

The drive to understand what has gone before us is innately human and springs from our need to know who we are. History serves this function of self-discovery in a variety of ways. Its subject matter is universal, dealing with all aspects of past human activity and belief. Among the many issues historians face in interpreting our complex and variegated historical heritage, two are fundamental: continuity and change. How and why do things change over time, and how and why do certain values and practices endure throughout a society's history? Answers to these questions, no matter how partial or tentative, reveal a culture's inner dynamics. When applied to the global community, historical perspective enables us to appreciate the richness of human experience and expression and the factors underlying the striking similarities and differences that exist among the world's peoples.

This collection of sources will help you discover some of the major lines of historical development within world history and understand the major cultural traditions and forces that shaped history around the globe. We will not hand you answers, however; you will have to work for them, for hard work lies at the heart of historical study. The word *history,* which is Greek in origin, means "learning through inquiry," and that is precisely what historians do. They discover and interpret the past by asking questions and conducting research. Their inquiry revolves around an examination of evidence left by the past. For lack of a better term, historians call that evidence *primary source material.*

Primary Sources: Their Value and Limitations

Primary sources for the most part are records that have been passed on in written form, thereby preserving the memory of past events. These written sources include, but are not limited to, official records, private correspondence, literature, religious texts, memoirs — the list goes on and on. None of these sources by itself contains unadulterated truth or the whole picture. Each gives us only a glimpse of reality, and it is the historian's task to fit these fragments of the past into a coherent picture.

Imagine for a moment that some historian in the late twenty-first century decides to write a history of your college class. Think about the primary sources that researcher would seek out: the school catalogue, the registrar's class lists, academic transcripts, and similar official documents; class lecture notes, course syllabi, exams, term papers, and textbooks; diaries and private letters; the school newspaper, yearbooks, and sports programs; handbills, posters, and even photographs of graffiti; recollections recorded by some of your classmates long after they have graduated. With some more thought you could add other items to the list, among them some nonwritten sources, such as recordings of popular music and photographs and videotapes of student life and activity. But let us confine ourselves, for the moment, to written records. What do all these documentary sources have in common?

As we examine this list of sources, we realize that, though numerous, these records do not and cannot present the past in its entirety. Where do we see among them the long telephone calls home, the all-night study groups, the afternoons spent at the student union? Someone may have recorded memories of some of these events, but how complete and trustworthy is that evidence? Also keep in mind that all the documents available to our twenty-first-century historian will be fortunate survivors. They will represent only a small percentage of the vast bulk of written material generated during your college career. Thanks to the wastebasket, the delete key, the disintegration of materials, and the inevitable loss of life's memorabilia as years slip by, the evidence available to the future historian will be fragmentary. This is always the case with historical evidence. We cannot preserve the records of the past in their totality. Clearly, the more remote the past, the more fragmentary our documentary evidence. Imagine the feeble chance any particular document from the twelfth century had of surviving the wars, wastebaskets, and worms of the past eight hundred years.

Now let us consider those many individual pieces of documentary evidence relating to your class's history that have survived. As we review the list, we see that not one of those primary sources gives us a pure, unvarnished, and complete picture. Each has its perspective, value, and limitations.

You certainly know that every college catalogue presents an idealized picture of campus life. Despite its flaws, however, that catalogue can be an important piece of evidence because it reflects the values of the faculty and administrators who composed it and provides useful information by listing rules and regulations, courses, instructors, school organizations, and similar items. That information, however, is the raw material of history, not history itself, and certainly it does not reflect the full historical reality of your class.

What is true of the catalogue is equally true of the student newspaper and every other piece of evidence generated by or pertinent to your class. Each primary source is a part of a larger whole, but as we have already seen, we do not have all the pieces. Think of your historical evidence in terms of a jigsaw puzzle. Many of the pieces are missing, but it is possible to put most, though probably not all, of the remaining pieces together in a reasonable fashion to form a fairly accurate and coherent picture. The picture that emerges may not be complete, but it is useful and valid. The keys to fitting these pieces together are hard work and imagination. Each is absolutely necessary.

Examining the Sources

Hard work speaks for itself, but students are often unaware that a historian also needs an imagination to reconstruct the past. After all, many students ask, doesn't history consist of strictly defined and irrefutable dates, names, and facts? Where does imagination enter into the process of learning these facts? Again, let us consider your class's history and its documentary sources. Many of those documents provide factual data — dates, names, grades, statistics — and these data are important, but individually and collectively they have no historical meaning until they are interpreted. Your college class is not a collection of statistics and facts. It is a group of individuals who, despite their differences, share and help mold a collective experience. It is a community evolving within a particular time and place. Influenced by its larger environment, it is, in turn, an influence on that world. Any valid or useful history must reach beyond a mere list of dates, names, and facts to interpret the historical characteristics and role of your class. What were its values? How did it change and why? What impact did it have? These are some of the important questions a historian asks of the evidence.

In order to arrive at answers the historian must examine each and every piece of evidence as fully as possible and wring from that evidence as many *inferences* as possible. Facts may be the foundation stones of history, but inferences are its edifices. An inference is a logical conclusion drawn from evidence, and it is the heart and soul of historical inquiry.

Every American schoolchild learns that Christopher Columbus "sailed the ocean blue in 1492." That fact is worthless, however, unless the student understands the motives, causes, and significance of this late fifteenth-century voyage. Certainly a historian must know when Columbus sailed west. After all, time is history's framework. Yet the questions historians ask go beyond simple chronology. Why did Columbus sail west? What factors made possible and almost inevitable Spain's involvement in such enterprises at this time? Why was Europe willing and able to exploit the "New World"? What were the short- and long-term consequences of the European presence in the Americas? These are some of the significant questions to which historians seek inferential answers, and those answers can only be found in the evidence.

One noted historian, Robin Winks, has written a book entitled *The Historian as Detective,* and the image is appropriate, although inexact. Like the detective, the historian examines clues in order to reconstruct events. However, the detective is essentially interested in discovering what happened, who did it, and why, while the historian goes one step beyond and asks what it all means.

Like the detective interrogating witnesses, the historian examines the testimony of sources, and both investigators ask similar questions. First and foremost, the historian must evaluate the *validity* of the source. Is it what it purports to be? Artful forgeries have misled many historians. Even if the source is authentic, and most are, it can still mislead the historian. The possibility always exists that the source's author is lying or otherwise deliberately misrepresenting reality. Even if this is not the case, the historian can easily be led astray by not fully understanding the *perspective* reflected in the document. As any detective who has examined a number of eyewitnesses to an event knows, viewpoints differ radically due to a number of factors. The police detective has the opportunity to reexamine witnesses and offer them the opportunity to change their testimony in the light of new evidence and deeper reflection. The historical researcher is usually not so fortunate. Even when the historian attempts to establish a creative interchange with documentary evidence by studying it in a probing manner and comparing it with other evidence, there is no way to cross-examine it in detail. What is written is written. Given this fact, it is absolutely necessary for the historian to understand, as fully as possible, the source's perspective. Thus, the historian must ask several key questions. *What* kind of document is this? *Who* wrote it? For *whom* and *why?* *Where* was it composed and *when?*

The *what* is important, because understanding the nature of the particular source can save the historian a great deal of frustration. Many historical sources simply do not directly address the questions a historian would like to ask of them. That twenty-first-century historian would be foolish to try to learn much about the academic quality of your school's courses from a study of the registrar's class lists and grade sheets. Student and faculty class notes, copies of old syllabi, exams, papers, and textbooks would be far more fruitful sources.

Who, for whom, and *why* are equally important questions. The official school catalogue undoubtedly addresses some issues pertaining to student social life. But should this document, designed to attract potential students and to place the school in the best possible light, be read and accepted uncritically? Obviously not. It should be tested against student testimony, discovered in such sources as private letters, memoirs, posters, the student newspapers, and the yearbook.

Where and *when* are also important questions to ask of a primary source. As a general rule, distance in space and time from an event colors perceptions and can adversely affect the validity of a source's testimony. The recollections of a person celebrating a twenty-fifth class reunion may prove quite insightful and valuable.

Conceivably, this graduate now has a perspective and even information that were absent a quarter of a century earlier. Just as conceivably, this person's memory might be playing tricks. A source can be so close to or so distant from the event it deals with that its view is distorted or totally erroneous. Even so, the source is not necessarily worthless. Often the blind spots and misinformation within a source reveal to the researcher much about the author's attitudes and sources of information.

The historical detective's task is not easy. In addition to constantly questioning the validity and perspectives of available sources, the historical researcher must often use whatever evidence is available in imaginative ways. Researchers must interpret these fragmentary and flawed glimpses of the past and piece together the resultant inferences as well as possible. While recognizing that a complete picture of the past is never possible, the historian assumes the responsibility of recreating a past that is valid and has meaning for the present.

You and the Sources

This book will involve you actively in the work of historical inquiry by asking you to draw inferences based on your careful analysis of primary source evidence. This is not an easy task, especially at first, but it is well within your capability. Moreover, we will help you all along the way.

You understand by now that historians do not base their conclusions on analysis of a single isolated source. Historical research consists of laborious sifting through mountains of documents. We have already done much of this work for you by selecting important sources that individually allow you to gain some significant insight into a particular historical culture or era. In doing this for you, we do not, however, relieve you of the responsibility of recognizing that no single source, no matter how rich it may appear, offers a complete picture of the society that produced it. Each source we ask you to analyze will provide valuable evidence, but it is only partial evidence.

You will analyze two types of evidence, documents and artifacts. Each source will be authentic, so you do not have to worry about validating it. We will supply you with the information necessary to place each piece of evidence into its proper context and will suggest questions you legitimately can and should ask of each source. If you carefully read the introductions and notes, the questions for analysis, and, most important of all, the sources themselves — and think about what you are doing — solid inferences will follow.

To illustrate how you should go about this task and what is expected of you, we have prepared a sample exercise, which we will take you through step by step. The exercise consists of analyzing two sources: a document from the pen of Christopher Columbus and a reproduction of an early sixteenth-century woodcut. First, we present the document, just as it would appear in any of the chapters of this book: introduction, suggested questions for analysis, and the source itself, with explanatory notes. (Because this source from Columbus is intended to introduce you to the art of historical inquiry, it is longer than most source excerpts that you will encounter in the text.) Then we show you how to read that document. The exercise will not draw every possible insight and inference from the document, but it will demonstrate how to set about answering several of the important questions you should ask of that source.

Following that, we introduce you to the art of "reading" a nonwritten piece of historical evidence. After a few general observations on how a historian uses artifacts as evidence, we present the piece of evidence just as it would appear in the book. Then we show you what we read in this picture. If you have worked closely with us, by the end of this exercise you should be ready to begin interpreting sources on your own.

Christopher Columbus, A LETTER CONCERNING RECENTLY DISCOVERED ISLANDS

There is no need to recount in detail the story of Christopher Columbus (1451–1506), a Genoese sea captain in the service of Isabella of Castile and Ferdinand of Aragon, who sailed westward into the Atlantic seeking a new route to the empires of East Asia described by Marco Polo, whose book of travels Columbus had read and copiously annotated. On October 12, 1492, his fleet of three ships dropped anchor at a small Bahamian island, which Columbus claimed for Spain and named San Salvador. The fleet then sailed to the major islands of Cuba, which he named Juana, and Hispaniola (where the modern nations of Haiti and the Dominican Republic are located), which he named Española. After exploring the two islands and establishing the post of Navidad del Señor on Española, Columbus departed for Spain in January 1493. On his way home Columbus prepared a public account of his expedition to the "Indies" and posted it from Lisbon, Portugal, where he landed in early March. As intended, the letter preceded Columbus to the Spanish royal court, which he entered in triumph in April.

As you analyze the document, you should be aware of several facts. The admiral was returning with only two of his vessels. He had lost his flagship, the *Santa Maria*, when it was wrecked on a reef off present-day Haiti on Christmas Day. Also, many of Columbus's facts and figures are based more on his enthusiasm than dispassionate analysis. His estimate of the dimensions of the two main islands he explored grossly exaggerates their sizes. His optimistic report of the abundance of such riches as gold, spices, cotton, and mastic (an aromatic gum) was not borne out by subsequent explorations and colonization. Gold was rare in the islands; the only indigenous "spice" proved to be the fiery chili pepper; the wild cotton was excellent but not plentiful; and mastic, native to eastern Mediterranean lands, was nonexistent in the Caribbean.

QUESTIONS FOR ANALYSIS

1. How does Columbus indicate that these lands deserve the careful attention of the Spanish monarchs?

2. What does Columbus's description of the physical attributes of the islands he explored suggest about some of the motives for his voyage?

3. Often the eyes see only what the mind prepares them to see. What evidence is there that Columbus saw what he wanted to see and discovered what he expected to discover? In other words, how had his cultural environment prepared Columbus to see and interpret what he encountered in the Caribbean?

4. What do the admiral's admitted actions regarding the natives and the ways in which he describes these people allow us to conclude about his attitudes toward these "Indians" and his plans for them?

5. What does this letter tell us about the culture of the Tainos on the eve of European expansion into their world? Is there anything that Columbus tells us about these people that does not seem to ring totally true?

6. What evidence suggests that Columbus's letter was a carefully crafted piece of self-promotion by a person determined to prove he had reached the Indies?

7. Notwithstanding the obvious self-promotion, is there any evidence that Columbus also attempted to present an objective and fairly accurate account of what he had seen and experienced? To what extent, if at all, can we trust his account?

8. How does this letter illustrate the fact that single historical sources read in isolation can mislead the researcher?

Knowing that it will afford you pleasure to learn that I have brought my undertaking to a successful termination, I have decided upon writing you this letter to acquaint you with all the events which have occurred in my voyage, and the discoveries which have resulted from it.

Thirty-three days after my departure . . . I reached the Indian sea, where I discovered many islands, thickly peopled,[1] of which I took possession without resistance in the name of our most illustrious Monarch, by public proclamation and with unfurled banners. To the first of these islands, which is called by the Indians Guanahani, I gave the name of the blessed Savior[2] (San Salvador), relying upon whose protection I had reached this as well as the other islands; to each of these I also gave a name, ordering that one should be called Santa Maria de la Concepción,[3] another Fernandina, the third Isabella, the fourth Juana,[4] and so with all the rest respectively. As soon as we arrived at that, which as I have said was named Juana, I proceeded along its coast a short distance westward, and found it to be so large and apparently without termination, that I could not suppose it to be an island, but the continental province of Cathay.[5] . . .

In the meantime I had learned from some Indians whom I had seized, that that country was

---

[1]The Tainos, a tribe that spoke a language belonging to the Arawak family. Arawak speakers inhabited an area from the Amazon River to the Caribbean.

[2]Jesus Christ.

[3]Holy Mary of the Immaculate Conception — Mary, mother of Jesus, who Catholics believe was so sinless she was conceived without the stain of Original Sin on her soul.

[4]Named for the daughter and heiress of Isabella and Ferdinand.

[5]Technically, Cathay was that area along China's northern frontier ruled by the Khitans, a people from Manchuria, between 907 and 1125. Columbus understood Cathay to be the entire Chinese empire of the Great Mongol Khan, not realizing that the Chinese had expelled the Mongols in the mid-fourteenth century. See Volume I, Chapter 12, sources 91–95, for additional information on the Mongols in China.

certainly an island: and therefore I sailed towards the east, coasting to the distance of three hundred and twenty-two miles, which brought us to the extremity of it; from this point I saw lying eastwards another island, fifty-four miles distant from Juana, to which I gave the name of Española. . . .

In . . . Española there are mountains of very great size and beauty, vast plains, groves, and very fruitful fields, admirably adapted for tillage, pasture, and habitation. The convenience and excellence of the harbors in this island, and the abundance of the rivers, so indispensable to the health of man, surpass anything that would be believed by one who had not seen it. The trees, herbage, and fruits of Española are very different from those of Juana, and moreover it abounds in various kinds of spices, gold, and other metals.

The inhabitants of both sexes in this island, and in all the others which I have seen, or of which I have received information, go always naked as they were born,[6] with the exception of some of the women, who use the covering of a leaf, or small bough, or an apron of cotton which they prepare for that purpose. None of them . . . are possessed of any iron, neither have they weapons, being unacquainted with, and indeed incompetent to use them, not from any deformity of body (for they are well-formed),[7] but because they are timid and full of fear. They carry however in place of arms, canes dried in the sun, on the ends of which they fix heads of dried wood sharpened to a point, and even these they dare not use habitually; for it

has often occurred when I have sent two or three of my men to any of the villages to speak with the natives, that they have come out in a disorderly troop, and have fled in such haste at the approach of our men, that the fathers forsook their children and the children their fathers. This timidity did not arise from any loss or injury that they had received from us; for, on the contrary, I gave to all I approached whatever articles I had about me, such as cloth and many other things, taking nothing of theirs in return: but they are naturally timid and fearful. As soon however as they see that they are safe, and have laid aside all fear, they are very simple and honest, and exceedingly liberal with all they have; none of them refusing any thing he may possess when he is asked for it, but on the contrary inviting us to ask them.

They exhibit great love towards all others in preference to themselves: they also give objects of great value for trifles, and content themselves with very little or nothing in return. I however forbade that these trifles and articles of no value (such as pieces of dishes, plates, and glass, keys, and leather straps) should be given to them, although if they could obtain them, they imagined themselves to be possessed of the most beautiful trinkets in the world. Thus they bartered, like idiots, cotton and gold for fragments of bows, glasses, bottles, and jars; which I forbade as being unjust, and myself gave them many beautiful and acceptable articles which I had brought with me, taking nothing from them in return; I did this in order that I might the more easily conciliate them, that they might be led to become Christians, and be inclined to entertain a regard for the King and Queen, our Princes and all Spaniards, and that I might induce them to take an interest in seeking out, and collecting, and delivering to us such things as they possessed in abundance, but which we greatly needed.

They practice no kind of idolatry,[8] but have a firm belief that all strength and power, and

---

[6]Marco Polo (Volume I, Chapter 12; source 93) described a number of islanders in South Asia who went naked. Compare also Columbus's description of this nudity with John Mandeville's account of the people of Sumatra in Volume I, Chapter 12, source 97.

[7]Europeans were prepared to find various races of "monster" humans and semihumans in the Indies. Such accepted travelogues as the fourteenth-century account of John Mandeville told of dog-headed people and a species of individuals who, lacking heads, had an eye on each shoulder. Columbus fully believed that such marvelous people resided somewhere in these islands (see note 10).

---

[8]Columbus claims they do not worship idols, or statues.

indeed all good things, are in heaven, and that I had descended from thence with these ships and sailors, and under this impression was I received after they had thrown aside their fears. Nor are they slow or stupid, but of very clear understanding; and those men who have crossed to the neighboring islands give an admirable description of everything they observed; but they never saw any people clothed, nor any ships like ours. On my arrival at that sea, I had taken some Indians by force from the first island that I came to, in order that they might learn our language, and communicate to us what they knew respecting the country; which plan succeeded excellently, and was a great advantage to us, for in a short time, either by gestures and signs, or by words, we were enabled to understand each other. These men are still traveling with me, and although they have been with us now a long time, they continue to entertain the idea that I have descended from heaven; and on our arrival at any new place they published this, crying out immediately with a loud voice to the other Indians, "Come, come and look upon beings of a celestial race": upon which both women and men, children and adults, young men and old, when they got rid of the fear they at first entertained, would come out in throngs, crowding the roads to see us, some bringing food, others drink, with astonishing affection and kindness.

Each of these islands has a great number of canoes, built of solid wood, narrow and not unlike our double-banked boats in length and shape, but swifter in their motion: they steer them only by the oar. These canoes are of various sizes, but the greater number are constructed with eighteen banks of oars, and with these they cross to the other islands, which are of countless number, to carry on traffic with the people. I saw some of these canoes that held as many as seventy-eight rowers. In all these islands there is no difference of physiognomy, of manners, or of language, but they all clearly understand each other, a circumstance very propitious for the realization of what I conceive to

be the principal wish of our most serene King, namely, the conversion of these people to the holy faith of Christ, to which indeed, as far as I can judge, they are very favorable and well-disposed. . . .

Juana . . . I can assert . . . is larger than England and Scotland united; . . . there are in the western part of the island two provinces which I did not visit; one of these is called by the Indians Anam,[9] and its inhabitants are born with tails.[10] . . . But the extent of Española is greater than all Spain from Catalonia to Fontarabia, which is easily proved, because one of its four sides which I myself coasted in a direct line, from west to east, measures five hundred and forty miles. This island is to be regarded with special interest, and not to be slighted; for although as I have said I took possession of all these islands in the name of our invincible King, and the government of them is unreservedly committed to his said Majesty, yet there was one large town in Española of which especially I took possession, situated in a remarkably favorable spot, and in every way convenient for the purposes of gain and commerce.

To this town I gave the name of Navidad del Señor,[11] and ordered a fortress to be built there, which must by this time be completed, in which I left as many men as I thought necessary, with all sorts of arms, and enough provisions for more than a year. I also left them one caravel,[12] and skillful workmen both in shipbuilding and other arts, and engaged the favor and friendship of the King of the island in their behalf, to a degree that would not be believed, for these people are so amiable and friendly that even the King took a pride in calling me his brother. But supposing their feelings should

---

[9]Havana.
[10]Marco Polo reported the existence of tailed humans (possibly orangutans) in the islands of Southeast Asia.
[11]The Lord's Nativity (Christmas).
[12]The wreck of the *Santa Maria,* which was totally useless to the garrison. He left thirty-nine men behind because there was no room for them in his two remaining ships.

become changed, and they should wish to injure those who have remained in the fortress, they could not do so, for they have no arms, they go naked, and are moreover too cowardly; so that those who hold the said fortress, can easily keep the whole island in check, without any pressing danger to themselves, provided they do not transgress the directions and regulations which I have given them.[13]

As far as I have learned, every man throughout these islands is united to but one wife, with the exception of the kings and princes, who are allowed to have twenty:[14] the women seem to work more than the men. I could not clearly understand whether the people possess any private property, for I observed that one man had the charge of distributing various things to the rest, but especially meat and provisions and the like. I did not find, as some of us had expected, any cannibals amongst them,[15] but on the contrary men of great deference and kindness. Neither are they black, like the Ethiopians: their hair is smooth and straight: for they do not dwell where the rays of the sun strike most vividly. . . . Thus, as I have already said, I saw no cannibals, nor did I hear of any, except in a certain island called Charis, which is the second from Española on the side towards India, where dwell a people who are considered by the neighboring islanders as most ferocious: and these feed upon human flesh.[16] The same people have many kinds of canoes, in which they cross to all the surrounding islands and rob and plunder wherever they can; they are not different from the other islanders, except that they wear their hair long, like women, and make use of the bows and javelins of cane, with sharpened spear-points fixed on the thickest end, which I have before described, and therefore they are looked upon as ferocious, and regarded by the other Indians with unbounded fear; but I think no more of them than of the rest. These are the men who form unions with certain women, who dwell alone in the island Matenin, which lies next to Española on the side towards India; these latter employ themselves in no labor suitable to their own sex, for they use bows and javelins as I have already described their paramours as doing, and for defensive armor have plates of brass, of which metal they possess great abundance.[17] They assure me that there is another island larger than Española, whose inhabitants have no hair,[18] and which abounds in gold more than any of the rest. I bring with me individuals of this island[19] and of the others that I have seen, who are proofs of the facts which I state.

Finally, to compress into few words the entire summary of my voyage and speedy return, and of the advantages derivable therefrom, I promise, that with a little assistance afforded me by our most invincible sovereigns, I will procure them as much gold as they need, as

---

[13]When Columbus returned in November 1493, he discovered the entire garrison had been killed by the native inhabitants in reaction to intolerable abuses. Columbus's actions before he departed for Europe, such as his staging a mock battle, suggest that he was uneasy about leaving these men behind and wanted to impress the Tainos with a display of Spanish firepower and fighting skills.

[14]Marco Polo had described a number of polygamous customs in Asia.

[15]Both Polo's late thirteenth-century travelogue and the equally popular mid-fourteenth-century *Travels* of John Mandeville reported numerous instances of Asian cannibalism.

[16]The Caribs, who shortly before the arrival of Columbus began to displace the peaceful Arawak peoples of the Lesser Antilles, the group of islands to the east and south of Hispaniola. Sixteenth-century Spanish writers unani-

mously agreed that the Caribs were cannibals, and there is no good reason to doubt their testimony.

[17]Columbus had read in Marco Polo of two islands, one inhabited solely by women, another exclusively by men. Mandeville, who probably never traveled to most of the Asiatic lands he so vividly described, wrote of the land of Amazonia, populated totally by warrior women. There is no evidence that this female society reported by Columbus ever existed in the Caribbean. Neither is there evidence that the Caribbean Amerindians used metal to any significant degree.

[18]John Mandeville described people with little body hair, and Marco Polo told of Buddhist monks whose heads and faces were shaved.

[19]Española.

great a quantity of spices, of cotton, and of mastic (which is only found in Chios),[20] and as many slaves for the service of the navy as their Majesties may require. I promise also rhubarb and other sorts of drugs, which I am persuaded the men whom I have left in the aforesaid fortress have found already and will continue to find. . . .

Although all I have related may appear to be wonderful and unheard of, yet the results of my voyage would have been more astonishing if I had had at my disposal such ships as I required. But these great and marvelous results are not to be attributed to any merit of mine, but to the holy Christian faith, and to the piety and religion of our Sovereigns; for that which the unaided intellect of man could not compass, the spirit of God has granted to human exertions, for God is wont to hear the prayers of his servants who love his precepts even to the performance of apparent impossibilities. Thus it has

happened to me in the present instance, who have accomplished a task to which the powers of mortal men had never hitherto attained; for if there have been those who have anywhere written or spoken of these islands, they have done so with doubts and conjectures, and no one has ever asserted that he has seen them, on which account their writings have been looked upon as little else than fables.

Therefore let the king and queen, our princes and their most happy kingdoms, and all the other provinces of Christendom, render thanks to our Lord and Savior Jesus Christ, who has granted us so great a victory and such prosperity. Let processions be made, and sacred feasts be held, and the temples be adorned with festive boughs. Let Christ rejoice on earth, as he rejoices in heaven in the prospect of the salvation of the souls of so many nations hitherto lost. Let us also rejoice, as well on account of the exaltation of our faith, as on account of the increase in our temporal prosperity, of which not only Spain, but all Christendom will be partakers.

[20]An island in the Aegean Sea (an arm of the Mediterranean, between Greece and Turkey).

Interpreting Columbus's Letter

This letter contains a number of interesting and potentially important facts. For example, the natives Columbus encountered on these islands were apparently homogeneous, were skilled sailors, and initially offered no resistance. Yet, as fascinating and important as these facts are, knowing them does not necessarily make a person a historian. Similarly, garnering such isolated items from a source does not constitute full historical analysis. True historical analysis consists of drawing as much inferential insight as possible from a source and trying to answer, at least in part, the central question of historical study: what does it all mean? This document allows us to do just that.

Historians use no secret method or magic formula to draw historical insights from documentary evidence. All one needs are attention to detail, thoroughness, common sense, and a willingness to enter imaginatively into the mind of the document's author as fully and honestly as possible while trying to set aside momentarily personal values and perspectives. Anyone who is willing to work at it can profitably interpret written primary sources. To prove that point, let us address all eight questions for analysis in an integrated manner. They suggest the important questions we should ask of the document, but we do not need to feel compelled to answer them slavishly in order.

As we begin our analysis, we have to confront the issue head-on: What evidence is there in this document that allows us to judge Columbus's reliability as an objective reporter? This question strikes at the heart of historical inquiry. The researcher always has to evaluate the worth of each source, and this means understanding its point of view and reliability. In this letter several things are obvious. Columbus believes he has reached Asian islands. Marco Polo's *Travels* and other accounts of Asia have provided a number of reference points by which he can recognize the Orient, and he believes he has found many of them. Equally obvious is the fact that Columbus is trying to present his discoveries in the best light possible. He is sending this letter ahead to the court of Ferdinand and Isabella to ensure that he will be received with due honor.

Certainly, there is exaggeration and error in this account. As the introduction informs us, Columbus greatly overestimates the size of several islands, and except for chilies, the spices he claims to have discovered proved eventually to be mirages.

We also find Columbus deliberately trying to mislead his reader. The *Santa Maria* has been lost, yet the admiral wants the reader to believe that he has left the ship in seaworthy condition with the sailors who remained in the garrison at Navidad del Señor. This is the only outright falsehood we can discover in the letter, although the admiral clearly is masking the less attractive aspects of his discoveries. For example, he does not mention the stinging insects that tormented so many Europeans who followed him there. Generally, however, despite Columbus's enthusiasm and understandable tendency to exaggerate, to conveniently neglect to mention anything negative, and to see what he wants to see, he seems to want to present a factual account.

Although he was prepared to encounter every sort of human monstrosity and undoubtedly would have enjoyed reporting such contacts, Columbus honestly reports that all the natives he has encountered are quite unmonstrous in appearance and temperament. He does report stories of people with tails, cannibals, and warlike women who live apart from men, but it is unlikely that the admiral was deliberately misleading anyone. The fierce Caribs were real enough, although Columbus did not encounter any on his first voyage. Rumors of tailed people and latter-day Amazons might have been the result of the natives' efforts to please Columbus. It is not difficult to imagine the admiral inquiring after the location of those various human curiosities whom Polo and others had placed in the islands of the Indian Ocean and the Tainos agreeably pointing across the waters to other islands. All things considered, Columbus's letter may be accepted as a generally honest, if not totally accurate, account of his discoveries and experiences.

That basic honesty, tempered by an understandable enthusiasm and desire to present his accomplishments in a positive and attractive manner, comes through in his attempt to describe the islands' physical qualities and the people he has encountered. The picture that emerges tells us a lot about the complex motives underlying his great adventure.

We notice that Columbus has matter-of-factly taken possession of these lands in the names of the monarchs of Spain and has even renamed the islands without once giving thought to anyone else's claims. Also, despite his avowed interest in protecting and winning over these native peoples, whom he apparently likes and admires, he thinks nothing of seizing some natives as soon as he arrives and of carrying several "Indians" back to Spain. Moreover, he remarks toward the end of his letter that he will procure from these islands as many slaves to serve in the navy as the monarchs of Spain desire. At the same time, and this may strike the modern student as curious, Columbus notes that he has acted kindly toward these natives so that they might become both Christians and loyal subjects of Ferdinand and Isabella. According to the admiral, the Indians' intelligence, timidity, naiveté, ignorance, sense of wonder at the Europeans, and ability to communicate freely among themselves make them prime candidates for conversion and subjugation. Is Columbus concerned with these people as humans, and is he interested in helping them achieve salvation through conversion? The tone of this letter suggests that he is, but there is a contrary note, which points up the tension that would exist within the entire Spanish colonial experience: Columbus believes it to be his and Catholic Spain's right and duty to rule and exploit these people.

Conquest of these people and their lands involved more than just a sense of divine mission and Christian altruism — as real as these motives were. Columbus, his royal patrons, and most others who joined overseas adventures expected to gain in earthly wealth as well. Even a superficial reading of his letter shows us the admiral's preoccupation with the riches of these islands. Gold, spices, cotton, aromatic mastic, and, of course, slaves are the material rewards that await Christian Europeans, and Columbus is fully interested in them.

Is he being cynical or hypocritical when, in his closing words, Columbus claims that Jesus Christ has provided this great victory to the Spanish monarchs and, indeed, to all Christians and from it will flow the dual benefits of worldly riches and the conversion of many people? It does not seem likely. Here was a man who saw no contradiction between spreading the faith and benefiting materially from that action, even if doing so meant exploiting those he had converted. He and most of his contemporaries generally perceived no inconsistency in converting a people to the freedom of an otherworldly faith and enslaving them in this world.

There are other questions we can ask of this source and other insights we can gather from it. Certainly, it tells us a lot about Taino culture, the issue raised in question 5 in the questions for analysis. Despite his cultural blinders, his own naiveté, and his tendency to see what he wanted to see, Columbus was an accurate and perceptive observer, and anyone interested in the culture of the Caribbean peoples before Europeans had much of a chance to influence it must necessarily look to this and similar accounts of first contacts. It would be good practice for you to try to answer more fully question 5, which we have considered only briefly.

We trust that by now you have a good idea of how a student of history should examine and mine a documentary source. Now let us look at an artifact.

Unwritten Sources

Historians distinguish between the prehistorical and historical past, with the chief characteristic of any historical culture being that it provides written records from which we can reconstruct its past. Without a large volume and variety of documentary sources it is impossible to write any society's history in detail. This is not to say that the unwritten relics of the past are worthless. The art and science of archeology proves the contrary, and historians, as we shall see, use such sources. As a rule of thumb, however, no matter how extensive its physical remains may be, if a culture has not left us records we can read, its history largely remains a closed book. The ancient civilizations of Harappan India and Minoan Crete, for example, knew and practiced the art of writing, but until we learn how to decipher their texts, we can draw only vague pictures of their respective histories.

Given the central role documents play in our reconstruction of the past, it should surprise no one to learn that most historians concentrate their research almost exclusively on written sources. Yet historians would be foolish to overlook *any* piece of evidence from the past. As we suggested earlier, photographs could be a rich source for anyone researching the history of your class. Our future historian might even want to study all the extant souvenirs and supplies sold in your school's bookstore. Examined properly, they probably could help fill in some gaps in the story of your class's cultural history.

Artifacts can be illuminating, particularly when used in conjunction with records. Coins tell us a lot about a society's ideals or its leaders' programs. Art in its many forms reveals the interests, attitudes, and mundane perceptions of various segments of society. More down-to-earth items, such as domestic utensils and tools, allow us to infer much about the lives of common individuals. In this book we concentrate on written sources, for reasons already outlined, but we include some examples of important artifactual evidence. Let us look at an example and proceed to "read" it.

AN ANONYMOUS WOODCUT OF 1511

Columbus arrived in Barcelona in April 1493 to learn not only had his letter arrived but it had already been published and publicly circulated. Within months the letter was translated into several languages, and the Latin translation alone went through nine editions, several of which were lavishly illustrated, before the end of 1494. Printers discovered that educated Europeans had an almost insatiable desire to learn about the peoples and lands Columbus and other explorers were "discovering," and they catered to that interest.

Their clientele wanted not only to read about the fascinating peoples, plants, and animals of these lands — they wanted also to see them. Consequently, as books proliferated on the new explorations, so did the number of printed illustrations, many of which are quite fanciful and tell us more about the Europeans who created them than the peoples and regions they supposedly portrayed. The woodcut print we have chosen appeared in a popular English pamphlet of 1511.

QUESTIONS FOR ANALYSIS

1. What scene has the artist set? What has the artist placed to the immediate right of the standing man, and what function does it have in this scene?
2. What do each person's actions, dress, and demeanor tell us about her or him?

3. What does this illustration tell us about popular European notions concerning the natives of the New World?

Interpreting the Woodcut

What a charming, even idyllic domestic scene. An attractive mother nurses an infant at her breast while amusing an older child with a feather. A well-muscled, equally attractive, and proud father stands nearby, holding the tools of his trade while next to him the family's dinner is slowly cooking. Dinner, of course, may strike us as macabre, as these are cannibals, and it looks like roast European is on the menu. The tools of the father's trade are weapons. Both children are naked, and the parents are virtually nude, save for what appear to be leaves that cover their loins, decorative necklaces, armbands and anklets of some indeterminate material, and feathers in their hair.

What is the message? What we have is a reprise of the image provided by Columbus in his letter of 1493 — the "noble savage." These are fully human beings with human bonds and affections. Yet they are still "savages," as their clothing (or lack of it), decorations, weapons, and choice of food would have suggested to most sixteenth-century Europeans. Here, as Columbus and many of those who followed agreed, were a people who could become Christians but who also, by virtue of their backwardness, were to be subjugated. There is something appealing about their innocent savagery, but what of that poor fellow whose severed leg and head are slowly roasting?

Have we read too much into the woodcut? It is arguable that we may have. The historian always faces this problem when trying to analyze an isolated piece of evidence, particularly when it is a nonverbal source. Yet this artifact is not completely isolated, for we brought to its analysis insight gained from documentary evidence — Columbus's letter. That is how we generally read the artifacts of historical cultures. We attempt to place them in the context of what we have already learned or inferred from documentary sources. Documents illuminate artifacts, and artifacts make more vivid and tangible the often shadowy world of words.

As you attempt to interpret the unwritten sources in this book, keep in mind what you have learned from the documents you have already read, your textbook, and class lectures. Remember that we have chosen these artifacts to illustrate broad themes and general trends. You should not find their messages overly subtle. As with the documents, always try to place each piece of nonverbal evidence into its proper context, and in that regard, read the introductions and questions for analysis very carefully. We will do our best to provide you with all the information and clues you need.

Good luck and have fun!

Part One

▼▼▼

The Ancient World

The term *ancient world* (literally, "the world that has gone before us") defies simple historical definition. Part of the problem lies in the fact that originally the term was coined by Western historians to encompass solely the early history of that relatively small region of the world which stretches from the northwest corner of the Indian subcontinent to Western Europe. Understood within this narrow context, ancient history involves the period from the rise of civilization in Southwest Asia (known today as the Middle East) to the collapse of the Roman Empire, approximately 3500 B.C. to A.D. 500. Within this occidental scheme of history, antiquity ended by the middle of the first millennium A.D., but not before it had laid the roots of Western civilization. Having spent itself, the ancient world was followed by the "Middle Ages" (500–1500), which in turn were followed by the modern world.

Such divisions of the past make little or no sense when history is studied globally. Nevertheless, the category "the ancient world" is useful for the global historian, if one redefines it in two ways: by expanding the term to include all of the world's primary or earliest civilizations that have "gone before us," and by distinguishing between the ancient Afro-Eurasian and American worlds.

Civilizations arose independently on two grand "world islands": the Afro-Eurasian landmass and the Americas. The first to witness this phenomenon was the Afro-Eurasian supercontinent, where separate primary civilizations appeared in the river valleys of Mesopotamia, Egypt, northwest India, and northern China between approximately 3500 and 1800 B.C. Although distinct and largely indigenous, these four early centers of civilization influenced one another to varying degrees. Mesopotamia, the world's first known civilization, had early contact with the nascent civilizations of Egypt and India, and by the middle of the second millennium B.C. (the 1000s) the cultivation of wheat and barley and the use of chariots had spread from Southwest Asia to northern China.

Across the Atlantic and Pacific oceans, unknown to and uninfluenced by the societies of Africa and Eurasia, civilizations appeared along the gulf coast of Mexico around 1200 B.C. and, at about the same time or shortly thereafter, along the Pacific coast and Andean highlands of Peru. As was the case in the Afro-Eurasian world island, the civilizations of the Americas cross-fertilized one another through their trade networks but were isolated from the rest of the world. As was also the case in the Afro-Eurasian hemisphere of the globe, the original centers of civilization in the Americas — namely, Mexico/Central America and the western highlands and shores of South America — served as the American hemisphere's dominant matrices of civilized culture for thousands of years and well beyond the period Europeans characterize as "antiquity."

The original nuclei of the Afro-Eurasian "system" of separate but connected civilizations were four fairly self-contained river valleys, but over the course of several millennia these centers spread outward to encompass large regions, each with its distinctive characteristics. By 300 B.C. the four major Afro-Eurasian cultural regions, or "pools," were Southwest Asia, the Mediterranean, India, and China. Of these, geography dictated that the culture of China would be the most singular and least stimulated by foreign influences because of China's relative isolation at the eastern end of the Eurasian landmass. Conversely, the culture of Southwest Asia — the crossroads of the Afro-Eurasian world of civilized peoples — was the most variegated and eclectic.

During the last few centuries B.C. and for the first several centuries A.D., the cultures at either end of the great Eurasian expanse of land, China and the Greco-Roman world, achieved political unity and consequently expanded at the expense of their less organized neighbors, such as Koreans and Southeast Asians in the East and various Celtic peoples in the West. The result was two massive empires linked by East African, Southwest Asian, Indian, and Central Asiatic intermediaries. Consequently, goods, ideas, and diseases were exchanged throughout Eurasia and portions of Africa more freely and quickly than ever before.

Between approximately A.D. 200 and 550 internal and external pressures, including diseases that had traveled along the trade routes, precipitated the collapse of empires in China, India, Southwest Asia, and the Roman Mediterranean, and with those disasters, which were neither totally contemporaneous nor equally severe, the ancient world, the first grand epoch of Afro-Eurasian history, was essentially at an end. The era that followed rested on the foundations of antiquity but was also quite different from the ancient world, in part because of three world religions, Mahayana Buddhism, Christianity, and Islam, which played major transforming roles throughout Eurasia and Africa between roughly A.D. 600 and 1500.

Across the waters, the civilizations of Mexico, Central, and South America continued their development in splendid isolation from the cares and trends of the eastern hemisphere. Cities and empires rose and fell, and societies continued to develop along cultural lines set down by their first civilizations. To be sure, changes took place. One important new trend between roughly A.D. 600 and 1200 was the rise of North American civilizations in what are today the deserts of the southwestern United States and the lands washed by the Mississippi and Ohio rivers. Despite these new centers of civilization, the Amerindian world was wrenched from its ancient patterns only when European invaders and colonists began arriving in significant numbers in the early sixteenth century.

Because of a relative lack of documentary evidence relating to preconquest Amerindian cultures and civilizations, the sources in Part I deal almost exclusively with ancient Afro-Eurasian history. We will more fully consider the story of antiquity in the western hemisphere in Part III, Chapter 11.

Chapter 1

▼▼▼

The First Civilizations

The word *civilization* is derived from the Latin adjective *civilis*, which means "political" or "civic." No matter how else one defines civilization, an organized state stands at the center of every society we call civilized, and the world's first civilizations were organized around sacred states. That means each early civilization produced rulers who governed by divine mandate. Religious beliefs, as well as political and social forms, varied according to time and place, but ultimately all power was unified and perceived as descending from the gods or, as was the case in China, Heaven.

Those who ruled were a minority and maintained power by exploiting the many. This was a fact of early civilized life largely because, until modern times, states could produce only severely limited surpluses due to the narrow agrarian base of their economies. That surplus, which is so necessary for the creation of a state, could be channeled into state-building activities only if rulers kept the majority of their subjects at a fairly low level of subsistence by exacting from them a major portion of the surplus through taxes, labor services, and military conscription. Consequently, the more agreeable benefits of civilization, such as literature and the other arts, were largely the exclusive property and tools of the few.

Most of the world's first civilizations evolved systems of writing, and in each case the art of writing served, at least initially, to strengthen the authority of a ruling elite. Whether writing was used to record temple possessions or taxes due, to give permanence to laws or to provide priests with a coherent body of sacred texts, writing set apart those who exercised power from those who were powerless.

Not all the records left behind by these first civilizations are open to us. We still cannot decipher the earliest texts of Minoan Crete or any of those of ancient Kush or Harappan

India. Happily, this is not the case with Mesopotamia, Egypt, and China. The written sources left behind by these three civilizations reveal societies that were strikingly different in perspective and structure, even as they shared characteristics common to all early civilizations.

▼▼▼

Mesopotamia: The Land of Two Rivers

According to the eminent historian Samuel N. Kramer, "History begins at Sumer," and there is a good deal of truth to this judgment. It is in Sumer, which lies just to the north of the Persian Gulf in an area encompassed by the southern regions of modern Iraq, that we find the first evidence of human civilization. By 3500 B.C. a number of Sumerian city-states had emerged, and humanity was embarked on the adventure of civilization.

Generally, we call the Sumerians, and the other peoples who succeeded them in this region of Southwest Asia, *Mesopotamians.* The term, which means "those who dwell between the rivers," acknowledges the origin of the world's first known civilization in the valley created by the Tigris and Euphrates rivers.

By approximately 1800 B.C. the Sumerians had been absorbed by waves of infiltrators and invaders and ceased to exist as an identifiable people. Moreover, the cultural center of gravity within Mesopotamia had shifted northward to the region of middle Mesopotamia, centering on the city of Babylon.

Despite their disappearance as a people, the Sumerians had laid the framework for what proved to be a dynamic Mesopotamian civilization that exercised profound cultural influence throughout West Asia and beyond for about three thousand years. Between roughly 3500 and 500 B.C. Mesopotamia was where much of the action was, so far as the history of West Asian civilization was concerned.

That action was both constructive and destructive. The Mesopotamians have been credited with such "firsts" as the world's first governments, schools, codes of law, ethical systems, and epic literature. Just as prominent in Mesopotamian life were disasters, both natural and human generated.

The geography of Mesopotamia provided its people with the challenge of harnessing the waters of its two great rivers, and from that necessary cooperative effort civilization arose. Yet those rivers also threatened to destroy the fragile fabric of civilized society, insofar as they were unpredictable and could easily turn into uncontrollable torrents. Moreover, most of southern Mesopotamia was covered by either arid wasteland or marsh. Consequently, Sumerian civilization was built upon heroic labor in the midst of a hostile environment.

Another significant geographical aspect of Mesopotamian life, which also proved to be an important factor throughout its history, is the land's openness to incursions. To the north and east lie the hills and mountains of Iran and Armenia, from which wave after wave of invaders descended into the inviting valley of cities. To the south and west lies the desert of Arabia, out of which came countless nomads century after century. In many instances these invaders toppled a preexisting state and then settled down to become, in turn, Mesopotamians.

Whether they came from the desert fringes, as did the Amorites, who established the first Babylonian empire around 1800 B.C., or were mountain folk, such as the Kassites, whose chariots toppled Babylon soon after 1700, they all eventually became part of a Mesopotamian cultural complex, with modes of life and thought the Sumerians had set in place at the dawn of human civilization.

The Search for Eternal Life in Mesopotamia
▼▼▼

1 ▼ THE EPIC OF GILGAMESH

Humans share many basic concerns. Two such concerns are finding meaning in life and confronting the reality of death. In Mesopotamia, where life and human fortune were so precarious, people deeply probed these issues and made them the subjects of numerous myths. Eventually, Mesopotamia evolved its classic answer to these questions in the form of its greatest work of literature, *The Epic of Gilgamesh*.

A myth is not a deliberate piece of fiction or simply a story told to amuse an audience. It represents an attempt by a prescientific society to make sense of the universe. Whereas the scientist objectifies nature, seeing the world as an "it," the myth-maker lives in a world where everything has a soul, a personality, and its own story. A raging river is not a body of water responding to physical laws but an angry or capricious god. In the same manner, the fortunes of human society are not the consequences of chance, history, or any laws discoverable by social scientists. Rather, the gods and other supernatural spirits intervene directly in human affairs, punishing and rewarding as they wish. The insight thus gained into the ways of the gods largely satisfies the emotional and intellectual needs of the myth-maker.

The most complete extant version of *The Epic of Gilgamesh* was discovered on twelve clay tablets in the ruins of the late seventh-century B.C. library of the Assyrian king Ashurbanipal. Other, earlier versions of the epic show, however, that the story, at least in its basic outline, is Sumerian in origin and goes back to the third millennium B.C. (2000s).

The hero, Gilgamesh, was a historic figure who ruled the city-state of Uruk sometime between 2700 and 2500 B.C. and was remembered as a great warrior, as well as the builder of Uruk's massive walls and temple. His exploits were so impressive that he became the focal point of a series of oral sagas that recounted his legendary heroic deeds. Around 2000 B.C. or shortly thereafter, an unknown Babylonian poet reworked some of these tales, along with other stories, such as the adventure of Utnapishtim which appears in the selection that follows, into an epic masterpiece that became widely popular and influential throughout Southwest Asia and beyond.

The epic contains a profound theme, the conflict between humanity's talents and aspirations and its mortal limitations. Gilgamesh, "two-thirds a god and one-third human," as the poem describes him, is a man of heroic proportions and appetites who still must face the inevitability of death.

As the epic opens, an arrogant Gilgamesh, not yet aware of his human limitations and his duties as king, is exhausting the people of Uruk with his manic energy. The people cry to Heaven for relief from his abuse of power, and the gods respond by creating Enkidu, a wild man who lives among the animals. Enkidu enters Uruk, where he challenges Gilgamesh to a contest of strength and fighting skill. When Gilgamesh triumphs, Enkidu embraces him as a brother, and the two heroes set out on a series of spectacular exploits.

In the course of several of their heroic adventures, they insult Ishtar, goddess of love and fertility, and for this a life is owed. The one chosen by the gods to die is Enkidu. As the selection opens, Enkidu, after having cursed his heroic past which has brought him to this fate, tells Gilgamesh of a vision he has had of the place Mesopotamians knew as "the land of no return."

QUESTIONS FOR ANALYSIS

1. What was the Mesopotamian view of the afterlife?
2. What is the message of Siduri's advice to Gilgamesh?
3. Consider Utnapishtim's initial response to Gilgamesh's request for the secret of eternal life. How does his message complement what Siduri has said? What do these two messages suggest about the Mesopotamian view of life?
4. Consider the story of Utnapishtim. What do the various actions of the gods and goddesses imply about how the Mesopotamians viewed their deities? Consider especially Ea's treatment of the truth. According to the epic, what are the roles of gods and humans? What do the Mesopotamian deities require of people? What do people expect of their gods?
5. Many epics revolve around the story of a quest in which a hero gains wisdom as a result of his toil. What wisdom has Gilgamesh brought back with him? How has he changed as a result of his quest?
6. Despite the apparent failure of his quest for eternal life, has Gilgamesh earned a type of immortality? If so, what is it?
7. Reconsider your answers to questions 2 and 3 in light of the epilogue, where the poet lays out for us the moral of the story. Basing your answer on the entire story, and especially the epilogue, what would you say was the Mesopotamian vision of the meaning of life?

As Enkidu slept alone in his sickness, in bitterness of spirit he poured out his heart to his friend. "It was I who cut down the cedar, I who leveled the forest, I who slew Humbaba[1] and now see what has become of me. Listen, my friend, this is the dream I dreamed last night. The heavens roared, and earth rumbled back an answer; between them stood I before an awful being, the sombre-faced manbird; he had directed on me his purpose. His was a vampire face, his foot was a lion's foot, his hand was an eagle's talon. He fell on me and his claws were in my hair, he held me fast and I smothered; then he transformed me so that my arms became wings covered with feathers. He turned his stare towards me, and he led me away to the palace of Irkalla, the Queen of Darkness,[2] to the house from which none who enters ever returns, down the road from which there is no coming back.

"There is the house whose people sit in darkness; dust is their food and clay their meat. They are clothed like birds with wings for covering, they see no light, they sit in darkness. I entered the house of dust and I saw the kings of the earth, their crowns put away forever; rulers and princes, all those who once wore kingly crowns and ruled the world in the days of old. They who had stood in the place of the gods like Anu and Enlil,[3] stood now like servants to fetch baked meats in the house of dust, to carry cooked meat and cold water from the waterskin. In the house of dust which I entered were high priests and acolytes, priests of the incantation and of ecstasy; there were servers of the temple, and there was Etana, that king of Kish whom the eagle carried to heaven in the days of old.[4] There was Ereshkigal[5] the Queen of the Underworld; and Belit-Sheri squatted in front of her, she who is recorder of the gods and keeps the book of death. She held a tablet from which she read. She raised her head, she saw me and spoke: 'Who has brought this one here?' Then I awoke like a man drained of blood who wanders alone in a waste of rushes; like one whom the bailiff has seized and his heart pounds with terror."

▷ Enkidu dies, and Gilgamesh now realizes that heroic fame is no substitute for life. Facing the reality of his own death, he begins a desperate search for immortality. In the course of his search, he meets Siduri, a goddess of wine, who advises him:

"Gilgamesh, where are you hurrying to? You will never find that life for which you are looking. When the gods created man they allotted to him death, but life they retained in their own keeping. As for you, Gilgamesh, fill your belly with good things; day and night, night and day, dance and be merry, feast and rejoice. Let your clothes be fresh, bathe yourself in water, cherish the little child that holds your hand, and make your wife happy in your embrace; for this too is the lot of man."

▷ Gilgamesh, however, refuses to be deflected from his quest. After a series of harrowing experiences, he finally reaches Utnapishtim, a former mortal whom the gods had placed in an eternal paradise, and addresses him.

"Oh, father Utnapishtim, you who have entered the assembly of the gods, I wish to question you concerning the living and the dead, how shall I find the life for which I am searching?"

---

[1]The giant who guarded the cedar forest and was slain by Enkidu and Gilgamesh.
[2]Goddess of the Underworld.
[3]Dead earthly kings. Anu was the supreme king of the gods and the source of all order and government, while Enlil was the storm god, who supported royal authority.

[4]A legendary king of the Sumerian city of Kish.
[5]Another name for Irkalla, goddess of the Underworld.

Utnapishtim said, "There is no permanence. Do we build a house to stand for ever, do we seal a contract to hold for all time? Do brothers divide an inheritance to keep forever, does the flood-time of rivers endure? It is only the nymph of the dragon-fly who sheds her larva and sees the sun in his glory. From the days of old there is no permanence. The sleeping and the dead, how alike they are, they are like a painted death. What is there between the master and the servant when both have fulfilled their doom? When the Anunnaki,[6] the judges, come together, and Mammetun[7] the mother of destinies, together they decree the fates of men. Life and death they allot but the day of death they do not disclose."

Then Gilgamesh said to Utnapishtim the Faraway, "I look at you now, Utnapishtim, and your appearance is no different from mine; there is nothing strange in your features. I thought I should find you like a hero prepared for battle, but you lie here taking your ease on your back. Tell me truly, how was it that you came to enter the company of the gods and to possess everlasting life?" Utnapishtim said to Gilgamesh, "I will reveal to you a mystery, I will tell you a secret of the gods."

"You know the city Shurrupak, it stands on the banks of Euphrates? That city grew old and the gods that were in it were old. There was Anu, lord of the firmament, their father, and warrior Enlil their counselor, Ninurta[8] the helper, and Ennugi[9] watcher over canals; and with them also was Ea.[10] In those days the world teemed, the people multiplied, the world bellowed like a wild bull, and the great god was aroused by the clamor. Enlil heard the clamor and he said to the gods in council, 'The uproar of mankind is intolerable and sleep is no longer possible by reason of the babel.' So the gods agreed to exterminate mankind. Enlil did this, but Ea because of his oath[11] warned me in a dream. He whispered their words to my house of reeds, 'Reed-house, reed-house! Wall, O wall, hearken reed-house, wall reflect; O man of Shurrupak, son of Ubara-Tutu; tear down your house and build a boat, abandon possessions and look for life, despise worldly goods and save your soul alive. Tear down your house, I say, and build a boat. . . . Then take up into the boat the seed of all living creatures.'

"When I had understood I said to my lord, 'Behold, what you have commanded I will honor and perform, but how shall I answer the people, the city, the elders?' Then Ea opened his mouth and said to me, his servant, 'Tell them this: I have learnt that Enlil is wrathful against me, I dare no longer walk in his land nor live in his city; I will go down to the Gulf to dwell with Ea my lord. But on you he will rain down abundance, rare fish and shy wildfowl, a rich harvest-tide. In the evening the rider of the storm will bring you wheat in torrents.'. . .

"On the seventh day the boat was complete. . . .

"I loaded into her all that I had of gold and of living things, my family, my kin, the beast of the field both wild and tame, and all the craftsmen. I sent them on board. . . . The time was fulfilled, the evening came, the rider of the storm sent down the rain. I looked out at the weather and it was terrible, so I too boarded the boat and battened her down. . . .

"For six days and six nights the winds blew, torrent and tempest and flood overwhelmed the world, tempest and flood raged together like warring hosts. When the seventh day dawned the storm from the south subsided, the sea grew calm, the flood was stilled; I looked at the face of the world and there was silence, all mankind was turned to clay. The surface of the sea stretched as flat as a roof-top; I opened a hatch and the light fell on my face. Then I bowed

---

[6]Gods of the Underworld who judge the dead.
[7]Goddess of fate.
[8]God of war.
[9]God of irrigation.

[10]God of wisdom and providence.
[11]Apparently an oath to protect humanity, because Ea was the god of life-giving water and good fortune.

low, I sat down and I wept, the tears streamed down my face, for on every side was the waste of water. I looked for land in vain, but fourteen leagues distant there appeared a mountain, and there the boat grounded; on the mountain of Nisir the boat held fast, she held fast and did not budge. . . . When the seventh day dawned I loosed a dove and let her go. She flew away, but finding no resting-place she returned. Then I loosed a swallow, and she flew away but finding no resting-place she returned. I loosed a raven, she saw that the waters had retreated, she ate, she flew around, she cawed, and she did not come back. Then I threw everything open to the four winds, I made a sacrifice and poured out a libation[12] on the mountain top. Seven and again seven cauldrons I set up on their stands, I heaped up wood and cane and cedar and myrtle. When the gods smelled the sweet savor, they gathered like flies over the sacrifice.[13] Then, at last, Ishtar also came, she lifted her necklace with the jewels of heaven that once Anu had made to please her. 'O you gods here present, by the lapis lazuli round my neck I shall remember these days as I remember the jewels of my throat; these last days I shall not forget.[14] Let all the gods gather round the sacrifice, except Enlil. He shall not approach this offering, for without reflection he brought the flood; he consigned my people to destruction.'

"When Enlil had come, when he saw the boat, he was wrath and swelled with anger at the gods, the host of heaven, 'Has any of these mortals escaped? Not one was to have survived the destruction.' Then the god of the wells and canals Ninurta opened his mouth and said to the warrior Enlil, 'Who is there of the gods that can devise without Ea? It is Ea alone who knows all things.' Then Ea opened his mouth and spoke to warrior Enlil, 'Wisest of gods, hero Enlil, how could you so senselessly bring down the flood?' . . . It was not that I revealed the secret of the gods; the wise man learned it in a dream. Now take your counsel what shall be done with him.

"Then Enlil went up into the boat, he took me by the hand and my wife and made us enter the boat and kneel down on either side, he standing between us. He touched our foreheads to bless us saying, 'In time past Utnapishtim was a mortal man; henceforth he and his wife shall live in the distance at the mouth of the rivers.' Thus it was that the gods took me and placed me here to live in the distance, at the mouth of the rivers."

Utnapishtim said, "As for you, Gilgamesh, who will assemble the gods for your sake, so that you may find that life for which you are searching?"

▷ After telling his story, Utnapishtim challenges Gilgamesh to resist sleep for six days and seven nights. When Gilgamesh fails the test, Utnapishtim points out how preposterous it is to search for immortality when one cannot even resist sleep. Out of kindness, Utnapishtim does tell Gilgamesh where he can find a submarine plant that will, at least, rejuvenate him. Consequently, the hero dives to the bottom of the sea and plucks it. However, humanity is to be denied even the blessing of forestalling old age and decrepitude, because the plant is stolen from Gilgamesh by a serpent. His mission a failure, Gilgamesh returns to Uruk.

The destiny was fulfilled which the father of the gods, Enlil of the mountain, had decreed for Gilgamesh: "In nether-earth the darkness will show him a light: of mankind, all that are known, none will leave a monument for generations to come to compare with his. The heroes, the wise men, like the new moon have their waxing and waning. Men will say, 'Who has ever ruled with might and with power like

---

[12]Poured out wine or some other beverage as an offering to the gods.
[13]Many myth-making people believe that the gods gain nourishment from the greasy smoke of burnt sacrifices.

[14]The necklace is a rainbow.

him?' As in the dark month, the month of shadows, so without him there is no light. O Gilgamesh, this was the meaning of your dream. You were given the kingship, such was your destiny, everlasting life was not your destiny. Because of this do not be sad at heart, do not be grieved or oppressed; he has given you power to bind and to loose, to be the darkness and the light of mankind. He has given unexampled supremacy over the people, victory in battle from which no fugitive returns, in forays and assaults from which there is no going back.

But do not abuse this power, deal justly with your servants in the palace, deal justly before the face of the Sun.". . .

Gilgamesh, the son of Ninsun, lies in the tomb. At the place of offerings he weighed the bread-offering, at the place of libation he poured out the wine. In those days the lord Gilgamesh departed, the son of Ninsun, the king, peerless, without an equal among men, who did not neglect Enlil his master. O Gilgamesh, lord of Kullab,[15] great is thy praise.

Bringing Order to an Uncertain World
▼▼▼

2 ▼ THE JUDGMENTS OF HAMMURABI

Mesopotamia's characteristic sense of insecurity resulted in its producing not only great philosophical literature but also detailed legal codes. The so-called *Code of Hammurabi* is the most famous but certainly not the earliest of the many collections of law that were produced throughout the first three thousand years of Mesopotamian civilization. Discovered in 1901, this eighteenth-century B.C. Babylonian code is inscribed on a stone pillar that measures over seven feet high and more than six feet in circumference.

Whether these compilations of law were Sumerian, Babylonian, Assyrian, or Chaldean, a number of common elements unite them. Chief among them is the expressed purpose, as the prologue to Hammurabi's collection declares, "to promote the welfare of the people . . . to cause justice to prevail in the land, to destroy the wicked and the evil, that the strong might not oppress the weak." There is good reason to believe that even conquerors such as Hammurabi (reigned ca 1792–1750 B.C.), who briefly united Mesopotamia and transformed Babylon into the capital of an empire, sought to promote justice through law.

Hammurabi's code is actually a collection of decisions or *misharum* (literally, "rightings" or "equity rulings") that the king made in response to specific cases and perceived injustices. Notwithstanding the fact that this is a compilation of judgments rather than a systematic code, the collection covers a wide variety of crimes and circumstances, thereby providing extensive insight into the structure and values of eighteenth-century Babylonian society.

[15]Part of Uruk.

QUESTIONS FOR ANALYSIS

1. What evidence is there of class distinctions in Babylon?
2. How are all members of this society made responsible for its good order?
3. How did Hammurabi seek to provide for the basic welfare of his subjects?
4. What was the status of women in this society? Did they enjoy any protection or liberties? What about children?
5. Mesopotamian society has been characterized as patriarchal (dominated by male heads of households). Does the evidence in this collection of decisions tend to support or refute that judgment?
6. The principle of "an eye for an eye and a tooth for a tooth" usually means in modern idiom a philosophy of retribution that is noted for its severity and lack of compassion. Does such a characterization do justice to the spirit behind Hammurabi's code?

PROLOGUE

When Marduk[1] had instituted me governor of men, to conduct and to direct, Right and Justice I established in the land, for the good of the people.

THE ADMINISTRATION OF JUSTICE

3. If in a lawsuit a man gives damning evidence, and his word that he has spoken is not justified, then, if the suit be a capital one,[2] that man shall be slain. . . .

5. If a judge has heard a case, and given a decision, and delivered a written verdict, and if afterward his case is disproved, and that judge is convicted as the cause of the misjudgment, then he shall pay twelve times the penalty awarded in that case. In public assembly he shall be thrown from the seat of judgment; he shall not return; and he shall not sit with the judges upon a case. . . .

FELONS AND VICTIMS

22. If a man has perpetrated brigandage, and has been caught, that man shall be slain.

23. If the brigand has not been taken, the man plundered shall claim before god[3] what he has lost; and the city and governor in whose land and boundary the theft has taken place shall restore to him all that he has lost.

24. If a life, the city and governor shall pay one mina[4] of silver to his people.[5] . . .

PROPERTY

29. If his son is under age, and unable to administer his [deceased] father's affairs, then a third part of the field and garden shall be given to his mother, and his mother shall bring him up. . . .

38. A captain, soldier, or official may not give his field, or garden, or house to his

---

[1] The chief god of Babylon.
[2] A case in which death is the penalty.
[3] The god of the city. Each city had its special protector deity.

[4] About 500 grams of silver. A mina was divided into 60 shekels.
[5] The family of the slain person.

wife or his daughter; neither can they be given as payment for debt.[6]

39. He may bequeath in writing to his wife or daughter a field, a garden, or a house that he may have bought, and may give it as payment for debt. . . .

WINESELLERS AND TAVERNS

109. If rebels meet in the house of a wineseller and she[7] does not seize them and take them to the palace, that wine-seller shall be slain.

110. If a priestess who has not remained in the temple,[8] shall open a wine-shop, or enter a wine-shop for drink, that woman shall be burned. . . .

DEBT SLAVERY

117. If a man has contracted a debt, and has given his wife, his son, his daughter for silver or for labor, three years they shall serve in the house of their purchaser or bondsmaster; in the fourth year they shall regain their original condition. . . .

MARRIAGE AND THE FAMILY

129. If the wife of a man is found lying with another male, they shall be bound and thrown into the water. If the husband lets his wife live, then the king shall let his servant live. . . .

134. If a man has been taken prisoner, and there is no food in his house, and his wife enters the house of another, then that woman bears no blame.

135. If a man has been taken prisoner, and there is no food before her, and his wife

has entered the house of another, and bears children, and afterward her husband returns and regains his city, then that woman shall return to her spouse. The children shall follow their father.

136. If a man has abandoned his city, and absconded, and after that his wife has entered the house of another, if that man comes back and claims his wife, because he had fled and deserted his city, the wife of the deserter shall not return to her husband.

137. If a man has decided to divorce . . . a wife who has presented him with children, then he shall give back to that woman her dowry,[9] and he shall give her the use of field, garden, and property, and she shall bring up her children. After she has brought up her children, she shall take a son's portion of all that is given to her children, and she may marry the husband of her heart.

138. If a man divorces his spouse who has not borne him children, he shall give to her all the silver of the bride-price,[10] and restore to her the dowry which she brought from the house of her father; and so he shall divorce her.

139. If there was no bride-price, he shall give her one mina of silver for the divorce.

140. If he is a peasant, he shall give her one-third of a mina of silver.

141. If a man's wife, dwelling in his house, has decided to leave, has been guilty of dissipation, has wasted her house, and has neglected her husband, then she shall be prosecuted. If her husband says she is divorced, he shall let her go her way; he shall give her nothing for divorce. If her husband says she is not divorced, her hus-

---

[6]The monarch retained ultimate ownership of the property that soldiers and vassals received as payment for their services.

[7]Women traditionally filled this role in ancient Mesopotamia, perhaps because the wine deity was the goddess Siduri (see *The Epic of Gilgamesh,* source 1).

[8]Thereby breaking her vow to devote her life to serving the temple deity.

[9]The required money or goods she brought to the marriage.

[10]The price he paid her family in order to marry her.

band may marry another woman, and that [first] woman shall remain a slave in the house of her husband.

142. If a woman hates her husband, and says "You shall not possess me," the reason for her dislike shall be inquired into. If she is careful, and has no fault, but her husband takes himself away and neglects her, then that woman is not to blame. She shall take her dowry and go back to her father's house. . . .

148. If a man has married a wife, and sickness has seized her, and he has decided to marry another, he may marry; but his wife whom the sickness has seized he shall not divorce. She shall dwell in the house he has built, and he shall support her while she lives. . . .

168. If a man has decided to disinherit his son, and has said to the judge, "I disown my son," then the judge shall look into his reasons. If the son has not been guilty of a serious offense which would justify his being disinherited, then the father shall not disown him.

169. If the son has committed a serious offense against his father which justifies his being disinherited, still the judge shall overlook this first offense. If the son commits a grave offense a second time, his father may disown him. . . .

PERSONAL INJURY

195. If a son has struck his father, his hands shall be cut off.

196. If a man has destroyed the eye of another free man, his own eye shall be destroyed.

197. If he has broken the bone of a free man, his bone shall be broken.

198. If he has destroyed the eye of a peasant, or broken a bone of a peasant, he shall pay one mina of silver.

199. If he has destroyed the eye of a man's slave, or broken a bone of a man's slave, he shall pay half his value.

200. If a man has knocked out the teeth of a man of the same rank, his own teeth shall be knocked out.

201. If he has knocked out the teeth of a peasant, he shall pay one-third of a mina of silver.

202. If a man strikes the body of a man who is superior in status, he shall publicly receive sixty lashes with a cowhide whip. . . .

206. If a man has struck another man in a dispute and wounded him, that man shall swear, "I did not strike him knowingly"; and he shall pay for the physician.

207. If he dies of his blows, he shall swear likewise; and if it is the son of a free man, he shall pay half a mina of silver.

208. If he is the son of a peasant, he shall pay a third of a mina of silver.

209. If a man strikes the daughter of a free man, and causes her fetus to abort, he shall pay ten shekels of silver for her fetus.

210. If that woman dies, his daughter shall be slain.

211. If he has caused the daughter of a peasant to let her fetus abort through blows, he shall pay five shekels of silver.

212. If that woman dies, he shall pay half a mina of silver. . . .

CONSUMER PROTECTION

215. If a physician has treated a man with a metal knife for a severe wound, and has cured the man, or has opened a man's tumor with a metal knife, and cured a man's eye, then he shall receive ten shekels of silver.

216. If the son of a peasant, he shall receive five shekels of silver. . . .

218. If a physician has treated a man with a metal knife for a severe wound, and has caused the man to die, or has opened a man's tumor with a metal knife, and destroyed the man's eye, his hands shall be cut off. . . .

229. If a builder has built a house for a man, and his work is not strong, and if the house he has built falls in and kills the householder, that builder shall be slain.
230. If the child of the householder is killed, the child of that builder shall be slain.
231. If the slave of the householder is killed, he shall give slave for slave to the householder.
232. If goods have been destroyed, he shall replace all that has been destroyed; and because the house that he built was not made strong, and it has fallen in, he shall restore the fallen house out of his own personal property.
233. If a builder has built a house for a man, and his work is not done properly, and a wall shifts, then that builder shall make that wall good with his own silver. . . .

EPILOGUE

The oppressed, who has a lawsuit, shall come before my image as king of justice. He shall read the writing on my pillar, he shall perceive my precious words. The word of my pillar shall explain to him his cause, and he shall find his right. His heart shall be glad [and he shall say,] "The Lord Hammurabi has risen up as a true father to his people; the will of Marduk, his god, he has made to be feared; he has achieved victory for Marduk above and below. He has rejoiced the heart of Marduk, his lord, and gladdened the flesh of his people for ever. And the land he has placed in order.". . .

In after days and for all time, the king who is in the land shall observe the words of justice which are written upon my pillar. He shall not alter the law of the land which I have formulated, or the statutes of the country that I have enacted. . . . If that man has wisdom, and desires to keep his land in order, he will heed the words which are written upon my pillar. . . . The . . . people he shall govern; their laws he shall pronounce, their statutes he shall decide. He shall root out of the land the perverse and the wicked; and the flesh of his people he shall delight.

Hammurabi, the king of justice, am I, to whom Shamash[11] has granted rectitude. My words are well weighed: my deeds have no equal, leveling the exalted, humbling the proud, expelling the haughty. If that man heeds my words that I have engraved upon my pillar, departs not from the laws, alters not my words, changes not my sculptures, then may Shamash make the scepter of that man to endure as long as I, the king of justice, and to lead his people with justice.

▼▼▼

Egypt: The Land of Two Lands

Civilization seems to have arisen in Egypt shortly after it first appeared in Sumer. Although there is evidence of early Sumerian contact with the Egyptians, Egypt's civilization was largely self-generated, and its history and cultural patterns followed courses that differed substantially from those of Mesopotamia. Egyptians, however, shared a myth-making way of perceiving reality.

An integral element of Egyptian myth was the belief that Egypt was the land of divine harmony ruled by a living god-king, or pharaoh, who balanced all

[11]The sun god, vindicator of the oppressed.

conflicting cosmic forces. Around 3100 B.C. the land of the Nile was unified into a single state, although culturally it remained two distinctive lands: the rich delta region of the north, known as Lower Egypt (because the Nile flows northward), and the long but narrow strip of green land that borders the Nile to the south, known as Upper Egypt. Before their unification, Lower and Upper Egypt had been separate kingdoms. As far as Egyptians were concerned, they were two antithetical yet complementary lands that were brought into harmony by a unifying king who was a god on earth.

The state that resulted from this union enjoyed about three thousand years of historically unparalleled prosperity and stability. Between approximately 3100 and 343 B.C. Egypt experienced only a handful of relatively short-lived periods of either major internal turmoil and the consequent breakdown of central authority or domination by foreign powers. This long history of centralized monarchy and native rule was due in large part to the blessings of geography. Egypt was fairly secure behind its barriers of sea and desert, and the Nile's annual flooding was predictable and beneficial.

The sense of security that followed from these geographic and historical circumstances was reflected in the life-affirming spirit that pervaded Egyptian religion and philosophy. It also left its imprint on Egypt's arts. Whether painting charming scenes of everyday activities or composing tender love poems, Egyptian artists celebrated the joys of life. At the same time, codes of law, which figure so prominently in the historical records of Mesopotamia, are not to be found in the literature of ancient Egypt. Though Egyptians were equally concerned with maintaining a well-ordered society, their avenue to this goal differed greatly from that of Mesopotamians.

The Search for Eternal Life in Egypt
▼▼▼

3 ▼ *THE BOOK OF THE DEAD*

Historians have traditionally divided the first two thousand years of Egyptian civilization into six ages: the Thinite Period (ca 3100–2700 B.C.), the Old Kingdom (ca 2700–2200), the Feudal or First Intermediate Period (ca 2200–2060), the Middle Kingdom (ca 2060–1785), the Second Intermediate Period or Age of the Hyksos (ca 1785–1570), and the New Kingdom or Empire (ca 1570–1086).

The Thinite Period was Egypt's age of initial unification and state building, which laid the foundation for the brilliant Old Kingdom. The Old Kingdom centered on Egypt's god-kings, whose mummified remains were reverently entombed in pyramids in preparation for the journey to eternal life in the "land of the west." During this age, Egyptians believed that all that was needed to ensure the king's safe journey was proper attention to the many details of the funeral ceremony. Egyptians would continue to bury their dead with great ceremony for thousands of years to come, but it was essentially only during the Old Kingdom that they constructed those few great pyramids that have so dazzled visitors for the past 4,500 years. The immense effort and cost expended on these pyramids are testimony to the power of Egypt's early god-kings, whose word was law. As the living embodiment of the union of Upper and Lower Egypt, the king was the divine embodiment of *Maat*, which, so far as the Old Kingdom was concerned, is best translated as "universal harmony."

The reign of Pepi II (ca 2275–2185 B.C.) marked the end of the Old Kingdom. Shortly after Pepi's death, pharaonic power collapsed, plunging Egypt into an era of internal turmoil. Eventually, the First Intermediate Period, an age of local rule and social upheaval, gave way to the Middle Kingdom, an era of revived central authority and a deepening awareness of social justice and individual morality. Moreover, the Egyptians now viewed eternal life, formerly the exclusive preserve of the divine pharaoh, the royal family, and certain favored royal servants, as available to all persons who met certain moral criteria.

Beginning in the Middle Kingdom, a great body of texts appeared in Egypt, which are collectively, and somewhat misleadingly, known as *The Book of the Dead*. These texts, painted on the walls of tombs, as well as written in various papyrus scrolls, deal with the search by individuals, both great and lowborn, for eternal bliss in the hereafter. The selection that appears here comes from the tomb of Nu, a high-ranking official of the Eighteenth Dynasty (1570–1305 B.C.), and his wife. Often called "The Negative Confession," this text represents the plea of Nu as he stands in judgment before Osiris, god of resurrection.

QUESTIONS FOR ANALYSIS

1. What does *Maat* mean in this text?
2. What does the new meaning of *Maat* suggest about changes that had taken place in Egypt?
3. What does this confession allow us to infer about Egyptian social values after the First Intermediate Period?
4. Compare this text with *The Epic of Gilgamesh* (source 1). What are their different messages? What do those messages suggest about the differences between these two civilizations?
5. Compare this confession with the judgments of Hammurabi (source 2). Do you perceive any differences in tone, style, or substance? Any similarities? What do their differences and similarities suggest about these two civilizations?

The following shall be said when the overseer of the palace, the chancellor-in-chief, Nu, triumphant, comes forth into the Hall of Double Maat[1] so that he can be separated from every sin which he has committed and may behold the faces of the gods. The Osiris Nu,[2] triumphant, says:

My homage to you, Great God,[3] Lord of Double Maat, I have come to you, my Lord, I have brought myself here to behold your beauty. I know you, and I know your name, and I know the names of the forty-two gods[4] who exist with you in this Hall of Double Maat, who live off of sinners and who feed upon their blood on the day when the lives of men are taken into account in the presence of the god Un-nefer [Osiris]; truly, "Ladies of Double Maat"[5] is your name. In truth, I have come to you; I have brought Maat to you; I have expelled deceit for you.

1. I have not done evil to humanity.
2. I have not oppressed the members of my family.
3. I have not committed sin in the place of right and truth.[6]
4. I have had no knowledge of that which is not [to be known by humans].
5. I have seen no evil. . . .
7. I have not advanced my name for exaltation to honors.
8. I have not ill treated servants.
9. I have not blasphemed a god.
10. I have not defrauded an oppressed person of his property.
11. I have not done that which the gods abominate.
12. I have not defamed a slave to his superior.
13. I have not caused pain.
14. I have not caused anyone to go hungry.
15. I have not caused anyone to weep.
16. I have not murdered.
17. I have not ordered any murder.
18. I have not inflicted pain upon humanity.
19. I have not defrauded temples of their income. . . .
22. I have not fornicated. . . .
26. I have not encroached upon the fields of others. . . .
29. I have not taken milk from the mouths of children. . . .
33. I have not dammed up the water [when it should flow]. . . .
36. I have not neglected the times of offering [to the gods].
37. I have not driven off cattle from the property of the gods.
38. I have not obstructed a god's procession.

I am pure! I am pure! I am pure! I am pure!

[1]The hall of justice presided over by Isis, goddess of Right, and Nephthys, goddess of Truth.
[2]In an involved ceremony the mummified corpse of Nu has been transformed into Osiris, god of resurrection, who through his own death and rebirth offers the promise of life after death to those who become him.
[3]Osiris, who serves as judge in the Hall of Double Maat. Nu, who has magically become Osiris, is addressing the god Osiris.
[4]Forty-two divine jurors and avengers of guilt.
[5]In this context the reference is to Osiris, who is identified with the "twin sisters with two eyes [of Maat]," Isis (Orisis's sister and wife) and Nephthys.
[6]He has not sinned in any holy place.

Divine Harmony in the Land of Two Lands
▼▼▼

4 ▼ *HYMN TO AMON-RE*

Between approximately 1785 and 1570 B.C. a group of hated foreign conquerors, known as the Hyksos, ruled Lower Egypt. Their expulsion was spearheaded by princes of Thebes who eventually instituted the eighteenth royal dynasty of Egypt and launched the Age of Empire or New Kingdom. During that period Egypt became a major power in Northeast Africa and Southwest Asia, driving deeply into Nubia, a region of the Upper (southern) Nile that the brown-skinned Egyptians termed "the land of the blacks," and battling the Hittites of Anatolia (modern Turkey) for control of Syria-Palestine. Imperial adventure and expansion produced temporary prosperity and growth at home, especially in the fifteenth century. The art and literature of the Eighteenth Dynasty reveal a world of opulence and a society whose elites enjoyed the good life to the fullest.

Over this society presided pharaoh, still revered as a god-king on earth, and over pharaoh ruled Amon-Re, a heavenly father. By the sixteenth century the chief god of Egypt was clearly Amon-Re, a composite of Amon (or Amun or Amen), a god of wind, and Re (or Ra), a sun deity and one of Egypt's oldest and most revered gods. Amon originally had been an obscure local god of Thebes, but the rise to power of a new ruling family from Thebes brought him to prominence and resulted in his identification with Re. The Hymn to Amon-Re that follows was composed between 1550 and 1350 B.C., at the height of Egypt's imperial greatness.

QUESTIONS FOR ANALYSIS

1. In what ways is Amon-Re distinguished from other gods? What do you infer from this?
2. Where is there evidence of Egypt's new imperialism in this hymn?
3. In what ways does this hymn reveal a society that sees the world as harmonious and the gods as beneficent?
4. Compare this Egyptian view of the world with that of Mesopotamia.

Adoration of Amon-Re, the Bull Residing in Heliopolis,[1] chief of all gods, the good god, the beloved who gives life to all that is warm and to all good cattle.

Hail to thee, Amon-Re,
Lord of the Thrones of the Two Lands,
    presiding over Karnak,[2]

---

[1] The "city of the sun." This city, sacred to Re, was located near Memphis, the ancient capital of the Old Kingdom.

[2] The great temple of Amon at Karnak was located across the Nile from Thebes. It is one of the world's most extensive religious complexes.

Bull of His Mother,³ Presiding over His
 Fields!
Far-reaching of stride, presiding over
 Upper Egypt,
The Lord of the Madjoi and ruler of Punt,⁴
Eldest of heaven, first-born of earth,
Lord of what is, enduring in all things,
 enduring in all things.
Unique in his nature like the fluid of the
 gods,⁵

The goodly bull of the Ennead,⁶ chief of all
 gods,
The lord of truth and father of the gods.
Who made mankind and created the
 beasts,
Lord of what is, who created the fruit tree,
Made herbage, and gave life to cattle.
The goodly daemon⁷ whom Ptah⁸ made,

The goodly beloved youth to whom the
 gods give praise,
Who made what is below and what is
 above,
Who illuminates the Two Lands
And crosses the heavens in peace:⁹
The King of Upper and Lower Egypt: Re,
 the triumphant,

Chief of the Two Lands,
Great of strength, lord of reverence,
The chief one, who made the entire earth.
More distinguished in nature than any
 other god,
In whose beauty the gods rejoice,
To whom is given jubilation in the
 Per-wer,¹⁰
Who is given ceremonial appearance in the
 Per-nezer.¹¹
Whose fragrance the gods love, when he
 comes from Punt,
Rich in perfume, when he comes down
 from Madjoi,
The Beautiful of Face who comes from
 God's Land.¹²
The gods fawn at his feet,
According as they recognize his majesty as
 their lord,
The lord of fear, great of dread,
Rich in might, terrible of appearances,
Flourishing in offerings and making
 provisions.
Jubilation to thee who made the gods,
Raised the heavens and laid down the
 ground!

Making a Living in Ancient Egypt
▼▼▼

5 ▼ THE SATIRE ON THE TRADES

**We would be greatly mistaken if we viewed the ancient Egyptians as a people
so preoccupied with death and the afterlife that they had little concern with the**

---

³As sun god, Amon-Re recreated himself daily.
⁴Regions of the south and southeast.
⁵According to one Egyptian creation myth, Re created the gods with his spittle.
⁶The nine chief deities of Heliopolis.
⁷God or spirit.
⁸The creator god of Memphis.
⁹Re sails across the heavens each day.

¹⁰Literally, the "Great House." This was the religious capital of Upper Egypt, where the god-king presided as priest. The word *pharaoh* is derived from this term.
¹¹Lower Egypt's counterpart to the Per-wer. Each land retained its separate identity. Hence the king had two official palaces, one in each land, and elaborate ceremonies for the king's coronation and death were held in each land, each with its own ritual and insignia.
¹²The east, land of the rising sun.

affairs of this world. The literature and art of Egypt provide many glimpses into everyday life, and one of the best in this regard is a standard exercise piece for student scribes known as *The Satire on the Trades*. The work, copied by generations of boys learning the craft of writing, originated in the Middle Kingdom or earlier. Despite its heavy-handed attempts at humor, this description of the wretchedness of all nonscribal activities gives a good overview of the types of employment in which Egyptians were engaged.

QUESTIONS FOR ANALYSIS

1. According to the father, what attributes do all these nonscribal trades share?
2. What are the presumed advantages of the scribe's profession?
3. Can you find evidence of primitive factories?
4. How labor intensive does work appear to be in this society?
5. Does this seem to be a fair picture of the dichotomy that existed in ancient society between the literate and the illiterate?
6. How would you characterize the economy of Egypt as revealed in this text?

The beginning of the instruction which a man of the ship's cabin, whose name was Duauf's son Khety, made for his son, whose name was Pepy, as he was journeying upstream to the Residence City, to put him into the Writing School among the children of officials, in the lower part of the Residence City.[1] Then he said to him:

"I have seen how the laborer is belabored — you should set your heart in pursuit of writing. And I have observed how one may be rescued from his duties — behold, there is nothing which surpasses writing. . . .

"I shall make you love writing more than your own mother. . . . It is greater than any other office; there is not its like in the land. If he[2] began to prosper when he was only a child, men greet him respectfully. . . .

"I have seen the metalworker at his work at the mouth of his furnace. His fingers were

somewhat like crocodiles,[3] he stank more than fish-roe."

Every craftsman that wields the adze,[4] he is wearier than a hoeman. His field is the wood, and his job is the metal. At night, though he is released, he does more than his arms can really do. . . .

The fashioner of costly stones seeks for skill in every kind of hard stone. When he has fully completed things, his arms are destroyed, and he is weary. When he sits down at the going in of Re,[5] his thighs and his back are cramped.

The barber is still shaving at the end of dusk. . . . He gives himself from street to street, to seek out those whom he may shave.[6] Thus if he is valiant his arms will fill his belly. . . .

The itinerant merchant sails downstream to the Delta[7] to get trade for himself. When he has done more than his arms can really do,

---

[1] The father, who seems to be of no high social or economic standing, and his son are traveling south to the capital of Thebes and its royal scribal school.
[2] A scribe.
[3] Tough and wrinkled.
[4] A carpenter.
[5] Sunset.
[6] He bears the burden of hustling around town to find people to shave.
[7] Sails north to Lower Egypt.

the gnats have slain him, the sand flies have made him miserably miserable. Then there is inflammation.[8]

The small building contractor carries mud.[9] . . . He is dirtier than vines or pigs, from treading under his mud. His clothes are stiff with clay; his leather belt is going to ruin. Entering into the wind, he is miserable. His lamp goes out, though still in good condition. He pounds with his feet; he crushes with his own self, muddying the court of every house, when the water of the streets has flooded.

Let me tell you also of the builder of walls. His sides ache, since he must be outside in a treacherous wind. . . . His arms are destroyed with technical work; every calculation of his is different.[10] What he eats is the bread of his fingers,[11] and he washes himself only once a season. He is simply wretched through and through. . . . As for food, he must give it to his house, for his children are very many.

The gardener brings vegetables . . . upon his neck. Early in the morning he must water the vegetables and in the evening the vines. . . . "The sand fly of his mother"[12] is his name. . . .

The tenant-farmer, his reckonings go on forever.[13] . . . Wearier is he than a wayfarer of the Delta. Yet he is a picked man: his safety is a safety from lions.[14] His sides ache, as if heaven and earth were in them. . . .

The weaver in the workshops, he is worse than a woman, with his thighs against his belly. He cannot breathe the open air. If he cuts short the day of weaving, he is beaten with fifty thongs. He must give food to the doorkeeper to let him see the light of day.

The arrow-maker, he is very miserable as he goes out into the desert.[15] Greater is that which he gives to his donkey than its work thereafter is worth. Great is that which he gives to him who is in the meadows, who sets him on the way. When he reaches his home in the evening, the traveling has cut him down.[16]

The courier goes out to a foreign country after he has made over his property to his children, being afraid of lions and Asiatics. And what of him, when he is in Egypt? When he arrives thence from the meadows and he reaches his home in the evening, the traveling has cut him down. His house is only an apron of brick.[17] He does not return happy of heart.

The embalmer, his fingers are foul, for the odor thereof is that of corpses. His eyes burn from the greatness of the heat. He could not oppose his own daughter.[18] He spends the day cutting up old rags[19] so that clothing is an abomination to him.

The cobbler, he is very badly off, carrying his equipment forever. His safety is a safety from corpses, as he bites into the leather.

The laundryman launders on the river bank, a neighbor of the crocodile. When a father[20] comes out of the greasy waters, he could not oppose his own daughter.[21] . . .

Let me tell you also of the fish-catcher. He is more miserable than any other profession. Behold, there is nothing in his work on the river, mingled with the crocodiles. . . . He cannot even say: "A crocodile is waiting there," for fear has made him blind. . . .[22]

Behold, there is no profession free of a boss — except for the scribe: he is the boss.

---

[8]Probably the insect-borne fever of the delta.
[9]To make mud bricks.
[10]He cannot keep proper count.
[11]He is so hungry he sucks on his fingers.
[12]A term of derision.
[13]He has to render account to the landlord forever. He is bound to the soil for life.
[14]A sarcastic jibe at the farmer who leads an "unmanly" life of peace.
[15]To gather flints.

[16]His traveling has worn him down and also cost him more than its worth.
[17]His house has been reduced to a shell.
[18]He is so weary from labor that his daughter could beat him in a fight.
[19]For strips with which to wrap the mummified corpses.
[20]The laundryman.
[21]See note 18.
[22]His fear of crocodiles severely hampers his efforts to gather his full quota of fish. But who is going to accept this as an excuse?

But if you know writing, then it will go better with you than in these professions which I have set before you. . . . A day in school is of advantage to you. The eternity of its work is like that of the mountains.[23]

▼▼▼

China: Xia, Shang, and Western Zhou

The study of history has been one of China's most revered and continuous traditions for well over two thousand years. By the time of their greatest historian, Sima Qian (ca 145–90 B.C.), the Chinese had evolved a detailed chronology for Chinese civilization that reached back into the early third millennium. According to this vision of their past, the Chinese traced their civilization to the Yellow Emperor, who established an organized state around 2700 B.C. He was followed by four other monarchs, each of whom was chosen for merit rather than by birth. Following these five predynastic "Sage Emperors," the Xia family established China's first royal dynasty and ruled from 2205 to 1766 B.C. After Xia's collapse, the Shang Dynasty (1766–1122 B.C.) held power, until it gave way to the Zhou Dynasty (1122–256 B.C.).

Until the late 1920s we had no irrefutable evidence of the Xia and Shang dynasties, and Western historians generally dismissed them as myths. The work of archeologists over the past sixty years, however, has proved beyond any shadow of a doubt that Shang royal rule was a historical reality, and some quite recent excavations strongly suggest that the Xia Dynasty also existed, possibly as early as 2200 or 2100 B.C. The most recent archeological evidence available seems to indicate that Xia, Shang, and Zhou were originally three coexisting centers of civilization in North China, and the Shang and Zhou "successions" of the eighteenth and twelfth centuries B.C. were shifts of military dominance from one state and family of royal warlords to another. The state of our current knowledge of earliest Chinese civilization is that northern China most likely had civilized centers of government as early as the late 2000s B.C., but the details still largely elude us. Most of the stories related by Sima Qian and other classical Chinese historians about the predynastic Sage Emperors and China's first royal dynasties still seem to most modern historians to be more the stuff of legend than the product of sober research.

Our knowledge of the Xia state and its age of predominance is exceedingly sketchy at best. We know much more about the Shang, thanks to modern archeologists who have unearthed magnificent bronze ceremonial vessels, two capital cities, and a primitive form of Chinese ideographic writing on what are known as *oracle bones*. Although scholars can read them, the oracle bones provide little detail about the social and political history of the Shang because they served only one purpose: magical divination of the future. China's earliest extant literary and political documents date from the age of Zhou rule.

---

[23]What is written lasts forever.

Because of these records we know much more about the Zhou Dynasty than about the Xia and Shang. The era of Zhou rule, which lasted approximately nine hundred years, fell into two periods: Western and Eastern Zhou. The age of Western Zhou witnessed a fairly strong feudal monarchy ruling a number of dependent vassal states. This ended in 771 B.C. when a group of rebellious northern nobles killed King Yu and overran the capital city, Xian. In 770 the royal heir and those members of the court who survived fled eastward to the auxiliary capital, Loyang, where the Zhou continued to reside as kings until 256 B.C. The kings of Eastern Zhou never enjoyed the power of their western forebears, and for five hundred years they reigned over but did not rule a kingdom in which real power resided in the hands of local lords.

The Mandate of Heaven
▼▼▼

6 ▼ *THE CLASSIC OF HISTORY*

The *Shu Jing*, or *Classic of History*, is the oldest complete work among what are known as the five Confucian classics. (See Chapter 4, source 25, for a biography of Confucius.) The five classics were canonized as the basic elements of the Confucian educational system during the second century B.C., when the books were reconstructed by order of several emperors of the Han Dynasty (202 B.C.– A.D. 220). Although Han scholars probably refashioned elements of the *Shu Jing*, the work was already ancient in Confucius's day, and the book, as we have received it, is probably essentially the same text that Confucius (551–479 B.C.) knew, studied, and accepted as an authentic record of Chinese civilization.

Despite its title, the *Classic of History* is not a work of historical interpretation or narration. Rather, it is a collection of documents spanning some seventeen hundred years of Chinese history and legend, from 2357 to 631 B.C. Many of the documents, however, are the spurious creations of much later periods and therefore reflect the attitudes of those subsequent eras.

The document that appears here was composed in the age of Zhou but purports to be the advice given by the faithful Yi Yin to King Tai Jia, second of the Shang kings. According to the story behind this document, when the first Shang king, Cheng Tang, died around 1753, his chief minister Yi Yin took it upon himself to instruct the new young king in the ways and duties of kingship and the workings of the Mandate of Heaven.

The Mandate of Heaven was a political-social philosophy that served as the basic Chinese explanation for the success and failure of monarchs and states down to the end of the empire in A.D. 1912. Whenever a dynasty fell, the reason invariably offered by China's sages was that it had lost the moral right to rule, which is given by Heaven alone. In this context Heaven did not mean a personal god but a cosmic all-pervading power. Most historians today agree that the theory of the Mandate of Heaven was an invention of the Zhou to justify their overthrow of the Shang. The king, after all, was the father of his people, and paternal authority was the basic cement of Chinese society from earliest times. Rebellion against a father, therefore, needed extraordinary justification.

QUESTIONS FOR ANALYSIS

1. How does a monarch lose the Mandate of Heaven, and what are the consequences of this loss?
2. What evidence can you find here of the Chinese cult of reverence for the ancestors?
3. What evidence can you find to support the conclusion that classical Chinese political philosophy perceived the state as an extended family?
4. What sort of harmony does the monarch maintain?
5. Would Yi Yin accept the notion that there can be a distinction between a ruler's private morality and public policies?
6. What does the theory of the Mandate of Heaven suggest about the nature of Chinese society?
7. American politicians often promise "innovative answers to the challenges of tomorrow." What would Yi Yin think about such an approach to statecraft? What would Yi Yin think about modern politicians who attempt to appear youthful? What would he think of popular opinion polls?
8. Compare the Chinese vision of its ideal monarch with Egyptian and Mesopotamian views of kingship. Despite all their obvious cultural differences, did each of these societies expect its king to perform essentially the same task? If so, what was that task?

In the twelfth month of the first year . . . Yi Yin sacrificed to the former king, and presented the heir-king reverently before the shrine of his grandfather. All the princes from the domain of the nobles and the royal domain were present; all the officers also, each continuing to discharge his particular duties, were there to receive the orders of the chief minister. Yi Yin then clearly described the complete virtue of the Meritorious Ancestor[1] for the instruction of the young king.

He said, "Oh! of old the former kings of Xia cultivated earnestly their virtue, and then there were no calamities from Heaven. The spirits of the hills and rivers likewise were all in tran-

quility; and the birds and beasts, the fishes and tortoises, all enjoyed their existence according to their nature. But their descendant did not follow their example, and great Heaven sent down calamities, employing the agency of our ruler[2] who was in possession of its favoring appointment. The attack on Xia may be traced to the orgies in Ming Tiao.[3] . . . Our king of Shang brilliantly displayed his sagely prowess; for oppression he substituted his generous gentleness; and the millions of the people gave him their hearts. Now your Majesty is entering on the inheritance of his virtue; — all depends on how you commence your reign. To set up love, it is for you to love your relations; to set

[1]Cheng Tang, founder of the Shang Dynasty.
[2]Cheng Tang (see note 1).

[3]According to legend, Jie, the last Xia king, held notorious orgies at Ming Tiao.

up respect, it is for you to respect your elders. The commencement is in the family and the state. . . .

"Oh! the former king began with careful attention to the bonds that hold men together. He listened to expostulation, and did not seek to resist it; he conformed to the wisdom of the ancients; occupying the highest position, he displayed intelligence; occupying an inferior position, he displayed his loyalty; he allowed the good qualities of the men whom he employed and did not seek that they should have every talent. . . .

"He extensively sought out wise men, who should be helpful to you, his descendant and heir. He laid down the punishments for officers, and warned those who were in authority, saying, 'If you dare to have constant dancing in your palaces, and drunken singing in your chambers, — that is called the fashion of sorcerers; if you dare to set your hearts on wealth and women, and abandon yourselves to wandering about or to the chase, — that is called the fashion of extravagance; if you dare to

despise sage words, to resist the loyal and upright, to put far from you the aged and virtuous, and to seek the company of . . . youths, — that is called the fashion of disorder. Now if a high noble or officer be addicted to one of these three fashions with their ten evil ways, his family will surely come to ruin; if the prince of a country be so addicted, his state will surely come to ruin. The minister who does not try to correct such vices in the sovereign shall be punished with branding.' . . .

"Oh! do you, who now succeed to the throne, revere these warnings in your person. Think of them! — sacred counsels of vast importance, admirable words forcibly set forth! The ways of Heaven are not invariable: — on the good-doer it sends down all blessings, and on the evil-doer it sends down all miseries. Do you but be virtuous, be it in small things or in large, and the myriad regions will have cause for rejoicing. If you not be virtuous, be it in large things or in small, it will bring the ruin of your ancestral temple."

Courtship and Marriage
▼▼▼

7 ▼ *THE CLASSIC OF ODES*

The *Shih Jing*, or *Classic of Odes*, is another of the five Confucian Classics that served as the basic texts of an educational system that molded China's leaders for more than two thousand years. The work consists of 305 poetic songs, covering a variety of topics from love to war, whose dates of composition largely fall into the period of about 900 to 600 B.C. The book ultimately became "Confucian" because Confucius and his many generations of disciples used the songs as texts for moral instruction. No good reason exists to believe that Confucius had a hand in crafting any of the poems or even in assembling the collection.

The following ballads reveal several important customs, attitudes, and realities relating to love, courtship, and marriage in early China. Traditional Chinese society revolved around the family to the point that all larger social and political units were viewed as its extensions. In any society in which family ties are the primary bond, courtship and marriage assume great significance, and as far back as the record goes, the Chinese have consistently exhibited a preoccupation with the proper rites of courtship and maintaining stable marriages.

The first ode concerns a woman who resists the attempt of a man to marry her and argues her case before a court of law; the second poem is analogous, insofar as it is a widow's protest against being urged to remarry. The third ballad recounts the affection a husband feels for his bride. The fourth song reveals a woman's change of mood upon her husband's return. In the fifth ode a man compares his middle-aged spouse with some young women whom he encounters.

QUESTIONS FOR ANALYSIS

1. On what apparent grounds has the woman in poem 1 refused to marry her suitor? Does she believe she has a good case? What do you infer from this?
2. From what you can infer from poem 1, how seriously were betrothal vows taken normally?
3. Why does the widow in poem 2 refuse to remarry? What does her refusal suggest about the power and status of widows in Zhou society?
4. What does poem 3 tell us about the traditional Chinese formula for a successful marriage?
5. Normally, first marriages in traditional China were arranged between the families of the bride and groom. Notwithstanding this, was it possible for the prospective partners to have some control over whom they would marry?
6. Women of high class tended to have more power and freedom in the ages of Shang and Zhou than did Chinese women a thousand years later. What evidence is there in these poems of female power?
7. Did the Chinese believe that love was possible within an arranged marriage? What is the evidence for your answer?

1. I WILL NOT MARRY YOU

The dew thick on the wet paths lay;
Thither at early dawn my way
I might have taken; but I said, "Nay.
The dew is thick, at home I'll stay." . . .

You say this trial is a proof
That I exchanged betrothal vows.
But though you've made me here appear in
    court,
Yet at betrothal what you did fell
    short. . . .

You say this trial proves my vows
Of plighted troth were perfect all.
But though to court you've forced me here
    to come,

My will is firm; — I'll not with you go
home.

2. NO SECOND MARRIAGE FOR ME

In the mid river that cypress boat floats
    free,
While friends a second marriage press on
    me,
I see my husband's youthful forehead there,
And on it the twin tufts of falling hair.
Rather than wed again I'll die, I swear!
O mother dear, O Heaven supreme, why
    should

You not allow my vow, and aid my purpose
good?

Near to the bank that cypress boat floats
free,
While friends a second marriage press on
me.
He was my only one, with forehead fair,
And on it the twin tufts of falling hair.
Till death to shun the evil thing I swear!
O mother dear, O Heaven supreme, why
should
You not allow my vow, and aid my purpose
good?

3. YOUNG LOVE

With axle creaking, all on fire I went,
To fetch my young and lovely bride.
No thirst or hunger pangs my bosom rent,
I only longed to have *her* by my side.
I feast with her, whose virtue fame had
told,
Nor need we friends our rapture to behold.

The long-tailed pheasants surest cover find,
Amid the forest on the plain.
Here from my virtuous bride, of noble
mind,
And person tall, I wisdom gain.
I praise her while we feast, and to her say,
"The love I bear you ne'er will know decay.

"Poor we may be; spirits and foods fine
My humble means will not afford.
But what we have, we'll taste and not
repine;[1]
From us will come no grumbling word.
And though to you no virtue I can add,
Yet we will sing and dance, in spirit glad.

"I oft ascend that lofty ridge with toil,
And hew large branches from the oaks;
Then of their leafy glory them I spoil,
And fagots form with vigorous strokes.
Returning tired, your matchless grace I
see,

And my whole soul dissolves in ecstasy.

"To the high hills I looked, and urged each
steed;
The great road next was smooth and plain.
Up hill, o'er dale, I never slackened speed;
Like lutestring sounded every rein.
I knew, my journey ended, I should come
To you, sweet bride, the comfort of my
home."

4. MY BELOVED RETURNS

Cold is the wind, fast falls the rain,
The cock aye shrilly crows.
But I have seen my lord again; —
Now must my heart repose.

Whistles the wind, patters the rain,
The cock's crow far resounds.
But I have seen my lord again,
And healed are my heart's wounds.

All's dark amid the wind and rain,
Ceaseless the cock's clear voice!
But I have seen my lord again; —
Should not my heart rejoice?

5. MATURE LOVE

My path forth from the east gate lay,
Where cloudlike moved the girls at play.
Numerous are they, as clouds so bright,
But not on them my heart's thoughts light.
Dressed in a thin white silk, with coiffure
gray,
Is she, my wife, my joy in life's low way.

Forth by the covering wall's high tower,
I went, and saw, like rush in flower,
Each flaunting girl. Brilliant are they,
But not with them my heart's thoughts
stay.
In thin white silk, with headdress madder-
dyed,
Is she, my sole delight, 'foretime my bride.

---

[1]Complain.

▼▼▼

Mute Testimony

Some of the world's earliest civilizations have left written records that we cannot yet decipher and may never be able to read. These include India's Harappan civilization, which was centered in the Indus valley from before 2500 to some time after 1700 B.C.; the Minoan civilization of the Aegean island of Crete, which flourished from roughly 2500 to about 1400 B.C.; and the African civilization of Kush, located directly south of Egypt, which reached its age of greatness after 800 B.C. but with much earlier origins as a state. For many other early civilizations and cultures we have as yet uncovered no written records. This is the case of the mysterious peoples who, between approximately 6000 B.C. and the first century A.D., painted and carved thousands of pieces of art on the rocks of Tassili n' Ajjer in what is today the central Sahara Desert. It is also true of the Moche state of the northwest coast of South America that appeared around the first century A.D.

The following pieces of artifactual evidence provide glimpses into these often forgotten cultures. As is always the case when dealing with nonverbal sources, however, the historian discovers that such clues from the past raise more questions than they answer.

Bringing in the Sheaves
▼▼▼

8 ▼ A TASSILI ROCK PAINTING

Tassili n' Ajjer is today a desiccated, largely uninhabited plateau deep in the heart of southern Algeria's Sahara Desert. Its name, however, which translates as "plateau of the rivers," suggests a past quite different from its current condition. Before the Sahara crept into the region about two thousand years ago, Tassili n' Ajjer was a lush area that supported a wide variety of animal species and human cultures. The latter left behind a rich artistic record of over six thousand years of human habitation on the plateau.

In 1956 an expedition of French scholars studied and copied more than four thousand rock paintings at Tassili and an equally impressive number of rock carvings. The art they recorded reflects the four major cultural epochs of the people who lived there. The earliest examples of rock paintings reach back to before 6000 B.C. and were the products of a pre-agricultural, hunter-gatherer society. The rock art produced from about 5000 to around 1200 B.C. was the work of a pastoral people whose cattle figure prominently in their paintings.

Tassili Rock Painting: Grain Harvesters

Around 1200 B.C. the horse and chariot appear in Tassili's rock art, evidence of significant new equine technology due to influences from the Mediterranean. Finally, as the desert was expanding, the domesticated single-humped Arabian camel appears on the faces of these rocks, signifying yet another and now final stage of cultural development for the terminally endangered people of this area.

The painting that appears here is generally interpreted as portraying a group of people harvesting wild grains. It might date anywhere from 4000 to 1500 B.C.

QUESTIONS FOR ANALYSIS

1. What appears to be the sex of the harvesters?
2. What does your answer suggest about gender roles in this society?
3. If these are wild grains that are being gathered, what would be the next cultural step?
4. Based on your answer to question 3, what do you think was the likelihood that agriculture developed indigenously at Tassili?

Cultural Impressions
▼▼▼

9 ▼ *INDUS, MESOPOTAMIAN, AND*
   CRETAN SEALS

The stamps and seals that grace the many documents certifying who we are and what we have attained have their origins in the carved magic amulets of prehistory. As official signatures and tokens of authority, seals and stamps have been used by individuals and states since the dawn of civilization. In Mesopotamia carved stone cylinder seals that were rolled into soft clay were used at Uruk and other Sumerian cities as early as 3500 B.C. and continued to be produced in large numbers throughout Southwest Asia for the next three thousand years. As papyrus and parchment came to replace clay as preferred writing surfaces, stamps and stamp seals replaced cylinder seals.

Ancient Southwest Asians did not have a monopoly on the use of these marks of ownership, authenticity, and official approval. More than two thousand stamp seals and seal impressions have been found at Harappan sites in the Indus Valley of what is today the nation of Pakistan. Collectively, the seals contain some four hundred different characters of what appears to be a pictographic form of writing. However, scholars have been unable to crack the code represented by these signs. Happily, the seals contain more than undecipherable words; they contain carved images, and those images allow us to infer something about this largely mysterious civilization of ancient India.

The first grouping contains six modern drawings of Indus seal impressions that date from the period 2100–1750 B.C., the age of Harappan cultural maturity. Seal 1 depicts a hairy person holding two tigers by the throat. Seal 2 portrays a horned, tailed, and cloven-footed individual grappling with a horned tiger under a tree. Seal 3 depicts two unicorn (single-horned) animal heads twisted around what appears to be a stylized pipal, or fig, tree, the sacred tree of India. Seal 4 shows four human figures somersaulting forward and backward over the raised horns of a bull. Seal 5 shows a humped bull, often called a Brahman bull. Seal 6 presents a male individual with a deeply furrowed or painted face who is wearing a water buffalo-horn headdress, numerous bangles, bracelets, and a V-shaped collar or necklace. The individual is sitting with his knees angled to either side and the soles of his feet pressed together in front of him. His arms extend away from his body and his hands rest on his knees, with fingers pointed downward. Surrounding this individual are wild animals: a rhinoceros and water buffalo to his left, an elephant and tiger to his right; beneath him are two antelopelike creatures (one is largely broken off; only its horns remain). A stick-figure human also stands or walks to his right.

For reasons of comparison, consider the second group of four seal impressions. Impression 7 is taken from a southern Mesopotamian cylinder seal that dates to somewhere between 2600 and 2350 B.C. It shows a hairy hero, probably Enkidu, Gilgamesh's companion (source 1), holding two vanquished lions. Item

8 is also southern Mesopotamian and from the same period. It depicts a creature that is half bull and half human grasping two lions. Impression 9 is of a cylinder seal from Agade (Akkad) in central Mesopotamia that was crafted in the period 2340–2180 B.C. It presents the image of a bull-man on the left and a hairy hero on the right. Each holds a rampant bull by the mane and tail. The forelegs of each bull touch the top of a stylized mountain and what might be a sacred tree on the mountain. The final impression (10) is of a seal from the island civilization of Crete that dates to roughly 1550–1500 B.C. and depicts two bulls and two acrobats. One athlete has just vaulted over a bull, while the second bull-leaper stands ready to vault.

QUESTIONS FOR ANALYSIS

1. Seals 2–10 contain horned figures. What do you suppose the horn symbolized to these societies? Why, of all horned creatures, do you think the bull figures so prominently in these seals? Based on your answers, what can you infer about the religious and social values of these societies?
2. Consider the hairy males in seals 1, 7, and 9. What does hairiness seem to symbolize in each instance? Again, what do you infer about their religious and social values from this?
3. Consider the central figure in seal 6. Does his posture seem casual or natural to you? What does your answer suggest about the individual and his function? Consider his dress and the figures that surround him. Do these suggest humanity or divinity? If a human, what is his class? If a god, what sort of god?
4. What can you infer from these seals about cultural contacts and influences? Who *might* have influenced whom, and how? On a map, trace the plausible routes of cultural exchange.

Sacred Kingship Along the Nile
▼▼▼

10 ▼ TWO TEMPLE RELIEFS

It is unclear whether several of the Indus seals we have studied portray humans or deities, but this is not the case with the two temple reliefs (raised carvings on flat backgrounds) that follow. The piece on the left is Egyptian and dates from the thirteenth century B.C. Located at the temple of King Seti I at Abydos in Upper Egypt, it portrays, from right to left, Horus the falcon god, King Seti, and the goddess Isis (see source 3). We will use it solely for comparison with the relief on the right. This piece of religious art is Kushite and dates from after 300 B.C. It is a small fragment (6½ inches) of a temple tablet from Meroë, a Nubian city considerably distant from Abydos. It portrays a Nubian king of Kush and the lion god Apedemak.

Indus Seals

Mesopotamian Seals

Cretan Seal

Temple Relief: Seti I and Horus

The Nubians, who were black Africans inhabiting the region directly south of Egypt, were drawn into the orbit of their powerful neighbor to the north at an early date. Yet, while they borrowed from the Egyptians, the Nubians managed to retain their indigenous culture. Around 800 B.C. the Nubians created the independent kingdom of Kush and around 730 B.C. were strong enough to conquer Egypt, which Kushite pharaohs ruled for nearly a century. After being driven out of Egypt by the Assyrians, the Kushites eventually established a new capital for their kingdom at Meroë on the Middle Nile. Between about 350 B.C. and the early fourth century A.D., Kush was a major economic power in Northeast Africa, largely because of Meroë's rich iron deposits.

In the relief on the right, one of those mighty monarchs of Kush stands face to face with the Nubians' most powerful deity. Unfortunately, we cannot decipher the writing above each figure, so we can only guess at the meaning of this scene. Perhaps the relief of Seti I provides a vital clue. There, Horus, the divine son of Isis, is handing the scepter of power to Seti, who as long as he lives on earth will be identified with Horus, upon whose throne he sits. Note that the Meroitic tablet also portrays both god and king with what appear to be scepters.

QUESTIONS FOR ANALYSIS

1. Do these two artifactual clues allow us to infer anything about the nature of royal power in Kush?

Temple Relief: Kushite King and Apedemak

2. What do they tell us about the balance the Kushites struck between accepting Egyptian influences and retaining traditional Nubian ways?

The God Who Descended from the Mountains
▼▼▼

11 ▼ A MOCHE CERAMIC

To most educated people, pre-Columbian civilization in Peru is synonymous with the Inca culture of the Andean highlands. Actually, the Incas, whom the Spanish conquistadors met and conquered, were newcomers and only the most

Moche Effigy Pot

recent participants in what was already some 2,500 years of Peruvian civilization. More than a thousand years before the rise of the Inca Empire, a people whom we call the Moche, or Mochica, constructed a highly developed civilization along the coastal desert plain of northern Peru. This region is one of the driest places on the face of the earth, receiving an average of far less than an inch of annual rainfall. It is fed, however, by a number of rivers that rise in the towering Andes to the east and flow down to the Pacific Ocean. One of those rivers is the Rio Moche. The fertility of the Moche Valley allowed its inhabitants to carve out a powerful state and a distinctive civilization that was at the height of its creativity in the period A.D. 200–750.

Moche artisans perfected the craft of casting and alloying a variety of soft metals, allowing them to create some of the finest gold, silver, and copper artifacts ever produced in antiquity. The most distinctive and brilliant artistic products of this culture, however, were made from a humbler material — clay. The Moche people produced vast numbers of finely crafted ceramics, particularly effigy vessels that represented a wide variety of deities, humans, animals, vegetables, and structures, and large numbers of these have survived. More than 90 percent of all Moche art and craftwork uncovered by modern archeologists consists of these magnificent ceramics — all made without benefit of the potter's wheel.

No effigy pot, by itself, tells the historian much about Moche culture, but cumulatively they tell a compelling story of the daily lives, beliefs, and ceremonies of the people who created these earthenware masterpieces. Although a single example of Moche art might more easily confuse than illuminate, the artifact that appears here does provide some interesting insights into the Moche vision of the world.

This vessel is molded into a stylized mountain from which two deities emerge. In the center is a Moche god, who wears a sunrise headdress from which a snake's head projects, and he is flanked by two snakes. To his right is a fanged god in jaguar headdress and wearing a living snake belt that curls beneath him.

QUESTIONS FOR ANALYSIS

1. Note the indentation or cave from which the god on the right emerges. What is his apparent relationship with the mountain?
2. Consider this same god's headdress. What is the message? (Keep in mind the geographic relationship of the mountains to the Moche Valley.)
3. Does the geographic situation of the Moche Valley provide any clue to what the four snakes that flow from the mountain represent?
4. Based on your answers to questions 1–3, what do you conclude this god's main functions were?
5. What about the feline qualities of the god on the far left? What does he seem to represent?
6. Which of these two gods seems more remote and lofty? Why? Which seems more active and closer to humanity? Why? Which of these is the creator god? What are the apparent functions of the other god?
7. Which deity was probably more loved and prayed to? Why?

Chapter 2

▼▼▼

New Peoples

The oldest town yet excavated by archeologists is Jericho, which has been inhabited, almost continuously, for the past 11,000 years. Around 8000 B.C. this site, immediately west of the River Jordan in lands today occupied by the state of Israel, covered more than eight acres and supported a population of more than 3,000. Most impressive of all are the town's massive watchtower, walls, and encircling ditch, which serve as silent evidence of the residents' fear of outsiders.

That fear was well based. Archeological evidence shows that Jericho suffered destruction on several occasions, and it is easy to imagine that some of those catastrophes were the handiwork of invading nomads, attracted by the city's wealth.

The tension between wandering pastoral people, tending herds of domesticated animals, and settled farmers, who became the backbone of civilization, is as old as agriculture itself, and it continued to be a major factor in global history into the fifteenth century A.D. To be sure, there were many mutually beneficial relationships between civilized communities and the pastoralists who wandered their borders. However, fringe peoples who served as mercenary soldiers, traders, and carriers of new ideas could also be formidable foes, threatening the very existence of some civilizations.

Afro-Eurasian civilizations were subjected to two periods of especially intense pressure from nomadic outsiders prior to 1000 B.C. Around 1800 B.C. nomads living on the Iranian plateau perfected the two-wheeled chariot. Within the relatively short span of several centuries, groups of pastoralists used this new master weapon to establish a number of warrior kingdoms as far west as Greece and at least as far east as northern India. These peoples included the Greeks of Mycenae, the Hittites of Anatolia, the Kassites and Mitanni of Mesopotamia, the Hyksos of Egypt, and the Aryans of India.

The second age of major nomadic disturbance took place around 1200 B.C. as an expanding knowledge of iron metallurgy made it possible for new fringe groups to challenge many of the now old and tired chariot kingdoms. With plentiful and therefore cheap weapons available to both their external and internal enemies, a number of these civilized societies found themselves fighting for their very survival, and several succumbed. Mycenaean Greece slipped back into a precivilized state, as it was overwhelmed by waves of ruder Greek cousins; the mighty Hittite empire was wiped out and soon became a faded memory. Other regions rode out these invasions with greater resilience. Egypt successfully fought off the invaders but only at great cost. The land of Syria-Palestine experienced invasion and settlement by Philistines, Hebrews, and others, but in the end it managed to absorb all without losing the essential elements of civilization.

Geographic isolation protected China from these Iron Age migrations. Iron would not arrive in China until the sixth century B.C. Around 1200 B.C., however, the chariot made its appearance in China and was used to great effect by the Zhou in their toppling of the Shang.

Around 1000 B.C. the general level of nomadic violence subsided for a while across Eurasia and North Africa, but the previous eight centuries had seen successive waves of nomads challenge, at times overwhelm, and in a few isolated instances eradicate centers of civilization.

▼▼▼

The Indo-Europeans

Sometime around 2000 B.C. pastoral people living on the steppes of western Asia, roughly in the area that lies north of the Caucasus Mountains, between the Black and Caspian seas, began to migrate out of their traditional grazing lands and, in successive waves, wandered into Europe, Asia Minor, Mesopotamia, Iran, and India. These bronze-armed nomads spoke a variety of related languages that shared a common origin in a prehistoric tongue scholars call *proto-Indo-European*. Through their migrations, these people eventually spread their family of languages from northern India to the British Isles. The fact that *Aryan*, *Eire* (the Gaelic name for the Republic of Ireland), and *Iran* derive from the common archaic root word *aryo*, which means "lord," eloquently attests to the extent of the ancient Indo-European wanderings and settlements.

Among the many significant waves of Indo-European newcomers, there were those whose tongue was Sanskrit and those who spoke an early form of Greek. The Sanskrit speakers moved eastward across the Hindu Kush mountain range and into the fertile Indus valley, where they encountered Harappan civilization. The Greek speakers moved westward into the Balkans, absorbing or displacing the native agricultural people they encountered.

Life from Death in Aryan India
▼▼▼

12 ▼ *THE RIG VEDA*

It is not totally clear whether the Aryans conquered and destroyed a vigorous Harappan civilization or, what seems more likely, took over a society already in eclipse. Whatever the case, by 1500 B.C. the Aryans were ruling northwest India as an illiterate warrior aristocracy, and the Harappan arts of writing and state-craft had disappeared. India would not reemerge into the light of history until around 600 B.C.

Because the early Aryans were a preliterate people, what little we know about them we derive from their oral tradition, which survives chiefly in four great collections of priestly hymns, chants, incantations, and ritual formulas known as the *Vedas*. *Veda* means "wisdom" or "knowledge," and the Aryans accepted these collections of sacred poetry as the eternal word of the gods.

The most celebrated and earliest of the four is the *Rig Veda*, a collection of 1,028 songs, which probably was compiled for the most part between 1200 and 900 B.C., although it contains many elements that stretch back to a time long before the Aryans arrived in India. This Sanskrit masterpiece remains, even today, one of the sacred books of Hinduism. It is also the earliest extant major work of literature in an Indo-European tongue, predating by several centuries the Homeric Greek epics.

As is common in preliterate societies, Aryan priests, known as *brahmins*, were trained to perform prodigious feats of memory. Generation after generation, they sang these songs and passed them on to those who followed. As a result, although the Vedas would not be written down until long after 1000 B.C., many of their songs reflect the religious, social, and political realities of Aryan life around 1500 B.C. or earlier. Conversely, other Vedic hymns were the products of much later centuries and mirror the more sophisticated culture of an emerging Indo-Aryan civilization.

The following two poems illustrate this dichotomy. The first celebrates the victory over Vritra, the dragon of drought, by Indra, the most prominent god in the *Rig Veda*. The second, which certainly is one of the latest hymns in the

Rig Veda, explains how all forms of life were generated when Purusha, the all-pervading universal spirit, was sacrificed to himself.

QUESTIONS FOR ANALYSIS

1. What did Indra accomplish by slaying Vritra? How does the theme of this hymn hint at the fact that the Aryans were becoming a settled agrarian people? What does the use of cattle imagery suggest about the values and economic structure of Aryan society?
2. What sort of god is Indra, and how would you characterize the society that worshiped him as its chief deity?
3. What evidence is there in the hymn to Purusha for the emergence of what would become the Hindu caste system, and how is that system explained and justified?
4. Can you find in the hymn to Purusha evidence of the basic Hindu concept of the unity of all life?
5. If Purusha brings forth all life by self-sacrifice, what does this suggest about the Indo-Aryan view of life and death? Is death a negation of life? Are they mutually exclusive states?
6. Compare Indra and Purusha as deities. In what ways do they represent significant historical changes that took place within Indo-Aryan society?

TO INDRA

I will declare the manly deeds of Indra, the first that he achieved, the thunder-wielder.

He slew the dragon,[1] then disclosed the waters, and cleft the channels of the mountain torrents.

He slew the dragon lying on the mountain: his heavenly bolt of thunder Twashtar[2] fashioned.

Like lowing cows in rapid flow descending, the waters glided downward to the ocean.

Impetuous as a bull, he chose the Soma,[3] and quaffed in threefold sacrifice the juices.

Maghavan[4] grasped the thunder for his weapon, and smote to death this firstborn of the dragons.

When, Indra, you had slain the dragons' firstborn, and overcome the charms of the enchanters,

Then, giving life to sun and dawn and heaven, you found not one foe to stand against you.

Indra with his own great and deadly thunder smote into pieces Vritra worst of Vritras.[5]

As trunks of trees, what time the axe has felled them, low on the earth so lies the prostrate dragon.

---

[1]Vritra. In slaying the dragon (clouds), Indra releases the waters that fall down as rain.
[2]The artisan of the gods.
[3]An intoxicating drink reserved for the gods.
[4]Lord Bountiful — another name for Indra.
[5]"Dragon, worst of dragons."

He, like a mad weak warrior,
challenged Indra, the great impetuous
many-slaying hero.

He, brooking not the clashing of the
weapons, crushed — Indra's foe — the
shattered forts in falling,[6]

Footless and handless still[7] he challenged Indra, who smote him with his
bolt between the shoulders.

Emasculated yet claiming manly vigor,
thus Vritra lay with scattered limbs
dissevered. . . .

Nothing availed him lightning, nothing
thunder, hailstorm or mist which he
had spread around him.[8]

When Indra and the dragon strove in
battle, Maghavan gained the victory for
ever. . . .

Indra is king of all that moves and
moves not, of creatures tame and
horned, the thunder-wielder.

Over all living men he rules as sovereign, containing all as spokes within
a rim.

TO PURUSHA

A thousand heads had Purusha,[9] a
thousand eyes, a thousand feet.

He covered earth on every side, and
spread ten fingers' breadth beyond.

This Purusha is all that yet has been
and all that is to be;

The lord of immortality which waxes
greater still by food.

So mighty is his greatness; yea, greater
than this is Purusha.

All creatures are one-fourth of him,
three-fourths eternal life in heaven.[10]

With three-fourths Purusha went up:
one-fourth of him again was here.

Thence he strode out to every side over
what eats not and what eats.

From him Viraj[11] was born; again Purusha from Viraj was born.

As soon as he was born he spread eastward and westward o'er the earth.

When gods prepared the sacrifice with
Purusha as their offering,

Its oil was spring, the holy gift was autumn; summer was the wood.

They balmed as victim on the grass[12]
Purusha born in earliest time.

With him the deities and all Sadhyas[13]
and Rishis[14] sacrificed.

From that great general sacrifice the
dripping fat was gathered up.

He formed the creatures of the air, and
animals both wild and tame.

From that great general sacrifice Richas
and Samahymns[15] were born:

---

[6]The clouds are pictured as forts imprisoning moisture.
[7]Vritra is serpentlike, lacking feet and hands.
[8]Vritra used magic to surround himself with storms and mist, but they failed him.
[9]Purusha, the all-pervading universal spirit and source of all life, is conceived as a god with countless eyes, hands, and feet. Purusha is both limitless and able to be en-closed in the smallest of spaces. In an act celebrated by this poem, Purusha is simultaneously the sacrifice and the sacrificer.

[10]One-quarter of Purusha is found in all mortal creation; three-fourths of Purusha is divine and eternal.
[11]The female creative germ.
[12]Special grasses laid out during Vedic sacrifices for the gods to sit upon.
[13]A class of demigods.
[14]Sages.
[15]The constituent elements of the *Rig Veda*.

Therefrom the metres were produced,[16] the Yajus[17] had its birth from it.

From it were horses born, from it all creatures with two rows of teeth:

From it were generated cows, from it the goats and sheep were born.

When they divided Purusha how many portions did they make?

What do they call his mouth, his arms? What do they call his thighs and feet?

The Brahmin[18] was his mouth, of both his arms was the Rajanya[19] made.

His thighs became the Vaisya,[20] from his feet the Sudra[21] was produced.

The Moon was gendered from his mind, and from his eye the Sun had birth;

Indra and Agni[22] from his mouth were born, and Vayu[23] from his breath.

Forth from his navel came mid-air; the sky was fashioned from his head;

Earth from his feet, and from his ear the regions. Thus they formed the worlds.

Seven fencing-logs had he, thrice seven layers of fuel were prepared,[24]

When the gods, offering sacrifice, bound, as their victim, Purusha.

Gods, sacrificing, sacrificed the victim: these were the earliest holy ordinances.

The mighty ones attained the height of heaven, there where the Sadhyas, gods of old, are dwelling.

A Journey to the Underworld
▼▼▼

13 ▼ *Homer, THE ODYSSEY*

History's first identifiable Greeks called themselves *Achaeans*. By 1600 B.C. they had created a decentralized, warrior civilization, which we term *Mycenaean*, after Mycenae, a city that exercised a loose leadership over the petty principalities of southern and central Greece. Around 1450 B.C. the Achaeans were masters of the island civilization of Crete and a major force in the eastern Mediterranean. It is against this background that we must place the Achaean expedition against Troy, a city in Anatolia, that took place around 1260.

---

[16]The verses of the *Sama Veda*. The *Sama Veda* is largely a collection of elements from the *Rig Veda*, arranged for religious ceremonial use.

[17]The ritual formulas of the *Yajur Veda*. This Veda was compiled a century or two after the *Rig Veda* and served as a collection of sacrificial chants.

[18]Aryan priests.

[19]The rajanyas, or kshatriyas, comprised the ruling or warrior class.

[20]This class initially encompassed free herders and farmers; later it included traders and artisans.

[21]Slaves and servants. The term was originally applied to the native dark-skinned people whom the Aryans conquered and subjugated when they entered India. Later it ceased to have any skin color connotations.

[22]The god of fire and sacrifice. This Sanskrit word is cognate with *ignis*, the Latin word for "fire" (hence, "ignite" in English).

[23]The wind.

[24]For a sacrificial fire.

The sack of rival Troy was the high-water mark for the Achaeans. Within a century Mycenaean civilization was collapsing due to internecine wars among the various Achaean principalities and the weight of migrations of unlettered Greek cousins from the north. These ruder kinfolk, whom we collectively call the *Dorians* (after the Doric Greek dialect, which many of them spoke), effectively smothered whatever of this fragile civilization the Achaeans themselves had failed to destroy in their post–Trojan War conflicts. By 1100 B.C. Greek society was again illiterate and stateless. When Greek literacy and civilization reemerged around 750 B.C., it was centered along the western shores of Anatolia in a region known as *Ionia*. These Greek settlements across the Aegean had largely sprung up in the period of the so-called Dark Ages following the Dorian migrations. Here Greek colonists, benefiting from their contact with the far more developed civilizations of Southwest Asia and Egypt, produced the first Greek literature known to us (as opposed to the bureaucratic lists left behind by Mycenaean civilization). Of all this early literature, the most significant are two poems, the *Iliad* and the *Odyssey*, both ascribed to a bard called Homer.

The ancients had no doubt there was a historic Homer who had created both works. Modern scholars are less certain. The weight of academic opinion today is that two eighth-century Asiatic Greeks, living a generation or more apart, orally composed the epics. Each poet crafted a single, coherent work of art but, in so doing, drew heavily from a long tradition of poetic stories preserved in the memories of wandering professional bards. A century or more later, that is, after 650 and possibly closer to 550 B.C., the two poems were finally written down in basically the forms we know them today.

Despite their late composition and even later transcription, when used judiciously, they tell us a good deal about life in the thirteenth century B.C. — the age of the Trojan War. At the same time the epics provide insight into the values and modes of perception of later "Dark Age" society, especially that of the ninth and eighth centuries.

On one level both poems celebrate such warrior virtues as personal honor, bravery, and loyalty to one's comrades, and on a deeper level they probe the hidden recesses of human motivation and emotion. On a third level the poems address the issue of the meaning of human suffering. Why do humans experience pain and sorrow? Are they captive to the whims of the gods? Are they and the gods subject to an overarching destiny that neither can avoid?

More to human scale than the *Iliad*, the *Odyssey* tells two intertwined stories. One traces the ten-year-long homeward voyage, after the sack of Troy, of the Achaean hero Odysseus. This clever adventurer has to battle, with cunning and skill, the enmity of Poseidon, god of the sea, and a variety of superhuman opponents before arriving home to his island kingdom of Ithaca. The second story details the attempts of Odysseus's wife and son, Penelope and Telemachus, who, with equal cunning and skill, attempt to stall indefinitely the advances of a group of suitors who seek to marry the presumed widow. As the suitors impatiently wait to see whom she will marry, they despoil Odysseus and Penelope's home and waste Telemachus's patrimony. The two story lines merge when Odysseus returns and, with the aid of his son and several loyal servants, wreaks vengeance on the suitors by killing them all. Unlike most epics, the story ends happily with Penelope and Odysseus reunited and Telemachus assured of his inheritance.

The following selection describes one of Odysseus's most daring adventures on his troubled homeward journey — a visit to the land of the dead. Here he consults Teiresias, the blind Theban seer, and meets the shades of many famous women and men, including his old comrade-in-arms Achilles, the Achaeans' greatest warrior and the central character in the *Iliad*, who was killed prior to the fall of Troy.

QUESTIONS FOR ANALYSIS

1. What values did Odysseus's society hold in highest esteem?
2. How does Homer address the issue of human responsibility for ill fortune?
3. Is there a destiny humans cannot escape?
4. What role do the gods play in this destiny?
5. It is often stated that the Greeks focused on human beings and human concerns. Does this selection seem to support or contradict that judgment?
6. Compare Achilles's sentiment toward the land of the dead with Enkidu's vision in *The Epic of Gilgamesh* (Chapter 1, source 1). What do you conclude from your analysis?
7. Compare Achaean society with that of the Aryans. Which strike you as more significant, the similarities or the differences? What do you conclude from your answer?

Now the spirit of Teiresias of Thebes came forward, bearing a golden staff in his hand. Knowing who I am, he addressed me: "Son of Laertes, sprung from Zeus,[1] Odysseus, known for your many wiles, why, unhappy man, have you left the sunlight to behold the dead in this cheerless region? Step back from the trench and put aside your sharp sword so that I might drink the blood[2] and thereby prophesy the truth to you." Thus he spoke. I, stepping backward, drove my silver-studded sword into its scabbard. When he had drunk the black blood, this noble prophet addressed me with these words.

"Lord Odysseus, you seek a honey-sweet homeward journey, but a god will make your travels difficult. I do not think you can escape the notice of the Earth-shaker,[3] who has set his mind in enmity against you, enraged because you blinded his beloved son.[4] Even so, you still might be able to reach home, although in sorry circumstances, if you are willing to restrain your desires, and those of your comrades, beginning when your seaworthy ship leaves the deep blue waters and approaches the island of Thrinacie,[5] where you will see the grazing cattle and fat sheep of Helios,[6] who sees and hears everything. If you leave the animals untouched and concentrate solely on getting home, it is possible that all of you might reach Ithaca, although in sorry circumstances. If you injure these animals, however, I foresee destruction for your ship and its crew, and even if you yourself

---

[1]The greatest of the Hellenic gods. This title implies Odysseus's "godlike" heroic qualities.

[2]The spirits of the dead can communicate with Odysseus only after drinking blood from animals he has sacrificed.

[3]Poseidon, god of the sea and of earthquakes.

[4]The Cyclops, a son of Poseidon, was a one-eyed, cannibal giant whom Odysseus had blinded in self-defense.

[5]Identified by ancient Hellenes as the island of Sicily.

[6]The sun god.

manage to escape, you will return home late, in a sorry state, in an alien ship, having lost all your companions.[7] And even there at home you will find troubles. Overbearing men will be consuming your wealth, wooing your goddess-like wife, and offering her bridal gifts. Certainly, following your arrival, you will gain revenge on these suitors for their evil deeds. When you have slain the suitors in your halls, whether by stratagem or in an open fight with sharp bronze weapons, you must again set out on a journey. You must take a well-fashioned oar and travel until you reach a people who are ignorant of the sea and never eat food mixed with salt, and who know nothing about our purple-ribbed ships and the well-fashioned oars that serve as ships' wings. And I say you will receive a sign, a very clear one that you cannot miss. When, another traveler upon meeting you remarks that you are carrying a 'winnowing-fan' across your broad back,[8] plant your well-fashioned oar in the earth and offer Lord Poseidon the sacrifice of a ram, a bull,[9] and a boar, the mate of the wild she-swine. Then return home and there make sacred offerings to all the immortal gods who inhabit wide heaven, and do so to each in order of rank. As for death, it will come to you at last gently out of the sea in a comfortable old age when you are surrounded by a prosperous people. This I tell you truly." . . .

Next came the spirits of Achilles, son of Peleus, of Patroclus,[10] of noble Antilochus,[11] and of Aias,[12] who surpassed all the Danaans[13] in beauty of physique and manly bearing, except for the flawless son of Peleus.[14] The spirit of swift-footed Achilles of the house of Aeacus[15] recognized me, and mournfully spoke in winged words: "Son of Laertes, sprung from Zeus, Odysseus, known for your many wiles! Rash man, what greater deed than this remains for you to devise in your heart? How did you dare to descend to Hades'[16] realm, where the dead dwell as witless images of worn-out mortals?"

Thus he spoke, and I answered in return. "Achilles, son of Peleus, by far the mightiest of the Achaeans, I came to consult with Teiresias in the hope of his giving me a plan whereby I might reach rocky Ithaca. For I have not yet come near the land of Achaea,[17] nor yet set foot on my own island, but have been constantly beset by misfortunes. How different from your situation, Achilles, you who are more fortunate than any man whoever was or will be. For in the old days, when you were alive, we Argives[18] honored you as though you were a god, and now that you are here, you rule nobly among the dead. Therefore, grieve not, Achilles, that you are dead."

So I spoke, and he immediately answered, saying: "Do not endeavor to speak soothingly to me of death, Lord Odysseus. I would rather live on earth as the hired help of some landless man whose own livelihood was meager, than be lord over all the dead who have perished. Enough of that. Tell me about my son, that lordly young man. Did he follow me to war and play a leading role in it? And tell me about noble Peleus. . . . I am not there in the sunlight to aid Peleus with that great strength that

---

[7]The crew will kill and eat the sun god's flocks, and all, except Odysseus, will die as a result.

[8]That is, Odysseus is in a region where no one knows what an oar's function is.

[9]The bull was sacred to Poseidon. See Chapter 1, source 9, for examples of the popularity of the bull as a sacred animal.

[10]Achilles's best friend, who also died at Troy.

[11]An Achaean hero who fell at Troy while defending his father, King Nestor of Pylos (note 20).

[12]The Achaeans' second greatest warrior; he committed suicide at Troy.

[13]Another name for the Achaeans, or Hellenes.

[14]Achilles.

[15]The ancestor from whom Peleus and his son Achilles were descended. Homer's heroes always identified themselves by reference to their fathers and other notable ancestors.

[16]The god of the dead.

[17]The land of the Achaeans.

[18]Another name for the Achaeans.

was once mine on the broad plains of Troy, where I slew the best of the enemy's army in defense of the Argives. If, but for an hour, I could return to my father's house with such strength as I once had, I would give those who do him violence and dishonor him cause to rue my might and my invincible hands."

So he spoke, and I answered: "I have heard nothing about noble Peleus, but I will give you all the news you desire of your dear son, Neoptolemus. It was I who brought him from Scyros[19] in my well-fashioned, hollow ship to join the ranks of the well-armed Achaeans. Whenever we held a council meeting during the siege of Troy, he was always the first to speak, and his words never missed the mark. God-like Nestor[20] and I alone surpassed him. As often as we fought with bronze weapons on the Trojan plain, he never lagged behind in the ranks or crowd, but would always run far out in front, yielding first place to no one, and he slew many men in mortal combat. I could not name all whom he killed in defense of the Argives. . . . Again, when we, the best of the Argives, were about to enter into the horse that Epeus made,[21] and responsibility lay solely with me to either open or keep closed the door of our stout-built ambush, the other Danaan leaders and chieftains were wiping away tears from their eyes and each man's limbs shook beneath him. But never did my eyes see his fair face grow pale, nor did I see him wiping away tears from his cheeks. Rather, he earnestly begged me to allow him to sally forth from the horse, and he kept handling his sword-hilt and his heavy bronze spear in his eagerness to inflict harm on the Trojans. Following our sack of the lofty city of Priam,[22] he boarded his ship with a full share of the spoils and his special prize.[23] And he was unscathed, never cut by a sharp sword or wounded in close combat, as often happens in war, since Ares[24] rages in a confused fashion."

So I spoke, and the spirit of the son of Aeacus departed with long strides across the field of asphodel,[25] rejoicing that his son was preeminent among men.

▼▼▼

The Hebrews and Their Neighbors

Recent excavations at the site of the long-forgotten city of Ebla in the modern nation of Syria reveal that the land of Syria-Palestine, which serves as a land bridge between Egypt and Mesopotamia, has known civilization since about 3000 B.C. As is the fate of most small lands that lie next to more powerful neighbors, the region has historically been prey to invaders. Its earliest known conqueror was Sargon the Great of Akkad in Mesopotamia, who sacked Ebla sometime before 2300 B.C.

---

[19]The Aegean island where Achilles's son had been raised.
[20]The aged king of Pylos noted for his wisdom and sage advice.
[21]The so-called Trojan horse, through which the Achaeans finally were able to capture Troy.
[22]The last king of Troy.

[23]At the division of the Trojan survivors, Neoptolemus was awarded Andromache, widow of Hector, Troy's greatest hero, whom Achilles had killed in single combat.
[24]The god of war.
[25]A flower that carpeted the Elysian fields, where the spirits of dead heroes, such as Achilles, resided.

Around 1200 B.C., in the midst of the great nomadic upheavals that were testing all the civilizations of the Middle East, several different invaders penetrated the lands of Syria-Palestine and established themselves at the expense of the indigenous Canaanite population. One of these was a mixed group of invaders from the Mediterranean, who settled down in cities along the coast of what is today the state of Israel. These people, who included a large percentage of uprooted Greeks and Cretans, became known as the *Philistines.* A second major wave was comprised of another hybrid mass of people who spoke a language that belongs to a family of tongues we term *Semitic.* These people, known as the *Hebrews,* infiltrated the region from the southern and eastern deserts and settled the inland high ground overlooking the Philistine cities.

Prior to the waves of nomadic invaders of around 1200, the Hittite and Egyptian empires had fought one another for mastery over Syria-Palestine. With the destruction of Hittite civilization and the concurrent severe weakening of the Egyptian empire, a momentary power vacuum occurred along the eastern rim of the Mediterranean. In the absence of any outside imperial power, the various cultural groups of Syria-Palestine had several centuries of relative freedom in which to struggle with one another and to amalgamate.

For the Hebrews, amalgamation was both seductively easy and potentially disastrous. The vast majority of the various peoples who already inhabited this land known as *Canaan* were, like the Hebrews, Semites. Hebrews and Canaanites spoke related languages that had a common place of origin (probably the Arabian Peninsula before 3000 B.C.), and they shared many other cultural similarities. As the Hebrews coalesced as a people, however, they evolved the idea that they enjoyed the special protection of a god whom they called *Yahweh.* In return for that protection, this deity demanded their sole devotion. A corollary of that belief was the conviction that if the Hebrews were to prosper in Canaan, which Yahweh had promised them, they had to maintain religious (and, therefore, cultural) distance from all other people.

Establishing a Covenant with Humanity
▼▼▼

14 ▼ THE BOOK OF GENESIS

The major documentary source for both the process of cultural fusion and the fierce struggles that took place among the various groups of Iron Age settlers in Syria-Palestine is a collection of sacred Hebrew writings known as the Bible (from the Greek word *biblos,* which means "book"). The exclusively Hebrew or Jewish portion of the Bible, known to Jews as the *Tanakh* but called by Christians the "Old Testament," consists of a wide variety of different types of literature. These were mainly composed, edited, and reedited from roughly 1000 B.C. to possibly as late as the second century B.C., although Jewish religious authorities did not fix the *Tanakh*'s final canon, or official body of accepted texts, until after A.D. 100. This means that biblical accounts of early Hebrew history are, in many cases, centuries removed from the events they narrate. It is nevertheless clear that these later authors often used early written and oral sources that are now lost to us. Moreover, although these authors primarily wrote history from a theological perspective and consequently clothed their stories in myth, independent archeological evidence has often confirmed the basic historical outline of many of the biblical stories concerning the fortunes of the Hebrews in Canaan, the Promised Land.

The first book of the Bible is known as Genesis (the beginning) and recounts the story of humanity's relationship with Yahweh from Creation through the settlement of the Hebrew people, known as the *Children of Israel*, in Egypt. Tradition ascribes its authorship to Moses, who lived during the thirteenth century B.C., but within the context of the culture of ancient Israel this did not necessarily mean that Moses actually wrote or dictated the book. Rather, he was the one who provided the initial and pervading spirit behind the work. In all likelihood, a number of different authors composed and reworked Genesis over the period from before 900 to after 721 B.C.

The following selection recounts a popular Southwest Asian theme that we saw in Chapter 1 — the Flood. As you read it, be aware not only of the striking similarities between it and the story told by Utnapishtim but of the even more significant differences. Remember that the author is making a religious statement.

QUESTIONS FOR ANALYSIS

1. Can you find any inconsistencies in this text in regard to the numbers of animals brought into the ark? What does this suggest about the story's creation process?
2. Why does Yahweh destroy all humanity except Noah and his family? How does Yahweh's reasoning compare with the Mesopotamian gods' reason for wanting to destroy humans and Ea's decision to warn Utnapishtim (Chapter 1, source 1)?
3. Compare Yahweh's treatment of Noah and his descendants after the Flood with the Mesopotamian gods' treatment of Utnapishtim after the waters had receded.
4. What do the Mesopotamian gods demand of humans? What does Noah's God demand?
5. From these several comparisons, what picture emerges of the god of the Hebrews? In what ways is their deity similar to the gods of Mesopotamia? In what ways does their god differ?
6. God establishes a covenant, or agreement, with all humanity and, indeed, with all living creation, through Noah. What is that covenant?
7. Consider the story of Noah's curse on Canaan. What has Ham done to deserve such anger, and why is it that his son suffers as a consequence? Do your answers tell us anything about Hebrew social values and practices at

this time? How is the story of the curse relevant to the Hebrews' settlement in the land of Canaan? What does this suggest about the story's date of composition? How does this illustrate the Hebrews' use of myth to explain and justify historical events?

8. How might we explain the fact that both the Mesopotamians and the Hebrews had flood stories as part of their mythology? Does the Hebrews' belief that Abraham, father of all Hebrews, was born in the Sumerian city of Ur provide a clue?

The Lord saw that the wickedness of man was great in the earth, and that every imagination of the thoughts of his heart was only evil continually. And the Lord was sorry that he had made man on the earth, and it grieved him to his heart. So the Lord said, "I will blot out man whom I have created from the face of the ground, man and beast and creeping things and birds of the air, for I am sorry that I have made them." But Noah found favor in the eyes of the Lord. . . .

Noah was a righteous man, blameless in his generation; Noah walked with God. And Noah had three sons, Shem,[1] Ham, and Japheth.

Now the earth was corrupt in God's sight, and the earth was filled with violence. And God saw the earth, and behold, it was corrupt; for all flesh had corrupted their way upon the earth. And God said to Noah, "I have determined to make an end of all flesh; for the earth is filled with violence through them; behold, I will destroy them with the earth. Make yourself an ark of gopher wood; make rooms in the ark, and cover it inside and out with pitch. . . . For behold, I will bring a flood of waters upon the earth, to destroy all flesh in which is the breath of life from under heaven; everything that is on the earth shall die. But I will establish my covenant with you; and you shall come into the ark, you, your sons, your wife, and your sons' wives with you. And of every living thing of all

flesh, you shall bring two of every sort into the ark, to keep them alive with you; they shall be male and female. Of the birds according to their kinds, and of the animals according to their kinds, of every creeping thing of the ground according to its kind, two of every sort shall come in to you, to keep them alive. Also take with you every sort of food that is eaten, and store it up; and it shall serve as food for you and for them." Noah did this; he did all that God commanded him.

Then the Lord said to Noah, "Go into the ark, you and all your household, for I have seen that you are righteous before me in this generation. Take with you seven pairs of all clean animals,[2] the male and his mate; and a pair of the animals that are not clean, the male and his mate; and seven pairs of the birds of the air also, male and female, to keep their kind alive upon the face of all the earth. For in seven days I will send rain upon the earth forty days and forty nights; and every living thing that I have made will blot out from the face of the ground." And Noah did all that the Lord had commanded him.

Noah was six hundred years old when the flood of waters came upon the earth. And Noah and his sons and his wife and his sons' wives with him went into the ark, to escape the waters of the flood. Of clean animals, and of animals that are not clean, and of birds, and of

---

[1]Shem was the eldest of Noah's sons and the one from whom the Hebrews claimed direct descent. The term Semite (one who speaks any Semitic language, such as Hebrew, Akkadian, Assyrian, and Arabic) is derived from the name.

[2]A ritually clean animal, such as a sheep, was one worthy of sacrifice to Yahweh. An unclean animal, such as a predator or a scavenger, would never be offered in sacrifice.

everything that creeps on the ground, two and two, male and female, went into the ark with Noah, as God had commanded Noah. And after seven days the waters of the flood came upon the earth.

In the six hundredth year of Noah's life, in the second month, on the seventeenth day of the month, on that day all the fountains of the great deep burst forth, and the windows of the heavens were opened.[3] And rain fell upon the earth forty days and forty nights. . . .

. . . And the waters prevailed so mightily upon the earth that all the high mountains under the whole heaven were covered. . . . He blotted out every living thing that was upon the face of the ground, man and animals and creeping things and birds of the air; they were blotted out from the earth. Only Noah was left, and those that were with him in the ark. And the waters prevailed upon the earth a hundred and fifty days.

But God remembered Noah and all the beasts and all the cattle that were with him in the ark. And God made a wind blow over the earth, and the waters subsided; the fountains of the deep and the windows of the heavens were closed, the rain from the heavens was restrained, and the waters receded from the earth continually. At the end of a hundred and fifty days the waters had abated; and in the seventh month, on the seventeenth day of the month, the ark came to rest upon the mountains of Ararat. And the waters continued to abate until the tenth month; in the tenth month, on the first day of the month, the tops of the mountains were seen.

At the end of forty days Noah opened the window of the ark which he had made, and sent forth a raven; and it went to and fro until the waters were dried up from the earth. Then he sent forth a dove from him, to see if the waters had subsided from the face of the ground; but the dove found no place to set her foot, and she returned to him to the ark, for the waters were still on the face of the whole earth. So he put forth his hand and took her and brought her into the ark with him. He waited another seven days, and again he sent forth the dove out of the ark; and the dove came back to him in the evening, and lo, in her mouth a freshly plucked olive leaf; so Noah knew that the waters had subsided from the earth. Then he waited another seven days, and sent forth the dove; and she did not return to him any more.

In the six hundred and first year,[4] in the first month, the first day of the month, the waters were dried from off the earth; and Noah removed the covering of the ark, and looked, and behold, the face of the ground was dry. . . . Then God said to Noah, "Go forth from the ark, you and your wife, and your sons and your sons' wives with you. Bring forth with you every living thing that is with you of all flesh — birds and animals and every creeping thing that creeps on the earth — that they may breed abundantly on the earth, and be fruitful and multiply upon the earth." So Noah went forth, and his sons and his wife and his sons' wives with him. And every beast, every creeping thing, and every bird, everything that moves upon the earth, went forth by families out of the ark.

Then Noah built an altar to the Lord, and took of every clean animal and of every clean bird, and offered burnt offerings on the altar. And when the Lord smelled the pleasing odor, the Lord said in his heart, "I will never again curse the ground because of man, for the imagination of man's heart is evil from his youth; neither will I ever again destroy every living creature as I have done. While the earth remains, seedtime and harvest, cold and heat, summer and winter, day and night, shall not cease."

---

[3]The view of the world shared by the peoples of Southwest Asia at this time was that the world's firmament, or land, was totally surrounded, above and below, by water. The water above was normally kept in place by a translucent crystalline sphere. Rain was the seepage of water through that sphere.

[4]Of Noah's life.

And God blessed Noah and his sons, and said to them, "Be fruitful and multiply, and fill the earth. The fear of you and the dread of you shall be upon every beast of the earth, and upon every bird of the air, upon everything that creeps on the ground and all the fish of the sea; into your hand they are delivered. Every moving thing that lives shall be food for you; and as I gave you the green plants, I give you everything. Only you shall not eat flesh with its life, that is, its blood.[5] For your lifeblood I will surely require a reckoning; of every beast I will require it and of man; of every man's brother I will require the life of man. Whoever sheds the blood of man, by man shall his blood be shed; for God made man in his own image. And you, be fruitful and multiply, bring forth abundantly on the earth and multiply in it."

Then God said to Noah and to his sons with him, "Behold, I establish my covenant with you and your descendants after you, and with every living creature that is with you, the birds, the cattle, and every beast of the earth with you, as many as came out of the ark. I establish my covenant with you, that never again shall all flesh be cut off by the waters of a flood, and never again shall there be a flood to destroy the earth." And God said, "This is the sign of the covenant which I make between me and you and every living creature that is with you, for all future generations: I set my bow[6] in the cloud, and it shall be a sign of the covenant between me and the earth. When I bring clouds over the earth and the bow is seen in the clouds, I will remember my covenant which is between me and you and every living creature of all flesh; and the waters shall never again become a flood to destroy all flesh. When the bow is in the clouds, I will look upon it and remember the everlasting covenant between God and every living creature of all flesh that is upon the earth." God said to Noah, "This is the sign of the covenant which I have established between me and all flesh that is upon the earth."

The sons of Noah who went forth from the ark were Shem, Ham, and Japheth. Ham was the father of Canaan. These three were the sons of Noah; and from these the whole earth was peopled.

Noah was the first tiller of the soil. He planted a vineyard; and he drank of the wine, and became drunk, and lay uncovered in his tent. And Ham, the father of Canaan, saw the nakedness of his father, and told his two brothers outside. Then Shem and Japheth took a garment, laid it upon both their shoulders, and walked backward and covered the nakedness of their father; their faces were turned away, and they did not see their father's nakedness. When Noah awoke from his wine and knew what his youngest son had done to him, he said

"Cursed be Canaan;
a slave of slaves shall he be to his
    brothers."[7]
He also said,

"Blessed by the Lord my God be Shem;
and let Canaan be his slave.
God enlarge Japheth,
and let him dwell in the tents of Shem;[8]
and let Canaan be his slave."

After the flood Noah lived three hundred and fifty years. All the days of Noah were nine hundred and fifty years; and he died.

---

[5] Raw meat or meat dripping with blood could not be consumed.
[6] A rainbow. Compare this with Ishtar's rainbow (Chapter 1, source 1).
[7] According to Hebrew legend, Ham and his son Canaan were the direct ancestors of the Canaanites, the people whom the Hebrews were dispossessing of their lands.

[8] Japheth, according to Hebrew tradition, was the ancestor of the Indo-European peoples of northern Syria and beyond, such as the Hittites and Hurrians. From the Hebrew perspective the Hebrews and the northern Indo-Europeans were dividing up the land of Syria-Palestine between them.

Establishing a Covenant with a Chosen People
▼▼▼

15 ▼ THE BOOK OF DEUTERONOMY

The story of Noah tells of Yahweh's post-Deluge covenant with all living creatures; the story of the Hebrews *Exodus* (flight) from Egypt tells of their special covenant with this god and their becoming a Chosen People with a new identity. The Hebrews had probably entered Egypt in the time of the Hyksos' conquest of that land. With the overthrow of the Hyksos and the reestablishment of native Egyptian rule around 1570 B.C., significant numbers of Hebrews were enslaved. Probably during the reign of Ramesses the Great (r. 1279–1213 B.C.), a charismatic leader known as Moses led a band of these Hebrews out of Egypt into Canaan. In the process of this migration, he molded them into a people and wedded them to his god Yahweh. No longer a loose band of nomads, they were now the Israelites — descendants of the patriarchs Abraham, Isaac, and Jacob (also called Israel).

The story of this thirteenth-century transformation is told in several books of the Bible. This selection comes from Deuteronomy, which, in its present form, dates from the reign of King Josiah of Jerusalem (r. 640–609 B.C.). It was composed or, more likely, recast at a time of religious reformation, when Josiah was attempting to abolish all forms of pagan worship in his kingdom, especially the practices of the Assyrians. Although Deuteronomy, as we know it, is essentially a seventh-century creation, it is doubtlessly based on sources that date from the time of Moses.

The setting of our excerpt is the frontier of Canaan, which, according to the story of the Exodus, the Israelites reached after forty years of wandering in the desert. Moses, realizing he will die before his people cross the Jordan River into the Promised Land, delivers a final message to them.

QUESTIONS FOR ANALYSIS

1. What is the covenant between Yahweh and the people of Israel? What does God promise and demand in return? What does Yahweh threaten for those who break the covenant?
2. Consider Yahweh's promises again. What does Yahweh have to say about rewards after death? What do you infer from your answer?
3. Compare this covenant with that given after the Flood. How, if at all, do they differ, and what do those differences suggest?
4. Which elements of Moses' message would the religious reformers of seventh-century Jerusalem wish to emphasize?
5. Compare these Ten Commandments with the Egyptian "Negative Confession" (Chapter 1, source 3). Which strike you as more significant, the similarities or the differences? What do you conclude from your answer?

And Moses summoned all Israel,[1] and said to them, "Hear, O Israel, the statutes and the ordinances which I speak in your hearing this day, and you shall learn them and be careful to do them. The Lord our God made a covenant with us in Horeb.[2] Not with our fathers did the Lord make this covenant, but with us, who are all of us here alive this day. The Lord spoke with you face to face at the mountain, out of the midst of the fire, while I stood between the Lord and you at that time, to declare to you the word of the Lord; for you were afraid because of the fire, and you did not go up into the mountain. He said:

"'I am the Lord your God, who brought you out of the land of Egypt, out of the house of bondage.

"'You shall have no other gods before me.

"'You shall not make for yourself a graven image, or any likeness of anything that is in heaven above, or that is on the earth beneath, or that is in the water under the earth; you shall not bow down to them or serve them; for I the Lord your God am a jealous God, visiting the iniquity of the fathers upon the children to the third and fourth generation of those who hate me, but showing steadfast love to thousands of those who love me and keep my commandments.

"'You shall not take the name of the Lord your God in vain: for the Lord will not hold him guiltless who takes his name in vain.

"'Observe the sabbath day, to keep it holy, as the Lord your God commanded you. Six days you shall labor, and do all your work; but the seventh day is a sabbath to the Lord your God; in it you shall not do any work, you, or your son, or your daughter, or your manservant, or your maidservant, or your ox, or your ass, or any of your cattle, or the sojourner who is within your gates, that your manservant and your maidservant may rest as well as you. You shall remember that you were a servant in the land of Egypt, and the Lord your God brought you out thence with a mighty hand and an outstretched arm; therefore the Lord your God commanded you to keep the sabbath day.

"'Honor your father and your mother, as the Lord your God commanded you; that your days may be prolonged, and that it may go well with you, in the land which the Lord your God gives you.

"'You shall not kill.

"'Neither shall you commit adultery.

"'Neither shall you steal.

"'Neither shall you bear false witness against your neighbor.

"'Neither shall you covet your neighbor's wife; and you shall not desire your neighbor's house, his field, or his manservant, or his maidservant, his ox, or his ass, or anything that is your neighbor's.'

"These words the Lord spoke to all your assembly at the mountain out of the midst of the fire, the cloud, and the thick darkness, with a loud voice; and he added no more. And he wrote them upon two tables of stone, and gave them to me. . . .

"Now this is the commandment, the statutes and the ordinances which the Lord your God commanded me to teach you, that you may do them in the land to which you are going over, to possess it; that you may fear the Lord your God, you and your son and your son's son, by keeping all his statutes and his commandments, which I command you, all the days of your life; and that your days may be prolonged. Hear therefore, O Israel, and be careful to do

---

[1]The Hebrews were the Children of Israel, or the Israelites, because they traced their lineage back to Jacob, whose name God had changed to Israel (meaning "God rules"). Jacob, the grandson of Abraham and the son of Isaac, had twelve sons, each of whom became the patriarch of one of the twelve tribes of Israel.

[2]Also known as Mount Sinai. Here Moses had received the Law from Yahweh, during the period of desert wandering.

them; that it may go well with you, and that you may multiply greatly, as the Lord, the God of your fathers, has promised you, in a land flowing with milk and honey.

"Hear, O Israel: The Lord our God is one Lord; and you shall love the Lord your God with all your heart, and with all your soul, and with all your might. And these words which I command you this day shall be upon your heart; and you shall teach them diligently to your children, and shall talk of them when you sit in your house, and when you walk by the way, and when you lie down, and when you rise. And you shall bind them as a sign upon your hand, and they shall be as frontlets between your eyes. And you shall write them on the doorposts of your house and on your gates.

"And when the Lord your God brings you into the land which he swore to your fathers, to Abraham, to Isaac, and to Jacob, to give you, with great and goodly cities, which you did not build, and houses full of all good things, which you did not fill, and cisterns hewn out, which you did not hew, and vineyards and olive trees, which you did not plant, and when you eat and are full, then take heed lest you forget the Lord, who brought you out of the land of Egypt, out of the house of bondage. You shall fear the Lord your God; you shall serve him, and swear by his name. You shall not go after other gods, of the gods of the peoples who are round about you; for the Lord your God in the midst of you is a jealous God; lest the anger of the Lord your God be kindled against you, and he destroy you from off the face of the earth. . . .

"When the Lord your God brings you into the land which you are entering to take possession of it, and clears away many nations before you . . . seven nations greater and mightier than yourselves, and when the Lord your God gives them over to you, and you defeat them;

then you must utterly destroy them; you shall make no covenant with them, and show no mercy to them. You shall not make marriages with them, giving your daughters to their sons or taking their daughters for your sons. For they would turn away your sons from following me, to serve other gods; then the anger of the Lord would be kindled against you, and he would destroy you quickly. But thus shall you deal with them: you shall break down their altars, and dash in pieces their pillars, and hew down their Asherim,[3] and burn their graven images with fire.

"For you are a people holy to the Lord your God; the Lord your God has chosen you to be a people for his own possession, out of all the peoples that are on the face of the earth. It was not because you were more in number than any other people that the Lord set his love upon you and chose you, for you were the fewest of all peoples; but it is because the Lord loves you, and is keeping the oath which he swore to your fathers, that the Lord has brought you out with a mighty hand, and redeemed you from the house of bondage, from the hand of Pharaoh king of Egypt. Know therefore that the Lord your God is God, the faithful God who keeps covenant and steadfast love with those who love him and keep his commandments, to a thousand generations, and repays those who hate him, by destroying them; he will not be slack with him who hates him. . . . You shall therefore be careful to do the commandment, and the statutes, and the ordinances, which I command you this day.

"And because you hearken to these ordinances, and keep and do them, the Lord your God will keep with you the covenant and the steadfast love which he swore to your fathers to keep; he will love you, bless you, and multiply you; he will also bless the fruit of your body

---

[3]Sacred poles raised to Astarte or Asherah, the Canaanite counterpart of Ishtar, the Mesopotamian goddess of fertility and love.

and the fruit of your ground, your grain and your wine and your oil, the increase of your cattle and the young of your flock, in the land which he swore to your fathers to give you. You shall be blessed above all peoples; there shall not be male or female barren among you, or among your cattle. And the Lord will take away from you all sickness; and none of the evil diseases of Egypt, which you knew, will he inflict upon you, but he will lay them upon all who hate you. And you shall destroy all the peoples that the Lord your God will give over to you, your eye shall not pity them; neither shall you serve their gods, for that would be a snare to you.

Keeping and Breaking the Covenant
▼▼▼

16 ▼ *The Book of Judges*

Following Moses' death, Joshua led the Israelites into Canaan. Unable to wipe out or displace all the indigenous peoples, the Israelites settled in the hills and became one of several major cultural groups in the region. Between Joshua's death, which took place around 1150 B.C., and the rise of the kingdom of Israel around 1050 B.C., various leaders, known as judges, arose to lead the Israelites in times of crisis. These were not judges in a narrow juridical or institutional sense but men and women who were defenders of Yahweh's law and justice.

The following story from The Book of Judges tells why the first of the major judges, Othniel, was called to lead Israel. The book, which is based on a cycle of written epics that date to around 1000 B.C., was probably put into its final form by the same group of seventh-century reformers in Jerusalem who were recasting Deuteronomy.

QUESTIONS FOR ANALYSIS

1. In what ways did the Israelites break the covenant, and what were the consequences?
2. What was the message or lesson to be learned from this experience?
3. What does this source suggest about the historical realities of the Hebrew experience in the Promised Land?
4. What do you think happened after Othniel died?
5. Compare the troubles of the Israelites with the fall of the Xia and Shang dynasties in China as recorded in the *Classic of History* (Chapter 1, source 6). In what ways do these two explanations of history, the Mandate of Heaven and the covenant, parallel one another? In what ways do they differ? What are more significant, the similarities or the differences? What do you conclude from this?

When Joshua dismissed the people, the people of Israel went each to his inheritance to take possession of the land. And the people served the Lord all the days of Joshua, and all the days of the elders who outlived Joshua, who had seen all the great work which the Lord had done for Israel. And Joshua the son of Nun, the servant of the Lord, died. . . . And all that generation also were gathered to their fathers; and there arose another generation after them, who did not know the Lord or the work which he had done for Israel.

And the people of Israel did what was evil in the sight of the Lord and served the Baals;[1] and they forsook the Lord, the God of their fathers, who had brought them out of the land of Egypt; they went after other gods, from among the gods of the peoples who were round about them, and bowed down to them; and they provoked the Lord to anger. They forsook the Lord, and served the Baals and the Ashtaroth.[2] So the anger of the Lord was kindled against Israel, and he gave them over to plunderers, who plundered them; and he sold them into the power of their enemies round about, so that they could no longer withstand their enemies. Whenever they marched out, the hand of the Lord was against them for evil, as the Lord had warned, and as the Lord had sworn to them; and they were in sore straits.

Then the Lord raised up judges, who saved them out of the power of those who plundered them. And yet they did not listen to their judges; for they played the harlot after other gods and bowed down to them; they soon turned aside from the way in which their fathers had walked, who had obeyed the commandments of the Lord, and they did not do so. Whenever the Lord raised up judges for them, the Lord was with the judge, and he saved them from the hand of their enemies all the days of the judge; for the Lord was moved to pity by their groaning because of those who afflicted and oppressed them. But whenever the judge died, they turned back and behaved worse than their fathers, going after other gods, serving them and bowing down to them; they did not drop any of their practices or their stubborn ways. So the anger of the Lord was kindled against Israel; and he said, "Because this people have transgressed my covenant which I commanded their fathers, and have not obeyed my voice, I will not henceforth drive out before them any of the nations that Joshua left when he died, that by them I may test Israel, whether they will take care to walk in the way of the Lord as their fathers did, or not." So the Lord left those nations, not driving them out at once, and he did not give them into the power of Joshua.

Now these are the nations which the Lord left, to test Israel by them, that is, all in Israel who had no experience of any war in Canaan; it was only that the generations of the people of Israel might know war, that he might teach war to such at least as had not known it before. These are the nations: the five lords of the Philistines, and all the Canaanites, and the Sidonians, and the Hivites. . . . They were for the testing of Israel, to know whether Israel would obey the commandments of the Lord, which he commanded their fathers by Moses. So the people of Israel dwelt among the Canaanites, the Hittites, the Amorites, the Perizzites, the Hivites, and the Jebusites; and they took their daughters to themselves for wives, and their own daughters they gave to their sons; and they served their gods.

And the people of Israel did what was evil in the sight of the Lord, forgetting the Lord their God, and serving the Baals and the Asheroth. Therefore the anger of the Lord was kindled

---

[1]Baal was the chief Canaanite god, hence, the gods of the native people.

[2]All the native gods, not just Baal and Astarte.

against Israel, and he sold them into the hand of Cushanrishathaim[3] king of Mesopotamia and the people of Israel served Cushanrishathaim eight years. But when the people of Israel cried to the Lord, the Lord raised up a deliverer for the people of Israel, who delivered them, Othniel the son of Kenaz, Caleb's younger brother.

The Spirit of the Lord came upon him, and he judged Israel; he went out to war, and the Lord gave Cushanrishathaim king of Mesopotamia into his hand; and his hand prevailed over Cushanrishathaim. So the land had rest forty years. Then Othniel the son of Kenaz died.

---

[3]A king who held major portions of Syria.

Chapter 3

▼▼▼

Developing the Religious Traditions of India and Southwest Asia, 800–200 B.C.

Between about 800 and 200 B.C. profound changes in thought, belief, social organization, and government took place in China, India, Southwest Asia, and *Hellas* (the land of the Greeks). During these six centuries, the Chinese, Indians, Southwest Asians, and Greeks formulated distinctive traditions and institutions that became essential characteristics of their civilizations and the many societies they later influenced.

These developments became especially pronounced by the sixth century. It is no coincidence that Confucius, the Buddha, the Mahavira, several of the authors of the Upanishads, Zarathustra, Second Isaiah, and Thales all lived during or around the sixth century B.C. Moreover, the caste system, the Persian Empire, and the Greek city-states were thriving by the end of this century.

What might explain these parallel evolutions? The Age of Iron witnessed the development of considerably larger, more complex, and more competitive political and economic entities that challenged older social systems and values. This disruption of life was unsettling and led to the search for new answers to some fundamental questions: What is the meaning and goal of life? How does one relate to the natural world? How does one relate to other humans?

The historical environments of the various civilizations posing such questions often differed radically. Their respective answers consequently varied significantly. In one way, however, they displayed a striking similarity. Each emerging tradition challenged the myth-making notion that human-kind is held hostage by a capricious, god-infested nature.

India did this by denying the ultimate reality and impor-tance of the world of observable nature. China witnessed several other approaches. One school of thought sought mystical union with nature, and two other schools sought to control nature by imposing human discipline upon it. One of these latter schools saw the solution in a moral order of virtuous behavior, the other in the order of strict and dispassionately applied human law. In Southwest Asia free-dom from myth-laden nature was partially achieved through worship of and obedience to a totally spiritual yet personal God of the universe, who stood completely outside nature and yet imposed moral and historical order upon it. In Greece the attempt to master nature took the form of ra-tional philosophy and science. Here certain thinkers sought to control nature by studying it objectively, thereby discov-ering laws that would enable humans to define more surely their place in the universe. In this manner, four major world traditions emerged: Indian transcendental religion; China's distinctive blend of practical worldliness with a mystical appreciation of nature; Southwest Asia's preoccu-pation with ethical monotheism; and Greek rationalism, with its special focus on the human condition.

In this chapter we shall explore the religious traditions that took shape in India and Southwest Asia.

▼▼▼

The Emergence of Hinduism

The *Rig-Veda*'s hymn to Purusha, which appears in Chapter 2, illustrates the emergence of what eventually became one of Hinduism's major beliefs, the unity of all being. During the period spanning the tenth through fourth centuries B.C., most of the other elements of classical Hindu thought and practice took shape.

It is wrong to think of Hinduism, either modern or ancient, as a single set of beliefs and practices. To the contrary, it is a fluid mass of religious and social expressions, which collectively encompass the living faiths of all the diverse peoples of India who call themselves *Hindu*. Hinduism comfortably includes folk rituals and beliefs, which have changed little over many millennia, and the most abstract and speculative thought on the nature of God. It is polytheistic and monotheistic; it is simultaneously earthy and metaphysical. Indeed, Hindus can choose from a variety of beliefs and modes of worship dizzying to the Western observer, because ultimately the basic religious insight of Hinduism is that there are an infinite number of paths to and manifestations of the One. Thus Hindus, unlike Christians or Muslims, for example, do not believe that the fullness of religious truth can be summed up in a neat package of doctrinal statements, nor do they believe that religion consists of a clear-cut struggle of truth versus error. The Western notion that something either is or is not, but cannot be both, has no place in the Hindu world, where countless apparent contradictions exist comfortably alongside one another.

Hinduism is also more than just a family of often seemingly contradictory beliefs and religious rituals. It involves all the ways in which Hindus live and relate to one another. Therefore, as one studies Hinduism's historical evolution, it is necessary to put aside the modern Western notion of a meaningful dichotomy between religion and social organization. Hinduism is a total way of life, and this is best seen in the caste system.

Not all Hindus are members of a caste, but most are, which suggests that beneath the variety of beliefs and rituals we term Hindu, there are some fairly common elements. These include the notion of the oneness of the universe; a belief in the ultimate reality of the spiritual and the nonreality of the corporeal world; the caste system; and *dharma* (caste law), reincarnation, and *karma* (the fruits of action performed in a previous life).

The Hindu Search for Divine Reality
▼▼▼

17 ▼ *THE UPANISHADS*

Between about 700 and 500 B.C. Indo-Aryan religious teachers brought the Vedic age to a close in a most spectacular intellectual manner. Taking certain concepts that were implied in the later Vedic hymns, these teachers developed a vision of an all-inclusive Being, or Ultimate Reality, called *Brahman* and enunciated that theological breakthrough in a number of speculative treatises known as *Upanishads*.

Upanishad means "additional sitting near a teacher," and these texts often take the form of a dialogue between a teacher and a pupil who seek to go beyond the Vedas in their search for ultimate wisdom. As one might expect, there are many contradictions among the many Upanishadic texts, yet a fundamental message binds them: not only is there a Universal Soul, or Brahman, but the innermost essence of a person, the *atman*, or spiritual self, is one with Brahman, the Self. Humans, therefore, are not outside Divine Reality; they are part of it.

The first selection, which comes from the early and especially revered *Chandogya Upanishad*, presents two analogies to explain this theological message. The second excerpt, taken from the later but equally important *Brihadaranyaka Upanishad*, deals with the issue of how that spark of Brahman, the Self, which is contained within each mortal body, finally achieves release and rejoins the One. Here we see an early enunciation of what will become two essential elements of Hindu religious thought: reincarnation and the law of karma.

The third selection, also from the *Brihadaranyaka*, describes the state of consciousness of a person who is on the verge of attaining release from the cycle of rebirth and union with Brahman.

QUESTIONS FOR ANALYSIS

1. What sort of truth does Uddalaka offer his son when he instructs him in "that . . . by which we know what cannot be known"?
2. What does the father mean when he states: "You, Svetaketu, are it"?
3. What is the law of karma?
4. Why are souls reincarnated?
5. How does one end the cycle of rebirth?
6. How important or real is this world to the soul returning to Brahman?
7. Why do good and evil cease to have any meaning to the soul that has found Brahman?
8. How is the Upanishadic view of Brahman a logical development from the message of the hymn to Purusha (Chapter 2, source 12)?

There lived once Svetaketu. . . . To him his father Uddalaka . . . said: "Svetaketu, go to school; for no one belonging to our race, dear son, who, not having studied, is, as it were, a brahmin[1] by birth only."

Having begun his apprenticeship when he was twelve years of age, Svetaketu returned to his father, when he was twenty-four, having then studied all the Vedas, — conceited, considering himself well-read, and stern.

His father said to him: "Svetaketu, as you are so conceited, considering yourself so well-read, and so stern, my dear, have you ever asked for that instruction by which we hear what cannot be heard, by which we perceive what cannot be perceived, by which we know what cannot be known?"

"What is that instruction, Sir?" he asked. . . .

"Fetch me . . . a fruit of the Nyagrodha tree."

"Here is one, Sir."

"Break it."

"It is broken, Sir."

"What do you see there?"

"These seeds, almost infinitesimal."

"Break one of them."

"It is broken, Sir."

"What do you see there?"

"Not anything, Sir."

The father said: "My son, that subtle essence which you do not perceive there, of that very essence this great Nyagrodha tree exists.

"Believe it, my son. That which is the subtle essence, in it all that exists has its self. It is the True. It is the Self, and you, . . . Svetaketu, are it."

"Please, Sir, inform me still more," said the son.

"Be it so, my child," the father replied.

"Place this salt in water, and then wait on me in the morning."

The son did as he was commanded.

---

[1]A member of the priestly caste. Brahmin is a male gender variation of the neuter Brahman.

The father said to him: "Bring me the salt, which you placed in the water last night."

The son having looked for it, found it not, for, of course, it was melted.

The father said: "Taste it from the surface of the water. How is it?"

The son replied: "It is salt."

"Taste it from the middle. How is it?"

The son replied: "It is salt."

"Taste it from the bottom. How is it?"

The son replied: "It is salt."

The father said: "Throw it away and then wait on me."

He did so; but the salt exists forever.[2]

Then the father said: "Here also, in this body,[3] . . . you do not perceive the True, my son; but there indeed it is.

"That which is the subtle essence,[4] in it all that exists has its self. It is the True. It is the Self, and you, Svetaketu, are it."

    •   •   •

"And when the body grows weak through old age, or becomes weak through illness, at that time that person, after separating himself from his members, as a mango, or fig, or Pippala-fruit is separated from the stalk,[5] hastens back again as he came, to the place from which he started, to new life. . . .

"Then both his knowledge and his work take hold of him[6] and his acquaintance with former things.[7]

"And as a caterpillar, after having reached the end of a blade of grass, and after having made another approach to another blade, draws itself together towards it, thus does this Self, after having thrown off this body and dispelled all ignorance, and after making another approach to another body, draw himself together towards it.

"And as a goldsmith, taking a piece of gold, turns it into another, newer and more beautiful shape, so does this Self, after having thrown off this body and dispelled all ignorance, make unto himself another, newer and more beautiful shape. . . .

"Now as a man is like this or like that, according as he acts and according as he behaves, so will he be: — a man of good acts will become good, a man of bad acts, bad. He becomes pure by pure deeds, bad by bad deeds.

"And here they say that a person consists of desires. And as is his desire, so is his will; and as is his will, so is his deed; and whatever deed he does, that he will reap.

"And here there is this verse: 'To whatever object a man's own mind is attached, to that he goes strenuously together with his deed; and having obtained the consequences of whatever deed he does here on earth, he returns again from that world . . . to this world of action.[8]

"So much for the man who desires. But as to the man who does not desire, who, not desiring, freed from desires, is satisfied in his desires, or desires the Self only, his vital spirits do not depart elsewhere, — being Brahman, he goes to Brahman.

"On this there is this verse: 'When all desires which once entered his heart are undone, then does the mortal become immortal, then he obtains Brahman.'"

    •   •   •

"Now as a man, when embraced by a beloved wife, knows nothing that is without, nothing that is within, thus this person, when embraced by the intelligent Self, knows nothing that is without, nothing that is within. This indeed is his true form, in which his wishes are fulfilled, in which the Self only is his wish, in which no wish is left, — free from any sorrow.

"Then a father is not a father, a mother not a mother, the worlds not worlds, the gods not gods, the Vedas not Vedas. Then a thief is

---

[2]The salt, although invisible, remains forever in the water.

[3]The human body.

[4]The soul.

[5]The image is of a fruit that carries the seed of new life, even as it decays.

[6]The law of karma, which is defined more fully later in this document.

[7]One's acquaintance with things in a former life explains the peculiar talents and inclinations evident in a child.

[8]This, in essence, is the law of karma.

not a thief, a murderer not a murderer, a Kandala not a Kandala,[9] a Sramana not a Sramana,[10] a Tapasa not a Tapasa.[11] He is not followed by good, not followed by evil, for he has then overcome all the sorrows of the heart."

Dharma: The Imperative of Caste Law
▼▼▼

18 ▼ *THE BHAGAVAD GITA*

The *Bhagavad Gita* (*Song of the Blessed Lord*) is Hinduism's most beloved sacred text. The poem appears in its present form as an episode in the *Mahabharata* (*The Great Deeds of the Bharata Clan*), the world's longest epic, which was composed over a period from perhaps 500 B.C. to possibly A.D. 400 but which certainly drew from much earlier Aryan oral traditions. Like the Homeric Greek epics, the *Mahabharata* deals on one level with the clash of armies and the combat of individual heroes, and simultaneously on a higher plane it expounds theological and philosophical insights. Among all these spiritual interjections, the *Bhagavad Gita* is the most profound.

The *Gita's* date of final composition is uncertain; scholars fix it anywhere from 300 B.C. to A.D. 300. What is certain is that Hindu commentators have consistently considered the song to be the last and greatest of the Upanishadic texts, for they see it as the crystallization of all that was expressed and implied in the Upanishadic tradition.

The core question addressed in the *Bhagavad Gita* is how a person can become one with Brahman while still functioning in this world. The answer comes from Lord Krishna, the incarnation of Vishnu, the Divine Preserver. In this particular corporeal form, or *avatara*, Krishna/Vishnu serves as charioteer to the warrior hero Arjuna. Arjuna, a brave soldier, shrinks from entering battle when he realizes that he must fight close relatives. The hero god Krishna then proceeds to resolve Arjuna's quandary by explaining to him the moral imperative of caste-duty, or dharma.

QUESTIONS FOR ANALYSIS

1. Why should Arjuna not grieve for those whom he might kill?
2. According to Krishna, how "real" is the corporeal world?
3. Why has Vishnu had so many incarnations (avataras)? How do his incarnations differ from those of mortals such as Arjuna?
4. Why should one perform one's caste duty in a totally disinterested fashion?

---

[9]Kandalas were the lowest and most "unclean" of all casteless persons. See Chapter 5, sources 38 and 40.

[10]A holy beggar.
[11]A person performing penance.

Why is it better to perform one's caste duty poorly than to perform the duties of another caste well?

5. According to Krishna, what constitutes sin? What is evil?
6. What hope, if any, does Krishna's theological message hold for the lowest elements of Hindu society?
7. The Hindu caste system is based on several elemental religious beliefs. What are they?
8. In what ways is Krishna's message the same as that of the Upanishads?

The deity said, you have grieved for those who deserve no grief. . . . Learned men grieve not for the living nor the dead. Never did I not exist, nor you, nor these rulers of men; nor will any one of us ever hereafter cease to be. As in this body, infancy and youth and old age come to the embodied self, so does the acquisition of another body; a sensible man is not deceived about that. The contacts of the senses, O son of Kunti! which produce cold and heat, pleasure and pain, are not permanent, they are ever coming and going. Bear them, O descendant of Bharata! For, O chief of men! that sensible man whom they (pain and pleasure being alike to him) afflict not, he merits immortality. There is no existence for that which is unreal; there is no non-existence for that which is real. And the correct conclusion about both is perceived by those who perceive the truth. Know that to be indestructible which pervades all this. . . . He who thinks it[1] to be the killer and he who thinks it to be killed, both know nothing. It kills not, is not killed. It is not born, nor does it ever die, nor, having existed, does it exist no more. Unborn, everlasting, unchangeable, and primeval, it is not killed when the body is killed. O son of Pritha! how can that man who knows it thus to be indestructible, everlasting, unborn, and inexhaustible, how and whom can he kill, whom can he cause to be killed? As a man, casting off old clothes, puts on others and

new ones, so the embodied self casting off old bodies, goes to others and new ones. . . . It is everlasting, all-pervading, stable, firm, and eternal. It is said to be unperceived, to be unthinkable, to be unchangeable. Therefore knowing it to be such, you ought not to grieve. But even if you think that it is constantly born, and constantly dies, still, O you of mighty arms! you ought not to grieve thus. For to one that is born, death is certain; and to one that dies, birth is certain. . . . This embodied self, O descendant of Bharata! within every one's body is ever indestructible. Therefore you ought not to grieve for any being. Having regard to your own duty also, you ought not to falter, for there is nothing better for a kshatriya[2] than a righteous battle. Happy those kshatriyas, O son of Pritha! who can find such a battle . . . an open door to heaven! But if you will not fight this righteous battle, then you will have abandoned your own duty and your fame, and you will incur sin. . . . Your business is with action alone; not by any means with fruit. Let not the fruit of action be your motive to action. Let not your attachment be fixed on inaction. Having recourse to devotion . . . perform actions, casting off all attachment, and being equable in success or ill-success; such equability is called devotion. . . . The wise who have obtained devotion cast off the fruit of action,[3] and released from the shackles of re-

[1]The atman, or individual soul, and Brahman, which are one and the same.
[2]A member of the warrior caste.
[3]They do not concern themselves with the earthly con-

sequences of their actions and develop no attachments to the rewards of this world (fame, wealth, family) that might result from those actions.

peated births, repair to that seat where there is no unhappiness. . . . The man who, casting off all desires, lives free from attachments, who is free from egoism, and from the feeling that this or that is mine, obtains tranquility. This, O son of Pritha! is the Brahmic state; attaining to this, one is never deluded; and remaining in it in one's last moments, one attains the Brahmic bliss.[4] . . .

I have passed through many births, O Arjuna! and you also. I know them all, but you, O terror of your foes! do not know them. Even though I am unborn and inexhaustible in my essence, even though I am lord of all beings, still I am born by means of my delusive power. Whensoever, O descendant of Bharata! piety languishes, and impiety is in the ascendant, I create myself. I am born age after age, for the protection of the good, for the destruction of evil-doers, and the establishment of piety. . . . The fourfold division of castes was created by me according to the appointment of qualities and duties. . . . The duties of brahmins, kshatriyas, and vaisyas, and of sudras, too, O terror of your foes! are distinguished according to the qualities born of nature.[5] Tranquility, restraint of the senses, penance, purity, forgiveness, straightforwardness, also knowledge, experience, and belief in a future world, this is the natural duty of brahmins. Valor, glory, courage, dexterity, not slinking away from battle, gifts, exercise of lordly power, this is the natural duty of kshatriyas. Agriculture, tending cattle, trade, this is the natural duty of vaisyas.

And the natural duty of sudras, too, consists in service. Every man intent on his own respective duties obtains perfection. Listen, now, how one intent on one's own duty obtains perfection. Worshiping, by the performance of his own duty, him from whom all things proceed, and by whom all this is permeated, a man obtains perfection. One's duty, though defective, is better than another's duty well performed. Performing the duty prescribed by nature, one does not incur sin. O son of Kunti! one should not abandon a natural duty though tainted with evil; for all actions are enveloped by evil, as fire by smoke. One who is self-restrained, whose understanding is unattached everywhere, from whom affections have departed, obtains the supreme perfection of freedom from action by renunciation. Learn from me, only in brief, O son of Kunti! how one who has obtained perfection attains the Brahman, which is the highest culmination of knowledge. A man possessed of a pure understanding, controlling his self by courage, discarding sound and other objects of sense, casting off affection and aversion; who frequents clean places, who eats little, whose speech, body, and mind are restrained, who is always intent on meditation and mental abstraction, and has recourse to unconcern, who abandoning egoism, stubbornness, arrogance, desire, anger, and all belongings, has no thought that this or that is mine, and who is tranquil, becomes fit for assimilation with the Brahman.

[4]Brahma-nirvana, or merging with Brahman and release from the cycle of rebirth.
[5]Each caste consists of people born to that station by virtue of their nature. Each person's karma has made that person's nature suitable for a particular caste and only that caste. Brahmins teach and offer sacrifices; kshatriyas rule and fight; vaisyas work; and sudras serve. See *The Hymn to Purusha,* Chapter 2, source 12, and *The Laws of Manu,* Chapter 5, source 40.

▼▼▼

Challenges to the Caste System: The Mahavira and the Buddha

By 600 B.C. the central spiritual question in Indian society was how one finds liberation from karma and the cycle of rebirth. As we have seen, the Upanishadic teachers offered their answers. The eventual result by about 300 B.C. was establishment of the caste system throughout most of Indian society and fairly general acceptance of the notion that dharma (the law) meant caste-duty. This was not, however, the only answer.

Even as the brahmin, or priestly, class was in the process of turning itself into the dominant Hindu caste and defining what would become mainstream Hinduism, several teachers emerged from the kshatriya, or warrior, class to offer alternatives to the caste system. One of these was Nataputta Vardhamana (ca 599–527 B.C.), known to history as the *Mahavira* (the Great Hero). The other was Siddhartha Gautama (ca 563–483 B.C.), better known as the *Buddha* (the Enlightened One).

Each teacher and his doctrine is understandable only within the context of an Indo-Aryan cosmology. Although both formulated philosophies that denied certain concepts basic to what was emerging as classical, brahminical Hinduism, the questions each asked and the answers they offered were predicated upon the world-denying assumptions underlying all Indian religious thought.

Ironically, although both doctrines began as philosophies in which divinities played no role, they became in time theistic (god-centered) religions. *Jainism,* which developed out of the Mahavira's teachings, would win adherents only in India, but it has survived to the present. Half a millennium after the Buddha's release from the bonds of matter, his teachings had been transformed into a family of related religions, many of which worshiped the Buddha himself as a divine being. For well over two thousand years *Buddhism* in its various forms has profoundly shaped the lives of countless devotees throughout South and East Asia and remains a vital force today, but not in India, its original home.

A Call to the Heroic Life
▼▼▼

19 ▼ THE BOOK OF GOOD CONDUCT

Our picture of the Mahavira and his teachings is hazy because even the Jains acknowledge that the earliest written sources for the Great Hero's life and doctrine date no earlier than two centuries after his death. One of these sources is the *Acaranga Sutra* (*Book of Good Conduct*), which Jains revere as the first of their eleven major sacred texts.

Here we encounter reincarnation, karma, and dharma, but with a Jain twist, and we discover Jain *ahimsa*, or absolute nonviolence toward all life. The first excerpt defines dharma, the second tells how the Mahavira conquered karma, and the third outlines the five great Jain vows.

QUESTIONS FOR ANALYSIS

1. What is dharma, according to Jainism?
2. What is the Jain definition of karma?
3. What sort of "heroic" life does the Great Hero challenge his followers to lead?
4. The Mahavira was acknowledged as the *Jina*, or Conqueror. Consequently, his followers are Jains. What do Jains seek to conquer?
5. Compare Jain notions of dharma and karma with those of conventional Hinduism. Compare Jain notions of sin and evil with those articulated in the *Bhagavad Gita*. What strike you as more significant, the differences or the similarities? What do you conclude from this?
6. Both Lord Krishna in the *Bhagavad Gita* and the Mahavira teach a doctrine of nonattachment to this world. How do their teachings parallel one another? Where do they diverge? Which are more pronounced, the differences or the similarities? What do you conclude from this?
7. Compare the five Jain vows with the Hebrew Ten Commandments (Chapter 2, source 15). What are more pronounced, the differences or the similarities? What do you conclude from this?

The Arhats[1] . . . of the past, present, and future, all say thus, speak thus, declare thus, explain thus: all breathing, existing, living, sentient creatures[2] should not be slain, nor treated with violence, nor abused, nor tormented, nor driven away.

This is the pure, unchangeable, eternal law [dharma], which the clever ones, who understand the world, have declared: among the zealous and the not zealous, among the faithful and the not faithful, among the not cruel and the cruel, among those who have worldly weakness and those who have not, among those who like

social bonds and those who do not: "that is the truth, that is so, that is proclaimed in this."

Having adopted the law, one should not hide it, nor forsake it. Correctly understanding the law, one should arrive at indifference for the impressions of the senses, and "not act on the motives of the world." "He who is not of this mind, how should he come to the other?"[3]

. . .

Beings which are born in all states become individually sinners by their actions.[4]

The Venerable One[5] understands thus: he who is under the conditions of existence, that

[1]Perfect souls, or saints.
[2]Not only the "higher forms" of sentient life, such as humans and animals, but also insects, plants, seeds, lichens, and even beings known as *earth bodies, wind bodies, water bodies,* and *fire bodies.*

[3]How is it possible for a person to sin ("come to the other") who does not "act on the motives of the world"?
[4]The law of karma as understood by Jains.
[5]The Mahavira.

fool suffers pain. Thoroughly knowing karma, the Venerable One avoids sin.

The sage, perceiving the double karma,[6] proclaims the incomparable activity,[7] he, the knowing one; knowing the current of worldliness, the current of sinfulness, and the impulse.

Practicing the sinless abstinence from killing, he[8] did no acts, neither himself nor with the assistance of others; he to whom women were known as the causes of all sinful acts, he saw the true state of the world. . . .

He well saw that bondage comes through action. Whatever is sinful, the Venerable One left that undone: he consumed clean food.[9]

Knowing measure in eating and drinking, he was not desirous of delicious food, nor had he a longing for it. . . .

The Venerable One, exerting himself, did not seek sleep for the sake of pleasure; he waked up himself, and slept only a little, free from desires. . . .

Always well guarded, he bore the pains caused by grass, cold, fire, flies, and gnats; manifold pains.

He traveled in the pathless country of the Ladhas.[10] . . .

In Ladha natives attacked him; the dogs bit him, ran at him.

Few people kept off the attacking, biting dogs. . . .

Such were the inhabitants. Many other mendicants,[11] eating rough food . . . and carrying about a strong pole [to keep off the dogs], . . . lived there.

Even thus armed they were bitten by the dogs, torn by the dogs. It is difficult to travel in Ladha.

Ceasing to use the stick against living beings, abandoning the care of the body, the houseless, the Venerable One endures the thorns of the villages being perfectly enlightened.

As an elephant at the head of the battle, so was Mahavira there victorious. . . .

The Venerable One was able to abstain from indulgence of the flesh. . . .

Purgatives and emetics, anointing of the body and bathing, shampooing and cleansing of the teeth do not behoove him, after he learned [that the body is something unclean]. . . .

In summer he exposes himself to the heat, he sits squatting in the sun; he lives on rough food: rice, pounded jujube, and beans. . . .

Sometimes the Venerable One did not drink for half a month or even for a month.

Or he did not drink for more than two months, or even six months, day and night, without desire for drink. Sometimes he ate stale food. . . .

Having wisdom, Mahavira committed no sin himself, nor did he induce others to do so, nor did he consent to the sins of others.

Having entered a village or a town, he begged for food which had been prepared for somebody else. Having got clean food, he used it, restraining the impulses. . . . The Venerable One slowly wandered about, and, killing no creatures, he begged for his food.

Moist or dry or cold food, old beans, old pap, or bad grain, whether he did or did not get such food he was rich. . . .

Himself understanding the truth and restraining the impulses for the purification of the soul, finally liberated, and free from delusion, the Venerable One was well guarded during his whole life.

The Venerable Ascetic[12] Mahavira endowed with the highest knowledge and intuition taught the five great vows.

· · ·

The first great vow, Sir, runs thus:

I renounce all killing of living beings, whether subtle or gross, whether movable or

---

[6]The present and the future.
[7]The life of the true Jain.
[8]The Mahavira.
[9]Food that does the absolute minimum violence to sentient life in all its forms.

[10]Possibly western Bengal.
[11]Wandering holy people who beg for their food.
[12]A person who leads a life of rigorous self-denial for religious reasons.

immovable. Nor shall I myself kill living beings, nor cause others to do it, nor consent to it. As long as I live, I confess and blame, repent and exempt myself of these sins, in the thrice threefold way,[13] in mind, speech, and body. . . .

The second great vow runs thus:

I renounce all vices of lying speech arising from anger or greed or fear or mirth. I shall neither myself speak lies, nor cause others to speak lies, nor consent to the speaking of lies by others. . . .

The third great vow runs thus:

I renounce all taking of anything not given,[14]

either in a village or a town or a wood, either of little or much, of small or great, of living or lifeless things. I shall neither take myself what is not given, nor cause others to take it, nor consent to their taking it.

The fourth great vow runs thus:

I renounce all sexual pleasures, either with gods or men or animals. I shall not give way to sensuality. . . .

The fifth great vow runs thus:

I renounce all attachments, whether little or much, small or great, living or lifeless; neither shall I myself form such attachments, nor cause others to do so, nor consent to their doing so.

The Buddha's First Sermon
▼▼▼

20 ▼ *SETTING IN MOTION THE WHEEL OF THE LAW*

Many parallels exist between the legendary lives of the Mahavira and the Buddha, and several of their teachings are strikingly similar. Each rejected the special sanctity of Vedic literature, and each denied the meaningfulness of caste distinctions and duties. Yet a close investigation of their doctrines reveals substantial differences.

Like the Mahavira, young Prince Siddhartha Gautama, shrinking in horror at the many manifestations of misery in this world, fled his comfortable life and eventually became an ascetic. Where, however, the Mahavira found victory over karma in severe self-denial and total nonviolence, Prince Gautama found only severe disquiet. The ascetic life offered him no enlightenment as to how one might escape the sorrows of mortal existence. After abandoning extreme asceticism in favor of the *Middle Path* of self-restraint, Gautama achieved Enlightenment in a flash while meditating under a sacred pipal tree (see Chapter 1, source 9, seal 3). He was now the Buddha.

Legend tells us he then proceeded to share the path to Enlightenment by preaching a sermon in a deer park at Benares in northeastern India to five ascetics, who became his first disciples. Buddhists refer to that initial sermon as "Setting in Motion the Wheel of the Law," which means that the Buddha had

---

[13]Acting, commanding, consenting in mind, speech, or body, in the past, present, or future.

[14]The Jain must live as a beggar.

embarked on a journey (turning the wheel) on behalf of the law of Righteousness (dharma).

The following document is a reconstruction of that first sermon. Although composed at least several centuries after Siddhartha Gautama's death, it probably contains the essence of what the Buddha taught his earliest disciples.

QUESTIONS FOR ANALYSIS

1. What is the Middle Path? Why is it the proper path to Enlightenment?
2. What are the Four Noble Truths?
3. How has the Buddha reached the point of escaping the cycle of rebirth?
4. How does one free oneself from this world?
5. Buddhists call the law, or code, taught by the Buddha *dharma*. How does Buddhist dharma differ from that of Hinduism?
6. In what ways have both the Mahavira and the Buddha rejected the caste system, especially the primacy of the brahmins? Why might Jainism and Buddhism appeal to non-brahmins?
7. Both the Buddha and the Mahavira came from the warrior caste. Do their respective doctrines hint at this fact in any way?
8. What elements do Hinduism, Jainism, and Buddhism share? Where do they differ? What are more significant, the similarities or the differences? Is it correct to call Hinduism, Jainism, and Buddhism *world denying*?

And the Blessed One thus addressed the five Bhikkhus.[1] "There are two extremes, O Bhikkhus, which he who has given up the world, ought to avoid. What are these two extremes? A life given to pleasures, devoted to pleasures and lusts: this is degrading, sensual, vulgar, ignoble, and profitless; and a life given to mortifications: this is painful, ignoble, and profitless. By avoiding these two extremes, O Bhikkhus, the Tathagata[2] has gained the knowledge of the Middle Path which leads to insight, which leads to wisdom which conduces to calm, to knowledge, to the Sambodhi,[3] to Nirvana.[4]

"Which, O Bhikkhus, is this Middle Path the knowledge of which the Tathagata has gained, which leads to insight, which leads to wisdom, which conduces to calm, to knowledge, to the Sambodhi, to Nirvana? It is the Holy Eightfold Path, namely, Right Belief,[5] Right Aspiration,[6] Right Speech,[7] Right Conduct,[8] Right Means of Livelihood,[9] Right Endeavor,[10] Right Memory,[11] Right Meditation.[12] This, O Bhikkhus, is the Middle Path the knowledge of which the Tathagata has gained, which leads to insight, which leads to wisdom,

---

[1] Ascetics.
[2] One of the Buddha's titles, its derivation is not totally clear. It might mean "He who has arrived at the Truth."
[3] Total enlightenment.
[4] The state of release from the limitations of existence and rebirth.
[5] Understanding the truth about the universality of suffering and knowing the path leading to its extinction.
[6] A mind free of ill will, sensuous desire, and cruelty.
[7] Abstaining from lying, harsh language, and gossip.
[8] Avoiding killing, stealing, and unlawful sexual intercourse.
[9] Avoiding any occupation that brings harm directly or indirectly to any other living being.
[10] Avoiding unwholesome and evil things.
[11] Awareness in contemplation.
[12] Concentration that ultimately reaches the level of trance.

which conduces to calm, to knowledge, to the Sambodhi, to Nirvana.

"This, O Bhikkhus, is the Noble Truth of Suffering: Birth is suffering; decay is suffering; illness is suffering; death is suffering. Presence of objects we hate, is suffering; Separation from objects we love, is suffering; not to obtain what we desire, is suffering. Briefly, . . . clinging to existence is suffering.

"This, O Bhikkhus, is the Noble Truth of the Cause of suffering: Thirst, that leads to rebirth, accompanied by pleasure and lust, finding its delight here and there. This thirst is threefold, namely, thirst for pleasure, thirst for existence, thirst for prosperity.

"This, O Bhikkhus, is the Noble Truth of the Cessation of suffering: it ceases with the complete cessation of this thirst, — a cessation which consists in the absence of every passion — with the abandoning of this thirst, with the doing away with it, with the deliverance from it, with the destruction of desire.

"This, O Bhikkhus, is the Noble Truth of the Path which leads to the cessation of suffering: that Holy Eightfold Path, that is to say, Right Belief, Right Aspiration, Right Speech, Right Conduct, Right Means of Livelihood, Right Endeavor, Right Memory, Right Meditation. . . .

"As long, O Bhikkhus, as I did not possess with perfect purity this true knowledge and insight into these four Noble Truths . . . so long, O Bhikkhus, I knew that I had not yet obtained the highest, absolute Sambodhi in the world of men and gods. . . .

"But since I possessed, O Bhikkhus, with perfect purity this true knowledge and insight into these four Noble Truths . . . then I knew, O Bhikkhus, that I had obtained the highest, universal Sambodhi. . . .

"And this knowledge and insight arose in my mind: "The emancipation of my mind cannot be lost; this is my last birth; hence I shall not be born again!""

Admitting Women to the Mendicant Life
▼▼▼

21 ▼ THE DISCIPLINE

Although the Buddha originally preached his message of Enlightenment to a group of five male ascetics, his teachings soon attracted large numbers of people who desired to follow the Middle Path in the hope of achieving release from the shackles of existence. These aspirants to Buddhahood fell into two categories. An enthusiastic minority became mendicant, or begging, monks and attempted to live the Holy Eightfold Path to its fullest. They were known collectively as the *Sangha* or Order [of monks]. Most people attracted to the Buddha's message, however, remained enmeshed in the affairs of this world and constituted a class of faithful laity who supported the Sangha's holy beggars and attempted, in individual ways, to translate the Buddhist Middle Path into a code of conduct that enabled them to balance their attachments to this world with their desire to find in Buddhism a means of escaping the bonds of suffering.

This group of lay faithful contained from the start both men and women, whereas the Sangha appears to have originally been composed of only men. Soon, however, the question arose: What to do about women who wish to become monastic beggars? According to a venerable tradition, the first woman to challenge the Buddha on this issue was his maternal aunt and foster mother, Queen Maha-Prajapati, who had recently been widowed.

The following story of Maha-Prajapati's attempt to become a mendicant is preserved in a collection of documents relating to the earliest history of the Buddhist Sangha known as the *Vinaya (The Discipline)*. Although the *Vinaya* was assembled and written down in its present form more than a century after the Buddha's death, the stories contained within it probably are based on strong oral traditions and contain more than a germ of historical truth.

QUESTIONS FOR ANALYSIS

1. Why does the Buddha finally relent and allow his aunt and other women to embrace the mendicant life?
2. Even after giving his permission, what does he think about the wisdom of allowing women to enter monastic life?
3. Consider the eight special rules for Buddhist nuns. What is their combined effect?
4. What can you infer from this document about the general status of women in north India in the age of the Buddha?
5. Notwithstanding the special rules imposed on them, as well as the profession's natural rigor, why would some women find the mendicant monastic life attractive?

Now the Blessed Buddha was staying among the Sakyas[1] in Kapilavatthu. . . . And Maha-Prajapati the Gotami[2] went to the place where the Blessed One was, and on arriving there, bowed down before the Blessed One, and remained standing on one side. And so standing she spoke thus to the Blessed One:

"It would be well, lord, if women should be allowed to renounce their homes and enter the homeless state under the doctrine and discipline proclaimed by the Tathagata."[3]

"Enough, Gotami. Let it not please you that women should be allowed to do so."

[And a second and a third time Maha-Prajapati the Gotami made the same request in the same words, and received the same reply.]

Then Maha-Prajapati the Gotami, sad and sorrowful that the Blessed One would not permit women to enter the homeless state, bowed down before the Blessed One, and keeping him on her right hand as she passed him, departed . . . weeping and in tears.

Now when the Blessed One had remained at Kapilavatthu as long as he thought fit, he set out on his journey toward Vesali; and traveling

---

[1]The Buddha's clan.
[2]Her family name; before renouncing his patrimony, the Buddha had been surnamed Gautama.

[3]One of the Buddha's titles. See note 2 in the previous document.

straight on he in due course arrived there. And there at Vesali the Blessed One stayed. . . .

And Maha-Prajapati the Gotami cut off her hair, and put on orange-colored robes,[4] and set out, with a number of women of the Sakya clan, toward Vesali; and in due course she arrived at Vesali. . . . And Maha-Prajapati the Gotami, with swollen feet and covered with dust, sad and sorrowful, weeping and in tears, took her stand outside under the entrance porch.

And the venerable Ananda[5] saw her so standing there, and on seeing her so he said to Maha-Prajapati: "Why are you standing there, outside the porch, with swollen feet and covered with dust, sad and sorrowful, weeping and in tears?"

"Because Ananda, the lord, the Blessed One, does not permit women to renounce their homes and enter the homeless state under the doctrine and discipline proclaimed by the Tathagata."

Then the venerable Ananda went up to the place where the Blessed One was, and bowed down before the Blessed One, and took his seat on one side. And, so sitting, the venerable Ananda said to the Blessed One:

"Behold, lord, Maha-Prajapati the Gotami is standing outside under the entrance porch, with swollen feet and covered with dust, sad and sorrowful, weeping and in tears, because the Blessed One does not permit women to renounce their homes and enter the homeless state under the doctrine and discipline proclaimed by the Blessed One.

"It would be well, lord, if women were to have permission granted to them to do as she desires."

"Enough, Ananda. Let it not please you that women should be allowed to do so."

[And a second and a third time Ananda made the same request, in the same words, and received the same reply]. . .

Then the venerable Ananda thought: "The Blessed One does not give his permission, let me now ask the Blessed One on another ground." And the venerable Ananda said to the Blessed One:

"Are women, lord, capable when they have gone forth from the household life and entered the homeless state, under the doctrine and discipline proclaimed by the Blessed One — are they capable of realizing the fruit of conversion, or of the second path, or of the third path,[6] or of Arahantship?"[7]

"They are capable, Ananda."

"If then, lord, they are so capable, since Maha-Prajapati the Gotami has proved herself of great service to the Blessed One, when as aunt and nurse she nourished him and gave him milk, and on the death of his mother suckled the Blessed One at her own breast, it would be well, lord, that women should have permission to go forth from the household life and enter the homeless state under the doctrine and discipline proclaimed by the Tathagata."

"If then, Ananda, Maha-Prajapati the Gotami takes upon herself the eight chief rules, let that be reckoned as her ordination.[8] They are these:

1. "A nun, even if of a hundred years standing, shall make salutation to, shall rise up in the presence of, shall bow down before, and shall perform all proper duties toward a monk, even a newly initiated monk. This is a rule to be revered and reverenced, honored and observed, and her life long never to be transgressed.

[4]Orange robes are the distinguishing costume of Buddhist monks.
[5]The Buddha's beloved disciple and personal attendant.
[6]The three states that anticipate Enlightenment ("crossing the stream") once one has received and accepted the message of the Four Noble Truths: the fruit of entering the stream; the fruit of the once returner; the fruit of the nonreturner.
[7]*Arahant* is a Sanskrit word meaning "a worthy person." In a Buddhist context it means a perfected or enlightened person — a Buddha.
[8]By accepting these eight special rules, she is ordained to the monastic life.

2. "A nun is not to spend the rainy season[9] in a district in which there is no monk. This is a rule . . . never to be transgressed.

3. "Every half month a nun is to await from the order of Bhikkhus[10] two things, . . . the date of the uposatha ceremony,[11] and the time when the monk will come to give the exhortation. This is a rule . . . never to be transgressed.

4. "After keeping the rainy season the nun is to hold Pavarana,[12] to inquire whether any fault can be laid to her charge, before both orders — monks as well as nuns — with respect to three matters, namely, what has been seen, and what has been heard, and what has been suspected. This is a rule . . . never to be transgressed.

5. "A nun who has been guilty of a serious offense is to undergo suitable discipline toward both orders, monks and nuns. This is a rule . . . never to be transgressed.

6. "When a nun, as novice, has been trained for two years in the . . . rules, she is to ask leave for . . . ordination from both orders, monks as well as nuns. This is a rule . . . never to be transgressed.

7. "A nun is on no pretext to revile or abuse a monk. This is a rule . . . never to be transgressed.

8. "From henceforth official admonition by nuns of monks is forbidden, whereas the official admonition of nuns by monks is not forbidden. This is a rule . . . never to be transgressed.

"If, Ananda, Maha-Prajapati the Gotami take upon herself these eight chief rules, let that be reckoned . . . as her ordination."

Then the venerable Ananda, when he had learned from the Blessed One these eight chief rules, went to Maha-Prajapati the Gotami and told her all that the Blessed One had said, to which she replied: . . .

"I, Ananda, take upon me these eight chief rules never to be transgressed my life long."

Then the venerable Ananda returned to the Blessed One, and bowed down before him, and took his seat on one side. And, so sitting, the venerable Ananda said to the Blessed One: "Maha-Prajapati the Gotami, lord, has taken upon herself the eight chief rules, the aunt of the Blessed One has received . . . ordination."

"If, Ananda, women had not received permission to go out from the household life and enter the homeless state, under the doctrine and discipline proclaimed by the Tathagata, then would the pure religion, Ananda, have lasted long, the good law would have stood fast for a thousand years. But since, Ananda, women now have received that permission, the pure religion, Ananda, will not now last so long, the good law will now stand fast for only five hundred years. Just, Ananda, as houses in which there are many women and but few men, are easily violated by robbers, by burglars; just so, Ananda, under whatever doctrine and discipline women are allowed to go out from the household life into the homeless state, that religion will not last long.

"And just, Ananda, as when disease, called mildew, falls upon a field of rice in fine condition, that field of rice does not continue long; just so, Ananda, under whatsoever doctrine and discipline women are allowed to go forth from the household life into the homeless state, that religion will not last long. And just, Ananda, as when disease, called blight, falls upon a field of sugar-cane in good condition, that field of sugar-cane does not continue long; just so, Ananda, under whatsoever doctrine and discipline women are allowed to go forth from the household life into the homeless state, that religion does not last long. And just, Ananda, as a man

---

[9]The time of spiritual retreat.
[10]Male monks.
[11]The twice-monthly monastic meeting.

[12]The final ceremony of the religious retreat where one seeks to discover one's faults.

would in anticipation build an embankment to a great reservoir, beyond which the water should not overpass; just even so, Ananda, have

I in anticipation laid down these eight chief rules for the nuns, their life long not to be overpassed."

Persians, Israelites, and Their Gods of the Universe

By the sixth century B.C. two peoples of Southwest Asia, the Hebrews and the Persians, had evolved separate visions of a single God of the universe who demanded wholehearted devotion and imposed an uncompromising code of moral behavior upon all believers. Both the Persian Ahura Mazda (Wise Lord) and the Hebrew Yahweh (I Am Who I Am) were originally perceived as sky gods, existing among a multiplicity of other gods of nature; by the sixth century, however, their respective devotees worshiped each as the sole creator of the entire universe and envisioned each as transcending all material creation. This totally spiritual nature did not prevent either from also being a god of history. That is, each God used humans as agents to serve the Divine Will and thereby to assist in the realization of the Divine Plan for humanity. For both the Persians and Hebrews, human history had a purpose and a goal. By serving as agents in the unfolding of God's plan for creation, humans thus assumed a spiritual dignity and importance that they could otherwise never have hoped to attain.

The Fight Between Good and Evil
▼▼▼

22 ▼ *Zarathustra, GATHAS*

About the same time the Aryans were invading the Indian subcontinent, a closely related group of Indo-Europeans was settling the Iranian highlands. The religion and general culture of these people initially resembled that of the Vedic Aryans. For example, they celebrated the slaying of Verethra, the drought, by their war god Indara. The parallel with Indra's striking down Vritra, the dragon of drought, is obvious (see Chapter 2, source 12). In time, however, these settlers, of what is today largely Iran and the southern Caucasus region of the former Soviet Union, developed a civilization that differed radically from that of the Indo-Aryans. We call that ancient civilization Persian.

By the late sixth century B.C. the Persians possessed the largest empire the world had yet seen. For nearly two centuries they united Southwest Asia and portions of Central Asia, Northeast Africa, and the Balkan region of Europe into a politically centralized yet culturally diverse entity. During the reign of Darius the Great (r. 522–486 B.C.), who rightly styled himself King of Kings, the royal house of Persia officially adopted as its religion the teachings of a native son, Zarathustra. The highly ethical message of this Persian religious visionary appears to have been one of the major factors contributing to the empire's general policy of good government.

We know little about the life of Zarathustra. Apparently, he flourished in eastern Iran around 660 B.C. and taught his disciples to uphold, through ritual and moral conduct, the cause of Ahura Mazda, the sole deity of the universe. It is clear that Zarathustra claimed to be a prophet (a person speaking by divine inspiration, thereby revealing the will of God). It is equally clear that Zarathustra transmitted to his followers the message that Ahura Mazda required all humans to join in the cosmic struggle against Angra Mainyu (Enemy Spirit). Although in no way the equal of Ahura Mazda, Angra Mainyu, the Liar, afflicted human souls with evil and led them away from the path of righteousness.

Zarathustra's teachings took hold in Persia, evolving into a complex religion we call *Zoroastrianism* (after Zoroaster, the Greek version of Zarathustra). In the process, however, Zarathustra's strict monotheism was lost. From A.D. 224 to 651 Zoroastrianism was the official state religion of a revived Persian Empire under the Sassanian house, but Zoroastrianism had by then lapsed into polytheism. Moreover, Angra Mainyu was now seen as coeternal and coequal with Ahura Mazda. One deity was the creator of all goodness; the other was the origin of all evil.

The *Avesta*, the Zoroastrian collection of holy scripture, was compiled only in the early Sassanian era and strongly reflects this later dualism. It also contains, however, a few short devotional hymns, known as *Gathas*, which date to the age of Zarathustra and probably owe their composition to him or an early disciple. Essentially our only reliable sources for the teachings of the Persian prophet, they illustrate his vision and message.

QUESTIONS FOR ANALYSIS

1. Where and how does Zarathustra refer to Ahura Mazda's use of humanity and history to realize certain sacred purposes? How does each person's life become a microcosm of the battle between Ahura Mazda and the Liar?
2. What is promised to those who serve Ahura Mazda faithfully? Compare those promises with what Yahweh promised the Children of Israel for their faithful service (Chapter 2, source 15). What do you conclude from this comparison?
3. What does Zarathustra think of those persons who do not accept and serve Ahura Mazda?
4. How do we know that Zarathustra believed Ahura Mazda would ultimately triumph over evil?
5. What evidence indicates that Zarathustra saw Ahura Mazda as the sole creator of the universe?

6. Does Zarathustra see his faith as only one of many paths to the truth, or is it the Truth?
7. Compare the message proclaimed by Zarathustra with the messages of the Mahavira and the Buddha. Which strike you as more significant, their similarities or differences, and what do you conclude from your answer?

Then shall I recognize you as strong and holy, Mazda,[1] when by the hand in which you yourself hold the destinies that you will assign to the Liar and the Righteous . . . the might of Good Thought[2] shall come to me.

As the holy one I recognized you, Mazda Ahura,[3] when I saw you in the beginning at the birth of Life, when you made actions and words to have their reward — evil for the evil, a good Destiny for the good — through your wisdom when creation shall reach its goal.

At which goal you will come with your holy Spirit, O Mazda, with Dominion, at the same with Good Thought, by whose action the settlements[4] will prosper through Right. . . .

As the holy one I recognized you, Mazda Ahura, when Good Thought came to me and asked me, "Who are you? to whom do you belong? By what sign will you appoint the days for questioning about your possessions and yourself?"

Then I said to him: "To the first question, I am Zarathustra, a true foe to the Liar, to the utmost of my power, but a powerful support would I be to the Righteous, that I may attain the future things of the infinite Dominion, as I praise and proclaim you, Mazda.". . .

As the holy one I recognized you, Mazda Ahura, when Good Thought came to me, when the still mind taught me to declare what is best: "Let not a man seek again and again to please the Liars, for they make all the righteous enemies."

And thus Zarathustra himself, O Ahura, chooses that spirit of thine that is holiest, Mazda. May Right be embodied, full of life and strength! May Piety abide in the Dominion where the sun shines! May Good Thought give destiny to men according to their works!

· · ·

This I ask you, tell me truly, Ahura. Who is by generation the Father of Right, at the first? Who determined the path of sun and stars? Who is it by whom the moon waxes and wanes again? This, O Mazda, and yet more, I want to know.

This I ask you, tell me truly, Ahura. Who upheld the earth beneath and the firmament from falling? Who the waters and the plants? Who yoked swiftness to winds and clouds? Who is, O Mazda, creator of Good Thought?

This I ask you, tell me truly, Ahura. What artist made light and darkness? What artist made sleep and waking? Who made morning, noon, and night, that call the understanding man to his duty? . . .

This I ask you, tell me truly, Ahura. Who created together with Dominion the precious Piety? Who made by wisdom the son obedient to his father? I strive to recognize by these things you, O Mazda, creator of all things through the holy spirit. . . .

This I ask you, tell me truly, Ahura. The Religion which is the best for all that are, which in union with Right should make prosperous all that is mine, will they duly observe

---

[1]*Mazda* means "wise" or "wisdom."
[2]Zarathustra seems to have conceived of Good Thought, Piety, Right, and other such entities as angelic spirits and not simply abstract virtues.
[3]*Ahura* means "lord."
[4]Settled or civilized people.

it, the religion of my creed, with the words and action of Piety, in desire for your future good things, O Mazda?

This I ask you, tell me truly, Ahura — whether Piety will extend to those to whom your Religion shall be proclaimed? I was ordained at the first by you: all others I look upon with hatred of spirit.

This I ask you, tell me truly, Ahura. Who among those with whom I would speak is a righteous man, and who a liar? On which side is the enemy? . . .

This I ask you, tell me truly, Ahura — whether we shall drive the Lie away from us to those who being full of disobedience will not strive after fellowship with Right, nor trouble themselves with counsel of Good Thought. . . .

This I ask you, tell me truly, Ahura — whether through you I shall attain my goal . . . and that my voice may be effectual, that Welfare and Immortality may be ready to unite according to that promise with him who joins himself with Right.

This I ask you, tell me truly, Ahura — whether I shall indeed, O Right, earn that reward, even ten mares with a stallion and a camel,[5] which was promised to me, O Mazda, as well as through you the future gift of Welfare and Immortality.

⋅　⋅　⋅

I will speak of that which Mazda Ahura, the all-knowing, revealed to me first in this earthly life. Those of you that put not in practice this word as I think and utter it, to them shall be woe at the end of life. . . .

I will speak of that which the Holiest declared to me as the word that is best for mortals to obey: he, Mazda Ahura said, "They who at my bidding render him[6] obedience, shall all attain Welfare and Immortality by the actions of the Good Spirit.". . .

In immortality shall the soul of the righteous be joyful, in perpetuity shall be the torments of the Liars. All this does Mazda Ahura appoint by his Dominion.

A New Covenant for All Peoples
▼▼▼

23 ▼ THE BOOK OF ISAIAH

As we saw in Chapter 2, around 1200 B.C. the Israelites moved into the land of Canaan. Once settled there, they waged a continuing battle to retain their independence, cultural identity, and exclusive devotion to Yahweh. In the late eleventh century B.C., largely in response to Philistine pressure, the Israelites created a kingdom. Around 1020 B.C. their second king, David, captured Jerusalem and converted it into the religious and political capital of the Israelites.

The political stability of this kingdom was precarious at best. In 922 it was split into two independent entities: the larger kingdom of Israel in the north and the kingdom of Judah, centering on Jerusalem, in the south. In 722 the

---

[5]Symbols of wealth on earth.　　　　　　[6]Zarathustra.

Assyrians obliterated Israel. The more compact and remote kingdom of Judah survived until 586 B.C., when finally a Semitic people from Mesopotamia known as the Chaldeans captured and destroyed Jerusalem and carried off most of Judah's upper classes into exile in Babylon, an episode known forever after as the Babylonian Captivity.

Cultural and religious stability was equally precarious. The cult of Yahweh was in many ways more suitable to the life of the desert herder than to the settled farmer. As the Hebrews settled down, they adopted many of the religious practices of their Canaanite neighbors. This action occasioned angry protests from a group of religious reformers known as the *prophets*. The prophets, who claimed inspiration from Yahweh, now increasingly referred to simply as "the Lord," protested vehemently against debasement of the Mosaic religion, but in the process of their protest they broadened considerably the moral and theological scope of the worship of the Lord.

One of the greatest and last of these prophets was a person we know only as Second Isaiah. He served as the voice of a new faith that was born out of the anguish of the Babylonian Captivity. We call that faith *Judaism*.

The original Prophet Isaiah had towered over the religious scene of Jerusalem from the middle to late eighth century B.C. and left behind a rich legacy of teaching on the Lord's role as the God who controls the destinies of all people. Second Isaiah, who lived in the mid- and late sixth century B.C., carried on this tradition. Consequently, the prophecies of this otherwise unknown person were appended to the writings of the earlier Isaiah and appear as chapters 40 through 55 in the Bible's Book of Isaiah.

The following passages were composed around 538 B.C., when Cyrus the Great, king of Persia and conqueror of the Chaldean (Neo-Babylonian) Empire, released the Israelites from captivity. Here Second Isaiah metaphorically describes the people of Israel as Yahweh's "Suffering Servant" and delineates the historical role that the Lord has decreed for this servant.

QUESTIONS FOR ANALYSIS

1. Consider the opening lines of this selection. In what manner has Yahweh's special relationship with the people of Israel remained unchanged since the days of Moses?

2. Consider the Lord's relationship with King Cyrus and the Persians. Even though Cyrus does not know or honor Him, the Lord has chosen Cyrus as a servant. Why? In what ways does this represent a departure from the Israelites' traditional view of their neighbors?

3. What does Second Isaiah mean by the prophecy that the Lord will present Israel "as a light to the nations"? How will the Children of Israel's redemption from exile in Babylon serve a universal purpose?

4. What are the essential elements of Second Isaiah's vision of the Lord and this deity's chosen people?

5. In what way has the Lord's Covenant with Israel been given a new mean-

ing? How does this new interpretation of the Covenant relate to the covenant Yahweh entered into with Noah (Chapter 2, source 14)?

6. In what ways are Ahura Mazda and the Lord both universal gods of righteousness? How do their attitudes toward good and evil differ from that expressed by Lord Krishna in the *Bhagavad Gita* (source 18)? What do you conclude from this?

7. "For the Hebrews and Persians religion became the means of transforming the world, not negating it." What does the author of this statement mean? Do you agree or disagree? Why?

8. How do Ahura Mazda and the Lord differ from Brahman?

"But now hear, O Jacob[1] my servant,
Israel whom I have chosen!
Thus says the Lord who made you,
   who formed you from the womb
   and will help you:
Fear not, O Jacob my servant,
Jeshurun[2] whom I have chosen.
For I will pour water on the thirsty land,
and streams on the dry ground;
I will pour my Spirit upon your descendants,
and my blessing on your offspring.
They shall spring up like grass amid waters,
like willows by flowing streams;
This one will say, 'I am the Lord's,
another will call himself by the name of
   Jacob,
and another will write on his hand, 'The
   Lord's,'[3]
and surname himself by the name of Israel."
Thus says the Lord, the King of Israel[4]
and his Redeemer, the Lord of hosts:
"I am the first and I am the last;
besides me there is no God. . . .
Remember these things, O Jacob,
and Israel, for you are my servant;
I formed you, you are my servant;
O Israel, you will not be forgotten by me.
I have swept away your transgressions like a
   cloud,

and your sins like mist;
return to me, for I have redeemed you. . . .
I am the Lord, who made all things,
who stretched out the heavens alone,
who spread out the earth —
   Who was with me?—
who frustrates the omens of liars,
and makes fools of diviners;
who turns wise men back,
and makes their knowledge foolish;
who confirms the word of his servant,
and performs the counsel of his messengers;
who says of Jerusalem, 'She shall be
   inhabited,'
and of the cities of Judah, 'They shall be
   built,
and I will raise up their ruins,' . . .
who says of Cyrus, 'He is my shepherd,
and he shall fulfill all my purpose';
saying of Jerusalem, 'She shall be built,'
and of the temple, 'Your foundation shall be
   laid.'"
Thus says the Lord to his anointed, to Cyrus,
whose right hand I have grasped,
to subdue nations before him
and ungird the loins of kings,
to open doors before him
that gates may not be closed:
"I will go before you

---

[1]Here "Jacob" refers to all of Jacob's descendants — the Children of Israel.
[2]"Upright one" — a term of endearment.
[3]Compare this with Moses' command that the Israelites

tie the Law to their arms and wear it on their foreheads (Chapter 2, source 15).
[4]This refers to all the Israelites and should not be confused with the kingdom of Israel, which the Assyrians destroyed in 722 B.C.

and level the mountains,
I will break in pieces the doors of bronze
and cut asunder the bars of iron,[5]
I will give you the treasures of darkness
and the hoards in secret places,
that you may know that it is I, the Lord,
the God of Israel, who call you by your name.
For the sake of my servant Jacob,
and Israel my chosen,
I call you by your name,
I surname you,[6] though you do not know me.
I am the Lord, and there is no other,
besides me there is no God;
I gird you, though you do not know me,
that men may know, from the rising of the
    sun
and from the west, that there is none besides
    me;
I am the Lord, and there is no other. . . .
I made the earth,
and created man upon it;
it was my hands that stretched out the
    heavens,
and I commanded all their host.
I have aroused him[7] in righteousness,
and I will make straight all his ways;
he shall build my city[8]
and set my exiles free,
not for price or reward,"
says the Lord of hosts. . . .
"I the Lord speak the truth,
I declare what is right.
"Assemble yourselves and come,
draw near together,
you survivors of the nations![9]
They have no knowledge
who carry about their wooden idols,
and keep on praying to a god
that cannot save.
Declare and present your case;
let them take counsel together!

Who told this long ago?
Who declared it of old?
Was it not I, the Lord?
And there is no other god besides
    me, a righteous God and a Savior;
there is none besides me.
"Turn to me and be saved,
all the ends of the earth!
For I am God, and there is no other.
By myself I have sworn,
from my mouth has gone forth in
    righteousness
a word that shall not return:
'To me every knee shall bow,
every tongue shall swear.'
"Only in the Lord, it shall be said of me,
are righteousness and strength;
to him shall come and be ashamed,
all who were incensed against him.
In the Lord all the offspring of Israel
shall triumph and glory.". . .
Listen to me, O coastlands,
and hearken, you peoples from afar.
The Lord called me[10] from the womb,
from the body of my mother he named my
    name.
He made my mouth like a sharp sword,
in the shadow of his hand he hid me;
he made me a polished arrow,
in his quiver he hid me away.
And he said to me, "You are my servant,
Israel, in whom I will be glorified."
But I said, "I have labored in vain,
I have spent my strength for nothing and
    vanity;
yet surely my right is with the Lord,
and my recompense with my God."

And now the Lord says, . . .
"It is too light a thing that you should be my
    servant

---

[5]A reference to the great walls of Babylon.
[6]The Lord bestows on Cyrus the title "the Great."
[7]Cyrus.
[8]Jerusalem will be rebuilt.

[9]All peoples who survive the collapse of the Chaldean, or Neo-Babylonian, Empire.
[10]The Children of Israel.

to raise up the tribes of Jacob
and to restore the preserved of Israel;
I will give you as a light to the nations,
that my salvation may reach to the end of the
   earth."

Thus says the Lord,
the Redeemer of Israel and his Holy One,

to one deeply despised, abhorred by the
   nations,
the servant of rulers:
"Kings shall see and arise;
princes, and they shall prostrate themselves;
because of the Lord, who is faithful,
the Holy One of Israel, who has chosen you."

Chapter 4

▼▼▼

Developing the Secular Traditions of China and Hellas: 600–200 B.C.

The Chinese and the Greeks, who inhabited the eastern and western extremes of civilized Eurasia in the sixth century B.C., had deities for every imaginable function and a wide range of religious taboos and rituals. But religion in its narrowest sense — reverence for a supernatural being — offered these people relatively little in the way of either intellectual stimulation or emotional outlet. While contemporaries in India and Southwest Asia were raising religious speculation to high levels of abstract thought, religion for the Chinese and Greeks remained, for the most part, a practical affair. One sacrificed to the gods and spirits in order to assure their benevolence. Religion was a form of magical insurance and not a relationship with Ultimate Reality.

At the same time, the social and psychic crises of the Age of Iron were just as real in China and Greece as elsewhere. In fashioning responses to the questions occasioned by the dislocation of traditional ways of life, both the Chinese and the Greeks looked more toward this world than the Beyond and created cultures that were essentially secular in the sense that they focused on humanity's position within an observable universe of finite space and time. Social philosophy rather than theology engaged the intellectual energies of the Chinese and the Greeks as they endeavored to meet the challenges of the Iron Age.

In China various philosophers offered insights into how humans should behave in regard to their families, the state, and nature. These philosophers also struggled with the issue of personal excellence. They first inquired whether such a goal was achievable or even desirable, and many ultimately concluded that the cult of individuality that was inherent in such a quest for personal perfection threatened the harmony of the family, the state, and even the natural order. For those who accepted, however tentatively and reluctantly, even a modified search for personal excellence, several questions remained: How is it achieved and what purposes does it serve? Does one's cultivation of virtue have only personal value or is it subordinate to a higher social purpose?

Many of these same human-centered concerns preoccupied Greek rationalists. Two issues in particular dominated Greek social thought: how the individual achieves excellence, a quality the Greeks assumed was the natural goal of all human striving and termed *arete*, and how the individual functions as an effective citizen within the city-state. Most Greek social philosophers, at least during the fifth and fourth centuries B.C., assumed that cultivation of one's personal talents and good citizenship were complementary and not antithetical pursuits. Additionally, a small but highly influential group of Greek rationalists turned their attention to an objective study of the physical environment, thereby becoming the West's first natural scientists. Like its social philosophers, Greece's scientists attempted to explain the workings of the physical universe in response to human needs, the most basic of which was to provide information that would allow people to control their lives and environment.

With the possible exception of China's Daoists, the Chinese and the Greeks did not look to divine forces for direction and meaning in life. Rather, they fashioned cultures in which humanity and the natural world were the measures of all that was important.

▼▼▼

China: Three Ways of Thought

Ages of political and social unrest often prove to be periods of significant intellectual ferment, and this was certainly true of the era of Eastern Zhou (770–256

B.C.). The collapse of the Western Zhou monarchy in 771 signaled the end of royal power in China and ushered in a five hundred-year period when regional states held center stage. Zhou kings continued to perform their traditional religious roles and received tokens of nominal obedience from the great feudal lords. True power, however, lay in the hands of the regional lords, who developed bureaucratic governments and strong standing armies. With each local prince essentially a sovereign, military and diplomatic maneuvering among their states became a constant fact of life. As disruptive as this was at times, it also proved to be a stimulus to intellectual activity. Both the demands of statecraft at the regional level and the occasional social dislocation that resulted from the conflicts among these states encouraged the development of political theory and social philosophy.

This was especially true from the fifth century B.C. onward, as wars became more frequent and bitter. Chinese historians traditionally catalogue the period from 403 to 221 B.C. as the Age of Warring States. Innovations such as cavalry, iron weapons, and the crossbow broke the battlefield superiority of the chariot-driving aristocracy. Armies of conscripted foot and horse soldiers became larger and more deadly. Concomitantly, intellectuals sought to keep pace with this changing world.

Between 260 and 221 B.C., Qin, the most aggressive and best organized of the warring states, conquered all rival powers in China and established a new royal family, the short-lived but pivotal Qin Dynasty (221–206 B.C.). The triumph of the lord of Qin, the self-styled Qin Shi Huangdi (the First Emperor of Qin, r. 221–210 B.C.) not only inaugurated China's first age of empire, it brought with it the momentary victory of a political philosophy known as *Legalism*. In conforming to the principles of Legalism, the Qin regime was ruthless and brutal in its drive for complete centralization of authority. Undone by the harshness of its laws and policies, the Qin Dynasty collapsed in early 206 in the midst of rebellion and civil war. Within four years, however, a commoner general, Liu Bang, reformulated the empire by establishing the successful and long-lived Han Dynasty (202 B.C.–A.D. 220).

Although the extreme measures of the Qin regime discredited Legalism as a philosophy, Legalist-inspired organizational structures and administrative procedures served as the framework of the highly centralized Han empire. By the late second century B.C., however, the Han Dynasty adopted as its official ideology the gentler and more humane philosophy of *Confucianism,* which had also taken shape in the disturbing period of Eastern Zhou.

Han imperial policies and institutions were, therefore, the products of a Confucian-Legalist synthesis, but these were not the only modes of thought to play a prominent role both then and ever after in China. *Daoism,* an antirational, quite antipolitical, and somewhat antisocial philosophy, had also emerged from the confusion of Eastern Zhou and survived the hostility of Qin censors.

These three schools of Chinese thought, each of which claimed to offer the only correct Way, or path, to social harmony, were not the only important intellectual currents in China in the age of Han. They were, however, destined to become the philosophical tripod of Chinese civilization. Although they offered different answers to the social ills of their day and presented some striking differences of perspective, they were not mutually exclusive; indeed, they have served for more than two thousand years as the intertwined and complementary primary elements of Chinese thought and action.

Daoism: The Way That Is and Is Not
▼▼▼

24 ▾ *Laozi,* THE CLASSIC OF THE WAY AND VIRTUE

In 1939 the British statesman Winston Churchill characterized the Soviet Union as "a riddle wrapped in a mystery inside an enigma." He could have said the same of Daoism — the philosophy of the Way (*Dao*). The opening lines of this school's greatest masterpiece *The Classic of the Way and of Virtue (Dao De Jing)*, which is ascribed to the legendary Laozi, immediately confront the reader with Daoism's essential paradox: "The Way that can be trodden is not the enduring and unchanging Way. The name that can be named is not the enduring and unchanging name." Here is a philosophy that purports to teach *the* Way but simultaneously claims that this Way transcends human understanding and definition.

Like the Dao itself, Daoism has many origins and manifestations. No one knows when or where it originated, although it probably sprang, at least in part, from Chinese folk religion. Its early sages are equally shadowy. According to tradition, the author of Daoism's greatest classic was Laozi, who supposedly was born around 604 B.C. and died about 517. As one story has it, the aged Laozi decided to leave the state in which he lived, because he foresaw its imminent decay. At the frontier he was delayed by a customs official who implored him not to depart without first leaving behind his wisdom. In response, Laozi dashed off the *Dao De Jing* and left, never to be heard from again. The fact that Laozi means "Venerable Master" suggests to many that this sage was more a composite figure of legend and imagination than a historic individual of flesh and blood. Indeed, many scholars believe that the language and ideas contained within this classic indicate an intellectual and social environment closer to 300 than to 500 B.C.

Whatever its date and circumstances of composition, the *Dao De Jing* is one of the most profound and beautiful works ever written in Chinese. This book of only about five thousand words has exercised an incalculable influence on Chinese life and art through the centuries. There is a good deal of truth to the cliché that traditional Chinese upper-class males were Confucians in public and Daoists in private.

As you study the following selections, pay particular attention to the Daoist notion of *Nonaction,* or Nonstriving (*wuwei*). This idea underlies all Daoist thought and comes closest to being Daoism's universal principle and driving force, if such is possible.

QUESTIONS FOR ANALYSIS

1. How does one define the Way? How permanent is it? How limited is it? Is there anything it does not encompass?
2. Does the Way acknowledge absolute right and wrong?
3. How does a sage ruler who is in harmony with the Way govern?
4. What is wuwei, and how does it function? Why is it the greatest form of action?
5. What are Daoism's major criticisms of Confucianism and Legalism?
6. Why would Daoism appeal to some individuals in the Age of Warring States?
7. Compare wuwei with the teachings of the Mahavira and the Buddha (Chapter 3, sources 19 and 20). Do you see any similarities? What are more significant, the similarities or the differences?
8. Compare the Way with the Supreme Beings of India and Southwest Asia (Chapter 3, sources 17, 18, 22, and 23). Does it share any common characteristics with Brahman, Ahura Mazda, or Yahweh? Which are more significant, the similarities or the differences?

THE WAY

The Dao that can be trodden is not the enduring and unchanging Dao. The name that can be named is not the enduring and unchanging name.

Conceived of as having no name, it is the Originator of heaven and earth; conceived of as having a name, it is the Mother of all things.

. . .

The Dao produces all things and nourishes them; it produces them and does not claim them as its own; it does all, and yet does not boast of it; it presides over all, and yet does not control them. This is what is called "The mysterious quality" of the Dao.

. . .

When the Great Dao ceased to be observed, benevolence and righteousness came into vogue.

Then appeared wisdom and shrewdness, and there ensued great hypocrisy.[1]

. . .

Man takes his law from the Earth; the Earth takes its law from Heaven; Heaven takes its law from the Dao. The law of the Dao is its being what it is.

. . .

All-pervading is the Great Dao! It may be found on the left hand and on the right.

All things depend on it for their production, which it gives to them, not one refusing obedience to it. When its work is accomplished, it does not claim the name of having done it. It clothes all things as with a garment, and makes no assumption of being their lord; — it may be named in the smallest things; . . . it may be named in the greatest things.

. . . .

---

[1]This is a criticism of the "hypocrisy" of Confucians who claim to know and practice virtue. See source 25.

He who has in himself abundantly the attributes of the Dao is like an infant.

. . .

The Dao in its regular course does nothing, for the sake of doing it, and so there is nothing which it does not do.

THE WISE PERSON

When we renounce learning we have no troubles.[2]

. . .

If we could renounce our sageness and discard our wisdom, it would be better for the people a hundredfold. If we could renounce our benevolence and discard our righteousness, the people would again become filial and kindly.[3] If we could renounce our artful contrivances and discard our scheming for gain, there would be no thieves nor robbers.

. . .

The sage manages affairs without doing anything, and conveys his instructions without the use of speech.

. . .

Therefore the sage holds in his embrace the one thing of humility, and manifests it to all the world. He is free from self-display, and therefore he shines; from self-assertion, and therefore he is distinguished; from self-boasting, and therefore his merit is acknowledged; from self-complacency, and therefore he acquires superiority. It is because he is thus free from striving that therefore no one in the world is able to strive with him.

. . .

When gold and jade fill the hall, their possessor cannot keep them safe. When wealth and honors lead to arrogance, this brings its evil on itself. When the work is done, and one's name is becoming distinguished, to withdraw into obscurity is the way of Heaven.

THE IDEAL GOVERNMENT

A state may be ruled by measures of correction;[4] weapons of war may be used with crafty dexterity; but the kingdom is made one's own only by freedom from action and purpose.

How do I know that it is so? By these facts: — In the kingdom the multiplication of prohibitive enactments increases the poverty of the people; the more implements to add to their profit that the people have, the greater disorder is there in the state and clan; the more acts of crafty dexterity that men possess, the more do strange contrivances appear; the more display there is of legislation, the more thieves and robbers there are.

Therefore a sage has said, "I will do nothing, and the people will be transformed of themselves; I will be fond of keeping still, and the people will of themselves become correct. I will take no trouble about it, and the people will of themselves become rich; I will manifest no ambition, and the people will of themselves attain to the primitive simplicity."

. . .

Not to value and employ men of superior ability is the way to keep the people from rivalry among themselves; not to prize articles which are difficult to procure is the way to keep them from becoming thieves; not to show them what is likely to excite their desires is the way to keep their minds from disorder.

Therefore the sage, in the exercise of his government, empties their minds, fills their bellies, weakens their wills, and strengthens their bones.

He constantly tries to keep them without knowledge and without desire, and where there are those who have knowledge, to keep them from presuming to act on it. When there is this abstinence from action, good order is universal.

---

[2]According to the Confucians, careful study of the past is a primary avenue to harmony.

[3]These first two sentences reject the Confucian values of wisdom (saintliness), knowledge, human-heartedness, and righteousness, all of which, according to the Con-

fucians, will result in filial piety (proper devotion to one's parents and ancestors).

[4]This aphorism rejects the principles and methods of Legalism. See sources 26 and 27.

Confucianism: The Way of the Superior Man
▼▼▼

25 ▼ *Confucius, THE ANALECTS*

The Chinese refer to the period of Eastern Zhou as the age of "The Hundred Schools." Of the many schools of thought that flourished then, none has had a more substantial impact on Chinese culture than Confucianism.

Unlike the case of Laozi, we are certain there was a historical Confucius. According to tradition, he was born in 551 B.C. into the impoverished, lower aristocratic family of the Kong. He became a high-ranking civil servant in his native state of Lu but was forced into exile as a result of political intrigue. There followed ten years of wandering from state to state as he attempted without success to convince the princes of the states he visited to employ his theory of how to achieve a harmonious and just society. Disappointed at his inability to win over the lords of his day, Master Kong turned to teaching, seeking out students who showed promise of rising to eminent posts in the various states of feudal China. In this way he hoped his philosophy of life and government — his moral Way — would essentially transform Chinese society to the point that it returned to the values and practices of the age of the duke of Zhou, a twelfth-century B.C. legislator and consolidator of the Zhou Dynasty, whom Confucius deeply admired. For his educational efforts, posterity accorded him the elegant title *Kong Fuzi* (Kong the Philosopher), which Western scholars have Latinized into Confucius. Tradition records that he died in 479, a decade before the birth of his great Greek counterpart Socrates (ca 469–399 B.C.).

Somewhat like Socrates, who claimed that if he was wise it was because he recognized his own ignorance (source 31), Confucius claimed to possess no special genius or knowledge. He simply saw himself as someone who revered the old ways and followed them zealously. There is no question that much of what Confucius taught was already part of Chinese culture. However, he took such traditional values as *filial piety* (respect for one's parents and ancestors) and *propriety* (regard for proper decorum) and turned them into moral principles. He insisted that human beings are moral creatures with social obligations and are, by that fact, obliged to comport themselves humanely and with integrity. He also believed that humans, or at least men, are capable of perfecting themselves as upright individuals. His ideal moral agent was the superior man (*zhunzi*) who cultivated virtue through study and imitation of the moral Way of the past. By knowing the good, this person would choose the good. What is more, he would act as an example to others, who would irresistibly follow the path he set along the Way of Goodness.

Confucius's pupils were few; we know the names of only about twenty. Although Master Kong appears to have been a widely respected sage, he was only one of many itinerant teachers of his age and probably not the most popular. There is reason to conclude he died believing himself a failure. Such failure should happen to us all. In time Confucianism became virtually synonymous with Chinese culture and played an almost equally important role in shaping Korean and Japanese thought.

As is true of so many great teachers whose words and example have placed a permanent stamp on a civilization, Confucius was not a productive writer. As far as we know, nothing he wrote or edited survives. Early Confucian disciples, however, managed to transmit to posterity a number of sayings ascribed to Confucius and his immediate pupils. In time these were gathered into a book known as *The Analects* (*Lun You*). We do not know which of these maxims Confucius actually uttered, but collectively they provide us with the best available view of Kong Fuzi's teachings as remembered by those who knew and followed him.

As you study the following selections, note the role that propriety (*li*) plays in Confucius's system. For him propriety meant much more than good manners or proper etiquette. It was the primary interior quality that set the superior man apart from all other humans.

QUESTIONS FOR ANALYSIS

1. How does Confucius define *filial piety?*
2. What does Confucius mean by the term *propriety,* and how does it serve as the keystone of his philosophical system?
3. What is Confucius's concept of the ideal state?
4. What is the superior man? Is he born or made? If the latter, how?
5. According to Confucius, what was the most "practical" form of education, and what was its purpose? What do your answers suggest about Confucius's social views?
6. Consider the four topics on which Confucius did not talk. Why do you suppose this was the case? What does this suggest about the man and his philosophy?
7. Confucius, like Laozi, speaks of the Way and claims to teach it. How does his Way differ from that of Daoism? What do you think his attitude was toward those who preached either the way of Nonstriving or the idea that there are no absolute standards of behavior?

FILIAL PIETY

Zi, you asked what filial piety was. The Master said, "The filial piety of now-a-days means the support of one's parents. But dogs and horses likewise are able to do something in the way of support; — without reverence, what is there to distinguish the one support given from the other?"

. . .

The Master said, "In serving his parents, a son may remonstrate with them, but gently; when he sees that they do not incline to follow his advice, he shows an increased degree of reverence, but does not abandon his purpose; and should they punish him, he does not allow himself to murmur."

. . .

Mang I asked what filial piety was. The Master said, "It is not being disobedient."

Soon after, as Fan Chih was driving him, the Master told him, saying, "Mang Sun asked me what filial piety was, and I answered him, 'not being disobedient.'"

Fan Chih said, "What did you mean?" The Master replied, "That parents, when alive, should be served according to propriety; that, when dead, they should be buried according to propriety; and that they should be sacrificed to according to propriety."

PROPRIETY

The Master said, "Respectfulness, without the rules of propriety, becomes laborious bustle; carefulness, without the rules of propriety, becomes timidity; boldness, without the rules of propriety, becomes insubordination; straightforwardness, without the rules of propriety, becomes rudeness."

IDEAL GOVERNMENT

The Master said, "When rulers love to observe the rules of propriety, the people respond readily to the calls on them for service."

．　．　．

The Master said, "If the people be led by laws, and uniformity sought to be given them by punishments,[1] they will try to avoid the punishment, but have no sense of shame.

"If they be led by virtue, and uniformity sought to be given them by the rules of propriety, they will have the sense of shame, and moreover will become good."

．　．　．

The Master said, "He who exercises government by means of his virtue may be compared to the north polar star, which keeps its place and all the stars turn towards it."

．　．　．

The duke Ai[2] asked, saying, "What should be done in order to secure the submission of the people?" Confucius replied, "Advance the up-

right and set aside the crooked, then the people will submit. Advance the crooked and set aside the upright, then the people will not submit."

Ji Kang asked how to cause the people to reverence their ruler, to be faithful to him, and to go on to nerve themselves to virtue. The Master said, "Let him preside over them with gravity; — then they will reverence him. Let him be filial and kind to all; — then they will be faithful to him. Let him advance the good and teach the incompetent; — then they will eagerly seek to be virtuous."

．　．　．

Ji Kang asked Confucius about government. Confucius replied, "To govern means to rectify. If you lead on the people with correctness, who will dare not to be correct?"

．　．　．

The Master said, "If a minister make his own conduct correct, what difficulty will he have in assisting in government? If he cannot rectify himself, what has he to do with rectifying others?"

．　．　．

The Master said, '"If good men were to govern a country in succession for a hundred years, they would be able to transform the violently bad, and dispense with capital punishments.' True indeed is this saying!"

THE SUPERIOR MAN

Confucius said, "There are three things of which the superior man stands in awe. He stands in awe of the ordinances of Heaven. He stands in awe of great men. He stands in awe of the words of sages.

"The mean man does not know the ordinances of Heaven, and consequently does not stand in awe of them. He is disrespectful to great men. He makes sport of the words of sages."

．　．　．

---

[1]This was the "Way" of the Legalists (sources 26 and 27).

[2]The lord of the state of Lu (r. 494–468 B.C.), whom several of Confucius's disciples served.

Zi Gong asked what constituted the superior man. The Master said, "He acts before he speaks, and afterward speaks according to his actions."

•   •   •

The Master said, "The mind of the superior man is conversant with righteousness; the mind of the mean man is conversant with gain."

•   •   •

The Master said, "If the will be set on virtue, there will be no practice of wickedness."

The Master said, "Riches and honors are what men desire. If it cannot be obtained in the proper way, they should not be held. Poverty and meanness are what men dislike. If it cannot be obtained in the proper way, they should not be avoided.

"If a superior man abandon virtue, how can he fulfill the requirements of that name?

"The superior man does not, even for the space of a single meal, act contrary to virtue. In moments of haste, he cleaves to it. In seasons of danger, he cleaves to it."

•   •   •

The Master said, "By nature, men are nearly alike; by practice, they get to be wide apart."

•   •   •

The Master said, "By extensively studying all learning, and keeping himself under the restraint of the rules of propriety, one may thus likewise not err from what is right."

•   •   •

The Master said, "The accomplished scholar is not a utensil."[3]

SPIRITS

The subjects on which the Master did not talk, were extraordinary things,[4] feats of strength,[5] disorder, and spiritual beings.[6]

•   •   •

Ji Lu asked about serving the spirits of the dead. The Master said, "While you are not able to serve men, how can you serve their spirits?" Ji Lu added, "I venture to ask about death?" He was answered, "While you do not know life, how can you know about death?"

Legalism: The Way of the State
▼▼▼

26 ▼ Han Fei, THE WRITINGS OF MASTER HAN FEI

Daoism offered no active political program, whereas Confucius and his disciples preached a doctrine of benevolent reform based on virtuous imitation of the past. A third school of thought that emerged in the chaos of the late Zhou era was Legalism, which rejected both the Way of nature, as embraced by the Daoists, and Confucianism's emphasis on the primacy of the moral Way of antiquity. Legalist writers, to the contrary, emphasized law as government's formulative force and advocated a radical restructuring of society in ways that were totally rational and up-to-date.

---

[3]A specialist, or technician.
[4]Extraordinary phenomena that cause delight and wonder among the ignorant.
[5]Confucius and his disciples had only contempt for sol-

diers and all other people who exercised power by virtue of physical strength. The Confucians believed in the exclusive exercise of moral and intellectual power.
[6]The spirits of the ancestors.

Legalism reached its apogee in the late third century B.C. in the writings of Han Feizi (Master Han Fei) and the policies of Emperor Qin Shi Huangdi. Han Fei was a prince of the state of Han who defected to its chief rival, the state of Qin, but eventually he ran afoul of Qin's chief minister, Li Si (d. 208 B.C.), and was forced to commit suicide in 233 B.C. Before he died, he composed a number of essays on how to construct a stable and peaceful state. The following selections present Han Fei's major principles of political philosophy.

QUESTIONS FOR ANALYSIS

1. In Han Fei's ideal state what is the supreme governing authority, the will of the ruler or the law?
2. What are the "Two Handles" and how important are they to a Legalist state? Why must the sovereign never surrender control over the two handles?
3. What roles do individuality and private initiative play in Han Fei's ideal state?
4. Why do you think Legalism appealed to some people?
5. Imagine a series of conversations among a Daoist, a Confucian, and a Legalist. How would each respond on the following issues: What is the purpose of good government? What role does morality play in formulating law? What are the qualities of a superior ruler? The proposition "Might makes right."

HAVING REGULATIONS

No country is permanently strong. Nor is any country permanently weak. If conformers to law are strong, the country is strong; if conformers to law are weak, the country is weak. . . .

Any ruler able to expel private crookedness and uphold public law, finds the people safe and the state in order; and any ruler able to expunge private action and act on public law, finds his army strong and his enemy weak. So, find out men following the discipline of laws and regulations, and place them above the body of officials. Then the sovereign cannot be deceived by anybody with fraud and falsehood. . . .

Therefore, the intelligent sovereign makes the law select men and makes no arbitrary promotion himself. He makes the law measure merits and makes no arbitrary regulation himself. In consequence, able men cannot be obscured, bad characters cannot be disguised; falsely praised fellows cannot be advanced, wrongly defamed people cannot be degraded. . . .

To govern the state by law is to praise the right and blame the wrong.

The law does not fawn on the noble. . . . Whatever the law applies to, the wise cannot reject nor can the brave defy. Punishment for fault never skips ministers, reward for good never misses commoners. Therefore, to correct the faults of the high, to rebuke the vices of the low, to suppress disorders, to decide against mistakes, to subdue the arrogant, to straighten the crooked, and to unify the folkways of the masses, nothing could match the law. To warn the officials and overawe the people, to rebuke obscenity and danger, and to forbid falsehood and deceit, nothing could match penalty. If penalty is severe, the noble cannot discriminate against the humble. If law is definite, the superiors are esteemed and not violated. If the superiors are not violated, the sovereign will become strong and able to maintain the proper course of government. Such was the reason why the early kings esteemed Legalism and handed it down to posterity. Should the lord of men discard law and practice selfishness, high and low would have no distinction.

THE TWO HANDLES

The means whereby the intelligent ruler controls his ministers are two handles only. The two handles are chastisement and commendation. What are meant by chastisement and commendation? To inflict death or torture upon culprits, is called chastisement; to bestow encouragements or rewards on men of merit, is called commendation.

Ministers are afraid of censure and punishment but fond of encouragement and reward. Therefore, if the lord of men uses the handles of chastisement and commendation, all ministers will dread his severity and turn to his liberality. The villainous ministers of the age are different. To men they hate they would by securing the handle of chastisement from the sovereign ascribe crimes; on men they love they would by securing the handle of commendation from the sovereign bestow rewards. Now supposing the lord of men placed the authority of punishment and the profit of reward not in his hands but let the ministers administer the affairs of reward and punishment instead, then everybody in the country would fear the ministers and slight the ruler, and turn to the ministers and away from the ruler. This is the calamity of the ruler's loss of the handles of chastisement and commendation.

The Legalist Policies of Qin
▼▼▼

27 ▼ *Sima Qian, THE RECORDS OF THE GRAND HISTORIAN*

Born around 145 B.C., Sima Qian was educated in the classics, served his emperor on a variety of missions, and in 107 succeeded his father as Grand Historian of the Han court. Even before rising to this position, Sima Qian had avidly collected historical records during his travels on imperial service. Upon his appointment as Grand Historian, he embarked on the initial project of collecting additional sources, especially from the imperial library, and verifying his facts. Only in 104 was he ready to begin the process of composition, a labor that lasted until 91 B.C. The result was a history monumental in scope. In 130 chapters he traced the story of China from the age of the legendary Five Sage Emperors, who preceded the Xia and Shang dynasties, to his own day. In later years he made small additions and changes and probably continued to revise his masterpiece in minor ways until his death, which happened at an unknown date.

The result was well worth the effort. The Chinese rightly consider *The Records of the Grand Historian* to be traditional China's greatest piece of historical writing. Sima Qian aimed at telling the whole truth, insofar as he could discover it, and in pursuit of that truth he scoured all available archives. As he composed his work, he included verbatim many of the records he had found, thereby providing modern historians with a wealth of documentary evidence that would otherwise have been lost, for many of the sources Sima Qian quoted, paraphrased, and cited exist today only in his history.

In the first excerpt the Grand Historian quotes a memorial that the First Emperor, Qin Shi Huangdi (r. 221–210 B.C.), built to proclaim his accomplishments. The second selection tells of an edict of 213 that banned virtually all non-Legalist literature.

QUESTIONS FOR ANALYSIS

1. Of what accomplishments does the emperor boast?
2. In what ways does this memorial emphasize the government's standardization of society?
3. What general principles and policies underlie this memorial?
4. Does the inscription contain any claims that Confucius would have applauded? What claims would Confucius have found troubling?
5. What would a Daoist think of the emperor's policies?
6. How and for what reason did Li Si reject all non-Legalist schools of thought and especially Confucian principles? What does his rejection of the "Hundred Schools" and Confucianism in particular suggest about the way in which Legalists viewed the world and themselves?
7. Why do you think books on medicine, divination, and agriculture were exempted from the general prohibition of 213 B.C.? What does your answer suggest about Legalist policies?
8. Consider the Legalist view of the proper subject matter and purpose of education. How does it differ from the educational philosophy of the Confucians? How does it differ from the Daoist view of education?

The emperor had a tower built on Mount Langya and a stone inscription set up to praise the power of Qin and make clear his will. The inscription read:

A new age is inaugurated by the Emperor;
Rules and measures are rectified,
The myriad things set in order,
Human affairs are made clear
And there is harmony between fathers and
  sons.
The Emperor in his sagacity, benevolence
  and justice
Has made all laws and principles manifest.

He set forth to pacify the east,
To inspect officers and men;
This great task accomplished
He visited the coast.
Great are the Emperor's achievements,
Men attend diligently to basic tasks,
Farming is encouraged, secondary pursuits
  discouraged,
All the common people prosper;
All men under the sky
Toil with a single purpose;
Tools and measures are made uniform,
The written script is standardized;
Wherever the sun and moon shine,

Wherever one can go by boat or by
carriage,
Men carry out their orders
And satisfy their desires;
For our Emperor in accordance with the
time
Has regulated local customs,
Made waterways and divided up the land.
Caring for the common people,
He works day and night without rest;
He defines the laws, leaving nothing in
doubt,
Making known what is forbidden.
The local officials have their duties,
Administration is smoothly carried out,
All is done correctly, all according to plan.
The Emperor in his wisdom
Inspects all four quarters of his realm;
High and low, noble and humble,
None dare overshoot the mark;
No evil or impropriety is allowed,
All strive to be good men and true,
And exert themselves in tasks great and
small;
None dares to idle or ignore his duties,
But in far-off, remote places
Serious and decorous administrators
Work steadily, just and loyal.
Great is the virtue of our Emperor
Who pacifies all four corners of the earth,
Who punishes traitors, roots out evil men,
And with profitable measures brings
prosperity.
Tasks are done at the proper season,
All things flourish and grow;
The common people know peace
And have laid aside weapons and armor;
Kinsmen care for each other,
There are no robbers or thieves;
Men delight in his rule,
All understanding the law and discipline.
The universe entire
Is our Emperor's realm,

Extending west to the Desert,
South to where the houses face north,
East to the East Ocean,
North to beyond Daxia;
Wherever human life is found,
All acknowledge his suzerainty,
His achievements surpass those of the Five
Emperors,[1]
His kindness reaches even the beasts of the
field;
All creatures benefit from his virtue,
All live in peace at home.

• • •

Chunyu Yueh, a scholar of Chi . . . said, "I have yet to hear of anything able to endure that was not based on ancient precedents. . . ."

The emperor ordered his ministers to debate this question.

The prime minister Li Si said, "The Five Emperors did not emulate each other nor did the Three Dynasties[2] adopt each other's ways, yet all had good government. This is no paradox, because times had changed. Now Your Majesty has built up this great empire to endure for generations without end. Naturally this passes the comprehension of a foolish pedant. Chunyu Yueh spoke about the Three Dynasties, but they are hardly worth taking as examples. In times gone by different barons fought among themselves and gathered wandering scholars. Today, however, the empire is at peace, all laws and order come from one single source, the common people support themselves by farming and handicrafts, while students study the laws and prohibitions.

"Now these scholars learn only from the old, not from the new, and use their learning to oppose our rule and confuse the black-headed people.[3] As prime minister I must speak out on pain of death. In former times when the world, torn by chaos and disorder, could not be united, different states arose and argued from the past to condemn the present, using empty rhetoric

[1]The mythical Five Sage Emperors of predynastic China.
[2]Xia, Shang, and Zhou.
[3]The common people.

to cover up and confuse the real issues, and employing their learning to oppose what was established by authority. Now Your Majesty has conquered the whole world, distinguished between black and white, set unified standards. Yet these opinionated scholars get together to slander the laws and judge each new decree according to their own school of thought, opposing it secretly in their hearts while discussing it openly in the streets. They brag to the sovereign to win fame, put forward strange arguments to gain distinction, and incite the mob to spread rumors. If this is not prohibited, the sovereign's prestige will suffer and factions will be formed among his subjects. Far better put a stop to it!

"I humbly propose that all historical records but those of Qin be burned. If anyone who is not a court scholar dares to keep the ancient songs, historical records or writings of the hundred schools, these should be confiscated and burned by the provincial governor and army commander. Those who in conversation dare to quote the old songs and records[4] should be publicly executed; those who use old precedents to oppose the new order should have their families wiped out; and officers who know of such cases but fail to report them should be punished in the same way.

"If thirty days after the issuing of this order the owners of these books have still not had them destroyed, they should have their faces tattooed and be condemned to hard labor at the Great Wall.[5] The only books which need not be destroyed are those dealing with medicine, divination, and agriculture. Those who want to study the law can learn it from the officers." The emperor sanctioned this proposal.

▼▼▼

Hellenic Civilization: A Rational Inquiry into Life

Early in the sixth century B.C., a small group of Greek intellectuals, beginning, according to tradition, with a semilegendary figure known as Thales of Miletus (ca 640–562 B.C.), started to challenge age-old mythic ways of explaining the workings of the universe by looking at the world as an objective phenomenon that could be studied in a rational, systematic manner. These thinkers, who sought to discover the physical underpinnings of the universe, are acknowledged as ancient Hellas's first philosophers and scientists and the people who established the Greek intellectual tradition of rational inquiry into all aspects of the physical and moral world.

As important as reason was in the formation of Greek thought, it never threatened to totally displace myth, mysticism, and religion. We would very much misunderstand Greek civilization by concluding that rational inquiry dominated

---

[4]A reference to the *Classic of Odes* (Chapter 1, source 7) and the *Classic of History* (source 6).

[5]The First Emperor began the process of linking frontier fortresses to form the Great Wall. Labor on the Great Wall, which was tantamount to a death sentence, was a common penalty under Qin.

every element of Greek life from the sixth century onward. Indeed, the nonrational permeated Greek society. This fact should not be surprising, nor should it cause us to undervalue the achievements of Greek rationalists, whose modes of analysis became a hallmark of Greek civilization.

As we survey the development of Greek rationalism, it would be helpful to keep in mind the broad division of Greek history favored by historians. The period from about 750 B.C. down to the death of Alexander the Great in 323 B.C. is known as the *Hellenic Age* because the people we call *Greeks* referred to themselves as *Hellenes* and their land as *Hellas*. (It was the Romans who began the tradition of calling all Hellenes *Greeks*). The period from 323 to 30 B.C. is known as the *Hellenistic Age*. In this case, *Hellenist* means a non-Hellene who adopted the Greek language and culture.

During the Hellenic Age the Greek world was a frontier society along the western periphery of the ancient civilized world. As a result, the Greeks were able to draw from the experiences of their more deeply rooted neighbors while enjoying a certain amount of freedom to experiment culturally, especially in the areas of politics and thought. This age was characterized by general Greek independence from foreign domination, political decentralization, intense rivalry among Hellas's many city-states, and a deep-seated ethnocentrism and even contempt for the non-Hellenic world. The Hellenes coined the term *barbarian* to refer to all non-Greek speakers, even the most civilized, because their alien languages sounded to Greek ears like so much babble, or *bar-bar*. The two characteristic and dominating events of this period were the Persian Wars (499–450 B.C.) and the Peloponnesian War (431–404 B.C.). In the first, Greeks, under the leadership of Athens and Sparta, successfully withstood the threat of Persian domination. In the latter, again under Athenian and Spartan leadership, the whole Greek world was embroiled in a bitter family bloodletting.

Under the leadership of King Philip and his son Alexander (r. 336–323 B.C.) the Macedonians finally forced internal peace and unity on the Greeks. Alexander the Great's conquest of the Persian Empire and his penetration even into northwest India ushered in a new age for western Eurasia. Whereas the Hellenic world had been parochial, the Hellenistic world was cosmopolitan and culturally syncretic (the process of combining different cultural traditions to create new hybrid cultures). The armies of Alexander and the state builders who followed helped create a cultural amalgamation of Southwest Asian, North African, and even some Indian elements, over which lay a deep layer of Greek language, thought, and artistic expression. What emerged was, to use a Greek word, a cultural *ecumene* (a unity of diverse civilized peoples). This ecumenical culture stretched from Afghanistan and northwest India in the east to the regions of the central Mediterranean in the west, and much of it was Greek in form and inspiration. Greek science and philosophy matured during the Hellenistic Age. Although the Roman Empire later expanded the boundaries of this rich cultural ecumene into northwest Africa and portions of western Europe, it is convenient to date the end of the Hellenistic Age as 30 B.C., when Egypt, the last independent and arguably most brilliant of the Hellenistic kingdoms, passed into Roman hands.

The Science of Medicine
▼▼▼

28 ▼ *Hippocrates, ON THE SACRED DISEASE*

No matter how much they differed among themselves, early Greek scientists shared two basic assumptions: the world is a physical entity governed by regular, natural laws and not by mysterious supernatural forces or divine whims; and the human mind, unaided by magic or divine revelation, can understand how those laws function.

One area of Hellenic science that proved especially fruitful was medicine, especially as pioneered by the physicians of the island of Cos. Of all the healers of Cos, the most famous in history and legend was Hippocrates. For all of his fame and reputed dominance in his field, we know very little about Hippocrates' life. Born on Cos around 460, he served as a member of that community's Guild of Aesculapius, a group of physicians who traced their origin to the priesthood of the god of healing. Hippocrates' abilities as a practitioner and teacher of medicine eventually earned him a pan-Hellenic reputation, and he found himself traveling from city to city teaching his art and science. Plato (source 31) implies that ultimately, like most of Hellas's great teachers, Hippocrates made his way to Athens. While we cannot precisely place Hippocrates in Athens, it is clear that Hippocratic medical ideas were part of Athens's intellectual atmosphere by the end of the fifth century B.C. A very late tradition holds that the Master Physician died in Thessaly in northern Greece around 377 B.C.

Succeeding generations of physicians looked to Hippocrates as the preeminent figure in their profession, and consequently his legend and stature grew beyond simple human proportions as the years passed. By 300 B.C. some seventy-two books were ascribed to him, but this "Hippocratic" body of medical knowledge clearly shows the hands of many different authors. It is impossible to say precisely which, if any, of these books Hippocrates composed, but it is safe to assume that they represent the medical tradition that he and generations of his students practiced and taught.

Our document comes from one of the earliest treatises within this body of Hippocratic texts, *On the Sacred Disease*, in which the author, putatively Hippocrates, deals with the issue of epilepsy.

QUESTIONS FOR ANALYSIS

1. Why does Hippocrates reject the notion that epilepsy comes from the gods?
2. In his rejection of the idea that this is a "sacred" disease, does he show any atheistic tendencies?
3. How does he propose to cure this ailment?
4. Do you consider Hippocrates' explanation of the origins and treatment of epilepsy "scientific"? Why or why not?

In regard to the disease called "sacred," it seems to me to be no more divine or sacred than other diseases but has a natural cause from which it originates, like other afflictions. People regard its nature and cause as divine out of ignorance and credulity, because it is unlike other diseases. This notion of its divinity persists by virtue of people's inability to comprehend it and the simplicity of the means by which it is "cured," for those afflicted are supposedly freed from it by purifications and incantations. If people reckon it divine because it incites awe, then instead of one sacred disease there would be many. As I will show, other diseases are no less awe-inspiring and strange, yet no one considers them sacred. . . . For example, one can see people grow mad and demented for no apparent reason and doing many strange things. I have known many persons to groan and cry out in their sleep, . . . some jumping up and rushing out of doors, all deprived of their reason until they wake up. Afterward they are as healthy and rational as before, although pale and weak. And this will occur not once but frequently. There are many similar phenomena that it would be tedious to enumerate.

In my view, they who first associated this disease with the gods were people just like our present-day magicians, purifiers, charlatans, and quacks, who claim great piety and superior knowledge. Such persons, using superstition as camouflage for their own inability to offer any help, proclaimed the disease "sacred" . . . and instituted a method of treatment which protected them, namely purifications, incantations, and enforced abstinence from bathing and from many types of food. . . . Their course of treatment forbids the patient to have a black robe, because black is symbolic of death, or to sleep on a goatskin, or to wear one, or to put one foot on another, or one hand on another. All these things are reputed to be impediments to healing. . . . If the patient recovers they reap the honor and credit; if the patient dies, they have a perfect defense: the gods, not they, are to blame, seeing as they had administered nothing to eat or drink in the way of medicine, and they had not overheated the patient with baths. . . . To my way of thinking, if this course of treatment were correct, no Libyan living in the interior of Africa would be free of the disease, since they all sleep on goatskins and live on goat meat. . . . Then again, if such things, when administered as food, aggravate the disease, and if it is cured by abstinence from them, then the disease cannot be divine in origin, and the rites of purification provide no benefit. It is the food which is either beneficial or harmful. . . . Therefore, they who attempt to cure this disease in such a manner appear to me to be incapable of believing the disease is sacred or divine. . . .

Neither do I believe it to be a worthy opinion to maintain that a human body is polluted by the divine: the most impure substance being polluted by the most pure. . . . For it is the godhead that purifies, makes holy, and cleanses us from the greatest and most wicked of our offenses. . . . When we enter temples and the groves of gods we are sprinkled with holy water, not as a pollution but as a means of cleansing whatever pollution we had. And this principle seems to me to be the same in regard to purifications offered by charlatan healers.

Consequently, this disease seems to me to be no more divine than others. It has the same nature and cause as other diseases. It is also no less curable than other diseases. . . . The key to its origin, as is the case with other diseases, lies in heredity. . . . There is nothing to prevent it from happening that where one or the other parent suffers from this malady, some of their children likewise suffer from it. . . . Another strong proof that this disease is no more divine in origin than any other is that it afflicts those who are by nature phlegmatic,[1] but it does not attack the bilious.[2] If this disease were

---

[1] A calm, even sluggish, temperament. See note 3.

[2] A peevish, sour-tempered disposition. See note 3.

more divine than other diseases, it should afflict all groups equally, making no distinction between the bilious and the phlegmatic. . . .

Since the brain, as the primary center of sensation and of the spirits, perceives whatever occurs in the body, if any unusual change takes place in the air, due to the seasons, the brain is changed by the state of the air. . . . And the disease called "sacred" arises from . . . those things that enter and leave the body, such as cold, the sun, and winds, which are constantly changing and never at rest. . . . Therefore the physician should understand and distinguish each individual situation, so that at one time he might add nourishment, at another time with-

hold it. In this disease, as in all others, he must endeavor not to feed the disease, but he must attempt to wear it out by administering whatever is most contrary to each disease and not that which favors and is allied to it. For it grows vigorous and increases through that which is allied to it, but it wears out and disappears under the administration of whatever is opposed to it.[3] Whoever is knowledgeable enough to render a person humid or dry, hot or cold by regimen can also cure this disease, if the physician recognizes the proper season for administering remedies. The physician can do so without attention to purifications, spells, and all other forms of "hocus-pocus."

The Athenian as Citizen
▼▼▼

29 ▼ *Thucydides, THE HISTORY OF THE PELOPONNESIAN WAR*

During the eighth century B.C. Homer, the putative author of the *Iliad* and the *Odyssey* (Chapter 2, source 13), interpreted the past through the medium of poetic myth. By the mid-fifth century certain Hellenic researchers were recapturing and interpreting the past through the more prosaic but accurate medium of history. The word *historia* is Greek and means "knowledge achieved through inquiry." As we have seen, the Hebrews and Persians had already evolved a sense of divinely directed history (Chapter 2, sources 14 to 16, and Chapter 3, sources 22 and 23). However, it was the Greeks who became western Eurasia's first students of secular history, that is, researchers who systematically studied worldly affairs divorced from any consideration of divine intervention or control. The particular genius of Greek *historiography* (the writing of history) was that certain thinkers, largely beginning with Herodotus (ca 484–424 B.C.), be-

---

[3]The physicians of Cos believed the body contains four basic fluids or "humors": blood, phlegm, black bile, and yellow bile. They further believed that an excess of any humor, by reason of hereditary factors, environment, or accident, causes both psychic and physical imbalance. The patient becomes, depending on the humor that has thrown the body out of balance: sanguine, phlegmatic, melancholy, or bilious. Of course, no one is ever in perfect harmony; some humor always is dominant, and that

"fact" of humor dominance explains why there are different personality types. When, however, the imbalance becomes so great as to cause clinical illness, the physician must intervene. The Greek physician's art and science consisted of helping the body reestablish its natural harmony by administering or withholding foods and medicines that either reduced or increased one or more of the humors.

lieved that human events could be reconstructed and made comprehensible through careful research into the human record.

One such student of the human past was Thucydides (ca 460–400 B.C.), widely regarded as classical Hellas's greatest historian. Thucydides was a citizen of Athens in an age when Hellenic civilization was dominated by rivalry among its many different city-states, or *poleis* (the plural of *polis*). During Thucydides's youth and young manhood, Athens was led by Pericles, who from 461 to 429 B.C. presided over the final stages of the evolution of Athenian democracy. In 431 Pericles led democratic Athens into the Peloponnesian War against the oligarchic (ruled by a few) polis of Sparta and its allies. The war dragged on for a generation, ending in 404 with a Spartan victory. In the early stages of the conflict, it had seemed as though there was no way Athens could lose the war. In 430 a confident Athens paused to honor those citizens who had fallen in battle during the first year of fighting and called upon Pericles, its unofficial First Citizen, to deliver the eulogy. Pericles used the occasion to praise the polis for which those citizens had lived and died.

Thucydides undoubtedly attended that funeral, and perhaps dreamed of his own glorious service to Athens. Six years later Thucydides commanded a small naval squadron that failed to relieve a besieged Athenian infantry force, and for that failure he was forced into exile. An avid student of human affairs, especially politics, Thucydides used his enforced retirement to study the war and write its history. As he noted in the opening lines of his *History*, he had begun writing about the war from its outbreak because he believed it would prove to be the most memorable conflict in all of Hellenic history, outstripping even the Trojan and Persian wars in magnitude. His purpose was simple: to provide all Hellenes with "an everlasting possession," whose careful study would enable them to avoid similar errors in the future.

In his attempt to create an aura of dramatic verisimilitude, thereby assuring his work's being read and preserved, Thucydides used the convention of including large numbers of speeches in his *History*. As he admitted, the speeches were not verbatim accounts, but he did claim to preserve the sense of either what was said or what he judged should have been said on a particular occasion. Because Pericles' Funeral Oration was such a public and memorable speech, there is good reason to believe Thucydides has preserved the essence of Pericles' message. That message tells us a good deal about Hellenic secular culture in the fifth century B.C.

QUESTIONS FOR ANALYSIS

1. How does Pericles define Athenian democracy? According to him, what sort of citizens does this democracy breed? How does Athens help its citizens achieve their full potential? According to Pericles, what role should public affairs play in a citizen's life?
2. In his idealized portrait of Athens, Pericles contrasts Athens's spirit with that of Sparta. According to him, how do the Spartans live?
3. Why is Athens, in Pericles' words, "the school of Hellas"?

4. How does Pericles' speech provide evidence of Hellenic secularism, particularly its preoccupation with the individual, the life of the polis, and rational analysis?
5. Pericles claims that Athenians respect authority and the laws. How, if at all, does this reverence for the rule of law differ from China's Legalism? What would Qin Shi Huangdi have thought of this "ideal" polis?
6. What would Confucius have thought of this speech?

During the . . . winter, . . . the funeral of those who first fell in this war was celebrated by the Athenians at the public charge. . . . Over those who were the first buried Pericles was chosen to speak. At the fitting moment he advanced from the sepulcher to a lofty stage, which had been erected in order that he might be heard as far as possible by the multitude, and spoke as follows: . . .

"I will speak first of our ancestors, for it is right and becoming that now, when we are lamenting the dead, a tribute should be paid to their memory. There has never been a time when they did not inhabit this land, which by their valor they have handed down from generation to generation, and we have received from them a free state. But if they were worthy of praise, still more were our fathers, who added to their inheritance, and after many a struggle transmitted to us their sons this great empire. And we ourselves assembled here today, who are still most of us in the vigor of life, have chiefly done the work of improvement, and have richly endowed our city with all things, so that she is sufficient for herself both in peace and war. Of the military exploits by which our various possessions were acquired, or of the energy with which we or our fathers drove back the tide of war, Hellenic or Barbarian, I will not speak; for the tale would be long and is familiar to you. But before I praise the dead, I should like to point out by what principles of action we rose to power, and under what institutions and through what manner of life our empire became great. For I conceive

that such thoughts are not unsuited to the occasion, and that this numerous assembly of citizens and strangers may profitably listen to them.

"Our form of government does not enter into rivalry with the institutions of others. We do not copy our neighbors, but are an example to them. It is true that we are called a democracy, for the administration is in the hands of the many and not of the few. But while the law secures equal justice to all alike in their private disputes, the claim of excellence is also recognized; and when a citizen is in any way distinguished, he is preferred to the public service, not as a matter of privilege, but as the reward of merit. Neither is poverty a bar, but a man may benefit his country whatever be the obscurity of his condition. There is no exclusiveness in our public life, and in our private intercourse we are not suspicious of one another, nor angry with our neighbor if he does what he likes; we do not put on sour looks at him which, though harmless, are not pleasant. While we are thus unconstrained in our private intercourse, a spirit of reverence pervades our public acts; we are prevented from doing wrong by respect for authority and for the laws, having an especial regard to those which are ordained for the protection of the injured as well as to those unwritten laws which bring upon the transgressor of them the reprobation of the general sentiment.

"And we have not forgotten to provide for our weary spirits many relaxations from toil; we have regular games and sacrifices throughout the year; at home the style of our life is refined; and the delight which we daily feel in all these things helps to banish melancholy. Because of the greatness of our city the fruits of the whole earth flow in upon us; so that we enjoy the goods of other countries as freely as of our own.

"Then, again, our military training is in many respects superior to that of our adversaries. Our city is thrown open to the world, and we never expel a foreigner or prevent him from seeing or learning anything of which the secret if revealed to an enemy might profit him. We rely not upon management or trickery, but upon our own hearts and hands. And in the matter of education, whereas they from early youth are always undergoing laborious exercises which are to make them brave, we live at ease, and yet are equally ready to face the perils which they face. . . .

"If then we prefer to meet danger with a light heart but without laborious training, and with a courage which is gained by habit and not enforced by law, are we not greatly the gainers? Since we do not anticipate the pain, although, when the hour comes, we can be as brave as those who never allow themselves to rest; and thus too our city is equally admirable in peace and in war. For we are lovers of the beautiful, yet simple in our tastes, and we cultivate the mind without loss of manliness. Wealth we employ, not for talk and ostentation, but when there is a real use for it. To avow poverty with us is no disgrace; the true disgrace is in doing nothing to avoid it. An Athenian citizen does not neglect the state because he takes care of his own household; and even those of us who are engaged in business have a very fair idea of politics. We alone regard a man who takes no interest in public affairs, not as a harmless, but as a useless character; and if few of us are originators, we are all sound judges of a policy. The great impediment to action is, in our opinion, not discussion, but the want of that knowledge which is gained by discussion preparatory to action. For we have a peculiar power of thinking before we act and of acting too, whereas other men are courageous from ignorance but hesitate upon reflection. And they are surely to be esteemed the bravest spirits who, having the clearest sense both of the pains and pleasures of life, do not on that account shrink from danger. . . . To sum up: I say that Athens is the school of Hellas, and that the individual Athenian in his own person seems to have the power of adapting himself to the most varied forms of action with the utmost versatility and grace. This is no passing and idle word, but truth and fact; and the assertion is verified by the position to which these qualities have raised the state. For in the hour of trial Athens alone among her contemporaries is superior to the report of her. No enemy who comes against her is indignant at the reverses which he sustains at the hands of such a city; no subject complains that his masters are unworthy of him. And we shall assuredly not be without witnesses; there are mighty monuments of our power which will make us the wonder of this and of succeeding ages; we shall not need the praises of Homer or of any other panegyrist whose poetry may please for the moment, although his representation of the facts will not bear the light of day. For we have compelled every land and every sea to open a path for our valor, and have everywhere planted eternal memorials of our friendship and of our enmity. Such is the city for whose sake these men nobly fought and died; they could not bear the thought that she might be taken from them; and every one of us who survives should gladly toil on her behalf.

"I have dwelt upon the greatness of Athens because I want to show you that we are contending for a higher prize than those who enjoy none of these privileges, and to establish by manifest proof the merit of these men whom I am now commemorating. Their loftiest praise has been already spoken. For in magnifying the city I have magnified them, and men like them whose virtues made her glorious."

An Alienated Woman
▼▼▼

30 ▼ *Euripides, MEDEA*

Pericles concluded that Athens had become "the school of Hellas" because of the freedom its citizens enjoyed. As citizens with a vested interest in the polis, its people could develop independence and self-reliance easily and in many different directions. There is likely much truth to Pericles' conclusion, and undoubtedly this freedom contributed substantially to Athens's vitality as an intellectual and artistic center. Yet we must remember that in Pericles' day the benefits of citizenship were restricted to a minority of the population — free, native-born, male adults. Moreover, a number of Hellenic rationalists, including some Athenians, found the atmosphere of city-states that were dictatorships and oligarchies more attractive or less threatening than the often tumultuous democracy of Athens. One notable expatriate from Athens was the playwright Euripides (ca 480–406 B.C.).

While Hippocrates studied the clinical course of physical disease, Euripides specialized in diagnosing emotional disorders and mental breakdowns, especially those brought on by social ills. Deep compassion underlay his dissections of tortured human psyches. Although he sought more to understand than to judge, his extant plays show him to have been an outspoken critic of the indignities suffered by those whom Athenian society exploited: war victims, slaves, foreigners, and especially women.

Athenian women lived in a society that accorded them little status and less freedom. They dominate, however, most of Euripides' extant plays. His heroines differ in character and situation, but all share several qualities. Each is memorable and a powerful personality in her own right. Each also, in differing degrees, is a social victim and consequently displays the aberrant behavior of a person denied the full range of human expression.

Euripides possessed more than just a voice of indignation and a strong social conscience. He was able, through his art, to analyze rationally and coolly the terrible personal and social consequences of exploitation in works that his fellow citizens found fascinating but disturbing. His plays were always well attended, yet the playwright's more than ninety works, composed over a career of some fifty years, won only five first prizes, one of which was posthumous. Late in life the aged artist-psychologist was forced to leave Athens, probably because of his outspoken opposition to Athenian atrocities in the Peloponnesian War. Eventually, he took up residence in the wilds of far-off Macedon.

A quarter of a century earlier, on the eve of the outbreak of the Peloponnesian War, Euripides produced *Medea*, ironically a play revolving around a mythical exile. The story tells how Medea, a "barbarian" woman from the region of the Black Sea, had fallen in love with the adventurer Jason and resolved to assist him in his quest for the Golden Fleece, no matter the price. The price was high.

She killed her brother and betrayed her father. Eventually, she, Jason, and their two children arrived at Corinth as refugees. Here Jason abandoned Medea and became engaged to King Creon's daughter. Creon, perceiving Medea and her children as a threat and embarrassment, orders them to leave Corinth.

Love and hate, emotions so clearly allied, soon become one and the same in Medea. Eventually, she kills Creon, his daughter, and her own two children before magically escaping. Here, in the opening scene, Euripides establishes the play's theme and provides clear hints of the horrors to come.

QUESTIONS FOR ANALYSIS

1. Assuming that Euripides' play was a commentary on contemporary Athenian social issues, what does the evidence tell us specifically about the status of women and minors in Athens?
2. What does Medea's speech suggest about the status of foreigners and other noncitizens in Pericles' Athens?
3. What would Medea say in answer to Pericles' Funeral Oration?
4. All of Hellas's poleis were organized for and focused on war, and a citizen's status depended on his role as a warrior. What evidence do Thucydides and Euripides provide in support of this fact?

The scene is **Corinth***, in front of* **Medea's** *house.*

Enter aged **Nurse***, who accompanied* **Medea** *from Colchis and now serves as nurse of* **Medea's** *children*

NURSE. How I wish that the ship Argo[1] had never flown between the blue Clashing Rocks to Colchis,[2] that the pine had never been cut down to make oars for the hands of those princes who sought the Golden Fleece for Pelias![3] For then my mistress would never have fallen in love with Jason and sailed with him to the towers of Iolchus,[4] she would never have persuaded the daughters of Pelias to kill their father;[5] she would never have come to live in this land of Corinth[6] with her husband and children.

To be sure, the people here were pleased when she came. She helped Jason in every way. They never had arguments, and it's a happy home when husband and wife agree. But now love has sickened, and everything is hatred between them. Jason has betrayed his children and my mistress. He is taking to his bed the royal princess, and wretched Medea, outraged, cries aloud the promises he gave her, their right hands clasped in loyalty to each other, the greatest pledge there is, and summons the gods to witness how Jason repays all she did for him. She lies without food, her body smitten with grief, wasting away all the time in tears, brooding over the wrong done her by her husband. She doesn't lift her face from the floor, she's like a rock or a wave of the sea, deaf to her friends' advice, turning away from them as she moans

---

[1] The ship Jason captained in his search for the Golden Fleece.
[2] Medea's homeland along the eastern shores of the Black Sea.
[3] Jason's uncle, who sent Jason to Colchis to secure the Golden Fleece.

[4] Jason's homeland in Thessaly, northern Greece.
[5] Medea was a witch and dispatched the evil Pelias by duping his daughters through her magical arts.
[6] Because of Pelias's death, Jason, Medea, and their children sought refuge in Corinth, which is in the Peloponnesus.

for her father, her native land, and the home she deserted to follow a man who has now dishonored her.

Yes, poor woman, she has learned from disaster what it is to lose one's country. She even hates her children, they give her no joy when she looks at them. I'm afraid she has something terrible in mind, for in her sullen fury she won't put up with being insulted. I know her! What will she do? Will she go silently into a bedroom and drive a dagger through someone's heart? Or will she kill the King and the bridegroom and then pay for it with even greater suffering? A terrible woman she is, and no one will easily harm her and sing a song of triumph.

But here come the children, through with their morning sport. How little they know of their mother's troubles, for the mind of the young does not take to grief.

Enter Children *and* Attendant.

MEDEA (WITHIN THE HOUSE). O God!
Wretched am I and full of woe,
How I wish I were dead!
   NURSE. Do you hear that, dearest
   children? Your mother's
Heart is racked, her fury full.
Hasten quickly inside the house,
And don't approach within her sight,
Don't go near her, but guard against
The savage nature and raging hate
Of her self-willed heart.
Come now, go in as fast as you can.
For a cloud has arisen above the earth,
A cloud which will quickly burst into flame
With rising fury. What will she do,
That heart, proud and hard to control,
That spirit stung by injustice?
   MEDEA (WITHIN). How I have suffered,
   suffered things
Full of agony! O cursed children
Of a hated mother, I wish you were dead!
May your father and our home perish!
   NURSE. O God, O God, you pitiful woman!

What part have the children in their father's
   sin?
Why do you hate them? O my dears,
How I fear lest you will suffer!
For terrible are the moods of princes,
Ruled in few things, controlling many,
They find it hard to govern their wrath.
To learn to live as an equal with equals
Is better. In modest and quiet ways
May I come to life's end securely.
Best is the middle road. To use it
Is good for mortals, but any excess
Brings no advantage whatever to people.
Greater ruin, when he becomes outraged,
A god brings on prosperous homes.

As she finishes speaking, the **Chorus** *of women of Corinth, with their* **Leader**, *enter.*

   LEADER. I heard the voice, I heard the cry
Of the wretched
Woman of Colchis, savage still.
Tell me, old woman, why is she wailing
Within her home? I am unhappy
At the pain she suffers, for this home
I have come to regard with devotion.
   NURSE. It's a home no more, all that is
   gone.
He has a bed in the royal palace,
She wastes her life away in her room.
My mistress allows herself no comfort
In words that her friends would offer.
   MEDEA (WITHIN). O God,
Through my brain let a lightning bolt
   from heaven
Smite. What's the gain of living longer?
If only death would give me release
And I could leave hated life behind!
   CHORUS. Do you hear, Zeus,[7] Earth, and
   Light,
What a cry the unfortunate wife
Utters of woe?
Why, wretched one, long for the last
Bed on which all of us once must lie?
Death will hasten all too soon,

---

[7]Chief of the gods.

Do not beg for it.
If your husband
Rejoices in a new marriage
That is common. Do not be agonized,
Zeus will befriend you. Do not so bitterly
Waste away grieving over your husband.
    MEDEA (WITHIN). O great Themis[8] and
    Lady Artemis,[9]
You see what I suffer, after I bound
That cursed husband to me with great oaths.
Now may I see him and his bride
Crumble to dust in their new home,
They who dared wrong me without cause.
O father, O city, which I fled from
After I shamelessly slew my brother!
    NURSE. Do you hear what she says, and how
    she calls
On Themis and Zeus with her entreaties,
Zeus the trusted steward of promises?
Certainly no mild revenge
Will satisfy my lady's anger.
    CHORUS. If only she would let us see her,
Let us soothe her with comforting words,
Then she might lessen her fierce rage
And her frenzy of spirit.
I would never be alien to my friends.
So go to her,
Bring her forth from the house,
Tell her friends are here.
Hurry before she harms those within,
For great grief journeys fast.
    NURSE. I will do it, but I am afraid
I can never persuade my mistress.
Yet I will do this labor of love.
Like a lioness with her brood
She glares at us servants, whenever one
Approaches her with soothing words. . . .

Exit **Nurse** *into the house.*

CHORUS. I heard the cry weighted with woe
Of the woman grieving over betrayal
By the husband who forsook her bed,
And she calls on the gods to avenge the
    injustice,
On Themis, keeper of oaths for Zeus,
Who led her to Hellas over the sea,
The sea to the north, through the endless gate
Of the Hellespont.[10]

Medea *enters.*

MEDEA. Women of Corinth, I have come out of the house so that you will not blame me for keeping to myself. For I know that many people are too reserved toward others; they stay at home too much or are not friendly in company, and some by sheer laziness get the reputation of not caring for their neighbors. But it isn't fair to judge and dislike at first sight people who have done no wrong, without understanding them. A foreigner must be especially careful to conform to the customs of the city, but even a Greek who lives entirely to himself is criticized for it and becomes unpopular, because people do not know him.

As for me, you must be tolerant, because a totally unexpected blow has fallen on me and ruined my life. I go about with all joy in life gone, friends, wishing only to die. The man in whom all my happiness rested has turned out to be the basest of all men — my husband.

Of all things that live upon the earth and have intelligence we women are certainly the most wretched. First we must get a great amount of money to buy a husband, and then it's a master of our bodies that we take. Not to succeed in getting one brings even greater unhappiness. Then comes the greatest gamble of all —will he be kind or cruel to us? You know

---

[8]The handmaiden of the gods, who presides over justice and order and serves as Zeus's counselor. She was the protector of the oppressed and goddess of the rights of hospitality.
[9]Daughter of Zeus and Apollo's twin, she punished the wicked and impious with her arrows.

[10]The narrow strait separating Europe from Asia Minor, it connects the Aegean with the Sea of Marmara. Its modern name is the Dardanelles.

how hard it is for women to get a divorce, and it's impossible to reject a husband. So then, entering among new ways of life and customs, a bride must be a seer — she never learned those things at home — to get on well with this man who sleeps beside her. If by working our hardest we bring it about that our husbands stay with us without fretting, life is enviable, but if we fail we were better dead. When a man finds life unbearable at home he goes out to visit some friend, or to his club, and gets relief, but we have no one to look to but him. Then they say we lead a sheltered life at home, avoiding danger, while they go out to fight, but I say that's absurd. I'd sooner go three times into battle than bear one child.

But beyond these things we share in common, my situation is different from yours. You have this city and your father's homes, security, and the company of your friends. I am alone, without a city, and now I am outraged by the man who dragged me from a foreign country. I have no mother, no brother, no kin to take refuge with from this disaster.

There is only one thing I shall ask of you. If I find some way of repaying my husband for the way he has treated me, keep quiet about it. For you know that a woman is timid in other things, and is a coward in looking on cold steel, but whenever she is wronged in her marriage there is no heart so murderous as hers.

Reason on Trial
▼▼▼

31 ▼ *Plato, APOLOGIA*

The *Dialogues* of Plato (427–348 B.C.) are the major source for the life and teachings of Socrates of Athens (ca 469–399 B.C.). Although Socrates left behind only a small number of students and no writings, he served a pivotal role in the development of Greek philosophy. Indeed, modern students of ancient philosophy generally divide Greek thought into the pre- and post-Socratic periods.

Socrates' ultimate contribution was his refusal to accept easy answers as he searched after wisdom and virtue, which to him were the same. Like Confucius, Socrates had an implicit faith in the proposition that action inevitably follows knowledge. The moral person, for Socrates, was the one who knew the good and acted accordingly. Unlike Confucius, however, Socrates refused to accept the answers of tradition and the way of the past as infallible guides to wisdom and moral behavior.

Socrates' uncompromising search for truth and goodness of soul earned him a number of enemies, and he finally fell victim to the mood of bitter recrimination that followed Athens's defeat in the Peloponnesian War. In 399 a conservative politician charged Socrates with impiety against the gods and corruption of youth. On trial for his life, the seventy-year-old philosopher refused to defend himself against the charges, choosing instead to offer a justification of his life and methods of inquiry. He was found guilty and condemned to death by a jury that fully expected him to flee the city. Socrates, faithful to the end to his sense of morality, refused to avoid the sentence and went serenely to his death.

The best account of Socrates' *apologia*, or defense, at his trial comes to us from Plato, Socrates' brilliant pupil and arguably the most original of all of Hellas's great thinkers. It is impossible to say exactly where Socrates' ideas end and Plato's begin in the many philosophical dialogues Plato composed and in which his former master serves as hero. It is likely, however, that the *Apologia* is faithful to the concepts, if not the actual words, that Socrates presented in his defense of philosophy.

Following the death of his teacher, Plato withdrew from his native Athens and did not return for twelve years. Upon his return, he founded his own school of philosophy, the Academy, which he presided over for nearly forty years, although later he again left Athens, this time for six years. When he returned, he again took up residence in the Academy and there, for the rest of his life, instructed the men and women who attended in large numbers. The Academy continued to be a center of Greek rational philosophy until the Christian emperor Justinian ordered its closing in A.D. 529. For over nine hundred years the Academy served the cause of the unfettered pursuit of wisdom that Socrates so ably defended and for which he died.

QUESTIONS FOR ANALYSIS

1. What defense does Socrates offer against the charges of impiety and corruption of Athens's youth?
2. According to Socrates, what necessary social function does he serve?
3. What wisdom does Socrates claim to have?
4. What does he teach, and what is his method of instruction? Can you discover in this text what the "Socratic method" of analysis, argumentation, and education is?
5. According to Socrates, what is a human being's highest function and greatest responsibility?
6. How was it possible for people to perceive Socrates as guilty of all charges?
7. Hippocrates, Thucydides, Euripides, and Socrates: what basic cultural attitudes and assumptions did they share?
8. How does Socrates' definition of virtue parallel that of Confucius? How does it differ? Which are more significant, the similarities or differences?

Men of Athens, do not interrupt me with noise, even if I seem to you to be boasting; for the word which I speak is not mine, but the speaker to whom I shall refer it is a person of weight. For of my wisdom — if it is wisdom at all — and of its nature, I will offer you the god of Delphi[1] as a witness. You know Chaerephon, I fancy. He was my comrade from a youth and the comrade of your democratic party.[2] . . . Well, once he went to Delphi and made so bold as to ask the oracle this question; and, gentlemen, don't make a disturbance at what I say;

---

[1]The oracle, or prophetess, at Delphi spoke for the god Apollo.

[2]Socrates mistrusted the "unthinking masses" and consequently was not a supporter of Athens's democratic faction.

for he asked if there were anyone wiser than I. Now the Pythia[3] replied that there was no one wiser. And about these things his brother here will bear you witness, since Chaerephon is dead.

But see why I say these things; for I am going to tell you whence the prejudice against me has arisen. For when I heard this, I thought to myself: "What in the world does the god mean, and what riddle is he propounding? For I am conscious that I am not wise either much or little. What then does he mean by declaring that I am the wisest? He certainly cannot be lying, for that is not possible for him." And for a long time I was at a loss as to what he meant; then with great reluctance I proceeded to investigate him somewhat as follows.

I went to one of those who had a reputation for wisdom, thinking that there, if anywhere, I should prove the utterance wrong and should show the oracle "This man is wiser than I, but you said I was wisest." So examining this man — for I need not call him by name, but it was one of the public men with regard to whom I had this kind of experience, men of Athens — and conversing with him, this man seemed to me to seem to be wise to many other people and especially to himself, but not to be so; and then I tried to show him that he thought he was wise, but was not. As a result, I became hateful to him and to many of those present; and so, as I went away, I thought to myself, "I am wiser than this man; for neither of us really knows anything fine and good, but this man thinks he knows something when he does not, whereas I, as I do not know anything, do not think I do either. I seem, then, in just this little thing to be wiser than this man at any rate, that what I do not know I do not think I know either." From him I went to another of those who were reputed to be wiser than he, and these same things seemed to me to be true; and there I

became hateful both to him and to many others. . . .

Now from this investigation, men of Athens, many enmities have arisen against me, and such as are most harsh and grievous, so that many prejudices have resulted from them and I am called a wise man. For on each occasion those who are present think I am wise in the matters in which I confute someone else; but the fact is, gentlemen, it is likely that the god is really wise and by his oracle means this: "Human wisdom is of little or no value." And it appears that he does not really say this of Socrates, but merely uses my name, and makes me an example, as if he were to say: "This one of you, O human beings, is wisest, who, like Socrates, recognises that he is in truth of no account in respect to wisdom."

Therefore I am still even now going about and searching and investigating at the god's behest anyone, whether citizen or foreigner, who I think is wise; and when he does not seem so to me, I give aid to the god and show that he is not wise. And by reason of this occupation I have no leisure to attend to any of the affairs of the state worth mentioning, or of my own, but am in vast poverty on account of my service to the god.

And in addition to these things, the young men who have the most leisure, the sons of the richest men, accompany me of their own accord, find pleasure in hearing people being examined, and often imitate me themselves, and then they undertake to examine others; and then, I fancy, they find a great plenty of people who think they know something, but know little or nothing. As a result, therefore, those who are examined by them are angry with me, instead of being angry with themselves, and say that "Socrates is a most abominable person and is corrupting the youth."

And when anyone asks them "by doing or

---

[3]The priestess who acted as the vehicle for the sacred serpent (the python), who was believed to be the actual soothsayer at Delphi.

teaching what?" they have nothing to say, but they do not know, and that they may not seem to be at a loss, they say these things that are handy to say against all the philosophers, "the things in the air and the things beneath the earth" and "not to believe in the gods" and "to make the weaker argument the stronger." For they would not, I fancy, care to say the truth, that it is being made very clear that they pretend to know, but know nothing. . . . If you should say to me . . . : "Socrates, this time we will not do as Anytus[4] says, but we will let you go, on this condition, however, that you no longer spend your time in this investigation or in philosophy, and if you are caught doing so again you shall die"; if you should let me go on this condition which I have mentioned, I should say to you, "Men of Athens, I respect and love you, but I shall obey the god rather than you, and while I live and am able to continue, I shall never give up philosophy or stop exhorting you and pointing out the truth to any one of you whom I may meet, saying in my accustomed way: "Most excellent man, are you who are a citizen of Athens, the greatest of cities and the most famous for wisdom and power, not ashamed to care for the acquisition of wealth and for reputation and honor, when you neither care nor take thought for wisdom and truth and the perfection of your soul?" And if any of you argues the point, and says he does care, I shall not let him go at once, nor shall I go away, but I shall question and examine and cross-examine him, and if I find that he does not possess virtue, but says he does, I shall rebuke him for scorning the things that are of most importance and caring more for what is of less worth. This I shall do to whomever I meet, young and old, foreigner and citizen, but most to the citizens, inasmuch as you are more nearly related to me. For know that the god commands me to do this, and I believe that no greater good ever came to pass in the city than my service to the god. For I go about doing

nothing else than urging you, young and old, not to care for your persons or your property more than for the perfection of your souls, or even so much; and I tell you that virtue does not come from money, but from virtue comes money and all other good things to man, both to the individual and to the state. If by saying these things I corrupt the youth, these things must be injurious; but if anyone asserts that I say other things than these, he says what is untrue. Therefore I say to you, men of Athens, either do as Anytus tells you, or not, and either acquit me, or not, knowing that I shall not change my conduct even if I am to die many times over. . . .

For know that if you kill me, I being such a man as I say I am, you will not injure me so much as yourselves. . . . And so, men of Athens, I am now making my defence not for my own sake, as one might imagine, but far more for yours, that you may not by condemning me err in your treatment of the gift the god gave you. For if you put me to death, you will not easily find another, who, to use a rather absurd figure, attaches himself to the city as a gadfly to a horse, which, though large and well bred, is sluggish on account of his size and needs to be aroused by stinging. I think the god fastened me upon the city in some such capacity, and I go about arousing, and urging and reproaching each one of you, constantly alighting upon you everywhere the whole day long. Such another is not likely to come to you, gentlemen; but if you take my advice, you will spare me. But you, perhaps, might be angry, like people awakened from a nap, and might slap me, as Anytus advises, and easily kill me; then you would pass the rest of your lives in slumber, unless God, in his care for you, should send someone else to sting you. And that I am, as I say, a kind of gift from the god, you might understand from this; for I have neglected all my own affairs and have been enduring the neglect of my concerns all these years, but I am

---

[4]The person who introduced charges against Socrates.

always busy in your interest, coming to each one of you individually like a father or an elder brother and urging you to care for virtue; now that is not like human conduct. If I derived any profit from this and received pay for these exhortations, there would be some sense in it; but now you yourselves see that my accusers, though they accuse me of everything else in such a shameless way, have not been able to work themselves up to such a pitch of shamelessness as to produce a witness to testify that I ever exacted or asked pay of anyone. For I think I have a sufficient witness that I speak the truth, namely, my poverty. . . .

I was never any one's teacher. If any one, whether young or old, wishes to hear me speaking and pursuing my mission, I have never objected, nor do I converse only when I am paid and not otherwise, but I offer myself alike to rich and poor; I ask questions, and whoever wishes may answer and hear what I say. And whether any of them turns out well or ill, I should not justly be held responsible, since I never promised or gave any instruction to any of them; but if any man says that he ever learned or heard anything privately from me, which all the others did not, be assured that he is lying.

But why then do some people love to spend much of their time with me? You have heard the reason, men of Athens; for I told you the whole truth; it is because they like to listen when those are examined who think they are wise and are not so; for it is amusing.

Chapter 5

▼▼▼

Regional Empires and Afro-Eurasian Interchange: 300 B.C.– A.D. 500

Eurasia's four major cultural traditions were in place by 300 B.C., and for the next several centuries these religious, philosophical, and social systems expanded geographically, often as a consequence of conquest. The most dramatic early example of this phenomenon was the Hellenistic amalgamation brought about by Alexander the Great and his generals. Eventually, by the end of the first century B.C., four great regional empires linked the cultural traditions of China, India, Southwest Asia, and the Greco-Roman Mediterranean in a chain of civilization from the Pacific to the Atlantic. Han China dominated East Asia and reached deeply into Central Asia. India, which was not politically united, was joined to Central Asia by the Kushana Empire in its northern regions. The Parthian Empire controlled the Southwest Asian lands of Iran and Mesopotamia and aggressively butted up against the Roman Empire, which was centered on the Mediterranean.

Land and sea routes, most notably the fabled Silk Road, 5,000 rugged miles of camel caravan trails from western China to the eastern Mediterranean, now joined these civilized regions, creating the first age of Afro-Eurasian interchange. Historians often refer to such a grand linkage of peoples as an *ecumene,* a Greek word meaning "world community." However, the term and its image can be mislead-

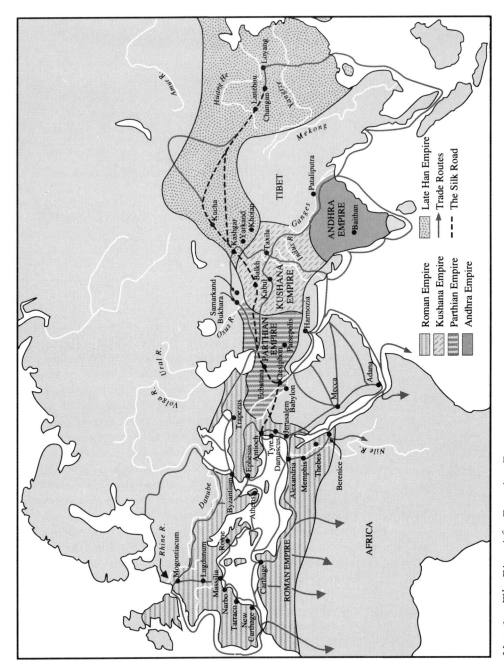

Map 1   The First Afro-Eurasian Ecumene

ing, because very few Mediterraneans traveled all the way to China, and fewer Chinese ventured even to the borders of the Roman Empire. Instead, a series of merchant intermediaries passed along the silk, cotton, spices, manufactured goods, gold, ideas, and even killing diseases that traveled from one end of this great network to the other.

Although most of the major routes of exchange traversed the waters and lands of Eurasia, Africa also shared in this unification to the extent that its northern regions were an integral part of the Roman Empire, and portions of its eastern coast were linked by regular trade with Arabia, India, and Southeast Asia.

This age of grand-scale linkage began to break down around A.D. 200, as both China and the Roman Empire entered periods of severe crisis. Although there was some interchange between East Asia and the West as late as the era of Emperor Justinian of Constantinople (r. 527–565), during whose reign the secret of silk production was smuggled into the West, by A.D. 500 trans-Eurasian commerce that regularly carried the goods of China into the Mediterranean was largely a memory. At its height, however, the first age of Afro-Eurasian interchange had witnessed the flourishing of some brilliant civilizations and empires. Indeed, it was a period during which several of the Afro-Eurasian world's classical civilizations reached the fullness of their cultural flowering.

▼▼▼

The Greco-Roman World

Alexander the Great died in Babylon in 323 B.C. Tradition claims that when questioned as to whom he bequeathed his empire, he replied, "To the strongest." No single would-be successor proved strong enough to seize the entire empire. Rather, rival generals eventually divided the Hellenistic world into a number of successor states. The two mightiest and most brilliant were the kingdom of the Seleucids, centered in Anatolia, Mesopotamia, and Syria, and the kingdom of Egypt, which fell to the family of Ptolemy, one of Alexander's younger Macedonian generals.

Ptolemy and his successors lavished money on their capital, Alexandria, transforming this new city, located in Egypt's northern delta region, into the most impressive cosmopolitan setting in the Hellenistic world. The city's twin crowning glories, at least in the opinion of scholars and scientists, were the Museum, which functioned as a center of advanced research, and the Library, which represented an attempt to gather under one roof the entire Hellenistic world's store of written knowledge and contained perhaps as many as 500,000 separate scrolls.

Both institutions enjoyed the continuous generous patronage of the Macedonian-Greek god-kings of Egypt and served as focal points for scientific and literary studies that were Greek in form and substance but cosmopolitan in scope and clientele. Educated Persians, Jews, Mesopotamians, Syrians, Italians, and members of many other ethnic groups flocked to Alexandria, where they formed an ecumenical community of scholars and artists whose common language and intellectual perspective were as Greek as that of their Ptolemaic hosts.

In 30 B.C. Cleopatra VII, the last Ptolemaic ruler of Egypt, died in Alexandria by her own hand, and Egypt passed under the direct authority of the rising imperial power of Rome. By this time Rome had already seized control of Italy, Greece, major portions of Anatolia (which it termed *Asia Minor*), Syria, most of North Africa, all the major Mediterranean islands, Spain, and the area north of the Alps and Pyrenees known as Gaul. The Mediterranean had truly become Rome's *Mare Nostrum* (Our Sea), and the Roman Empire now controlled a large portion of the Hellenistic world. As inheritor by conquest of eastern Mediterranean lands and culture, Rome would disseminate a Greco-Roman form of Hellenistic culture throughout the western Mediterranean, as well as among various "barbarian" peoples living in European lands well beyond the Mediterranean coastline. Within a century, Roman legions would be erecting Greek-style temples to the Persian god Mithras along the Rhine and in Britain, and Greek literature would be studied in schools throughout lands recently wrested from Gallic tribes.

The World According to Strabo
▼▼▼

32 ▼ *Strabo, GEOGRAPHY*

The life and work of the late Hellenistic historian and geographer Strabo (ca 64 B.C.–A.D. 25) reflect the hybrid nature and wide horizons of Hellenistic civilization. By descent Strabo was part Asian and part Greek. He was born in Amaseia in northeastern Asia Minor but studied and worked at length in Rome and Alexandria. He admired the Romans and their empire but composed his historical and geographical works in Greek, the common language of educated Hellenistic people.

His only surviving work is the *Geography*. Its seventeen books are largely a compilation of information (and misinformation) garnered from accounts and studies by earlier Hellenistic travelers and geographers of the known lands of Europe, Asia (up to and including India), and Africa. Because most of Strabo's sources were lost forever when the Library of Alexandria was destroyed in late Roman times, his *Geography* is our main source of information on the Hellenistic

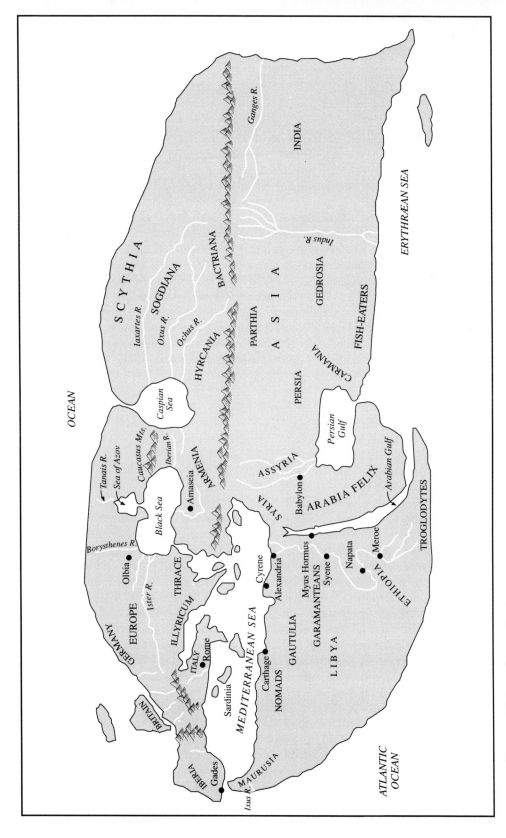

Map 2   *The World According to Strabo*

world's geographical knowledge and lore. In this selection Strabo discusses the
state of his society's knowledge of the world.

QUESTIONS FOR ANALYSIS

1. What kind of evidence did Strabo rely on?
2. Why does he prefer the accounts of contemporary to earlier writers and
   travelers, and what does this suggest about travel in his own day?
3. Using the map, trace that portion of the inhabited world Strabo knew from
   firsthand experience.
4. What level of contact did Strabo's society have with India? How did it compare with earlier exchanges in the age of the Ptolemies?
5. Consider the map and Strabo's account of Asia. What does he know about
   lands east of India, and what does this suggest about direct Greco-Roman
   knowledge of China?
6. What does Strabo tell us about the physical and human geography of North
   Africa? What evidence does Strabo present to allow us to conclude that
   North Africa was more fertile and less desiccated in his day than in our
   own? What does he know about Africa's interior? From what he tells us
   and does not tell us, what do you infer about Greco-Roman knowledge of
   Africa?

Now I shall tell what part of the land and sea I have myself visited and concerning what part I have trusted to accounts given by others by word of mouth or in writing. I have traveled westward from Armenia as far as the regions of Tyrrhenia[1] opposite Sardinia, and southward from the Euxine Sea[2] as far as the frontiers of Ethiopia.[3] And you could not find another person among the writers on geography who has traveled over much more of the distances just mentioned than I; indeed, those who have traveled more than I in the western regions have not covered as much ground in the east, and those who have traveled more in the eastern countries are behind me in the western; and the same holds true in regard to the regions towards the south and north. However, the greater part of our material both they and I receive by hear-

say and then form our ideas. . . . And men who are eager to learn proceed in just that way: they trust as organs of sense those who have seen or wandered over any region, no matter what, some in this and some in that part of the earth, and they form in one diagram their mental image of the whole inhabited world. . . . And he who claims that only those have knowledge who have actually seen abolishes the criterion of the sense of hearing, though this sense is much more important than sight for the purposes of science.

In particular the writers of the present time can give a better account of the Britons, the Germans, the peoples both north and south of the Ister, the Getans, the Tyregetans, the Bastarnians,[4] and, furthermore, the peoples in the regions of the Caucasus, such as the Albanians

[1]North central Italy.
[2]The Black Sea.
[3]Ethiopia meant all the land of Southeast Africa. See the map of Strabo's world.

[4]Tribes wandering through the Balkans, especially in Thrace.

and the Iberians.[5] Information has been given us also concerning Hyrcania and Bactriana by the writers of Parthian histories (Apollodorus of Artemita[6] and his school), in which they marked off those countries more definitely than many other writers. Again, since the Romans have recently invaded Arabia Felix with an army, of which Aelius Gallus,[7] my friend and companion, was the commander, and since the merchants of Alexandria are already sailing with fleets by way of the Nile and of the Arabian Gulf as far as India, these regions also have become far better known to us of to-day than to our predecessors. At any rate, when Gallus was prefect of Egypt, I accompanied him and ascended[8] the Nile as far as Syene and the frontiers of Ethiopia, and I learned that as many as one hundred and twenty vessels were sailing from Myos Hormos[9] to India, whereas formerly, under the Ptolemies, only a very few ventured to undertake the voyage and to carry on traffic in Indian merchandise. . . .

And Libya[10] is — as the others show, and indeed as Cnaeus Piso,[11] who was once the prefect of that country, told me — like a leopard's skin; for it is spotted with inhabited places that are surrounded by waterless and desert land. The Egyptians call such inhabited places "oases." But though Libya is thus peculiar, it has some other peculiarities, which give it a threefold division. In the first place, most of its coastline that lies opposite to us[12] is extremely fertile, and especially Cyrenaea and the country about Carthage up to Maurusia and to the Pillars of Heracles,[13] secondly, even its coastline on

the ocean[14] affords only moderate sustenance; and thirdly, its interior region, which produces silphium,[15] affords only a wretched sustenance, being, for the most part, a rocky and sandy desert; and the same is also true of the straight prolongation of this region through Ethiopia, the Troglodyte Country,[16] Arabia, and Gedrosia where the Fish-Eaters live. The most of the peoples of Libya are unknown to us; for not much of it is visited by armies, nor yet by men of outside tribes; and not only do very few of the natives from far inland ever visit us, but what they tell is not trustworthy or complete either. But still the following is based on what they say. They call the most southerly peoples Ethiopians; those who live next north of the Ethiopians they call, in the main, Garamantians, Pharusians, and Nigritans; those who live still north of these latter, Gaetulans; those who live near the sea, or even on the seacoast, next to Egypt and as far as Cyrenaea, Marmaridans; while they call those beyond Cyrenaea and the Syrtes, Psyllians, Nasamonians, and certain of the Gaetulans, and then Asbystians and Byzacians, whose territory reaches to that of Carthage. The territory of Carthage is large, and beyond it comes that of the Nomads,[17] the best known of these are called, some of them, Masylians, and others Masaesylians. And last of all come the Maurusians. The whole country from Carthage to the Pillars is fertile, though full of wild beasts, as is also the whole of the interior of Libya. So it is not unlikely that some of these peoples were also called Nomads for the reason that in early times they were not able to culti-

---

[5]These are the *eastern* Iberians, who resided in the region between the Black and Caspian seas. The western Iberians inhabited the land which is today Spain and Portugal.
[6]A second-century B.C. geographer of Alexandria and Athens.
[7]A Roman prefect of Egypt who led a disastrous two-year expedition into southern Arabia in 25–24 B.C.
[8]Sailed south. Because the Nile flows north, upstream lies to the south.
[9]An African port on the Red Sea.
[10]Libya here means all of Africa.

[11]Proconsul (governor) of the North African province of Africa in the early years following the birth of Jesus.
[12]The coast of North Africa.
[13]The Strait of Gibraltar.
[14]It is not clear which ocean he means here, the Indian or the Atlantic. Strabo knew and wrote about each. Quite possibly he refers to both ocean coastlines.
[15]An aromatic plant grown for export in Cyrene, on Africa's northeast coast; its resin was a popular medicine.
[16]A stone age people of sub-Saharan Africa.
[17]The Berber inhabitants of the North African Roman province of Numidia.

vate the soil on account of the multitude of wild animals. But the Nomads of today not only excel in the skill of hunting (and the Romans take a hand in this with them because of their fond- ness for fights with wild animals), but they have mastered farming as well as the chase. This, then, is what I have to say about the continents.

The Roman Peace
▼▼▼

33 ▼ *Caesar Augustus,*
THE ACCOMPLISHMENTS OF THE DEIFIED AUGUSTUS

Following its total victory over Carthage in the Second Punic War (218–201 B.C.), the Roman Republic was the major power in the Mediterranean and an empire in fact, if not in name. Rome's acquisition of an empire had major repercussions at home, and the resultant strains triggered more than a century of class discord and civil war. The civil wars ended in 30 B.C. when Octavian, the great-nephew and adopted son of Julius Caesar (ca 100–44 B.C.), defeated Mark Antony and became sole master of the Roman world. In 27 B.C. the Senate accorded him the title *Augustus* (Revered One), implying he possessed superhuman authority. Posterity remembers him as Caesar Augustus (63 B.C.–A.D. 14), the man who created and presided over the early years of the *Pax Romana* — the Roman Peace.

Augustus maintained the forms of traditional oligarchic republicanism while creating a political entity in which all real power was concentrated in the hands of a single individual — himself. The system he established, known as the *Principate* (from one of his favorite titles, *Princeps*, or First Citizen), worked fairly well for nearly two centuries.

It would be difficult to exaggerate the importance of Caesar Augustus's Roman Peace. The several centuries of relative stability that his system gave the empire proved to be an important incubation period for the quickening of Hellenistic culture in the West. Perhaps without the Roman Peace a new Southwest Asian religion, Christianity, would have had much less success in establishing itself in the western regions of the Mediterranean. The importance of the Pax Romana was not lost on the Romans, and this was especially true of Augustus. In A.D. 13 an aged Augustus deposited a number of documents with the vestal virgin priestesses of Rome. Among them was the following account of his accomplishments, which he ordered inscribed on two bronze pillars that were to stand before his mausoleum.

He died on 19 August of the next year, and on 17 September the Senate decreed he should be worshiped as one of the gods of the Roman state. The cult of the Deified Augustus was promoted throughout the empire and became especially popular in the East, particularly in Asia Minor, where there was a long tradition of worshiping god-kings. Over the centuries, Augustus's mausoleum pillars were lost, but copies of his last testament were preserved in eastern temples raised to his honor. The best extant copy comes from the temple of Rome and Augustus in what is now Ankara, Turkey.

QUESTIONS FOR ANALYSIS

1. What picture emerges of the Roman Empire's size, wealth, and power?
2. What evidence is there that the empire expanded under Augustus's leadership?
3. Is there any evidence of the empire's dark side?
4. How does Augustus manage to disguise the extent and nature of his power? Why would he want to do so? How extensive was his power?
5. What image does Augustus wish to project in his last testament?
6. Augustus established the model to be followed by his imperial successors for the next two centuries. Judging by what he claims to have done, what were a Roman emperor's chief responsibilities?
7. Augustus has been called a "conservative innovator." Based on this document, does that characterization seem appropriate?
8. What does this document tell us about Augustus's foreign policy and the empire's relations with the peoples of Kush, Germany, Arabia, the Parthian Empire, and India?
9. Compare Augustus's accomplishments with the claims of Qin Shi Huangdi (Chapter 4, source 27). Which strike you as more significant, the similarities or the differences? What do the similarities suggest about the common nature of ancient empires? What do the dissimilarities allow us to infer about the essential differences that separated these two civilizations?

At nineteen years of age, on my own authority and at my own cost, I raised the army with which I liberated the Republic from the oppression of a tyrannical faction.[1] . . . I waged civil and foreign wars on land and sea throughout the entire world; in victory I showed mercy to all surviving citizens, and I preferred sparing conquered foreigners, rather than wiping them out, whenever I could safely offer them pardon. About 500,000 Roman citizens were bound to me by military oath. . . .

In the consulship of Marcus Marcellus and Lucius Arruntius,[2] I refused the office of dictator[3] offered to me by the People and the Senate,[4] . . . At that same time, I refused the consulship when it was offered to me as an an-

---

[1]Mark Antony and his allies.
[2]In 22 B.C. The consuls were the Roman Republic's chief magistrates. Two were elected annually. Augustus retained the consulship as Rome's chief constitutional office. See note 5.

[3]The dictatorship was a constitutional office that carried with it unlimited power and was bestowed on an individual for a stipulated period of time, usually to meet an extraordinary crisis. Julius Caesar had been named dictator for life, and this was one of the reasons certain supporters of the Republic assassinated him in 44 B.C.
[4]In theory, sovereignty still lay in the hands of the Senate and Roman People.

nual office for life.[5] . . . Even though the Senate and Roman People were totally agreed that I should be elected superintendent of the laws and public morals with supreme authority, I declined to accept any office inconsistent with our ancestors' traditions. I achieved the domestic measures which the Senate desired that I carry out by virtue of the tribunician power.[6] To assist me in this power, five times I asked for and received a colleague from the Senate.[7] . . .

In my sixth consulship,[8] when Marcus Agrippa was my colleague, I carried out a census of the people. . . . In this count 4,063,000 Roman citizens were recorded. . . . A second time, in the consulship of Gaius Censorinus and Gaius Asinius,[9] I acted alone to take a census, invested as I was with consular authority,[10] and at this second census 4,233,000 Roman citizens were recorded. For a third time I completed a census . . . and 4,937,000 Roman citizens were recorded.[11] By passing new laws, I restored many of our ancestors' traditions which we were neglecting, and I personally handed down precedents in many areas for posterity to imitate. . . .

According to the records, the gateway of Janus Quirinus,[12] which our ancestors desired to be shut whenever victorious peace should be secured on sea and land throughout the entire empire of the Roman People, was closed only twice in the entire period from the founding of the city[13] to my birth. Three times during my principate the Senate decreed it should be shut. . . .

In accordance with the testament of my father,[14] I paid out to every Roman commoner 300 sesterces[15]; in my fifth consulship[16] I gave 400 sesterces to each person in my own name and out of the spoils of war; again, in my tenth consulship[17] I paid out a gratuity of 400 sesterces to every person from my own patrimony; in my eleventh consulship[18] I distributed twelve special allowances of grain purchased with my own funds; and in the twelfth year of my tribunician power,[19] for the third time, I gave everyone 400 sesterces. These gifts which I gave out never went to fewer than 250,000 persons. In the eighteenth year of my tribunician power and my twelfth consulship[20] I gave each of 320,000 urban commoners the sum of sixty *denarii*.[21] . . . Four times I came to the aid of the public treasury with my own money, transferring to the treasury officials 150,000,000 sesterces. . . . Out of my own patrimony I paid out 170,000,000 sesterces to the military treasury, which was established on my advice to provide bonuses for soldiers who had served twenty or more years.

I repaired the Capitol[22] and the theater of Pompey with an enormous outlay of funds on both projects, and without having my name in-

---

[5]Augustus personally held the consulship only thirteen times. After he was secure in his power, Augustus preferred to allow others to hold the office. See note 10.

[6]The tribune was the ancient protector of the common people. Augustus held this office continuously from 30 B.C., and it served as the constitutional basis for much of his power.

[7]Augustus, in other words, accepted the responsibility for establishing moral and social codes but did so only by virtue of his being a tribune, and he insisted on having cotribunes.

[8]28 B.C.

[9]8 B.C.

[10]Note that he exercises consular power, even though he does not hold the office.

[11]In A.D. 14. This indicates the account was reworked after Augustus deposited it with the Vestal Virgins.

[12]The ancient Italian two-faced god of gates (which have two sides) and beginnings and endings (hence, January

is his sacred month). A passageway dedicated to Janus stood in the Forum, or civic center, of Rome.

[13]According to Roman tradition, the year 753 B.C.

[14]Julius Caesar, his adopted father.

[15]Sesterces were small bronze coins, four of which equaled a silver *denarius,* the empire's basic monetary standard. A legionnaire earned 900 sesterces a year at this time, and in order to be eligible for admission to the Senate, a person needed wealth equal to one million sesterces.

[16]29 B.C.

[17]24 B.C.

[18]23 B.C.

[19]12 B.C.

[20]5 B.C.

[21]The plural of denarius. See note 15.

[22]The temple of Jupiter Capitolinus, Rome's chief civic deity.

scribed on either. I repaired the aqueduct[23] channels which in many spots were falling into decay because of age. . . . Three times I sponsored a gladiatorial show in my own name and five times in the names of my sons and grandsons; at these shows about 10,000 men fought. . . . Twenty-six times I provided the people . . . with hunting exhibitions of African wild animals . . . in which about 3,500 animals were killed. I gave the people the spectacle of a naval battle on the spot across the Tiber River where the grove of the Caesars now stands, excavating a site 1,800 feet in length and 1,200 feet wide. In this space thirty beaked ships, all triremes or biremes,[24] and a large number of smaller craft, fought one another. In addition to the rowers, there were about 3,000 combatants on board the contending fleets.

I pacified the sea by suppressing piracy. In that struggle I handed over to their masters for punishment nearly 30,000 fugitive slaves who had taken up arms against the state. . . . I extended the frontiers of all the provinces of the Roman People on whose boundaries were located peoples not subject to our rule. I restored peace to the provinces of Gaul and Spain and to Germany.[25] . . . My fleet sailed the ocean from the mouth of the Rhine as far east as the borders of the land of the Cimbrians,[26] where no Roman before that time had penetrated either by land or sea. The Cimbrians . . . and other German peoples of the region used envoys to seek my friendship and that of the Roman People. At my command and under my auspices, two ar-

mies were led almost simultaneously,[27] one into Ethiopia, the other into that part of Arabia called Felix.[28] Large numbers of enemies in each country were killed in battle, and numerous towns were taken. In Ethiopia the army advanced as far as the town of Napata, which is next to Meroë.[29] . . . I added Egypt to the empire of the Roman People. . . .

I established colonies of retired soldiers in Africa,[30] Sicily, Macedonia, both provinces in Spain, Achaea,[31] Asia,[32] Syria, Narbonese Gaul,[33] and Pisidia.[34] Italy, moreover, possesses twenty-eight colonies of retired soldiers established under my auspices, which grew large and prosperous in my lifetime.

I recovered a number of military standards lost by other leaders, after defeating enemies from Spain, Gaul, and Dalmatia.[35] I compelled the Parthians to restore to me the spoils and battle standards of three Roman armies and to seek the friendship of the Roman People as suppliants. . . .

Envoys from Indian kings, never before seen in the presence of any Roman military leader, were often sent to me. Our friendship was sought through ambassadors sent by the Bastarnians and Scythians and by the kings of the Sarmatae, who live on both sides of the Don River.[36] . . . During my principate, numerous other peoples, with whom previously there had existed no diplomatic ties or friendship, sampled the good faith of the Roman People. . . .

In my sixth and seventh consulships,[37] after I had ended the civil wars, having attained su-

---

[23]The massive brick structures that carried fresh water into Rome from the outlying highlands.

[24]Warships with three and two tiers of rowers, respectively.

[25]This is a convenient bending of the facts since the Germans had annihilated three Roman legions, some eighteen thousand soldiers, in the Teutoberg Forest in A.D. 9.

[26]In A.D. 5 a Roman fleet sailed to the coast of southern Denmark.

[27]Around 25–24 B.C.

[28]Southern Arabia.

[29]In the kingdom of Kush (Chapter 1, source 10). Nothing much came of these expeditions. See Strabo (source 32) for a note on the Arabian campaign.

[30]The region around ancient Carthage.

[31]Southern Greece.

[32]The westernmost province of Asia Minor (Anatolia).

[33]Southern, or Mediterranean, Gaul (today southern France).

[34]A western province of Asia Minor.

[35]Dalmatia is the northern half of the eastern shore of the Adriatic (largely modern Croatia and Bosnia-Herzegovina).

[36]Various western Asian peoples on the eastern fringe of the empire.

[37]28–27 B.C.

preme power by universal consent, I transferred the state from my own power to the free control of the Senate and Roman People. For this service I received the title *Augustus* by decree of the Senate, and the doorposts of my house were publicly decked with laurel leaves. The civic crown was fixed above my doorway, and a golden shield set up in the Julian senate chamber, which, as its inscription testifies, was granted to me by the Senate and Roman People to recognize my valor, clemency, justice, and devotion. From that time onward I excelled everyone in moral authority, but I possessed no more actual power than those who served as my colleagues in various magisterial offices.

The Pax Romana from Another Perspective
▼▼▼

34 ▼ *Tacitus, AGRICOLA*

The historian Cornelius Tacitus (ca A.D. 55–115) did not share Augustus's enthusiasm for the blessings of the Roman Peace. Tacitus's political career blossomed in the reign of Emperor Domitian (r. 81–96), but it is clear that Tacitus despised the emperor's policies of brutally crushing all aristocratic opposition and of accentuating the absolutist tendencies of his imperial predecessors. Tacitus looked back longingly to the "free" days of the Republic when, in his estimation, Romans possessed an independence, courage, and moral fiber that was sorely lacking in his own day.

In 98 Tacitus published his first historical work, a biography of his father-in-law, Gnaeus Julius Agricola, who, as governor of Britain, was responsible for completing the conquest of that island province. Tacitus admitted in his prologue that he intended to honor Agricola with "expressions of filial devotion," and he honored that promise by treating the man as a great Roman hero. Notwithstanding his family partisanship, Tacitus also exhibited sympathy and fair-mindedness toward Agricola's British foes.

The following excerpt purports to be a speech uttered by Calgacus, a Celtic chieftain, who harangues his followers before the decisive battle of Mount Graupius (A.D. 83), in which the army of Agricola will crush the last effective resistance to Roman power in northern Britain. Created in the tradition of classical Greco-Roman history-writing, this speech is a pure fabrication by Tacitus. It does, however, show us what one well-placed Roman aristocrat believed to be the sentiments of a significant element of the conquered British people.

QUESTIONS FOR ANALYSIS

1. According to Calgacus (Tacitus), what are the evils of the Roman imperial system?
2. How does the conquest of Britain, in "Calgacus's" mind, exhibit the sheer rapacity and greed of the Roman Empire?

3. How does Calgacus evaluate the much-vaunted Roman Peace?
4. What, according to Calgacus, was the key flaw in the Roman military system?
5. Given what Calgacus/Tacitus tells us about the Roman Empire, what do you think could possibly have happened to that empire once it reached the peak of its expansion?
6. How would Caesar Augustus (source 33) have answered Calgacus's charges?

"Whenever I reflect on the causes of this war and the events leading up to our present crisis, I have a feeling of confidence that your united effort today will be the beginning of freedom for all Britain. As freemen you have mustered to a man. There are no lands beyond us,[1] and even the sea is unsafe, menaced as it is by a Roman fleet. The clash of battle, where the brave find glory, has become even the coward's place of refuge. Earlier battles were fought with Rome. Some were lost and some were won. Whatever the case, we[2] remained the last great hope, insofar as we are the flower of the British people, dwelling as we do in the very heart of the land. Living beyond sight of the conquered shores,[3] we were able to keep even our eyes unpolluted by the contagion of slavery. We who dwell in the most distant corner of the world, we the last of the free, have been kept safe, until today, by the remoteness and seclusion for which we are famous. Now, however, the most remote region of Britain lies exposed, and everything that lay hidden is now marveled at. There are no tribes beyond us. There is nothing but rocks and waves and, more dangerous than either, the Romans, whose tyranny cannot be escaped by any act of reasonable submission. These brigands of the world have exhausted the land by their rapacity, so they now ransack the sea. When their enemy is rich, they lust after wealth; when their enemy is poor, they lust after power. Neither East nor West has satisfied their hunger. They are unique among humanity insofar as they equally covet the rich and the poor. They refer to robbery, butchery, and rapine by the lying name of 'Empire,' and where they create a desert, they call it 'Peace.'

"We naturally love our children and family above all else. Yet they are torn away from us, conscripted to be slaves in foreign lands. If our wives and sisters manage to escape being raped, they are seduced by the Romans under the guise of friendship and hospitality. The Romans collect our possessions and fortunes as tribute; they seize our fields and harvests for their own food. Under the weight of insults and beatings, our very bodies and hands are worn down clearing forests and swamps. People born into slavery are sold but once and, furthermore, are fed by their masters. Britain, however, is daily paying for its own enslavement and daily feeding its own slave masters. As is true in a private household where the latest slave is always the object of his fellow slaves' mockery, so it is that in this already ancient state of global slavery, we, the newest and cheapest slaves, are picked out for destruction. We do not have fruitful fields, mines, or harbors, for which we might be spared to work. Moreover, courage and a warlike spirit in a subject people offend a master. Even our remoteness and seclusion, while providing protection, expose us to suspicion. Since you cannot hope for mercy, at least take courage, regardless of whether it is personal safety or honor that you prize the most. Under a woman's leadership, the Brigantes were able to burn a colony, storm a camp, and might have thrown off the Roman yoke, had not success

---

[1]That might provide sanctuary.
[2]The British of the north.

[3]Of Britain. The Romans had initially conquered only the eastern coastal region of Britain.

turned them foolish.[4] Let us, therefore, an uncorrupted and unconquered people who demand freedom but never regret failure, show at the first clash of arms what heroes Caledonia[5] has held in reserve.

Do you think the Romans will be as courageous in war as they are unrestrained in peace? They owe their fame to our quarrels and disharmony; they use the enemy's errors to gain fame for their army. The Roman army, composed as it is of soldiers from a wide variety of ethnic groups, is held together by success and will disintegrate in the face of disaster. These Gauls and Germans, and, I am sorry to say, these numerous Britons, though they offer their life blood in support of a stranger's rule, have been Rome's enemies longer than its subjects. Do you really think they are bound to Rome by loyalty and love? Fear and terror are weak bonds of attachment. Remove them, and they who

have ceased fearing will begin to hate. . . . Do not be alarmed by external appearances, by the glitter of gold and silver, which neither protect nor wound. In the enemy's own ranks we shall find allies. The Britons will recognize our cause as their cause; the Gauls will remember their previous freedom; the . . . Germans will desert them. . . . To the "Roman" army's rear there is nothing we need fear. . . . The towns with their disloyal subjects and oppressive governors are filled with discontentment and are strife-ridden. Here before you is their general, and here is his army; to your rear are tribute, quarries,[6] and all the other burdens of an enslaved people. This field of battle will decide whether you endure these forever or, in an instant, gain vengeance. As you advance into battle, think of your ancestors and of those who will come after you."

▼▼▼

Han China

In A.D. 2 an imperial census counted 12,233,062 families, or approximately 60 million people, residing in China. As we have seen, Rome's census of A.D. 14 recorded 4,937,000 Roman citizens. Full-fledged citizens of Rome probably constituted less than 10 percent of the empire's total population at that time, so it is reasonable to conclude that the Roman Empire contained 50 to 60 million people in the early decades of the first century A.D. Therefore, as we look at Eurasia around the turn of the millennium, we see two massive empires of about the same size and population at each end of this great land mass. For the next two centuries Han China and Rome dominated their respective regions and, although each experienced periods of crisis, each also offered its subjects fairly stable government and a degree of prosperity.

A measure of Rome's and China's greatness can be seen in their powerful mythic influences on those who followed. Well into the modern period, European emperors and kings claimed to be legitimate heirs of Roman authority. As

[4]Queen Boudicca (Boadicea) led an uprising in A.D. 60 that resulted in the destruction of a Roman legion and the deaths of large numbers of Roman colonists. When a Roman army finally defeated her followers, she took her own life.

[5]Scotland.
[6]Criminals and dissidents were sent as slaves to work in mines and quarries.

late as the early twentieth century, German and Russian monarchs styled themselves Kaiser and Tsar, variations on the title *Caesar*. In China today, all ethnic Chinese — 97 percent of the population of the People's Republic — proudly call themselves *Han*.

The Han Dynasty reigned during one of China's golden ages, creating a political and social order based on a synthesis of Legalist and Confucian principles. It expanded China's influence into Korea, Vietnam, and across the reaches of Central Asia, presided over a general economic upswing, and witnessed a period of rich cultural productivity. Han China flourished for nearly four centuries, but in the end, like the Roman Empire, the dynasty and its empire collapsed due to internal instabilities and invasions.

The age of Han was not one period but two. From 202 B.C. to A.D. 9 the Former Han ruled China, and its most powerful and important emperor was Han Wudi, the Martial Emperor of Han, who reigned from 141 to 87 B.C. His domestic and foreign policies provided his successors for the next two thousand years with *the* model of aggressive imperial greatness. Following an interlude in which Wang Mang (A.D. 9–23) wrested the imperial throne temporarily from the Han family, the dynasty returned to power as the Later, or Eastern, Han (A.D. 25–220). After the first century, however, domestic and frontier conditions deteriorated. From A.D. 88 onward a series of ineffective rulers plagued the family.

By 220, when the Han Dynasty formally came to an end, local lords and invaders from the steppes ruled China. The stability of the earlier Han was only a memory as China plunged into a social, economic, and political chaos that would last for almost four centuries. This period has often been compared with the so-called Dark Ages that ensued after the disintegration of Roman imperial unity in the West, although the differences between the two are more significant than any superficial parallels.

Zhang Qian's Western Expedition
▼▼▼

35 ▼ Sima Qian,
THE RECORDS OF THE GRAND HISTORIAN

One of the most impressive achievements of Emperor Han Wudi (r. 141–87 B.C.) was his extension of imperial power far beyond China's traditional borders. Under his leadership, China entered into an age of confident military expansion, pushing vigorously against its neighbors to the north, west, and south. The emperor's aggressive foreign policy brought China into conflict with the *Xiongnu,* a nomadic Turkish people of the steppes whose mounted archers proved to be formidable foes. Searching for allies against the Xiongnu, the emperor dispatched one of his courtiers, Zhang Qian, in 138 B.C. to the court of the Yuezhi, another Turkish steppe people. After a series of harrowing adventures the indomitable Zhang Qian caught up with the Yuezhi in Daxia (which the West knew as Bactria and today is northern Afghanistan) but was unable to convince them to ally with China against their common foe, the Xiongnu. Although his mission ended in apparent failure, Zhang Qian returned to the Chinese imperial court in 126 with exciting information about West and South Asia, areas with which China had not had much direct contact previously. Zhang Qian's travels ushered in a fruitful period of interchange between China and West Asia, and he is rightly remembered as one of the pioneers who blazed the trail of what became the Silk Road.

In this selection Sima Qian, whom we saw in Chapter 4 (source 27), writes about events that occurred during his own youth and young manhood. Remember, the Chinese place family names first, so these two Qians shared given names but were not related.

QUESTIONS FOR ANALYSIS

1. What evidence is there that at least some of the western "barbarians" desired closer contacts with China?
2. What evidence is there in this account for the existence of at least indirect trade between China and West Asia before Zhang Qian's travels? What Chinese goods made their way west, and how did they get there?
3. How safe was it to travel from China to West Asia in the late second century B.C.?
4. What was there about Zhang Qian's report that particularly caught the interest of Han Wudi?
5. How did Zhang Qian propose to establish contact between China and Daxia? What was the result of the emperor's following his proposal?
6. In addition to hostile tribes, what else made Zhang Qian's suggested new route to Daxia (Bactria) so impractical? Map 1 shows the Silk Road. Do you now see why it followed the route that it eventually did?
7. After studying this account, what do you conclude that China had to do before there could be a Silk Road between East and West Asia?

Zhang Qian was the first person to bring back a clear account of Dayuan.[1] . . . At this time [139 B.C.] the emperor questioned various Xiongnu[2] who had surrendered to the Han, and they all reported that the Xiongnu had defeated the king of the Yuezhi people and had made his skull into a drinking vessel. As a result the Yuezhi had fled and bore a constant grudge against the Xiongnu, though as yet they had been unable to find anyone to join them in an attack on their enemy.

The Han at this time were engaged in a concerted effort to destroy the Xiongnu, and therefore, when the emperor heard this, he decided

[1] A steppe kingdom to China's northwest, located in a region that today encompasses portions of Kyrgystan and Uzbekistan, two of the Central Asiatic members of the Commonwealth of Independent States (the former Soviet Union).

[2] The Xiongnu were possibly the ancestors of the Huns who devastated the Roman Empire in the fifth century A.D.

to try to send an envoy to establish relations with the Yuezhi. To reach them, however, an envoy would inevitably have to pass through Xiongnu territory. The emperor accordingly sent out a summons for men capable of undertaking such a mission. Zhang Qian, who was a palace attendant at the time, answered the summons and was appointed as envoy.

He set out . . . , accompanied by Kanfu, a Xiongnu slave. . . . They traveled west through the territory of the Xiongnu and were captured by the Xiongnu and taken before the Shanyu.[3] The Shanyu detained them and refused to let them proceed. "The Yuezhi people live north of me," he said. "What does the Han mean by trying to send an envoy to them! Do you suppose . . . the Han would let my men pass through China?"

The Xiongnu detained Zhang Qian for over ten years and gave him a wife from their own people, by whom he had a son. Zhang Qian never once relinquished the imperial credentials that marked him as an envoy of the Han, and after he had lived in Xiongnu territory for some time and was less closely watched than at first, he and his party finally managed to escape and resume their journey toward the Yuezhi.

After hastening west for twenty or thirty days, they reached the kingdom of Dayuan.[4] The king of Dayuan had heard of the wealth of the Han empire and wished to establish communication with it, though as yet he had been unable to do so. When he met Zhang Qian he was overjoyed and asked where Zhang Qian wished to go.

"I was dispatched as envoy of the Han to the Yuezhi, but the Xiongnu blocked my way and I have only just now managed to escape," he replied. "I beg Your Highness to give me some guides to show me the way. If I can reach my destination and return to the Han to make my report, the Han will reward you with countless gifts!"

The king of Dayuan trusted his words and sent him on his way, giving him guides and interpreters to take him to the state of Kangju.[5] From there he was able to make his way to the land of the Great Yuezhi.

Since the king of the Great Yuezhi had been killed by the Xiongnu, his son had succeeded him as ruler and had forced the kingdom of Daxia [Bactria] to recognize his sovereignty.[6] The region he ruled was rich and fertile and seldom troubled by invaders, and the king thought only of his own enjoyment. He considered the Han too far away to bother with and had no particular intention of avenging his father's death by attacking the Xiongnu. . . .

After spending a year or so in the area, Zhang Qian began to journey back, . . . but he was once more captured by the Xiongnu and detained over a year. Just at this time the Shanyu died and the . . . King of the Left[7] attacked the Shanyu's heir and set himself up as the new Shanyu [126 B.C.]. As a result of this the whole Xiongnu nation was in turmoil and Zhang Qian, along with his Xiongnu wife and the former slave Kanfu, was able to escape and return to China.

The emperor honored Zhang Qian with the post of palace counselor and awarded Kanfu the title of "Lord Who Carries Out His Mission." . . . When Zhang Qian first set out on his mission, he was accompanied by over 100 men, but after thirteen years abroad, only he and Kanfu managed to make their way back to China. Zhang Qian in person visited the lands of Dayuan, the Great Yuezhi, Daxia, and

---

[3]The Xiongnu king.

[4]See note 1.

[5]A steppe kingdom, whose territory lay southeast of the Aral Sea and directly north of Bactria (note 6). Today the region forms part of Kazakhstan of the Commonwealth of Independent States.

[6]Around 139 B.C. the Yuezhi conquered Bactria (Daxia), which was located in northern Afghanistan and the southern portions of Turkmenistan and Uzbekistan. Bactria was a West Asian remnant of the Hellenistic ecumene forged by Alexander the Great and his generals and, until its conquest by the Yuezhi, was governed by Greek rulers. The Yuezhi later used Bactria as the launching area from which they carved out the Kushana Empire during the late first century B.C.

[7]A formerly subordinate Xiongnu prince.

Kangju, and in addition he gathered reports on five or six other large states in the neighborhood. All of this information he related to the emperor on his return.

▷   Zhang Qian's report contained the following types of information. In this selection he describes Parthian Persia [Anxi], Mesopotamia [Tiaozhi], and India [Shendu], none of which he had personally visited:

Anxi [Parthian Persia] is situated several thousand *li*[8] west of the region of the Great Yuezhi. The people are settled on the land, cultivating the fields and growing rice and wheat. They also make wine out of grapes.[9] They have walled cities . . . , the region containing several hundred cities of various sizes. The kingdom . . . is very large, measuring several thousand square li. Some of the inhabitants are merchants who travel by carts or boats to neighboring countries, sometimes journeying several thousand li. The coins of the country are made of silver and bear the face of the king. When the king dies, the currency is immediately changed and new coins issued with the face of his successor. . . . To the west lies Tiaozhi [Mesopotamia]. . . .

Tiaozhi is situated several thousand li west of Anxi and borders the Western Sea [Persian Gulf]. It is hot and damp, and the people live by cultivating the fields and planting rice. . . . The people are very numerous and are ruled by many petty chiefs. The ruler of Anxi[10] gives orders to these chiefs and regards them as his vassals. . . .

Southeast of Daxia is the kingdom of Shendu [India]. "When I was in Daxia," Zhang Qian reported, "I saw bamboo canes from Qiong[11] and cloth made in the province of Shu.[12] When I asked the people how they had gotten such articles, they replied, 'Our merchants go to buy them in the markets of Shendu.' Shendu, they told me, lies several thousand li southeast of Daxia. The people cultivate the land and live much like the people of Daxia. The region is said to be hot and damp. The inhabitants ride elephants when they go into battle. The kingdom is situated on a great river.[13]

"We know that Daxia is located 12,000 li southwest of China. Now if the kingdom of Shendu is situated several thousand li southeast of Daxia and obtains goods which are produced in Shu, it seems to me that it must not be very far from Shu. At present, if we try to send envoys to Daxia by way of the mountain trails that lead through the territory of the Qiang people,[14] they will be molested by the Qiang, while if we send them a little farther north, they will be captured by the Xiongnu. It would seem that the most direct route, as well as the safest, would be that out of Shu."[15]

Thus the emperor learned of Dayuan, Daxia, Anxi, and the others, all great states rich in unusual products whose people cultivated the land and made their living in much the same way as the Chinese. All these states, he was told, were militarily weak and prized Han goods and wealth. He also learned that to the north of them live the Yuezhi and Kangju[16]

---

[8]A *li* is a bit more than a third of a mile.

[9]Grape wine was, up to this point, apparently unknown in China. Tradition credits Zhang Qian with introducing the grapevine into China. Later Chinese envoys to the West apparently brought back for Chinese cultivation the chive, coriander, cucumbers, figs, sesame, safflower, and walnuts. In return, China sent westward knowledge of how to grow pears, peaches, oranges, roses, peonies, azaleas, camellias, and chrysanthemums. By the mid sixth century A.D. even the secret of silk manufacture had made its way to the eastern Mediterranean.

[10]The Parthian monarchs Phraates II (r. 138–127 B.C.) and Artabanus I (r. 127–124).

[11]Qiongzhou in Szechwan province in southwest China.

[12]China's Szechwan province.

[13]Probably a reference to the Indus River.

[14]A Tibetan mountain people.

[15]In other words, in order to avoid the Xiongnu and the Qiang, Zhang Qian proposes traveling to Daxia by way of India.

[16]Another nomadic people. See note 5.

people who were strong in arms but who could be persuaded by gifts and the prospect of gain to acknowledge allegiance to the Han court. If it were only possible to win over these states by peaceful means, the emperor thought, he could then extend his domain 10,000 li, attract to his court men of strange customs who would come translating and retranslating their languages,[17] and his might would become known to all the lands within the four seas.

The emperor was therefore delighted, and approved Zhang Qian's suggestion. He ordered Zhang Qian to start out from . . . Shu on a secret mission to search for Daxia. The party broke into four groups. . . . All the groups managed to advance one or two thousand li, but were blocked on the north by the Di and Tso tribes and on the south by the Sui and Kunming tribes. The Kunming tribes have no rulers but devote themselves to plunder and robbery, and as soon as they seized any of the Han envoys they immediately murdered them. Thus none of the parties was ever able to get through to its destination. They did learn, however, that some 1,000 or more li to the west there was a state called Tianyue[18] whose people rode elephants and that the merchants from Shu sometimes went there with their goods on unofficial trading missions.[19] In this way the Han, while searching for a route to Daxia, first came into contact with the kingdom of Tian.

Earlier the Han had tried to establish relations with the barbarians of the southwest, but the expense proved too great and no road could be found through the region and so the project was abandoned. After Zhang Qian reported that it was possible to reach Daxia by traveling through the region of the southwestern barbarians, the Han once more began efforts to establish relations with the tribes in the area.

Establishing an Imperial Confucian Academy
▼▼▼

36 ▼ Sima Qian,
THE RECORDS OF THE GRAND HISTORIAN

During its short existence the Qin Dynasty had experimented with various recruitment procedures for filling bureaucratic offices with competent and loyal officials. The early emperors of Former Han and their chief ministers continued the search for rational ways of discovering people of ability. In 124 B.C. Emperor Han Wudi established an important precedent when he decreed that proven knowledge of one of the Confucian classics would be a basis for promotion to the imperial civil service and created a rudimentary imperial academy for educating aspiring scholar-officials in the various fields of Confucian learning. By this act he set in motion a process whereby centuries later Confucianism became the empire's ideological framework.

---

[17]Having no knowledge of Chinese, they would need to communicate through a series of intermediary languages.

[18]Probably Burma (Myanmar), which today borders China's Yunnan province, but in the late second century B.C. Yunnan was not yet fully part of China and would not be for centuries to come. Burma, therefore, was a distant and mysterious land.

[19]Smuggling.

What began modestly as an academy designed to educate fifty young men became an institution that numbered upward of thirty thousand students in the last days of Later Han. Relatively few of these scholars, however, were called to the emperor's service, and the examinations Han Wudi initiated were held irregularly under his Han successors. Government office was still largely the privilege of the landed aristocracy right to the end of the Later Han era. Only in the age of the Tang Dynasty (618–907) did a regular system of civil service examinations emerge as a consequence of the imperial court's successful attempt to break the power of the traditional landed aristocracy by creating a new class of salaried imperial officials. By the early tenth century education in all the Confucian classics was virtually the only route to civil office. China had not only established the world's first known civil service examination system, it had also, for the most part, conferred civil authority on a class of people who shared a common education and philosophy. This class of Confucian *literarchs,* or literary rulers, would, more often than not, control China into the twentieth century.

In the following selection Sima Qian, one of Former Han's greatest Confucian scholars, traces the vicissitudes of Confucianism as a practiced political doctrine from the days of Master Kong to the time of the contemporary emperor, Han Wudi.

QUESTIONS FOR ANALYSIS

1. What vicissitudes did the school of Confucius experience in the four centuries following his death?
2. How were students selected for admission to the academy, and what sort of person was to be admitted? What do these standards for admission tell us of the values and purposes of Confucian education in the era of Han Wudi?
3. By approving this proposal, how has Han Wudi joined Confucianism with Legalism?
4. Consider what Confucius says in *The Analects* about government and the superior man (Chapter 4, source 25). How do you think he would respond to this academy, its students, curriculum, and purpose for existence? What would Confucius have thought about the tone of the imperial edict?

After the death of Confucius, his band of seventy disciples broke up and scattered among the feudal lords, the more important ones becoming tutors and high ministers to the rulers, the lesser ones acting as friends and teachers to the lower officials, while some went into retirement and were never seen again. . . . Among the feudal lords, however, only Marquis Wen of Wei had any fondness for literature. Conditions continued to deteriorate until the time of the First Emperor of the Qin; the empire was divided among a number of states, all warring with each other, and no one had any use for the arts of the Confucians. Only in Qi and Lu[1] did

---

[1] Two of the warring states.

scholars appear to carry on the teachings and save them from oblivion. During the reigns of Kings Wei and Xuan of Qi (378–323 B.C.), Mencius[2] and Xun Qing[3] and their respective groups both honored the doctrines of the Master and worked to expand and enrich them, winning prominence among the men of the time by their learning.

Then followed the twilight[4] days of the Qin emperor, who burned the *Odes* and *Documents* and buried the scholars alive,[5] and from this time on the texts of the Six Classics[6] of the Confucians were damaged and incomplete. . . .

Later, when Gaozu[7] had defeated Xiang Yu,[8] he marched north and surrounded the state of Lu with his troops, but the Confucian scholars of Lu went on as always, reciting and discussing their books, practicing rites and music, and never allowing the sound of strings and voices to die out.[9] . . . And when the Han came to power, these scholars were at last allowed to study and teach their Classics freely and to demonstrate the proper rituals. . . .

Shusun Tong[10] drew up the ceremonial for the Han court and was rewarded with the post of master of ritual, while all the other scholars who assisted him were likewise given preferential treatment in the government. The emperor sighed over the neglected state of learning and would have done more to encourage its revival, but at the time there was still considerable turmoil within the empire and the region within the four seas had not yet been set at peace. Likewise, during the reigns of Emperor Zu[11] and Empress Lü[12] there was still no leisure to attend to the matter of government schools. Moreover, the high officials at this time were all military men who had won their distinction in battle.

With the accession of Emperor Wen,[13] Confucian scholars began little by little to be summoned and employed in the government, although Emperor Wen himself rather favored the Legalist teachings on personnel organization and control. Emperor Jing[14] made no effort to employ Confucian scholars, and his mother, Empress Dowager Dou,[15] was an advocate of the

---

[2]Mencius (the Latinized form of *Mengzi,* or Master Meng), lived from around 372 to about 289 B.C. and, after Confucius, was the single most important thinker in the evolution of Confucian ideology. His basic doctrines were that humans are innately good and that each person has the potential to become a sage. From these two principles he evolved a political philosophy of benevolent government.

[3]Master Xun Qing (ca 300–235 B.C.) was the last great philosopher in the formative age of Confucian classical thought. Unlike Confucius and Mencius, he set his ideas down systematically in a detailed book. Although he may have been the most original and systematic of the three great Confucian sages, the Chinese valued his teachings far less than those of Confucius and Mencius, because he was too much of a free thinker, rejecting the existence of spirits, and he also doubted that humans are innately good.

[4]"Twilight" because, in Han Confucian eyes, this brief and evil reign was more the last stage of Zhou than a full-fledged dynasty itself. It had not followed the classic pattern, established in the first three dynasties, of vigorous growth, maturity, and decay (see The Mandate of Heaven, Chapter 1, source 6).

[5]Chapter 4, source 27.

[6]*The Classic of History, The Classic of Odes* (Chapter 1, sources 6 and 7), *The Analects* (Chapter 4, source 25), *The Classic of Changes, The Classic of Rites,* and *The Spring and Autumn Annals. The Classic of Changes,* or *Yi Jing,* is

a work of divination that enjoys popularity today among Western readers; *The Classic of Rites* is a compilation of proper rituals. See note 18 for a description of *The Spring and Autumn Annals.* Although *The Analects* always remained a revered book of Confucian wisdom, the other five classics assumed greater importance during the age of Later Han and collectively emerged as the *Wu Jing* — the core of the Confucian canon.

[7]*Gaozu* means "high ancestor" and was the throne name of Liu Bang, the first Han emperor (r. 202–195 B.C.).

[8]The brilliant but erratic noble whom the commoner Liu Bang defeated in contest for the empire after the fall of Qin.

[9]Confucians emphasize music because it is the art of creating harmony out of dissonance.

[10]A Confucian scholar who served both the Qin and early Han rulers.

[11]Known as the Filial Emperor, he reigned from 195 to 188 B.C., but his mother, the Empress Dowager Lü, held all real power. See note 12.

[12]The widow of Han Gaozu (note 7), she ruled China as the power behind the throne from 195 to 180 B.C.

[13]Wen the Filial (r. 180–157 B.C.), the fourth son of Han Gaozu and the first strong emperor since his father's death fifteen years earlier.

[14]Wen's successor, who ruled from 157 to 141 B.C.

[15]This powerful woman, who died in 135 B.C., sponsored the study of Daoist teachings at the courts of her husband and son.

teachings of the Yellow Emperor[16] and Laozi. Thus various scholars were appointed to fill the posts of court councilor and to answer questions, but they had no prospects of advancement.

When the present emperor came to the throne there were a number of enlightened Confucian scholars . . . at court. The emperor was much attracted by their ideas and accordingly sent out a summons for scholars of moral worth and literary ability to take service in the government.

After Empress Dowager Dou passed away, the marquis of Wuan, Tianfan,[17] became chancellor. He rejected the doctrines of the Daoists, the Legalists, and the other philosophical schools, and invited several hundred Confucian scholars and literary men to take service in the government. Among them was Gongsun Hong who, because of his knowledge of the *Spring and Autumn Annals*,[18] advanced from the rank of commoner to that of one of the three highest ministers in the government and was installed as marquis of Pingjin. Scholars throughout the empire saw which way the wind was blowing and did all they could to follow his example.

As a scholar official, Gongsun Hong, who held the post of imperial secretary, was disturbed that the teachings of Confucius were being neglected and not put into greater practice and he therefore submitted the following memorial:

The chancellor and the imperial secretary wish to make this statement. Your Majesty has issued an edict which reads:

"I have heard that the people are to be guided by rites and led to the practice of virtue through music, and that the insti-

tution of marriage is the basis of the family. Yet at the present time rites have fallen into disuse and music has declined, a fact which grieves me deeply. Therefore I have invited men of outstanding moral worth and wide learning from all over the empire to come and take service at court. Let the officials in charge of ritual encourage learning, hold discussions, and gather all the information they can to encourage the revival of rites in order to act as leaders of the empire. Let the master of ritual consult with the erudites[19] and their students on how to promote the spread of virtue in the countryside and open the way for men of outstanding talent."

In accordance with this edict we have respectfully discussed the matter with the master of ritual Kong Zang, the erudit Ping, and others, and they have told us that, according to their information, it was the custom under the Three Dynasties of antiquity to set up schools for instruction in the villages. In the Xia dynasty these were called *xiao*, in the Shang dynasty *xu*, and in the Zhou dynasty *xiang*. These schools encouraged goodness by making it known to the court and censured evil by applying punishments. Thus it was the officials of the capital who took the initiative in instructing and educating the people, and virtue spread from the court outwards to the provinces.

Now Your Majesty, manifesting supreme virtue and displaying a profound intelligence worthy to rank with that of heaven and earth, has sought to rectify human relations, encourage learning, revive the former rites, promote instruction in goodness, and open the way for men of worth so that the people of the four

---

[16]Huang Di (the Yellow Emperor), one of the five legendary predynastic Sage Emperors, supposedly reigned during the mid-third millennium B.C. He was believed to be, along with Laozi, the founder of Daoism.
[17]Maternal uncle of Han Wudi.
[18]A terse chronicle of events covering the period of 722 to 481 B.C. and written from the perspective of the state

of Lu, Confucius's home state. This Confucian classic was also ascribed to the Great Master. There is no reason to believe he had a hand in composing it, but apparently he did study and admire the work.
[19]Erudites (*boshi*) were scholar-advisers to the imperial court by virtue of the fact that each was a specialist in one of the Confucian classics.

directions[20] may be swayed to virtue. This is indeed the way to lay the foundations for an era of great peace.

In earlier times, however, the instruction provided by the government was incomplete and the rites were not fully carried out. We therefore beg that the previous official system be utilized to increase the spread of instruction. In order to fill the offices of erudit we suggest that fifty additional students be selected and declared exempt from the usual labor services. The master of ritual shall be charged with the selection of these students from among men of the people who are eighteen years of age or older and who are of good character and upright behavior. In order to supply candidates for the selection, the governors, prime ministers, heads, and magistrates of the various provinces, kingdoms, districts, marches,[21] and feudal cities shall recommend to the two thousand picul officials[22] in their respective regions any men who are fond of learning, show respect for their superiors, adhere to the teachings of the government, and honor the customs of their village, and whose actions in no way reflect discredit upon their reputations. The two thousand picul officials shall in turn make a careful examination of the men recommended; those found worthy shall then be sent in company with the local accounting officials when the latter come to the capital to make their reports, and shall there be presented to the master of ritual. They shall then receive instruction in the same manner as the regular students of the erudits.

At the end of a year, all of them shall be examined. Those who have mastered one or more of the Classics shall be assigned to fill vacancies among the scholar officials in the provinces or among the officers . . . who serve under the master of ritual. If there are any outstanding students who qualify for the post of palace attendant, the master of ritual shall present their names to the throne. In this way men of exceptional talent and ability will be brought at once to the attention of the ruler. If, on the contrary, there are any who have not applied themselves to their studies, whose ability is inferior, or who have failed to master even one Classic, they shall be summarily dismissed. In addition, if there are any among the recommending officials who have failed to carry out their duties properly, we suggest that they be punished. . . .

The emperor signified his approval of this proposal, and from this time on the number of literary men who held positions as ministers and high officials in the government increased remarkably.

▼▼▼

India in the Age of Empires

More often than not, in its long history India has been divided into political fragments, and modern study of its past has consequently centered far more on its cultural developments than on its transitory political structures. During these

---

[20]That is, throughout all China.
[21]Frontier regions.
[22]A picul was 133.33 pounds of grain. Every office was graded according to its annual salary, and most ranged from 2,000 to 100 piculs a year, although the emperor's chief counselor received 10,000 piculs. Salaries were paid partly in grain and partly in silk and cash equivalents.

centuries of Afro-Eurasian interaction, however, India witnessed the creation of two significant native empires that command our attention.

First there was the mighty Mauryan Empire (ca 315–183 B.C.), which controlled all but the most southern portions of the subcontinent. Centuries later the Gupta Empire (A.D. 320–ca 550) arose, centered on the Ganges River in the northeast but exercising authority over most of northern and central India. Although neither equaled the Han and Roman Empires in size, military power, and longevity, both Indian empires provided peace and a general prosperity based in part on energetic administration and benign social intervention. At the height of the Gupta Empire under Chandragupta II (r. ca A.D. 376–415), India may well have been the most prosperous and peaceful society in all of Eurasia. China was then immersed in its interdynastic time of troubles; Greco-Roman civilization was undergoing severe stresses at every level; and the powerful Sassanian Empire of Persia was embroiled in internal religious turmoil and wars on its frontiers.

Between these two homebred imperial periods, India underwent a series of invasions from the northwest that resulted in portions of northern India falling under the domination of alien rulers and being joined to important Central Asian kingdoms and empires. The first of these invaders were Greeks from Bactria, essentially northern Afghanistan, who arrived in the early second century B.C. and established a number of competing kingdoms in northern India. The Greco-Bactrians did not remain in India long and soon gave way to various nomadic invaders from East Asia.

The most significant of the new invaders were the Yuezhi (source 35), who created the Kushana Empire toward the end of the first century B.C. The Kushana, whose imperial focus was always Central Asia, lasted into the third century A.D., and during their centuries of empire provided India with connections to Southwest Asia and China. Much of that interaction consisted of the peaceful exchange of goods and ideas, but Chinese annals also tell how General Ban Chao, brother of the historians Ban Gu and Ban Zhao (source 39), destroyed a Yuezhi army in A.D. 90 when the Kushana emperor launched a retaliatory strike against the Chinese after he was refused the hand of a Han princess.

All of these important political developments should not blind us to the fact that the most significant developments taking place in India during the period 300 B.C.–A.D. 500 were cultural. The Gupta era is especially important in this regard and is rightly acknowledged as one of traditional India's golden ages.

The Softening Effects of Dharma
▼▼▼

37 ▼ *Asoka, ROCK AND PILLAR EDICTS*

As Alexander the Great and his Macedonian generals pulled back from northwest India, a local lord, Chandragupta Maurya (r. ca 315–281 B.C.), began the

process of carving out what would become the greatest of India's ancient empires. Under the founder and his son, Bindusara, the empire expanded and functioned with brutal efficiency. Around 269 B.C. Bindusara's son Asoka (r. ca 269–232) inherited the throne and initially continued his family's tradition of imperial aggression.

In the eighth year of his reign, however, he underwent a spiritual conversion when he beheld the bloodshed and misery that resulted from his conquest of the land of Kalinga, along India's southeastern flank. As a consequence, Asoka embraced the teachings of the Buddha and embarked on a new policy of government. Probably inspired by the public monuments of the kings of Persia, Asoka publicized his change of heart and new imperial policies in a series of engraved rock and pillar inscriptions scattered throughout his lands.

QUESTIONS FOR ANALYSIS

1. What evidence is there in these edicts of India's contacts with the outside world?
2. What evidence is there that Asoka attempted to export Buddhist teachings to his western neighbors?
3. Following his conversion, what did Asoka consider to be the purpose of good government? What structures and policies did he institute in order to achieve his vision?
4. What was Asoka's attitude and policy toward all non-Buddhist religions and ceremonies?
5. How did Asoka define *dharma*? Can you find any Hindu or Jain influences on his understanding of dharma?
6. Asoka saw himself as a follower of the Buddha's Law of Righteousness (dharma). Review the Buddha's First Sermon on the Law (Chapter 3, source 20). Where would the Buddha agree with Asoka's policies and beliefs? Where would he disagree with Asoka? What would be the Buddha's overall evaluation of Asoka's Buddhism?
7. Imagine that several Chinese travelers, a Confucian, a Legalist, and a Daoist, read these inscriptions. What would be their reactions?
8. Imagine a debate between Asoka and Caesar Augustus over the issue of an emperor's proper responsibilities. What major points would each man raise?

ROCK EDICT XIII

The Kalinga country was conquered by King Priyadarsi,[1] Beloved of the Gods, in the eighth year of his reign. One hundred and fifty thousand persons were carried away captive, one hundred thousand were slain, and many times that number died.

Immediately after the Kalingas had been conquered, King Priyadarsi became intensely devoted to the study of Dharma,[2] to the love of Dharma, and to the inculcation of Dharma.

---

[1]Asoka's throne name, it means "one who sees to the good of others."

[2]Sources 18, 19, and 20 in Chapter 3 provide three different definitions of *dharma*.

The Beloved of the Gods, conqueror of the Kalingas, is moved to remorse now. For he has felt profound sorrow and regret because the conquest of a people previously unconquered involves slaughter, death, and deportation.

But there is a more important reason for the King's remorse. The Brahmanas[3] and Sramanas[4] as well as the followers of other religions and householders — who all practiced obedience to superiors, parents, and teachers, and proper courtesy and firm devotion to friends, acquaintances, companions, relatives, slaves, and servants — all suffer from the injury, slaughter, and deportation inflicted on their loved ones. Even those who escaped calamity themselves are deeply afflicted by the misfortunes suffered by those friends, acquaintances, companions, and relatives for whom they feel an undiminished affection. Thus all men share in the misfortune, and this weighs on King Priyadarsi's mind. . . .

Therefore, even if the number of people who were killed or who died or who were carried away in the Kalinga war had been only one one-hundredth or one one-thousandth of what it actually was, this would still have weighed on the King's mind.

King Priyadarsi now thinks that even a person who wrongs him must be forgiven for wrongs that can be forgiven.

King Priyadarsi seeks to induce even the forest peoples who have come under his dominion[5] to adopt this way of life and this ideal. He reminds them, however, that he exercises the power to punish, despite his repentance, in order to induce them to desist from their crimes and escape execution.

For King Priyadarsi desires security, self-control, impartiality, and cheerfulness for all living creatures.

King Priyadarsi considers moral conquest the most important conquest. He has achieved this moral conquest repeatedly both here and among the peoples living beyond the borders of his kingdom, even as far away as six hundred *yojanas*[6], where the Yona [Greek] king Antiyoka[7] rules, and even beyond Antiyoka in the realms of the four kings named Turamaya, Antikini, Maka, and Alikasudara,[8] and to the south among the Cholas and Pandyas[9] as far as Ceylon.[10]

Here in the King's dominion also, . . . everywhere people heed his instructions in Dharma.

Even in countries which King Priyadarsi's envoys have not reached, people have heard about Dharma and about his Majesty's ordinances and instructions in Dharma, and they themselves conform to Dharma and will continue to do so.

Wherever conquest is achieved by Dharma, it produces satisfaction. Satisfaction is firmly established by conquest by Dharma. Even satisfaction, however, is of little importance. King Priyadarsi attaches value ultimately only to consequences of action in the other world.

This edict on Dharma has been inscribed so that my sons and great-grandsons who may come after me should not think new conquests worth achieving. If they do conquer, let them take pleasure in moderation and mild punishments. Let them consider moral conquest the only true conquest.

---

[3]Hindu ascetics who were members of the brahmin caste. They were divided into many sects.
[4]Another group of ascetics. In the context of this edict, "Brahmanas and Sramanas" means all Hindu and Buddhist holy people.
[5]The primitive, largely uncivilized folk of the southern jungle.
[6]About three thousand miles.
[7]Antiochus II Theos (r. 261–246 B.C.), a member of the Macedonian family of Seleucus and king of Syria.

[8]Ptolemy II Philadelphus of Egypt (r. 285–247 B.C.); Antigonos Gonatas of Macedonia (r. 278–239 B.C.); Magos of Cyrene in North Africa (r. 300–258 B.C.); and Alexander of Epirus in the northwest region of Greece (r. ca 272–258 B.C.).
[9]People of the southern tip of India.
[10]The major island off the southeast coast of India, today it is the nation of Sri Lanka.

This is good, here and hereafter. Let their pleasure be pleasure in morality. For this alone is good, here and hereafter.

PILLAR EDICT VII

King Priyadarsi, the Beloved of the Gods, speaks as follows: . . .

How can the people be induced to follow Dharma strictly? How can progress in morality be increased sufficiently? How can I raise them up by the promotion of Dharma? . . . This occurred to me. I shall issue proclamations on Dharma, and I shall order instruction in Dharma to be given to the people. Hearing these proclamations and instructions, the people will conform to Dharma; they will raise themselves up and will make progress by the promotion of Dharma. To this end I have issued proclamations on Dharma, and I have instituted various kinds of moral and religious instruction.

My highest officials, who have authority over large numbers of people, will expound and spread the precepts of Dharma. I have instructed the provincial governors, too, who are in charge of many hundred thousand people, concerning how to guide people devoted to Dharma. . . .

My officers charged with the spread of Dharma are occupied with various kinds of services beneficial to ascetics and householders, and they are empowered to concern themselves with all sects. I have ordered some of them to look after the affairs of the Sangha[11], some to take care of the brahmin . . . ascetics, some to work among the Nirgranthas,[12] and some among the various other religious sects. Different officials are thus assigned specifically to the affairs of different religions, but my officers for spreading Dharma are occupied with all sects. . . .

These and many other high officials take care of the distribution of gifts from myself as well

as from the queens. They report in various ways . . . worthy recipients of charity. . . . I also ordered some of them to supervise the distribution of gifts from my sons and the sons of other queens, in order to promote noble deeds of Dharma and conformity to the precepts of Dharma. These noble deeds and this conformity consist in promoting compassion, liberality, truthfulness, purity, gentleness, and goodness. . . .

Whatever good deeds I have done the people have imitated, and they have followed them as a model. In doing so, they have progressed and will progress in obedience to parents and teachers, in respect for elders, in courtesy to priests and ascetics, to the poor and distressed, and even to slaves and servants. . . .

The people can be induced to advance in Dharma by only two means, by moral prescriptions and by meditation. Of the two, moral prescriptions are of little consequence, but meditation is of great importance. The moral prescriptions I have promulgated include rules making certain animals inviolable, and many others. But even in the case of abstention from injuring and from killing living creatures, it is by meditation that people have progressed in Dharma most.

This edict on Dharma has been inscribed in order that it may endure and be followed as long as my sons and great-grandsons shall reign and as long as the sun and moon shall shine. For one who adheres to it will attain happiness in this world and hereafter. . . .

This edict on morality should be engraved wherever stone pillars or stone slabs are available, in order that it may endure forever.

PILLAR EDICT II

King Priyadarsi says:

Dharma is good. But what does Dharma consist of? It consists of few sins and many good

---

[11]Buddhist monastic groups. See Chapter 3, source 21.

[12]Jain ascetics. See Chapter 3, source 19.

deeds, of kindness, liberality, truthfulness, and purity.

I have bestowed even the gift of spiritual insight on men in various ways. I have decreed many kindnesses, including even the grant of life, to living creatures, two-footed and four-footed as well as birds and aquatic animals. I have also performed many other good deeds.

I have ordered this edict on Dharma to be inscribed in order that people may act according to it and that it may endure for a long time. And he who follows it completely will do good deeds.

ROCK EDICT IX

King Priyadarsi, the Beloved of the Gods, says:

People perform various ceremonies. Among the occasions on which ceremonies are performed are sicknesses, marriages of sons or daughters, children's births, and departures on journeys. Women in particular have recourse to many diverse, trivial, and meaningless ceremonies.

It is right that ceremonies be performed. But this kind bears little fruit. The ceremony of Dharma,[13] on the contrary, is very fruitful. It consists in proper treatment of slaves and servants, reverence to teachers, restraint of violence toward living creatures, and liberality to priests and ascetics. These and like actions are called the ceremonies of Dharma.

Therefore, a father, son, brother, master, friend, acquaintance, or even neighbor ought to say about such actions, "These are good; they should be performed until their purpose is achieved. I shall observe them."

Other ceremonies are of doubtful value. They may achieve their purpose, or they may not. Moreover the purposes for which they are performed are limited to this world.

The ceremony of Dharma, on the other hand, is not limited to time. Even if it does not achieve its object in this world, it produces un-

limited merit in the next world. But if it produces its object in this world, it achieves both effects: the purpose desired in this world and unlimited merit in the next.

It has also been said that liberality is commendable. But there is no greater liberality than the gift of Dharma or the benefit of Dharma. Therefore, a friend, well-wisher, relative, or companion should urge one when the occasion arises, saying, "You should do this; this is commendable. By doing this you may attain heaven." And what is more worth doing than attaining heaven?

ROCK EDICT VII

King Priyadarsi wishes members of all faiths to live everywhere in his kingdom.

For they will seek mastery of the senses and purity of mind. Men are different in their inclinations and passions, however, and they may perform the whole of their duties or only part.

Even if one is not able to make lavish gifts, mastery of the senses, purity of mind, gratitude, and steadfast devotion are commendable and essential.

PILLAR EDICT IV

Impartiality is desirable in legal procedures and in punishments. I have therefore decreed that henceforth prisoners who have been convicted and sentenced to death shall be granted a respite of three days. During this period their relatives may appeal to the officials for the prisoners' lives; or, if no one makes an appeal, the prisoners may prepare for the other world by distributing gifts or by fasting.

For I desire that, when the period of respite has expired, they may attain happiness in the next world, and that various ways of practicing Dharma by self-control and the distribution of gifts may be increased among the people.

[13]Ceremony should be understood in a metaphorical sense — meditation and the good works of dharma.

Gupta India As Seen by a Chinese Monk
▼▼▼

38 ▼ Faxian, TRAVELS IN INDIA AND CEYLON

During the age of the Later, or Eastern, Han Dynasty (A.D. 25–220) Buddhist missionaries traveled to China along the overland routes of Central Asia and the oceanic trade routes of Southeast Asia. As China underwent increasing stresses during the last stages of the Han Empire, a form of salvationist Buddhism known as the *Mahayana doctrine* became particularly popular (Chapter 6, source 50). In the post-Han period of disunity it provided many Chinese with a comforting refuge from the evils of the world.

As Buddhism expanded in China, devotees of the new religion, particularly monks, avidly sought to add to the available body of Buddhist literature, which often meant tracking down various Buddhist holy books in their original homeland, India, and translating them into Chinese. This search for a complete and authentic library of Buddhist scripture, together with the desire of many Chinese Buddhists to make pilgrimages to sites made sacred by the Buddha and his early disciples, meant that Chinese travel to India for religious purposes became a fairly common practice during India's Gupta age and thereafter.

The earliest known Chinese pilgrim to travel to India and return with sacred books was the monk Faxian. Between 399 and 413 he journeyed overland from northern China to visit all of Buddhism's holy shrines in India. From India, he sailed to the island of Ceylon, which, according to tradition, had received Buddhism through the efforts of Asoka and his missionary son, Mahendra. From there Faxian traveled to Java and eventually reached home, where he spent the rest of his days translating the texts he had obtained in India.

In addition to these translations, Faxian left behind a record of his travels in which he described Indian society in the reign of Chandragupta II (r. ca 376–415). Although this Chinese monk was much more concerned with pilgrimage sites and holy books than with providing detailed descriptions of Indian culture, his travelogue is important because it provides an outsider's view of India at the height of Gupta prosperity.

QUESTIONS FOR ANALYSIS

1. According to Faxian, how strong was Buddhism in northern India in his day?
2. How well or poorly did the Hindu and Buddhist communities interact?
3. How prosperous and well governed do the land and its people appear to have been? Do they appear to have been intensively governed and restricted?
4. How did Buddhist principles influence the various social practices and values of Gupta India?
5. How had the Buddha's original teaching, which denied the existence of

spirits, the soul, and gods and rejected all ritual, merged with folk beliefs and customs? Reread the Rock and Pillar Edicts. Can you find evidence of this same phenomenon in Asoka's time?

6. In describing Indian society, Faxian indirectly tells us a lot about China. What can we reasonably infer about Chinese culture from this account?

7. What would Asoka have thought about the Gupta Empire as described by Faxian?

From this place they[1] traveled southeast, passing by a succession of very many monasteries, with a multitude of monks, who might be counted by myriads. After passing all these places, they came to a . . . river on the banks of which, left and right, there were twenty monasteries, which might contain three thousand monks; and here the Law of Buddha was still more flourishing. Everywhere, from the Sandy Desert, in all the countries of India, the kings had been firm believers in that Law. When they make their offerings to a community of monks, they take off their royal caps, and along with their relatives and ministers, supply them with food with their own hands. That done, the king has a carpet spread for himself on the ground, and sits down on it in front of the leader of the monastery; — they dare not presume to sit on couches in front of the community. The laws and ways, according to which the kings presented their offerings when Buddha was in the world, have been handed down to the present day.

All south from this is named the Middle Kingdom. In it the cold and heat are finely tempered, and there is neither hoarfrost nor snow. The people are numerous and happy; they have not to register their households, or attend to any magistrates and their rules; only those who cultivate the royal land have to pay a portion of the gain from it. If they want to go, they go; if they want to stay on, they stay. The king governs without decapitation or other corporal punishments. Criminals are simply fined, lightly or heavily, according to the circumstances of each case. Even in cases of repeated attempts at wicked rebellion, they only have their right hands cut off. The king's bodyguards and attendants all have salaries. Throughout the whole country the people do not kill any living creature, nor drink intoxicating liquor, nor eat onions or garlic. The only exception is that of the kandalas.[2] That is the name for those who are held to be wicked men, and live apart from others. When they enter the gate of a city or a market-place, they strike a piece of wood to make themselves known, so that men know and avoid them, and do not come into contact with them. In that country they do not keep pigs and fowls, and do not sell live cattle; in the markets there are no butchers' shops and no dealers in intoxicating drink. . . . Only the kandalas are fishermen and hunters, and sell flesh meat.

After Buddha attained to pari-nirvana[3] the kings of the various countries and the heads of the vaisyas[4] built viharas[5] for the monks,[6] and endowed them with fields, houses, gardens, and orchards, along with the resident populations and their cattle, the grants being engraved on plates of metal, so that afterwards they were handed down from king to king, without any one daring to annul them, and they remain even to the present time.

---

[1]Faxian and his fellow pilgrims.
[2]The lowest group of "untouchables." See *The Laws of Manu* (source 40) for a fuller description of the kandalas.
[3]The Buddha's release from life.
[4]The caste of merchants and prosperous farmers. See *The Laws of Manu* (source 40).
[5]A hermitage for a recluse or a little house built for a holy person.
[6]Chapter 3, source 21.

The regular business of the monks is to perform acts of meritorious virtue, and to recite their Sutras[7] and sit wrapt in meditation. When stranger monks arrive at any monastery, the old residents meet and receive them, carry for them their clothes and alms-bowl, give them water to wash their feet, oil with which to anoint them, and the liquid food permitted out of the regular hours.[8] When the stranger has enjoyed a very brief rest, they further ask the number of years that he has been a monk, after which he receives a sleeping apartment with its appurtenances, according to his regular order, and everything is done for him which the rules prescribe.

Where a community of monks resides, they erect stupas[9] to Sariputtra, to Mahamaudgalyayana, and to Ananda,[10] and also stupas in honor of the Abhidharma, the Vinaya, and the Sutras.[11] A month after the annual season of rest, the families which are looking out for blessing stimulate one another to make offerings to the monks, and send round to them the liquid food which may be taken out of the ordinary hours. All the monks come together in a great assembly, and preach the Law; after which offerings are presented at the stupa of Sariputtra, with all kinds of flowers and incense. All through the night lamps are kept burning, and skillful musicians are employed to perform. . . .

Having crossed the river, and descended south . . . the travelers came to the town of Pataliputtra,[12] in the kingdom of Magadha, the city where king Asoka ruled. . . .

By the side of the stupa of Asoka, there has been made a mahayana monastery, very grand and beautiful; there is also a hinayana[13] one; the two together containing six hundred or seven hundred monks. The rules of demeanor and the scholastic arrangements in them are worthy of observation.

Shamans[14] of the highest virtue from all quarters, and students, inquirers wishing to find out truth and the grounds of it, all resort to these monasteries. There also resides in this monastery a brahmin teacher, whose name also is Manjusri, whom the shamans of greatest virtue in the kingdom, and the mahayana bhikshus[15] honor and look up to.

The cities and towns of this country are the greatest of all in the Middle Kingdom. The inhabitants are rich and prosperous, and vie with one another in the practice of benevolence and righteousness. Every year on the eighth day of the second month they celebrate a procession of images. They make a four-wheeled car, and on it erect a structure of five stories by means of bamboos tied together. This is supported by a king-post, with poles and lances slanting from it, and is rather more than twenty cubits high, having the shape of a stupa. White and silk-like cloth of hair is wrapped all round it, which is then painted in various colors. They make figures of devas[16] with gold, silver, and lapis lazuli grandly blended and having silken streamers and canopies hung out over them. On the four sides are niches, with a Buddha seated in each, and a Bodhisattva[17] standing in attendance on him. There may be twenty cars, all grand and imposing, but each one different from the others. On the day mentioned, the monks and laity within the borders all come

---

[7] Sacred texts.
[8] Solid food was prohibited between sunrise and noon.
[9] A *stupa* was a large domed structure built to house some relic of the Buddha or one of his early disciples. Asoka had commissioned the construction of a large number of these holy sites throughout his empire, and they continued to be built and refined architecturally long after the collapse of the Mauryan Empire.
[10] Three of the Buddha's principal disciples.
[11] The three major collections of Buddhist sacred literature.
[12] Modern Patna.

[13] The *Hinayana* (Small Vehicle), or, more correctly, *Theravada,* school was the second of Buddhism's two major sects at this time. Both it and the *Mahayana* (Great Vehicle) school are treated in Chapter 6.
[14] He probably means Hindu yogis and other holy persons.
[15] Buddhist monks.
[16] Gods and goddesses.
[17] A saint who voluntarily postpones Nirvana, or escape from this world, in order to work for the salvation of others. See Chapter 6, source 50.

together; they have singers and skillful musicians; they pay their devotions with flowers and incense. The brahmins come and invite the Buddhas to enter the city. These do so in order, and remain two nights in it. All through the night they keep lamps burning, have skillful music, and present offerings. This is the practice in all the other kingdoms as well. The heads of the vaisya families in them establish in the cities houses for dispensing charity and medicines. All the poor and destitute in the country, orphans, widowers, and childless men, maimed people and cripples, and all who are diseased, go to those houses, and are provided with every kind of help, and doctors examine their diseases. They get the food and medicines which their cases require, and are made to feel at ease; and when they are better, they go away of themselves.

▼▼▼

The Ties That Bind: Social Relations Across the Afro-Eurasian Ecumene

Political activity, exploration, wars, and empire building provide much of history's drama, but exclusive concentration on such phenomena leaves us ignorant of the ways in which the vast majority of humans viewed the world and related to one another. Our innate human need to understand and touch the lives of the people who have gone before us is, after all, the ultimate reason we study the past. If we are to connect with these ancestors and, by learning of their many different value systems and modes of life, learn more about ourselves as members of a richly variegated human family, we must look at evidence that deals with much more than just past politics. The three documents that appear here focus on gender relations, class distinctions, and the search for psychic and social certainty in a most uncertain world. The three cultures represented are China, India, and the Greco-Roman Mediterranean world.

The Views of a Female Confucian
▼▼▼

39 ▼ Ban Zhao, *LESSONS FOR WOMEN*

Education in the Confucian classics increasingly became one of several avenues to a position of social and political power in Han China. Confucian doctrine, however, did not accord women a status equal to that of men, because women were generally regarded as unworthy or incapable of a literary education. In fact, the Confucian classics say little about women, which shows how little they mattered in the scheme of Confucian values. Most Confucians accepted the subservience of women to men as natural and proper. In their view, failure to maintain a proper relationship between two such obviously unequal people as husband and wife or brother and sister would result in social disharmony and a breakdown of all the rules of propriety.

Yet this was only part of the traditional Chinese view of women. Both Confucian doctrine and Chinese society at large accorded women, as both mothers and mothers-in-law, a good deal of honor, and with that honor came power within the family structure. In every age, moreover, a handful of extraordinary women managed to acquire literary educations or otherwise achieve positions of far-ranging influence and authority despite social constraints. The foremost female Confucian of the age of Han was Ban Zhao (ca A.D. 45–116), younger sister of the court historian Ban Gu (A.D. 32–92). Upon Gu's death, Zhao served as imperial historian under Emperor Han Hedi (r. 88–105) and completed her brother's *Han Annals*, a history of the Former Han Dynasty, which is generally regarded as second only to the historical work of Sima Qian (sources 27, 35, and 36). Ban Zhao also served as an adviser on state matters to the Empress Deng, who assumed power as regent for her infant son in 106.

Madame Ban was the daughter of the widely respected writer and administrator Ban Biao (A.D. 3–54) and received her elementary education from her literate mother while still a child in her father's house. Otherwise, her early life appears to have been quite conventional. She married at the age of fourteen, thereby becoming the lowest-ranking member of her husband's family, and bore children. Although her husband died young, Ban Zhao never remarried, devoting herself instead to literary pursuits and acquiring a reputation for scholarship and compositional grace that eventually brought her to the imperial court.

Among her many literary works, Ban Zhao composed a commentary on the popular *Lives of Admirable Women* by Liu Xiang (ca 77–6 B.C.) and later in life produced her most famous work, the *Nü Jie*, or *Lessons for Women*, which purports to be an instructional manual on feminine behavior and virtue for her daughters. In fact, she intended it for a much wider audience. Realizing that Confucian texts contained little in the way of specific and practical guidelines for a woman's everyday life, Ban Zhao sought to fill that void with a coherent set of rules for women, especially young women.

QUESTIONS FOR ANALYSIS

1. What does Ban Zhao tell us about the status of daughters-in-law? How has she escaped from the fears of such servitude?
2. According to Ban Zhao, what rules of propriety should govern a marriage?
3. What does Ban Zhao consider the principal duty of a husband? of a wife? How and why are they complementary parts of the natural order of the universe?
4. What sort of education does she advocate for women, and what is its purpose? Why are we able to infer that her daughters also received at least a rudimentary education in Confucian literature?
5. In what way and why does Ban Zhao advocate a departure from tradition?

6. What does her claim to lack of intelligence suggest? Do you think she was sincere in this claim?
7. What was there about Ban Zhao's essay that caused it to be so highly regarded by Confucian scholars over the following centuries?
8. Would it be correct to call Ban Zhao a feminist?

I, the unworthy writer, am unsophisticated, unenlightened, and by nature unintelligent, but I am fortunate both to have received not a little favor from my scholarly father, and to have had a cultured mother and instructresses upon whom to rely for a literary education as well as for training in good manners. More than forty years have passed since at the age of fourteen I took up the dustpan and the broom in the Cao family.[1] During this time with trembling heart I feared constantly that I might disgrace my parents, and that I might multiply difficulties for both the women and the men of my husband's family. Day and night I was distressed in heart, but I labored without confessing weariness. Now and hereafter, however, I know how to escape from such fears.

Being careless, and by nature stupid, I taught and trained my children without system. Consequently I fear that my son Gu may bring disgrace upon the Imperial Dynasty by whose Holy Grace he has unprecedentedly received the extraordinary privilege of wearing the Gold and the Purple, a privilege for the attainment of which by my son, I a humble subject never even hoped. Nevertheless, now that he is a man and able to plan his own life, I need not again have concern for him. But I do grieve that you, my daughters, just now at the age for marriage, have not at this time had gradual training and advice; that you still have not learned the proper customs for married women. I fear that by failure in good manners in other families you will humiliate both your ancestors and your clan. I am now seriously ill, life is uncertain. As I have thought of you all in so untrained a state, I have been uneasy many a time for you. At hours of leisure I have composed . . . these instructions under the title, "Lessons for Women." In order that you may have something wherewith to benefit your persons, I wish every one of you, my daughters, each to write out a copy for yourself.

From this time on every one of you strive to practice these lessons.

HUMILITY

On the third day after the birth of a girl the ancients observed three customs: first to place the baby below the bed; second to give her a potsherd[2] with which to play; and third to announce her birth to her ancestors by an offering. Now to lay the baby below the bed plainly indicated that she is lowly and weak, and should regard it as her primary duty to humble herself before others. To give her potsherds with which to play indubitably signified that she should practice labor and consider it her primary duty to be industrious. To announce her birth before her ancestors clearly meant that she ought to esteem as her primary duty the continuation of the observance of worship in the home.

These three ancient customs epitomize a woman's ordinary way of life and the teachings of the traditional ceremonial rites and regulations. Let a woman modestly yield to others; let her respect others; let her put others first, herself last. Should she do something good, let her not mention it; should she do something bad, let her not deny it. Let her bear disgrace; let her even endure when others speak or do evil to her. Always let her seem to tremble and to fear. When a woman follows such maxims as these, then she may be said to humble herself before others.

[1] The family into which she married.

[2] A piece of broken pottery.

Let a woman retire late to bed, but rise early to duties; let her not dread tasks by day or by night. Let her not refuse to perform domestic duties whether easy or difficult. That which must be done, let her finish completely, tidily, and systematically. When a woman follows such rules as these, then she may be said to be industrious.

Let a woman be correct in manner and upright in character in order to serve her husband. Let her live in purity and quietness of spirit, and attend to her own affairs. Let her love not gossip and silly laughter. Let her cleanse and purify and arrange in order the wine and the food for the offerings to the ancestors. When a woman observes such principles as these, then she may be said to continue ancestral worship.

No woman who observes these three fundamentals of life has ever had a bad reputation or has fallen into disgrace. If a woman fail to observe them, how can her name be honored; how can she but bring disgrace upon herself?

HUSBAND AND WIFE

The Way of husband and wife is intimately connected with *Yin* and *Yang*,[3] and relates the individual to gods and ancestors. Truly it is the great principle of Heaven and Earth, and the great basis of human relationships. Therefore the "Rites"[4] honor union of man and woman; and in the "Book of Poetry"[5] the "First Ode" manifests the principle of marriage. For these reasons the relationships cannot but be an important one.

If a husband be unworthy, then he possesses nothing by which to control his wife. If a wife be unworthy, then she possesses nothing with which to serve her husband. If a husband does not control his wife, then the rules of conduct manifesting his authority are abandoned and broken. If a wife does not serve her husband,

then the proper relationship between men and women and the natural order of things are neglected and destroyed. As a matter of fact the purpose of these two [the controlling of women by men, and the serving of men by women] is the same.

Now examine the gentlemen of the present age. They only know that wives must be controlled, and that the husband's rules of conduct manifesting his authority must be established. They therefore teach their boys to read books and study histories. But they do not in the least understand that husbands and masters must also be served, and that the proper relationship and the rites should be maintained.

Yet only to teach men and not to teach women — is that not ignoring the essential relation between them? According to the "Rites," it is the rule to begin to teach children to read at the age of eight years, and by the age of fifteen years they ought then to be ready for cultural training. Only why should it not be that girls' education as well as boys' be according to this principle?

RESPECT AND CAUTION

As *Yin* and *Yang* are not of the same nature, so man and woman have different characteristics. The distinctive quality of the *Yang* is rigidity; the function of the *Yin* is yielding. Man is honored for strength; a woman is beautiful on account of her gentleness. Hence there arose the common saying: "A man though born like a wolf may, it is feared, become a weak monstrosity; a woman though born like a mouse may, it is feared, become a tiger."

Now for self-culture nothing equals respect for others. To counteract firmness nothing equals compliance. Consequently it can be said that the Way of respect and acquiescence is woman's most important principle of conduct.

[3]According to Chinese cosmology these were the two basic elements of the universe: Yin, the soft, yielding, feminine element; and Yang, the hard, aggressive, male element. Every substance contains both elements in varying proportions. As one element increases within a

substance or being, the other decreases, but neither is ever eliminated.
[4]*The Classic of Rites* (page 137, note 6).
[5]*The Classic of Odes* (Chapter 1, source 7).

So respect may be defined as nothing other than holding on to that which is permanent; and acquiescence nothing other than being liberal and generous. Those who are steadfast in devotion know that they should stay in their proper places; those who are liberal and generous esteem others, and honor and serve them.

If husband and wife have the habit of staying together, never leaving one another, and following each other around within the limited space of their own rooms, then they will lust after and take liberties with one another. From such action improper language will arise between the two. This kind of discussion may lead to licentiousness. Out of licentiousness will be born a heart of disrespect to the husband. Such a result comes from not knowing that one should stay in one's proper place.

Furthermore, affairs may be either crooked or straight; words may be either right or wrong. Straightforwardness cannot but lead to quarreling; crookedness cannot but lead to accusation. If there are really accusations and quarrels, then undoubtedly there will be angry affairs. Such a result comes from not esteeming others, and not honoring and serving them.

If wives suppress not contempt for husbands, then it follows that such wives rebuke and scold their husbands. If husbands stop not short of anger, then they are certain to beat their wives. The correct relationship between husband and wife is based upon harmony and intimacy, and conjugal love is grounded in proper union. Should actual blows be dealt, how could matrimonial relationship be preserved? Should sharp words be spoken, how could conjugal love exist? If love and proper relationship both be destroyed, then husband and wife are divided.

WOMANLY QUALIFICATIONS

A woman ought to have four qualifications: (1) womanly virtue; (2) womanly words; (3) womanly bearing; and (4) womanly work. Now what is called womanly virtue need not be brilliant ability, exceptionally different from others. Womanly words need be neither clever in debate nor keen in conversation. Womanly appearance requires neither a pretty nor a perfect face and form. Womanly work need not be work done more skillfully than that of others.

To guard carefully her chastity; to control circumspectly her behavior; in every motion to exhibit modesty; and to model each act on the best usage, this is womanly virtue.

To choose her words with care; to avoid vulgar language; to speak at appropriate times; and not to weary others with much conversation, may be called the characteristics of womanly words.

To wash and scrub filth away; to keep clothes and ornaments fresh and clean; to wash the head and bathe the body regularly, and to keep the person free from disgraceful filth, may be called the characteristics of womanly bearing.

With whole-hearted devotion to sew and to weave; to love not gossip and silly laughter; in cleanliness and order to prepare the wine and food for serving guests, may be called the characteristics of womanly work.

These four qualifications characterize the greatest virtue of a woman. No woman can afford to be without them. In fact they are very easy to possess if a woman only treasure them in her heart. The ancients had a saying: "Is Love afar off? If I desire love, then love is at hand!" So can it be said of these qualifications. . . .

IMPLICIT OBEDIENCE

Whenever the mother-in-law says, "Do not do that," and if what she says is right, unquestionably the daughter-in-law obeys. Whenever the mother-in-law says, "Do that," even if what she says is wrong, still the daughter-in-law submits unfailingly to the command.

Let a woman not act contrary to the wishes and the opinions of parents-in-law about right and wrong; let her not dispute with them what is straight and what is crooked. Such docility may be called obedience which sacrifices personal opinion. Therefore the ancient book, "A

Pattern for Women," says: "If a daughter-in-law who follows the wishes of her parents-in-law is like an echo and a shadow, how could she not be praised?"

Sacred Law in Classical India
▼▼▼

40 ▼ *THE LAWS OF MANU*

Despite Asoka's promotion of the Buddhist principle of dharma, or the Law of Righteousness, the majority of classical India's population seems to have remained true to more traditional Hindu ways and beliefs, which included acceptance of the caste system and the concept that dharma defined one's caste duties. Hindus, like Buddhists, believed that dharma was the moral law of the universe and the highest good upon which all reality was founded. Yet, for Hindus dharma was not an abstract, impersonal code of righteousness; it was Sacred Law and, as such, governed all of a person's social and religious activities. For most Hindus, dharma became concrete in the innumerable rituals that Asoka found so useless and in Indian civilization's numerous forms of mandated social behavior. Faith, worship, and social duty all sprang from dharma.

The earliest extant codification of the Sacred Law of dharma is *The Laws of Manu*, which was compiled between the first century B.C. and the second or third century A.D. In Hindu mythology Manu was the primeval human being, the father of humanity, and its first king. In the Vedas he appears as the founder of all human social order and the original teacher of dharma, having been instructed in the Sacred Law by Brahman. Tradition also regarded him as an Indian Utnapishtim or Noah, the sole survivor of a catastrophic flood, after which he created a woman, through whom he generated the human species. The anonymous compilers of *The Laws of Manu* claimed that the rules and regulations contained in this code were universal and timeless. Each law was believed to be a manifestation of dharma, passed down uncorrupted from Brahman through Manu. In reality, this collection mirrors 2,500 years of Indian social history and consequently contains what seem to a Western viewer to be numerous contradictions. These apparent discrepancies, however, are readily integrated in a cultural complex predicated on the idea that truth has infinite manifestations.

The selections here illustrate the two major determinants of classical Indian society: caste and gender. As far as we can ascertain, gender and class distinctions of one sort or another were common to all ancient civilizations, but the Hindu caste system was unique to India. The English word *caste* is derived from the Portuguese *casta*, which means "pure." Hindus use two different Sanskrit words for caste: *varna* (color) and *jati* (birth). Varna refers only to the four major social-religious divisions that "The Hymn to Purusha" (Chapter 2, source 12) enumerates: brahmins (priests), kshatriyas (warriors), vaisyas (farmers, artisans, and merchants), and sudras (workers). These classifications of Indian society clearly resulted from the Aryans' attempt to separate themselves from the darker-skinned natives they had conquered. The jati system, which today includes more than three thousand identifiable groupings, was not fully developed until around the Gupta period, long after the Aryans had disappeared into India's general population. Jatis are hereditary occupations, each with its own dharma. Hindus generally classify jatis as subdivisions of the varna system and steps in the ladder of reincarnation.

QUESTIONS FOR ANALYSIS

1. The lowest-ranking jatis are composed of people known as *untouchables*. Why are they called that, and what manner of life do they lead? What is there about their occupations that other Hindus find so offensive? To what extent does Faxian's account of the life led by members of the kandala jati (source 38) agree with the evidence from the *Laws of Manu*?
2. Under what circumstances might a person engage in work appropriate to a lower varna? How far may one go in this regard, and what are the consequences? May one legitimately assume the duties of a higher varna? Is intermarriage among the castes considered acceptable?
3. Each varna and jati has its own dharma. Is there, additionally, a universal dharma common to all Hindus?
4. Can you see from this evidence why the Portuguese concluded that purity was the essential component of the varna and jati systems? What forms of purity are most important?
5. How might the caste system make political and social unification difficult, if not impossible?
6. Why are women denied access to ceremonies where the vedic texts are recited? Notwithstanding this prohibition, do women perform any necessary religious functions? If so, what are they, and what do these functions tell us about the status of women?
7. What constraints are placed on women, and why? What freedoms, if any, does a woman enjoy? How and why, if at all, are women protected and honored? What are the duties of their fathers and husbands?
8. Compare the status of Hindu women with that of women in Han China (source 39). How do their respective situations reflect the different cultures in which they live? Notwithstanding cultural differences, are their positions comparable, or does one seem to enjoy greater freedom and power? Is one better protected than the other?

VARNA

The brahmin, the kshatriya, and the vaisya castes are the twice-born ones,[1] but the fourth, the sudra, has one birth only; there is no fifth caste. . . .

To brahmins he[2] assigned teaching and studying the Vedas, sacrificing for their own

---

[1]One's second birth was initiation into the recitation of the Vedas. Only men could be "twice born."

[2]Brahman.

benefit and for others, giving and accepting of alms.

The kshatriya he commanded to protect the people, to bestow gifts, to offer sacrifices, to study the Vedas, and to abstain from attaching himself to sensual pleasures;

The vaisya to tend cattle, to bestow gifts, to offer sacrifices, to study the Vedas, to trade, to lend money, and to cultivate land.

One occupation only the lord prescribed to the sudra, to serve meekly . . . these other three castes.

JATIS

From a male sudra are born an ayogava, a kshattri, and a kandala, the lowest of men, by vaisya, kshatriya, and brahmin females respectively, sons who owe their origin to a confusion of the castes.[3] . . .

Killing fish to nishadas; carpenters' work to the ayogava; to medas, andhras, kunkus, and madgus, the slaughter of wild animals. . . .

But the dwellings of kandalas . . . shall be outside the village. . . .

Their dress shall be the garments of the dead, they shall eat their food from broken dishes, black iron shall be their ornaments, and they must always wander from place to place.

A man who fulfills a religious duty, shall not seek intercourse with them; their {kandala] transactions shall be among themselves, and their marriages with their equals. . . .

At night they shall not walk about in villages and in towns.

By day they may go about for the purpose of their work, distinguished by marks at the king's command, and they shall carry out the corpses of persons who have no relatives; that is a settled rule.

By the king's order they shall always execute the criminals, in accordance with the law, and they shall take for themselves the clothes, the beds, and the ornaments of such criminals.

DHARMA

A king who knows the sacred law must inquire into the laws of castes [jatis], of districts, of guilds, and of families, and settle the peculiar law of each. . . .

Among the several occupations the most commendable are, teaching the Veda for a brahmin, protecting the people for a kshatriya, and trade for a vaisya.

But a brahmin, unable to subsist by his peculiar occupations just mentioned, may live according to the law applicable to kshatriyas; for the latter is next to him in rank. . . .

A man of low caste [varna] who through covetousness lives by the occupations of a higher one, the king shall deprive of his property and banish.

It is better to discharge one's own duty incompletely than to perform completely that of another; for he who lives according to the law of another caste is instantly excluded from his own.

A vaisya who is unable to subsist by his own duties, may even maintain himself by a sudra's mode of life, avoiding however acts forbidden to him, and he should give it up, when he is able to do so. . . .

Abstention from injuring creatures, veracity, abstention from unlawfully appropriating the goods of others, purity, and control of the organs,[4] Manu has declared to be the summary of the law for the four castes.

THE NATURE OF WOMEN

It is the nature of women to seduce men in this world; for that reason the wise are never unguarded in the company of females. . . .

---

[3]This is a mythic explanation for the existence of certain low-born, or "unclean," jatis: they originated in mythic time as the result of illicit unions between people of different castes. The greatest profanation of all was when a male sudra "defiled" a female brahmin, and the conse-

quence was the origin of the kandala jati —the basest of all jatis.

[4]Control of all the senses and especially one's sexual drives.

For women no rite is performed with sacred texts, thus the law is settled; women who are destitute of strength and destitute of the knowledge of Vedic texts are as impure as falsehood itself; that is a fixed rule.

HONORING WOMEN

Where women are honored, there the gods are pleased; but where they are not honored, no sacred rite yields rewards.

Where the female relations live in grief, the family soon wholly perishes; but that family where they are not unhappy ever prospers.

FEMALE PROPERTY RIGHTS

A wife, a son, and a slave, these three are declared to have no property; the wealth which they earn is acquired for him to whom they belong. . . .

What was given before the nuptial fire, what was given on the bridal procession, what was given in token of love, and what was received from her brother, mother, or father, that is called the six-fold property of a woman.

Such property, as well as a gift subsequent and what was given to her by her affectionate husband, shall go to her offspring, even if she dies in the lifetime of her husband. . . .

But when the mother has died, all the uterine[5] brothers and the uterine sisters shall equally divide the mother's estate.

A WOMAN'S DEPENDENCE

In childhood a female must be subject to her father, in youth to her husband, when her lord is dead to her sons; a woman must never be independent.

She must not seek to separate herself from her father, husband, or sons; by leaving them she would make both her own and her husband's families contemptible. . . .

Him to whom her father may give her, or her brother with the father's permission, she shall obey as long as he lives, and when he is dead, she must not insult his memory.

BETROTHAL

No father who knows the law must take even the smallest gratuity for his daughter; for a man who, through avarice, takes a gratuity, is a seller of his offspring. . . .

Three years let a damsel wait,[6] though she be marriageable,[7] but after that time let her choose for herself a bridegroom of equal caste and rank.

If, being not given in marriage, she herself seeks a husband, she incurs no guilt, nor does he whom she weds.

MARRIAGE AND ITS DUTIES

To be mothers were women created, and to be fathers men; religious rites, therefore, are ordained in the Veda to be performed by the husband together with the wife. . . .

No sacrifice, no vow, no fast must be performed by women apart from their husbands; if a wife obeys her husband, she will for that reason alone be exalted in heaven. . . .

By violating her duty towards her husband, a wife is disgraced in this world, after death she enters the womb of a jackal, and is tormented by diseases as punishment for her sin. . . .

Let the husband employ his wife in the collection and expenditure of his wealth, in keeping everything clean, in the fulfilment of religious duties, in the preparation of his food, and in looking after the household utensils. . . .

Drinking spirituous liquor, associating with wicked people, separation from the husband, rambling abroad, sleeping at unseasonable hours, and dwelling in other men's houses, are the six causes of the ruin of women. . . .

Offspring, religious rites, faithful service, highest conjugal happiness and heavenly bliss

---

[5] All natural siblings (born from her uterus).
[6] To be offered in marriage by her father or brother.

[7] Twelve was a common age of marriage for women; men tended to wait until their twenties.

for the ancestors and oneself, depend on one's wife alone. . . .

"Let mutual fidelity continue until death," . . . may be considered as the summary of the highest law for husband and wife.

Let man and woman, united in marriage, constantly exert themselves, that they may not be disunited and may not violate their mutual fidelity.

DIVORCE

For one year let a husband bear with a wife who hates him; but after a year let him deprive her of her property and cease to cohabit with her. . . .

But she who shows aversion towards a mad or outcaste[8] husband, a eunuch,[9] one destitute of manly strength, or one afflicted with such diseases as punish crimes,[10] shall neither be cast off nor be deprived of her property. . . .

A barren[11] wife may be superseded[12] in the eighth year, she whose children all die in the tenth, she who bears only daughters in the eleventh, but she who is quarrelsome without delay.

But a sick wife who is kind to her husband and virtuous in her conduct, may be superseded only with her own consent and must never be disgraced.

Isis: The Goddess Who Saves
▼▼▼

41 ▼ *Lucius Apuleius, METAMORPHOSES*

Very much like China, early Roman religion centered on each family's *paterfamilias,* the male head of the household who embodied that family's *genius,* or unique living spirit, and, as its chief priest, communicated with the spirits of the family's ancestors. These ceremonies, it was believed, assured familial harmony and prosperity. As was true also in China, religion that had begun as family ancestor worship was raised to a civic level in order to assure the state's harmony and prosperity. Such religion stressed public ceremony over private belief and was centered on worldly concerns. Rome's civic cults, which were presided over by the emperor who served as *pontifex maximus,* or chief priest (source 42), were designed to learn the will of the gods and to curry their favor. The rationale was that if the rituals were performed properly, Rome would prosper.

Such practical approaches to religion failed to satisfy many individuals who desired religious experiences that offered personal comfort in an often hostile world and private relief from the ills and sorrows that attend all humans. Just

---

[8]One who has so egregiously violated the dharma of his caste (varna) that he has been made an outcaste. For example, a brahmin who knowingly receives food or a gift from a kandala or other "unclean" person.

[9]Sexually impotent.

[10]A disease incurred by reason of a sin in a previous in-

carnation (the law of karma). Hindu society evolved complex and lengthy lists of diseases and their corresponding sins.

[11]Childless.

[12]Replaced as primary wife by a second wife.

as Mahayana Buddhism, a foreign import, provided solace to many millions of Chinese who sought a deeper and more personal spiritual experience than was provided by traditional household and state religious rituals (Chapter 6, source 51), so also many of the so-called *mystery cults* of the eastern Mediterranean and Southwest Asia helped Romans to cope with the stresses of life. The attraction of these religions from the East became pronounced in the first century A.D. when the Greco-Roman world became increasingly vast and complex, thereby contributing to a high level of anxiety and alienation. As the empire began to undergo frightening challenges from the late second century onward, conversions to the empire's many mystery religions multiplied many times over.

Members of these various mystery religions believed that, through a process of conversion and ritual initiation, a devotee was transformed into a new person. By virtue of that transformation, or rebirth, the new member was admitted to a particular religion's ceremonies and its mysteries, or secret knowledge that led to everlasting tranquility. Membership in this select body of initiates provided a believer with the immediate support of a cohesive community of like-minded individuals and the promise of personal salvation. The various savior deities who offered such aid to their worshipers included Mithras, an Iranian sun god whose cult was open only to males, and Cybele, or the Great Mother, a fertility goddess from Asia Minor. Most popular of all was the ancient Egyptian goddess Isis (Chapter 1, sources 3 and 10), the loving mother of humanity whose temples could be found throughout the empire. Save for the fact that Isis's followers were not prevented from worshiping other deities, the cult of this goddess might almost be termed monotheistic, so all-powerful was she believed to be.

The *Metamorphoses*, also known as *The Golden Ass*, is a multilayered, allegorical novel by Lucius Apuleius (ca A.D. 123–185), a native of the city of Madauros in North Africa (modern Algeria) who, through a sophisticated blending of bawdy comedy and moral instruction, traced his personal spiritual journey to Isis. In the following selection the goddess miraculously appears to the novel's hero, Lucius, and promises him relief from his miseries.

QUESTIONS FOR ANALYSIS

1. What forms of service does Isis demand of her devotees?
2. What does Isis promise her faithful devotees? By implication, what happens to those not devoted to her?
3. *Syncretism* is the combination or reconciliation of differing cultural values, traditions, and modes of belief or opinion. What evidence is there of this phenomenon in this document? What does the evidence of syncretism in this source suggest about the Greco-Roman ecumene of the second century A.D.?
4. There was a tendency in the Greco-Roman world of late antiquity for many pious individuals to search for a common, unifying Divine Reality behind all the different religious beliefs and practices of their day. Can you find evidence of this phenomenon here? Why do you think people had this tendency?

5. Compare the views of life and the afterlife presented in this work with those of *The Odyssey* (Chapter 2, source 13). What has changed, and what has remained the same? Which seem more significant, the continuities or the changes? What factors do you think might have influenced the changes?
6. Compare this Isis with the Isis we saw in *The Book of the Dead* (Chapter 1, source 3). Are they essentially the same goddess? Are there any significant differences? What do you conclude from your answers to those questions?

"Behold, Lucius, here I am, moved by your prayers. I am the Mother of all Nature, the Mistress of all the elements, the First-born of the ages, the Supreme Deity, Queen of the dead, the foremost heavenly being, the unchanging manifestation of all the gods and goddesses. By my will, I govern the lofty stars of heaven, the health-giving breezes of the sea, and the bitter silence of those in the underworld. My single godhead is worshiped worldwide in various forms, in different rites, and under a variety of names. Thus the Phrygians,[1] the earliest race of people, call me Pessinuntia, Mother of the gods; the aboriginal natives of Attica[2] call me Cecropian Minerva[3]; the people of Cyprus, who travel the sea, call me Paphian Venus[4]; the archer Cretans call me Diana of Mount Dictys[5]; the trilingual[6] inhabitants of Sicily call me Ortygian Proserpina[7]; the Eleusinians know me as the ancient goddess Ceres[8]; some know me as Juno,[9] others as Bellona.[10] . . . Those, however, who are illuminated by the first rays of the rising sun-god, the

Ethiopians, the Africans, and those who excel in ancient lore, the Egyptians,[11] all these do me honor with my distinctive rites and call me by my true name, Queen Isis.

Here I am, taking pity on your miseries; here I am, benevolent and protective. Put aside your tears. Cease your lamentations. Stop grieving. Through my providence, a day of salvation is now dawning for you. . . . But above all remember and understand deep in the recesses of your heart that the remaining course of your life, right to the limit of your last breath, is pledged to me. It is not wrong that you render to her, through whose favor you shall return to human company,[12] the remainder of your life. You shall live as one of the blessed. You will live in full glory under my protection, and when you have completed the span of time alloted to you, you will pass down to the underworld. There also, in that subterranean hemisphere, you shall often worship me, whom you now see as the one who favors you, shining amid the dark gloom of Acheron[13] and reigning

---

[1] A people of Asia Minor (modern Turkey).
[2] The peninsula in Greece on which Athens is located.
[3] Cecrops was the legendary founder and first king of Athens who devoted the city to the goddess of wisdom, Athena (Minerva in Latin).
[4] Paphos, a seaside town on Cyprus, was the reputed birthplace and center of the cult of Aphrodite (Venus in Latin), goddess of love.
[5] Artemis (Diana in Latin) was the Greco-Roman goddess of light, the moon, and hunting.
[6] Greek, Latin, and their native language.
[7] Proserpina (Persephone in Greek) was queen of the underworld; Ortygia was an island off the Sicilian city of Syracuse.
[8] Eleusis was a town on the Attic peninsula dedicated to

Demeter (Ceres in Latin), goddess of agriculture and mother of Persephone/Proserpina.
[9] Juno (Hera in Greek) was sister, consort, and female counterpart to Jupiter (Zeus in Greek), king of the gods. Hence, she was queen of heaven.
[10] Roman goddess of war.
[11] Apuleius distinguishes among the black-skinned peoples of the south (the Ethiopians), the Mediterranean peoples of North Africa (the Africans), and the Egyptians.
[12] In this allegory Lucius had been magically metamorphosed into an ass, the symbol of sexual debauchery and an unspiritual life. Now, through Isis's intervention he is being returned to human form.
[13] Several rivers that were believed to be connected in the lower world.

in the Stygian[14] depths, while you dwell amidst the Elysian fields.[15] If by diligent obedience, pious service, and steadfast purity[16] you prove worthy of Our godhead, know that I alone have the power to prolong your life even beyond the span prescribed by your destiny.

▼▼▼

The Transit of Images Along the Silk Road

The most visible manifestation of this age of Afro-Eurasian interchange was the manner in which artistic motifs and styles traveled across the four major cultural pools, especially from west to east. As these ideas and forms moved from one region to another, they were reshaped and merged with native elements to produce striking examples of syncretic art. The four selections that appear here illustrate the way in which a Greco-Roman sculptural style traveled from the Mediterranean to China between the late first century B.C. and the fifth century A.D. and, in the process, how it was changed by the various cultures that adopted it.

The Revered Emperor
▼▼▼

42 ▼ *CAESAR AUGUSTUS AS CHIEF PRIEST*

Every human society seeks to express in its art the force of sacred authority. In this sculpture, crafted by an unknown eastern Mediterranean artist around 20 B.C., Caesar Augustus is portrayed in the fullness of his civil and religious power. As head of the Roman state, Augustus held the office of *Pontifex Maximus* (Chief Priest) and was responsible for presiding over Rome's major religious ceremonies. His very title, *Augustus* (Revered One), imparted an aura of sanctity to him, and throughout the empire temples were erected for the worship of his divine spirit even while he lived (source 33).

This work is typical of late Hellenistic sculpture in its idealized naturalism, evocative use of drapery, and sense of drama and mystery. At the same time, its stolidity, restraint, and soberness mark it as Roman. Augustus's appearance, especially his attire, pose, and facial expression, conform to accepted Hellenistic norms for portraying deities, priests, and other sacred persons.

---

[14]The Styx was the river that encircled the nether regions seven times.

[15]The area of the underworld reserved for heroes and others beloved by the gods; see Chapter 2, source 13, note 25.

[16]Keep in mind that Isis is saving the suppliant Lucius from a life of meaningless carnal pleasures (note 12).

QUESTION FOR ANALYSIS

1. Consider Augustus's expression, posture, and dress. How has the sculptor evoke a sense of sacred authority?

Caesar Augustus

A Woman of Authority
▼▼▼

43 ▼ A PARTHIAN NOBLEWOMAN

In 171 B.C. the Parthians, an Iranian steppe people, replaced the Macedonian Seleucids as masters of Persia and Mesopotamia and established an empire that lasted to A.D. 226. Although creative in military and administrative matters, the Parthians seem to have been content to be inheritors rather than innovators in the fine arts. As a result, their rise did not result in any immediate repudiation of the Hellenistic forms of artistic expression that had been part of the fabric of Persian civilization since the late fourth century B.C. The Parthian Empire, however, was the Greco-Roman world's link to Central Asia. As a result, its culture was a rich combination of many elements, of which Mediterranean Hellenism was only one.

The sculpture represented here of a woman in Iranian dress dates from the late second or early third century A.D. and illustrates a typical Parthian blend of Greco-Roman and Iranian components. It is one of over a hundred similar votive statues discovered at the many shrines of the city of Hatra in northern Mesopotamia. The unknown noblewoman whom it portrays offered it in devotion to an equally unknown deity. The statue, which is more than six feet high, affirms the importance of this woman, who stands with her hand raised in reverence.

QUESTIONS FOR ANALYSIS

1. Consider the woman's expression, posture, and dress. How has the sculptor evoked a sense of her authority?
2. Compare this statue with that of Caesar Augustus. What common elements do you find in each? Do you perceive any differences? Which are more significant?

The First Buddha Images
▼▼▼

44 ▼ A GANDHARAN BUDDHA

Early Buddhists believed it was wrong to depict the Buddha artistically in human form since he had broken the chains of matter and had achieved Nirvana. For over five hundred years Buddhist artists used such symbols as a wheel, a pipal tree, a throne, a footprint, and a stupa to symbolize his last earthly body. Toward the end of the first century A.D., artists in the Kushana province of

Parthian Noblewoman

Gandharan Buddha

Gandhara, which today comprises Afghanistan and northwest Pakistan, began representing the Buddha as a human. The sculpture of the standing Buddha that appears here is typical of the many carvings that have survived from this period and place. The setting is the Buddha's first sermon on the Law of Dharma (Chapter 3, source 20).

Many of the features are distinctively Buddhist. The knot on the top of the Buddha's head is known as the *ushnisha* and represents his cosmic consciousness; the garment he wears is the *sanghati*, or monk's robe. His missing right hand undoubtedly was raised palm outward in the gesture of blessing. It is interesting to compare this statue with the preceding Roman and Parthian sculptures. Scholars claim that the style and majesty of the Roman imperial sculpture from the workshops of the eastern Mediterranean deeply influenced the creators of the early Gandharan statues of the Buddha.

QUESTIONS FOR ANALYSIS

1. Consider the Buddha's expression, posture, and dress. How has the sculptor evoked a sense of his authority?
2. Compare this statue with those of Caesar Augustus and the Parthian noblewoman. What common elements do you find in all three pieces of art? Do you perceive any differences? Which are more significant?

The Buddha in East Asia
▼▼▼

45 ▼ A CHINESE BUDDHA

During the age of Later Han and for several centuries thereafter, Buddhism made deep inroads into China through the Silk Road. Here we have an early northern Chinese relief sculpture of the Buddha dating to around A.D. 500. This work, which deals with the same theme and setting as the Gandharan Buddha, has been characterized as an example of a fully developed Chinese style of Buddhist art.

QUESTIONS FOR ANALYSIS

1. Consider the Buddha's expression and posture. What responses does the sculptor seem to hope to elicit from the viewer?
2. Compare this Buddha with the Gandharan Buddha. In what ways are they similar, and how do they differ? Which are more significant — the similari-

Chinese Buddha

ties or the differences? Which of the two seems to be closer to the message of the Buddha's First Sermon (Chapter 3, source 20)?

3. Compare this Buddha with the statues of Caesar Augustus and the Parthian noblewoman. What styles and motifs has the sculptor borrowed from the Hellenistic West? In what ways does this Buddha differ from these Greco-Roman and Parthian prototypes? Which seem to be more important to the sculptor's message — these borrowed elements or the differences?

Part Two

▼▼▼

Faith, Devotion, and Salvation: Great World Religions to A.D. *1500*

By about 200 B.C. two overarching religious traditions had taken shape in Eurasia. Indian civilization produced Buddhism and Hinduism, both of which denied the reality of this world and sought release from it. In Southwest Asia two monotheistic faiths emerged — Judaism and Zoroastrianism — whose believers saw themselves as agents in the transformation of this world according to precepts decreed by their God.

During the next fifteen hundred years these four religions evolved significantly. Zoroastrianism virtually disappeared after the ninth century A.D., but Judaism survived, continued its historical evolution, and served as the source for the world's two most aggressive and expansionistic faiths: Christianity and Islam. Meanwhile, one school of Buddhist thought, the Mahayana sect, evolved into a faith that offered its believers personal salvation. Mainstream Hinduism never developed such a clearly articulated doctrine of heavenly salvation, as it is understood in the religious traditions of Southwest Asia, but it did evolve a form of worship centered on an intensely personal and deeply emotional devotion to a single, select deity.

Three of these five faiths — Buddhism, Christianity, and Islam — became universal religions. That is, they found homes in a wide variety of cultural settings and claimed to offer salvation to all humanity. Of the three, Buddhism was the most regional, confined largely to the vast and heavily populated regions of South and East Asia. Islam became the most global. Muslim communities dominated the east coast of Africa and the trading empires of interior West Africa. Islam stretched across North Africa, Southwest Asia, and the northern and central portions of India. It spread through much of Central Asia, the island and coastal regions of Southeast Asia, and even touched many parts of China. Christianity in its various forms could be found in Ethiopia, in the lands that bordered the eastern rim of the Mediterranean, among the Slavs of Eastern and Central Europe, and throughout Western Europe. In addition, small groups of Christians inhabited portions of Central Asia, north China, and even the western shores of India. With the new age of European transoceanic explorations that was getting under

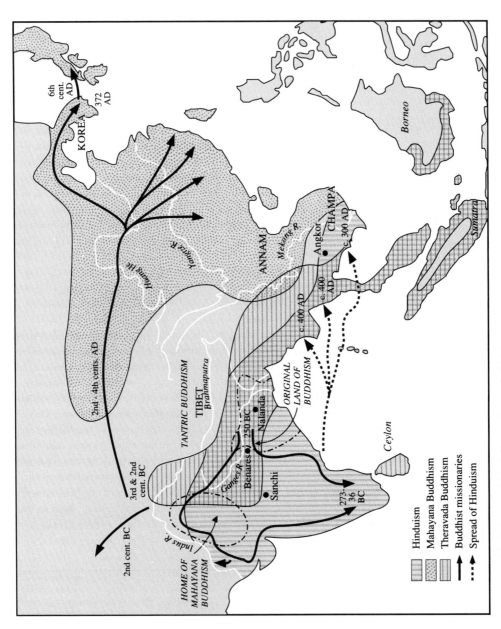

Map 3   Hinduism and Buddhism Around 1200

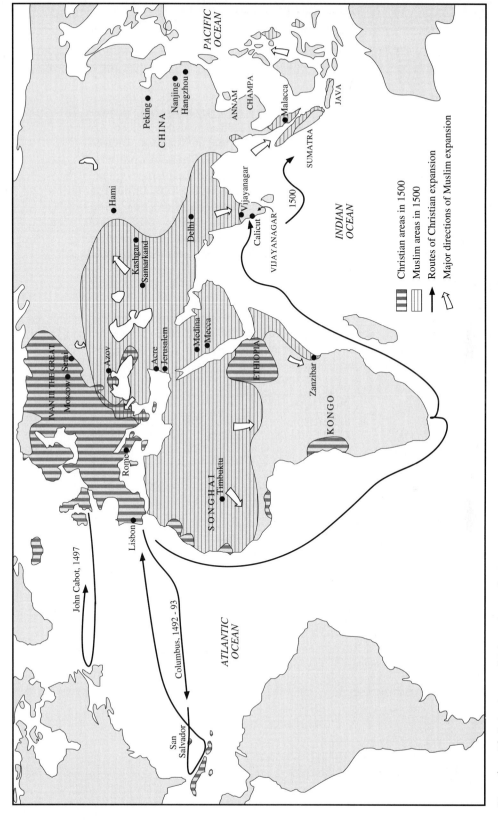

Map 4 Christianity and Islam Around 1500

way by 1500, Westerners would in time transplant Christianity throughout the Americas, along the Atlantic and Indian coasts of Africa, and in various parts of East and South Asia.

Meanwhile, Judaism and Hinduism also expanded beyond the confines of their ethnic and geographic origins. In addition to the *Diaspora*, or dispersion, of Jewish communities throughout much of Eurasia and northern Africa, Jews also welcomed gentile converts into their midst. The most notable example of such conversion was when the Khazars, a Turkic people who inhabited the upper Volga region between the Black and Caspian seas, embraced Judaism toward the middle of the eighth century, possibly under the influence of Jewish refugees from Persia. Yet conversions of this sort were rare in Jewish history, and generally Jews did not attempt to spread their religion beyond their ethnic boundaries. Indian merchants and brahmin teachers were more active disseminators of culture and religion than their Jewish counterparts. Between especially the first and sixth centuries A.D. Indians traveled in significant numbers across the waters of the Bay of Bengal bringing Hindu culture, particularly that of southern India, to the coastal regions of Southeast Asia. The cults of Shiva and Vishnu found especially fertile soil in these lands across the sea. Despite this expansion, however, both Judaism and Hinduism remained far less universal in scope or appeal than Buddhism, Christianity, and Islam.

Chapter 6

▼▼▼

New Developments in Three Ancient Religions

During the first age of Afro-Eurasian interchange (Chapter 5), Hinduism, Judaism, and Buddhism all experienced important changes that profoundly affected their historical development. Within Hinduism a new movement known as *bhakti*, or the Way of Devotion, challenged the caste system without actually rejecting it. At the same time, it was this new form of Hindu religion, not the caste system, that Indian merchants transplanted among the emerging civilizations of Southeast Asia in the early centuries A.D. Without the Way of Devotion Hinduism would probably not have spread significantly beyond the Indian subcontinent.

Hinduism and Judaism have historically been "family" religions, in the sense that each has been largely confined to the heirs of a single civilization. Normally, their adherents are born into these religious-social complexes and are not converts. At the same time, both religions have occasionally reached out beyond their cultural matrices. This was particularly so in the case of Judaism because of the Diaspora, or Great Dispersion, which scattered Jewish communities all over the Afro-Eurasian "world island." While Jews remained conscious of being a people apart from their gentile (non-Jewish) neighbors, Jewish communities could not totally avoid cultural interchange with the societies among which they were settled.

Cultural exchange also contributed significantly to the development of a new form of Buddhist belief and devotion — the Mahayana sect. This school moved radically away from the Buddha's original teachings, which rejected all notions of God and personal immortality, by offering the promise of personal salvation. This message attracted many people suffering from the chaos of the breakdown of the first Afro-Eurasian ecumene. As early as the first century A.D., Mahayana Buddhist ideas were entering China, and in the centuries that followed Buddhism in its many different forms swept through East Asia.

▼▼▼

Hinduism: The Way of Devotion

In one of the *Bhagavad Gita*'s more famous scenes, which does not appear in the excerpt quoted in Chapter 3, source 18, the hero god Krishna (Vishnu) teaches Arjuna that bhakti, or unconditional devotion to a god, is one of several ways a person can win release (*moksha*) from the cycle of rebirth. Such an approach to liberation appealed to many low-caste and casteless persons, including women, who found strict and selfless conformity to the laws of dharma (the Way of Works) unattractive. It also appealed to people who lacked the temperament or leisure to attain release from the shackles of matter through asceticism, study of the sacred scriptures, and meditation (the Way of Knowledge). The Way of Devotion, in which one passionately adored a savior god, offered a promise of immediate liberation to everyone.

In the Gupta period and thereafter, many Hindus tended to reduce the myriad divine personifications of Brahman, the One, to three: Brahma the Creator, Vishnu the Preserver, and Shiva the Destroyer. Of this trinity, Brahma (not to be confused with Brahman) was the least widely worshiped, because he was perceived as a remote kingly god who, after completing the process of creation, had retired from concerning himself with worldly affairs. Hindus widely adored Vishnu and Shiva, however, and they became two of the great gods of Asia. The cult of Shiva was especially popular in Southeast Asia, where he merged with several local deities.

Hindus who concentrated their worship on Vishnu or Shiva did not deny the existence of the many other divine and semidivine personalities who were part of the traditional pantheon. They chose Shiva or Vishnu as gods of special devotion because each, in his way, was a loving personification of the totality of Divine Reality. Vishnu's worshipers, for example, believed he had selflessly blessed and taught humanity on a number of critical occasions in descents (*avataras*) from heaven. On each occasion he took on either human or animal form and intervened on behalf of the forces of goodness to redress the equilibrium between good and evil. In fact, Vishnu's worshipers regarded the Buddha as one of Vishnu's nine chief avataras. Of all his various incarnations, however, the warriors Krishna and Rama enjoyed the widest devotional popularity. As Lord Krishna exemplified in the *Bhagavad Gita*, Vishnu's emergence into this world provided humanity with a model of divine perfection. By offering such a god exclusive and unqualified devotion, a worshiper hoped to share in that perfection.

The religious development of bhakti, which met so many needs of the members of Hindu India's lower social levels, helped Hinduism to counter successfully the challenges of Buddhism, especially that of the Mahayana school. Indeed, Hinduism was more than able to hold its own against that faith, and by A.D. 1500 Buddhism had largely disappeared from the land of its origin.

Vishnu, Destroyer of Sin
▼▼▼

46 ▼ THE VISHNU PURANA

Between approximately A.D. 300 and 1000 a new sacred literature known as the *Puranas* (stories of ancient times) developed to give voice to bhakti. Composed for popular consumption, each of the eighteen major Puranas was a long, rambling collection of myth and folklore that brought home to its largely unsophisticated audience the central message that a particular god — Brahma, Vishnu, or Shiva — deserved worship without reservation. The following selection comes from the closing lines of the *Vishnu Purana*.

QUESTIONS FOR ANALYSIS

1. What power does the very name of Vishnu have?
2. What traditional avenues to liberation are referred to in this passage, and how does worship of Vishnu allow one to bypass or transcend them?
3. How does Vishnu, of and by himself, encompass all the powers of the Hindu trinity? How is he equated with Brahman, the World Soul? Was the author of this passage a monotheist?
4. How does the theological message of this Purana represent a departure from the spirit that pervades *The Laws of Manu* (Chapter 5, source 40)?

I have related to you this Purana, which is equal to the Vedas in sanctity, and by hearing which all faults and sins whatever are expiated. . . .

By hearing this, all sins are at once obliterated. In this also the glorious Hari[1] has been revealed, the cause of the creation, preserva- tion, and destruction of the world; the soul of all things, and himself all things: by the repetition of whose name man is undoubtedly liberated from all sins, which fly like wolves that are frightened by a lion. The repetition of his name with devout faith is the best remover of

---
[1]Another name for Vishnu.

all sins, destroying them as fire purifies the metal from the dross. The stain of the Kali age,[2] which ensures to men sharp punishments in hell,[3] is at once effaced by a single invocation of Hari. He who is all that is, the whole egg of Brahma[4] . . . he who is all things, who knows all things, who is the form of all things, being without form himself, and of whom whatever is, from mount Meru[5] to an atom, all consists — he, the glorious Vishnu, the destroyer of all sin — is described in this Purana. By hearing this Purana an equal recompense is obtained to that which is derived from the performance of an Asvamedha sacrifice,[6] or from fasting at the holy places. . . . This Purana is the best of all preservatives for those who are afraid of worldly existence, a certain alleviation of the sufferings of men, and remover of all imperfections. . . . Whoever hears this great mystery, which removes the contamination of the Kali, shall be freed from all his sins. He who hears this every day acquits himself of his daily obligations to ancestors, gods and men. . . . What marvel therefore is it that the sins of one who repeats the name of Achyuta[7] should be wiped away? Should not that Hari be heard of, whom those devoted to acts[8] worship with sacrifices continually as the god of sacrifice; whom those devoted to meditation[9] contemplate . . . , who, as the gods, accepts the offerings addressed to them; the glorious being who is without beginning or end; . . . who is the abode of all spiri-

tual power; in whom the limits of finite things cannot be measured; and who, when he enters the ear, destroys all sin?

I adore him, that first of gods, Purushottama,[10] who is without end and without beginning, without growth, without decay, without death; who is substance that knows not change. I adore that ever inexhaustible spirit, who assumed sensible qualities;[11] who, though one, became many; who, though pure, became as if impure, by appearing in many and various shapes; who is endowed with divine wisdom, and is the author of the preservation of all creatures. I adore him, who is the one conjoined essence and object of both meditative wisdom and active virtue; who is watchful in providing for human enjoyments; who is one with the three qualities;[12] who, without undergoing change, is the cause of the evolution of the world; who exists of his own essence, ever exempt from decay. I constantly adore him, who is entitled heaven, air, fire, water, earth, and ether; who is the bestower of all the objects which give gratification to the senses; who benefits mankind with the instruments of fruition; who is perceptible, who is subtle, who is imperceptible. May that unborn, eternal Hari, whose form is manifold, and whose essence is composed of both nature and spirit, bestow upon all mankind that blessed state which knows neither birth nor decay!

---

[2]The Kali Age receives its name from Kali, goddess of destruction and consort of Shiva. It is 360,000 years of evil and the last of an eternal cycle of four repetitive ages. Following the Kali Age's dissolution, a period of new birth and virtue will commence again. The authors of the Puranas assumed they were living in a Kali Age.
[3]There are many hells (one Purana enumerates twenty-one) where the servants of Yama, god of death, punish people for their social sins, especially sins against caste restrictions. This punishment is not eternal; eventually, each soul is reborn into a lower caste, or life form, depending on the weight of one's karma.
[4]All creation.
[5]The central mountain of the earth and the home of the gods.

[6]A horse sacrifice, which was a carryover from Aryan times.
[7]"The Unfallen One," another of Vishnu's titles.
[8]Those who seek moksha (release) through the Way or Yoga (discipline) of Works.
[9]Those who seek release through the Way or Yoga of Knowledge.
[10]Another name for Vishnu — the sacrificial substance from which the world was created (see The Hymn to Purusha, Chapter 2, source 12).
[11]Who had many incarnations, or avataras, such as Krishna (Chapter 3, source 18).
[12]Creation, preservation, destruction.

Shiva, Auspicious Destroyer
▼▼▼

47 ▼ SHIVA NATARAJA

Many people, especially those whose religions spring from the Southwest Asian tradition of ethical monotheism, might find it hard to accept the notion that a god whose primary function is destruction and death is regarded as a loving deity. The name *Shiva*, in fact, means "auspicious" and, among his many functions, Shiva serves as the patron of ascetics and other holy people.

The artifact illustrated here is a bronze statue of Shiva Nataraja (Lord of the Dance) from the Chola kingdom of southern India (ca 850–1250), an area of fervent devotion to Shiva from which the cult of Shiva spread across the Bay of Bengal to Southeast Asia. The statue represents the god engaged in an ecstatic cosmic dance. The statue's iconographic symbols offer numerous clues to how his worshipers perceive Shiva. Here he is dancing within a circle of fire. His hair is piled up in a crownlike style; flowing from the sides of his head are strands of hair intertwined with flowers and forming the shape of wings. His upper left hand holds a devouring flame; his upper right hand clasps a drum for beating out the rhythm of the universe. The lower right arm is entwined by a cobra, but the hand is raised in the silent "fear not" gesture (compare this with the Buddha's right hand in Chapter 5, sources 44 and 45). The lower left hand points to his raised left foot as a sign of "release." The other foot is planted firmly on the writhing body of Apasamara, the demon of ignorance and heedlessness.

QUESTIONS FOR ANALYSIS

1. What double function does fire serve, especially in an agricultural society?
2. Keeping in mind your answer to question 1 and also the fact that Shiva uses a drum to beat out the rhythm of the universe, what do you think the circle of fire and the flame in his left hand represent?
3. If fire presents a double message, what other symbols in this statue give a similar double message? Consider particularly Shiva's body language.
4. Consider Shiva's hair. According to one tradition, the sacred River Ganges flows from Shiva's head. What do this tradition and the manner in which the god's hair is represented suggest about this deity?
5. Why do you think the artist has depicted Shiva with four arms instead of the standard two?
6. We saw in source 46 that Vishnu's devotees believed that their savior god exercised all the primary functions of the godhead — creation, destruction, regeneration, preservation, and release (moksha). Can you find the appropriate symbols in this statue that illustrate a similar belief on the part of Shiva's followers?
7. Consider the demon of ignorance. How would an "ignorant" person regard death? What do you think Shiva's triumph over this demon represents?

Shiva Nataraja

▼▼▼

Diaspora Judaism

In A.D. 66 Palestine broke out in general rebellion against Roman occupation, and it took the Roman armies seven bloody years to root out the last vestiges of insurgency. In the process, Jerusalem and its Temple were destroyed in A.D. 70. In A.D. 132 another Jewish revolt against Roman authority flared up, and when it was finally suppressed in 135, the rebuilt remnants of ancient Jerusalem had been transformed into a Roman military camp that was closed to Jewish habitation. Long before the destruction of the Temple and their sacred city, Jews had established prosperous communities throughout the Greco-Roman, Persian, and Arabic worlds. After these two unsuccessful rebellions, however, the Jewish flight from Palestine reached the proportions of a folk migration. The Great Dispersion, or Diaspora, was under way. For nineteen hundred years Jews would be strangers in a variety of foreign lands — a people without a homeland.

In spite of these travails, Judaism survived as a living faith and culture, because wherever Jews settled, they remained faithful to the memory of their special covenant with God and their dream of returning to the Promised Land. Moreover, despite its innate conservatism, born of a need to maintain contact with the ways of the past, Judaism remained flexible. Jews proved adaptable to a variety of alien settings, and over the centuries Judaism continued its historical development in response to the needs of its various scattered communities.

Jewish Life in Twelfth-Century Baghdad
▼▼▼

48 ▼ *Benjamin of Tudela, BOOK OF TRAVELS*

Rabbi Benjamin ben Jonah of Tudela provides the best eyewitness account of twelfth-century Jewish life in Europe, Asia, and North Africa. This scholar and traveler, whose birth and death dates are unknown, departed his native northern Spain around 1159 and spent the next thirteen or fourteen years visiting several hundred Jewish communities from the Mediterranean, to perhaps as far east as India (see Map 5 in Chapter 12). The purpose of his journey seems to have been to establish contact with these scattered remnants of Israel (which he tells us were flourishing even in China) and to report on the quality of Jewish life throughout the world. The Christian *Reconquista*, or reconquest of the Iberian Peninsula, already had been under way in Spain for a century, and Tudela, which had a large Jewish population, was now located in Christian territory. It is conceivable that because crusader lords had replaced the generally more tolerant Muslim rulers of northern Spain, Rabbi Benjamin decided it was time to seek out regions where Jews lived in greater security.

In the following excerpt he describes the quality of life for Jews under Muslim rule in Baghdad on the Tigris (in modern Iraq). As we shall see in Chapter 8, source 64, the Abbasid caliphs (750–1258), who ruled Baghdad and much of Southwest Asia, claimed (but never exercised) authority over all Islam.

QUESTIONS FOR ANALYSIS

1. Who was Daniel the son of Hisdai, and what function did he serve under the caliph?
2. Trace on a map the region supposedly under the Head of the Captivity's authority. What does this suggest about the extent of the Diaspora?
3. What was the status of Jews within the lands ruled by the caliph, and how would you characterize Muslim-Jewish relations in the reign of al-Abbasi?
4. What aspects of Baghdad's Jewish community most interested Rabbi Benjamin, and what does his interest in them suggest about the reasons why Judaism managed to flourish as a religion and a culture?

Baghdad [is] . . . the royal residence of the Caliph Emir al-Muminin al-Abbasi[1] of the family of Muhammad.[2] He is at the head of the Muslim religion, and all the kings of Islam obey him; he occupies a similar position to that held by the Pope over the Christians.[3] He has a palace in Baghdad three miles in extent, wherein is a great park with all varieties of trees, fruit-bearing and otherwise, and all manner of animals. . . . There the great king, al–Abbasi the Caliph holds his court, and he is kind unto Israel, and many belonging to the people of Israel are his attendants; he knows all languages, and is well versed in the law of Israel. He reads and writes the holy language [Hebrew]. . . . He is truthful and trusty, speaking peace to all men. . . .

In Baghdad there are about 40,000 Jews, and they dwell in security, prosperity, and honor under the great Caliph, and among them are great sages, the heads of Academies engaged in the study of the law. In this city there are ten Academies.[4] . . . And at the head of them all is Daniel the son of Hisdai, who is styled "Our Lord the Head of the Captivity of all Israel." He possesses a book of pedigrees going back as far as David, King of Israel.[5] The Jews call him "Our Lord, Head of the Captivity," and the Muslims call him "Saidna ben Daoud,"[6] and he has been invested with authority over all the congregations of Israel at the hands of the Emir al-Muminin, the Lord of Islam. For thus Muhammad[7] commanded concerning him and his descendants; and he granted him a seal of office over all the congregations that dwell under his rule, and ordered that every one, whether Muslim or Jew, or belonging to any other nation in his dominion, should rise up

---

[1]Also known as al-Mustanjid (r. 1160–1170).
[2]The Prophet of Islam. See Chapter 8.
[3]See Chapter 7, source 59.
[4]Academies for the study of scripture and post-biblical law (the Talmud; see note 20). These scholars served as the chief teachers and judges of their community.

[5]King of Israel around 1000 B.C.
[6]"The Lord son of David."
[7]Not the Prophet Muhammad but possibly al-Abbasi's predecessor Muhammad el-Moktafi.

before him and salute him, and that any one who should refuse to rise up should receive one hundred stripes.

And every fifth day when he goes to pay a visit to the great Caliph, horsemen, Gentiles as well as Jews, escort him, and heralds proclaim in advance, "Make way before our Lord, the son of David, as is due unto him," the Arabic words being "Amilu tarik la Saidna ben Daud." He is mounted on a horse, and is attired in robes of silk and embroidery with a large turban on his head. . . . Then he appears before the Caliph and kisses his hand, and the Caliph rises and places him on a throne which Muhammad had ordered to be made for him, and all the Muslim princes who attend the court of the Caliph rise up before him. And the Head of the Captivity is seated on his throne opposite to the Caliph, in compliance with the command of Muhammad. . . . The authority of the Head of the Captivity extends over all the communities of Shinar,[8] Persia, Khurasan[9] and Sheba which is El-Yemen,[10] and Diyar Kalach[11] and the land of Aram Naharaim,[12] and over the dwellers in the mountains of Ararat[13] and the land of the Alans.[14] . . . His authority extends also over the land of Siberia,[15] and the communities in the land of the Togarmim[16] unto the mountains of Asveh and the land of Gurgan, the inhabitants of which are called Gurganim who dwell by the river Gihon, and these are the Girgashites who follow the Christian religion.[17] Further

it extends to the gates of Samarkand,[18] the land of Tibet, and the land of India. In respect of all these countries the Head of the Captivity gives the communities power to appoint Rabbis and Ministers who come unto him to be consecrated and to receive his authority. They bring him offerings and gifts from the ends of the earth. He owns hospices, gardens, and plantations in Babylon,[19] and much land inherited from his fathers, and no one can take his possessions from him by force. He has a fixed weekly revenue arising from the hospices of the Jews, the markets and the merchants, apart from that which is brought to him from far-off lands. The man is very rich, and wise in the Scriptures as well as in the Talmud,[20] and many Israelites dine at his table every day.

At his installation, the Head of the Captivity gives much money to the Caliph, to the Princes, and to the Ministers. On the day that the Caliph performs the ceremony of investing him with authority, he rides in the second of the royal carriages, and is escorted from the palace of the Caliph to his own house with timbrels and fifes. The Exilarch[21] appoints the Chiefs of the Academies by placing his hand upon their heads, thus installing them in their office. The Jews of the city are learned men and very rich.

In Baghdad there are twenty-eight Jewish Synagogues, situated either in the city itself or in al-Karkh on the other side of the Tigris; for

---

[8]Southern Mesopotamia (ancient Sumer and Agade).
[9]Northeastern Iran.
[10]Southern Arabia.
[11]Asia Minor, or Anatolia (modern Turkey).
[12]Northern Mesopotamia (modern north Syria).
[13]Armenia.
[14]An Indo-European people inhabiting the Caucasus mountain region of Georgia.
[15]He probably means Iberia, not Siberia. If the reference is to Iberia, he does not mean the Iberian Peninsula, where the modern nations of Spain and Portugal are located, but rather the land that today roughly corresponds to the nation of Georgia (note 14).
[16]One of a number of people of the central Euphrates in biblical times (The Bible, Genesis: 10).
[17]Apparently he means the African Christian civilizations of the Sudan (Kush) and Ethiopia (Chapter 11,

source 86). Gihon was one of the four biblical rivers of the Garden of Eden and usually refers to the Nile. The Girgashites were one of the seven people who inhabited Canaan before its conquest by the Hebrews under Joshua.
[18]A major city that today is located in Uzbekistan, one of the Central Asian nations comprising the Commonwealth of Independent States (the former Soviet Union).
[19]The region around Baghdad.
[20]Collections of legal opinions touching every aspect of Jewish life that scholars compiled in Palestine and Mesopotamia between approximately A.D. 100 and 500. Diaspora Jews generally regarded the Talmud as the highest source of legal authority after the Torah (the first five books of the Bible).
[21]The "Ruler of the Exile" — Daniel the son of Hisdai.

the river divides the metropolis into two parts. The great synagogue of the Head of the Captivity has columns of marble of various colors overlaid with silver and gold, and on these columns are sentences of the Psalms in golden letters. And in front of the ark are about ten steps of marble; on the topmost step are the seats of the Head of the Captivity and of the Princes of the House of David. The city of Baghdad is twenty miles in circumference, situated in a land of palms, gardens and plantations, the like of which is not to be found in the whole land of Shinar.

Jacob's Seed
▼▼▼

49 ▼ *Moses ben Maimon, SELECTED WRITINGS*

As Rabbi Benjamin bears witness, many medieval Jewish congregations located in Muslim and Christian lands enjoyed varying degrees of self-government in local affairs. The two most notable examples of prosperous, semiautonomous Jewish communities were the late twelfth-century Jews of Baghdad and of Cairo in Egypt. Under the tolerant rule of the caliph of Baghdad and the sultan of Egypt, the Jews of both cities achieved a deserved reputation for piety and scholarship. Even when Jews lived under less benign rulers, and most did, their communities generally fostered scholarship, especially in the areas of theological and legal studies. Jewish biblical scholars of twelfth-century Paris, for example, played an important role in upgrading the level of understanding of the ancient biblical texts among their Christian counterparts, until the Jews were expelled from France in 1182.

Whenever medieval Jewish scholarship is the topic, one name inevitably arises: Rabbi Moses ben Maimon (1135–1204), known in the West as Maimonides. Maimonides possessed the most comprehensive and original intellect of medieval Jewry and composed works that deeply influenced Jewish, Muslim, and Christian contemporaries. His scholarship was immense; he composed works in both Arabic and Hebrew on such topics as the Bible, astronomy, mathematics, jurisprudence, medicine, ethics, and metaphysics. Born in Cordova, Spain, when the city was still a seat of Muslim power, Maimonides and his family were compelled to flee to Morocco in North Africa while he was a teenager. At the age of thirty he again had to take flight, from potential persecution in Morocco, and landed in Palestine, then the scene of the crusades. Finding the Promised Land bitterly disappointing, he immigrated the following year to the tolerant land of Muslim Egypt, where he became physician at the court of Sultan Saladin (1138–1193) and spent the rest of his life engaged in a ceaseless round of duties that would have destroyed a lesser person. He was one of the most popular and widely published physicians of his day. For thirty years he served as head of the Jewish congregation of Cairo, and in this capacity he enjoyed wide prestige among Jewish communities throughout North Africa and Southwest

Asia. As an acknowledged authority, he carried on an extensive correspondence in which he answered questions on a wide variety of issues. Impelled by his own inner drives, he wrote voluminous treatises on every imaginable topic of Jewish religion and law. The sheer volume, scope, and depth of his writings earned him the sobriquet *the Great Eagle.*

The following selections from Rabbi Moses, all written in response to burning late twelfth-century issues, reveal Judaism's dual sense of universality and exclusivity.

QUESTIONS FOR ANALYSIS

1. In Maimonides's view, how are Jews to treat one another?
2. According to Maimonides, why were Jews persecuted, and how were they to respond to that persecution? How would those persecutions affect Judaism?
3. Does Rabbi Moses consider a convert to Judaism to be fully a Jew? Why or why not?
4. According to Maimonides, what place does the Promised Land hold in a Jew's life?
5. How does Rabbi Moses see King Messiah — as a spiritual or a political leader? In the rabbi's view, what will be the consequences of the Messiah's coming?
6. As Maimonides envisions it, what is the World-to-Come, and who will enjoy it? How will it differ from the Messianic Era?
7. Does Rabbi Moses agree with Second Isaiah (Chapter 3, source 23) that, as a Chosen People, the Jews have a special role to play in human history? If so, what is that role?
8. Can you discover any evidence provided by rabbis Benjamin and Moses that suggests why Jews were able to maintain their cultural identity despite being so widely scattered?

RELATIONS AMONG JEWS

It is incumbent on every one to love each individual Israelite as himself, as it is said, "Thou shalt love thy neighbor as thyself." Hence a person ought to speak in praise of his neighbor and be careful of his neighbor's property as he is careful of his own property and solicitous about his own honor. Whoever glorifies himself by humiliating another person, will have no portion in the World-to-Come. . . .

The house of Israel that bears the name of Jacob[1] and upholds the religion of Moses our

teacher, must be one united community. Nothing whatsoever should create dissension. You are wise and understanding people and you must know how serious are the consequences of discord and to what misfortunes it leads.

WHY ARE JEWS PERSECUTED?

The antagonism of the nations toward us is due to our unique position as a people of faith. This is why their kings oppress us and visit upon us hatred and hostility. But the Creator endowed

[1]Jacob was the son of Isaac, who in turn was the son of Abraham, the father of the Hebrews. Yahweh blessed Jacob, changed his name to Israel, and promised that he would be "the father of nations."

us with confidence, so that whenever the fury of persecution arises against Israel, it will surely be endured. The power of the kings presses down upon us and they exercise a hard rule over us; they persecute and torment us with oppressive decrees, but they cannot destroy us or wipe out our name. . . .

Therefore, brethren, be strong and of good courage. If persecutions arise, let them not disconcert you. Let not the mighty hand of the enemy and the weakness of our nation frighten you. These events are but trial and proof of your faith and your love. By holding firm to the law of truth in times like these, you prove that you belong to those of Jacob's seed who fear God and who are named "the remnant whom the Lord shall call."[2]

CONVERTS

I received the question of the master Obadiah, the wise and learned proselyte,[3] may the Lord reward him for his work, may a perfect recompense be bestowed upon him by the Lord of Israel, under whose wings he has sought cover.

You ask me if you, too, are allowed to say in the blessings and prayers you offer alone or in the congregation: *"Our* God" and "God of *our* Fathers," . . . "Thou who hast brought *us* out of the land of Egypt," Thou who hast worked miracles for *our* fathers," and more of this kind.

Yes, you may say all this in the described order and not change it in the least. In the same way as every Jew by birth says his blessing and prayer, you, too, shall bless and pray alike, whether you are alone or pray in the congregation. The reason for this is that Abraham, our father, taught the people, opened their minds, and revealed to them the truth, faith, and the unity of God; he rejected the idols and abolished their adoration; he brought many chil-

dren under the wings of the Divine Presence; he gave them counsel and advice, and ordered his sons and the members of his household after him to keep the ways of the Lord forever. . . . Ever since then whoever adopts Judaism and confesses the unity of the Divine Name, as it is prescribed in the Torah,[4] is counted among the disciples of Abraham, our father, peace be with him. These men are Abraham's household, and he it is who converted them to righteousness. . . .

For the Creator, may He be extolled, has indeed chosen you and separated you from the nations[5] and given you the Torah. For the Torah has been given to us *and* to the proselytes.

RIGHTEOUS GENTILES

As to your question about the nations, know that the Lord desires the heart, and that the intention of the heart is the measure of all things. That is why our sages say, "The pious men among the Gentiles have a share in the World-to-Come," namely, if they have acquired what can be acquired of the knowledge of God, and if they ennoble their souls with worthy qualities. There is no doubt that every man who ennobles his soul with excellent morals and wisdom based on the faith in God, certainly belongs to the men of the World-to-Come.

THE PROMISED LAND

At all times one should live in Palestine even in a place the majority of whose population is heathen, and not live outside Palestine even in a place the majority of whose population is Jewish. . . .

It is forbidden to emigrate from Palestine and go abroad, unless one goes to study the Law, or to marry a wife, or to rescue property

---

[2]The Bible, Joel 2:32. This biblical prophet of the fifth or fourth century B.C. continued the theme of Second Isaiah and spoke of the coming Day of the Lord, when God would judge all humanity.

[3]A convert.
[4]The basic law of Judaism, comprising the first five books of the Bible.
[5]The nations of other (non-Jewish) peoples.

from heathens and then returns to Palestine.[6] So, too, one may leave on business. . . . But though one is permitted to emigrate, if one does, the act is not in conformity with the law of saintliness. . . .

When the Temple was destroyed, the Sages of the time ruled that a Jew should not build a painted and wainscoted house, but daub it with clay, wash it with lime, and leave about the entrance a square cubit's spot unwashed. The Sages likewise ordained: Whoever sets his table for a feast should let something be missing on it, and should leave one place empty without the service plate that otherwise would have been put there. When a woman orders ornaments of silver or gold, she should omit one of the details so that it should not appear perfect. When a man takes a wife, he should strew hearth-ashes on his head. All this one should do in remembrance of Jerusalem. As it is said: "If I forget thee, O Jerusalem, let my right hand forget her cunning. Let my tongue cleave to the roof of my mouth if I remember thee not; if I set not Jerusalem above my chiefest joy."

THE MESSIAH

King Messiah[7] will arise and restore the kingdom of David to its former state and original sovereignty. He will rebuild the sanctuary[8] and gather the dispersed of Israel. All the ancient laws will be reinstated in his days. . . .

He who does not believe in the restoration or does not look forward to the coming of the Messiah denies not only the teachings of the Prophets but also those of the Law of Moses, our teacher. . . .

The ultimate and perfect reward, the final bliss which will suffer neither interruption nor diminution is the life in the World-to-Come. The Messianic Era, on the other hand, will be realized in this world; which will continue in its normal course except that independent sovereignty will be restored to Israel. The ancient Sages already said, "The only difference between the present and the Messianic Era is that political oppression will then cease." . . .

Let no one think that in the days of the Messiah any of the laws of nature will be set aside, or any innovations be introduced into creation. The world will follow its normal course. The words of Isaiah: And the wolf shall dwell with the lamb, and the leopard shall lie down with the kid are to be understood figuratively, meaning that Israel will live securely among the wicked of the heathens who are likened to wolves and leopards. . . . They will all accept the true religion, and will neither plunder nor destroy, and together with Israel earn a comfortable living in a legitimate way.

Said the Rabbis: "The sole difference between the present and the Messianic days is deliverance from servitude to foreign powers." . . .

The Sages and Prophets did not long for the days of the Messiah that Israel might exercise dominion over the world, or rule over the heathens or be exalted by the nations, or that it might eat and drink and rejoice. Their aspiration was that Israel be free to devote itself to the Law and its wisdom, with no one to oppress or disturb it, and thus be worthy of the life of the world to come.

In that era will be neither famine nor war, neither jealousy nor strife. Blessings will be abundant, comforts within the reach of all. The one preoccupation of the whole world will be to know the Lord. Hence Israelites will be very wise; they will know the things that are now concealed, and will attain an understanding of their Creator to the utmost capacity of the human mind.

---

[6]Rabbi Moses left Palestine for Egypt because he found, to his dismay, that it was intellectually and spiritually a wasteland, and in this age of the crusader Latin kingdom of Jerusalem, there was no place for Jews in Judea. He never returned.

[7]The Anointed One. The Messiah was the deliverer promised through the prophets. Christians believed Jesus Christ was the Messiah; Jews were still awaiting the deliverer's coming.

[8]The sanctuary of the Temple that was destroyed in A.D. 70.

▼▼▼

Buddhism: A Religion of Infinite Compassion

Asoka's Buddhism (Chapter 5, source 37) was idealistic, but it was also practical, insofar as he endeavored to make the Law of Righteousness a living reality for his people. Withdrawal from the world to live the life of a mendicant monk who sought Nirvana through meditation (Chapter 3, source 21) was not for Asoka. While he revered and patronized Buddhist monks, he practiced social activism based on his understanding of Buddhist principles. Moreover, by sending missionaries to neighboring and distant regions he affirmed his belief in Buddhism's universality. As his edicts indicate, Asoka also did not abandon belief in the gods or a heavenly hereafter.

All the qualities of Asoka's Buddhism became more pronounced in the generations that followed. Eventually they helped engender a new interpretation of Buddhism known as the *Mahayana*, or the Great Vehicle. The title is metaphorical: Mahayana sectarians picture their form of Buddhism as a great ferry which, under the guidance of enlightened pilots, carries all humanity simultaneously across the river of life to salvation on the opposite shore.

Conversely, Mahayanists term the older, more traditional form of Buddhism the *Hinayana*, or the Small Vehicle. The image is of a one-person raft, since Hinayana Buddhism centers on the single *arahat*, or perfected disciple, who through solitary meditation, normally within a monastic setting, individually attains Nirvana, or an Enlightenment that results in the cessation of all desires. Followers of this form of Buddhism, which today predominates in the island nation of Sri Lanka and the countries of mainland Southeast Asia, especially Burma and Thailand, generally dislike the term Hinayana because it implies inferiority, and call their sect *Theravada* (the Teaching of the Elders).

Evidence indicates that Mahayana Buddhism emerged in northwest India during the age of the Kushana Empire (first century B.C.–third century A.D.) and probably did so in part as a result of certain Southwest Asian influences, primarily the notion of a savior god. According to Mahayana belief, Siddhartha Gautama the Buddha (Chapter 3, source 20) was not unique. There had been many buddhas, or enlightened ones, before and after Gautama. These buddhas or, more properly, *bodhisattvas* (Sanskrit for "one whose essence is enlightenment") are compassionate saints. Having achieved full illumination, or buddahood, they delay entry into Nirvana, which most Mahayana Buddhists understand to be a heaven of eternal bliss, in order to act as pilots of the Great Vehicle, leading others from all walks of life to salvation through the countless merits they have accumulated in their perfect lives of selflessness. Those whom they save become, in turn, bodhisattvas who then delay their entry into Nirvana in order to help others. Through this pyramid of selfless compassion, ultimately all humanity will cross into Nirvana together.

This comforting, unexclusive doctrine was destined to become the basis of a world religion. As early as the reign of Emperor Han Mingdi (r. A.D. 58–75), Buddhist ideas were entering China. At first Buddhism made little progress there because its practices, especially monasticism, and such basic principles as its otherworldliness ran counter to two central Chinese qualities: the centrality of the family and preoccupation with this world. The few early inroads Buddhism made in China occurred because some Chinese initially were able to equate it with Daoism. In the time of troubles that followed the collapse of Later Han, however, Buddhism, especially in its Mahayana form, won a place alongside Daoism and Confucianism as a doctrine that offered comfort in the face of affliction.

Buddhism continued to grow at a rapid rate in China until the middle of the ninth century, when it suffered a severe setback due to imperial confiscation of monastic properties. Although it never regained its former strength, it did not die out and has remained an element of Chinese civilization to the present. At the same time, with their remarkable ability to sinicize (make Chinese) virtually all foreign elements, the Chinese reshaped Buddhism in their own image, creating a variety of schools, most of which were deeply affected by Daoist principles.

From China, Buddhist ideas were introduced into Korea by the fourth century, into Japan in the sixth, and later into Tibet, Mongolia, and northern regions of Southeast Asia. Meanwhile, perhaps because Hinduism in all its diversity was proving able to meet so many different religious needs, Buddhism was in decline in India by the seventh century. Between the twelfth and fourteenth centuries zealous Muslim warriors administered the final blow to Buddhist monasticism, and Buddhism essentially disappeared in India, save for a few scattered remnants, largely in the northeast.

The Bodhisattva: A Suffering Savior
▼▼▼

50 ▼ Shantideva, *A COMPENDIUM OF DOCTRINE*

The seventh-century Indian poet-philosopher Shantideva compiled excerpts from over a hundred Mahayana works, many of which would otherwise be lost to us, to create a summary of that sect's basic doctrines. One essential theme of his compendium was the superiority of the selfless bodhisattva over the Theravadan monk. The following passages describe a bodhisattva's attributes.

QUESTIONS FOR ANALYSIS

1. What are the consequences of human sin?
2. Why does the bodhisattva assume the burden of the sins of the world?

3. What are the consequences of the bodhisattva's assumptions of this burden?
4. Siddhartha Gautama apparently rejected the notions of rebirth and personal salvation since he denied the existence of a soul, or real "Self." How does Mahayana belief differ from the Buddha's teaching?
5. Compare the bodhisattva with Second Isaiah's Suffering Servant (Chapter 3, source 23). What are their similarities? Their differences? Which are more significant, the similarities or the differences? What do you conclude from these answers?

The bodhisattva is lonely, with no . . . companion, and he puts on the armor of supreme wisdom. He acts himself, and leaves nothing to others, working with a will steeled with courage and strength. He is strong in his own strength . . . and he resolves thus:

"Whatever all beings should obtain, I will help them to obtain. . . . The virtue of generosity is not my helper — I am the helper of generosity. Nor do the virtues of morality, patience, courage, meditation and wisdom help me — it is I who help them. The perfections of the bodhisattva do not support me — it is I who support them. . . . I alone . . . must subdue Mara,[1] with all his hosts and chariots, and develop supreme enlightenment with the wisdom of instantaneous insight! . . .

"All creatures are in pain," he resolves, "all suffer from bad and hindering karma[2] . . . so that they cannot see the Buddhas or hear the Law of Righteousness. . . . All that mass of pain and evil karma I take in my own body. . . . I take upon myself the burden of sorrow; I resolve to do so; I endure it all. I do not turn back or run away, I do not tremble . . . I am not afraid . . . nor do I despair. Assuredly I must bear the burdens of all beings . . . for I have resolved to save them all. I must set them all free, I must save the whole world from the forest of birth, old age, disease, and rebirth, from misfortune and sin, from the round of birth and death, ... For all beings are caught in the net of craving, encompassed by ignorance, held by the desire for existence; they are doomed to destruction, shut in a cage of pain . . . they are ignorant, untrustworthy, full of doubts, always at loggerheads one with another, always prone to see evil; they cannot find a refuge in the ocean of existence; they are all on the edge of the gulf of destruction.

"I work to establish the kingdom of perfect wisdom for all beings. I care not at all for my own deliverance. I must save all beings from the torrent of rebirth with the raft of my omniscient mind. I must pull them back from the great precipice. I must free them from all misfortune, ferry them over the stream of rebirth.

"For I have taken upon myself, by my own will, the whole of the pain of all things living. Thus I dare try every abode of pain, in . . . every part of the universe, for I must not defraud the world of the root of good. I resolve to dwell in each state of misfortune through countless ages . . . for the salvation of all beings . . . for it is better that I alone suffer than that all beings sink to the worlds of misfortune. There I shall give myself into bondage, to redeem all the world from the forest of purgatory,[3] from rebirth as beasts, from the realm of death. I shall bear all grief and pain in my own body, for the good of all things living. I venture to stand surety for all beings, speaking

[1]The lord of the realm of sense; the Tempter, or Evil One.
[2]The fruit of actions performed in a previous life. See Chapter 3, source 18.

[3]A world where souls suffer in order to be purged of evil karma acquired in previous lives.

the truth, trustworthy, not breaking my word. I shall not forsake them. . . . I must so bring to fruition the root of goodness that all beings find the utmost joy, unheard of joy, the joy of omniscience. I must be their charioteer. I must be their leader, I must be their torchbearer. I must be their guide to safety. . . . I must not wait for the help of another, nor must I lose my resolution and leave my tasks to another. I must not turn back in my efforts to save all beings nor cease to use my merit[4] for the destruction of all pain. And I must not be satisfied with small successes."

Buddhism in Tang China: A Conflict of Values
▼▼▼

51 ▼ Han Yu, MEMORIAL ON BUDDHISM

Chinese Buddhism reached its high point of popularity and influence during the initial stages of the Tang Dynasty (618–907), an age of renewed imperial unity and prosperity. Buddhist monasteries and sects proliferated, and the early Tang imperial court often patronized Buddhism in one form or another. However, because so many aspects of Buddhism were at variance with the traditional culture of China, especially Confucian values, conflict was inevitable.

One of the leaders in the Confucian counterattack on Buddhism was the classical prose stylist and poet Han Yu (768–824), who in 819 composed a vitriolic polemic attacking Buddhism. The emperor was so enraged that initially he wanted to execute the author, but eventually he contented himself with banishing this impudent civil servant to a frontier outpost.

Later Confucians considered Han Yu a pioneer of a Confucian intellectual revival that culminated in the eleventh and twelfth centuries with the rise of Neo-Confucianism, a movement that wedded metaphysical speculation (concern with matters that transcend the senses) to traditional Confucian practicality. In so doing, the Neo-Confucians offered a metaphysical alternative to the other-worldliness of Daoism and Buddhism and undercut them severely. More immediately, Han Yu's essay foreshadowed by only a generation a nativist reaction against "foreign" religions.

A champion of rationalism, Han Yu wished to suppress Daoism as well as Buddhism, yet ironically it was due to Daoist influence that Emperor Wuzong initiated a policy of state suppression of a number of foreign religious establishments between 841 and 845. Buddhist monasteries were hard hit by these events, and Chinese Buddhism consequently suffered a major reversal of fortune. Buddhism still remained strong at the popular level, where it increasingly merged with folk magic and other forms of religious Daoism, but from the mid-

---

[4]The infinite merit which the bodhisattva has earned in numerous lives and which is sufficient to save all humanity.

ninth century on it declined rapidly as a powerful rival to Confucianism for the allegiance of China's ruling class.

Han Yu's *Memorial to Buddhism*, which he composed in protest over the emperor's devotion to a relic of the Buddha's finger bone, reveals why so many Chinese ultimately found Buddhism unacceptable.

QUESTIONS FOR ANALYSIS

1. How does Han Yu imply that those emperors who have espoused Buddhism have lost the Mandate of Heaven (Chapter 1, source 6)?
2. How does he imply that this religion is not Chinese?
3. What aspect of Buddhism most repels Han Yu?
4. In Han Yu's mind, what are the social and political dangers of Buddhism?
5. Keeping in mind the Chinese cult of ancestors, why would a Confucian find the practice of venerating the Buddha's finger bone especially disgusting?

Your servant submits that Buddhism is but one of the practices of barbarians which has filtered into China since the Later Han. In ancient times there was no such thing. . . . In those times the empire was at peace, and the people, contented and happy, lived out their full complement of years. . . . The Buddhist doctrine had still not reached China, so this could not have been the result of serving the Buddha.

The Buddhist doctrine first appeared in the time of the Emperor Ming[1] of the Han Dynasty, and the Emperor Ming was a scant eighteen years on the throne. Afterwards followed a succession of disorders and revolutions, when dynasties did not long endure. From the time of the dynasties Song, Qi, Liang, Chen, and Wei,[2] as they grew more zealous in the service of the Buddha, the reigns of kings became shorter. There was only the Emperor Wu of the Liang who was on the throne for forty-eight years. First and last, he thrice abandoned the world and dedicated himself to the service of the Buddha. He refused to use animals in the

sacrifices in his own ancestral temple. His single meal a day was limited to fruits and vegetables. In the end he was driven out and died of hunger. His dynasty likewise came to an untimely end. In serving the Buddha he was seeking good fortune, but the disaster that overtook him was only the greater. Viewed in the light of this, it is obvious that the Buddha is not worth serving.

When Gaozu[3] first succeeded to the throne of the Sui,[4] he planned to do away with Buddhism, but his ministers and advisors were short-sighted men incapable of any real understanding of the Way of the Former Kings, or of what is fitting for past and present; they were unable to apply the Emperor's ideas so as to remedy this evil, and the matter subsequently came to naught — many the times your servant has regretted it. I venture to consider that Your Imperial Majesty, shrewd and wise in peace and war, with divine wisdom and heroic courage, is without an equal through the centuries. When first you came to the throne, you would not per-

---

[1]Han Mingdi (r. A.D. 57–75).
[2]Five fairly short-lived dynasties of the troubled fourth through sixth centuries.
[3]Literally, "high (or great) ancestor," an honorific title

bestowed posthumously on several Chinese emperors (see Chapter 5, source 36, note 7). This high ancestor was Li Yuan (r. 618–626), the first Tang emperor.
[4]The Sui Dynasty (581–618) reunited China in 589.

mit laymen to become monks or nuns or Daoist priests,[5] nor would you allow the founding of temples or cloisters. It constantly struck me that the intention of Gaozu was to be fulfilled by Your Majesty. Now even though it has not been possible to put it into effect immediately, it is surely not right to remove all restrictions and turn around and actively encourage them.

Now I hear that by Your Majesty's command a troupe of monks went to Fengxiang[6] to get the Buddha-bone, and that you viewed it from a tower as it was carried into the Imperial Palace; also that you have ordered that it be received and honored in all the temples in turn. Although your servant[7] is stupid, he cannot help knowing that Your Majesty is not misled by this Buddha, and that you do not perform these devotions to pray for good luck. But just because the harvest has been good and the people are happy, you are complying with the general desire by putting on for the citizens of the capital this extraordinary spectacle which is nothing more than a sort of theatrical amusement. How could a sublime intelligence like yours consent to believe in this sort of thing?

But the people are stupid and ignorant; they are easily deceived and with difficulty enlightened. If they see Your Majesty behaving in this fashion, they are going to think you serve the Buddha in all sincerity. All will say, "The Emperor is wisest of all, and yet he is a sincere believer. What are we common people that we still should grudge our lives?" Burning heads and searing fingers by the tens and hundreds, throwing away their clothes and scattering their money, from morning to night emulating one another and fearing only to be last, old and young rush about, abandoning their work and place; and if restrictions are not immediately imposed, they will increasingly make the rounds of temples and some will inevitably

cut off their arms and slice their flesh in the way of offerings. Thus to violate decency and draw the ridicule of the whole world is no light matter.

Now the Buddha was of barbarian origin. His language differed from Chinese speech; his clothes were of a different cut; his mouth did not pronounce the prescribed words of the Former Kings, his body was not clad in the garments prescribed by the Former Kings. He did not recognize the relationship between prince and subject, nor the sentiments of father and son. Let us suppose him to be living today, and that he come to court at the capital as an emissary of his country. Your Majesty would receive him courteously. But only one interview in the audience chamber, one banquet in his honor, one gift of clothing, and he would be escorted under guard to the border that he might not mislead the masses.

How much the less, now that he has long been dead, is it fitting that his decayed and rotten bone, his ill-omened and filthy remains, should be allowed to enter in the forbidden precincts of the Palace? Confucius said, "Respect ghosts and spirits, but keep away from them."[8] The feudal lords of ancient times, when they went to pay a visit of condolence in their states, made it their practice to have exorcists go before with rush-brooms and peachwood branches to dispel unlucky influences. Only after such precautions did they make their visit of condolence. Now without reason you have taken up an unclean thing and examined it in person when no exorcist had gone before, when neither rush-broom nor peachwood branch had been employed. But your ministers did not speak of the wrong nor did the censors call attention to the impropriety; I am in truth ashamed of them. I pray that Your Majesty will turn this bone over to the officials that it may be cast into

---

[5]By the second century A.D. a polytheistic Daoist Church, which practiced congregational worship, preached immortality, and used drugs and magic, had emerged.

[6]A western city.
[7]Han Yu.
[8]From *The Analects*. See Chapter 4, source 25, for similar aphorisms.

water or fire, cutting off for all time the root and so dispelling the suspicions of the empire and preventing the befuddlement of later generations. Thereby men may know in what manner a great sage acts who a million times surpasses ordinary men. Could this be anything but ground for prosperity? Could it be anything but a cause for rejoicing?

If the Buddha has supernatural power and can wreak harm and evil, may any blame or retribution fittingly fall on my person. Heaven be my witness: I will not regret it. Unbearably disturbed and with the utmost sincerity I respectfully present my petition that these things may be known.

Your servant is truly alarmed, truly afraid.

Zen Buddhism in Japan
▼▼▼

52 ▼ Dogen, ON LIFE AND DEATH

Chan (meditation) Buddhism emerged in China during the seventh century as a fusion of Buddhist and Daoist principles. For Chan practitioners, meditation was not an avenue to insight; it *was* insight. Disdaining all learning and logic, Chan masters sought to lead their students to a state in which they suspended all normal forms of reasoning and intuitively grasped the Buddha nature that lies within each person and thing. This Enlightenment, or Awakening, would be a blinding and unexpected flash that could be triggered by any nonrational activity or external stimulus: contemplating a rock or the jolt of a clap of thunder. To prepare their students for this moment of Awakening, Chan masters presented them with puzzles for meditation that had no logical answers. One of the classic conundrums Chan students wrestled with was: "What is the sound of one hand clapping?"

Because Chan monks mostly remained aloof from imperial patronage in the early Tang era, their sect suffered far less than others in the persecutions of the mid-ninth century. By the Song Dynasty (960–1279) Chan was the only Buddhist school in China that still showed intellectual and artistic vitality, and it thus deeply influenced Song art, literature, and philosophy. During the age of Song, Chan Buddhism also took root in Japan because of the efforts of two Japanese masters who had studied in China: Eisei (1141–1215) and Dogen (1200–1253). Characteristically, the Japanese converted this import, which they pronounced *Zen*, into something distinctly Japanese.

Zen's austerity and discipline, as well as its emphasis on intuitive action as opposed to logical thought, appealed to Japan's feudal warrior class, the emerging *samurai*. Many fused Zen philosophy to their military skills, attempting to break down the artificial and "logical" duality between warrior and weapon. For example, a form of archery in which the archer sought to become one with the bow and arrow became part of Zen training. The archer did not consciously aim; instead, the arrow projected itself from the bow into the target. In a similar manner, Zen profoundly influenced all other forms of Japanese culture, especially its sense of beauty and proper ceremony. The tea ceremony becomes a moment of Zen meditation and a potential Awakening, as one intuits how this common herb and the lump of clay are things of serene delicacy and comfort. The Buddha-reality of the beverage and the cup is revealed to the person open to receiving this insight.

One of the pioneers of the tea ceremony was Dogen, who, on a visit to China in 1222, brought with him a potter to study the art of Chinese porcelain. The potter later established a thriving center for the production of tea vessel ceramics in Japan. In the following sermon Dogen talks not about tea but about life and death, important issues to a Zen master, but no more so than the proper preparation and drinking of tea. Here Dogen addresses the issue of how both life and death are equally expressions of Buddha-reality.

QUESTIONS FOR ANALYSIS

1. What does Dogen mean when he states that one should neither renounce nor covet life and death?
2. What does he mean when he states that life and death must be regarded as identical to Nirvana?
3. Is Buddhahood something to be attained in another life? Is it even something to be achieved? What do your answers mean?
4. Reread Laozi in Chapter 4, source 24. Can you find any Daoist elements in Dogen's thought?
5. Why would the Zen approach to life and death be especially attractive to a warrior?
6. Can you see any germs of a code of warrior conduct in this philosophy?
7. Why would Dogen agree with the saying, "Do not anticipate, be"?

'Since there is Buddhahood in both life and death," says Kassan, "neither exists." Jozan says, "Since there is no Buddhahood in life or death, one is not led astray by either." So go the sayings of the enlightened masters, and he who wishes to free himself of the life-and-death bondage must grasp their seemingly contradictory sense.

To seek Buddhahood outside of life and death is to ride north to reach Southern Etsu or face south to glimpse the North Star. Not only are you traveling the wrong way on the road to emancipation, you are increasing the links in your karma-chain. To find release you must begin to regard life and death as identical to nirvana, neither loathing the former nor coveting the latter.

It is fallacious to think that you simply move from birth to death. Birth, from the Buddhist point of view, is a temporary point between the preceding and the succeeding; hence it can be called birthlessness. The same holds for death and deathlessness. In life there is nothing more than life, in death nothing more than death: we are being born and are dying at every moment.

Now, to conduct: in life identify yourself with life, at death with death. Abstain from yielding and craving. Life and death constitute the very being of Buddha. Thus, should you renounce life and death, you will lose; and you can expect no more if you cling to either. You must neither loathe, then, nor covet, neither think nor speak of these things. Forgetting body and mind, by placing them together in Buddha's hands and letting him lead you on, you will without design or effort gain freedom, attain Buddhahood.

There is an easy road to Buddhahood: avoid evil, do nothing about life-and-death, be merciful to all sentient things, respect superiors and sympathize with inferiors, have neither likes nor dislikes, and dismiss idle thoughts and worries. Only then will you become a Buddha.

Chapter 7

▼▼▼

The Growth
of Christianity

Mainstream Jewish thought perceived no meaningful distinction between Church and State, because Judaism's special covenant with God bound it body and soul to the Lord of the universe. Jews therefore believed that, as God's people, they had been given a sanctified homeland. When they were dispossessed of that inheritance and scattered among the Gentiles, they believed it was because of their sins. Should they reform their ways and fully observe their special covenant with God, they would regain sovereign possession of Palestine. By right, this Holy Land and its Chosen People should be ruled strictly according to the laws given them by God through Moses and incorporated in the Torah (the first five books of the Bible).

Not all Jewish sects, however, accepted this interpretation of the Covenant. One such dissident element was a small body of religious Jews who coalesced around a prophet from Nazareth called Jesus (ca 4 B.C.–A.D. 33). The heart of Jesus' message was that the promised messianic Kingdom of God was at hand. The *Messiah,* God's anointed deliverer whose coming the prophets had foretold, was generally expected to be a political and military leader who would reestablish Israel as a free state. Jesus, to the contrary, expanding upon certain themes in the teachings of Second Isaiah, preached that the Messiah would usher in a spiritual age of universal judgment and redemption, whereby God's holy reign would extend to all lands and peoples.

As his ministry developed, Jesus' disciples became convinced he was the Messiah. Although he claimed, "My kingdom is not of this earth," local Roman and Jewish authorities were disquieted by the threat to the establishment that Jesus and his followers seemed to offer, and they conspired successfully to execute him by crucifixion. Jesus' followers believed, however, that he rose from the dead, appeared to a number of his friends, and then ascended to heaven with the promise of returning soon to sit in judgment of all humanity. Believing that his resurrection proved Jesus' divinity, his disciples proceeded to spread the *Gospel* (Good News) of redemption.

At first these disciples preached only to Jews. Within a short time, however, they spread the faith throughout the entire Roman Empire and beyond. Before the first century A.D. was over, Christians (so called because of Jesus' title *Christos*, which is Greek for Messiah, or "the anointed one") had established the faith in every major city of the Roman Empire and had penetrated the Persian Empire, Africa, Arabia, and the west coast of India. In the early fourth century Christianity was adopted as the state religion of the Axumite kingdom of Ethiopia, became the favored religion of the Roman Emperor Constantine I (r. 306–337), and took root among a number of German tribes beyond the northeast frontiers of the Roman Empire. In the seventh century a group of dissident Christians known as *Nestorians* established themselves in western China. This otherworldly faith was conquering a fair portion of the world.

Despite Jesus' claim that the Kingdom of God was a purely spiritual entity, evidence shows that even the earliest Christians were ambivalent when it came to defining their relationship with the world. Some wanted to reach an accommodation with it; others wanted nothing to do with it. Out of this conflict within Christianity several different traditions emerged. One was the Western notion of separation of Church and State, which was still not fully delineated by 1500. Another was the Eastern Christian tradition that the Church is a community of all God's people, an indivisible entity ruled jointly by priests and lay officials, all of whom are subject to the Orthodox (right-believing) Emperor.

Between 330 and 1453 the Eastern branch of Christianity was centered on imperial Constantinople. The Western Church's center of gravity was Rome, which from about A.D. 400 onward increasingly evolved into the spiritual capital of Europe. Despite growing differences, particularly in their visions of how to govern the Church, Eastern and Western Christians agreed on most basic doctrinal issues. They also shared the belief, inherited from their common Judaic origin, that they were God's Chosen People who had a divine mission to battle the forces of unbelief and evil and to win over the world for Christ. Each branch of Christendom was active in spreading the faith and otherwise acting to help accomplish its understanding of the Divine Plan for humanity.

▼▼▼

The Early Centuries

Christianity's first five hundred years were filled with challenges and changes. First, and most basic, was the ministry of Jesus of Nazareth, whose call for spiritual perfection has been the foundation of the Christian faith for almost two thousand years. Following Jesus' departure from the world, his followers had to grapple with many still unresolved questions: Who was Jesus? What was his relationship with God and humanity? What was the nature of the community he had left behind? Were they Jews, or something else? Among the many teachers who tried to answer these questions, none was more influential than Paul of Tarsus, who laid down the basic theological framework for this emerging church. The next major developmental period in Christian history was when the Roman Empire adopted Christianity as its own in the fourth century. This new status forced Christians to face, more squarely than ever before, the issue of how they, as both individuals and a church, related to the world.

Never was there unanimity on any answer to any of these questions. By the year 500 Christianity was divided into a wide variety of often hostile sects and schools. At the same time, the essential outlines of medieval Christendom's two major traditions — the cultures of Constantinople and Rome — were in place.

Becoming Spiritually Perfect
▼▼▼

53 ▼ THE GOSPEL OF SAINT MATTHEW

Tradition ascribes authorship of the Gospels, the four major accounts of Jesus of Nazareth's life and teachings, to authors known as Matthew, Mark, Luke, and John. The early Christian Church believed that Matthew had been one of Jesus' twelve apostles, or major companions, and accepted his Gospel as authoritative. Modern scholarship dates the work, as we know it, to around A.D. 85, or approximately fifty years after Jesus' ministry. This late date does not preclude authorship by the Apostle Matthew or one of his disciples, because evidence strongly indicates that the Greek version of this Gospel, the only version extant today, is a translation, or even revision, of a long-lost original in Aramaic, the language of Jesus and his companions. The author appears to have been a Palestinian Jewish Christian who had been trained in the rabbinical tradition of Jewish law and scripture and who was writing specifically for other Christian converts from Judaism.

The central theme of the Gospel of Matthew is that Jesus is the Messiah and the fulfillment of the promises made by God through Abraham, Moses, and the prophets. For Matthew, Second Isaiah was the greatest of the prophets, the one who most clearly foretold Jesus' mission of salvation. In the following selection Matthew presents what is commonly known as the Sermon on the Mount. Second Isaiah (Chapter 3, source 23) had preached that the universal reign of the Lord was imminent. Jesus now instructs his followers about what the Kingdom of God requires of all its members. In all likelihood, what Matthew presents here is not a verbatim account of a specific sermon but a distillation of the essence of Jesus' moral and theological teachings.

QUESTIONS FOR ANALYSIS

1. Jesus establishes priorities for his followers. What are they?
2. In what ways does Jesus emphasize the spiritual relationship of each believer to God?
3. How does Jesus regard Judaism and especially the Law of Moses? In what ways does he claim that his teachings complete, or perfect, the Law of Moses?
4. What does Matthew mean when he says that Jesus taught with authority and was not like the scribal teachers of the Law? What is the basis of Jesus' authority?
5. To whom would Jesus' message especially appeal?
6. Compare the message and spirit behind the Sermon on the Mount with that of the Buddha's First Sermon on the Law (Chapter 3, source 20). Which strike you as more pronounced, their differences or similarities? What do you conclude from that?

Seeing the crowds, he went up on the mountain, and when he sat down his disciples came to him. And he opened his mouth and taught them, saying:

"Blessed are the poor in spirit, for theirs is the kingdom of heaven.

"Blessed are those who mourn, for they shall be comforted.

"Blessed are the meek, for they shall inherit the earth.

"Blessed are those who hunger and thirst for righteousness, for they shall be satisfied.

"Blessed are the merciful, for they shall obtain mercy.

"Blessed are the pure in heart, for they shall see God.

"Blessed are the peacemakers, for they shall be called sons of God.

"Blessed are those who are persecuted for righteousness' sake, for theirs is the kingdom of heaven.

"Blessed are you when men revile you and persecute you and utter all kinds of evil against you falsely on my account. Rejoice and be glad, for your reward is great in heaven, for so men persecuted the prophets who were before you. . . .

"Think not that I have come to abolish the law and the prophets; I have come not to abolish them but to fulfill them. For truly, I say to you, till heaven and earth pass away, not an iota, not a dot, will pass from the law until all is accomplished. Whoever then relaxes one of the least of these commandments and teaches men so, shall be called least in the kingdom of heaven; but he who does them and teaches them shall be called great in the kingdom of heaven. For I tell you, unless your righteousness exceeds that of the scribes and the Pharisees,[1] you will never enter the kingdom of heaven.

"You have heard that it was said to the men of old, 'You shall not kill; and whoever kills shall be liable to judgment.' But I say to you that every one who is angry with his brother shall be liable to judgment; whoever insults his brother shall be liable to the council,[2] and whoever says, 'You fool!' shall be liable to the hell of fire. So if you are offering your gift at the altar, and there remember that your brother has something against you, leave your gift there before the altar and go; first be reconciled to your brother, and then come and offer your gift. . . . You have heard that it was said, 'An eye for an eye and a tooth for a tooth.' But I say to you, Do not resist one who is evil. But if any one strikes you on the right cheek, turn to him the other also. . . . You have heard that it was said, 'You shall love your neighbor and hate your enemy.' But I say to you, Love your enemies and pray for those who persecute you, so that you may be sons of your Father who is in heaven; for he makes his sun rise on the evil and on the good, and sends rain on the just and on the unjust. For if you love those who love you,

what reward have you? . . . You, therefore, must be perfect, as your heavenly Father is perfect. . . .

"And in praying do not heap up empty phrases as the Gentiles do; for they think that they will be heard for their many words. Do not be like them, for your Father knows what you need before you ask him. Pray then like this:

Our Father who art in heaven,
Hallowed be thy name.
Thy kingdom come,
Thy will be done,
    On earth as it is in heaven.
Give us this day our daily bread;
And forgive us our debts,
    As we also have forgiven our debtors;
And lead us not into temptation,
    But deliver us from evil.

For if you forgive men their trespasses, your heavenly Father also will forgive you; but if you do not forgive men their trespasses, neither will your Father forgive your trespasses. . . .

"Do not lay up for yourselves treasures on earth, where moth and rust consume and where thieves break in and steal, but lay up for yourselves treasures in heaven, where neither moth nor rust consumes and where thieves do not break in and steal. For where your treasure is, there will your heart be also. . . . Therefore do not be anxious, saying, 'What shall we eat?' or 'What shall we drink?' or 'What shall we wear?' For the Gentiles seek all these things; and your heavenly Father knows that you need them all. But seek first his kingdom and his righteousness, and all these things shall be yours as well. . . .

"Judge not, that you be not judged. For with the judgment you pronounce you will be judged, and the measure you give will be the measure you get. . . .

---

[1]Members of a Jewish religious party who stressed that the written Law of Moses and all the nonscriptural traditions of Judaism had to be equally and fully observed.

[2]The Sanhedrin, Judaism's chief religious and judicial body.

"Every one then who hears these words of mine and does them will be like a wise man who built his house upon the rock; and the rain fell, and the floods came, and the winds blew and beat upon that house, but it did not fall, because it had been founded on the rock. And every one who hears these words of mine and does not do them will be like a foolish man who built his house upon the sand; and the rain fell, and the floods came, and the winds blew and beat against that house, and it fell; and great was the fall of it."

And when Jesus finished these sayings, the crowds were astonished at his teaching, for he taught them as one who had authority, and not as their scribes.

The Path to Righteousness
▼▼▼

54 ▼ *Saint Paul, EPISTLE TO THE ROMANS*

Paul (ca 3 B.C.–A.D. 64 or 67), a Hellenized Jew from Tarsus in Asia Minor, has often been called "the second founder of Christianity." His was the leading voice opposing certain conservatives who wished to keep Christianity within the boundaries of Judaism. From roughly A.D. 47 to his death in Rome in either 64 or 67 (ancient authorities differ on the date), Paul was an indefatigable missionary, converting Gentiles and Jews alike throughout the Mediterranean region. Most important of all, Paul transformed Jesus' messianic message into a faith centering on Jesus as Lord and Savior.

Paul developed his distinctive theology in a series of letters, or *epistles,* which he sent to various Christian communities throughout the Greco-Roman world. Although each epistle was addressed to a specific group of Christians and often dealt with local issues, they were revered as authoritative pronouncements of general interest for all believers. As a result, copies were circulated, and in time a number of his letters (as well as some Paul never composed but that were ascribed to him) were incorporated into the body of scriptural books known to Christians as the *New Testament* (the Old Testament being the pre-Christian, or Jewish, portion of the Bible).

Around A.D. 57, probably while residing in Corinth, Greece, Paul planned to establish a mission in Spain and decided to make Rome his base of operations. In preparation, he wrote to the Christians at Rome to inform them of his plans and to instruct them in the faith. The result was the Epistle to the Romans, the most fully articulated expression of Paul's theology of salvation.

QUESTIONS FOR ANALYSIS

1. According to Paul, who was Jesus?
2. This epistle focuses on how one becomes "righteous" in the eyes of God. What role does faith play in putting one right with God? Faith in what or

whom? Can the Law of Moses or any other body of law put one right with God?

3. For Paul, what two virtues, or qualities, must dominate a Christian's life?

4. What do you infer from the evidence about the role of women in the early Church?

5. Like Second Isaiah (Chapter 3, source 23), Paul believes that God has a master plan for all humanity. How does Paul's understanding of that plan differ from that of his sixth-century B.C. predecessor?

6. Compare this epistle with the Sermon on the Mount. Do they agree, disagree, or complement one another?

7. What parallels can you discover between Christian devotion to Jesus, as taught by Paul, and similar contemporary forms of piety and belief in the Hindu and Buddhist traditions? In answering this question, consider the sources in Chapter 6.

8. On what points would Rabbi Moses ben Maimon (Chapter 6, source 49) and Paul agree? Where would they disagree? Which are more pronounced, the areas of agreement or disagreement?

Paul, a servant of Jesus Christ, called to be an apostle,[1] set apart for the gospel of God which he promised beforehand through his prophets in the holy scriptures, the gospel concerning his Son, who was descended from David[2] according to the flesh and designated Son of God in power according to the Spirit of holiness by his resurrection from the dead, Jesus Christ our Lord, through whom we have received grace and apostleship to bring about obedience to the faith for the sake of his name among all the nations, including yourselves who are called to belong to Jesus Christ;

To all God's beloved in Rome, who are called to be saints: . . . I am eager to preach the gospel to you also who are in Rome.

For I am not ashamed of the gospel: it is the power of God for salvation to every one who has faith, to the Jew first and also to the Greek.[3] For in it the righteousness of God is revealed through faith for faith; as it is written, "He who through faith is righteous shall live." . . . For we hold that a man is justified[4] by faith apart from works of law.[5] Or is God the God of Jews only? Is he not the God of Gentiles also? Yes, of Gentiles also, since God is one; and he will justify the circumcised[6] on the ground of their faith and the uncircumcised because of their faith. . . . The promise to Abraham[7] and his descendants, that they should inherit the world, did not come through the law but through the righteousness of faith. If it is the

---

[1]Paul was not one of the original twelve apostles, Jesus' closest companions. He claimed apostolic status because he believed he had been miraculously called and converted by the Risen Christ, who appeared to him in a vision.

[2]The prophetic tradition maintained that the Messiah would be descended from the line of King David, Israel's greatest monarch, who flourished around 1000 B.C. Consequently, Christian Jews stressed Jesus' Davidic lineage.

[3]*Greek* here means any non-Jew, or Gentile, because Greek was the common tongue of educated people in the eastern half of the Roman Empire.

[4]Made "just," or righteous, in the eyes of God.

[5]The Law, or Torah, of Judaism.

[6]The Law of Moses prescribes circumcision for all Jewish males; Gentiles are, therefore, the "uncircumcised."

[7]The "father" of the Jews. See Chapter 6, source 49.

adherents of the law who are to be the heirs, faith is null and the promise is void. . . . That is why it depends on faith, in order that the promise may rest on grace and be guaranteed to all his descendants — not only to the adherents of the law but also to those who share the faith of Abraham, for he is the father of us all, as it is written, "I have made you the father of many nations.". . .

Therefore, since we are justified by faith, we have peace with God through our Lord Jesus Christ. Through him we have obtained access to this grace in which we stand, and we rejoice in our hope of sharing the glory of God. . . . God shows his love for us in that while we were yet sinners Christ died for us. Since, therefore, we are now justified by his blood, much more shall we be saved by him from the wrath of God. For if while we were enemies we were reconciled to God by the death of his Son, much more, now that we are reconciled, shall we be saved by his life. . . . There is therefore now no condemnation for those who are in Christ Jesus. For the law of the Spirit of life in Christ Jesus has set me free from the law of sin and death. . . .

If you confess with your lips that Jesus is Lord and believe in your heart that God raised him from the dead, you will be saved. For man believes with his heart and so is justified, and he confesses with his lips and so is saved. The scripture says, "No one who believes in him will be put to shame." For there is no distinction between Jew and Greek; the same Lord is Lord of all and bestows his riches upon all who call upon him. For, "every one who calls upon the name of the Lord will be saved.". . .

I appeal to you therefore, brethren, by the mercies of God, to present your bodies as a living sacrifice, holy and acceptable to God, which is your spiritual worship. . . . Let love be genuine; hate what is evil, hold fast to what is good; love one another with brotherly affection; outdo one another in showing honor. Never flag in zeal, be aglow with the Spirit, serve the Lord. Rejoice in your hope, be patient in tribulation, be constant in prayer. Contribute to the needs of the saints, practice hospitality.

Bless those who persecute you; bless and do not curse them. Rejoice with those who rejoice, weep with those who weep. Live in harmony with one another; do not be haughty, but associate with the lowly; never be conceited. Repay no one evil for evil, but take thought for what is noble in the sight of all. If possible, so far as it depends upon you, live peaceably with all. Beloved, never avenge yourselves, but leave it to the wrath of God; for it is written, "Vengeance is mine, I will repay, says the Lord." No, "if your enemy is hungry, feed him; if he is thirsty, give him drink; for by so doing you will heap burning coals upon his head." Do not be overcome by evil, but overcome evil with good. . . .

Owe no one anything, except to love one another; for he who loves his neighbor has fulfilled the law. The commandments, "You shall not commit adultery, You shall not kill, You shall not steal, You shall not covet," and any other commandment, are summed up in this sentence, "You shall love your neighbor as yourself." Love does no wrong to a neighbor; therefore love is the fulfilling of the law. . . .

I commend to you to our sister Phoebe, a deaconess of the church at Cenchreae,[8] that you may receive her in the Lord as befits the saints, and help her in whatever she may require from you, for she has been a helper of many and of myself as well.

Greet Prisca and Aquila,[9] my fellow workers in Christ Jesus, who risked their necks for my life, to whom not only I but also all the churches of the Gentiles give thanks; greet also the church in their house.

---

[8]A community in the Greek Peloponnesus. Deaconesses and deacons were assistants to the presbyters, or elders. Their duties consisted of baptizing, preaching, and dispensing charity.

[9]A married couple of Jewish Christians from Asia Minor who figured prominently in the Church of Rome. Priscilla was the wife, Aquila the husband.

The New Christian Imperial Order
▼▼▼

55 ▼ *THE THEODOSIAN CODE*

Paul eventually arrived at Rome, where he was martyred for his faith around A.D. 64 or 67. For the next two-and-a-half centuries Roman authorities treated Christianity as an illegal religion. While persecutions were sporadic and localized until the middle of the third century, Christians lived and worshiped under a cloud and were often convenient scapegoats when crops failed or other disasters occurred. Life became increasingly precarious for Christians in the face of the empire-wide crises of the third century, and between 303 and 311 the Church was rocked by a major assault known as the Great Persecution.

After 305 this persecution was largely confined to the eastern half of an empire that was now officially divided between two co-emperors. In the West a general named Constantine claimed the imperial crown in 306 and by 312 had secured control over the western half of the empire. In 313 Emperor Constantine (r. 306–337) and his eastern colleague granted freedom of worship to all people in the empire, Christians included. In the years that followed, Constantine became an increasingly enthusiastic patron of Christianity, especially from 324 onward when he assumed control of the entire empire. In 330 he dedicated a new imperial capital, Constantinople, which was to serve as the center for the new imperial Christian order.

All Roman emperors from Constantine onward were baptized Christians, and most were generous patrons of the Church. Only one of them, Emperor Julian the Apostate (r. 361–363), ever turned against the new faith, and his attempts to return the empire to its pre-Christian ways proved totally futile. It was almost an anticlimax when Emperor Theodosius I (r. 379–395) and his two co-emperors declared Catholic Christianity to be the imperial state religion in 380.

The following documents are from *The Theodosian Code*, a collection of late imperial law gathered and published under the direction of Emperor Theodosius II (r. 408–450) in 438. They provide us with a panorama of the first century of imperial Christianity.

QUESTIONS FOR ANALYSIS

1. According to the edicts of February 380 and May 391, what is the status of heretical Christians, those who do not accept the *orthodox* (correctly taught) form of Christianity?
2. What do you think distinguished a *heretic* from an orthodox Catholic Christian in this imperial Church? What policies did the empire adopt in regard to heretics?
3. Compare the legal status of Jews, pagans, and heretics by the end of the fourth century. Which of these groups was tolerated? Can you hazard a guess as to why? How would you characterize this toleration? Which group

was perceived as the greatest threat to the faith and imperial authority? Why? How was it treated?

4. How did the Christian emperors treat the Christian clergy? Can you think of any reasons for this policy?

5. Compare Asoka's edicts in favor of the Law of Righteousness (Chapter 5, source 37) with these laws. Which seem to you to be more significant, the similarities or the differences, and what do those similarities and differences tell us about these two societies?

THE IMPERIAL CHURCH

[February 28, 380]

Edict to the people of the Constantinopolitan city.

All peoples, whom the moderation of our Clemency rules, we wish to be engaged in that religion, which the divine Peter,[1] the apostle, is declared — by the religion which has descended even to the present from him — to have transmitted to the Romans and which, it is clear the pontiff Damasus[2] and Peter,[3] bishop of Alexandria, a man of apostolic sanctity, follow: this is, that according to apostolic discipline[4] and evangelic doctrine[5] we should believe the sole Deity of the Father and of the Son and of the Holy Spirit under an equal Majesty[6] and under a pious Trinity.

We order those following this law to assume the name of Catholic[7] Christians, but the rest, since we judge them demented and insane, to sustain the infamy of heretical[8] dogma and their conventicles[9] not to take the name of churches, to be smitten first by divine vengeance, then also by the punishment of our authority, which we have claimed in accordance with the celestial will.

HERETICS

[May 11, 391]

Those who shall have betrayed the holy faith and shall have profaned holy baptism[10] should be segregated from all persons' association, should be debarred from testifying,[11] should not have . . . [the right of] making a will, should succeed to no one in an inheritance, should be written by no one as heirs.

And these also we should have commanded to be banished to a distance and to be removed rather far away, if it had not seemed to be a

---

[1]Saint Peter the apostle (d. ca A.D. 64).

[2]Damasus I, bishop of Rome (r. 366–384). By the end of the first century A.D. the office of bishop had evolved from that of the earlier presbyter, and each bishop ruled over the Christian community of a particular city and its suburbs. See the introductions to sources 58 and 59 for an explanation of the claims of the bishops of Rome.

[3]Peter II (r. 373–381). The bishop, or patriarch, of Alexandria was one of the most honored leaders in the Church by virtue of the importance of Alexandria as an imperial city. Like the bishop of Rome, he claimed the title of *papa* (father), or pope.

[4]According to the practices of the apostles.

[5]According to the faith as revealed in the Gospels.

[6]Here Theodosius I and his co-emperors reject the teaching of the Arian branch of Christianity, which taught that the Son, the Second Person of the Divine Trinity, was God only by adoption and was not, therefore, equal in majesty or nature to God the Father. The majority of

the Church accepted an explanation of the doctrine of the Holy Trinity which recognizes three separate, totally equal, and coeternal divine persons in a single, indivisible God: God the Father, the Creator; God the Son (Jesus), the Redeemer; and God the Holy Spirit, the Sanctifier.

[7]*Catholic* means universal. Here it means the Church of the entire empire.

[8]*Heresy* here means wrong Christian belief, or dogma: for example, the Arians.

[9]Secret religious meeting places.

[10]It is not clear whether this condemnation extended to all heretics, who profaned their baptism (the rite through which they were initiated into the Church) by their heresy, or only those heretics who insisted on re-baptizing people who had previously been baptized as orthodox, or Catholic, Christians.

[11]In a court of law.

greater penalty for them to dwell among men and to lack men's approbation.

But they never shall return to their previous status, the shame of their conduct shall not be obliterated by penitence and shall not be concealed by any shade of elaborate defense or protection, since things which are fabricated and fashioned cannot protect indeed those who have polluted the faith which they had vowed to God and who, betraying the divine mystery,[12] have turned to profanations. And indeed for the lapsed[13] and the errant[14] there is help, but for the lost — that is, the profaners of holy baptism — there is no aid through any remedy of penitence, which is wont to be available for other crimes.

[May 19, 391]

We order the heretics' polluted contagions to be driven from cities, to be ejected from villages, and the communities not at all to be available for any meetings, lest in any place a sacrilegious company of such persons should be collected. Neither public meeting places to their perversity nor more hidden retreats to their errors should be granted.

PAGANS

[August 7, 395]

We ordain that none may have the liberty of approaching any shrine or temple whatever or of performing abominable sacrifices at any place or time whatever.

JEWS

[May 29, 408]

Governors of provinces should forbid Jews, in a certain ceremony of their festival Aman[15] for re-

membrance of a former punishment, to ignite and to burn for contempt of the Christian faith with sacrilegious mind a simulated appearance of the Holy Cross[16] lest they should connect our faith's sign with their sports; but they should retain their rites without contempt of the Christian law,[17] because without doubt they shall lose privileges previously permitted to them, unless they shall have abstained from illicit acts.

[August 6, 412 or 418]

No one, on the ground that he is a Jew, when he is innocent, should be condemned nor any religion whatsoever should cause a person to be exposed to abuse.

Their synagogues or habitations should not be burned indiscriminately or should not be damaged wrongfully without any reason, since, moreover, even if anyone should be implicated in crimes, yet the vigor of the law-courts and the protection of the public law appear to have been established in our midst, lest anyone should have the power to venture on vengeance for himself.

But as we desire this to be provided for the persons of the Jews, so we decree also that the following warning ought to be made: that Jews perchance should not become insolent and, elated by their own security, should not commit anything rash against reverence for the Christian worship.

THE CLERGY

[June 23, 318]

Pursuant to his own duty a judge shall be bound to observe that, if there should be an appeal to an episcopal court,[18] silence should be applied[19] and that, if anyone shall have wished

---

[12]The sacrament of baptism. See Chapter 5, source 41 for an interesting comparison.
[13]Those who no longer practice the faith but are not heretics.
[14]Non-Christians.
[15]The feast of Purim, which commemorates the deliverance of Persian Jews from the evil designs of Haman, a fifth-century B.C. Persian official.

[16]Haman was hanged for his machinations. In celebrating the feast, Jews burned an effigy of Haman suspended from a gallows that vaguely resembled a cross.
[17]The Christian religion.
[18]A bishop's court.
[19]The civil judge cannot object.

to transfer a matter to the Christian law and to observe that sort of court, he should be heard, even if the matter has been begun before the judge. . . .

[*October 21, 319*]

Whoever devote to divine worship the services of religion, that is, those who are called cler-

gymen, should be excused entirely from all public services, lest through certain persons' sacrilegious malice they should be diverted from divine services.

The Origins of Christian Monasticism
▼▼▼

56 ▼ *Saint Ephraem of Edessa,*
THE LIFE OF SAINT MARY THE HARLOT

During the fourth and fifth centuries many pious men and women sought escape from the new Christian imperial order and what they perceived to be a corrupt and decaying society by going into the wastelands of Egypt, Syria-Palestine, and Anatolia. These desert elders included such colorful and unconventional characters as Abbot John the Dwarf, Abbot Moses the Black, and Mary the Harlot, the heroine of this story. Despite their many differences, they shared a number of characteristics. Chief among these was a desire to live the spirit of the Gospels in a totally uncompromising manner.

This flight to the desert became the foundation of Christian monasticism. The first desert elders were usually hermits (also known as *anchorites*), who elected to live solitary lives in their desert refuges. The desert oases could support only a limited number of hermitages, however, and in time many former hermits chose to join together in communities. Those who elected to live communally were known as *cenobites*. By the end of the sixth century, cenobitic communities had become the Christian monastic norm, but they never totally displaced hermits. Moreover, the lives and legends of the first desert hermits continued to inspire Christian monasticism through the ages. Whether anchorite or cenobite, Christian monks of every variety have universally claimed that their ways of life continue the tradition of the flight to the desert.

Our source comes from the pen of a Syrian anchorite and scholar, Saint Ephraem of Edessa (d. 373), a friend of the monk Abraham who figures so prominently in this tale. Ephraem, much like Abraham, preferred the solitude of his monastic cell to the bustle of the world. Late in his life, however, he left his monastic isolation in order to found and preside over a hospital that cared for the victims of a plague that was devastating the region around Edessa, a site in the southeastern region of modern Turkey. When the plague passed, he returned to his hermitage.

The story that Ephraem tells revolves around two well-known fourth-century holy people, Abraham and his niece Mary. Upon being orphaned, Mary joined her paternal uncle as an anchorite. After twenty years of monastic austerity, Mary was seduced by a monk who visited her uncle under the pretense of seeking religious instruction. In her horror and shame, she fled the hermitage and joined a brothel in a distant city. After several years had passed, Abraham had a vision of his niece's location and left his cell in disguise to rescue her. The rest of the tale illustrates why these eccentric holy people, who were a small percentage of the population, became folk heroes of such magnitude that they, more than any other single group, were responsible for turning Christianity into a mass religion.

QUESTIONS FOR ANALYSIS

1. When reminded of her former monastic life, Mary suddenly realizes how lonely she is, even though she has left her hermitage for a city. What is Ephraem's message?
2. How, if at all, does this story reflect the message of the Sermon on the Mount?
3. In his Epistle to the Romans (source 54) Paul writes of the primacy of love over all other religious obligations. In what ways do Abraham's actions during his rescue of Mary illustrate this principle?
4. The desert hermits have often been characterized as self-centered dropouts. Judging from this story, is that how their society perceived them? How did it perceive them?
5. The pre-Christian Greco-Roman world had tended to think and worship in terms of holy places, such as temples and natural sites sacred to various deities. During the fourth and fifth centuries, Christian holy people, who, it was believed, possessed special religious powers, began replacing "holy spaces" as the new focal point of people's religious imagination. How does this story illustrate that development?
6. Compare Abraham's treatment of Mary with the Buddha's treatment of his aunt (Chapter 3, source 21). Which strike you as more pronounced, the parallels or the differences? What do you conclude from your answer?

Abraham went forth to battle the Evil One and, once he had defeated him, to achieve the greater victory of bringing his niece home again. When he arrived at the city, he entered the tavern where she worked as a prostitute and anxiously looked around, glancing this way and that way, hoping to see her. Time went by, and he still had not caught sight of her. Finally he addressed the innkeeper in a joking manner: "They tell me, my friend," he said, "that you have an excellent 'working girl' here. If it is all right with you, I would like to have a look at her."

The innkeeper . . . replied that everything he had heard was true. She was unusually beautiful. . . . The old man asked her name and was told they called her Mary. Beaming merrily, he then said: "Come on, bring her in and show her to me, and let me buy her a fine dinner, for I have heard her praises sung everywhere." So they called her. When she came in and the holy old man saw her in her prostitute's clothes, his entire body came close to collapsing in grief. However he hid his heartache behind the facade of a cheerful face, and heroically held back the tears that welled up in his eyes, lest the young woman recognize him and flee.

As they sat down and drank their wine, this magnificent old man began to joke around with her. She rose, put her arms around his neck, and teased him with kisses. As she was kissing him, she smelled the fragrant austerity that his lean body exuded, and she thought back to the days when she had lived as an ascetic. Struck as though a spear had pierced her soul, she began to weep. Unable to bear the pain in her heart, she cried out: "Ah, the pain at being alone and unhappy."

The innkeeper was amazed and asked: "What is troubling you, Mary, that suddenly you burst out into this sorrowful lament? You have been here two years to the day, and no one in that time ever heard a sigh or sad word from you. I have no idea of what has overcome you."

The young woman replied: "I would have been happy had I died three years ago.". . .

The holy old man then produced the gold coin he had brought with him and gave it to the innkeeper, saying: "Now, friend, make us a good dinner, so that I can have some fun with the young woman. I have come a long distance in my love for her." O divine-like wisdom! O wise understanding of the spirit! O remarkable discretion for the sake of salvation! During fifty years of abstinence he had never tasted bread; now without hesitation he eats meat to save a lost soul. . . . Marvel at such madness, such a reversal of form, when an upright, wise, discreet, and prudent man becomes a reckless fool in order to snatch a soul from the jaws of the lion, and set free a captive. . . .

Once they had feasted, the young woman began to tease him to come to her room to lie with her. "Let us go," he said. Entering the room, he saw a high bed prepared for them and immediately he sat on it in a light-hearted manner.

What should I call you, O perfect athlete of Christ?[1] I really do not know. Should I say you are continent or incontinent, wise or foolish, discreet or reckless? During the fifty years of your monastic profession you have slept on a straw mat. How is it that you can so indifferently climb onto such a bed? The long journey with its many stops along the way, your eating meat and drinking wine, your entering a brothel — you have done all of this in order to praise and glorify Christ by saving a soul. On our part, if we have to say one useful word to a neighbor, we are upset by the prospect of the task. . . .

"Come close to me, Mary," said the old man. When she was next to him, he took her by the hand, as though to kiss her. Then taking off his hat, and with a voice cracking with tears, he said: "Mary, my daughter, do you not know me? My heart, was I not the one who raised you? . . . Who was it who destroyed you? Where is that angelic garb you used to wear?[2] Where is your chastity? Your tears? Your vigils? Your bed on the ground? My daughter, how did you fall from the height of heaven into this pit? Why, when you lapsed into sin, did you not tell me? Why did you not come to me then and there? I would have done your penance for you, so also would have my beloved friend Ephraem.[3] Why did you desert me, and bring this intolerable sorrow on me? For who is sinless, except God Himself? . . . Have pity on my old age. Grieve for the burden placed on my white head. I beg you. Get up and come home with me. Do not be afraid. A human is given to slipping, but if one falls down swiftly, one can also rise again swiftly with God's help. God does not desire a sinner's death but, rather, that the sinner is healed and lives."

---

[1] Abraham. Monastic ascetics were often called *athletes*, because they were involved in painful competition (*agonia* in Greek) for spiritual perfection.

[2] Her simple, rough-spun monastic robe.

[3] Probably Ephraem of Edessa.

She replied: "If you are sure that I can do penance and that God will accept my atonement, I will come as you request." . . . And they rose up and went away . . . and so the blessed Abraham, his heart filled with joy, journeyed along the road with his niece.

When they arrived home, he placed her in the inner cell that had previously been his, and he remained in the outer cell.[4] She, clad in a hair shirt, resided there in humility of soul, weeping in her heart and through her eyes, disciplining herself with vigils and the stern burden of abstinence . . . ceaselessly calling on God and bewailing her sin but with a sure hope of pardon. . . . And God the compassionate, who desires that no person perishes but that all come to repentance, so accepted her penance that after three years He restored many

ill people to health through her prayers. Crowds flocked to her, and she would pray to God for their healing, and her prayers were granted.

The blessed Abraham, after living for another ten years in this earthly life, and seeing her blessed repentance, and giving glory to God, rested in peace in his seventieth year. . . . Mary lived another five years, ever more devoutly disciplining her life and persevering night and day in tearful and sorrowful prayer to God, so that many a person passing by that place at night and hearing her grief-filled voice would be turned to weeping and add his tears to hers. When the hour of her sleeping came, in which she was taken from this life, all that saw her gave glory to God for the look of happiness on her face.

▼▼▼

The Medieval Centuries

Western historians often refer to the period from about 500 to 1500 as the *medieval era* (from the Latin *Media Aeva* — the Middle Ages). Although the term is inappropriate for world history and misleading even when applied to Western Europe, there is good reason to view this era as Christianity's Middle Ages. By A.D. 500 Christianity was ready to play a major role in both Byzantium and Western Europe, and the thousand years that followed would be *the* Christian millennium for each. After 1500 the situation was different. The Byzantine world was, for the most part, swallowed up by Islam, while serious challenges to medieval forms of Christian expression and organization arose on several fronts in Western Europe.

One element of Western Europe's medieval Christian civilization that suffered severe diminution after 1500 was the Roman papacy. Between approximately 1050 and 1300, however, the papacy was at the height of its powers, and its aggressive claim to be the moral center of Christendom occasioned several significant shifts in Christian history during this period. Popes quarreled with emperors and kings over their respective powers and areas of authority, and two

[4]Originally she had inhabited the outer cell, or room. Being closer to the world, she had fallen into sin. In his greater solitude, Abraham had been unaware of what was happening to Mary and for several days was not even aware of her flight. He was now going to be her buffer against the world.

major consequences followed from those controversies. A bitter estrangement developed between the Churches of Rome and Constantinople, and that schism has persisted to our own day. Also, certain political thinkers in the West began to articulate the idea that it is necessary for the well-being of society to separate the functions of Church and State. This concept would become a reality and a hallmark of Western civilization centuries later.

Bringing Christianity to the Rus'
▼▼▼

57 ▼ THE RUSSIAN PRIMARY CHRONICLE

During the sixth century the Roman Empire underwent a metamorphosis. The western half was divided into a number of German kingdoms, with circumstances causing it to sever most ties with the old Mediterranean ecumene and to fall back on its own resources.

While the West was in the midst of a painful process of cultural transformation, the East was evolving a new Hellenistic synthesis, which we call *Byzantine* civilization, a term created by modern historians to refer to the Eastern Christian civilization centered at Constantinople, the site of the ancient Greek city of Byzantion. This new civilization resulted from the amalgamation of three key elements: the autocratic structure of the late Roman Empire, Eastern Orthodox Christianity, and the cultural heritage of the Hellenistic past.

In true Hellenistic fashion, the entire Byzantine world revolved around the orthodox emperor, who in theory was answerable to no one on earth. As a Christian, he could not play the part of a god-king, but he was the next best thing: the living image of God on Earth, insofar as his imperial majesty was a pale reflection of the glory of God. As such, the emperor was the link between the Chosen People and their God.

Under the leadership of these emperors, who bore the title "peer of the Apostles," the Eastern Christian Empire defended itself against a number of pagan enemies on its northern frontiers, eventually converting many of them to Byzantine Christianity. The most notable example of Constantinople's successful blending of imperial foreign policy with Christian missionary fervor was its conversion of the Rus' of Kiev, a people of mixed Scandinavian and Slavic origins, beginning in the late tenth century.

The following account, which blends fact and fiction into a charming pastiche, presents the conversion of Prince Vladimir I (r. 978–1015) from a Kievan perspective. Compiled by a single monastic author around 1113 from earlier written sources and oral traditions, *The Russian Primary Chronicle* is the single most important source for the history of the state of Kiev from the mid-ninth to the early twelfth century.

QUESTIONS FOR ANALYSIS

1. **The tale of Prince Vladimir's study of various religions may not be literally true, but what deeper truth does it reveal about why Byzantine Christianity was so attractive to the Rus' and other pagans on the empire's frontiers?**
2. **What did Vladimir gain from his conversion?**
3. **What did the Byzantine Empire gain from Vladimir's conversion?**
4. **This account was composed by a Kievan monk in the early twelfth century. Judging from the tone of the chronicle, how deeply had Byzantine Christianity penetrated Kievan lands in a little more than a century?**

6495 (987).[1] Vladimir summoned together his boyars[2] and the city-elders, and said to them, "Behold, the Bulgars[3] came before me urging me to accept their religion. Then came the Germans and praised their own faith[4]; and after them came the Jews.[5] Finally the Greeks[6] appeared, criticizing all other faiths but commending their own, and they spoke at length, telling the history of the whole world from its beginning. Their words were artful, and it was wondrous to listen and pleasant to hear them. They preach the existence of another world. 'Whoever adopts our religion and then dies shall arise and live forever. But whosoever embraces another faith, shall be consumed with fire in the next world.' What is your opinion on this subject, and what do you answer?" The boyars and the elders replied, "You know, oh Prince, that no man condemns his own possessions, but praises them instead. If you desire to make certain, you have servants at your disposal. Send them to inquire about the ritual of each and how he worships God."

Their counsel pleased the prince and all the people, so that they chose good and wise men to the number of ten, and directed them to go first among the Bulgars and inspect their faith. The emissaries went their way, and when they arrived at their destination they beheld the disgraceful actions of the Bulgars and their worship in the mosque[7]; then they returned to their country. Vladimir then instructed them to go likewise among the Germans, and examine their faith, and finally to visit the Greeks. They thus went into Germany, and after viewing the German ceremonial, they proceeded to Tsar'grad,[8] where they appeared before the Emperor.[9] He inquired on what mission they had come, and they reported to him all that had occurred. When the Emperor heard their words, he rejoiced, and did them great honor on that very day.

On the morrow, the Emperor sent a message to the Patriarch[10] to inform him that a Russian delegation had arrived to examine the Greek faith, and directed him to prepare the church

---

[1]By Byzantine reckoning the world was created in 5508 B.C. Consequently, the year A.D. 987 was the 6495th year since Creation.
[2]Rus' nobles.
[3]The Bulgars of the Volga, a Turkic people who had inhabited the upper Volga since about the fifth century A.D.
[4]Both the Roman papacy and the Western emperors, who also happened to be the kings of Germany, were actively attempting to convert the Rus' of Kiev and Novgorod to Roman Catholic Christianity at this time.
[5]These Jews were the Khazars. See p. 170.
[6]The Byzantines, whose language was Greek.

[7]A Muslim place of communal worship; see Chapter 8. Unlike the Bulgars of the Balkans, who had accepted Christianity, the Volga Bulgars were Muslims.
[8]"The Imperial City" — the Russian term for Constantinople.
[9]Basil II (r. 976–1025), known as "the Bulgar-Slayer."
[10]The patriarch of Constantinople, at this moment Nicholas II (r. 979–991), was the chief bishop of the Byzantine Church. The patriarch was usually an imperial appointee, and his authority should not be equated with that of the pope of Rome.

and the clergy, and to array himself in his sacerdotal robes, so that the Rus' might behold the glory of the God of the Greeks. When the Patriarch received these commands, he bade the clergy assemble, and they performed the customary rites. They burned incense, and the choirs sang hymns. The Emperor accompanied the Rus' to the church, and placed them in a wide space, calling their attention to the beauty of the edifice, the chanting, and the pontifical services and the ministry of the deacons, while he explained to them the worship of his God. The Rus' were astonished, and in their wonder praised the Greek ceremonial. Then the Emperors Basil and Constantine[11] invited the envoys to their presence, and said, "Go hence to your native country," and dismissed them with valuable presents and great honor.

Thus they returned to their own country, and the Prince called together his boyars and the elders. Vladimir then announced the return of the envoys who had been sent out, and suggested that their report be heard. He thus commanded them to speak out before his retinue. The envoys reported, "When we journeyed among the Bulgars, we beheld how they worship in their temple, called a mosque, while they stand ungirt. The Bulgar bows, sits down, looks hither and thither like one possessed, and there is no happiness among them, but instead only sorrow and a dreadful stench. Their religion is not good. Then we went among the Germans, and saw them performing many ceremonies in their temples; but we beheld no glory there. Then we went to Greece, and the Greeks led us to the edifices where they worship their God, and we knew not whether we were in heaven or on earth. For on earth there is no such splendor or such beauty, and we are at a loss how to describe it. We only know that God

dwells there among men, and their service is fairer than the ceremonies of other nations. For we cannot forget that beauty. Every man, after tasting something sweet, is afterward unwilling to accept that which is bitter, and therefore we cannot dwell longer here." Then the boyars spoke and said, "If the Greek faith were evil, it would not have been adopted by your grandmother Olga[12] who was wiser than all other men." Vladimir then inquired where they should all accept baptism, and they replied that the decision rested with him.

After a year had passed, in 6496 (988), Vladimir proceeded with an armed force against Kherson, a Greek city,[13] and the people of Kherson barricaded themselves therein. Vladimir halted at the farther side of the city beside the harbor, a bowshot from the town, and the inhabitants resisted energetically while Vladimir besieged the town. Eventually, however, they became exhausted, and Vladimir warned them that if they did not surrender, he would remain on the spot for three years. When they failed to heed this threat, Vladimir marshalled his troops and ordered the construction of an earthwork in the direction of the city. While this work was under construction, the inhabitants dug a tunnel under the city-wall, stole the heaped-up earth, and carried it into the city, where they piled it up in the center of the town. But the soldiers kept on building, and Vladimir persisted. Then a man of Kherson, Anastasius by name, shot into the Rus' camp an arrow on which he had written, "There are springs behind you to the east, from which water flows in pipes. Dig down and cut them off." When Vladimir received this information, he raised his eyes to heaven and vowed that if this hope was realized, he would be baptized. He gave orders straightway to dig down above

---

[11]The future of Emperor Constantine VIII (r. 1025–1028), Basil II's brother and successor.

[12]Olga, widow of Prince Igor and regent of Kiev from 945 to 964, traveled to Constantinople in 957 where she was baptized a Christian. This act laid the foundation for her grandson's work in introducing Christianity to the Rus'.

[13]Kherson was a Byzantine city located in the Crimea, the peninsula that juts into the northern regions of the Black Sea and the object of fierce competition between the Kievans and the Byzantines.

the pipes, and the water-supply was thus cut off. The inhabitants were accordingly overcome by thirst, and surrendered.

Vladimir and his retinue entered the city, and he sent messages to the Emperors Basil and Constantine, saying, "Behold, I have captured your glorious city. I have also heard that you have an unwedded sister. Unless you give her to me to wife, I shall deal with your own city as I have with Kherson." When the Emperors heard this message they were troubled, and replied, "It is not proper for Christians to give in marriage to pagans. If you are baptized, you shall have her to wife, inherit the kingdom of God, and be our companion in the faith. Unless you do so, however, we cannot give you our sister in marriage." When Vladimir learned their response, he directed the envoys of the Emperors to report to the latter that he was willing to accept baptism, having already given some study to their religion, and that the Greek faith and ritual, as described by the emissaries sent to examine it, had pleased him well. When the Emperors heard this report, they rejoiced, and persuaded their sister Anna to consent to the match. They then requested Vladimir to submit to baptism before they should send their sister to him, but Vladimir desired that the Princess should herself bring priests to baptize him. The Emperors complied with his request, and sent forth their sister, accompanied by some dignitaries and priests. Anna, however, departed with reluctance. "It is as if I were set-

ting out into captivity," she lamented; "better were it for me to die at home." But her brothers protested, "Through your agency God turns the land of Rus' to repentance, and you will relieve Greece from the danger of grievous war. Do you not see how much harm the Rus' have already brought upon the Greeks? If you do not set out, they may bring on us the same misfortunes." It was thus that they overcame her hesitation only with great difficulty. The Princess embarked upon a ship, and after tearfully embracing her kinfolk, she set forth across the sea and arrived at Kherson. The natives came forth to greet her, and conducted her into the city, where they settled her in the palace.

By divine agency, Vladimir was suffering at that moment from a disease of the eyes, and could see nothing, being in great distress. The Princess declared to him that if he desired to be relieved of this disease, he should be baptized with all speed, otherwise it could not be cured. When Vladimir heard her message, he said, "If this proves true, then of a surety is the God of the Christians great," and gave order that he should be baptized. The Bishop of Kherson, together with the Princess's priests, after announcing the tidings, baptized Vladimir, and as the Bishop laid his hand upon him, he straightway received his sight. Upon experiencing this miraculous cure, Vladimir glorified God, saying, "I have now perceived the one true God." When his followers beheld this miracle, many of them were also baptized.

A Byzantine View of Western Christianity
▼▼▼

58 ▾ *Anna Comnena,* THE ALEXIAD

While the city of Rome was losing its political importance during the period from roughly 300 to 600, its spiritual authority was on the rise. The bishop who presided over Rome's Christian community held a unique position in the Church. His bishopric alone could claim the bodies and, therefore, the inherited

powers of Saints Peter and Paul, the Church's two greatest apostles. From the fourth century onward the bishops of Rome increasingly claimed to be the heirs of Saint Peter, whom they believed had received special powers of governance over the Church directly from Jesus. They thus assumed the title *Pope*, or Father (*Papa* in Latin), thereby claiming the right to govern the Church with an authority analogous to the almost absolute power of a traditional Roman paterfamilias, or head of a household. At this time few people were ready to accept or even acknowledge the implications of the claims of the bishops of Rome, but the foundations had been laid for what would become the medieval papacy.

Toward the middle of the eleventh century the Roman papacy had achieved a level of independence, moral authority, and institutional strength whereby it could and did successfully push forward its claims to primacy within the Western Church. These claims, however, failed to impress the Byzantines.

The following document comes from the pen of a Byzantine princess, Anna Comnena (1083–after 1148), daughter of Emperor Alexius I (r. 1081–1118). Anna, who had received an extensive education in classical Greek literature and philosophy, undertook to write the history of her father's eventful reign following the death of her husband in 1137. The fact that she entitled the work *The Alexiad*, in imitation of Homer's epic poem *The Iliad*, clearly indicates the view she held of her father's place in history. Anna's protestations of historical objectivity notwithstanding, this is partisan history, but its very partisanship allows us to see the world through Byzantine eyes.

In the first selection Anna comments on the Investiture Controversy, a half-century-long dispute between the Roman papacy and the Western emperors over the issue of who was the God-appointed head of the Christian people, the pope or the emperor. The second selection deals with the arrival on Byzantine soil in 1096 of the lead elements of the First Crusade, a holy war launched by Pope Urban II (r. 1088–1099), in large part to rescue Eastern Christians, including the Byzantines, from the threat posed by a resurgent Islam.

QUESTIONS FOR ANALYSIS

1. What does Anna think of Pope Gregory VII's actions in the Investiture Controversy?
2. What does she think of the Roman papacy's claims?
3. To her mind, who is the Church's chief priest, and what is the source of his authority?
4. Pope Urban II called for a holy war in the East partly in response to appeals from Alexius I for aid against the Seljuk Turks. What was Anna's view of those Western Christians who had responded to the pope's call?
5. The age of the crusades (1095–1291) witnessed a growing estrangement between the societies of Western Europe and Byzantium. Judging from Anna's account, what do you think contributed to that rift?

Meanwhile, an event occurred which is worth relating, as it, too, contributed to this man's [Emperor Alexius] reputation and good fortune. . . . Now it happened that the Pope of Rome[1] had a difference with Henry, King of Germany,[2] . . . The Pope is a very high dignitary, and is protected by troops of various nationalities. The dispute between the King and the Pope was this: the latter accused Henry of not bestowing livings[3] as free gifts, but selling them for money,[4] and occasionally entrusting archbishoprics to unworthy recipients,[5] and he also brought further charges of a similar nature against him. The King of Germany on his side indicted the Pope of usurpation, as he had seized the apostolic chair without his consent.[6] Moreover, he had the effrontery to utter reckless threats against the Pope, saying that if he did not resign his self-elected office, he should be expelled from it. . . . When these words reached the Pope's ears, he vented his rage upon Henry's ambassadors; first he tortured them inhumanly, then clipped their hair with scissors, and sheared their beards with a razor, and finally committed a most indecent outrage upon them, which transcended even the insolence of barbarians, and so sent them away. My womanly and princely dignity forbids my naming

the outrage inflicted on them, for it was not only unworthy a high priest, but of anyone who bears the name of a Christian. I abhor this barbarian's idea, and more still the deed, and I should have defiled both my pen and my paper had I described it explicitly.[7] But as a display of barbaric insolence, and a proof that time in its flow produces men with shameless morals, ripe for any wickedness, this alone will suffice, if I say, that I could not bear to disclose or relate even the tiniest word about what he did. And this was the work of a high priest. Oh, justice! The deed of the supreme high priest! nay, of one who claimed to be the president of the whole world, as indeed the Latins assert and believe, but this, too, is a bit of their boasting. For when the imperial seat was transferred from Rome hither to our native Queen of Cities, and the senate, and the whole administration, there was also transferred the arch-hieratical primacy.[8] And the Emperors from the very beginning have given the supreme right to the episcopacy[9] of Constantinople, and the Council of Chalcedon emphatically raised the Bishop of Constantinople to the highest position, and placed all the dioceses of the inhabited world under his jurisdiction.[10] There can be no doubt that the insult done to the ambassadors was

---

[1]The dispute began in 1075 in the reign of Pope Gregory VII (r. 1073–1085) and continued to 1122 and the pontificate of Calixtus II (r. 1119–1124).
[2]Henry IV (r. 1056–1106). As king of Germany, Henry was also emperor-elect of the Western Roman Empire.
[3]A "living," also known as a *prebend,* was the income a cleric received in order to support him in his clerical office and duties.
[4]The papacy claimed that lay rulers, such as Henry, were guilty of the sin of *simony* — the selling of sacred clerical offices and other holy items.
[5]According to the papal reformers, this was another abuse of the system known as *lay investiture* — the tradition whereby lay (nonclerical) rulers chose and invested church people with their offices. Because the papal reformers attacked this tradition, this half-century-long struggle between the papacy and the German empire is known as the Investiture Controversy.
[6]A charge Henry raised in his letter of 24 January 1076. By tradition, the pope-elect applied for imperial approval of his election.

[7]Anna seems to imply that Gregory had the envoys castrated. There is no credible evidence of his having abused Henry's legates in this manner.
[8]Chief patriarch of the universal Church.
[9]Another term for *bishopric.* A bishop was the chief priest of a city or large town and its surrounding lands. An archbishop was the bishop of a major city and exercised authority over a number of subordinate, or suffragan, bishops. A patriarch was the bishop of such an exceptionally important city that he claimed authority over vast areas and large numbers of subordinate archbishops and bishops. The question was: Who was the chief patriarch of the Church — the bishop of Rome or the bishop of Constantinople?
[10]Wrong. The Council of Chalcedon of 451 stipulated in canon (regulation) 28 that the bishop of Constantinople enjoyed a primacy of honor second only to that of the bishop of Rome because Constantinople was the "New Rome."

aimed at the king who sent them; not only because he scourged them, but also because he
was the first to invent this new kind of outrage.
For by his actions, the Pope suggested, I think,
that the power of the King was despicable, and
by this horrible outrage on his ambassadors that
he, a demi-god, as it were, was treating with a
demi-ass! The Pope consequently, by wreaking
his insolence on the ambassadors, and sending
them back to the King in the state I have mentioned, provoked a very great war.

·   ·   ·

Before he[11] had enjoyed even a short rest, he
heard a report of the approach of innumerable
Frankish[12] armies. Now he dreaded their arrival
for he knew their irresistible manner of attack,
their unstable and mobile character and all the
peculiar natural and concomitant characteristics
which the Frank retains throughout; and he also
knew that they were always agape for money,
and seemed to disregard their truces readily for
any reason that cropped up. For he had always
heard this reported of them, and found it very
true. However, he did not lose heart, but prepared himself in every way so that, when the
occasion called, he would be ready for battle.
And indeed the actual facts were far greater and
more terrible than rumor made them. For the
whole of the West and all the barbarian tribes
which dwell between the further side of the

Adriatic and the pillars of Heracles,[13] had all
migrated in a body and were marching into
Asia through the intervening Europe, and
were making the journey with all their household. . . . And they were all so zealous and
eager that every highroad was full of them.
And those Frankish soldiers were accompanied
by an unarmed host more numerous than the
sand or the stars, carrying palms and crosses
on their shoulders; women and children, too,
came away from their countries.[14] And the
sight of them was like many rivers streaming
from all sides, and they were advancing towards us through Dacia[15] generally with all
their hosts. . . .

The incidents of the barbarians' approach followed in the order I have described, and persons
of intelligence could feel that they were wit-
nessing a strange occurrence. The arrival of
these multitudes did not take place at the same
time nor by the same road (for how indeed
could such masses starting from different places
have crossed the straits of Lombardy all together?) Some first, some next, others after
them and thus successively all accomplished the
transit, and then marched through the continent. Each army was preceded, as we said, by
an unspeakable number of locusts; and all who
saw this more than once recognized them as
forerunners of the Frankish armies.

The Primacy of Rome
▼▼▼

59 ▼ *Pope Boniface VIII, UNAM SANCTAM*

The tradition of imperial governance of the Christian Church, which some historians term *caesaropapism* (a caesar acting as a pope), was not unique to Con-

---

[11]Emperor Alexius.
[12]*Frank* was a term used in the eastern Mediterranean to
refer to any Westerner. See Chapter 9, source 77.
[13]The Strait of Gibraltar.

[14]This was the so-called, and misnamed, Peasants' Crusade of 1096.
[15]Hungary and Romania.

stantinople. When Pope Leo III (r. 795–816) crowned Charlemagne (r. 768–814) emperor on Christmas Day, 800, the West once again had its own "Roman" emperor. Even before he became emperor, Charles controlled the churches within his lands and felt no hesitation in instructing the pope on points of theology. Needless to say, he and his imperial successors continued this tradition after 800.

Between 800 and 1050, the Roman papacy at times acquiesced in and at other times resisted this imperial direction. When popes resisted, they did so on a variety of grounds but chiefly on the basis of their Petrine claim that they alone were the successors of Saint Peter, the Rock of the Church, to whom Christ had committed stewardship over all Christians.

From the age of the Investiture Controversy (source 58) onward, a self-confident papacy took on Western emperors and kings in a series of struggles over the issue of their respective powers and areas of authority. In 1302, in the midst of a nasty conflict of wills between the papacy and King Philip IV of France (r. 1285–1314), Pope Boniface VIII (r. 1294–1303) issued the following bull (an official document of such importance that it had a lead *bulla*, or seal, attached to it) known as *Unam Sanctam*, from its initial two words, "One holy [Church]." Although the pope ultimately lost his contest with King Philip, he was able in this letter to let loose a salvo of claims that some historians interpret as the medieval papacy's most extreme expression of papal supremacy.

As you read this source, keep several points in mind. None of Boniface's claims of papal power was new. Many of these statements were borrowed from the correspondence of Boniface's papal predecessors, especially Pope Innocent III (r. 1198–1216). We should also not be misled into believing that any medieval pope ever exercised such wide powers over Christian Europe as Boniface seemed to claim. In the end, Philip IV prevailed in his struggle with the papacy, and Boniface probably understood when he issued this bull that his political position was precarious.

QUESTIONS FOR ANALYSIS

1. What was Boniface VIII's view of the power wielded by princes and all other secular rulers?
2. What was his view of papal power?
3. Did Boniface believe in the separation of Church and State?
4. What would a Byzantine emperor have thought of *Unam Sanctam*?
5. What do you suppose King Philip IV's reaction was to this papal bull?

One holy, Catholic,[1] and Apostolic Church! This we are bound by faith to believe and hold, and this we firmly believe and simply confess. Moreover, outside this Church there is no sal- vation or remission of sins. . . . Within this Church there is one Lord, one faith, one baptism. At the time of the flood there was one ark, which symbolizes the one Church. It . . .

---

[1]Universal.

had one pilot, Noah, and we read that everything on earth that was outside of the ark was destroyed.[2]

We venerate this Church and it alone. . . . This Church is the seamless garment of the Lord. . . . There is, accordingly, one body and one head of this one and only Church, not two heads as a monster would have.[3] This single head is Christ, and Christ's deputy Peter, and Peter's successor, for the Lord said to Peter: "Feed my sheep."[4] He said, "My sheep" encompassing all, not limiting it to these or those. From this we conclude he committed them all to Peter's care. If the Greeks or any other people claim they were not committed to the care of Peter and his successors, it follows that they admit they are not members of Christ's flock, for the Lord says in the Gospel of John that there is one sheepfold and one shepherd.

We learn from the words of the Gospel that within this Church and within its power are two swords, a spiritual sword and a secular sword. When the apostles said, "Here are two swords,"[5] they referred to the Church, since it was the apostles who spoke. The Lord did not reply that two were too many but were enough. Certainly anyone who denies that the secular sword is in the power of Peter has not paid attention to the Lord's words: "Put your sword back in its sheath."[6] Both, therefore, are under the Church's power, the secular sword and the spiritual sword. One, however, is wielded *for* the Church, the other is wielded *by* the Church. The latter is in the priest's hand; the former is in the hands of kings and soldiers, but it is used

at the will and by the allowance of the priest. One sword ought to be subordinate to the other, just as secular authority is subject to spiritual power. As the Apostle [Paul] says, "There is no power save that which comes from God, and those who are ordained by God."[7] They would not be ordained unless one sword was subordinate to the other and, being inferior, was led by the other to the highest ends. . . . Spiritual power exceeds all secular power in dignity and nobility in direct proportion to the manner in which spiritual matters outweigh worldly concerns. . . . The truth bears witness that spiritual power has to institute secular power and stand in judgment of it if it has not been moral. The prophecy of Jeremiah verifies the nature and power of the Church: "Lo, today I have set you over the nations and over kingdoms."[8]

It follows from this that if the secular power errs, it shall be judged by the spiritual power; if a lesser spiritual power errs, it shall be judged by its superior; but if the supreme spiritual power errs, it can be judged solely by God and not by any human, as the Apostle [Paul] bears witness: "The spiritual person judges all things and is, in turn, judged by no one."[9] Although this authority was given to a man and is exercised by a man, it is not human but rather it is divine, given as it was to Peter from God's mouth and confirmed to him and his successors. Peter was the Rock whom the Lord acknowledged when he said to Peter himself: "Whatsoever you bind on earth will be bound also in heaven; whatsoever you loose on earth will be

---

[2]Chapter 2, source 14.
[3]If pope and emperor (or king) jointly ruled the Church, it would be a two-headed monster.
[4]The Bible, John 21:17.
[5]The Bible, Luke 22:38. This is a reference to that moment at the close of the Last Supper when Jesus foretells his coming death and notes, perhaps in an ironic effort to underscore the confusion that is about to occur: "Whoever does not have a sword must sell his coat and purchase one." When the apostles reply, "Look, Lord, here are two swords," Jesus answers, "That is enough."

Medieval Catholic commentators, vexed by this curious passage, generally interpreted it as an allegorical reference to the fact that there were two powers in the world: spiritual (priestly) power and worldly (royal) power.
[6]The Bible, John 18:11. A reference to Jesus' instructions to Peter after Peter had cut off the ear of the high priest while attempting to protect Jesus from arrest.
[7]The Bible, Romans 13:1.
[8]The Bible, Jeremiah 1:10.
[9]The Bible, 1 Corinthians 2:15.

loosed in heaven."[10] Whoever, therefore, resists this power so ordained by God resists God's ordinance. . . . Therefore we declare, state, define, and pronounce that it is absolutely necessary for salvation that every human being be subject to the Roman Pontiff.

Two Thirteenth-Century Representations of the Virgin
▼▼▼

60 ▼ THE DORMITION OF THE CATHEDRAL OF STRASBOURG AND THE DORMITION OF THE CHURCH OF SAINT MARY PERIBLEPTOS

By the thirteenth century, Eastern and Western Christians disagreed over many issues, but they equally regarded Mary, the mother of Jesus, as the most lovable and loving of all God's saints. Both Byzantine and Latin Christians revered Mary as the fully human yet sinless Mother of God who served as advocate for all humanity before her Son's throne.

The cult of Mary resulted in a massive volume of paintings and statues in East and West of the Virgin Mother, as she was also known. One of the more popular themes, especially in Byzantium, was the Dormition, or "Falling Asleep," of Mary. According to a tradition accepted equally in East and West, when Mary died, her incorruptible body was assumed into heaven. With body and soul reunited, she was crowned Queen of Heaven.

Our two illustrations represent typical thirteenth-century High Gothic (Western) and Late Byzantine renderings of the Dormition. The first is a carving at the Rhineland cathedral of Strasbourg, which today is located in eastern France, and dates from around 1230. The other is a wall painting from the Serbian Church of Saint Mary Peribleptos and dates to around 1295. During the thirteenth century Serbia, which is located in the central Balkans, was culturally part of Byzantine civilization, whereas its immediate Balkan neighbor to the north, Croatia, had accepted Roman Catholicism.

Both pieces of art employ many of the same features. A "sleeping" Virgin is surrounded by mourning apostles. Saint Peter is at the far left, at the head of the bed, and Saint Paul is at the far right, at the foot of the bed. Jesus dominates the central background where he tenderly holds his mother's winged soul in his arms. In the Strasbourg sculpture a kneeling Saint Mary Magdalene, one of Je-

---

[10]The Bible, Matthew 16:19. The whole passage, 16:17–19, is the primary scriptural text on which the Roman papacy bases its claims of Petrine primacy.

Dormition, Cathedral of Strasbourg

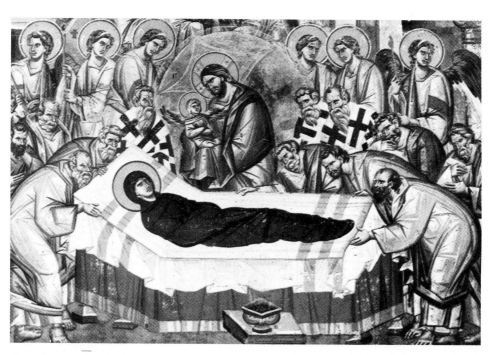

Dormition, Church of Saint Mary Peribleptos

sus' most important female disciples, grieves at the bedside, but she is absent in the Serbian painting. Just as these iconographic similarities suggest an essential theological agreement between these two separated branches of Christendom, the differences in style may help us understand better the ways in which these two Christian civilizations had parted.

QUESTIONS FOR ANALYSIS

1. In which scene do Mary and Jesus appear more serenely detached from this world? Do they seem approachable? Do the figures in the other scene appear more human, or more like common folks?
2. In which scene do the mourners appear more to be paying court than grieving? Compare it with the other scene. Which is more awe-inspiring? Why?
3. Which scene seems more naturalistic? Why? Which scene seems to emphasize more the mystery, or otherworldliness, of the faith?
4. Judging from these scenes, which Christian tradition emphasized the cult of the Risen, Glorified Christ? Which emphasized the suffering Jesus? Which tradition probably placed greater emphasis on the Nativity (Christmas)?
5. If each does represent a different devotional emphasis and a different way of perceiving humanity's relationship with the Divine, what can you say about the two Christian cultures that produced them?

Chapter 8

▼▼▼

Islam: Universal Submission to God

The last of the great monotheistic faiths to arise in Southwest Asia was Islam, which emerged in Arabia during the early seventh century. *Islam* means "submission" in Arabic, and a *Muslim* is one who submits to the will of God.

The Prophet of Islam was a merchant of Mecca called Muhammad (ca 571–632), who around 610 began to receive visions in which he was called by God (*Allah* in Arabic) to preach God's Oneness, the imminence of the resurrection of the dead, a Day of Judgment, an all-consuming hell fire for the unjust and unbelievers, and a paradise of bliss for the faithful. Muhammad believed that just as Jews and Christians had their divine revelations from God, now the Arabs were receiving the full and final word of God through him, the last and greatest of the prophets but still only a man. Abraham, Moses, Jesus, and the other prophets had been earlier messengers of God. Muhammad was the "seal" of these forerunners.

Most of Meccan society was initially unmoved by Muhammad's message, so in 622 Muhammad journeyed to the city of Yathrib, where he was able to establish a theocratic (ruled by God) Muslim community. In his honor the city was renamed *Medinat al-Nabi* (City of the Prophet), or, more simply, Medina. From Medina Muhammad and his followers initiated a holy war against Mecca, and in 630 Muhammad was able to reenter Mecca in triumph. The Prophet of Allah was now the most powerful chieftain in Arabia, and the various tribes of the peninsula soon were united under his leadership. When Muhammad died in 632, his closest friend Abu Bakr, assumed the title and office of *caliph* (deputy, or successor, of the Prophet), thereby accepting leadership of the family of Islam. Thanks to his efforts at destroying secessionist elements, Islam under Abu Bakr's stewardship (632–634) remained a unified community ready to explode out of its homeland, which it did under the second caliph, Umar (r. 634–644).

When Umar's Muslims began raiding the territories of their neighbors, they discovered lands ripe for conquest. Both the Sassanian Persian and Byzantine empires had exhausted each other in a series of destructive wars that ran from 503 to 627. In addition, the Byzantine Empire was rent by ethnic and religious dissension, especially in Syria-Palestine and Egypt. Before Umar's death the Byzantines had lost all of Syria-Palestine and Egypt to the green flag of Islam, and the Arab conquest of the Persian Empire was virtually completed. By 750 Muslim territory reached from the Pyrenees and Atlantic coast in Spain to the Indus Valley of India and Tang China's far-western borders.

Originally the Arabs considered Islam their special revelation and had no intention of sharing the faith with their non-Arab subjects, but several factors combined to attract large numbers of converts. These included Islam's uncompromising monotheism and the straightforwardness of its other central doctrines; the sense of security offered by membership in a totally integrated Muslim community, where one's entire life is subject to God's Word; and the desire to escape the second-class status of Islam's non-Muslim subjects. When the Abbasid caliphs (r. 750–1258) established their court at Baghdad on the Tigris in 762, they claimed dominion over a multiethnic ecumene bound together by one of the fastest growing religions in the history of humanity. The culture of this world community was a combination of many different elements, of which the most important were Arabic, Persian, and Hellenistic.

Later, other peoples, especially the Turks from the tenth century onward, would convert to Islam and carry it farther afield, especially into the heart of India. Arab and East African merchants would transport the faith across the Indian Ocean to the ports of Southeast Asia, and Berbers from North Africa would introduce Islam into western sub-Saharan Africa.

▼▼▼

The Foundations of Muslim Life

Like the Buddha and Jesus, Muhammad was a teacher who spoke rather than wrote his message, but also like Buddhism and Christianity, following its Messenger's death Islam quickly became a religious culture centered on a body of sacred texts, and it has remained so to the present. Islam's text without equal is the *Qur'an* (the Recitations), which Muslims believe contains, word for word, absolutely everything that God revealed to Muhammad and nothing else. As the full and final revelation of God, the Qur'an encompasses everything that any human needs to know. Its verses, each a poetically perfect proclamation from heaven, are both doctrine and law, governing essentially every aspect of a Muslim's life. Islam without the Qur'an is unimaginable.

A second source of guidance for most Muslims is *al-Hadith* (Tradition), a vast body of transmitted stories of what the Prophet said or did or what was said or done in his presence and, therefore, approved by him. Unlike the Qur'an, these stories, individually known as hadiths (literally, "tales," or "instructions"), are not assembled in a single, absolutely accepted text. Rather, there are many collections of Hadith, some more authoritative than others, some even largely dismissed as spurious. Most Muslims believe that authentic hadiths enshrine the *sunna* (the beaten track), or traditions, of the Prophet and the first Muslim community and thereby provide perfect models for behavior in all aspects of life, especially those not expressly covered in the precepts of the Qur'an.

The Word of God
▼▼▼

61 ▼ *The Qur'an*

As long as the Prophet was alive, there was no compelling reason to set his messages down in some definitive form. However, following Muhammad's sudden death in 632, Caliph Abu Bakr ordered one of the Prophet's companions, Zayd ibn Thabit, to collect from both oral and written sources all of Muhammad's inspired utterances. Subsequently, Caliph Uthman (r. 644–656) promulgated an official collection of these Recitations and ordered all other versions destroyed.

This standard text became the basis for every pious Muslim's education. As Islam spread beyond Arab ethnic boundaries, Muslims all over the world learned Arabic in order to study and recite (usually from memory) the sacred *surahs* (chapters) of this holy book. Because of the Qur'an's centrality, Arabic literacy became the hallmark of Muslims from sub-Saharan West Africa to Southeast Asia.

The following excerpts come from the second of the Qur'an's 114 surahs. Known as "The Cow" (*al-Baqarah*) because portions of it tell the story of how the ancient Israelites had sacrificed a cow to God, this surah illustrates several of Islam's major doctrinal tenets, religious obligations, and moral principles.

QUESTIONS FOR ANALYSIS

1. What are the basic tenets of faith enjoined on all Muslims?
2. What are a Muslim's basic moral obligations?
3. What specific religious rites and practices must every observant Muslim perform?
4. How are Muslims to deal with those who attack them?
5. What evidence is there that Muhammad was experiencing difficulty converting Jewish and Christian Arabs?
6. How does the Qur'an portray Jews and Christians, and what is Islam's relationship with these two faiths?
7. "For members of the Muslim community, there is no distinction between what one believes and the manner in which one lives and conducts one's affairs." After reading these passages from the Qur'an, do you agree or disagree with this statement? Why?
8. Compare these passages with the readings from Second Isaiah (Chapter 3, source 23) and the Sermon on the Mount (Chapter 7, source 53). Which strike you as more pronounced, the similarities or the differences in message and tone? What do you conclude from your answer?

Those unbelievers of the People of the Book[1]
and the idolaters[2] wish not that any good
should be sent down upon you from your
  Lord;
but God singles out for His mercy whom he
  will;
    God is of bounty abounding. . . .

Many of the People of the Book wish they
  might
restore you as unbelievers, after you have
  believed,
in the jealousy of their souls, after the truth
has become clear to them; yet do you pardon

and be forgiving, till God brings His
  command;
truly God is powerful over everything.
And perform the prayer, and pay the alms;[3]
whatever good you shall forward to your souls'
  account,
you shall find it with God; assuredly God
    sees the things you do.
And they say, "None shall enter Paradise
except that they be Jews or Christians."
Such are their fancies. Say: "Produce your
  proof, if you speak truly."
Nay, but whosoever submits his will to God,
being a good-doer, his wage is with his Lord,

---

[1] Jews and Christians who have their own sacred scriptures from God through such prophets as Moses and Jesus.

[2] Pagans who worship idols.
[3] The *zakat*, or obligatory alms payment, which supports the poor within the Muslim community.

and no fear shall be on them, neither shall
they sorrow.

The Jews say, "The Christians stand not on
anything";
the Christians say, "The Jews stand not on
anything";
yet they recite the Book. So too the ignorant
say the like of them. God shall decide
between them on the Day of Resurrection
touching their differences.
And who does greater evil than he who bars
God's places of worship, so that His Name
be not rehearsed in them, and strives to
destroy them?
Such men might never enter them, save in
fear;
for them is degradation in the present world,
and in the world to come a mighty
chastisement.

To God belong the East and the West;
whithersoever you turn, there is the Face of
God;
God is All-embracing, All-knowing. . . .

Children of Israel,[4] remember My blessing
wherewith I blessed you, and that I
have preferred you above all beings. . . .

And when his Lord tested Abraham[5]
with certain words, and he fulfilled them.
He said, "Behold, I make you a leader
for the people." Said he, "And of my seed?"

He said "My covenant shall not reach
the evildoers."
And when We appointed the House[6] to be
a place of visitation for the people,
and a sanctuary,
and: "Take to yourselves Abraham's station
for a place of prayer." And We made covenant
with Abraham and Ishmael,[7] "Purify
My House for those that shall go about it
and those that cleave to it, to those who bow
and prostrate themselves."[8] . . .

When his Lord said to him, "Surrender,"
he said, "I have surrendered me to
the Lord of all Being."
And Abraham charged his sons with this
and Jacob[9] likewise: "My sons, God has
chosen for you the religion;
see that you die not
save in surrender."[10]

Why, were you witnesses, when death came
to Jacob? When he said to his sons,
"What will you serve after me?" They said,
"We will serve thy God and the God of thy
fathers
Abraham, Ishmael, and Isaac, One God;
to Him we surrender."
That is a nation that has passed away;[11]
there awaits them that they have earned,
and there awaits you that you have earned;
you shall not be questioned concerning
the things they did.

---

[4]Jews–the offspring of Israel, or Jacob, the son of Isaac
and grandson of Abraham.
[5]According to both Arabic and Jewish traditions, Abraham (ca 1800 B.C.) was the father of both the Arabic and
Jewish people.
[6]The Ka'bah, a cube-shaped shrine at the heart of the
Great Mosque of Mecca. Associated with both Adam and
Abraham, it is the focal point of Muslim daily prayer
and the sacred spot around which pilgrims on *hajj* (see
note 19) circulate in a series of ritual ceremonies.
[7]Both Muslim and Jewish tradition see Ishmael, the son
of Abraham and half-brother of Isaac (from whom the
Jews are descended), as the forefather of the Arabs.

[8]Purify it from idols, whose worship Muslims consider
to be the worst of all possible sins. Muhammad cleansed
the Ka'bah of its idols following his triumphant reentry
into Mecca.
[9]See note 4.
[10]By surrendering to God, Abraham and his sons and
grandsons were Muslims.
[11]Jews (the progeny of Jacob) who surrender to God, and
are Muslims by reason of that submission, no longer
exist.

And they say, "Be Jews or Christians and
you shall be guided." Say thou: "Nay, rather
the creed of Abraham, a man of pure faith;
    he was no idolater."
Say you: "We believe in God, and
in that which has been sent down on us
and sent down on Abraham, Ishmael,
Isaac and Jacob, and the Tribes,[12]
and that which was given to Moses and Jesus
and the Prophets, of their Lord; we
make no division between any of them, and
    to Him we surrender."
And if they believe in the like of that you
believe in, then they are truly guided; but if
they turn away, then they are clearly in
    schism;[13]
God will suffice you for them; He is
    the All-hearing, the All-knowing;
the baptism of God; and who is there
that baptizes fairer than God?[14]
    Him we are serving.
Say: "Would you then dispute with us
concerning God, who is our Lord
and your Lord? Our deeds belong to us,
and to you belong your deeds; Him
    we serve sincerely. . . .

It is not piety, that you turn your faces
    to the East and to the West.[15]
    True piety is this:
to believe in God, and the Last Day,
the angels, the Book, and the Prophets,
to give of one's substance, however cherished,
    to kinsmen, and orphans,
the needy, the traveler, beggars,
    and to ransom the slave,
to perform the prayer,[16] to pay the alms.
And they who fulfill their covenant
when they have engaged in a covenant,

and endure with fortitude
misfortune, hardship, and peril,
these are they who are true in their faith,
    these are the truly godfearing. . . .

O believers, prescribed for you is
the Fast,[17] even as it was prescribed for
those that were before you — haply you
    will be godfearing —
for days numbered; and if any of you
be sick, or if he be on a journey,
then a number of other days. . . .

And fight in the way of God with those
who fight with you, but aggress not: God
    loves not the aggressors.
And slay them wherever you come upon them,
and expel them from where they expelled you;
persecution is more grievous than slaying.
But fight them not by the Holy Mosque[18]
until they should fight you there;
then, if they fight you, slay them —
such is the recompense of unbelievers —
but if they give over, surely God is
All-forgiving, All-compassionate.
Fight them, till there is no persecution
and the religion is God's; then if they
give over, there shall be no enmity
    save for evildoers.
The holy month for the holy month;
holy things demand retaliation.
Whoso commits aggression against you,
do you commit aggression against him
like as he has committed against you;
and fear you God, and know that God is
    with the godfearing.

And expend in the way of God;
and cast not yourselves by your own hands

---

[12]The Twelve Tribes of the Israelites whom Moses led out of Egypt.

[13]Schism means separation. They have separated themselves from Islam.

[14]Here the Qur'an juxtaposes the Christian sacrament of baptism, the ceremony of initiation into the Christian faith, with God's baptism of the Word.

[15]In prayer.

[16]The ritual prayer performed five times daily by all observant Muslims.

[17]The annual fast during the month of Ramadan when observant Muslims refrain from all food, drink, sexual intercourse, and other physical pleasures from sunrise to sunset.

[18]The Great Mosque of Mecca.

into destruction, but be good-doers; God
   loves the good-doers.

Fulfill the Pilgrimage[19] and the Visitation
unto God; but if you are prevented,
then such offering as may be feasible. . . .
And when you have performed your holy rites
remember God, as you remember your fathers
or yet more devoutly. . . .

God

   there is no god but He, the
      Living, the Everlasting.
   Slumber seizes Him not, neither sleep;
         to Him belongs
   all that is in the heavens and the earth.
   Who is there that shall intercede with Him
         save by His leave?
   He knows what lies before them and
         what is after them,
      and they comprehend not anything of
         His knowledge save such as He
         wills.
   His Throne comprises the heavens and
         earth;
   the preserving of them oppresses Him not;
   He is the All-high, the All-glorious.

No compulsion is there in religion.
Rectitude has become clear from error.
So whosoever disbelieves in idols
and believes in God, has laid hold of

the most firm handle, unbreaking; God is
      All-hearing, All-knowing.

God is the Protector of the believers;
He brings them forth from the shadows
         into the light. . . .

Those who believe and do deeds of
      righteousness,
and perform the prayer, and pay the alms —
their wage awaits them with their Lord,
and no fear shall be on them, neither shall
      they sorrow. . . .

God charges no soul save to its capacity;
standing to its account is what it has earned,
and against its account what it has merited.

      Our Lord,
         take us not to task
      if we forget, or make mistake.
         Our Lord,
      charge us not with a load such
   as Thou didst lay upon those before us.
         Our Lord,
         do Thou not burden us
   beyond what we have the strength to bear.
         And pardon us,
            and forgive us,
            and have mercy on us;
         Thou art our Protector.
      And help us against the people
         of the unbelievers.

The Tales of Tradition
▼▼▼

62 ▼ *Imam Nawawi, GARDENS OF THE RIGHTEOUS*

**Although earlier Muslims, such as Malik ibn-Anas (d. 795), had collected stories
about the Prophet, it was not until about two centuries after Muhammad's death**

---

[19]All adult Muslims who are able to make the journey
must embark on the *hajj,* or pilgrimage to Mecca, at
least once before death. See source 66.

that Muslim scholars began to catalogue systematically the traditions that circulated about the Prophet and his first followers. The most important individual in this effort was the Persian lawyer Ismail al-Bokhari (810–870), who reportedly collected some 600,000 tales (undoubtedly many were variations of common themes) and memorized more than 200,000 of them. From this vast body of material he identified a little over 7,000 tales as genuine, which he then preserved. The second great editor of Hadith was Bokhari's younger contemporary, Abul Husain Muslim (819–875), whose collection is almost identical to Bokhari's. Slightly less important than the work of these two scholarly giants were the collections of Abu Daud (d. 889), al-Tirmidhi (d. 892), Ibn Majah (d. 896), and al-Nisai (d. 915). The combined efforts of these six individuals are known as the *Sahih Sitta (The Six Authentic Compilations).*

The sheer bulk of these canonical texts, as well as the discrepancies among them and the existence of many other less universally accepted compendia of such tales, necessitated continued editing and digesting of Muslim tradition by legions of Islamic jurists and religious scholars in every generation. One of the most significant of these later scholars was the Syrian *imam* (religious teacher) Nawawi (1233–1278), whose *Gardens of the Righteous* provided an analytical digest of the spiritual values enshrined in the *Six Authentic Compilations* and several lesser collections of Hadith.

As the following texts show, Nawawi's usual method of exposition was to set out a relevant passage or series of passages from the Qur'an and then to list a number of variant stories and sayings, largely as remembered by the Prophet's Companions, that illustrate the spiritual message contained in that qur'anic text.

QUESTIONS FOR ANALYSIS

1. What virtues do these selections emphasize? Which of these are also part of the Judeo-Christian tradition?
2. The Arabic word used for "striving" in both the Qur'an and Hadith is *jihad,* which is often translated as "holy war." In the light of these excerpts, does this translation seem correct and complete?
3. What gives Hadith its authority, since, unlike the Qur'an, Muslims do not regard it as the literal word of God?
4. How does Hadith allow for a certain diversity within the context of religious uniformity?
5. "Hadith is a living commentary on the Qur'an, insofar as it makes explicit all that is implicit in that book." What does this statement mean? Does it appear to be a fair statement of how a Muslim would regard Hadith?
6. What picture emerges of the place of women in Muslim society? Compare the status of Muslim women with that of Hindu women as illustrated in the *Laws of Manu* (Chapter 5, source 40). Which are more striking, the differences or the parallels? What do you conclude from this answer?

ON MAKING PEACE
BETWEEN PEOPLE

Allah, the Exalted, has said:

Most of their conferrings together are devoid of good, except such as enjoin charity, or the promotion of public welfare or of public peace (4.115).
Reconciliation is best (4.129).
Be mindful of your duty to Allah and try to promote accord between yourselves (8.2).
All believers are brothers; so make peace between your brothers (49.11).

Abu Hurairah relates that the Honorable Prophet said: Charity is incumbent upon every human limb every day on which the sun rises. To bring about just reconciliation between two contestants is charity. Helping a person to mount his animal, or to load his baggage on to it is charity. A good word is charity. Every step taken towards the mosque for *salat*[1] is charity. To remove anything from the street that causes inconvenience is charity (Bokhari and Muslim).
Umm Kulthum relates that she heard the Honorable Prophet say: He who brings about peace between people and attains good or says that which is good is not a liar (Bokhari and Muslim). Muslim's version adds: I did not hear him let people have a latitude in what they said except in three situations: war, making peace, and talk between husband and wife.

ON THE SUPERIORITY OF
THE POOR AND WEAK
AMONG MUSLIMS

Allah, the Exalted, has said:

Continue thy companionship with those who call on their Lord, morning and evening, seeking His pleasure, and look not beyond them (18.29).

Haritha ibn Wahb relates that he heard the Honorable Prophet say: Shall I tell you who are the dwellers of Paradise? It is every weak one who is accounted weak and is looked down upon, who if he takes an oath relying upon Allah He would fulfill it. Now shall I tell you who are the denizens of the Fire? It is every ignorant, impertinent, prideful, and arrogant one (Bokhari and Muslim). . . .
Usamah relates that the Honorable Prophet said: I stood at the gate of Paradise and observed that the generality of those who entered it were the lowly. The wealthy had been held back from it. Then those condemned to the Fire were ordered to it and I stood at the gate of the Fire and observed that the generality of those who entered it were women (Bokhari and Muslim).

ON KIND TREATMENT OF
ORPHANS, GIRLS, THE WEAK, THE
POOR, AND THE LOWLY

Allah, the Exalted, has said:

Continue to be kindly gracious towards the believers (15.89).
Continue thy companionship with those who call on their Lord, morning and evening, seeking His pleasure, and look not beyond them, for if thou dost that thou wouldst be seeking the values of this life (18.29).
Oppress not the orphan and chide not him who asks (93.10–11).
Knowest thou him who rejects the faith? That is the one who drives away the orphan and urges not the feeding of the poor (107.2–4). . . .

---

[1]Ritual prayer. Observant Muslims pray five times daily and on Friday attend community prayer services at a mosque.

Abu Hurairah relates that the Honorable Prophet said: He who exerts himself on behalf of widows and the indigent is like one who strives[2] in the cause of Allah; and the narrator thinks he added: and like the guardian who never retreats, and like one who observes the fast and does not break it (Bokhari and Muslim). . . .

Anas relates that the Honorable Prophet said: He who brings up two girls through their childhood will appear on the Day of Judgment attached to me like two fingers of a hand (Muslim). . . .

Ayesha[3] relates: A poor woman came to me with her two daughters. I gave her three dates. She gave one to each girl and raised the third to her own mouth to eat. The girls asked her for it. So she broke it into two parts and gave one to each of the girls. I was much struck by her action and mentioned what she had done to the Honorable Prophet. He said: Allah appointed Paradise for her in consequence of it; or he said: Allah freed her from the Fire on account of it.

Abu Shuraih Khuwailad ibn Amr Khuza'i relates that the Honorable Prophet said: Allah, I declare sinful any failure to safeguard the rights of two weak ones; orphans and women (Nisai).

ON A HUSBAND'S RIGHT CONCERNING HIS WIFE

Allah, the Exalted, has said:

Men are appointed guardians over women, because of that in respect of which Allah has made some of them excel others, and because the men spend their wealth. So virtuous women are obedient and safeguard, with Allah's help, matters the knowledge of which is shared by them with their husbands (4.35). . . .

Ibn Umar relates that the Honorable Prophet said: Every one of you is a steward and is accountable for that which is committed to his charge. The ruler is a steward and is accountable for his charge, a man is a steward in respect of his household, a woman is a steward in respect of her husband's house and his children. Thus everyone of you is a steward and is accountable for that which is committed to his charge (Bokhari and Muslim).

Abu Ali Talq ibn Ali relates that the Honorable Prophet said: When a man calls his wife for his need, she should go to him even if she is occupied in baking bread (Tirmidhi and Nisai). . . .

Umm Salamah relates that the Honorable Prophet said: If a woman dies and her husband is pleased with her she will enter Paradise (Tirmidhi).

Mu'az ibn Jabal relates that the Honorable Prophet said: Whenever a woman distresses her husband his mate from among the *houris*[4] of Paradise says to her: Allah ruin thee, do not cause him distress for he is only thy guest and will soon part from thee to come to us (Tirmidhi).

Usamah ibn Zaid relates that the Honorable Prophet said: I am not leaving a more harmful trial for men than woman (Bokhari and Muslim).

ON STRIVING IN THE CAUSE OF ALLAH

Allah, the Exalted, has said:

Fight the idolators all together, as they fight you all together, and know that Allah is with the righteous (9.36). . . .

Allah has purchased of the believers their persons and their belongings in return for the promise that they shall have

---

[2]*Jihad.* See question 2.
[3]One of the Prophet's wives and a major source of hadiths.

[4]Beautiful virgins who serve the saved in Paradise.

Paradise, for they fight in the cause of Allah and they slay the enemy or are themselves slain. This is a promise that He has made incumbent upon Himself as set out in the Torah, and the Gospel and the Qur'an; and who is more faithful to his promises than Allah? Rejoice, then, in the bargain that you have made with Him; that indeed is the supreme triumph (9.111). . . .

O ye who believe, shall I guide you to a commerce that will deliver you from a painful chastisement? It is that you believe in Allah and His Messenger, and strive in the cause of Allah with your belongings and your persons, that is the better for you, did you but know. He will forgive you your sins and will admit you to gardens beneath which rivers flow, and to pure and pleasant dwellings in Gardens of Eternity. That is the supreme triumph (61.11–14). . . .

Anas relates that the Honorable Prophet said: To be occupied in the cause of Allah a morning or evening is better than the world and all it contains (Bokhari and Muslim). . . .

Sahl ibn Sa'ad relates that the Honorable Prophet said: Patroling the frontier for a day is better than the world and all it contains. Your being allotted a strip in Paradise no wider than your horse-whip is better than the world and all it contains. Being occupied with striving in the cause of Allah for a morning or an evening is better than the world and all it contains (Bokhari and Muslim). . . .

Fuzalah ibn Ubaid relates that the Honorable Prophet said: Death puts an end to all action, except in the case of one who patrols the frontier in the cause of Allah, for his activity continues to grow till the Day of Judgment and he is shielded against the trials of the grave (Abu Daud and Tirmidhi).

Uthman relates that he heard the Honorable Prophet say: Patroling the frontier for a day in the cause of Allah is better than a thousand days of other good works (Tirmidhi). . . .

Abu Bakr ibn Abu Musa Ash'ari relates that he heard his father say in the face of the enemy: The Honorable Prophet said: The gates of Paradise are under the shadow of swords. Thereupon a man of lowly condition stood up and inquired: Abu Musa, did you indeed hear the Honorable Prophet say that? He answered: Yes. The man then turned towards his companions and saluted them in farewell. He then broke the scabbard of his sword and threw it away and walked with his sword into the enemy ranks and fought till he was killed (Muslim).

Abdullah ibn Jubair relates that the Honorable Prophet said: The Fire[5] will not touch one whose feet are covered with dust in striving for the cause of Allah (Bokhari). . . .

Anas relates that the Honorable Prophet said: He who supplicates sincerely for martyrdom is granted it, even though he is not slain (Muslim).

Abu Hurairah relates that the Honorable Prophet said: A martyr does not suffer when he is slain anymore than one of you suffers from being bitten by an ant (Tirmidhi). . . .

Abu Hurairah relates that the Honorable Prophet said: He who observes the fast for a day in the cause of Allah will find that Allah has dug a moat between him and the Fire as wide as the distance between heaven and earth (Tirmidhi).

Abu Hurairah relates that the Honorable Prophet said: He who dies without having fought in the cause of Allah and without having thought of it in his mind dies with one characteristic of hypocrisy within him (Muslim). . . .

Abu Hurairah relates that a man asked the Honorable Prophet's permission to travel and he told him: The travel for my people is striv-

---

[5]Hell.

ing in the cause of Allah, the Lord of honor and glory (Abu Daud). . . .

Anas relates that the Honorable Prophet said: Strive against the idolators with your be-

longings, your persons and your tongues (Abu Daud).

▼▼▼

Variety and Unity in Islam

Ideally, Islam is a single community united in its submission and service to God. In fact, however, it has been fragmented into a wide variety of sects and schools. Chief among these are the Sunni and Shi'ite traditions and various forms of Sufi mysticism.

Despite these divisions, Muslims have maintained a degree of unity because of the centrality of the Qur'an in the life of every practicing Muslim, regardless of sect, and most Muslims' acceptance of certain fundamental religious obligations. Most basic of all are the Five Pillars of Islam: to say with absolute conviction, "There is no God but God, and Muhammad is the Prophet of God"; to offer prescribed prayers at five stipulated times during the day; to give alms in charity to poorer members of the Islamic community; to fast from sunrise to sunset during the month of Ramadan; and to make a pilgrimage to Mecca at least once in one's lifetime. Some Muslims add a sixth pillar, jihad, which is understood in many different senses (source 62, question 2).

God's Martyrs: The Party of Ali
▼▼▼

63 ▼ Ibn Babawayh al-Saduq, *CREED CONCERNING THE IMAMS*

The Six Authentic Compilations preserve traditions sacred to that majority element of Islam known as *Sunni* Muslims, who claim to follow the correct path (*sunna*) of tradition as it evolved from the day of the Prophet and his Companions to the present. Underlying the Sunni self-image is the belief that God's community can never err; consequently, the practices and institutions of mainstream Islam are always correct. Another major faction of Islam, which claims its own Hadith as the authentic record of the Prophet's words and actions, is the *Shi'at Ali*, or Party of Ali. Members of this branch of Islam, known popularly as *Shi'ites*, today comprise almost all of Iran's population, are a slight majority in Iraq, and also inhabit portions of Syria, Lebanon, and the Indian subcontinent.

The Shi'ite break with other Muslims dates back to the mid-seventh century. Partisans of Ali, Muhammad's cousin and son-in-law, managed to have him installed as fourth caliph (r. 656–661) following the murder of Caliph Uthman (r. 644–656). Many of Uthman's followers did not recognize Ali, however, and civil war ensued. The result was Ali's eventual assassination in 661, establishment of the rival Umayyad Dynasty as caliphs (r. 661–750), and the martyrdom of Ali's son, al-Husayn, the Prophet's sole surviving grandson, in 680. Supporters of the family of Ali, who included many of the original Muslims of Medina, refused to accept the Umayyads as rightful successors of the Prophet. Following the patriarchal traditions of the desert, they claimed that only a member of Muhammad's family could succeed him as imam, or religious leader, of Islam. The result was a schism in Islam, and to this day the annual commemoration of al-Husayn's martyrdom is the most sorrowful event in the Shi'ite religious calendar.

Often persecuted as religious dissidents and driven underground, the Shi'ites evolved a theology of history. They not only traced the rightful succession of leadership over the community of Islam from Muhammad and Ali through a number of subsequent imams, whom the Sunnis did not accept as legitimate, but they also developed the notion of a messianic "hidden imam," or *Mahdi* (the Guided One). According to this religious vision, the line of visible imams ended at an early point in time (here the various Shi'ite sects disagree as to who was the last visible imam). The imamate, however, was not destroyed. Rather, the last visible imam had simply withdrawn from sight and would at some future time reappear to gather his faithful, persecuted followers around him, usher in a Muslim holy age, and herald the Last Judgment.

The largest of all Shi'ite sects is the Twelver Shia, which developed around A.D. 900. These Shi'ites, who predominate in Iran, accept a line of twelve infallible imams divinely appointed from birth and believe that the twelfth and last of these visible imams disappeared in the late ninth century. The following selection from the creed, or statement of belief, of Muhammad ibn Ali ibn Babawayh, known as Sheik al-Saduq (d. 991), one of the greatest of the early Twelver theologians, illustrates several major Twelver beliefs.

QUESTIONS FOR ANALYSIS

1. Who is Muhammad al-Qa'im, and what will he accomplish?
2. What happened to the Prophet Muhammad and each of the first eleven imams?
3. What is *taqiya,* and why is it obligatory for a Shi'ite? In what ways does a follower of the imams follow the model of al-Qa'im by practicing taqiya?
4. How does al-Saduq view Sunnis? Can you find any suggestion that Shi'ites believe they possess a secret religious truth denied Sunnis? What would be the source of that truth?

5. **Shi'ites are said to see themselves as the persecuted, righteous remnant of Islam. Is there any evidence in this document to support such a conclusion?**

Our belief concerning the number of the prophets is that there have been one hundred and twenty-four thousand prophets and a like number of plenipotentiaries. Each prophet had a plenipotentiary to whom he gave instructions by the command of God. And concerning them we believe that they brought the truth from God and their word is the word of God, their command God's command, and obedience to them obedience to God. . . .

The leaders of the prophets are five (on whom all depends): Noah, Abraham, Moses, Jesus, and Muhammad. Muhammad is their leader . . . he confirmed the (other) apostles.

It is necessary to believe that God did not create anything more excellent than Muhammad and the Imams. . . . After His Prophet,[1] the proofs of God for the people are the Twelve Imams. . . .

We believe that the Proof of Allah in His earth and His viceregent among His slaves in this age of ours is the Upholder [*al-Qa'im*] [of the law of God], the Expected One, Muhammad ibn al-Hasan al-'Askari.[2] He it is concerning whose name and descent the Prophet was informed by God, and he it is who WILL FILL THE EARTH WITH JUSTICE AND EQUITY JUST AS IT IS NOW FULL OF OPPRESSION AND WRONG. He it is whom God will make victorious over the whole world until from every place the call to prayer is heard and religion will belong entirely to God, exalted be He. He is the rightly guided *Mahdi* about whom the prophet gave information that when

he appears, Jesus, son of Mary, will descend upon the earth and pray behind him.[3] We believe there can be no other *Qa'im* than him; he may live in the state of occultation[4] (as long as he likes); were it the space of the existence of this world, there would be no *Qa'im* other than him.

Our belief concerning prophets, apostles, Imams, and angels is that they are infallible . . . and do not commit any sin, minor or major . . . he who denies infallibility to them in any matter . . . is a *kafir*, an infidel. . . .

Our belief concerning the Prophet [Muhammad] is that he was poisoned by Jews during the expedition to Khaybar. The poison continued to be noxious until he died of its effects.

1. Imam: And the Prince of Believers ['Ali], on whom be peace, was murdered by . . . Ibn Muljam al-Muradi, may God curse him, and was buried in Ghari.
2. Imam: Hasan ibn 'Ali,[5] on whom be peace, was poisoned by his wife Ja'da bint Ash'ath of Kinda, may God curse her and her father.
3. Imam: Husayn ibn 'Ali[6] was slain at Karbala. His murderer was Sinan ibn-Anas al-Nakha'i, may God curse him and his father. [Al-Saduq then lists the fourth through eleventh imams and identifies the murderers of each.] . . .

And verily the Prophet and Imams, on whom be peace, had informed the people that they would be murdered. He who says that they were not has given them the lie and has

---

[1]The Prophet Muhammad.
[2]The twelfth imam. Al-Hasan al'-Askari, the eleventh imam, died around 1 January 874. Twelvers believe that he was succeeded by a young son, Muhammad al-Qa'im (the Upholder of God's Law), who went into concealment around 878. Muhammad ibn al-Hasan al-'Askari means Muhammad, the son of al-Hasan al-'Askari.

[3]Sunni and Shi'ite Muslims believe that the return to earth of the prophet Jesus will signal the Last Judgment.
[4]Invisible to earthly eyes.
[5]Hasan, the son of (*ibn*) Ali, was Ali's elder son.
[6]Al-Husayn, Ali's younger son.

imputed falsehood to God the Mighty and Glorious.

Our belief concerning *taqiya* [permissible dissimulation of one's true beliefs] is that it is obligatory, and he who forsakes it is in the same position as he who forsakes prayer. . . . Now until the time when the Imam al-Qa'im appears, *taqiya* is obligatory and it is not permissible to dispense with it. He who does . . . has verily gone out of the religion of God. And God has described the showing of friendship to unbelievers as being possible only in the state of *taqiya*.

And the Imam Ja'far[7] said, "Mix with enemies openly but oppose them inwardly, so long as authority is a matter of question."[8] . . . And he said, "He who prays with hypocrites [Sunnis], standing in the first row, it is as though he prayed with the Prophet standing in the first row." And he said, "Visit their sick and attend their funerals and pray in their mosques." . . .

Our belief concerning the 'Alawiya [descendants of 'Ali] is that they are the progeny of the Messenger of God and devotion to them is obligatory.

God's Viceregent on Earth
▼▼▼

64 ▾ Al-Mawardi, *BOOK OF THE PRINCIPLES OF GOVERNMENT*

In the Shi'ite tradition the title *imam* could be applied to either *the* infallible imam or any lesser but acknowledged religious leader. Sunnis generally accorded this title only to local religious leaders and until the mid-thirteenth century preferred to bestow the title of *caliph,* or deputy, on the person who claimed authority over all Islam. For Abu Bakr, the first caliph, the title meant that he was Muhammad's deputy and served as first among equals within the Muslim community. The Umayyads, however, altered the nature of the caliphate by claiming the title *khalifat Allah* (God's Deputy). The implication was that whoever disobeyed them in any matter was an enemy of God and an unbeliever. The Abbasids expanded this tradition, assumed the title "Shadow of God on Earth," and transformed the caliphate into a Persian-style autocracy.

In the following document, al-Mawardi (d. 1058), a jurist and political philosopher who resided in eleventh-century Baghdad, describes the office and qualities of the ideal caliph. His use of the term imam for the caliph stems from the fact that, beginning in the reign of Caliph al-Mahdi (r. 775–785), the Abbasids claimed that the Prophet directly conferred the office of imam on their ancestor al-Abbas. This claim, as well as the caliph's assuming the throne name al-Mahdi (the Guided One; see source 63), was motivated, at least partially, by the Abbasids' desire to counter the charismatic appeal of their Shi'ite rivals. It

---

[7]The sixth imam.

[8]As long as there are Sunni rulers.

also served as a way of demonstrating the Abbasids' piety, thereby distancing themselves from their predecessors, the Umayyads, who had a reputation for irreligiosity.

QUESTIONS FOR ANALYSIS

1. How does al-Mawardi describe the ideal caliph and his office? What are his most important attributes? What are his chief duties?
2. Does al-Mawardi emphasize more the caliph's duties or his powers and prerogatives? What do you infer from your answer?
3. What is the caliph's relationship, in theory, with the Muslim community at large?
4. Which of Muhammad's special powers or functions are not attributed to the caliph? What do you infer from your answer?
5. How does the Sunni caliph, or imam, differ from the Shi'ite imam (source 63)? What do you infer from your answer?

The office of Iman was set up in order to replace the office of Prophet in the defense of the faith and the government of the world. . . . There is disagreement as to whether this obligation [to elect an Imam] derives from reason or from Holy Law. One group says it derives from reason, since it is in the nature of reasonable men to submit to a leader who will prevent them from injuring one another and who will settle quarrels and disputes, for without rulers men would live in anarchy and heedlessness like benighted savages. . . .

Another group says that the obligation derives from the Holy Law and not from reason, since the Imam deals with matters of Holy Law. . . . All that reason requires is that a reasonable man should refrain from mutual injury and conflict with his neighbor and act equitably in mutual fairness and good relations, conducting himself in accordance with his own reason, and not with someone else's. But it is the Holy Law which intervenes to entrust these affairs to its religious representative. God said, "O you who believe, obey God, obey the Prophet, and obey those among you who are in authority" [Qur'an, iv, 62]. He thus explicitly enjoined us

to obey those among us who are in authority, and they are the Imams who hold sway over us. . . .

The conditions of eligibility for the Imamate are seven:

1. Rectitude in all respects.
2. The knowledge to exercise personal judgment in cases and decisions.
3. Soundness of hearing, sight, and tongue so that he may deal accurately with those matters which can only be attained by them.
4. Soundness of limb so that he has no defect which would prevent him from moving freely and rising quickly.
5. The discernment needed to govern the subjects and conduct public affairs.
6. The courage and vigor to defend the lands of Islam and to wage holy war against the enemy.
7. Descent, that is to say, he must be of the tribe of Quraysh.[1] . . .

The duties of the Imam in the conduct of public affairs are ten:

1. To maintain the religion according to established principles and the consensus of

---

[1]The Arabs of Mecca and the Prophet's own tribe.

the first generation of Muslims. If an innovator appears or if some dubious person deviates from it, the Imam must clarify the proofs of religion to him, expound that which is correct, and apply to him the proper rules and penalties so that religion may be protected from injury and the community safeguarded from error.

2. To execute judgments given between litigants and to settle disputes between contestants so that justice may prevail and so that none commit or suffer injustice.

3. To defend the lands of Islam and to protect them from intrusion so that people may earn their livelihood and travel at will without danger to life or property.

4. To enforce the legal penalties for the protection of God's commandments from violation and for the preservation of the rights of his servants from injury or destruction.

5. To maintain the frontier fortresses with adequate supplies and effective force for their defense so that the enemy may not take them by surprise, commit profanation there, or shed the blood, either of a Muslim or an ally.

6. To wage holy war [*jihad*] against those who, after having been invited to accept Islam, persist in rejecting it, until they either become Muslims or enter the Pact [*dhimma*][2] so that God's truth may prevail over every religion.

7. To collect the booty and the alms in conformity with the prescriptions of the Holy Law, as defined by explicit texts and by independent judgment, and this without terror or oppression.

8. To determine the salaries and other sums due from the treasury, without extravagance and without parsimony, and to make payment at the proper time, neither in advance nor in arrears.

9. To employ capable and trustworthy men and appoint sincere men for the tasks which he delegates to them and for the money which he entrusts to them so that the tasks may be competently discharged and the money honestly safeguarded.

10. To concern himself directly with the supervision of affairs and the scrutiny of conditions so that he may personally govern the community, safeguard the faith, and not resort to delegation in order to free himself either for pleasure or for worship, for even the trustworthy may betray and the sincere may deceive. God said, "O David,[3] we have made you our viceregent[4] [*khalifa*] on earth; therefore, judge justly among men and do not follow your caprice, which will lead you astray from God's path." [Qur'an, *xxxviii*, 25]. In this, God was not content with delegation, but required a personal performance and did not excuse the following of passions, which, He says, lead astray from His path, and this, though He considered David worthy to judge in religion and to hold His vicegerency. This is one of the duties of government of any shepherd. The Prophet of God, may God bless and save him, said, "You are all shepherds, and you are all answerable for your flocks." . . .

---

[2]A compact by which non-Muslims accept the rule of Islam and become, thereby, *dhimmis,* or protected subject people, and pay *jizya,* or tribute.

[3]King of Israel ca 1000 B.C.
[4]A viceregent is the deputy of a ruler or sovereign.

Sufi Mysticism
▼▼▼

65 ▼ *Abu Hamid Muhammad al-Ghazali,* *THE ALCHEMY OF HAPPINESS*

Islam enjoins all its faithful to live a life centered on God. Those who have taken this injunction most literally, to the point of seeking mystical union with the Divine, are known as *Sufis.* The term's origins are obscure. It might derive from the rough wool (*suf*) clothes worn by Sufi ascetics; it could also refer to the reputed purity (*safa*) of their lives. Whatever the etymology of their title, Sufis have been part of Islam from its early days.

   As is often the case with mystics and similar holy people, Sufis, although few in number, enjoyed widespread popularity among the masses and, like their Christian monastic counterparts (Chapter 7, source 56), proved to be great ambassadors of the faith. Also like the Christian desert hermits, Sufi mystics were more than just a little disturbing to many theologians, jurists, and state builders. Sufi emphasis on one's attaining a personal relationship, and even union, with God by means of a variety of meditative exercises struck many Muslim traditionalists as extremely suspicious. Sufis, however, had a champion in the person of Abu Hamid Muhammad al-Ghazali (1058–1111), Islam's most brilliant and respected theologian. This Persian Sunni managed in both his life and writings to create a synthesis of Sufi devotion and Sunni tradition and intellectualism. As a result, Sufis became more acceptable to Islam's learned religious teachers.

   The following excerpts come from al-Ghazali's *The Alchemy of Happiness,* a treatise composed in the final years of his life. The title derives from al-Ghazali's contention that the mystic, by turning away from carnal pleasures in favor of contemplating Eternal Beauty, finds heaven while still on earth and is transmuted from base matter into spiritual gold.

QUESTIONS FOR ANALYSIS

1. According to al-Ghazali, what is the key element in a person's spiritual transformation?
2. Why does al-Ghazali claim that Muslims do not have a monopoly on eternal life with God?
3. Consider the central message of this selection. Is it consistent with the messages of the Qur'an and Hadith? What do you conclude from your answer?
4. Is the message of this selection consistent with the tone and message of al-Mawardi's treatise (source 64)? What do you conclude from your answer?
5. Assuming al-Ghazali reflects mainstream Sufi thought, how do you imagine most Sufis would understand the religious duty of jihad (source 62, question 2)?

6. How do you imagine most Sufis would react to the issues that separated Shi'ites and Sunnis?

7. Compare these excerpts to Jesus' Sermon on the Mount (Chapter 7, source 53). Which seem more striking, the differences or the similarities? What do you conclude from that answer?

ON THE LOVE OF GOD

O traveler on the way and seeker after the love of God! know that the love of God is a sure and perfect method for the believer to attain the object of his desires. It is a highly exalted station of rest, during the journey of the celestial traveler. It is the consummation of the desires and longings of those who seek divine truth. It is the foundation of the vision of the beauty of the Lord.

The love of God is of the most binding obligation upon every one. It is indeed the spirit of the body, and the light of the eye. The Prophet of God declares that the faith of the believer is not complete, unless he loves God and his Prophet more than all the world besides. The Prophet was once asked, what is faith? He replied, "It is to love God and his Prophet more than wife, children, and property." And the Prophet was continually in the habit of praying, "O my God! I ask for your love, I ask that I may love whomsoever loves you, and that I may perform whatsoever your love makes incumbent upon me."

On the resurrection day all sects will be addressed by the name of the prophet whom each followed, "O people of Moses! O people of Jesus! O people of Muhammad!" even to all the beloved servants of God, and it will be proclaimed to them, "O Friends and beloved of God, come to the blessed union and society of God! Come to Paradise and partake of the grace of your beloved!" When they hear this proclamation, their hearts will leap out of their places, and they will almost lose their reason. Yahya ben Moa'z says, "It is better to have as much love of God, even if only as much as a grain of mustard seed, than seventy years of devotion and obedience without love." Hassan of Basra says, "Whoever knows God, will certainly love him, and whoever knows the world, will shun it."

O you who seek the love of God! know that this love is founded upon two things: one is Beauty, and the other is Beneficence. Beauty acts as a cause to produce love, because the being, the attributes and the works of God possess beauty, and every one loves that which is beautiful. There is a tradition which says "Verily, God is beautiful and he loves beauty." And the Prophet says, "Desire to transact your affairs with those who have beautiful countenances." It is on this account that the spirit in man has been created in accordance with the image of beauty, so that whenever it either hears or sees anything beautiful, it may have a propensity towards it, and seek for communion with it. . . .

O inquirer after the love of God! The love of God exists in every heart, though it lies concealed, just as fire exists in the flint stone, until it is drawn out. If you take the steel of desire and affection into your hands, and with it strike the heart, you obtain fire by the means, and your soul will be filled with light. The malice, deceitfulness, hatred, vileness, envy, and strife that are in the heart will be burned up, and it will be freed and purified from sensual perturbations. But if you are careless and do nothing and pass several days without seeking, the heart will again become like fire covered over with ashes, which by remaining a long time unused will finally be extinguished. So at last the heart becomes encased with sensual impurities and with the blackness of the passions, and is no longer capable of being enlightened with the light of truth. Our refuge is in God!

O, faithful friend, you who are worthy to be loved! Know, that the love of God is a standard that leads to victory. Whoever seeks refuge under it, will be a sovereign in two worlds, and lord of a throne at the king's court. This love is a universal solvent to secure happiness. Whoever secures it, is richer than in the possession of both worlds. God is always rich. . . . The heart which bears no traces of the love of God, is like a dead corpse, which knows nothing of its own spirit.

An African Pilgrim to Mecca
▼▼▼

66 ▼ *Mahmud Kati,*
THE CHRONICLE OF THE SEEKER

Despite their differences, all Muslims accept certain basic beliefs, such as the Oneness of God, and perform a number of common religious obligations that serve as powerful forces for Islamic unification. Among these is the pilgrimage, or hajj, to Mecca. Every Muslim adult is expected, unless it is impossible, to travel once in a lifetime to Mecca, arriving during the sacred month of *Dhu-al-Hijja,* and join a vast multitude of other pilgrims in a mass celebration of devotional activities. Here Muslims of all sects, races, and social levels mingle without distinction and join in affirming the unity of the family of Islam.

The following document describes the famous pilgrimage that Mansa (King) Musa (Moses) of Mali (r. 1312–1327) made to Mecca in 1324–1325. The sheer size of Mansa Musa's entourage and the generosity this king of sub-Saharan West Africa exhibited to Muslims along the route guaranteed that the memory of his pilgrimage would not be lost. Several written accounts exist. This particular record is ascribed to the family of Mahmud Kati (1468?–1593), a native scholar and Islamic judge of Timbuktu. Kati, who according to tradition lived for 125 years, began to compose his history around 1519, and continued it until his death almost seventy-five years later. His sons and grandsons carried on his labors, bringing the story of Islam in West Africa down to 1655. As was the case with all contemporary writers in that region of the world, Kati and his family composed the work in Arabic.

QUESTIONS FOR ANALYSIS

1. What does Mansa Musa's alleged reason for undertaking the pilgrimage suggest about the hajj and pilgrimages in general?
2. How did his going on pilgrimage make Mansa Musa a better Muslim? What does this suggest about the role of hajj?
3. Is there any evidence in this story to suggest that Islam, though a world religion, still retained strong Arabic connections and flavor?
4. What evidence is there that this particular story was composed in its final form by one of Kati's successors?

5. What evidence suggests that the author used a source dated earlier than the end of the fifteenth century?
6. What role did oral tradition apparently play in sub-Saharan West African society?

We shall now relate some of what we have been able to discover about the history of the Mali-koy Kankan Musa.[1]

This Mali-koy was an upright, godly, and devout Sultan.[2] His dominion stretched from the limits of Mali as far as Sibiridugu, and all the peoples in these lands, Songhay[3] and others, obeyed him. Among the signs of his virtue are that he used to emancipate a slave every day, that he made the pilgrimage to the sacred house of God,[4] and that in the course of his pilgrimage he built the great mosque of Timbuktu[5] as well as the mosques of Dukurey, Gundam, Direy, Wanko, and Bako.

His mother Kankan was a native woman, though some say she was of Arab origin. The cause of his pilgrimage was related to me as follows by the scholar Muhammad Quma, may God have mercy on him, who had memorized the traditions of the ancients. He said that the Mali-koy Kankan Musa had killed his mother, Nana Kankan, by mistake. For this he felt deep regret and remorse and feared retribution. In expiation he gave great sums of money in alms and resolved on a life-long fast.

He asked one of the ulema[6] of his time what he could do to expiate this terrible crime, and he replied, "You should seek refuge with the Prophet of God, may God bless and save him. Flee to him, place yourself under his protection, and ask him to intercede for you with God, and God will accept his intercession. That is my view."

Kankan Musa made up his mind that very day and began to collect the money and equipment needed for the journey. He sent proclamations to all parts of his realm asking for supplies and support and went to one of his shaykhs[7] and asked him to choose the day of his departure. "You should wait," said the shaykh, "for the Saturday which falls on the twelfth day of the month. Set forth on that day, and you will not die before you return safe and sound to your residence, please God."

He therefore delayed and waited until these two coincided, and it was not until nine months later that the twelfth of the month fell on a Saturday. He set forth when the head of his caravan had already reached Timbuktu, while he himself was still in his residence in Mali.

Since that time travelers of that people believe it is lucky to set out on a journey on a Saturday which falls on the twelfth of a month. It has become proverbial that when a traveler returns in a bad state, they say of him, "Here is one who did not set out on the Mali-koy's Saturday of departure!"

Kankan Musa set out in force, with much money and a numerous army. A scholar told me that he heard from our shaykh, the very learned qadi[8] Abu'l-Abbas Sidi Ahmad ibn Ahmad ibn

---

[1]Titles meaning "King of Mali, Lord Musa."
[2]An Arabic term meaning "one who wields authority."
[3]Songhay lay to the east of Mali and centered on the trading city of Gao. Mansa Musa's armies conquered Gao around 1325, and Mali maintained control over Songhay until about 1375. By the late fifteenth century Songhay had replaced Mali as West Africa's major sub-Saharan trading kingdom and held this position of primacy until it was conquered in 1591 by invaders from Morocco.
[4]The Ka'bah in Mecca, Islam's holiest site.
[5]Timbuktu was the major trading city of the kingdom of Mali from 1325 to 1433. Its mosque school became the chief center of Muslim learning in sub-Saharan West Africa.
[6]Religious authorities by virtue of their learning.
[7]An Arabic title of respect meaning "elder."
[8]An Islamic judge.

Anda-ag-Muhammad, may God have mercy on him and be pleased with him, that on the day when the pasha[9] Ali ibn al-Qadir[10] left for Twat, announcing that he was going on the pilgrimage to Mecca, he asked how many persons were going with him and was told that the total number of armed men the pasha had with him was about eighty. "God is great! Praise be to God!," said the qadi. "Everything in the world grows less. When Kankan Musa left here to go on pilgrimage he had with him 8,000 men. The Askia Muhammad[11] made the pilgrimage later with 800 men, that is, one-tenth of that. Third after them came 'Ali ibn 'Abd al-Qadir, with 80 men, one-tenth of 800." And he added, "Praise be to God, other than Whom there is no God! 'Ali ibn 'Abd al-Qadir did not even achieve his purpose."

Kankan Musa went on his journey, about which there are many stories. Most of them are untrue and the mind refuses to accept them. One such story is that in every town where he stopped on Friday between here and Egypt he built a mosque on that very day. It is said that the mosques of Gundam and Dukurey were among those he built. Both at lunch and at dinner, from when he left his residence until he returned, he ate fresh fish and fresh vegetables.

I was told that his wife, called Inari Konte, went with him, accompanied by 500 of her women and serving women.

Our shaykh, the Mori Bukar ibn Salih, . . . may God have mercy on him, told me that Kankan Musa took forty mule-loads of gold with him when he went on his pilgrimage and visited the tomb of the Prophet.[12]

It is said that he asked the skaykh of the noble and holy city of Mecca, may Almighty God protect it, to give him two, three, or four

sharifs[13] of the kin of the Prophet of God, may God bless him and save him, to go with him to his country, so that the people of these parts might be blessed by the sight of them and by the blessing of their footsteps in these lands. But the shaykh refused, it being generally agreed that such things should be prevented and refused out of respect and regard for the noble blood of the *sharifs* and for fear lest one of them fall into the hands of the infidels and be lost or go astray. But he persisted in his request and urged them very strongly, until the shaykh said, "I will not do it, but I will neither command nor forbid it. If anyone wishes, let him follow you. His fate is in his own hands, I am not responsible."

The Mali-koy then sent a crier to the mosques to say, "Whoever wishes to have a thousand *mithqals*[14] of gold, let him follow me to my country, and the thousand is ready for him." Four men of the tribe of Quraysh[15] came to him, but it is claimed that they were freedmen[16] of Quraysh and not real Qurayshis. He gave them 4,000, 1,000 each,[17] and they followed him, with their families, when he returned to his country.

When the Mali-koy reached Timbuktu on his way back, he collected ships and small boats on which he transported their families and luggage, together with his own women, as far as his country, for the riding animals were too exhausted to use. When the ships, carrying the *sharifs* from Mecca, reached the town of Kami, the Dienné-koy[18] . . . attacked the ships and plundered all that they contained. They took the *sharifs* ashore and revolted against the Mali-koy. But when the people of the ships told them about the *sharifs* and informed them of their high station, they attended them, and in-

---

[9]A Turkish title meaning "chief."
[10]Governor of Timbuktu, 1628–1632.
[11]Askia (Emperor) Muhammad Ture the Great (r. 1492–1528), lord of Songhay. The askia undertook his pilgrimage in 1495–1496, accompanied by Mahmud Kati, who was one of his chief advisers.
[12]The Prophet's tomb is in Medina.
[13]An Arabic title meaning "exalted one."

[14]A weight of precious metal that varied by region.
[15]The tribe of the Prophet.
[16]Freed former slaves, therefore Qurayshis by adoption, not birth.
[17]He gave each of four men 1,000 mithqals of gold.
[18]The lord of Dienné, technically one of Mansa Musa's vassals.

stalled them in a nearby place called Shinshin. It is said that the *sharifs* of the town of Kay are descended from them.

This is the end of the story of the pilgrimage of the Mali-koy Kankan Musa. . . .

As for Mali, it is a vast region and an immense country, containing many towns and villages. The authority of the Sultan of Mali extends over all with force and might. We have heard the common people of our time say that there are four sultans in the world, not counting the supreme Sultan,[19] and they are the Sultan of Baghdad,[20] the Sultan of Egypt, the Sultan of Bornu,[21] and the Sultan of Mali.

---

[19]The Ottoman sultan of Constantinople.
[20]The last caliph of Baghdad died in 1258.

[21]A West African trading rival of Songhay located in the region of Lake Chad, along the border of modern Chad and Nigeria.

Part Three

▼▼▼

Continuity, Change, and Interchange, 500–1500

Hinduism, Buddhism, Confucianism, Greek rationalism, imperial systems of government and bureaucracy, Christianity, and many other major world traditions were firmly in place by A.D. 500 and, despite changes, they remained integral elements of global civilization for the next thousand years and beyond. The continuity of culture, especially in China and India, is one of the major features of the period 500 to 1500. A Chinese of the Han Dynasty would have found much that was familiar in Ming China (1368–1644), and while Islam was making an impact on northern India after 1000, Hindu culture continued to flourish and develop along lines that reached back at least to Indo-Aryan antiquity. At the same time, this millennium witnessed radical changes from which even the essentially conservative societies of China and India were not immune.

Many of these changes were due to the movement and interchange of people. Germans and other fringe groups infiltrated the western regions of the Roman Empire, thereby serving as a major factor in the radical transformation of society in Western Europe. The rise and spread of Islam in the seventh and eighth centuries created a new cultural bloc that stretched from western North Africa and Spain to Central Asia. The later movement of Turkish and Mongol nomads out of Central Asia resulted in empires that severely strained but also richly cross-pollinated virtually all of Eurasia's older civilized societies. Hindu, Chinese, and Arab merchants greatly influenced the development of civilization in Southeast Asia, their common meeting ground. It is almost impossible to exaggerate the impact China had on the development of Korean and Japanese cultures. The Byzantine world became the model and civilizer of the Eastern Slavs, most notably the Russians. Western Christian Europe expanded into Ireland, Scandinavia, Germany, the lands of the Baltic Sea, Poland, and Hungary. By 1500 Christianity, in both its Latin and Byzantine forms, provided spiritual direction to Europeans from Iceland to the Volga. Long before 1500, major portions of sub-Saharan Africa had become integral parts of the Muslim world, and toward the end of the fifteenth century Europeans were making their presence known along the African coast.

Of all Eurasia's civilizations, Western Europe underwent the most radical changes during this thousand-year period. Out of the chaos that ensued following the collapse of Roman society in the West, a new civilization emerged — Western Christian Europe. By 1100 it was an aggressive, expansionistic power, as the crusades bear witness. Despite a number of crises in the fourteenth century, which occasioned a momentary retrenchment, Western Europe never abandoned its spirit of expansion. In 1492 it was ready to resume explorations across the Atlantic. The eventual result was the virtual destruction of almost all Amerindian cultures and their absorption into the fabric of European civilization.

Chapter 9

▼▼▼

Asia

Asia was home to the world's oldest and most complex civilizations, and as such, its deeply rooted cultures were the most tradition-bound. Even Asia's newer civilizations, such as Japan, exhibited an innate conservatism, in part because they had borrowed so heavily from their well-established neighbors.

Change, of course, comes to all societies, old and new, and Asia was no exception. Occasionally, it arrived in dramatic fashion, as in the destruction of the Abbasid caliphate in 1258 or the establishment of the hated Yuan Dynasty (1264–1368) in China. More often than not, however, change arrived clothed in the guise of tradition. Even Kubilai Khan, Mongol emperor of China (r. 1260–1294), adopted a Chinese name for his dynasty, performed the Confucian imperial rites, and tried to reestablish the civil service examination system. When in 1192 Minamoto Yoritomo (1147–1199) transferred all real political and military power to himself as *shogun*, he left Japan's imperial court and structure in place and allowed local lords to retain a good measure of their old feudal autonomy.

A reverence for tradition did not mean a lack of dynamism. The great urban centers of Asia — Baghdad, Cambay, Delhi, Hangzhou, Nara — were prosperous and cosmopolitan. China in the eleventh century had several cities with populations of a million or more, and the volume of commerce in those urban centers eventually necessitated the creation of imperially guaranteed paper money. Economic prosperity also meant artistic patronage, and as a result artistic expression flourished from Southwest Asia to Japan. As European travelers learned, the riches of Asia were no empty fable.

▼▼▼

Japan

Japan was a late addition to the society of East Asian civilizations. Agriculture based on rice cultivation seems to have arrived from South China not much before 300 B.C., and Japan's first identifiable state arose no earlier than the third century A.D. when the chieftains of a clan devoted to the sun goddess established their hegemony on the Yamato Plain in the western regions of the island of Honshu. To the sophisticated Chinese, Japan in this period was the rustic land of Wa, which they represented with an ideograph that meant dwarf. The Japanese themselves were illiterate until a Korean scribe named Wani arrived in A.D. 405 to offer instruction in Chinese script, which the Japanese quickly adapted to their language. In the mid-sixth century a Chinese form of Mahayana Buddhism made its way to Japan from Korea, and in 646 it was officially acknowledged as the religion of the aristocracy. The coming of Buddhism sharpened the desire of Japan's leaders to adopt Chinese culture, and during the seventh and eighth centuries the imperial court of Japan dispatched large numbers of students to China, where they could observe the governmental system of the Tang Dynasty (618–907) at first hand before returning home to assume important official positions. These scholars brought back with them not only the forms of Chinese government but also some of the spirit that infused Chinese culture. Confucianism, Buddhism, and Daoism were woven into the fabric of Japanese civilization during these centuries of tutelage.

Although the Japanese borrowed extensively from China, their separation from the mainland of Asia enabled them to absorb foreign influences in a manner that did not destroy native culture. During the Heian period (794–1185), when the culture of the imperial court at Heian-kyo, or Kyoto as it came to be known, soared to unprecedented levels of refinement, Japanese civilization reached a level of mature independence it would never relinquish. The Japanese became more selective in their assimilation of Chinese influences and increasingly discovered inspiration for creative expression in their own land and people. By the early eleventh century Japan had evolved a distinctive civilization that set it apart from its two ancient mentors — Korea and China.

The Constitution of Prince Shotoku
▼▼▼

67 ▾ CHRONICLES OF JAPAN

Japan is unique in the fact that a single imperial dynasty has reigned over the land and its people for the past 1,700 years. This family, known as the Sun Line, claims descent from the sun goddess Ameterasu through her great-great-grandson Jimmu Tennu (Divine Warrior), the mythic first emperor of Japan, who, according to legend, began to rule in 660 B.C. The historical truth is less grand. The Yamato clan, which became the Sun Line, seems to have established its dominance in western Japan no earlier than the third century A.D. Whatever the origins of their dynasty, the range of the Yamato clan's authority grew in the course of its first several centuries of state building, thanks to fortunate alliances, conquests, and the development of a literate bureaucracy. By the sixth century the Yamato emperors and empresses had become living symbols of Japanese religious and cultural unity. However, even though it claimed divine origins and, by virtue of that claim, held a monopoly on the imperial throne, the Yamamoto family could not control several of Japan's powerful clan chieftains. Indeed, the opposite was more the case. Several powerful clans vied to control the imperial family.

One of the most powerful of Japan's late sixth-century clans, or *uji*, was the Soga family headed by Soga no Umako. In addition to struggling successfully against the rival Nakatomi and Mononobe clans for influence over the imperial court, Soga no Umako supported the policy of actively welcoming Chinese influences on a massive scale into Japan as a way of increasing the power of this island empire.

After engineering the assassination of one emperor, Soga no Umako chose a woman, Empress Suiko (r. 592–628), as nominal ruler. To guide her along proper lines, Soga designated an imperial prince to serve as regent. Under the direction of this crown prince, known as Shotoku (Sovereign Moral Power), Japan embarked on a course of deliberate cultural borrowing that was unprecedented in history. In 604 Prince Shotoku issued the so-called Constitution of Seventeen Articles, which laid out the ideological basis for the reforms that he, Empress Suiko, and Soga no Umako were championing.

Our knowledge of Shotoku's constitution comes from the *Nihongi*, or *Chronicles of Japan*, one of Japan's two oldest collections of legend and history. Composed in its final form in A.D. 720, the *Nihongi* traces the history of Japan back to the mythological age of the gods. By the time the *Nihongi* reaches the sixth century A.D., its narrative has largely left the realm of myth and become more reliable history.

QUESTIONS FOR ANALYSIS

1. What kind of constitution is this? Is it a code of institutional rules and regulations, or is it something else? What does your answer suggest?
2. What does this constitution allow you to infer about Shotoku's ideals and goals?
3. Review Chapter 4. What Confucian elements do you find in this document? Can you find any Daoist elements? What about Legalist elements?
4. What central principles of Chinese political philosophy do you see in this document? (See Chapters 1 and 4.)
5. What native, or non-Chinese, elements do you find in this document? What do they suggest about Japanese society?

The Prince Imperial in person prepared for the first time laws. There were seventeen clauses as follows:—

1. Harmony is to be valued, and an avoidance of wanton opposition to be honored. All men are influenced by class-feelings, and there are few who are intelligent. Hence there are some who disobey their lords and fathers, or who maintain feuds with the neighboring villages. But when those above are harmonious and those below are friendly, and there is concord in the discussion of business, right views of things spontaneously gain acceptance. Then what is there which cannot be accomplished!

2. Sincerely reverence the three treasures. The three treasures: the Buddha, the Law, and the Priesthood,[1] are the final refuge . . . and are the supreme objects of faith in all countries. What man in what age can fail to reverence this law? Few men are utterly bad. They may be taught to follow it. But if they do not go to the three treasures, how shall their crookedness be made straight?

3. When you receive the Imperial commands, fail not scrupulously to obey them. The lord is Heaven, the vassal is Earth. Heaven overspreads, and Earth upbears. When this is so, the four seasons follow their due course, and the powers of Nature obtain their efficacy. If the Earth attempted to overspread, Heaven would simply fall in ruin. Therefore is it that when the lord speaks, the vassal listens; when the superior acts, the inferior yields compliance. Consequently when you receive the Imperial commands, fail not to carry them out scrupulously. Let there be a want of care in this matter, and ruin is the natural consequence.

4. The Ministers and functionaries should make decorous behavior their leading principle, for the leading principle of the government of the people consists in decorous behavior. If the superiors do not behave with decorum, the inferiors are disorderly: if inferiors are wanting in proper behavior, there must necessarily be offenses. Therefore it is that when lord and vassal behave with propriety, the distinctions of rank are

[1]The Buddha, the Law of Dharma, and the Sangha, or order of male and female monks, are the three treasures, or key elements, of Buddhism. See Chapter 3, sources 20 and 21.

not confused: when the people behave with propriety, the Government of the Commonwealth proceeds of itself. . . .

6. Chastise that which is evil and encourage that which is good. This was the excellent rule of antiquity. Conceal not, therefore, the good qualities of others, and fail not to correct that which is wrong when you see it. Flatterers and deceivers are a sharp weapon for the overthrow of the State, and a pointed sword for the destruction of the people. Sycophants are also fond, when they meet, of speaking at length to their superiors on the errors of their inferiors; to their inferiors, they censure the faults of their superiors. Men of this kind are all wanting in fidelity to their lord, and in benevolence toward the people. From such an origin great civil disturbances arise.

7. Let every man have his own charge, and let not the spheres of duty be confused. When wise men are entrusted with office, the sound of praise arises. If unprincipled men hold office, disasters and tumults are multiplied. In this world, few are born with knowledge: wisdom is the product of earnest meditation. In all things, whether great or small, find the right man, and they will surely be well managed: on all occasions, be they urgent or the reverse, meet but with a wise man, and they will of themselves be amenable. In this way will the State be lasting and the Temples of the Earth and of Grain will be free from danger. Therefore did the wise sovereigns of antiquity seek the man to fill the office, and not the office for the sake of the man. . . .

10. Let us cease from wrath, and refrain from angry looks. Nor let us be resentful when others differ from us. For all men have hearts, and each heart has its own leanings.

Their right is our wrong, and our right is their wrong. We are not unquestionably sages, nor are they unquestionably fools. Both of us are simply ordinary men. How can any one lay down a rule by which to distinguish right from wrong? For we are all, one with another, wise and foolish, like a ring which has no end. Therefore, although others give way to anger, let us on the contrary dread our own faults, and though we alone may be in the right, let us follow the multitude and act like them.

11. Give clear appreciation to merit and demerit, and deal out to each its sure reward or punishment. In these days, reward does not attend upon merit, nor punishment upon crime. You high functionaries who have charge of public affairs, let it be your task to make clear rewards and punishments. . . .

15. To turn away from that which is private, and to set our faces toward that which is public — this is the path of a Minister. Now if a man is influenced by private motives, he will assuredly feel resentments, and if he is influenced by resentful feelings, he will assuredly fail to act harmoniously with others. If he fails to act harmoniously with others, he will assuredly sacrifice the public interests to his private feelings. When resentment arises, it interferes with order, and is subversive of law. . . .

16. Let the people be employed [in forced labor] at seasonable times. This is an ancient and excellent rule. Let them be employed, therefore, in the winter months, when they are at leisure. But from Spring to Autumn, when they are engaged in agriculture or with the mulberry trees,[2] the people should not be so employed. For if they do not attend to agriculture, what will

---

[2]The cultivation of silk worms that ate mulberry leaves. The technique of silk production was an import from China.

they have to eat? If they do not attend to the mulberry trees, what will they do for clothing?

17. Decisions on important matters should not be made by one person alone. They should be discussed with many. But small matters are of less consequence. It is unnecessary to consult a number of people. It is only in the case of the discussion of weighty affairs, when there is a suspicion that they may miscarry, that one should arrange matters in concert with others, so as to arrive at the right conclusion.

The Life of an Aristocratic Woman in Eleventh-Century Japan
▼▼▼

68 ▼ *Murasaki Shikibu, DIARY*

When Prince Shotoku died in 622, the process of restructuring Japan along Chinese lines was far from complete, but the foundation had been laid. The next stage in Japan's adoption of Chinese values and modes of imperial administration was the *Taika*, or Great Transformation, that began in 645, ironically with the wholesale destruction of the Soga clan by a cabal of pro-Chinese reformers.

The centralized administrative system established in the Great Transformation failed, however, to function as intended, and by the mid-ninth century true power in the provinces rested in the hands of local clan chiefs and a new element, Buddhist monasteries (see source 69). At the same time, the organs of Taika government remained in place, even though provincial governors largely resided at the imperial court at Kyoto. The court itself became an increasingly elegant setting for emperors and empresses, who were regarded as sacred beings and theoretically stood at the summit of all power. The elaborate ceremony that surrounded these people, who claimed to rule the world, masked, at least at close hand, the fact that effective power lay elsewhere.

While the imperial court was increasingly losing touch with the center of political authority, a group of aristocratic women at court were developing Japan's first native literature. Unlike many of Japan's Confucian scholars, who continued to study the Chinese classics along fairly rigid lines established a millennium earlier in a foreign land, these court women gave free play in their prose and poetry to their imaginations, emotions, and powers of analysis.

Japan's greatest literary artist of the Heian period was Murasaki Shikibu (978–after 1010), a lady-in-waiting at the court of Second Empress Akiko. Her masterpiece is the massive *The Tale of Genji*, a romance whose psychological insights and realistic portraits of life have earned it universal recognition as the single greatest piece of classical Japanese literature and one of the world's immortal novels. Like many other imperial ladies-in-waiting, Lady Murasaki kept a diary in which she recorded, with the same level of insight and narrative ability she displayed in *The Tale of Genji*, her observations on court life and her deepest reflections.

QUESTIONS FOR ANALYSIS

1. What was expected of court women? How did male aristocrats look upon and treat women of their class? As equals? As servants? As ornaments? As something else?
2. What did this aristocratic society think of literary accomplishment?
3. How important was Chinese literature to Japanese literary artists?
4. What does this diary tell us about the level of refinement and sophistication among Japan's aristocracy? What does it suggest about the Japanese sense of beauty?
5. How Confucian was Lady Murasaki in her values and way of life? Does the diary contain any non-Confucian tones? What do you infer from your answers to these two questions?
6. Would Lady Murasaki ever think of herself as "liberated"? Would she understand such a concept? What seems to be her view of women in general and herself in particular?
7. Compare Murasaki Shikibu's vision of what it means to be a woman with that of Madame Ban Zhao (Chapter 5, source 39). What do you conclude from that comparison?

As the autumn season approaches the Tsuchimikado[1] becomes inexpressibly smile-giving. The tree-tops near the pond, the bushes near the stream, are dyed in varying tints whose colors grow deeper in the mellow light of evening. The murmuring sound of waters mingles all the night through with the never-ceasing recitation of sutras[2] which appeal more to one's heart as the breezes grow cooler.

The ladies waiting upon her honored presence are talking idly. The Queen hears them; she must find them annoying, but she conceals it calmly. Her beauty needs no words of mine to praise it, but I cannot help feeling that to be near so beautiful a queen will be the only relief from my sorrow.[3] So in spite of my better desires [for a religious life] I am here. Nothing else dispels my grief — it is wonderful! . . .

I can see the garden from my room beside the entrance to the gallery. The air is misty, the dew is still on the leaves. The Lord Prime Minister is walking there; he orders his men to cleanse the brook. He breaks off a stalk of omenaishi [flower maiden] which is in full bloom by the south end of the bridge. He peeps in over my screen! His noble appearance embarrasses us, and I am ashamed of my morning [not yet painted and powdered] face. He says, "Your poem on this! If you delay so much the fun is gone!" and I seize the chance to run away to the writing-box, hiding my face—

Flower-maiden in bloom—
Even more beautiful for the bright dew,
Which is partial, and never favors me.

---

[1] The residence of Prime Minister Fujiwara Michinaga, father of Second Empress Akiko, who has returned to her father's home to give birth to Prince Atsusada.

[2] Buddhist texts.
[3] Her husband, whom she had married in 999, had died in 1001. It is now 1007.

"So prompt!" said he, smiling, and ordered a writing-box to be brought for himself.

His answer:

The silver dew is never partial.
From her heart
The flower-maiden's beauty.

One wet and calm evening I was talking with Lady Saisho. The young Lord[4] of the Third Rank sat with the misu[5] partly rolled up. He seemed maturer than his age and was very graceful. Even in light conversation such expressions as "Fair soul is rarer than fair face" come gently to his lips, covering us with confusion. It is a mistake to treat him like a young boy. He keeps his dignity among ladies, and I saw in him a much-sought-after romantic hero when once he walked off reciting to himself:

Linger in the field where flower-maidens
    are blooming
And your name will be tarnished with tales
    of gallantry.

Some such trifle as that sometimes lingers in my mind when really interesting things are soon forgotten — why? . . .

On the fifth night the Lord Prime Minister celebrated the birth.[6] The full moon on the fifteenth day was clear and beautiful. Torches were lighted under the trees and tables were put there with rice-balls on them. Even the uncouth humble servants who were walking about chattering seemed to enhance the joyful scene. All minor officials were there burning torches, making it as bright as day. Even the attendants of the nobles, who gathered behind the rocks and under the trees, talked of nothing but the new light which had come into the world, and

were smiling and seemed happy as if their own private wishes had been fulfilled. . . .

This time, as they chose only the best-looking young ladies, the rest who used to tie their hair on ordinary occasions to serve the Queen's dinner wept bitterly; it was shocking to see them. . . .

To serve at the Queen's dinner eight ladies tied their hair with white cords, and in that dress brought in Her Majesty's dining-table. The chief lady-in-waiting for that night was Miya-no-Naishi. She was brilliantly dressed with great formality, and her hair was made more charming by the white cords which enhanced her beauty. I got a side glance of her when her face was not screened by her fan.[7] She wore a look of extreme purity. . . .

The court nobles rose from their seats and went to the steps [descending from the balcony]. His Lordship the Prime Minister and others cast da.[8] It was shocking to see them quarreling about paper. Some others composed poems. A lady said, "What response shall we make if some one offers to drink saké with us?"[9] We tried to think of something.

Shijo-no-Dainagon is a man of varied accomplishments. No ladies can rival him in repartee, much less compete with him in poetry, so they were all afraid of him, but this evening he did not give a cup to any particular lady to make her compose poems. Perhaps that was because he had many things to do and it was getting late. . . .

The Great Adviser[10] is displeased to be received by ladies of low rank, so when he comes to the Queen's court to make some report and suitable ladies to receive him are not available, he goes away without seeing Her Majesty. Other court nobles, who often come to make reports, have each a favorite lady, and when that one is away they are displeased, and go

---

[4]The prime minister's son Yorimichi, who was sixteen years old.
[5]A bamboo curtain used to hide distinguished people from view.
[6]Of his imperial grandson.

[7]Women were expected to hide their faces behind fans.
[8]A game of dice.
[9]Thereby challenging the person to compose an impromptu poem.
[10]Fujiwara Michitaka, the prime minister's brother.

away saying to other people that the Queen's ladies are quite unsatisfactory. . . .

Lady Izumi Shikibu[11] corresponds charmingly, but her behavior is improper indeed. She writes with grace and ease and with a flashing wit. There is fragrance even in her smallest words. Her poems are attractive, but they are only improvisations which drop from her mouth spontaneously. Every one of them has some interesting point, and she is acquainted with ancient literature also, but she is not like a true artist who is filled with the genuine spirit of poetry. Yet I think even she cannot presume to pass judgment on the poems of others.

The wife of the Governor of Tamba Province is called by the Queen and Prime Minister Masa Hira Emon. Though she is not of noble birth, her poems are very satisfying. She does not compose and scatter them about on every occasion, but so far as we know them, even her miscellaneous poems shame us. Those who compose poems whose loins are all but broken, yet who are infinitely self-exalted and vain, deserve our contempt and pity.

Lady Seishonagon.[12] A very proud person. She values herself highly, and scatters her Chinese writings all about. Yet should we study her closely, we should find that she is still imperfect. She tries to be exceptional, but naturally persons of that sort give offense. She is piling up trouble for her future. One who is too richly gifted, who indulges too much in emotion, even when she ought to be reserved, and cannot turn aside from anything she is interested in, in spite of herself will lose self-control. How can such a vain and reckless person end her days happily?

▷ Here there is a sudden change from the Court to her own home.

---

[11]One of Japan's greatest poets.
[12]One of the leading literary figures of her day and a rival of Murasaki Shikibu. Lady Seishonagon served at the court of the First Empress, who was a rival of her cousin, the Second Empress.

Having no excellence within myself, I have passed my days without making any special impression on anyone. Especially the fact that I have no man who will look out for my future makes me comfortless. I do not wish to bury myself in dreariness. Is it because of my worldly mind that I feel lonely? On moonlight nights in autumn, when I am hopelessly sad, I often go out on the balcony and gaze dreamily at the moon. It makes me think of days gone by. People say that it is dangerous to look at the moon in solitude, but something impels me, and sitting a little withdrawn I muse there. In the wind-cooled evening I play on the koto,[13] though others may not care to hear it. I fear that my playing betrays the sorrow which becomes more intense, and I become disgusted with myself — so foolish and miserable am I. . . .

A pair of big bookcases have in them all the books they can hold. In one of them are placed old poems and romances. They are the homes of worms which come frightening us when we turn the pages, so none ever wished to read them. [Perhaps her own writings, she speaks so slightingly of them.] As to the other cabinet, since the person[14] who placed his own books [there] no hand has touched it. When I am bored to death I take out one or two of them; then my maids gather around me and say: "Your life will not be favored with old age if you do such a thing! Why do you read Chinese? Formerly even the reading of sutras was not encouraged for women." They rebuke me in the shade [i.e., behind my back]. I have heard of it and have wished to say, "It is far from certain that he who does no forbidden thing enjoys a long life," but it would be a lack of reserve to say it [to the maids]. Our deeds vary with our age and deeds vary with the individual. Some are proud [to read books], others look over old cast-away writings because they are bored with

---

[13]A stringed instrument.
[14]Her deceased husband, who had been a scholar of Chinese literature.

having nothing to do. It would not be becoming for such a one to chatter away about religious thoughts, noisily shaking a rosary.[15] I feel this, and before my women keep myself from doing what otherwise I could do easily. But after all, when I was among the ladies of the Court I did not say what I wanted to say either,

for it is useless to talk with those who do not understand one and troublesome to talk with those who criticize from a feeling of superiority. Especially one-sided persons are troublesome. Few are accomplished in many arts and most cling narrowly to their own opinion.

The Ideal Samurai
▼▼▼

69 ▾ *CHRONICLE OF THE GRAND PACIFICATION*

While imperial courtiers at Kyoto composed exquisite poems that extolled the beauty of nature, Japan's warlords were engaged in carving out independent principalities backed by the might of their private armies of *samurai* (those who serve). Between 1180 and 1185 a conflict known as the Gempei War devastated the heartland of the main island of Honshu as the mighty Taira and Minimoto clans fought for control of the imperial family and its court. In 1185 the Minimoto house destroyed the Taira faction, thereby becoming the supreme military power in Japan.

Rather than seizing the imperial office for himself, the leader of the victorious Minimoto family accepted the title of *shogun,* or imperial commander-in-chief, and elected to rule over a number of military governors from his remote base at Kamakura, while a puppet emperor reigned at Kyoto. This feudal system, known as the *bakufu* (tent headquarters), shaped the politics and culture of Japan for centuries to come.

Toward the early fourteenth century the Kamakura shogunate began to show signs of weakening, which in turn encouraged Emperor Go-Daigo (r. 1318–1336) to lead a coup in an attempt to destroy the shogunate and reestablish the primacy of the emperor. This rebel emperor became the nucleus of a full-scale feudal uprising by wide numbers of dissatisfied warlords, samurai, and warrior-monks. The warrior-monks were members of great landholding Buddhist monasteries which already for many centuries had been centers of independent political, economic, and military power. The rebellion resulted in the destruction of Kamakura and the death of its last shogun.

Go-Daigo's victory was brief, however. Within a few years he was deposed by another warlord, who installed his own emperor and received back from him the title of shogun, thereby establishing the Ashikaga Shogunate (1338–1573).

---

[15]Literally, a garland of roses. The rosary is an aid to prayer consisting of beads strung together in a circle allowing a person to count prayers. Begun by Hindus, the rosary spread among Buddhists and later to Muslims and Christians.

Japanese government and society, therefore, continued to be dominated by its feudal warriors.

The story of the last several years of the Kamakura Shogunate is recorded in the pages of the *Taiheiki*, or *Chronicle of the Grand Pacification*. Composed by a number of largely anonymous Buddhist monks between about 1333 and maybe as late as 1370, this chronicle recounts the battles and intrigues of the period 1318–1333. Its title refers to Go-Daigo's momentarily successful attempt to destroy, or "pacify," the shogunate.

Our excerpt tells the story of the defense in 1331 of Akasaka castle by Kusunoki Masashige, one of the emperor's most fervent supporters. This was a dark moment for the imperial forces. The emperor, along with many followers, had recently been captured at Kasagi, a fortified monastic temple. The imperial cause needed a victory, even a moral one, and this heretofore obscure warrior was about to provide new hope with his inspired defense of this stronghold.

Killed in 1333 in a battle he knew he could not win, Masashige has been revered through the centuries as a paragon of samurai virtues. The *kamikaze* (divine wind) suicide pilots whom Japan launched against the U.S. Navy in 1945 were called "chrysanthemum warriors" in reference to the Kusunoki family's flowered crest.

QUESTIONS FOR ANALYSIS

1. Why do the warriors assaulting Akasaka hope that Kusunoki will be able to hold out for at least one day? What does this suggest?
2. Bravery is naturally expected of all warriors, but which other samurai virtues does Kusunoki Masashige exemplify?
3. Which samurai virtues do his foes exhibit? In what ways did they show themselves to be less than ideal warriors?
4. Thinking their enemy dead, the shogun's warriors pause to remember Kusunoki Masashige. What does this suggest?
5. Based on this account, what picture emerges of the ideals and realities of fourteenth-century Japanese feudal warfare?

No man of the mighty host from the distant eastern lands was willing to enter the capital, so sorely were their spirits mortified because Kasagi castle had fallen.[1] . . . All took their way instead toward Akasaka castle, where Kusunoki Hyoe Masashige was shut up. . . .

When these had passed beyond the Ishi River, they beheld the castle. Surely this was a stronghold of hasty devising! The ditch was not a proper ditch, and there was but a single wooden wall, plastered over with mud. Likewise in size the castle was not more than one hundred or two hundred yards around, with but twenty or thirty towers within, made ready in haste. Of those who saw it, not one but thought:

[1]This force of Kamakura supporters from the east was dispirited because it had arrived too late to participate in the capture of Kasagi.

"Ah, what a pitiable spectacle the enemy presents! Even if we were to hold this castle in one hand and throw, we would be able to throw it! Let us hope that in some strange manner Kusunoki will endure for at least a day, that by taking booty and winning honor we may obtain future rewards."

Drawing near, the three hundred thousand riders[2] got down from their horses, one after another, jumped into the ditch, stood below the towers, and competed to be the first to enter the castle.

Now by nature Masashige was a man who would "scheme in his tent to defeat an enemy a thousand leagues distant," one whose counsels were as subtle as though sprung from the brain of Chenping or Zhang Liang.[3] Wherefore had he kept two hundred mighty archers within the castle, and had given three hundred riders to his brother Shichiro and Wada Goro Masato outside in the mountains. Yet the attackers, all unwitting, rushed forward together to the banks of the ditch on the four sides, resolved to bring down the castle in a single assault.

Then from tower tops and windows the archers shot furiously with arrowheads aligned together, smiting more than a thousand men in an instant. And greatly amazed, the eastern warriors said:

"No, no! From the look of things at this castle, it will never fall in a day or two. Let us take time before going against it, that we may establish camps and battle-offices and form separate parties."

They drew back from the attack a little, took off their horses' saddles, cast aside their armor, and rested in their camps.

In the mountains Kusunoki Shichiro and Wada Goro said, "The time is right." They made two parties of the three hundred horsemen, came out from the shelter of the trees on the eastern and western slopes with two fluttering banners, whereon were depicted the chrysanthemum and water crest of the Kusunoki house, and advanced quietly toward the enemy, urging their horses forward in the swirling mist.

The attackers hesitated doubtfully.

"Are they enemies or friends?" they thought.

Then suddenly from both sides the three hundred attacked, shouting, in wedge-shaped formations. They smote the center of the three hundred thousand horsemen spread out like clouds or mist, broke into them in all directions, and cut them down on every side. And the attackers' hosts were powerless to form to give battle, so great was their bewilderment.

Next within the castle three gates opened all together, wherefrom two hundred horsemen galloped forth side by side to let fly a multitude of arrows from bows pulled back to the utmost limits. Although the attackers were a mighty host, they were confounded utterly by these few enemies, so that they clamored aloud. Some mounted tethered horses and beat them with their stirrups, seeking to advance; others fixed arrows to unstrung bows and tried vainly to shoot. Two or three men took up a single piece of armor and disputed it, pulling against each other. Though a lord was killed, his vassals knew nothing of it; though a father was killed, his sons aided him not, but like scattered spiders they retreated to the Ishi River. For half a league along their way there was no space where a foot might tread, by reason of their abandoned horses and arms. To be sure, great gains came suddenly to the common folk of Tojo district![4]

Perhaps the proud eastern warriors thought in their hearts that Kusunoki's strategy could not be despised, since blundering unexpectedly they had been defeated in the first battle. For

---

[2]The *Taiheiki* grossly exaggerates the number of pro-Kamakura fighters.

[3]Two ministers of the first Han emperor of China. The quotation is from Ban Gu and Ban Zhao's *History of the Former Han Dynasty*.

[4]Commoners would scavenge battlefields.

though they went forth against Handa and Narahara,[5] they did not seek to attack the castle again quickly, but consulted together and made a resolution, saying:

"Let us remain awhile in this place, that led by men acquainted with the home provinces we may cut down trees on the mountains, burn houses, and guard thereby against warriors waiting in reserve to fall upon us. Then may we attack the castle with tranquil spirits."

But there were many . . . who had lost fathers and sons in the fighting. These roused themselves up, saying:

"What is the use of living? Though we go alone, let us gallop forth to die in battle!"

And thereupon all the others took heart as well, and galloped forward eagerly.

Now Akasaka castle might not be attacked easily on the east, where terraced rice fields extended far up the mountainside. But on three sides the land was flat; likewise there was but a single ditch and wall. All the attackers were contemptuous, thinking, "No matter what demons may be inside, it cannot be much of an affair." When they drew near again, they went forward quickly into the ditch to the opposite bank, pulled away the obstacles and made ready to enter. Yet within the castle there was no sound.

Then the attackers thought in their hearts:

"As it was yesterday, so will it be today. After wounding many men with arrows to confuse us, they will send other warriors to fight in our midst."

They counted out a hundred thousand riders to go to the mountains in the rear, while the remaining two hundred thousand compassed the castle round about like thickly growing rice, hemp, bamboo, or reeds. Yet from within the castle not an arrow was released, nor was any man seen.

At last the attackers laid hold of the wall on the four sides to climb over it, filled with excitement. But thereupon men within the castle cut the ropes supporting that wall, all at the same time, for it was a double wall, built to let the outside fall down. More than a thousand of the attackers became as though crushed by a weight, so that only their eyes moved as the defenders threw down logs and boulders onto them. And in this day's fighting more than seven hundred of them were slain.

Unwilling to attack again because of the bitterness of the first two days of fighting, for four or five days the eastern hosts merely besieged the castle from camps hard by. Truly were they without pride, to watch thus idly from a nearby place! How mortifying it was that men of the future would make a mock of them, saying, "Although the enemy were no more than four or five hundred persons shut up in a flatland castle not five hundred yards around, the hosts of the eight eastern provinces would not attack them, but shamefully laid down a siege from a distance!"

At last the attackers spoke among themselves, saying:

"Previously we attacked in the fierceness of our valor, not carrying shields or preparing weapons of assault, wherefore we suffered unforeseen injury. Let us go against them now with a different method."

All commanded the making of shields with toughened hide on their faces, such as might not be smashed through easily, and with these upheld they went against the castle once more, saying:

"There can be no difficulty about jumping across to the wall, since the banks are not high, nor is the ditch deep. Yet will not this wall also drop down upon us?"

They spoke with fearful hearts, reluctant to seize upon the wall lightly. All went down into the water of the ditch, laid hold upon the wall with grapnels, and pulled at it. But when the wall was about to fall, those within the castle took ladles with handles ten or twenty feet long, dipped up boiling water, and poured it

---

[5]Settlements near Akasaka.

onto them. The hot water passed through the holes in their helmet tops, ran down from the edges of their shoulder-guards, and burned their bodies so grievously that they fled panic-stricken, throwing down their shields and grapnels. How shameful it was! Although no man of them was slain, there were as many as two or three hundred persons who could not stand up from the burns on their hands and feet, or who lay down with sick bodies.

So it was that whenever the attackers advanced with new devisings, those within the castle defended against them with changed stratagems. Wherefore in consultation together the attackers said, "From this time on, let us starve them, for we can do no other." They forbore utterly to do battle, but only built towers in their camps, lined up obstacles, and laid down a siege.

Soon the warriors in the castle grew weary of spirit, since there was no diversion for them. Nor was their food sufficient, since Kusunoki had built the castle in haste. The battle having begun and the siege commenced, within twenty days the stores were eaten up; nor did food remain for more than four or five days.

Then Masashige spoke a word to his men, saying:

"In various battles of late have we overreached the foe, whose slain are beyond counting, but these things are as nothing in the eyes of so mighty a host. Moreover, the castle's food is eaten up, and no other warriors will come to deliver us.

"Assuredly I will not cherish life in the hour of need, from the beginning having been steadfast for His Majesty's sake . . . But the true man of courage 'is cautious in the face of difficulties, and deliberates before acting.'[6] I will flee this castle for a time, causing the enemy to believe that I have taken my life, so that they may go away rejoicing. When they are gone I will come forward to fight; and if they return I

will go deep into the mountains. When I have harassed the eastern hosts four or five times in this manner, will they not grow weary? This is a plan for destroying the enemy in safety. What are your views?"

All agreed, "It ought to be so."

Then quickly within the castle they dug a mighty hole seven feet deep, filling it with twenty or thirty bodies of the slain (who were fallen down dead into the ditch in great numbers), whereon they piled up charcoal and firewood. And they awaited a night of pouring rain and driving wind.

Perhaps because Masashige had found favor in the sight of heaven, suddenly a harsh wind came raising the sand, accompanied by a rain violent enough to pierce bamboo. The night was exceedingly dark, and all the enemy in their camps were sheltered behind curtains. This indeed was the awaited night!

Leaving a man in the castle to light a blaze when they were fled away safely five or six hundred yards, the defenders cast off their armor, assumed the guise of attackers, and fled away calmly by threes and fives, passing in front of the enemy battle-offices and beside enemy sleeping places.

It came about that the eyes of an enemy fell upon Masashige, where he passed before the stables of Nagasaki. The man challenged him, saying, "What person passes before this battle-office in stealth, not announcing himself?"

In haste Masashige passed beyond that place, calling back, "I am a follower of the grand marshal who has taken the wrong road."

"A suspicious fellow indeed!" thought the man. "Assuredly he is a stealer of horses! I shall shoot him down."

He ran up close and shot Masashige full in the body. But although the arrow looked to have driven deep at the height of the elbow-joint, it turned over and flew back again without touching the naked flesh.

---

[6]A quotation from Confucius's *Analects* (Chapter 4, source 25).

Later, when that arrow's track was observed, men saw that it had struck an amulet wherein was preserved the *Kannon Sutra,*[7] which Masashige had trusted and read for many years. Its arrowhead had stopped in the two-line poem, "Wholeheartedly praising the name." How strange it was!

When in this manner Masashige had escaped death from a certain-death arrowhead, he fled to a safe place more than half a league distant. And looking back he saw that the warrior had lighted fires in the castle's battle-offices, faithful to his covenant.

The hosts of the attackers were seized with amazement at the sight of the flames.

"Aha! The castle has fallen!" they shouted exultantly. "Let no man be spared! Let none escape!"

When the flames died away, they saw a mighty hole inside the castle, piled up with charcoal, wherein lay the burned bodies of many men. And then not a man of them but spoke words of praise, saying:

"How pitiful! Masashige had ended his life! Though he was an enemy, his was a glorious death, well befitting a warrior."

▼▼▼

China

The period from 500 to 1500 witnessed a variety of momentous developments in China: renewed imperial greatness, philosophical and technological innovation, economic expansion and a rapidly growing population, new modes of artistic expression, conquest by Mongol invaders, and eventual recovery and retrenchment. Through it all, Chinese civilization managed to retain intact its basic institutions and way of life.

The Time of Troubles that followed the fall of the house of Han was over by the end of the sixth century, and under the Tang Dynasty (618–907) China was again a great imperial power, with a restored Confucian civil service firmly in power. At the end of the seventh century China's borders reached to the Aral Sea in the western regions of Central Asia, Korea and Manchuria in the northeast, and Vietnam to the south. The Tang era was also an age of artistic brilliance. Sculpture, particularly the representation of magnificent horses and camels, poetry, and painting became Tang hallmarks.

Fifty-three years of disunity followed the Tang collapse. The Song Dynasty (960–1279) eventually reunited most of the Chinese heartland, but geographically and militarily Song China was a truncated shadow of former Tang greatness. Despite its external weakness, China under the Song achieved levels of political stability, economic prosperity, technological advancement, and cultural maturity unequaled anywhere else on earth at the time. By the mid-eleventh century the production of printed books had become such an important industry that artisans were experimenting with movable type—four hundred years before the introduction of a similar printing process in Europe. The thousands of books

---

[7]A holy book dedicated to the female bodhisattva Kannon, who was known as Guanyin in China. See Chapter 6, source 50.

and millions of pages printed in Song China are evidence that a remarkably high degree of its population was literate. In addition to this dramatic rise in basic literacy, there were significant developments in advanced philosophy. Intellectuals reinvigorated Confucian thought by injecting into it metaphysical concepts borrowed from Buddhism and Daoism. This new Study of the Way, or Neo-Confucianism, provided fresh philosophical insights clothed in traditional forms and enabled Confucianism to topple Buddhism from its position of intellectual preeminence.

The fine arts also reached new levels of achievement. Landscape painting, particularly during the period known as Southern Song (1127–1279), expressed in two dimensions the mystical visions of Daoism and Chan Buddhism. On a three dimensional plane, the craft of porcelain-making became a high art, and large numbers of exquisitely delicate pieces of fine "Chinaware" were traded from Japan to East Africa.

Advanced ships and navigational aids enabled Chinese traders to take to the sea in unprecedented numbers, especially in the direction of Southeast Asia, thereby transforming their homeland into the world's greatest merchant marine power of its day. Rapid-maturing strains of rice were introduced from Champa in Southeast Asia, making it possible to feed a population that exceeded 100 million, about double that of the Age of Tang. Although most of this massive population was engaged in traditional, labor-intensive agriculture, some Chinese were employed in industries, such as mining, iron and steel production, and textile manufacture, that used advanced technologies unequaled anywhere else in the world.

Song's age of greatness was brought to a close by Mongol invaders, who by 1279 had joined all of China to the largest land empire in world history. Mongol rule during what is known as the Yuan Dynasty (1264–1368) was unmitigated military occupation. Both the Mongols and the many foreigners whom they admitted to their service essentially exploited and oppressed the Chinese. While the Mongols encouraged agriculture and trade, few Chinese benefited from a prosperity that was largely confined to a small circle of landlords.

By the mid-fourteenth century China was in rebellion, and in 1368 a commoner, Zhu Yuan-zhang, reestablished native rule in the form of the Ming Dynasty (1368–1644). This new imperial family restored Chinese prestige and influence in East Asia to levels enjoyed under Tang and provided China with stability and prosperity until the late sixteenth century. Under the Ming traditional Chinese civilization attained full maturity. Toward the middle of the Age of Ming, however, China reluctantly established relations with seaborne Western European merchants and missionaries, and the resultant challenge of the West would result, centuries later, in major transformations in Chinese life.

Troubles in Late Tang
▼▼▼

70 ▼ *Du Fu, POEMS*

The Chinese consider the eighth century their golden age of classical poetry. Among the century's many great poets, three are universally recognized as China's preeminent poetic geniuses: the Buddhist Wang Wei (699–759), the Daoist Li Bo (701–762), and the Confucian Du Fu (712–770). Despite their differences in personality and perspective, they knew, deeply respected, and genuinely liked one another. Of the three, the Chinese most esteem Du Fu, primarily for the tone of compassion for the downtrodden that pervades his poetry.

Du Fu himself knew adversity. Despite his extraordinary erudition, he was denied a position of public responsibility and spent much of his adult life as an impoverished wanderer and farmer. He lived to see one of his children die of starvation and suffered through the destruction of General An Lushan's rebellion (755–763), a civil war from which the Tang regime never recovered. Despite these adversities, Du Fu never lost his love for humanity or his belief in the innate goodness of the common person.

QUESTIONS FOR ANALYSIS

1. According to Du Fu, what costs have the Chinese paid for their empire? Has it been worth it? What does he think of military glory?
2. From a Confucian perspective, what is wrong with eighth-century China?
3. Can you find any Daoist sentiments in these poems?
4. What do the second and third poems tell us about the economic and social consequences of An Lushan's rebellion?
5. In what ways do the first two poems seem to suggest that Du Fu believed that the Tang emperor might be losing the Mandate of Heaven (Chapter 1, source 6)?
6. One of the prime virtues of Confucianism is *ren,* which is best translated as "humaneness." The character for this word is composed of two elements: the signs for "person" and "two." In what ways do these poems, especially the third poem, exemplify the qualities of ren?

BALLAD OF THE WAR CHARIOTS

The jingle of war chariots,
Horses neighing, men marching,
Bows and arrows slung over hips;
Beside them stumbling, running
The mass of parents, wives and children

Clogging up the road, their rising dust
Obscuring the great bridge at Hsienyang;
Stamping their feet, weeping
In utter desperation with cries
That seem to reach the clouds;

Ask a soldier: Why do you go?
Would simply bring the answer:

Today men are conscripted often;
Fifteen-year-olds sent up the Yellow River
To fight; men of forty marched away
To colonize the western frontier;
Village elders take young boys,
Do up their hair like adults
To get them off; if they return
It will be white with age, but even then
They may be sent off to the frontier again;

Frontiers on which enough blood has
      flowed
To make a sea, yet our Emperor still would
Expand his authority! Have you not heard
How east of Huashan[1] many counties
Are desolate with weeds and thorns?
The strongest women till the fields,
Yet crops come not as well as before;

Lads from around here are well known
For their bravery, but hate to be driven
Like dogs or chickens; only because
You kindly ask me do I dare give vent
To grievances; now for instance
With the men from the western frontier
Still not returned, the government
Demands immediate payment of taxes,
But how can we pay when so little
Has been produced?

Now, we peasants have learnt one thing:
To have a son is not so good as having
A daughter who can marry a neighbor
And still be near us, while a son
Will be taken away to die in some
Wild place, his bones joining those
That lie bleached white on the shores
Of Lake Kokonor,[2] where voices of new
      spirits
Join with the old, heard sadly through
The murmur of falling rain.

THINKING OF OTHER DAYS

In those prosperous times
Of the period of Kai Yuan,[3]
Even a small county city
Would be crowded with the rich;
Rice flowed like oil and both
Public and private granaries
Were stuffed with grain; all
Through the nine provinces
There were no robbers on
The roads; traveling from home
Needless to pick an auspicious
Day to start; everywhere carriages
With folk wearing silk or brocade;
Farmers ploughed, women picked
Mulberries, nothing that did
Not run smoothly; in court
Was a good Emperor for whom
The finest music was played;
Friends were honest with each other
And for long there had been
No kind of disaster; great days with
Rites and songs, the best of other times,
Laws the most just; who could
Have dreamed that later a bolt
Of silk would cost ten thousand
Cash? Now the fields farmers
Tilled have become covered
With bloodshed; palaces at Loyang[4]
Are burnt, and temples to
The imperial ancestors are full
Of foxes and rabbit burrows!
Now I am too sad to ask
Questions of the old people,
Fearing to hear tales
Of horror and strife;
I am not able, but yet
The Emperor[5] has given me
A post, I hoping that he

---

[1]The land back home, east of the western frontier.
[2]A lake west of the Great Wall.
[3]A title of Emperor Xuanzong's (r. 712–756). Also known as Minghuang, or Brilliant Monarch, he was the last effective Tang emperor. An Lushan's rebellion broke out during the last years of his forty-four-year reign.

[4]The auxiliary capital and one of China's most sacred and ancient cities.
[5]Xuanzong's son and successor.

Can make the country
Rise again like King Xuan
Of Zhou,[6] though for myself
I simply grieve that now age
And sickness take their toll.

ON ASKING MR. WU
FOR THE SECOND TIME

Do please let your neighbor
Who lives to the west of you
Pick up the dates in front of

Your home; for she is a woman
Without food or children; only
Her condition brings her to
This necessity; surely she
Ought not to fear you, because
You are not a local man, yet
It would be good of you to try
And help her, and save her
Feelings; so do not fence off
Your fruit; heavy taxation is
The cause of her misery; the
Effect of war on the helpless
Brings us unending sorrow.

The Dao of Agriculture in Song China
▼▼▼

71 ▼ *Chen Pu, THE CRAFT OF FARMING*

China has continually faced the problem of producing sufficient food to meet the needs of an expanding population. During the Song era the Chinese met this challenge with reasonable success, despite a dramatic population increase. The following selections from a popular treatise written in 1149 by the otherwise unknown Chen Pu provide insight into some of the factors behind that agrarian success.

QUESTIONS FOR ANALYSIS

1. What does Chen Pu assume is more scarce, and consequently more valuable, labor or land? What do you infer from your answer?
2. Chen Pu focuses on several key elements that contributed to Song China's success in feeding its people. What are they?
3. According to Chen Pu, what qualities set the superior farmer apart from all others?
4. It has been said that this treatise focuses more on producing a superior farmer than a superior farm. What does this mean, and do you agree? If you agree, what do you find distinctly "Chinese" about such a goal?

---

[6]The last effective king of the Western Zhou Dynasty, he spent most of his reign (827–781 B.C.) fighting defensive wars against non-Chinese to the north.

5. Traditional Chinese agriculture has often been characterized as "family market gardening." What do you think this means, and does this treatise support such a conclusion?

6. In what way is this treatise a combination of agricultural science, folk wisdom, Confucian learning, and Daoist ideology? Can you find any Legalist elements, or influences, in the essay?

7. Some have characterized this work as an essay on the Dao of farming. What do they mean? Do you agree?

FINANCE AND LABOR

All those who engage in business should do so in accordance with their own capacity. They should refrain from careless investment and excessive greed, lest in the end they achieve nothing. . . . In the farming business, which is the most difficult business to manage, how can you afford not to calculate your financial and labor capacities carefully? Only when you are certain that you have sufficient funds and labor to assure success should you launch an enterprise. Anyone who covets more than he can manage is likely to fall into carelessness and irresponsibility. . . . Thus, to procure more land is to increase trouble, not profit.

On the other hand, anyone who plans carefully, begins with good methods, and continues in the same way can reasonably expect success and does not have to rely on luck. The proverb says, "Owning a great deal of emptiness is less desirable than reaping from a narrow patch of land." . . . For the farmer who is engaged in the management of fields, the secret lies not in expanding the farmland, but in balancing finance and labor. If the farmer can achieve that, he can expect prosperity and abundance. . . .

PLOWING

Early and late plowing both have their advantages. For the early rice crop, as soon as the reaping is completed, immediately plow the fields and expose the stalks to glaring sunlight. Then add manure and bury the stalks to nourish the soil. Next, plant beans, wheat, and vegetables to ripen and fertilize the soil so as to minimize the next year's labor. In addition, when the harvest is good, these extra crops can add to the yearly income. For late crops, however, do not plow until spring. Because the rice stalks are soft but tough, it is necessary to wait until they have fully decayed to plow satisfactorily. . . .

THE SIX KINDS OF CROPS

There is an order to the planting of different crops. Anyone who knows the right timing and follows the order can cultivate one thing after another, and use one to assist the others. Then there will not be a day without planting, nor a month without harvest, and money will be coming in throughout the year. How can there then be any worry about cold, hunger, or lack of funds?

Plant the nettle-hemp in the first month. Apply manure in intervals of ten days and by the fifth or sixth month it will be time for reaping. The women should take charge of knotting and spinning cloth out of the hemp.

Plant millet in the second month. It is necessary to sow the seeds sparsely and then roll cart wheels over the soil to firm it up; this will make the millet grow luxuriantly, its stalks long and its grains full. In the seventh month the millet will be harvested, easing any temporary financial difficulties.

There are two crops of oil-hemp. The early crop is planted in the third month. Rake the field to spread out the seedlings. Repeat the raking process three times a month and the hemp will grow well. It can be harvested in the seventh or the eighth month.

In the fourth month plant beans. Rake as with hemp. They will be ripe by the seventh month.

In mid-fifth month plant the late oil-hemp. Proceed as with the early crop. The ninth month will be reaping time.

After the 7th day of the seventh month, plant radishes and cabbage.

In the eighth month, before the autumn sacrifice to the god of the earth, wheat can be planted. It is advisable to apply manure and remove weeds frequently. When wheat grows from the autumn through the spring sacrifices to the god of the earth, the harvest will double and the grains will be full and solid.

The *Book of Poetry* says, "The tenth month is the time to harvest crops." You will have a large variety of crops, including millet, rice, beans, hemp, and wheat and will lack nothing needed through the year. Will you ever be concerned for want of resources? . . .

FERTILIZER

At the side of the farm house, erect a compost hut. Make the eaves low to prevent the wind and rain from entering it, for when the compost is exposed to the moon and the stars, it will lose its fertility. In this hut, dig a deep pit and line it with bricks to prevent leakage. Collect waste, ashes, chaff, broken stalks, and fallen leaves and burn them in the pit; then pour manure over them to make them fertile. In this way considerable quantities of compost are acquired over time. Then, whenever sowing is to be done, sieve and discard stones and tiles, mix the fine compost with the seeds, and plant them sparsely in pinches. When the seedlings have grown tall, again sprinkle the compost and bank it up against the roots. These methods will ensure a double yield.

Some people say that when the soil is exhausted, grass and trees will not grow; that when the *qi* [material force] is weak, all living things will be stunted; and that after three to five years of continuous planting, the soil of any field will be exhausted. This theory is erroneous because it fails to recognize one factor: by adding new, fertile soil, enriched with compost, the land can be reinforced in strength. If this is so, where can the alleged exhaustion come from?

WEEDING

The *Book of Poetry* says, "Root out the weeds. Where the weeds decay, there the grains will grow luxuriantly." The author of the *Record of Ritual* also remarks, "The months of mid-summer are advantageous for weeding. Weeds can fertilize the fields and improve the land." Modern farmers, ignorant of these principles, throw the weeds away. They do not know that, if mixed with soil and buried deep under the roots of rice seedlings, the weeds will eventually decay and the soil will be enriched; the harvest, as a result, will be abundant and of superior quality. . . .

CONCENTRATION

If something is thought out carefully, it will succeed; if not, it will fail; this is a universal truth. It is very rare that a person works and yet gains nothing. On the other hand, there is never any harm in trying too hard.

In farming it is especially appropriate to be concerned about what you are doing. Mencius said, "Will a farmer discard his plow when he leaves his land?" Ordinary people will become idle if they have leisure and prosperity. Only those who love farming, who behave in harmony with it, who take pleasure in talking about it and think about it all the time will manage it without a moment's negligence. For these people a day's work results in a day's gain, a year's work in a year's gain. How can they escape affluence?

Thirteenth-Century Hangzhou
▼▼▼

72 ▼ *A RECORD OF MUSINGS ON THE EASTERN CAPITAL*

When Jurchen steppe people overran all of northern China in the early twelfth century and established the rival Jin Dynasty (1115–1234) with its capital at Beijing, the Song imperial court moved to the port city of Hangzhou, just south of the Yangtze River. From here the Song ruled the southern remnants of their mutilated empire until Mongols captured the city in 1276.

The Southern Song Dynasty (1127–1279) presided over territory that in the age of Tang had been a pestilential borderland. By the twelfth century, however, it was China's most densely populated region and the newest hub of Chinese culture. Its heart was Hangzhou, which was more than merely an administrative center. In the thirteenth century it was home to well over one million people, who inhabited an area of seven to eight square miles, making it the largest and richest city in the world.

The following account, composed anonymously in 1235, describes the city and its residents.

QUESTIONS FOR ANALYSIS

1. How prosperous and varied does the city's economy appear to be?
2. What adjectives would you use to characterize this city?
3. Compare life in Hangzhou with that in a modern metropolis, such as New York or Los Angeles. What would a modern urban dweller or visitor recognize as familiar in this thirteenth-century city?

MARKETS

During the morning hours, markets extend from Tranquility Gate of the palace all the way to the north and south sides of the New Boulevard. Here we find pearl, jade, talismans, exotic plants and fruits, seasonal catches from the sea, wild game — all the rarities of the world seem to be gathered here. The food and commodity markets at the Heavenly-View Gate, River Market Place, Central Square, Ba Creek, the end of Superior Lane, Tent Place, and Universal Peace Bridge are all crowded and full of traffic.

In the evening, with the exception of the square in front of the palace, the markets are as busy as during the day. The most attractive one is at Central Square, where all sorts of exquisite artifacts, instruments, containers, and hundreds of varieties of goods are for sale. In other marketplaces, sales, auctions, and exchanges go on constantly. In the wine shops and inns business also thrives. Only after the fourth drum[1] does the city gradually quiet down, but by the fifth drum, court officials already start preparing for audiences and merchants are getting ready for the morning market again. This cycle goes on all year round without respite. . . .

On the lot in front of the wall of the city building, there are always various acting troupes performing, and this usually attracts a large crowd. The same kind of activity is seen in almost any vacant lot, including those at the meat market of the Great Common, the herb market at Charcoal Bridge, the book market at Orange Grove, the vegetable market on the east side of the city, and the rice market on the north side. There are many more interesting markets, such as the candy center at the Five Buildings, but I cannot name them all.

COMMERCIAL ESTABLISHMENTS

In general, the capital attracts the greatest variety of goods and has the best craftsmen. For instance, the flower company at Superior Lane does a truly excellent job of flower arrangement, and its caps, hairpins, and collars are unsurpassed in craftsmanship. Some of the most famous specialties of the capital are the sweet-bean soup at the Miscellaneous Market, the pickled dates of the Ge family, the thick soup of the Guang family at Superior Lane, the fruit at the Great Commons marketplace, the cooked meats in front of Eternal Mercy Temple, Sister Song's fish broth at Penny Pond Gate, the juicy lungs at Flowing Gold Gate, the "lamb rice" of the Zhi family at Central Square, the boots of the Peng family, the fine clothing of the Xuan family at Southern Commons, the sticky rice pastry of the Zhang family, the flutes made by Gu the Fourth, and the Qiu family's Tatar whistles at the Great Commons.

WINE SHOPS

Among the various kinds of wine shops, the tea-and-food shops sell not only wine, but also various foods to go with it. However, to get seasonal delicacies not available in these shops, one should go to the inns, for they also have a menu from which one can make selections. The pastry-and-wine shops sell pastries with duckling and goose fillings, various fixings of pig tripe, intestines and blood, fish fat and spawn; but they are rather expensive. The mansion-style inns are either decorated in the same way as officials' mansions or are actually remodeled from such mansions. The garden-style inns are often located in the suburbs, though some are also situated in town. Their decoration is usually an imitation of a studio-garden combination. Among other kinds of wine shops are the straight ones which do not sell food. There are also the small retail wine shops which sell house wine as well as wine from other stores. Instead of the common emblem — a painted branching twig — used by all other winehouses, they have bamboo fences and canvas awnings. To go drinking in such a place is called "hitting the cup," meaning that a person drinks only one cup; it is therefore not the most respectable place and is unfit for polite company.

The "luxuriant inns" have prostitutes residing in them, and the wine chambers are equipped with beds. At the gate of such an inn, on top of the red gardenia lantern, there is always a cover made of bamboo leaves. Rain or shine, this cover is always present, serving as a trademark. In other inns, the girls only keep the guests company. If a guest has other wishes, he has to go to the girl's place. . . .

The expenses incurred on visiting an inn can vary widely. If you order food, but no drinks, it is called "having the lowly soup-and-stuff," and is quite inexpensive. If your order of wine

---

[1]The night was divided into five watches, each of which was signaled by a drumbeat.

and food falls within the range of 100–5000 cash,[2] it is called a small order. However, if you ask for female company, then it is most likely that the girls will order the most expensive delicacies. You are well advised to appear shrewd and experienced, so as not to be robbed. One trick, for instance, in ordering wines is to give a large order, of say, ten bottles, but open them one by one. In the end, you will probably have used only five or six bottles of the best. You can then return the rest. . . .

TEAHOUSES

In large teahouses there are usually paintings and calligraphies by famous artists on display. In the old capital,[3] only restaurants had them, to enable their patrons to while away the time as the food was being prepared, but now it is customary for teahouses as well to display paintings and the like. . . .

Often many young men gather in teahouses to practice singing or playing musical instruments. To give such amateur performances is called "getting posted."

A "social teahouse" is more of a community gathering place than a mere place that sells tea. Often tea-drinking is but an excuse, and people are rather generous when it comes to the tips.

There is a special kind of teahouse where pimps and gigolos hang out. Another kind is occupied by people from various trades and crafts who use them as places to hire help, buy apprentices, and conduct business. These teahouses are called "trade heads."

"Water teahouses" are in fact pleasure houses, the tea being a cover. Some youths are quite willing to spend their money there, which is called "dry tea money.". . .

SPECIALTY STORES

The commercial area of the capital extends from the old Qing River Market to the Southern Commons on the south and to the border on the north. It includes the Central Square, which is also called the Center of Five Flowers. From the north side of the Five Buildings to South Imperial Boulevard, there are more than one hundred gold, silver, and money exchanges. On the short walls in front of these stores, there are piles of gold, silver, and copper cash: these are called "the money that watches over the store." Around these exchanges there are also numerous gold and silversmiths. The pearl marts are situated between the north side of Cordial Marketplace and Southtown Marketplace. Most deals made here involve over 10,000 cash. A score of pawnshops are scattered in between, all owned by very wealthy people and dealing only in the most valuable objects.

Some famous fabric stores sell exquisite brocade and fine silk which are unsurpassed elsewhere in the country. Along the river, close to the Peaceful Ford Bridge, there are numerous fabric stores, fan shops, and lacquerware and porcelain shops. Most other cities can only boast of one special product; what makes the capital unique is that it gathers goods from all places. Furthermore, because of the large population and busy commercial traffic, there is a demand for everything. There are even shops that deal exclusively in used paper or in feathers, for instance.

WAREHOUSES

In Liu Yong's (ca 1045) poem on Qiantang, we read that there were about ten thousand families residing here; but that was before the

---

[2]The basic unit of currency was the "cash," a copper coin with a square hole in the middle. These were strung together in groups of hundreds and thousands. Late in the century the government was circulating bank notes, backed by gold and silver, ranging in value from 1,000 to 100,000 cash coins.

[3]Kaifeng, which was captured in 1126.

Yuanfeng reign (1078–1085). Today, having been the "temporary capital" for more than a hundred years,[4] the city has over a million households. The suburbs extend to the south, west, and north; all are densely populated and prosperous in commerce as well as in agriculture. The size of the suburbs is comparable to a small county or prefecture, and it takes several days to travel through them. This again reflects the prosperity of the capital.

In the middle of the city, enclosed by the Northern Pass Dam, is White Ocean Lake. Its water spreads over several tens of *li*.[5] Wealthy families have built scores of warehouse complexes along this waterfront. Each of these consists of several hundred to over a thousand rooms for the storage needs of the various businesses in the capital and of traveling merchants. Because these warehouses are surrounded by water, they are not endangered by fires or thieves, and therefore they offer a special convenience.

HUSTLERS

Some of these hustlers are students who failed to achieve any literary distinction. Though able to read and write, and play musical instruments and chess, they are not highly skilled in any art. They end up being a kind of guide for young men from wealthy families, accompanying them in their pleasure-seeking activities. Some also serve as guides or assistants to officials on business from other parts of the country. The lowliest of these people actually engage themselves in writing and delivering invitation cards and the like for brothels. . . .

There are also professional go-betweens, nicknamed "water-treaders," whose principal targets are pleasure houses, where they flatter the wealthy young patrons, run errands for them, and help make business deals. Some gather at brothels or scenic attractions and accost the visitors. They beg for donations for "religious purposes," but in fact use the money to make a living for themselves and their families. If you pay attention to them, they will become greedy; if you ignore them, they will force themselves on you and will not stop until you give in. It requires art to deal with these people appropriately.

▼▼▼

India

Invasions from Central Asia by a nomadic people known as the Hunas, or White Huns, precipitated the collapse of the Gupta Empire around the middle of the sixth century. Northern India was again politically fragmented, but Hindu culture, having reached maturity in the Gupta period, continued to develop vigorously. Indeed, the history of classical India is largely the story of cultural continuity and evolution, in which political events and their chronology have little

---

[4]The Song emperors never gave up hope of recovering Kaifeng and the northern part of the empire. Kaifeng thus remained the official capital, and Hangzhou was designated only "temporary capital."

[5]A *li* is a bit more than a third of a mile.

relevance. The one significant exception to this rule in the period 500–1500 was the coming of Islam. Its impact was profound and permanent.

Early in the eighth century Arabs conquered the northwest corner of the Indian subcontinent, a region known as Sind, but advanced no farther. While Hindu civilization moved to its own rhythms, its Arab neighbors traded with it and freely borrowed whatever they found useful and nonthreatening to their Islamic faith. This included India's decimal mathematics and the misnamed "Arabic" system of numeration.

Islam did not make a significant impact on Indian life until the appearance of the Turks. These recent converts to the faith, whose origins lay in Central Asia, conducted a series of raids out of Afghanistan between 986 and 1030. After a respite of about 150 years, they turned to conquest. In 1192 the army of Muhammad of Ghor crushed a coalition of Indian princes, and the whole Ganges basin lay defenseless before his generals. By 1206 the Turkish sultanate of Delhi dominated all of northern India, and by 1327 it had extended its power over virtually the entire peninsula. Although these Turkish sultans lost the south to the native Hindu state of Vijayanagar (1336–1565), they controlled India's northern and central regions until the arrival of other Muslim conquerors: first, Timur the Lame's plundering horde in 1398; then Babur, who established the great Mughal Dynasty (1526–1857), which ruled most of India until the mid-eighteenth century.

As the modern Muslim states of Pakistan and Bangladesh bear witness, Islam became an important element in Indian society, but in the end Hinduism prevailed as the way of life for the Indian subcontinent's majority. The coming and going of armies destroyed the vital remnants of Buddhist monasticism in mainland India, although it continued to flourish on the island of Ceylon. Nothing, however, could root out the hold that the many varieties of Hindu belief and practice had upon Indian life.

The Perfect Wife
▼▼▼

73 ▼ Dandin, TALES OF THE TEN PRINCES

India's earliest known prose fiction dates from the sixth and seventh centuries, and the first acknowledged master of this art form was Dandin, who lived around 600. His *Tales of Ten Princes* is an ingenious interweaving of numerous subplots and stories around the central theme of the adventures of Prince Rajavahana. All of these stories celebrate the three things Dandin believed all people hold most dear in this life: virtue, wealth, and love. As such, they illustrate the other side of the Hindu vision of the physical world. Although one of the basic insights of Hindu religion is that all material existence is transitory and "unreal," as a practical matter Hindus accept *kama*, or delight in the sensual pleasures of life, and *artha*, pursuit of riches and power, as valid human responses to the attractions of this world. Like many of the stories told by Dandin, the following vignette sheds light on everyday life and values.

QUESTIONS FOR ANALYSIS

1. What qualities does the ideal wife possess?
2. What does a man expect to receive in an ideal marriage? What is he expected to give in return?
3. Compare this story with the view of women provided by *The Laws of Manu* (Chapter 5, source 40). Are they similar or different? Together, what do they allow us to infer about the role and status of women in Hindu society?

"In the land of the Dravidians[1] is a city called Kanci. Therein dwelt the very wealthy son of a merchant, by name Saktikumara. When he was nearly eighteen he thought: 'There's no pleasure in living without a wife or with one of bad character. Now how can I find a really good one?' So, dubious of his chance of finding wedded bliss with a woman taken at the word of others, he became a fortune-teller, and roamed the land with a measure of unhusked rice tied in the skirts of his robe; and parents, taking him for an interpreter of birthmarks, showed their daughters to him. Whenever he saw a girl of his own class, whatever her birthmarks, he would say to her: 'My dear girl, can you cook me a good meal from this measure of rice?' And so, ridiculed and rejected, he wandered from house to house.

"One day in the land of the Sibis, in a city on the banks of the Kaveri, he examined a girl who was shown to him by her nurse. She wore little jewelry, for her parents had spent their fortune, and had nothing left but their dilapidated mansion. As soon as he set eyes on her he thought: 'This girl is shapely and smooth in all her members. Not one limb is too fat or too thin, too short or too long. Her fingers are pink; her hands are marked with auspicious lines — the barleycorn, the fish, the lotus, and

the vase; her ankles are shapely; her feet are plump and the veins are not prominent; her thighs curve smoothly; her knees can barely be seen, for they merge into her rounded thighs; her buttocks are dimpled and round as chariot wheels; her naval is small, flat, and deep; her stomach is adorned with three lines; the nipples stand out from her large breasts, which cover her whole chest; her palms are marked with signs which promise corn, wealth, and sons; her nails are smooth and polished like jewels; her fingers are straight and tapering and pink; her arms curve sweetly from the shoulder, and are smoothly jointed; her slender neck is curved like a conch-shell; her lips are rounded and of even red; her pretty chin does not recede; her cheeks are round, full and firm; her eyebrows do not join above her nose, and are curved, dark and even; her nose is like a half-blown sesamum flower; her wide eyes are large and gentle and flash with three colors, black, white, and brown; her brow is fair as the new moon; her curls are lovely as a mine of sapphires; her long ears are adorned doubly, with earrings and charming lotuses, hanging limply; her abundant hair is not brown, even at the tips, but long, smooth, glossy, and fragrant. The character of such a girl cannot but correspond to her appearance, and my heart is fixed upon her, so

---

[1]The dark-skinned people of the south, whose language differs radically from that of the northerners.

I'll test her and marry her. For one regret after another is sure to fall on the heads of people who don't take precautions!' So, looking at her affectionately, he said, 'Dear girl, can you cook a good meal for me with this measure of rice?'

"Then the girl glanced at her old servant, who took the measure of rice from his hand and seated him on the veranda, which had been well sprinkled and swept, giving him water to cool his feet. Meanwhile the girl bruised the fragrant rice, dried it a little at a time in the sun, turned it repeatedly, and beat it with a hollow cane on a firm flat spot, very gently, so as to separate the grain without crushing the husk. Then she said to the nurse, 'Mother, goldsmiths can make good use of these husks for polishing jewelry. Take them, and, with the coppers you get for them, buy some firewood, not too green and not too dry, a small cooking pot, and two earthen dishes.'

"When this was done she put the grains of rice in a shallow, wide-mouthed, round-bellied mortar, and took a long and heavy pestle of acacia-wood, its head shod with a plate of iron. . . . With skill and grace she exerted her arms, as the grains jumped up and down in the mortar. Repeatedly she stirred them and pressed them down with her fingers; then she shook the grains in a winnowing basket to remove the beard, rinsed them several times, worshiped the hearth, and placed them in water which had been five times brought to the boil. When the rice softened, bubbled, and swelled, she drew the embers of the fire together, put a lid on the cooking pot, and strained off the gruel. Then she patted the rice with a ladle and scooped it out a little at a time; and when she found that it was thoroughly cooked she put the cooking pot on one side, mouth downward. Next she damped down those sticks which were not burnt through, and when the fire was quite out she sent them to the dealers to be sold as char-

coal, saying, 'With the coppers that you get for them, buy as much as you can of green vegetables, ghee,[2] curds, sesamum oil, myrobalans[3] and tamarind.'[4]

"When this was done she offered him a few savories. Next she put the rice-gruel in a new dish immersed in damp sand, and cooled it with the soft breeze of a palm-leaf fan. She added a little salt, and flavored it with the scent of the embers; she ground the myrobalans to a smooth powder, until they smelt like a lotus; and then, by the lips of the nurse, she invited him to take a bath. This he did, and when she too had bathed she gave him oil and myrobalans (as an unguent).

"After he had bathed he sat on a bench in the paved courtyard, which had been thoroughly sprinkled and swept. She stirred the gruel in the two dishes, which she set before him on a piece of pale green plantain leaf, cut from a tree in the courtyard. He drank it and felt rested and happy, relaxed in every limb. Next she gave him two ladlefuls of the boiled rice, served with a little ghee and condiments. She served the rest of the rice with curds, three spices (mace, cardamom, and cinnamon), and fragrant and refreshing buttermilk and gruel. He enjoyed the meal to the last mouthful.

"When he asked for a drink she poured him water in a steady stream from the spout of a new pitcher — it was fragrant with incense, and smelt of fresh trumpet-flowers and the perfume of full-blown lotuses. He put the bowl to his lips, and his eyelashes sparkled with rosy drops as cool as snow; his ears delighted in the sound of the trickling water; his rough cheeks thrilled and tingled at its pleasant contact; his nostrils opened wide at its sweet fragrance; and his tongue delighted in its lovely flavor, as he drank the pure water in great gulps. Then, at his nod, the girl gave him a mouthwash in another bowl. The old woman took away the re-

[2]Clarified butter.
[3]Edible seed from the so-called Indian almond tree.

[4]A pungent spice.

mains of his meal, and he slept awhile in his ragged cloak, on the pavement plastered with fresh cowdung.

"Wholly pleased with the girl, he married her with due rites, and took her home. Later he neglected her awhile and took a mistress, but the wife treated her as a dear friend. She served her husband indefatigably, as she would a god, and never neglected her household duties; and she won the loyalty of her servants by her great kindness. In the end her husband was so enslaved by her goodness that he put the whole household in her charge, made her sole mistress of his life and person, and enjoyed the three aims of life — virtue, wealth, and love. So I maintain that virtuous wives make their lords happy and virtuous."

A Sati's Sacrifice
▼▼▼

74 ▼ VIKRAMA'S ADVENTURES

Early English visitors to India mistakenly believed that *sati* (a virtuous woman), which they mistermed *suttee,* referred to the practice of a widow's self-immolation on her late husband's funeral pyre, rather than to the woman herself. By tradition, a widow, no matter what her caste, could not remarry, for this would entail her breaking her marriage vow and endangering her husband's spiritual welfare. She was expected to live out her life in severe austerity, shunned by all but her children, in the hope of remarrying her husband in some future incarnation. In such circumstances it seemed logical to many that a woman would prefer to join her deceased husband sooner rather than later and end her present life on his funeral day. Undoubtedly, some satis committed suicide willingly. Probably far greater numbers were forced by their husbands' relatives, for social and economic reasons, to perform this ultimate act of loyalty. Whatever their motivation, widows who committed this act of ritual suicide were common in traditional Hindu society until the British suppressed the custom during the nineteenth century.

Our text comes from an anonymous collection of stories recounting the adventures and wisdom of the semilegendary King Vikrama, or Vikramaditya, who may have lived around 58 B.C. The stories, as we have received them, were probably collected between the eleventh and thirteenth centuries.

QUESTIONS FOR ANALYSIS

1. Can a widow who refuses to immolate herself achieve moksha (release)?
2. What proprietary interest do the families to which the sati belongs have in her sacrifice?
3. What impact does her act have on her husband's soul? on her own?
4. What social and psychological factors make suicide appear so attractive?

5. Compare this story with the preceding one told by Dandin. In what ways was the wife in that story a sati? What does she have in common with this sati?

6. "By her perfect selflessness, a sati perfects and redeems her husband." What does this statement mean, and how do both this and Dandin's story illustrate that attitude?

7. Some have argued that these two stories are predicated upon the assumption that wives and husbands fulfill one another, and without the other each is incomplete. Do you agree with this analysis?

Once King Vikrama, attended by all his vassal princes, had ascended his throne. At this time a certain magician came in, and blessing him with the words "Live forever!" said: "Sire, you are skilled in all the arts; many magicians have come into your presence and exhibited their tricks. So today be so good as to behold an exhibition of my dexterity." The king said: "I have not time now; it is the time to bathe and eat. Tomorrow I will behold it." So on the morrow the juggler came into the king's assembly as a stately man, with a mighty beard and glorious countenance, holding a sword in his hand, and accompanied by a lovely woman; and he bowed to the king. Then the ministers who were present, seeing the stately man, were astonished, and asked: "O hero, who are you, and whence do you come?" He said: "I am a servant of Great Indra; I was cursed once by my lord, and was cast down to earth; and now I dwell here. And this is my wife. Today a great battle has begun between the gods and the Daityas [demons], so I am going thither. This King Vikramaditya treats other men's wives as his sisters, so before going to the battle I wish to leave my wife with him." Hearing this the king also was greatly amazed. And the man left his wife with the king and delivered her over to him, and sword in hand flew up into heaven. Then a great and terrible shouting was heard in the sky: "Ho there, kill them, kill them, smite them, smite them!" were the words they heard. And all the people who sat in the court, with upturned faces, gazed in amazement. After this, when a moment had passed by, one of the man's arms, holding his sword and stained with blood, fell from the sky into the king's assembly. Then all the people, seeing it, said: "Ah, this great hero has been killed in battle by his opponents; his sword and one arm have fallen." While the people who sat in the court were even saying this, again his head fell also; and then his trunk fell too. And seeing this his wife said: "Sire, my husband, fighting on the field of battle, has been slain by the enemy. His head, his arm, his sword, and his trunk have fallen down here. So, that this my beloved may not be wooed by the heavenly nymphs, I will go to where he is. Let fire be provided for me." Hearing her words the king said: "My daughter, why will you enter the fire? I will guard you even as my own daughter; preserve your body." She said: "Sire, what is this you say? My lord, for whom this body of mine exists, has been slain on the battlefield by his foes. Now for whose sake shall I preserve this body? Moreover, you should not say this, since even fools know that wives should follow their husbands. For thus it is said:

1. Moonlight goes with the moon, the lightning clings to the cloud, and women follow their husbands; even fools know this.

   And so, as the learned tradition has it:

2. The wife who enters into the fire when her husband dies, imitating Arundhati [a star, regarded as the

wife of one of the Seven Rishis (the Dipper), and as a typical faithful spouse] in her behavior, enjoys bliss in heaven.

3. Until a wife burns herself in the fire after the death of her husband, so long that woman can in no way be permanently freed from the body.

4. A woman who follows after her husband shall surely purify three families: her mother's, her father's, and that into which she was given in marriage.

And so:

5. Three and a half crores[1] is the number of the hairs on the human body; so many years shall a wife who follows her husband dwell in heaven.

6. As a snake-charmer powerfully draws a snake out of a hole, so a wife draws her husband upward [by burning herself] and enjoys bliss with him.

7. A wife who abides by the law of righteousness [in burning herself] saves her husband, whether he be good or wicked; yes, even if he be guilty of all crimes.

Furthermore, O king, a woman who is bereft of her husband has no use for her life. And it is said:

8. What profit is there in the life of a wretched woman who has lost her husband? Her body is as useless as a banyan tree in a cemetery.

9. Surely father, brother, and son measure their gifts; what woman would not honor her husband, who gives without measure?

Moreover:

10. Though a woman be surrounded by kinsfolk, though she have many sons, and be endowed with excellent qualities, she is miserable, poor wretched creature, when deprived of her husband.

And so:

11. What shall a widow do with perfumes, garlands, and incense, or with manifold ornaments, or garments and couches of ease?

12. A lute does not sound without strings, a wagon does not go without wheels, and a wife does not obtain happiness without her husband, not even with a hundred kinsfolk.

13. Woman's highest refuge is her husband, even if he be poor, vicious, old, infirm, crippled, outcast, and stingy.

14. There is no kinsman, no friend, no protector, no refuge for a woman like her husband.

15. There is no other misery for women like widowhood. Happy is she among women who dies before her husband.

Thus speaking she fell at the king's feet, begging that a fire be provided for her. And when the king heard her words, his heart being tender with genuine compassion, he caused a pyre to be erected of sandalwood and the like, and gave her leave. So she took leave of the king, and in his presence entered the fire together with her husband's body.

[1]A crore is ten million. Therefore, thirty-five million.

A Sultan's Memoirs
▼▼▼

75 ▼ THE DEEDS OF SULTAN FIRUZ SHAH

Firuz Shah Tughluq, who reigned from 1351 to 1388, enjoyed the reputation of being the most humane and generous of the sultans of Delhi. Toward the end of his life he prepared an account of the accomplishments in which he took the greatest pride. This sincere and pious ruler little realized that he had presided over the sultanate's last period of prosperity. Ten years to the day after Firuz Shah's death, Timur the Lame (ca 1336–1405) was encamped on the Indus, preparing to invade the heartland of India.

QUESTIONS FOR ANALYSIS

1. How did Firuz Shah define his general duties?
2. What, in his mind, were his responsibilities toward Muslims?
3. What did he see as his responsibility to his Hindu subjects?
4. What did he believe were his greatest responsibilities and achievements?
5. Compare Firuz Shah's policies with those of Asoka (Chapter 5, source 37). On what points would they agree and disagree?

Praises without end, and infinite thanks to that merciful Creator who gave to me his poor abject creature Firuz. . . . His impulse for the maintenance of the laws of His religion, for the repression of heresy, the prevention of crime, and the prohibition of things forbidden; who gave me also a disposition for discharging my lawful duties and my moral obligations. My desire is that, to the best of my human power, I should recount and pay my thanks for the many blessings He has bestowed upon me, so that I may be found among the number of His grateful servants. First I would praise Him because when irreligion and sins opposed to the Law prevailed in Hindustan,[1] and mens' habits and dispositions were inclined towards them, and were averse to the restraints of religion, He in-

spired me His humble servant with an earnest desire to repress irreligion and wickedness, so that I was able to labor diligently until with His blessing the vanities of the world, and things repugnant to religion, were set aside, and the true was distinguished from the false.

In the reigns of former kings[2] the blood of many Muslims had been shed, and many varieties of torture employed. Amputation of hands and feet, ears and noses; tearing out the eyes, pouring molten lead into the throat, crushing the bones of the hands and feet with mallets, burning the body with fire, driving iron nails into the hands, feet, and bosom, cutting the sinews, sawing men asunder; these and many similar tortures were practiced. The great and merciful God made me, His servant, hope and

---

[1]The north central region of India inhabited largely by Hindus.

[2]Muhammad ben Tughluq (r. 1325–1351), his predecessor, had been noted for his cruelty.

seek for His mercy by devoting myself to prevent the unlawful killing of Muslims, and the infliction of any kind of torture upon them or upon any men. . . .

By God's help I determined that the lives of Muslims and true believers should be in perfect immunity, and whoever transgressed the Law should receive the punishment prescribed by the book[3] and the decrees of judges. . . .

The sect of Shi'as . . . had endeavored to make proselytes.[4] They wrote treatises and books, and gave instruction and lectures upon the tenets of their sect, and traduced and reviled the first chiefs of our religion (on whom be the peace of God!). I seized them all and I convicted them of their errors and perversions. On the most zealous I inflicted punishment, and the rest I visited with censure and threats of public punishment. Their books I burnt in public, and so by the grace of God the influence of this sect was entirely suppressed. . . .

The Hindus and idol-worshipers had agreed to pay the money for toleration, and had consented to the poll tax,[5] in return for which they and their families enjoyed security. These people now erected new idol temples[6] in the city and the environs in opposition to the Law of the Prophet which declares that such temples are not to be tolerated. Under Divine guidance I destroyed these edifices, and I killed those leaders of infidelity who seduced others into error, and the lower orders I subjected to stripes and chastisement, until this abuse was entirely abolished. . . . I forbade the infliction of any severe punishment on the Hindus in general, but I destroyed their idol temples, and instead thereof raised mosques. . . . Where infidels and idolaters worshiped idols, Muslims now, by God's mercy, perform their devotions to the true God. Praises of God and the summons to prayer are now heard there, and that place

which was formerly the home of infidels has become the habitation of the faithful, who there repeat their creed and offer up their praises to God. . . .

In former times it had been the custom to wear ornamented garments, and men received robes as tokens of honor from kings' courts. Figures and devices were painted and displayed on saddles, bridles, and collars, on censers, on goblets and cups, and flagons, on dishes and ewers, in tents, on curtains and on chairs, and upon all articles and utensils. Under Divine guidance and favor I ordered all pictures and portraits to be removed from these things, and that such articles only should be made as are approved and recognized by the Law. Those pictures and portraits which were painted on the doors and walls of palaces I ordered to be effaced.[7]

Formerly the garments of great men were generally made of silk and gold brocades, beautiful but unlawful. Under Divine guidance I ordered that such garments should be worn as are approved by the Law of the Prophet, and that choice should be made of such trimmings of gold brocade, embroidery, or braiding as did not exceed four inches in breadth. Whatever was unlawful and forbidden by, or opposed to, the Law was set aside.

Among the gifts which God bestowed upon me, His humble servant, was a desire to erect public buildings. So I built many mosques and colleges and monasteries, that the learned and the elders, the devout and the holy, might worship God in these edifices, and aid the kind builder with their prayers. The digging of canals, the planting of trees, and the endowing with lands are in accordance with the directions of the Law. The learned doctors of the Law of Islam have many troubles; of this there is no doubt. I settled allowances upon them in pro-

---

[3]The Qur'an.
[4]Converts.
[5]The *jizya*, a tax paid by all non-Muslim subjects as a token of their submission.

[6]Presumably, previously constructed non-Muslim places of worship were tolerated.
[7]Most Muslims regard the representation of human or animal figures to be blasphemy.

portion to their necessary expenses, so that they might regularly receive the income. . . .

For the benefit of travelers and pilgrims resorting to the tombs of illustrious kings and celebrated saints, and for providing the things necessary in these holy places, I confirmed and gave effect to the grants of villages, lands, and other endowments which had been conferred upon them in olden times. In those cases where no endowment or provision has been settled, I made an endowment, so that these establishments might for ever be secure of an income, to afford comfort to travelers and wayfarers, to holy men and learned men. May they remember those ancient benefactors and me in their prayers.

I was enabled by God's help to build a . . . Hospital, for the benefit of every one of high or low degree, who was suddenly attacked by illness and overcome by suffering. Physicians attend there to ascertain the disease, to look after the cure, to regulate the diet, and to administer medicine. The cost of the medicines and the food is defrayed from my endowments. All sick persons, residents and travelers, gentle and simple, bond and free, resort thither; their maladies are treated, and, under God's blessing, they are cured. . . .

I encouraged my infidel subjects to embrace the religion of the prophet, and I proclaimed that every one who repeated the creed[8] and became a Muslim should be exempt from the jizya, or poll-tax. Information of this came to the ears of the people at large, and great numbers of Hindus presented themselves, and were admitted to the honor of Islam. Thus they came forward day by day from every quarter, and, adopting the faith, were exonerated from the jizya, and were favored with presents and honors. . . .

Whenever a person had completed the natural term of life and had become full of years, after providing for his support, I advised and admonished him to direct his thoughts to making preparation for the life to come, and to repent of all things which he had done contrary to the Law and religion in his youth; to wean his affections from this world, and to fix them on the next. . . .

My object in writing this book has been to express my gratitude to the All-bountiful God for the many and various blessings He has bestowed upon me. Secondly, that men who desire to be good and prosperous may read this and learn what is the proper course. There is this concise maxim, by observing which, a man may obtain God's guidance: Men will be judged according to their works, and rewarded for the good that they have done.

▼▼▼

Southwest Asia

Of all the significant developments that took place in Southwest Asia during this thousand-year period, the two most far-reaching were the rise and spread of Islam and the arrival of Turkish, European, and Mongol invaders after A.D. 1000. By approximately A.D. 750 Islam was firmly in control of most of Southwest Asia, except for the Anatolian peninsula, which remained the heart of the East Roman, or Byzantine, Empire until late in the eleventh century, when Muslim Turkish forces began the process of transforming this land into Turkey.

---

[8]"There is no God but God, and Muhammad is the Prophet of God."

Seljuk and Ottoman Turks, European crusaders, Mongols, and the armies of Timur the Lame would invade and contest Southwest Asia for much of the period from 1000 to 1500.

Around the early sixteenth century a clear pattern emerged. Europe's Christian crusaders had been expelled from the eastern Mediterranean, except for their precarious possession of a handful of island strongholds, such as Cyprus and Crete; the Mongol Empire was only a fading memory; and Timur the Lame's empire had crumbled upon his death in 1405. Two Turkish Muslim empires dominated Southwest Asia — the Shi'ite Safavids of Persia and the Sunni Ottomans, whose base of power was Anatolia, but who also controlled Syria-Palestine, Egypt, and western Arabia and were even driving deeply into Europe's Balkan Peninsula. Although these two empires would quarrel viciously for control of Islam, and Sunnis and Shi'ites would continue to shed one another's blood, Turkish domination of Southwest Asia was secure for the foreseeable future. European attempts to counter the Turkish menace by launching new crusades in the eastern Mediterranean generally proved feeble, and the Ottomans' and Safavids' pastoral cousins on the steppes of Inner Asia had finally ceased to be a major threat to the stability of Eurasia's civilizations.

Sindbad's First Voyage
▼▼▼

76 ▼ A THOUSAND AND ONE ARABIAN NIGHTS

A Thousand and One Arabian Nights is one of the most celebrated collections of stories in the world. Loosely arranged around the theme of a series of nightly stories told by Shahrazad in order to forestall decapitation by the order of her disturbed husband, Shahriyar, king of India and China, *The Arabian Nights* is a rich pastiche of Persian, Arabic, Greco-Roman, Indian, and Egyptian fables and legends. Its core is a now-lost ancient Persian collection known as *A Thousand Tales*, which tenth-century Arab commentators tell us was similarly structured around Queen Shahrazad's ingenious filibuster. This Persian work served as the matrix around which numerous anonymous Arab storytellers wove additional tales, especially out of the rich folk traditions of Iraq and Egypt, to create, by the fourteenth century, *The Arabian Nights* as we more or less know it today.

A major Arab addition to this constantly changing treasury of tales was the Sindbad cycle — seven stories that related the merchant voyages of one of literature's most celebrated adventurers. In the course of his seven voyages into the Indian Ocean, Sindbad narrowly escaped death at the hands of pirates and cannibals, monster birds and huge serpents, storms and whirlpools, and the murderous one-eyed Cyclops and the Old Man of the Sea. In his travels he discovered such fabled places as the valley of diamonds, the land where living people were buried alive with their deceased spouses, and the ivory-rich elephant burying ground. Not only did he survive to tell his tales, but each voyage left him wealthier than before.

Doubtless, the professional storytellers who recounted the adventures of this fictional merchant-sailor deliberately employed hyperbolic flights of fancy because their purpose was to present thrilling entertainment, much in the manner of an Indiana Jones movie. Yet the more fantastic elements within the stories also hint at some of the ways in which the world of the Indian Ocean was viewed from the perspective of Iraq.

One ninth-century Arab geographer described Iraq as "the center of the world, the navel of the earth." Iraq's centrality, and its consequent prosperity, was a function of its lying at the head of the Persian Gulf. The Persian Gulf afforded the merchants of Baghdad and Basra access to the Indian Ocean and the rich markets of East Africa, India, the Spice Islands of Southeast Asia, and South China. The potential for wealth was great for any Iraqi merchant who was sufficiently enterprising, courageous, skilled, and lucky. Danger, however, lay around every corner, as the following tale suggests.

QUESTIONS FOR ANALYSIS

1. How did an Arab merchant of modest means undertake the expense of outfitting a ship and filling it with cargo?
2. What do the goods that Sindbad brought back with him suggest about the nature of commerce in the Indian Ocean?
3. Consider the wonders that Sindbad reported. What do they suggest about the level of Arab knowledge of the more distant regions of the Indian Ocean? What do they suggest about Arab attitudes toward the eastern Indian Ocean?
4. How does this tale illustrate the ambivalence of the Iraqi world toward the vast region of the Indian Ocean?
5. What might we infer from this story about the role and status of merchants in Arabic society?

I dissipated the greatest part of my paternal inheritance in the excesses of my youth; but at length, seeing my folly, I became convinced that riches were not of much use when applied to such purposes as I had employed them in; and I moreover reflected that the time I spent in dissipation was of still greater value than gold, and that nothing could be more truly deplorable than poverty in old age. I recollected the words of the wise Solomon, which my father had often repeated to me, that it is better to be in the grave than poor. Feeling the truth of all these reflections, I resolved to collect the small remains of my patrimony and to sell my goods by auction. I then formed connections with some merchants who had negotiations by sea, and consulted those who appeared best able to give me advice. In short, I determined to employ to some profit the small sum I had remaining, and no sooner was this resolution formed than I put it into execution. I went to Basra,[1] where I embarked with several merchants in a vessel which had been equipped at our united expense.

We set sail and steered toward the East Indies by the Persian Gulf, which is formed by the coast of Arabia on the right, and by that of Persia on the left, and is commonly supposed to be seventy leagues[2] in breadth in the widest part; beyond this gulf the Western Sea, or Indian Ocean, is very spacious, and is bounded by the coast of Abyssinia,[3] extending in length four thousand five hundred leagues to the island of Vakvak.[4] I was at first rather incommoded with what is termed sea-sickness, but I soon recovered my health; and from that period I have never been subject to that malady. In the course of our voyage we touched at several islands, and sold or exchanged our merchandise. One day, when in full sail, we were unexpectedly becalmed before a small island appearing just above the water, and which, from its green color, resembled a beautiful meadow. The captain ordered the sails to be lowered, and gave permission to those who wished it to go ashore, of which number I formed one. But during the time that we were regaling ourselves with eating and drinking, by way of relaxation from the fatigues we had endured at sea, the island suddenly trembled, and we felt a severe shock.

They who were in the ship perceived the earthquake in the island, and immediately called to us to re-embark as soon as possible, or we should all perish, for what we supposed to be an island was no more than the back of a whale. The most active of the party jumped into the boat, whilst others threw themselves into the water to swim to the ship: as for me, I was still on the island, or, more properly speaking, on the whale, when it plunged into the sea, and I had only time to seize hold of a piece

of wood which had been brought to make a fire with. Meantime the captain, willing to avail himself of a fair breeze which had sprung up, set sail with those who had reached his vessel, and left me to the mercy of the waves. I remained in this situation the whole of that day and the following night; and on the return of morning I had neither strength nor hope left, when a breaker happily dashed me on an island. The shore was high and steep, and I should have found great difficulty in landing, had not some roots of trees, which fortune seemed to have furnished for my preservation, assisted me. I threw myself on the ground, where I continued, more than half dead, till the sun rose.

Although I was extremely enfeebled by the fatigues I had undergone, I tried to creep about in search of some herb or fruit that might satisfy my hunger. I found some, and had also the good luck to meet with a stream of excellent water, which contributed not a little to my recovery. Having in a great measure regained my strength, I began to explore the island, and entered a beautiful plain, where I perceived at some distance a horse that was grazing. I bent my steps that way, trembling between fear and joy, for I could not ascertain whether I was advancing to safety or perdition. I remarked, as I approached, that it was a mare tied to a stake: her beauty attracted my attention; but whilst I was admiring her, I heard a voice underground of a man, who shortly after appeared, and coming to me, asked me who I was. I related my adventure to him; after which he took me by the hand and led me into a cave, where there were some other persons, who were not less astonished to see me than I was to find them there.

I ate some food which they offered me; and having asked them what they did in a place which appeared so barren, they replied that

[1]Basra, located at the northern tip of the Persian Gulf and connected to Baghdad by the Tigris River, is Iraq's entryway to the Persian Gulf and Indian Ocean.
[2]A league is three miles.

[3]The horn of Africa: the region of the modern nations of Ethiopia and Somalia.
[4]This is possibly a reference to Sumatra.

they were grooms to King Mihrage, who was the sovereign of that isle, and that they came every year about that time with some mares belonging to the king, for the purpose of having a breed between them and a sea-horse which came on shore at that spot. They tied the mares in that manner, because they were obliged almost immediately, by their cries, to drive back the sea-horse, otherwise he began to tear them in pieces. As soon as the mares were with foal they carried them back, and these colts were called sea-colts, and set apart for the king's use. To-morrow, they added, was the day fixed for their departure, and if I had been one day later I must certainly have perished, because they lived so far off that it was impossible to reach their habitations without a guide.

Whilst they were talking to me, the horse rose out of the sea as they had described, and immediately attacked the mares. He would then have torn them to pieces, but the grooms began to make such a noise that he let go his prey, and again plunged into the ocean.

The following day they returned to the capital of the island with the mares, whither I accompanied them. On our arrival, King Mihrage, to whom I was presented, asked me who I was, and by what chance I had reached his dominions; and when I had satisfied his curiosity, he expressed pity at my misfortune. At the same time, he gave orders that I should be taken care of and have everything I might want. These orders were executed in a manner that proved the king's generosity, as well as the exactness of his officers.

As I was a merchant, I associated with persons of my own profession. I sought, in particular, such as were foreigners, as much to hear some intelligence of Baghdad, as with the hope of meeting with some one whom I could return

with; for the capital of King Mihrage is situated on the sea-coast, and has a beautiful port, where vessels from all parts of the world daily arrive. I also sought the society of the Indian sages, and found great pleasure in their conversation; this, however, did not prevent me from attending at court very regularly, nor from conversing with the governors of provinces, and some less powerful kings, tributaries of Mihrage, who were about his person. They asked me a thousand questions about my country; and I, on my part, was not less inquisitive about the laws and customs of their different states, or whatever appeared to merit my curiosity.

In the dominions of King Mihrage there is an island called Cassel. I had been told that in that island there was heard every night the sound of cymbals, which had given rise to the sailors' opinion, that al-Dajjal[5] had chosen that spot for his residence. I felt a great desire to witness these wonders, and during my voyage I saw some fish of one and two hundred cubits in length,[6] which occasion much fear, but do no harm; they are so timid that they are frightened away by beating on a board. I remarked also some other fish that were not above a cubit long, and whose heads resembled that of an owl.

After I returned, as I was standing one day near the port, I saw a ship come toward the land; when they had cast anchor, they began to unload its goods, and the merchants, to whom they belonged, took them away to their warehouses. Happening to cast my eyes on some of the packages, I saw my name written, and, having attentively examined them, I concluded them to be those which I had embarked in the ship in which I left Basra. I also recollected the captain; but as I was persuaded that he thought me dead, I went up to him, and asked him to

---

[5]The "deceiver," or "imposter," al-Dajjal is the false messiah who, according to Muslim belief, will appear shortly before Jesus returns to earth to usher in the end of time. Jesus will destroy al-Dajjal, and the Day of Judgment will follow.

[6]A cubit varies from seventeen to twenty-two inches.

whom those parcels belonged. "I had on board with me," replied he, "a merchant of Baghdad, named Sindbad. One day, when we were near an island, at least such it appeared to be, he, with some other passengers, went ashore on this supposed island, which was no other than an enormous whale, that had fallen asleep on the surface of the water. The fish no sooner felt the heat of the fire they had lighted on its back, to cook their provisions, than it began to move and flounce about in the sea. The greatest part of the persons who were on it were drowned, and the unfortunate Sindbad was one of the number. These parcels belonged to him, and I have resolved to sell them, that, if I meet with any of his family, I may be able to return them the profit I shall have made of the principal." "Captain," said I then, "I am that Sindbad, whom you supposed dead, but who is still alive, and these parcels are my property and merchandise."

When the captain of the vessel heard me speak thus, he exclaimed, "Great God! whom shall I trust? There is no longer truth in man. I with my own eyes saw Sindbad perish; the passengers I had on board were also witnesses of it; and you have the assurance to say that you are the same Sindbad? what audacity! At first sight you appeared a man of probity and honor, yet you assert an impious falsity to possess yourself of some merchandise which does not belong to you." "Have patience," replied I, "and have the goodness to listen to what I have to say." "Well," said he, "what can you have to say? speak, and I will attend." I then related in what manner I had been saved, and by what accident I had met with King Mihrage's grooms, who had brought me to his court.

He was rather staggered at my discourse, but was soon convinced that I was not an impostor; for some people arriving from his ship knew

me, and began to congratulate me on my fortunate escape. At last he recollected me himself, and embracing me, "Heaven be praised," said he, "that you have thus happily avoided so great a danger; I cannot express the pleasure I feel on the occasion. Here are your goods, take them, for they are yours, and do with them as you like." I thanked him, and praised his honorable conduct, and by way of recompense I begged him to accept part of the merchandise, but that he refused.

I selected the most precious and valuable things in my bales, as presents for King Mihrage. As this prince had been informed of my misfortunes, he asked me where I had obtained such rare curiosities. I related to him the manner in which I had recovered my property, and he had the complaisance to express his joy on the occasion; he accepted my presents, and gave me others of far greater value. After that, I took my leave of him, and re-embarked in the same vessel, having first exchanged what merchandise remained with that of the country, which consisted of aloes and sandal-wood,[7] camphor,[8] nutmegs, cloves, pepper, and ginger. We touched at several islands, and at last landed at Basra, from whence I came here, having realized about a hundred thousand sequins.[9] I returned to my family, and was received by them with the joy which a true and sincere friendship inspires. I purchased slaves of each sex, and bought a magnificent house and grounds. I thus established myself, determined to forget the disagreeable things I had endured, and to enjoy the pleasures of life. . . .

I had resolved after my first voyage, to pass the rest of my days in tranquility at Baghdad. . . . But I soon grew weary of an idle life; the desire of seeing foreign countries, and carrying on some negotiations by sea returned: I bought some merchandise, which I thought

---

[7]Both are woods noted for their aromatic and medicinal properties.
[8]A medicinal drug and aromatic made from camphor wood.

[9]Gold coins.

likely to answer in the traffic I meditated; and
I set off a second time with some merchants,
upon whose probity I could rely. We embarked
in a good vessel, and having recommended ourselves to the care of the Almighty, we began our
voyage. . . .

▷   And so the second voyage begins.

An Arab View of Western Crusaders
▼▼▼

77 ▼ Usamah ibn Munqidh, THE BOOK OF REFLECTIONS

In 1095 Pope Urban II (r. 1088–1099) attempted to harness the martial values
of Europe's warrior classes to service to the Church by calling for a holy war
against Islam in the eastern Mediterranean, specifically to assist the Christian
empire of Constantinople in its struggles with the Seljuk Turks and to liberate
Jerusalem and other sites in the Holy Land from Islam. Christian Western Europeans had been fighting Islam intermittently since the eighth century when
Muslim armies had invaded the Iberian peninsula and conquered the Visigothic
kingdom of Spain. During the eleventh century the struggles between Christian
and Islamic forces in Iberia had heated up to a flashpoint whereby the *Reconquista,* or Christian reconquest, of the entire peninsula was well under way by
mid-century, although the process would not be completed until 1492. It was
against this background that Pope Urban set in motion an expedition known as
the First Crusade (1096–1099).

That crusade inaugurated close to five hundred years of Western Christian
involvement in the ancient lands of the *Levant,* or eastern Mediterranean. Moreover, the crusades launched Western Europe on its first great age of overseas
colonization. The later transoceanic voyages of Columbus, da Gama, and those
who followed were in many ways a continuation of the crusade tradition.

From an eastern Mediterranean perspective, however, the crusades were barbarian invasions. Princess Anna Comnena of Constantinople (Chapter 7, source
58) characterized these Western coreligionists as unstable, greedy for money,
and always ready to break their word. Imagine what the Muslims thought.

One of the most telling commentaries on crusader behavior in Syria-Palestine
comes from the memoirs of Usamah ibn Munqidh (1095–1188), a warrior and
gentleman of Syria. Born in the year in which the First Crusade was called,
Usamah lived long enough to see Jerusalem reconquered in 1187 by his friend
and patron Saladin, sultan of Egypt and Syria. Late in life, sometime past his
ninetieth birthday, Usamah undertook the narration of his memoirs. Although
his descriptions of the Western "Franks" constitute only a small segment of this

amiably rambling work, they are among the autobiography's more fascinating and insightful sections.

QUESTIONS FOR ANALYSIS

1. What does Usamah identify as the major deficiencies of the Franks?
2. Does he acknowledge any virtues or positive qualities on their part?
3. *Acculturation* is the process of one ethnic group's adopting the cultural traits of another group. Can you find any evidence of this phenomenon in Usamah's account?
4. Can you discover any evidence of friendly, or at least peaceful, relations between the crusaders and the Muslims of Syria-Palestine? To what do you ascribe such relations?
5. Despite such relations, what were the elements that separated crusaders and Muslims?
6. What is the general tone and overall message of Usamah's commentary on the Franks?

AN APPRECIATION OF THE FRANKISH CHARACTER
Their Lack of Sense

Mysterious are the works of the Creator, the author of all things! When one comes to recount cases regarding the Franks,[1] he cannot but glorify Allah (exalted is he!) and sanctify him, for he sees them as animals possessing the virtues of courage and fighting, but nothing else; just as animals have only the virtues of strength and carrying loads. I shall now give some instances of their doings and their curious mentality.

In the army of King Fulk,[2] son of Fulk, was a Frankish reverend knight who had just arrived from their land in order to make the holy pilgrimage and then return home. He was of my intimate fellowship and kept such constant company with me that he began to call me "my brother." Between us were mutual bonds of amity and friendship. When he resolved to return by sea to his homeland, he said to me:

My brother, I am leaving for my country and I want you to send with me your son (my son, who was then fourteen years old, was at that time in my company) to our country, where he can see the knights and learn wisdom and chivalry. When he returns, he will be like a wise man.

Thus there fell upon my ears words which would never come out of the head of a sensible man; for even if my son were to be taken captive, his captivity could not bring him a worse misfortune than carrying him into the lands of the Franks. However, I said to the man:

By your life, this has exactly been my idea. But the only thing that prevented me from carrying it out was the fact that his grandmother, my mother, is so fond of him and did not this time let him come out with me until she exacted an oath from me to the effect that I would return him to her.

Thereupon he asked, "Is your mother still alive?" "Yes," I replied. "Well," said he, "disobey her not.". . .

Newly Arrived Franks are Especially Rough: One Insists That Usamah Should Pray Eastward

Everyone who is a fresh emigrant from the Frankish lands is ruder in character than those who have become acclimatized and have held long association with the Muslims. Here is an illustration of their rude character.

Whenever I visited Jerusalem I always entered the Aqsa Mosque,[3] beside which stood a small mosque which the Franks had converted into a church. When I used to enter the Aqsa Mosque, which was occupied by the Templars, who were my friends, the Templars would evacuate the little adjoining mosque so that I might pray in it. One day[4] I entered this mosque, repeated the first formula, "Allah is great," and stood up in the act of praying, upon which one of the Franks rushed on me, got hold of me and turned my face eastward saying, "This is the way you should pray!" A group of Templars hastened to him, seized him, and repelled him from me. I resumed my prayer. The same man, while the others were otherwise busy, rushed

once more on me and turned my face eastward, saying, "This is the way you should pray!" The Templars again came in to him and expelled him. They apologized to me, saying, "This is a stranger who has only recently arrived from the land of the Franks and he has never before seen anyone praying except eastward." Thereupon I said to myself, "I have had enough prayer." So I went out and have ever been surprised at the conduct of this devil of a man, at the change in the color of his face, his trembling and his sentiment at the sight of one praying towards the *qiblah*.[5]

Another Wants to Show to a Muslim God As a Child

I saw one of the Franks come to al-Amir[6] Mu'in-al-Din (may Allah's mercy rest upon his soul!) when he was in the Dome of the Rock[7] and say to him, "Do you want to see God as a child?" Mu'in-al-Din said, "Yes." The Frank walked ahead of us until he showed us the picture of Mary with Christ (may peace be upon him!) as an infant in her lap. He then said, "This is God as a child." But Allah is exalted far above what the infidels say about him! . . .

Their Judicial Trials: A Duel

I attended one day a duel in Nablus between two Franks. The reason for this was that certain Muslim thieves took by surprise one of the vil-

[3]The mosque of al-Aqsa is located on the Temple Mount, the site of the ancient temples of Solomon and Herod the Great. Following the crusader capture of Jerusalem in 1099, the mosque had been converted into a palace of the Latin king of Jerusalem. Subsequently, King Baldwin II (r. 1118–1131) handed over a portion of this mosque-palace to a community of knights who proposed to live a semimonastic life while serving in defense of the Christian kingdom of Jerusalem. As a consequence, this new elite fighting force became known as the Knights of the Temple, the Knights Templar, or simply the Templars.
[4]Around 1140.

[5]The niche in every mosque that indicates the direction of Mecca, toward which all Muslims pray. Depending on where a mosque is in relation to Mecca, the *qiblah* can point in any direction of the compass. In Christian Europe, however, it was the custom to build all altars so that the priest and worshipers standing before them faced east, the general direction of Jerusalem from Western Europe. Ironically, the church of the Holy Sepulcher, the site in Jerusalem toward which European Christians prayed, lies about four hundred yards northwest of al-Aqsa.
[6]*Amir* (commander) was a title bestowed on military leaders and local lords.
[7]Also located on the Temple Mount, this late seventh-century, octagonal Muslim shrine is located above the rock tip of Mount Moriah, the site tradition identifies as the holy of holies of the temple of Solomon.

lages of Nablus. One of the peasants of that village was charged with having acted as guide for the thieves when they fell upon the village. So he fled away. The king sent and arrested his children. The peasant thereupon came back to the king and said, "Let justice be done in my case. I challenge to a duel the man who claimed that I guided the thieves to the village." The king then said to the tenant who held the village in fief, "Bring forth someone to fight the duel with him." The tenant went to his village, where a blacksmith lived, took hold of him and ordered him to fight the duel. The tenant became thus sure of the safety of his own peasants, none of whom would be killed and his estate ruined.

I saw this blacksmith. He was a physically strong young man, but his heart failed him. He would walk a few steps and then sit down and ask for a drink. The one who had made the challenge was an old man, but he was strong in spirit and he would rub the nail of his thumb against that of the forefinger in defiance, as if he was not worrying over the duel. Then came the viscount, i.e., the lord of the town, and gave each one of the two contestants a cudgel and a shield and arranged the people in a circle around them.

The two met. The old man would press the blacksmith backward until he would get him as far as the circle, then he would come back to the middle of the arena. They went on exchanging blows until they looked like pillars smeared with blood. The contest was prolonged and the viscount began to urge them to hurry, saying, "Hurry on." The fact that the smith was given to the use of the hammer proved now of great advantage to him. The old man was worn out and the smith gave him a blow which made him fall. His cudgel fell under his back. The smith knelt down over him and tried to stick his fingers into the eyes of his adversary, but could not do it because of the great quantity of blood flowing out. Then he rose up and hit his

head with the cudgel until he killed him. They then fastened a rope around the neck of the dead person, dragged him away and hanged him. The lord who brought the smith now came, gave the smith his own mantle, made him mount the horse behind him and rode off with him. This case illustrates the kind of jurisprudence and legal decisions the Franks have — may Allah's curse be upon them!

Ordeal By Water

I once went in the company of al-Amir Mu'in-al-Din (may Allah's mercy rest upon his soul!) to Jerusalem. We stopped at Nablus. There a blind man, a Muslim, who was still young and was well dressed, presented himself before al-amir carrying fruits for him and asked permission to be admitted into his service in Damascus.[8] The amir consented. I inquired about this man and was informed that his mother had been married to a Frank whom she had killed. Her son used to practice ruses against the Frankish pilgrims and cooperate with his mother in assassinating them. They finally brought charges against him and tried his case according to the Frankish way of procedure.

They installed a huge cask and filled it with water. Across it they set a board of wood. They then bound the arms of the man charged with the act, tied a rope around his shoulders and dropped him into the cask, their idea being that in case he was innocent, he would sink in the water and they would then lift him up with the rope so that he might not die in the water; and in case he was guilty, he would not sink in the water. This man did his best to sink when they dropped him into the water, but he could not do it. So he had to submit to their sentence against him — may Allah's curse be upon them! They pierced his eyeballs with red-hot awls.

Later the same man arrived in Damascus. Al-Amir Mu'in-al-Din (may Allah's mercy rest upon his soul!) assigned him a stipend large

---

[8]One of the two major Muslim-held cities in Syria.

enough to meet all his needs and said to a slave of his, "Conduct him to Burhan-al-Din al-Balkhi (may Allah's mercy rest upon his soul!) and ask him on my behalf to order somebody to teach this man the Qur'an and something of Muslim jurisprudence. . . .

A Frank Domesticated in Syria Abstains From Eating Pork

Among the Franks are those who have become acclimatized and have associated long with the Muslims. These are much better than the recent comers from the Frankish lands. But they constitute the exception and cannot be treated as a rule.

Here is an illustration. I dispatched one of my men to Antioch[9] on business. There was in Antioch at that time al-Ra'is Theodoros Sophianos,[10] to whom I was bound by mutual ties of amity. His influence in Antioch was supreme. One day he said to my man, "I am invited by a friend of mine who is a Frank. You should come with me so that you may see their fashions." My man related the story in the following words:

> I went along with him and we came to the home of a knight who belonged to the old category of knights who came with the early expeditions of the Franks. He had been by that time stricken off the register and exempted from service, and possessed in Antioch an estate on the income of which he lived. The knight presented an excellent table, with food extraordinarily clean and delicious. Seeing me abstaining from food, he said, "Eat, be of good cheer! I never eat Frankish dishes, but I have Egyptian women cooks and never eat except their cooking. Besides, pork never enters my home."[11]

I ate, but guardedly, and after that we departed.

As I was passing in the market place, a Frankish woman all of a sudden hung to my clothes and began to mutter words in their language, and I could not understand what she was saying. This made me immediately the center of a big crowd of Franks. I was convinced that death was at hand. But all of a sudden that same knight approached. On seeing me, he came and said to that woman, "What is the matter between you and this Muslim?" She replied, "This is he who has killed my brother Hurso." This Hurso was a knight in Afamiyah who was killed by someone of the army of Hamah. The Christian knight shouted at her, saying, "This is a bourgeois [i.e., a merchant] who neither fights nor attends a fight." He also yelled at the people who had assembled, and they all dispersed. Then he took me by the hand and went away. Thus the effect of that meal was my deliverance from certain death.

---

[9]The chief Christian city of Syria, which fell to the crusaders in 1098.
[10]The name indicates he was a Greek.

[11]Muslim law prohibits the eating of pork, because it is an "unclean" food.

Chapter 10

▼▼▼

Western Europe

The story of the birth of a new civilization on the frontiers of western Eurasia — a civilization variously termed *the Medieval West*, or *the First Europe* — begins at a close of the fourth century A.D., when Rome, by then a Christian state, still ruled an empire stretching from the Atlantic Ocean to Mesopotamia, from the Scottish lowlands to the Sahara. In the centuries that immediately followed, this Mediterranean-centered ecumene underwent a transformation. Like several civilizations to the east, most notably Gupta India and Han China, the Roman Empire entered a time of troubles. Unlike those Eastern cultures, the Roman world changed irrevocably. Centuries of upheaval, caused by internal weaknesses and invasions by various fringe peoples, resulted in radical mutations of its political, social, and cultural forms. By about A.D. 700 the empire and its civilization had passed away, succeeded by three heirs — Byzantine Christendom, Islam, and Latin-Christian Europe.

Of the three, the Latin West seemed the least promising. It had been the civilization most severely beset by late antiquity's economic and political problems and was fast becoming a society whose apparent weakness and low level of culture stood in stark contrast to the magnificence of Byzantium and Islam. While its two more powerful siblings jockeyed for power in the Mediterranean, Latin Christendom had to look northward, beyond the Alps, to still untamed lands and recently converted peoples, especially a Germanic people known as the Franks. The eighth-century marriage of convenience between the Roman Church and the Franks, who received official recognition from Europe's leading spiritual power in return for offering the papacy military protection, shows that the West was following a path of historical development that differed radically from those of its eastern coheirs.

Yet, as backward as this society appears to have been during the Early Middle Ages (500–1000), these centuries were proving to be the formative period of a tenacious and revolutionary civilization, with technology, ideas, and institutions that would in time transform the world. All this lay in the distant future, but by the eleventh century Christian Europe was ready to take its place as a major power in western Eurasia. A dramatic turnaround in Europe's economy, a rise in its general level of political stability, and a new religious vitality provided the necessary impetus for the Age of the Crusades. This first period of Western European overseas expansion resulted in crusader colonial states in the Holy Land by 1100.

The twelfth and thirteenth centuries were a period of overall growth and prosperity for Latin Europe. Among other developments, this age witnessed the emergence of numerous new towns and cities, which served as centers of trade, industry, learning, and religious change. Those who dwelt in these urban settings, the *bourgeoisie,* proved to be one of the West's major dynamic forces, despite their relatively small numbers. As towns of about three thousand to six thousand inhabitants and cities of perhaps five times that size on average sprang up throughout Europe, often in areas that had recently been forest or marginal land, churches and civic buildings proliferated. Toward the end of the twelfth century a new form of urban ecclesiastical architecture developed in the region around Paris that symbolized the new importance of Europe's urban centers and the many forces that drove this new civilization. This was the Gothic cathedral.

The essence of Gothic construction is the opposition of contrary forces to create a soaring edifice that seems to defy gravity. Thrust and counterthrust, particularly through use of a serendipitous architectural device known as the flying buttress, result in a complex structure whose sheer beauty and size reflect the faith of the society that created it. Such an achievement is fitting for a civilization that was the product of many creative tensions, and it is these tensions that explain the revolutionary changes taking place in Europe and Europeans' great adaptability for change.

Tension lay at the heart of Europe's new dynamism. There was the tension of political pluralism. Not only was Europe divided into a number of separate states, but within these states different orders competed for supremacy or independence. Nobles struggled with monarchs, and townspeople sought freedom from feudal constraints. One result was the drafting of *Magna Carta*, the "Great Charter" of English liberties, in 1215. Another was the emergence of powerful urban centers, such as Milan and Paris. There were tensions between Church and State, as popes and kings vied for control over one another and the loyalties of all Europeans. Because neither priests nor secular rulers were ever able to dominate the other totally, their subjects' opportunities for choice and freedom multiplied substantially. In the field of human inquiry and knowledge there were similar fruitful tensions. As heirs of both the mystical religious traditions of Southwest Asia and the rationalism of Hellenic philosophy, the West's teachers, intellectuals, and visionaries had to seek a balance between faith and reason.

On a more mundane level, Western Europeans had to accommodate their warrior ethic and spirit of adventure to an increasingly complex society's need for internal peace and stability. One answer was to export violence in the forms of crusades and frontier expansion. As Eurasia's "Wild West," Europe was a frontier society, and its people struggled against an often hostile environment. The drive to clear forests, drain swamps, and "civilize" the fringe peoples on their borders by converting them to Christianity left Europeans with the notion that the world is a place for humans to tame, settle, and remake in their own image. Because this European frontier was land-rich and people-poor, Europeans became fascinated by technology and every form of labor-saving device. Tools developed in China and elsewhere, particularly the stirrup and horse collar, water and windmills, the compass, gunpowder, and the printing press, often became instruments of radical change in the hands of Westerners.

Europe's first great age of cultural flowering is known as the *High Middle Ages* (1000–1300). Without ever losing their adaptability and readiness for change, Europeans fashioned in these three centuries a "Gothic" equilibrium out of their society's many contradictory forces. By 1300, however, this synthesis appeared to be in danger of total disintegration. Internal stresses, such as war, rebellion, and religious dissent, combined with natural disasters like climatic change and the Black Death (1347–1350), produced an age of crisis in the fourteenth and fifteenth centuries.

European civilization, however, was neither destroyed nor fundamentally transformed during these centuries. Most of medieval Europe's core ideas and institutions turned out to be amazingly resilient, and those that were decaying, such as the ideal of a united Christian commonwealth, were giving way to creative new forces. The simultaneous vitality of traditional and new forms of expression in art, literature, and philosophy have given these two centuries a dual identity: as the Later Middle Ages and as the Early Renaissance (1300–1500). By the end of this period Europe was ready for another age of expansion, and in the last decade of the fifteenth century European sailors reached the shores of East Africa, the Americas, and India.

▼▼▼

Establishing a New Order

With the passing of Roman imperial order, Western Europeans were thrown back on their own resources and forced to create new social and political structures and a new civilization. In fashioning this new society, Westerners melded three elements: the vestiges of Roman civilization; the moral and organizational leadership of the Roman Catholic Church; and the vigor and cultures of the various new peoples, such as the Visigoths and Franks, who carved out kingdoms in Europe from the fifth century onward. The single act most vividly symbolizing the new order that emerged from that fusion was Pope Leo III's crowning of the Frankish king Charlemagne, or Charles the Great, as "Roman" emperor on Christmas Day, 800.

Charles the Great's empire was short-lived, and Europe was again thrown on the defensive as it was invaded by new fringe peoples during the ninth and tenth centuries. As serious as these new challenges were, Europe's emerging civilization did not collapse. Rather, its people produced a variety of military and political expedients that allowed them to get on with the task of building a new society. One of the most important of these was a system known as *feudalism*, in which a class of heavily armed cavalry, or knights, dominated a fair portion of the western European mainland and British Isles.

Feudal warriors were one more source of tension in European society because they were forces for both anarchy and order. This paradox was not lost on medieval Westerners, who, toward the end of the eleventh century, had achieved a sufficiently stable level of society to export some of this feudal violence in the form of crusades (Chapter 9, source 77). At home, feudalism was a fruitful element in fashioning new political structures, but feudal government was not medieval Europe's only answer to the problem of instability. From the eleventh century onward towns and cities proliferated, offering Europeans opportunities not only for survival but prosperity.

The Feudal Perspective
▼▼▼

78 ▼ *THE SONG OF ROLAND*

By 1000, warrior-landholders in northwest Europe had evolved a system of governance that modern historians termed feudalism. Like Japan's samurai, the feudal *vassal* (both terms mean "one who serves") was a warrior who served a lord and enjoyed in return a variety of political, social, and economic benefits. One of the major reasons a soldier became a vassal was to receive a *fief* (*feudum* in Latin, hence the term feudalism) as payment for services rendered. Originally, this fief, or *fee*, was anything of value, but increasingly it became a grant of land that the vassal ruled in the lord's name. During the eleventh century these fiefs tended to become hereditary, passing to the vassal's oldest surviving male heir. Therefore, feudal soldiers, who several generations earlier had been hired thugs in the employ of warlords, were becoming landed nobles. In the process they articulated a set of shared values that became known as the Code of Chivalry. Ideally, these principles and customs governed the life and conduct of the *chevalier*, or mounted knight. Reality, however, often diverged from the ideal.

One of the earliest and most popular literary articulations of the chivalric code is the anonymous *Song of Roland*, an epic *chanson de geste*, or "song of heroic deeds," written in Old French. Composed about 1100, the *Song of Roland* is saturated with the ideology of the French warrior class at the time of the First Crusade. This narrative poem, which relates the legendary last battle of Count Roland and his companions, is loosely based on a minor disaster suffered by Charlemagne (r. 768–814) in 778. While his army was returning from an expedition in northern Spain, Christian Basques ambushed and wiped out his baggage train and rear guard in the mountain pass of Roncesvalles. Among the fallen was Roland, lord of the Breton frontier. We know little else about this skirmish or the historical Roland. However, when Roland reemerges several centuries later, he has been transformed into Charlemagne's nephew and the greatest champion in the emperor's holy war against Islam: the Basque bandits have become an enormous Muslim army. Charlemagne, who was only thirty-six at the time of the ambush and twenty-two years shy of his eventual coronation as emperor, has been metamorphosed into a Moses-like patriarch more than two hundred years old, who rules as God's sole agent on earth over a united Christian world. He, his nephew, and his nephew's companions are now Frenchmen, even though there had been no France or French culture in Charlemagne's day. Likewise, feudalism was in its infancy when Charles the Great's Frankish kingdom served as western Christendom's focal point, yet the *Song of Roland* assumes a society pervaded by feudal relationships and values.

The story revolves around the themes of feudal loyalty and honor. Roland has unwittingly offended his stepfather, Ganelon, who in revenge enters into a conspiracy with the Saracen (Muslim) king, Marsilion, to deliver up Roland and the rest of the flower of French knighthood. Ganelon then arranges for Roland to command the emperor's rear guard, knowing that the Saracens plan to ambush it and that Roland will be too proud to sound his horn for reinforcements. Such is the case. Despite the entreaties of Oliver, his closest friend, Roland does not sound the horn until the battle is lost and twenty thousand Christian soldiers lie dead. The emperor returns too late to prevent his nephew's death but manages to exact revenge by destroying all Muslim forces in Spain and consigning Ganelon to death by torture. Our selection describes the opening and final stages of Roland's last fight.

QUESTIONS FOR ANALYSIS

1. Why does Roland not wish to sound his horn? Why does Oliver initially urge Roland to blow the horn but later tells him that it would be shameful to do so?
2. How does Roland define a vassal's duty? Would Oliver remove or add anything to that list?
3. How does the author express the salvation of Roland's soul in feudal terms?
4. Consider the words and actions of Roland, Oliver, and Turpin, and from them draw up a list of the Code of Chivalry's components. Do you see any potentially contradictory values or practices? What do their words and actions allow us to infer about Western Europe's crusade ideology?
5. Students often confuse feudal vassals with *serfs*, the semifree tenant farmers who worked the estates of Europe's landed lords. What evidence is there in this poem that by the mid-eleventh century, feudal vassals were enjoying a status far higher than that of peasants?
6. Which of these two warriors, Roland or Oliver, would Kusunoki Masashige (Chapter 9, source 69) admire more? Why?
7. Compare this poem with the *Taiheiki* (*Chronicle of the Grand Pacification*). Which values do these two warrior societies share? Can you discern any significant differences between the two? What role does religion play in each? Are those roles similar or different? What does your answer suggest?
8. Compose Usamah ibn Munqidh's commentary on the *Song of Roland* (see Chapter 9, source 77). Keep in mind that he also was a warrior.

The pagans[1] arm themselves with Saracen[2] coats of triple-layered chain mail.[3] They buckle on helmets made in Saragossa[4] and strap on swords of Viennese steel. Their shields are handsome, and their lances, crafted in Valencia,[5] are tipped with white, blue, and scarlet streamers. They leave behind their pack mules and riding horses and, mounting their war-horses, ride forth in tight formation. The day is fair and the sun bright, and all their gear glistens in the light.

---

[1]At the time of the First Crusade, European Christians were generally ignorant of the fact that Muslims are monotheists and, therefore, not "pagans."
[2]Originally, *Saracen* was a term the Romans used to designate an inhabitant of Arabia; later it became a general Western synonym for Muslim.

[3]Knee-length garments of interconnected iron rings (chain mail) that protected the torso and thighs.
[4]A city in northeast Spain that Christian forces captured from Islam in 1118.
[5]A region in eastern Spain.

To add to the splendor, they sound a thousand trumpets. So great is the clamor, the sound carries to the Franks.[6]

Upon hearing it, Oliver says to Count Roland: "Sir comrade, I think we are now going to battle the Saracens." Roland answers: "May God so grant it. If we make a stand here for our monarch, we are only doing what is expected of good men. A man ought to be willing to suffer pain and loss for his lord. He should endure extremes of heat and cold and should be ever ready to lose hide and hair in his lord's service. Let each of us now be sure to strike hard blows, so that no bard may sing ill of us in his songs. Pagans are wrong, and Christians are right. On my part, I will not set a bad example."

Oliver says: "The heathen army is massive, and our numbers are few. Roland, my good friend, sound your horn. Charles will hear it and return with his whole army." Roland replies: "That would be a foolish act, for by so doing I would lose all fame in sweet France. I prefer to strike hard blows with Durendal,[7] so that its blade is bloodied right up to the hilt. These foul pagans made a mistake in coming to this mountain pass. I pledge that they have not long to live."

"Roland, my comrade, blow your horn. Charles will hear it, return with his army, and the king and his barons will aid us." Roland answers: "God forbid that my family be shamed by my actions or any dishonor fall on fair France. No, I will fight with Durendal, the good sword girded here at my side, and you will see its blade fully reddened. The pagans asked for trouble when they gathered their army. I pledge that all of them will die.". . .

Oliver says: "I see no shame here. I have seen the Saracens of Spain, they cover the hills and

valleys, the scrubland and the plains. Numerous are the ranks of this hostile people, and we are but a small band of comrades." Roland answers: "This only inflames my desire. May God and His angels forbid that France should suffer any loss because of me. I would rather die than dishonor myself. The more we act like warriors, the more the emperor loves us."

Roland is valiant, Oliver is wise, and both are courageous. Once armed and on their horses, they would rather die than flee the battlefield. . . .

Close at hand is Archbishop Turpin.[8] He now spurs his horse to the crest of a knoll and delivers a sermon to the Franks: "Lord barons, Charles placed us here, and it is a man's duty to die for his monarch. Now help defend Christianity. It is certain you will have to fight, for here are the Saracens. Confess your sins and beg God's mercy. For the salvation of your souls, I will absolve your sins. Should you die, you will die as holy martyrs, and you will have exalted seats in Paradise." The Franks dismount and kneel, and the archbishop blesses them. As their penance,[9] he commands them to use their swords.

▷ Despite a courageous stand, the rear guard is overwhelmed.

Count Roland, aware of the great slaughter of his men, turns to Oliver, saying: "Noble comrade, for God's sake, what do you think? See how many good men lie on the ground. We ought to weep for sweet France, the fair, that has lost such barons. Ah, my king and friend, would that you were here now! Oliver, my

[6]The Christian army.
[7]The name of Roland's sword.
[8]Archbishop of the church of Reims and, along with Roland and Oliver, one of the Twelve Peers of France. *Peer* means equal; these twelve champions were socially the Emperor Charlemagne's equals by virtue of their birth, prowess, and worth to him. Although a priest, Turpin is also a fighter.

[9]After receiving absolution of one's sins from God through the agency of a priest, the penitent was required by the priest to perform some penitential act as a token of contrition. Depending on the severity of the sins forgiven, the act could range from simple prayers to a pilgrimage to the Holy Land.

brother, what should we do? How shall we send the king news of this?" "I do not know," says Oliver, "but I would prefer to die than dishonor myself." Then Roland says: "I will blow my horn, and Charles, as he crosses the mountains, will hear it. I swear that the Franks will return." Oliver then replies: "That would be shameful for you to do and would dishonor your family. It would be a disgrace they would carry to their graves. You would not blow the horn when I told you to do so, now I advise you not to sound it. To do so now would be useless.". . .

Roland asks: "Why are you angry with me?" Oliver answers: "Comrade, you have no one to blame but yourself. Valor tempered by wisdom is not foolishness, and prudence is better than pride. Because of your folly these Franks have died. Never again will King Charles enjoy our service. Had you taken my advice, my lord Charles would have been here, and this battle would have ended differently. King Marsilion would have been captured or killed. Your valor, Roland, has been our undoing. We shall never again fight for the great Emperor Charles, who will have no equal till the end of time. Now you must die, and France will be shamed by its loss. Today our loyal friendship will be ended; before night falls we will be sorrowfully parted."

The archbishop, hearing them quarrel, goads his horse with spurs of pure gold, rides to them, and rebukes them both, saying: "Sir Roland, and you, Sir Oliver, in God's name, I pray you, stop this strife. Your horn will give us little help now, yet it is better if you blow it. Should the king come, he will avenge us, and the pagans will not depart from here rejoicing. Our Frankish comrades will dismount and find

us dead and mutilated. They will lay us on stretchers placed on the backs of pack mules and will mourn us in sorrow and pity. They will bury us in churches, so that our corpses are not eaten by wolves, swine, and dogs."

"Sir, you speak well and correctly," says Roland. Whereupon he sets his horn to his lips and blows it with all his might. . . . A good thirty leagues away they hear it resound. Charles and his whole army hear it, and the king remarks: "Our men are engaged in battle." . . . With anguish and deep torment, Count Roland blows his horn with all his might, to the point that bright blood spurts out of his mouth, and the vessels of his brain are ruptured. . . .

Roland knows his time is over. . . . He has laid himself down beneath a pine tree, his face turned toward Spain. He begins to remember many things: all the lands he has conquered, sweet France, the noble lineage from which he is descended, and Charlemagne, his lord, who raised him in his own household. He cannot keep back his tears and sighs. But not forgetting himself, he confesses his sins and begs God's mercy: "Father, You who are truth itself, who raised Lazarus from the dead[10] and saved Daniel from the lions,[11] preserve my soul from all the dangers that beset it because of the sins I have committed throughout my life." He holds out his right glove to God, and Saint Gabriel[12] takes it from his hand. His head sinks down to rest on his arm. With clasped hands he meets his end. God sends down His cherubim[13] and Saint Michael,[14] who saves us from the perils of the sea, and with them comes Saint Gabriel, and they carry the soul of the count to paradise.

---

[10]A friend whom Jesus raised from the dead.
[11]A Jewish prophet protected by God while in a lion's den.
[12]An archangel and messenger of God.

[13]An order of angels.
[14]St. Michael the Archangel, a warrior saint. The island monastery of Mont-Saint-Michel off the Breton coast is dedicated to St. Michael.

Limitations on Royal Power
▼▼▼

79 ▼ *MAGNA CARTA*

The essence of the feudal bond between lord and vassal was the principle of reciprocal obligations and rights. Just as the vassal was expected to serve the lord faithfully, even unto death, the lord was obligated to protect every vassal's honor, status, and well-being. A lord's failure to honor such commitments justified a vassal's rebellion. This built-in tension within feudalism often resulted in a fair amount of violence between parties who, rightly or wrongly, believed themselves aggrieved. It also gave rise to significant constitutional developments in England and elsewhere. Following his conquest of England in 1066, William I (r. 1066–1087) strengthened the English monarchy by imposing a modified Norman-French feudal system on his realm and emphasizing the feudal obligations all the lords and knights of the realm owed him. Several generations later the kings of France and Germany would use similar means to expand their power. As fruitful as this strategy was for decreasing the level of feudal anarchy and increasing the range of royal authority, it carried with it certain inherent dangers for those kings.

Early in the thirteenth century many of the great lords of England believed that King John (r. 1199–1216) was abusing his feudal privileges and generally treating all his subjects, but especially the nobles, in a shoddy manner. The result was a baronial revolt in which the rebels sought not to depose or injure John, their lord, but to force him to acknowledge that he was equally subject to all the customs and laws of England, even though he was the source of justice and law. With the aid of the burghers of London, who also were disenchanted with the king's heavy-handedness, the rebels forced John in 1215 to agree to a list of reforms that eventually became known as *Magna Carta*, or the Great Charter.

Beginning with Henry III (r. 1216–1272) in 1216, 1217, and 1225, subsequent English kings were required to reissue the Great Charter in return for baronial support and financial assistance. As a result *Magna Carta* remained a living reminder of the limits of royal power in England.

QUESTIONS FOR ANALYSIS

1. How did the barons propose to prevent John from extorting uncustomary or unreasonable sums of money from them in the future?
2. What did the burghers of London get for their support of the rebellion?
3. Judging from the guarantees John was forced to give, in what ways had he abused his royal and feudal rights?

4. Can you guess what the common council of the kingdom, mentioned in article 12 and elsewhere, evolved into?
5. Which of the charter's clauses seem the most familiar to you? Why? What do you infer from your answer?
6. Some historians have characterized the Great Charter as a document that protects only the narrow class interests of the baronage. What do you think of this judgment?

John, by the grace of God, king of England, lord of Ireland, duke of Normandy and Aquitaine, count of Anjou, to the archbishops, bishops, abbots, earls, barons, justiciars, foresters, sheriffs, reeves, servants, and all bailiffs and his faithful people greeting.

1. In the first place we have granted to God, and by this our present charter confirmed, for us and our heirs forever, that the English church shall be free, and shall hold its rights entire and its liberties uninjured. . . .

   We have granted moreover to all free men of our kingdom for us and our heirs forever all the liberties written below, to be had and holden by themselves and their heirs from us and our heirs.

2. If any of our earls or barons, or others holding from us in chief[1] by military service shall have died, and when he has died his heir shall be of full age and owe relief,[2] he shall have his inheritance by the ancient relief; that is to say, the heir or heirs of an earl for the whole barony of an earl a hundred pounds; the heir or heirs of a baron for a whole barony a hundred pounds; the heir or heirs of a knight, for a whole knight's fee, a hundred shillings at most; and who owes less let him give

less according to the ancient custom of fiefs.

3. If moreover the heir of any one of such shall be under age, and shall be in wardship,[3] when he comes of age he shall have his inheritance without relief and without a fine.

4. The custodian of the land of such a minor heir shall not take from the land of the heir any except reasonable products, reasonable customary payments, and reasonable services, and this without destruction or waste of men or of property; and if we shall have committed the custody of the land of any such a one to the sheriff or to any other who is to be responsible to us for its proceeds, and that man shall have caused destruction or waste from his custody we will recover damages from him, and the land shall be committed to two legal and discreet men of that fief, who shall be responsible for its proceeds to us or to him to whom we have assigned them; and if we shall have given or sold to any one the custody of any such land, and he has caused destruction or waste there, he shall lose that custody, and it shall be handed over to two legal and discreet men of that fief who shall be in like manner responsible to us as is said above. . . .

[1]Any vassal who held a fief directly from the king, as opposed to a rear vassal, who was a vassal of a vassal.
[2]The tax paid to a lord by any vassal inheriting a fief.
[3]The lord had the right and responsibility to act as guardian for any underage heir or heiress of a deceased vassal. During the period of wardship the lord was ex-

pected to protect the rights and status of the minor but was also allowed to dispose of the income from the fief as he saw fit. When the child came of age, the lord was expected to pass on the complete and unspoiled fief to this former ward without charging any relief (note 2).

7. A widow, after the death of her husband, shall have her marriage portion and her inheritance immediately and without obstruction, nor shall she give anything for her dowry or for her marriage portion, or for her inheritance which inheritance her husband and she held on the day of the death of her husband; and she may remain in the house of her husband for forty days after his death, within which time her dowry shall be assigned to her.

8. No widow shall be compelled to marry so long as she prefers to live without a husband, provided she gives security that she will not marry without our consent, if she holds from us, or without the consent of her lord from whom she holds, if she holds from another.[4] . . .

12. No scutage[5] or aid[6] shall be imposed in our kingdom except by the common council of our kingdom,[7] except for the ransoming of our body, for the making of our oldest son a knight, and for once marrying our oldest daughter, and for these purposes it shall be only a reasonable aid; in the same way it shall be done concerning the aids of the city of London.

13. And the city of London shall have all its ancient liberties and free customs, as well by land as by water. Moreover, we will and grant that all other cities and boroughs and villages and ports shall have all their liberties and free customs.[8]

14. And for holding a common council of the kingdoms concerning the assessment of an aid otherwise than in the three cases mentioned above, or concerning the assessment of a scutage we shall cause to be summoned the archbishops, bishops, abbots, earls, and greater barons by our letters under seal; and besides we shall cause to be summoned generally, by our sheriffs and bailiffs all those who hold from us in chief, for a certain day, that is at the end of forty days at least, and for a certain place; and in all the letters of that summons, we will express the cause of the summons, and when the summons has thus been given the business shall proceed on the appointed day, on the advice of those who shall be present, even if not all of those who were summoned have come. . . .

20. A free man shall not be fined for a small offense, except in proportion to the measure of the offense; and for a great offense he shall be fined in proportion to the magnitude of the offense, saving his freehold; and a merchant in the same way, saving his merchandise; and the villain shall be fined in the same way, saving his wainage,[9] if he shall be at our mercy; and none of the above fines shall be imposed except by the oaths of honest men of the neighborhood.

21. Earls and barons shall only be fined by their peers,[10] and only in proportion to their offense. . . .

28. No constable or other bailiff of ours shall take anyone's grain or other chattels, without immediately paying for them in money, unless he is able to obtain a postponement at the good-will of the seller. . . .

---

[4] A lord had the right to deny a vassal's widow permission to marry a specific person if he believed such a marriage would place an enemy or other undesirable person in charge of the deceased vassal's fief. As the widow's guardian he faced the temptation to marry her (and her late husband's fief) off to the highest bidder or some lackey.
[5] Money paid in place of required military service. Generally, John preferred to collect scutage so that he could hire mercenaries, while his vassals preferred to meet their obligations by going into the field.
[6] Any levy paid by vassals to a lord.
[7] The feudal council of all his tenants-in-chief.
[8] Customs and privileges that have been secured by royal charter.
[9] Here *villain* means an unfree peasant, or serf. Wainage was that portion of the harvest that the serf was allowed to keep for food and seed.
[10] Their equals, that is, other vassals. Every vassal had the right to trial by the lord's council of vassals.

39. No free man shall be taken or imprisoned or dispossessed, or outlawed, or banished, or in any way destroyed, nor will we go upon him, nor send upon him, except by the legal judgment of his peers or by the law of the land.[11]

40. To no one will we sell, to no one will we deny, or delay right or justice.

41. All merchants shall be safe and secure in going out from England and coming into England and in remaining and going through England, as well by land as by water, for buying and selling, free from all evil tolls, by the ancient and rightful customs, except in time of war, and if they are of a land at war with us; and if such are found in our land at the beginning of war, they shall be attached without injury to their bodies or goods, until it shall be known from us or from our principal justiciar in what way the merchants of our land are treated who shall be then found in the country which is at war with us; and if ours are safe there, the others shall be safe in our land. . . .

60. Moreover, all those customs and franchises mentioned above which we have conceded in our kingdom, and which are to be fulfilled, as far as pertains to us, in respect to our men; all men of our kingdom as well as clergy as laymen, shall observe as far as pertains to them, in respect to their men.

The Medieval City
▼▼▼

80 ▼ *John of Viterbo,*
BOOK ON THE GOVERNMENT OF CITIES

Western Europe's feudal nobility never totally dominated medieval society and did not even enjoy a military monopoly. Mercenary footsoldiers often proved to be more than a match for mounted knights, and even urban militias were capable of defeating feudal levies, as Emperor Frederick I (r. 1152–1190) discovered in Italy and King Philip IV of France (r. 1285–1314) learned in Flanders. Moreover, townspeople frequently served as royal officials and enjoyed the privilege of administering their own urban governments.

Overall, towns and townspeople served as effective counterweights to the feudal nobility. While early medieval society usually saw its members engaged in three primary tasks — prayer, fighting, and agricultural labor — Europe from the eleventh century onward fostered an emerging class of free men and women who, unhampered by the servile bonds of serfdom, were employed in commerce and production. These *bourgeoisie*, or urban dwellers, were not only personally free but also enjoyed a large measure of self-government. At the very least, a

---

[11]Feudal vassals have the right to trial by their peers; everyone else will be tried according to the customs and laws governing his or her group and the alleged offense.

town would secure from the local lord or the king a charter of liberties that limited the extent to which any external authority could intervene in the town's fiscal, political, and judicial affairs. Some towns and cities, especially in northern Italy, went further and became independent of all outside control. While Song China's prosperous and far more numerous urban dwellers also possessed personal freedom, their cities were not self-governing but were instead centers of imperial administration. It was only in far less developed Europe that cities and towns, of modest size by Asiatic standards, achieved a degree of corporate independence, thereby challenging successfully the landed nobility's dominance.

If townsfolk were to govern themselves, they needed to understand the nature of government and how it functioned. Consequently, schools of law proliferated from the late eleventh century onward, and jurists composed a number of treatises on the theory and practice of good government. One of the most famous is the thirteenth-century *Book on the Government of Cities* by the Italian lawyer John of Viterbo. We know little about the author, and even the date of the work's composition is uncertain. Some scholars have dated it as early as 1228 and others as late as sometime after 1261.

In the following excerpts John, quoting from Roman law, explains why cities exist and defines the role of the *podesta*, the chief municipal official in many northern Italian city-states of the thirteenth century. Podestas were often professional, salaried magistrates brought in from outside and given a short-term contract (one year or less and generally renewable upon review) to govern the city. Because many cities suffered from family and class conflicts, they often recruited foreign chief executives on the theory that only an outsider could treat all persons and groups in an evenhanded manner.

QUESTIONS FOR ANALYSIS

1. The word *bourg*, from which we derive such terms for townspeople as burgher and bourgeoisie, originally meant a fortified site. Consider what John tells us about the primary function of a city. What does this suggest about medieval towns?
2. Are the podesta's powers absolute or limited? Compare his oath with *Magna Carta*. Can you discover any parallels? What do they suggest?
3. What evidence is there to support the judgment that thirteenth-century Italian cities tended to employ foreign-born podestas because they alone seemed to promise evenhanded governance?
4. Is there any evidence that merchants played a prominent role in creating and governing these urban centers?
5. John refers to the inhabitants of a city as "citizens." Why is that significant?
6. According to John, "Matters that touch all must be approved by all." What does this mean? Does he envision the ideal commune as a democracy? If not, what is his understanding of a commune's constitution and reason for existence?

THE MEANING OF "CITY"

A city, indeed, is said to be the liberty of its citizens or the defense of its inhabitants, as is said of a fortified town, for its walls are constructed to serve as a bulwark for those dwelling within. This word *civitas* [city] is syncopated, and so its aforementioned meaning comes from the three syllables that *civitas* contains within itself: namely, *ci, vi,* and *tas. Ci* stands for *citra* [apart from]; *vi* stands for *vim* [oppression]; *tas* stands for *habitas* [you dwell]. It follows that *civitas* means "you dwell apart from oppression." One resides there without oppression, because the governor of the city will protect men of more humble station so that they do not suffer injury at the hands of more powerful men (for, "We cannot be the equals of the more powerful").[1] Likewise, "it is not right for anyone to be oppressed by his adversary's might; if this is the case, it certainly reflects the ill-will of the person governing the province." Likewise, because everyone's house is his most secure refuge and place of shelter, no one ought to drag him from there against his will, nor is it natural that anyone in a city be constrained by violent fear, etc. Likewise, one speaks correctly of immunity, because inhabitants are made immune by the walls and towers of their city and are protected within it from hostile foreigners and personal enemies.

THE CREATION OF CITIES

Cities, indeed, were created or founded for a particular purpose. I do not speak of the holy, celestial city of Jerusalem, called "the Great City," the city of our God, whose explanation I leave to theologians and prophets, because it is not my intention to consider heaven. Rather, I speak of cities in this world, which have been founded so that anyone may hold on to his possessions and his guardianship of his belongings will not be disturbed. . . .

THE PODESTA'S OATH

The podesta's oath is, in fact, normally administered by a judge: "You, Lord B., shall swear on the Holy Gospels, which you hold in your hands, to administer the affairs and business of this city pertaining to your office and to rule, unite, govern, maintain, and hold safe this city, its surrounding countryside and district, and all people and every person, the small as well as the great, foot soldiers as well as knights,[2] and to maintain and protect their rights and to preserve and assure the observance of the established law regarding minors and adults, especially little children, orphans, widows, and other people worthy of pity, and everyone else who will come to petition or answer charges under your jurisdiction and that of your judges. Likewise, to defend, preserve, and maintain churches, shrines, hospitals, and other revered places, roads, pilgrims, and merchants; to keep inviolate the constitution of this city, on which you are swearing with a sound and pure conscience, saving exceptions, if any exceptions have been made, putting aside hatred, love, fraud, favor, and every sort of deceit, according to our sound and pure common understanding, from the next first day of January for one year and the whole day of the first of January." Having said these words, let him who has administered the oath say, "Just as I have administered, so you, Lord B., will swear; and you promise to respect the commune of Florence,[3]

---

[1]This and the following quotation come from the *Digest,* one of four collections of Roman law compiled in the reign of Justinian I (r. 526–565) that comprise the *Body of Civil Law.* Medieval European lawyers assumed Roman law was still valid because they believed their society was a natural and legal continuation of the Roman Empire.

[2]Only the well-to-do could afford a knight's armor, weapons, and horses. Poorer citizens served as infantry.
[3]A commune was a self-governing town or city that possessed a constitutional charter. Florence, an industrial and commercial city in the northern Italian region of Tuscany, had been a commune since at least 1200.

and you will honor it in good faith and without fraud, guile, and any sort of deceit. So may God and these holy Gospels of God aid you." Following this, the judges, notaries, chamberlains, the podesta's knight or knights, and even his squires[4] swear oaths. . . .

THE PODESTA'S CONSULTATION WITH THE COUNCIL ON COMPLEX ISSUES

To be sure, in those situations that are complex or serious or pertain to the essential interests of the city, he ought to confer with the council,[5] once it has been assembled, and should do so again and again if the nature of the matter demands it. . . . For then the podesta can act decisively with the knowledge and advice of the city council. . . . If the gravity of the situation requires greater counsel, others from among the wiser element of the citizenry should be summoned to render advice, after they have been elected by the city at large. To wit: representatives of the judges and those experienced in the law, representatives from the consuls of merchants and bankers[6] and from the priors of the trades,[7] and other appropriate persons. . . . For matters that touch all should be approved by all, and let unanimous agreement determine what benefits everyone.

The Two Ends of Humanity
▼▼▼

81 ▼ *John of Paris,*
A TREATISE ON ROYAL AND PAPAL POWER

The struggle for power and independence was not confined to monarchs, feudal nobles, and the bourgeoisie. As we saw in Chapter 7 (sources 58 and 59), the leaders of the Church also entered the fray. Initially popes and emperors, and later popes and the kings of Europe's new nation-states, struggled with one another to control the lives of their Christian subjects. The fact that neither popes nor secular rulers were ever able to overwhelm the other resulted in a growing feeling among some observers that perhaps there are two powers, Church and State, which have legitimate but different claims upon a subject's loyalty. The clearest medieval articulator of this position was John of Paris, a French priest and scholar of the Dominican order of friars, who around 1302 composed *A Treatise on Royal and Papal Power*, in which he argued that civil government and the priesthood have separate roles to play in guiding human conduct.

---

[4]Podestas generally brought with them a large retinue of their own trained assistants, who would be given positions of responsibility within the commune during the podesta's term of office. They included notaries (legal secretaries), chamberlains (financial officers), knights (the podesta's bodyguard), and squires (personal attendants).

[5]City councils, composed of aristocrats and rich merchants, were the usual governing bodies of Italy's early communes. During the thirteenth century many of these councils found it necessary to surrender executive power to podestas.
[6]The elected heads of the merchant-banker associations, or guilds.
[7]The elected heads of the other trade and artisan guilds.

QUESTIONS FOR ANALYSIS

1. According to John of Paris, what are humanity's two ends, or goals, and how is each attained?
2. Why is civil government natural and necessary?
3. Why is the priesthood higher in dignity than secular authority?
4. In what ways is secular authority greater than priestly authority?
5. Compose responses to John of Paris's views by both Anna Comnena and Pope Boniface VIII (Chapter 7, sources 58 and 59).
6. Compare John of Paris's political theories with those of al-Mawardi (Chapter 8, source 64). Where do they agree and/or disagree? What do their respective political philosophies suggest about their different cultures?

First it should be shown that kingship, properly understood, can be defined as the rule of one man over a perfect multitude so ordered as to promote the public good. . . . Such a government is based on natural law and the law of nations. For, since man is naturally a civil or political creature . . . it is essential for a man to live in a multitude and in such a multitude as is self-sufficient for life. The community of a household or village is not of this sort, but the community of a city or kingdom is, for in a household or village there is not found everything necessary for food, clothing, and defense through a whole life as there is in a city or kingdom. But every multitude scatters and disintegrates as each man pursues his own ends unless it is ordered to the common good by some one man who has charge of this common good. . . .

Next it must be borne in mind that man is not ordered only to such a good as can be acquired by nature, which is to live virtuously, but is further ordered to a supernatural end which is eternal life, and the whole multitude of men living virtuously is ordered to this. Therefore it is necessary that there be some one man to direct the multitude to this end. If in-

deed this end could be attained by the power of human nature, it would necessarily pertain to the office of the human king to direct men to this end, for we call a human king him to whom is committed the highest duty of government in human affairs. But since man does not come to eternal life by human power but by divine . . . this kind of rule pertains to a king who is not only man but also God, namely Jesus Christ . . . and because Christ was to withdraw his corporal presence from the church it was necessary for him to institute others as ministers who would administer the sacraments[1] to men, and these are called priests. . . . Hence priesthood may be defined in this fashion. Priesthood is a spiritual power of administering sacraments to the faithful conferred by Christ on ministers of the church. . . .

From the foregoing material it is easy to see which is first in dignity, the kingship or the priesthood. . . . A kingdom is ordered to this end, that an assembled multitude may live virtuously, as has been said, and it is further ordered to a higher end which is the enjoyment of God; and responsibility for this end belongs to Christ, whose ministers and vicars are the priests. Therefore the priestly power is of

---

[1]The seven major rites, or ceremonies (baptism, penance, the Eucharist, confirmation, matrimony, holy orders, and the last blessing), that the Catholic Church's priests administer as channels of God's grace. See source 112 of Chapter 14.

greater dignity than the secular and this is commonly conceded. . . .

But if the priest is greater in himself than the prince and is greater in dignity, it does not follow that he is greater in all respects. For the lesser secular power is not related to the greater spiritual power as having its origin from it or being derived from it as the power of a proconsul is related to that of the emperor, which is greater in all respects since the power of the former is derived from the latter. The relationship is rather like that of a head of a household to a general of armies, since one is not derived from the other but both from a superior power. And so the secular power is greater than the spiritual in some things, namely in temporal affairs, and in such affairs it is not subject to the spiritual power in any way because it does not have its origin from it but rather both have

their origin immediately from the one supreme power, namely the divine. Accordingly the inferior power is not subject to the superior in all things but only in those where the supreme power has subordinated it to the greater. A teacher of literature or an instructor in morals directs the members of a household to a nobler end, namely the knowledge of truth, than a doctor who is concerned with a lower end, namely the health of bodies, but who would say therefore the doctor should be subjected to the teacher in preparing his medicines? For this is not fitting, since the head of the household who established both in his house did not subordinate the lesser to the greater in this respect. Therefore the priest is greater than the prince in spiritual affairs and, on the other hand, the prince is greater in temporal affairs.

▼▼▼

Mind and Spirit

As religious cultures based on books of divine revelation, Judaism, Christianity, and Islam have all had to wrestle with the issue of the proper relationship of faith to reason. What legitimate role, if any, does human reason have in shedding light upon God's revealed truths and the mysteries of the faith? Is it illicit for a believer to pursue secular scholarship and science? If rational studies and religious doctrine seem to contradict each other, which is to be preferred?

From the middle of the twelfth century onward, European schoolmasters and students avidly collected and studied Latin translations of all the available works of the Greek scientist and philosopher Aristotle (384–322 B.C.) and several of his Muslim commentators. This swift influx of Greek rationalism, particularly the more advanced levels of Aristotelian logic, revolutionized education and had a profound effect on Latin Christianity's approach to theology. Europe's schoolmasters inaugurated an exciting period of intellectual flowering that historians term the *Renaissance of the Twelfth Century.*

The work of thirteenth-century intellectuals was no less impressive. Not only did they carry forward the breakthroughs of the twelfth century, but the best of them constructed encyclopedic syntheses in various fields, especially theology and law. Early twelfth-century scholars for the most part had been wandering students and teachers, but thirteenth-century academicians gravitated toward Europe's newest intellectual arenas — the universities. Although these universities attracted thinkers representing many schools of thought and approaches to learning, their means of investigation and instruction were refined variations on the methods of rational analysis championed by so many twelfth-century predecessors.

During the fourteenth century Europe dramatically shifted its intellectual and spiritual orientation, largely in response to a series of catastrophes that seemed to threaten its very survival. Famine, international war, civil discord and rebellion, and plague racked the West. To many, it seemed as though the last days of the world were at hand. These blows had a profound impact on the psyches of Western Europeans. Large numbers of Christians increasingly turned to more mystical and emotional forms of expression for solace, and death and decay became favorite artistic and literary themes.

Western civilization, however, did not decay or die. Its foundations had been firmly built over the previous thousand years, and by the end of the fourteenth century Europe was already beginning to show signs of recovery. The resiliency of Western European civilization was probably best expressed in new forms of literature and art that appeared toward the end of the century. By the fifteenth century European artists were producing works that again breathed an optimistic view of humanity's place in the cosmos. Europe had entered another "Renaissance."

Faith and Reason
▼▼▼

82 ▼ *John of Salisbury, METALOGICON*

One of twelfth-century Europe's foremost humanists and patrons of learning was John of Salisbury (ca 1115-20–1180), an Englishman who studied at two of France's preeminent centers of scholarship, Paris and Chartres, who spent a half-dozen or more years working at the papal court in Rome, served as secretary to the archbishop of Canterbury, and ultimately became bishop of Chartres, site of his youthful studies. In the midst of all this activity John wrote voluminously. His more important works include the *Policratus*, or *Statesman's Book*, a treatise of political theory in which he argued that it is legitimate to assassinate a tyrant, and the *Metalogicon*, a treatise that championed the arts of verbal expression and rational analysis. Both appeared in 1159.

The curious title *Metalogicon* was John's own creation, coined from two Greek words and understood as meaning "a plea for the arts that relate to words and reasoning." The work is a spirited defense of three of the Seven Liberal Arts. Basic education in twelfth-century Europe centered on the Seven Liberal Arts, which were divided into the *trivium* and the *quadrivium*. The trivium, which literally means "the confluence of three roads," consisted of Latin grammar (largely the study of classical Latin poetry), rhetoric, or the art of persuasion (largely the study of classical Latin prose authors), and *dialectic*, or logic, the art of analyzing words and arguments. Whereas the trivium centered on verbal analysis, the quadrivium, which literally means "the intersection of four roads," was concerned with quantitative analysis and mathematical relationships. Its four subjects were arithmetic, geometry, astronomy, and music. It was the trivium that captured John's attention, especially the art of logic.

The *Metalogicon* deserves a special place in the history of both Western educational theory and European philosophy. In the following selections John addresses the arguments of a group of philosophers he calls the "Cornificians," who claimed that the dialectical method of laboriously analyzing the meaning of words and propositions was a sterile pursuit.

QUESTIONS FOR ANALYSIS

1. According to John, what essential role do the arts play?
2. John presents two possible etymological origins of the term *liberal arts*. Which one does he favor? Why do you conclude this?
3. To John's mind, why is logic the most important of the liberal arts?
4. As John sees it, what is the relationship of reason to truth?
5. How, according to John, do reason and the pursuit of truth help one become a more virtuous person?
6. According to John, what are reason's limitations? Are there certain truths not attainable by reason alone? What are they? How then does one reach these truths?
7. Why does John see no essential conflict between faith and reason? Indeed, how does reason help one become a better Christian? Conversely, how do one's moral qualities and the certitudes of revealed religious truth help one become a better rationalist?
8. Medieval Europe is often characterized as the "Dark Ages," when reason was enslaved to faith and religious authority. Based on this selection, what do you think of this characterization?

Behold, the Cornificians disclose their objective, and advance to attack logic, although, of course, they are equally violent persecutors of all philosophical pursuits. They have to begin somewhere, and so they have singled out that branch of philosophy which is the most widely known and seems the most familiar to their heretical sect. First, bear with me while we define what "logic" is. Logic (in its broadest sense) is the science of verbal expression and argumentative reasoning. Sometimes the term "logic" is used with more restricted extension, and limited to rules of argumentative reasoning. Whether logic teaches only the ways of reasoning, or embraces all rules relative to words, surely those who claim that it is useless are deluded. For either of these services may be proved by incontrovertible arguments to be very necessary. The twofold meaning of "logic" stems from its Greek etymology, for in the latter language *"logos"* means both "word" and "reason." For the present let us concede to logic its widest meaning, according to which it includes all instruction relative to words, in which case it can never be convicted of futility. In this more general sense, there can be no doubt that all logic is both highly useful and necessary. . . .

Art is a system that reason has devised in order to expedite, by its own short cut, our ability to do things within our natural capabilities. Reason neither provides nor professes to provide the accomplishment of the impossible. Rather, it substitutes for the spendthrift and roundabout ways of nature a concise, direct method of doing things that are possible. It further begets (so to speak) a faculty of accomplishing what is difficult. Wherefore the Greeks also call it *methodon,* that is, so to speak, an efficient plan, which avoids nature's wastefulness, and straightens out her circuitous wanderings. . . .

While there are many sorts of arts, the first to proffer their services to the natural abilities of those who philosophize are the liberal arts. All of the latter are included in the courses of the Trivium and Quadrivium. The liberal arts are said to have become so efficacious among our ancestors, who studied them diligently, that they enabled them to comprehend everything they read, elevated their understanding to all things, and empowered them to cut through the knots of all problems possible of solution. Those to whom the system of the Trivium has disclosed the significance of all words, or the rules of the Quadrivium have unveiled the secrets of all nature, do not need the help of a teacher in order to understand the meaning of books and to find the solutions of questions. . . . These arts are called "liberal," either because the ancients took care to have their children instructed in them,[1] or because their object is to effect man's liberation, so that, freed from cares, he may devote himself to wisdom. More often than not, they liberate us from cares incompatible with wisdom. They often even free us from worry about material necessities, so that the mind may have still greater liberty to apply itself to philosophy. . . .

Among all the liberal arts, the first is logic. . . . In its narrower sense, logic is the science of argumentative reasoning, which provides a solid basis for the whole activity of prudence. Of all things the most desirable is wisdom, whose fruit consists in the love of what is good and the practice of virtue. Consequently the human mind must apply itself to the quest of wisdom, and thoroughly study and investigate questions in order to formulate clear and sound judgments concerning each. Logic is exercised in inquiry into the truth. . . . Truth is the subject matter of prudence, as well as the fountainhead of all the virtues. One who comprehends truth is wise, one who loves it good, one who orders his life in accordance with it happy. . . . Happy is the man who possesses the gift of understanding. On the one hand, the more intimately what is transitory and momentary comes to be known, the cheaper that which is thus doomed to perish becomes in the estimation of a sensible mind. On the other hand, the truth will set us free, and will lead us from slavery to liberty, relieving us of the oppressive yoke of vice. For it is impossible that one who seeks and embraces the truth with his whole heart should remain a suitor and servant of vanity. . . .

Let us now, with all reverence, contemplate the happy and intimate connection between reason and truth. And let us, at the same time, implore the assistance of these two, without which we are powerless to comprehend or even to investigate them. Reason is, in a way, the eye of the mind. Or to put it more broadly, reason is the instrument whereby the mind effects all its cognition. Reason's special function is to investigate and apprehend the truth. The contrary of the virtue of reason is imbecility and consequent lack of the power to investigate and determine the truth. The contrary of the activity of investigating the truth, which we have above called "reason," is error. . . . Truth is both the light of the mind and the subject matter of reason. God and the angels see truth directly, God beholding universal truth, and the angels particular truths. But man, no matter how perfect, glimpses the truth only in part,

---

[1]A pun. The Latin word for children used here is *liberos.*

and to a definitely limited degree. However, the more perfect a man is, the more ardently he desires to comprehend the truth. For truth is the basis of certitude, in which reason's investigations flourish and thrive. In the absence of light and of solid objects our senses of sight and touch cannot operate. Our other senses are put in a similar plight if sound and scent and flavor are not present. In like manner, reason's perception is frustrated when truth is withdrawn. The contrary of truth is vanity, falsity, or emptiness, all of which are proved by philosophy to be nothing. . . . Original truth is found in the divine majesty. There is also other truth, which consists in an image or likeness of the divinity. The truth of anything is directly dependent on the degree in which it faithfully reflects the likeness of God. The more deficient anything is in this respect, the more it fades into falsity and nothingness. . . . One who walks in darkness falters and knows not whither he is going. Truth properly fosters, enlightens, and corroborates reason, just as reason properly seeks, attains, and embraces truth. As has been said, external light nourishes vision; and solid objects provide an object for the sense of touch. In God, however, reason and truth are one. He, Who is both the Reason and the Word eternal, says of Himself: "I am the truth." He is self-sufficient, and has need of nothing external. His reason illumines itself, and His truth contemplates itself. In creation, on the other hand, truth is one thing, reason another. For in creation, truth is an image of the divinity, which is sought and found by reason in created things. Reason is a virtue or activity of the mind, whose object is to discern truth. . . .

Many things exceed our comprehension: some because of their august dignity, some because of their great number or vast extent, some because of their mutability and instability. Accordingly, Ecclesiasticus instructs us as what should be our principal concern, and what is to our greatest advantage. "Seek not" he says, "things that are beyond your reach, and do not fret over questions that exceed your comprehension."[2] Note how he restrains the rashness of those who, with irreverent garrulity, discuss the secrets of the Divine Trinity and mysteries whose vision is reserved for eternal life. While the impression may be created that knowledge is increased by such a procedure, devotion is certainly diminished. "Refrain" Ecclesiasticus warns us, "from being inquisitive about numerous unnecessary things, and do not be curious about too many of the divine works. . . . For consideration of such things has caused the fall of many, and has enslaved their minds to vanity."[3] The holy writer represses the audacity of those who stick their nose into everything, and want to account for all things. We know, on the authority of Solomon in Ecclesiastes, that man cannot fully explain the least object on earth, much less give a complete account of heavenly and supracelestial things.[4] The son of Sirac makes clear to what the philosopher should direct his mental abilities: "Ever bear in mind God's commandments, and you will not be curious about too many of his works."[5] We know that our knowledge flows ultimately from our senses, which are frequently misled, and that faltering human infirmity is at a loss to know what is expedient. Accordingly, God, in His mercy, has given us a law, to make evident what is useful, to disclose how much we may know about Him, and to indicate how far we may go in our inquiries concerning Him. This law displays the divine power in the creation, the divine wisdom in the orderly plan, and the divine goodness in the conservation of the world. The latter attributes of God are especially evident in the redemption of man. This law further clearly discloses God's will, so that everyone may be certain about what he should do. Since not only man's senses, but even his reason frequently err, the law of God has made faith the primary and fundamental prerequisite for understanding of the truth. . . .

---

[2]Bible, Ecclesiasticus, 3:22.
[3]*Ibid.,* 3:24 and 26.

[4]Bible, Ecclesiasticus, 7:17.
[5]Bible, Ecclesiasticus, 3:22.

Fourteenth-Century Troubles
▼▼▼

83 ▼ *Jean de Venette, CHRONICLE*

Jean de Venette (ca 1307–1368), priest, master of theology at the University of Paris, and head of the French province of the order of Carmelite Friars, composed a graphic account of French history covering the years 1340 to 1368 and concentrating on the disasters and devastations that seemed to characterize his age. Of peasant origin himself, he displayed genuine concern for the sufferings of France's lower classes, who bore such a disproportionate amount of the pain. Our selections deal with the famine of 1315–1317 and the onslaught of the Black Death in 1348–1349.

QUESTIONS FOR ANALYSIS

1. What is Venette's attitude toward visions, prophecies, and other supernatural phenomena?
2. Consider his treatment of the presumed causes of the Black Death. What does his analysis tell you about his methods of analysis and world view? How scientific is his attempt to understand and describe the cause, course, and consequences of this pestilence?
3. According to Venette, what were the most serious consequences of the plague? What does this tell us about the man and the purpose behind his history?
4. What does the flagellant movement suggest about the psychological effects of the plague? Compare it with the age's persecution of the Jews. Were they connected in any way?
5. What does the attitude of the masters of theology at Paris, the pope, and Venette toward the flagellants suggest?
6. Was Jean de Venette a rationalist? If so, what sort?
7. What is the general tone of this history, and what does it tell us about the fourteenth century?

Let anyone who wishes to be reminded of most of the noteworthy events which happened in the kingdom of France from 1340 on read this present work in which I, a friar[1] at Paris, have written them down briefly, in great measure as I have seen and heard them. I shall begin with some hitherto unknown prognostications or prophecies which have come to hand. What

---

[1]Literally, a brother. The Roman Church had four major orders of mendicant, or begging, friars who ministered to the spiritual needs of urban populations: the Franciscans, the Dominicans, the Augustinians, and the Carmelites.

they mean is not altogether known. Whether they speak truth or not I do not say but leave to the decision of the reader. This is one such. A priest of the diocese of Tours, freed in A.D. 1309 from the hands of the Saracens, who had held him captive for the space of thirteen years and three months, was saying mass in Bethlehem where the Lord was born. While he was praying for all Christian people . . . there appeared to him letters of gold written in this wise:

> In the year of the Lord 1315, on the fifteenth day of the month of March, shall begin so great a famine on earth that the people of low degree shall strive and struggle against the mighty and rich of this world. Also the wreath of the mightiest boxer shall fall to the ground very quickly afterwards. Also its flowers and its branches shall be broken and crushed. Also a noble and free city shall be seized and taken by slaves. Also strangers shall dwell there. Also the Church shall totter and the line of Saint Peter shall be execrated. Also the blood of many shall be poured out on the ground. Also a red cross shall appear and shall be lifted up. Therefore, good Christians, watch.

These are the words of this vision, but what they mean is not known.

Yet you must know that I, at the age of seven or eight, saw this great and mighty famine begin the very year foretold, 1315. It was so severe in France that most of the population died of hunger and want. And this famine lasted two years and more, for it began in 1315 and ceased in 1318. . . . Now, as I promised, I come to some of the noteworthy events, though not to all, which took place in the kingdom of France, and to a few which took place elsewhere, about A.D. 1340 and thereafter. I shall narrate them

truthfully, as I saw them or heard about them. . . .

In A.D. 1348, the people of France and of almost the whole world were struck by a blow other than war. For in addition to the famine which I described in the beginning and to the wars which I described in the course of this narrative, pestilence and its attendant tribulations appeared again in various parts of the world. In the month of August, 1348, after Vespers[2] when the sun was beginning to set, a big and very bright star appeared above Paris, toward the west. It did not seem, as stars usually do, to be very high above our hemisphere, but rather near. As the sun set and night came on, this star did not seem to me or to many other friars who were watching it to move from one place. At length, when night had come, this big star, to the amazement of all of us who were watching, broke into many different rays and, as it shed these rays over Paris toward the east, totally disappeared and was completely annihilated. Whether it was a comet or not, whether it was composed of airy exhalations and was finally resolved into vapor, I leave to the decision of astronomers. It is, however, possible that it was a presage of the amazing pestilence to come, which, in fact, followed very shortly in Paris and throughout France and elsewhere, as I shall tell. All this year and the next, the mortality of men and women, of the young even more than of the old, in Paris and in the kingdom of France, and also, it is said, in other parts of the world, was so great that it was almost impossible to bury the dead. People lay ill little more than two or three days and died suddenly, as it were in full health. He who was well one day was dead the next and being carried to his grave. Swellings appeared suddenly in the armpit or in the groin — in many cases both — and they were infallible signs of death. This sickness or pestilence was called an epidemic by the doctors. Nothing like the great

---

[2]A time of day set aside for prayer in the late afternoon or early evening.

numbers who died in the years 1348 and 1349 has been heard of or seen or read of in times past. This plague and disease came from . . . association and contagion, for if a well man visited the sick he only rarely evaded the risk of death. Wherefore in many towns timid priests withdrew, leaving the exercise of their ministry to such of the religious as were more daring. In many places not two out of twenty remained alive. So high was the mortality at the Hôtel-Dieu[3] in Paris that for a long time, more than five hundred dead were carried daily with great devotion in carts to the cemetery of the Holy Innocents in Paris for burial. A very great number of the saintly sisters of the Hôtel-Dieu who, not fearing to die, nursed the sick in all sweetness and humility, with no thought of honor, a number too often renewed by death, rest in peace with Christ, as we may piously believe. . . .

Some said that this pestilence was caused by infection of the air and waters, since there was at this time no famine nor lack of food supplies, but on the contrary great abundance. As a result of this theory of infected water and air as the source of the plague the Jews were suddenly and violently charged with infecting wells and water and corrupting the air. The whole world rose up against them cruelly on this account. In Germany and other parts of the world where Jews lived, they were massacred and slaughtered by Christians, and many thousands were burned everywhere, indiscriminately. The unshaken, if fatuous, constancy of the [Jewish] men and their wives was remarkable. For mothers hurled their children first into the fire that they might not be baptized and then leaped in after them to burn with their husbands and children. It is said that many bad Christians were found who in a like manner put poison into wells. But in truth, such poisonings, . . . [if] . . . they actually were perpetrated, could

not have caused so great a plague nor have infected so many people. There were other causes; for example, the will of God and the corrupt humors and evil inherent in air and earth.[4] Perhaps the poisonings, if they actually took place in some localities, reinforced these causes. The plague lasted in France for the greater part of the years 1348 and 1349 and then ceased. Many country villages and many houses in good towns remained empty and deserted.

After the cessation of the epidemic, pestilence, or plague, the men and women who survived married each other. There was no sterility among the women, but on the contrary fertility beyond the ordinary. Pregnant women were seen on every side. Many twins were born and even three children at once. But the most surprising fact is that children born after the plague, when they became of an age for teeth, had only twenty or twenty-two teeth, though before that time men commonly had thirty-two in their upper and lower jaws together. What this diminution in the number of teeth signified I wonder greatly, unless it be a new era resulting from the destruction of one human generation by the plague and its replacement by another. But woe is me! the world was not changed for the better but for the worse by this renewal of population. For men were more avaricious and grasping than before, even though they had far greater possessions. They were more covetous and disturbed each other more frequently with suits, brawls, disputes, and pleas. Nor by the mortality resulting from this terrible plague inflicted by God was peace between kings and lords established. On the contrary, the enemies of the king of France and of the Church were stronger and wickeder than before and stirred up wars on sea and on land. Greater evils than before populated everywhere in the world. And this fact was very remarkable. Although there was an abundance of all

---

[3]The House of God — Paris's largest hospital.
[4]Until the triumph of the germ theory in the late nineteenth century, one widely held explanation for disease was that it originates from miasma, the poisonous fumes arising from swamps and other putrefying matter. For an explanation of the humor theory, which remained the dominant Western explanation for disease for several millennia, see Chapter 4, source 28, note 3.

goods, yet everything was twice as dear, whether it were utensils, victuals, or merchandise, hired helpers or peasants and serfs, except for some hereditary domains which remained abundantly stocked with everything. Charity began to cool, and iniquity with ignorance and sin to abound, for few could be found in the good towns and castles who knew how or were willing to instruct children in the rudiments of grammar. . . .

In the year 1349, while the plague was still active and spreading from town to town, men in Germany, Flanders, Hainaut, and Lorraine[5] uprose and began a new sect on their own authority. Stripped to the waist, they gathered in large groups and bands and marched in procession through the crossroads and squares of cities and good towns. There they formed circles and beat upon their backs with weighted scourges, rejoicing as they did so in loud voices and singing hymns suitable to their rite and newly composed for it. Thus for thirty-three days[6] they marched through many towns doing their penance and affording a great spectacle to the wondering people. They flogged their shoulders and arms with scourges tipped with iron points so zealously as to draw blood. But they did not come to Paris nor to any part of France, for they were forbidden to do so by the king of France, who did not want them. He acted on the advice of the masters of theology of the University of Paris, who said that this new sect had been formed contrary to the will of God, to the rites of Holy Mother Church, and to the salvation of all their souls. That indeed this was and is true appeared shortly. For Pope Clement VI was fully informed concerning this fatuous new rite by the masters of Paris through emissaries reverently sent to him and, on the grounds that it had been damnably formed, contrary to law, he forbade the Flagellants under threat of anathema[7] to practice in the future the public penance which they had so presumptuously undertaken. His prohibition was just, for the Flagellants, supported by certain fatuous priests and monks, were enunciating doctrines and opinions which were beyond measure evil, erroneous, and fallacious. For example, they said that their blood thus drawn by the scourge and poured out was mingled with the blood of Christ. Their many errors showed how little they knew of the Catholic faith. Wherefore, as they had begun fatuously of themselves and not of God, so in a short time they were reduced to nothing. On being warned, they desisted and humbly received absolution and penance at the hands of their prelates as the pope's representatives. Many honorable women and devout matrons, it must be added, had done this penance with scourges, marching and singing through towns and churches like the men, but after a little like the others they desisted.

Joan of Arc: Witch, Rebel, or Saint?
▼▼▼

84 ▼ Johann Nider, THE HIVE OF ACTIVITY

Europe's witch hunt, which witnessed the executions and murders of possibly as many as several tens of thousands of accused witches and sorcerers, was

---

[5]Regions in modern Belgium, northwest Germany, eastern France, and Luxembourg.
[6]Medieval Christians believed Jesus had lived on earth for thirty-three years.

[7]Excommunication, or exclusion, from the community and rites of the Church.

largely a sixteenth- and seventeenth-century phenomenon, reaching its peak of intensity between 1560 and 1680 in both Catholic and Protestant lands. Indeed, it was not until the fifteenth century, when Europe was still in the throes of its "crisis of the Late Middle Ages," that the fervor of witch hunters began to make any substantial impression on Western society.

In both the popular imagination and the teachings of Catholic and Protestant theologians, witchcraft was any formal alliance with the devil. By virtue of this pact with Satan, the witch, or sorcerer, received supernatural powers for evil purposes, thereby making her or him a major danger to society. Cutting out such dangerous "tumors" from the body of Christian Europe became, therefore, a necessary act of self-survival in the eyes of many.

Although Europe did not become obsessed with rooting out witches until the 1500s, the previous century had its zealous witch hunters and several highly publicized witch trials and executions. The fifteenth century's most famous execution is that of Joan of Arc (ca 1412–1431), a French heroine who almost single-handedly rallied France around King Charles VII (r. 1422–1461) and destroyed the myth of English invincibility during the latter stages of the Hundred Years' War, thereby setting the stage for France's eventual recovery and victory. Taken prisoner in 1430, this pious teenage peasant woman, who claimed divine guidance, was executed as a witch, essentially for political and not religious reasons, in 1431.

Our selection comes from the pages of the *Formicarius* of Johann Nider (ca 1380–1438), a work whose curious title, which means "ant hill," is best understood as meaning "a hive of activity," a reference to the fact that it is a lengthy collection of anecdotes and dialogues relating to the religious life of fifteenth-century Europe. Nider, a priest and member of the Dominican Order, was a professor of theology at the University of Vienna and an active preacher against heresy in the region around Prague. A life-long foe of heresy, or incorrect religious belief, and every other form of what he perceived as devilish error, Nider included long discourses on contemporary diabolical activities in the *Formicarius*, which he completed only shortly before his death. In the following excerpt, Nider, in a stylized dialogue between himself and a fictional pupil, relates the story of Joan of Arc.

QUESTIONS FOR ANALYSIS

1. On what grounds was Joan of Arc judged to be a witch?
2. What qualities did all four "witches" have in common?
3. Why were they perceived as such a threat to society?
4. Two of these four "witches" escaped execution. How did they manage that, and what do you infer from the means they used to escape this penalty?
5. Consider Johann Nider's final comments about women in general in the light of the story of Saint Mary the Harlot (Chapter 7, source 56). It has been said that Christian ecclesiastics tended to portray women as either saints or seductresses. On the basis of the evidence, what do you think of this judgment?

6. Consider this story in the light of Hindu attitudes toward women (Chapter 5, source 40; Chapter 9, sources 73 and 74). Can you see any parallels?

PUPIL: In your opinion, have some good people been deceived by sorceresses and witches in our own day?

MASTER: I suspend judgment concerning the truth of the story that follows, but I will tell you what is related by public rumor and report. We have in our days the distinguished professor of divinity, Brother Heinrich Kaltyseren, Inquisitor of Heretical Activity.[1] As he told me himself, last year, while performing his inquisitorial office in Cologne,[2] he discovered in the region a certain young woman who always went around in male clothing, bore weapons, and wore the type of degenerate garments that are favored by courtiers.[3] She danced with men and was so given to feasting and drinking that she seemed to overstep totally the boundaries of her sex, which she did not conceal. Because the bishopric of Trier[4] was at that time gravely beset by two rivals contending for the office of bishop (as unfortunately is also the case today), she boasted that she could and would set one of the claimants on the throne, just as Maid Joan, of whom I will presently speak, had done shortly before with King Charles of France, by confirming him in his royal office.[5] In fact, this woman claimed to be that same Joan, raised from the dead by God! One day, when she had come into Cologne with the youthful count of Württemberg, who protected and favored her, and there, in the presence of the nobility, had

performed marvels that seemed magical, she was at last diligently scrutinized and publicly cited by the aforesaid inquisitor, in order that she might be formally examined. She was said to have cut a napkin into pieces and suddenly have restored it whole in the sight of the people; to have thrown a glass against the wall, thereby breaking it, and to have repaired it in a moment; and to have shown many similar idle devices. The wretched woman, however, would not obey the Church's commands. The count protected her from arrest and sneaked her out of Cologne. In this way she escaped the inquisitor's hands but did not elude the sentence of excommunication.[6] Bound by this curse, she left Germany for France, where she married a knight, in order to protect herself from ecclesiastical penalty and the sword [of secular punishment].[7] Then a priest, or rather pimp, seduced this witch with talk of love. Finally she ran away with him and went to Metz,[8] where she lived as his concubine and openly showed everyone by what spirit she was led.

Moreover, there was in France, within the past ten years, a maid named Joan, about whom I have already spoken, who was distinguished, so it was thought, for her prophetic spirit and the power of her miracles. She always wore men's clothes, and none of the arguments of the learned doctors[9] convinced her to put them aside and to content herself with feminine

---

[1]An inquisitor was a papally appointed cleric who was charged with "inquiring" into heresy and other forms of religious dissidence in a region and effecting its suppression through both ecclesiastical and civil means.
[2]A German city on the Rhine River.
[3]Tight-fitting doublets and hose worn at the courts of kings and other lords by their male attendants, or courtiers.
[4]A German city on the Mosel River.
[5]Joan of Arc had secured Charles VII's official coronation in 1429.
[6]A sentence of exclusion from the community and pro-

tection of the Church. It was believed that: "Outside of the Church there is no salvation."
[7]Church and State generally worked in harmony in attempting to root out heresy and witchcraft. The Church's inquisitors tried and condemned heretics and similar nonconformists, but it was secular governments that punished and executed them.
[8]A city in eastern France, not too far from Joan of Arc's home region.
[9]Doctor etymologically means teacher, and the word is used here in that sense — doctors of theology and church law.

dress, even though she openly professed her womanhood and virginity. She said: "I have been sent by God in these masculine garments, that serve as a token of future victory, to preach by both word and attire, to help Charles, the true king of France, and to set Charles firmly upon his throne, from which the king of England and the duke of Burgundy are striving to chase him." At that time those two men were allied and were oppressing France grievously with war and carnage.[10] Joan, therefore, rode constantly around like a knight with her lord, predicted many successes to come, was present in the field at some victories, and performed many other wonders that elicited a sense of marvel not only in France but in every realm in Christendom. Finally this Joan reached such a level of presumption that, before France had yet recovered, she was already sending threatening letters to the Bohemians, among whom there were a host of heretics.[11] From that period onward both lay people and clerics began to have doubts about the spirit that ruled her, wondering whether it was diabolical or divine. Then certain learned men wrote treatises concerning her, in which they expressed not only diverse but even adverse opinions concerning the Maid. Then following that, after she had given Charles tremendous assistance and had confirmed his hold on the throne for some years, by God's will, as it is believed, she was captured in battle by the English and cast into prison.[12] Large numbers of masters of both canon and civil law[13] were summoned, and she was examined for many days. As I have heard from Master Nicholas Midi, Master of Theology, who represented the University of Paris,

she finally confessed that she had a personal angel from God. Based on many conjectures and proofs, and the opinion of the most learned men, this "angel" was judged to be an evil spirit. Consequently, this spirit made her a sorceress. For this reason they permitted her to be burned at the stake by the common executioner. . . .

At this same time two women sprang up near Paris, publicly preaching that God had sent them to aid Maid Joan, and, as I heard from the lips of the aforesaid Master Nicholas, they were immediately arrested as witches or sorcerers by the Inquisitor for France, examined by many doctors of theology, and found at last to have been deceived by the ravings of an evil spirit. When, therefore, one of these women perceived she had been misled by an angel of Satan, she followed the advice of her masters, abandoned that which she had begun, and, as was her duty, immediately renounced her error. The other one, however, remained obstinate and was burned.

PUPIL: I cannot marvel enough how the frail sex can dare to rush into such presumptuous matters.

MASTER: These matters are marvelous to simple folk like you, but they are not rare in the eyes of wise men. For there are three things in nature, which, if they transgress the limits of their own condition, whether by diminution or excess, attain to the highest pinnacles of goodness and evil. They are the tongue, the cleric, and woman. All are commonly best of all, as long as they are guided by a good spirit, but worst of all if guided by an evil spirit.

---

[10]King Henry VI (r. 1422–1461) of England claimed to be the rightful monarch of France and at this period was allied with the duke of Burgundy against Charles VII.
[11]Bohemia, especially its capital city of Prague, was a hotbed of religious dissent and heresy in the fifteenth century. Nider himself had preached against these dissidents, who were inspired by the teachings of John Huss (1370–1415) and collectively known as *Hussites*.

[12]Actually, she was captured by the Burgundians and later turned over to the English.
[13]The two branches of law studied and practiced in continental Europe were canon (church) law and civil law. Civil law was based on the sixth-century *Body of Civil Law* of Emperor Justinian (r. 527–565).

Chapter 11

▼▼▼

Africa and
the Americas

As we saw in Chapter 5, toward the end of the first century B.C. the dominant civilizations of Eurasia and North Africa were loosely linked through a series of trade networks and imperialistic adventures. The result was the first Afro-Eurasian ecumene, or world community, whose heyday extended to about A.D. 200. The term is somewhat misleading, however, since most of Africa south of the Sahara Desert lay outside this first "Old World" ecumene, as Strabo's *Geography* (Chapter 5, source 32) showed.

The cultures of the Americas also did not participate in that first age of Afro-Eurasian linkage nor in the second, which peaked between A.D. 1250 and 1350 (Chapter 12). A few adventurers and lost sailors from Africa and Eurasia undoubtedly stumbled across the lands of America before 1492, as was the case with a handful of Vikings who set up a short-lived colony in northern Newfoundland around A.D. 1000. Nevertheless, there is no convincing evidence that any of these occasional visitors established meaningful links between the Americas and the outside world, nor is there reason to believe that they had a substantial impact on the development of Amerindian cultures. Prior to the late fifteenth century A.D., the American peoples developed their societies and civilizations in essential isolation from the lands that lay across the Pacific and Atlantic oceans. Isolated though they may have been from the rest of the world, most Amerindian peoples were linked, although loosely, in an American ecumene that allowed for the spread of goods and cultural influences over vast expanses. Maize, for example, initially domesticated as early as 4000 B.C. in the highlands of central Mexico, had spread to Peru by 2000 B.C. and Canada by A.D. 1000.

Sub-Saharan Africa also had its early cultural and trade networks that made possible a widespread diffusion of such technologies as agriculture and iron metallurgy. Moreover, despite the continued growth of the Sahara Desert from around 2500 B.C. to the present (Chapter 1, source 8), interior Africa has never been totally cut off from the rest of the Afro-Eurasian "world island," even in the most ancient times. However, the volume of traffic across the Sahara began to achieve significant proportions only after the introduction into North Africa of the Arabian, or single-humped, camel as a beast of burden during the early centuries A.D., ironically just as the first Afro-Eurasian ecumene was beginning to break down due to crises in China and the Greco-Roman West. Conquest of western North Africa by Muslim Arabs in the seventh century provided another major boost to trans-Saharan trade, so that by about the year 1000, four major commercial routes connected the north with western sub-Saharan Africa. Our first document relating to Africa sheds light on some of the consequences of that commerce.

Trade and the development of trade-based states in the western sub-Saharan grasslands constitute a major chapter in Africa's history, but they are not the whole story of what was happening in this richly diverse continent during the millennium from A.D. 500 to 1500. As our second and third sources suggest, Africa was a land of many cultures.

▼▼▼

Africa

Africa commands a special place in the history of humanity because it is the home of the earliest protohumans, *Homo habilis* and *Homo erectus*, direct ancestors of modern *Homo sapiens sapiens*. Nothing, short of the total destruction of humanity, will likely ever rival that historical "first" in scope, but Africa's place in human history hardly stopped there.

During the millennium under present consideration Africa witnessed a number of important historical developments. Chief among these were the Bantu migration, the coming of Islam, the creation of trade empires in the western Sudan, the rise of a Swahili culture in East Africa, and the arrival of Europeans toward the end of this period.

The four hundred or so languages belonging to the Bantu linguistic family that are spoken today throughout most of the southern half of the continent are traceable to a common place of origin in West Africa, probably the Benue River valley in present eastern Nigeria. Around the first century A.D. the Bantu-speaking people of this region, who were agriculturalists and workers of iron, began the slow process of moving east and southward, thereby introducing the crafts of farming and iron metallurgy wherever they settled. Within a few centuries Bantu speakers had pushed as far south as the region today occupied by the nation of Zimbabwe, where by the late thirteenth century they constructed a gold-trade civilization centered on the now famous Great Zimbabwe stone citadel, from which the modern state took its name in 1979.

Another great migration that profoundly influenced the course of history in Africa was the influx of Islam in the wake of the conquering Arab armies that swept through North Africa in the seventh century. These conquests, and the conversions that followed, transformed what had been Christian North Africa into an integral part of the Islamic world, thereby wrenching it from the orbits of Constantinople and Rome and tying it culturally to Mecca, Damascus, and Baghdad.

From North Africa the faith and culture of Islam penetrated the trade empires of the western grassland states south of the Sahara after A.D. 1000. The empires of Ghana (source 85), Mali (Chapter 8, source 66; Chapter 12, source 96), and Songhay became progressively more Islamic and, therefore, more closely tied to North Africa and a greater Muslim world beyond Africa by reason of a shared religious culture, as well as by commercial interests.

On the east coast of Africa a similar process was at work. In the ninth and tenth centuries Arabian sailor-merchants like the legendary Sindbad (Chapter 9, source 76) established trading settlements far down the coast of East Africa — the land of Zanj, as the Arabs called it. The culture that emerged from the interchange between the Arab and East African peoples who traded and intermarried here is known as *Swahili* (from the Arabic *Sahel*, "coast"). Like the language that bears the same name, Swahili culture was at this time a coastal trade culture consisting of an indigenous Bantu base with strong Arabic influences. From about 1200 to the early sixteenth century, the port city of Kilwa, today located in the nation of Tanzania, served as the Swahili coast's main emporium.

Kilwa's position of commercial prominence along Africa's eastern shore ended with its sack and destruction by the Portuguese in 1505. With the arrival in force of the Portuguese, first on Africa's west coast in the fifteenth century (Chapter 12, source 100) and then on the east coast in the early sixteenth century, the age of direct European contact with sub-Saharan Africa had begun, with all the consequences that would follow from that interchange (Chapter 13).

Despite the impact of Islam and Europe on Africa south of the Sahara, in most cases older ways of life proved resilient to these outside influences. Ethiopia, for example, successfully resisted both Islamic (source 86) and later Portuguese attempts at conquest and conversion to retain its autonomy and its ancient native Christian culture. Likewise, the coastal states of West Africa (source 87) retained their essentially African features, even after their leaders received the faith of Islam, and maintained autonomy, extensive political authority, and widespread economic interests, even in the face of the European presence along their coastline.

Eleventh-Century Western Sudan
▼▼▼

85 ▼ Al-Bakri,
THE BOOK OF ROUTES AND REALMS

Located south of the Sahara Desert is a broad expanse of grasslands, or savanna, that stretches across the breadth of the African continent from the Atlantic Ocean to the Red Sea. To the Arabs, this region was known as *Bilad al-Sudan*, "the country of the blacks." Arab and Berber merchants were especially interested in West Africa's Sudan, insofar as its inhabitants were advantageously located between the markets of North Africa and the cultures farther south toward the tropical rain forests of the coast. From the southern peoples of the Niger and Senegal river valleys the inhabitants of the savanna obtained gold and slaves which they traded for manufactured goods, horses, and salt with Arab and Berber merchants who arrived in camel caravans from the north. In time, this trans-Saharan commerce became the basis for the development of a series of significant trading states in the region that connected West Africa's gold fields with the cities of Mediterranean North Africa.

One of the earliest important trading empires to emerge was Ghana (not to be confused with its modern namesake, the nation of Ghana), which was located essentially in territory encompassed today by the nations of Mauritania and Mali. The origins of Ghana are lost in the shadows of the past, probably going back as far as the fourth century A.D. When in the early ninth century it finally came to the attention of Arab commentators, who knew it as "the land of gold," Ghana was already a well-established state.

In 1067/1068 Abu 'Ubaydallah al-Bakri (d. 1094), a resident of the city of Cordova in what is today Spain but then the Muslim land of al-Andalus, penned a detailed description of this fabled region. Although he never traveled to nearby Africa and probably never even left his native land, al-Bakri provides us with one of the most important sources for the early history of the western Sudan. As was the accepted practice among Muslim geographers of this era, al-Bakri drew heavily from the writings of predecessors, whose works are now otherwise lost, and he also collected oral testimony from merchants who had traveled to the area. These interviews made it possible for al-Bakri to present up-to-date information on Ghana at a crucial moment in its history.

In 1076/1077 a Muslim Berber people known as the *Almoravids* swept down from Morocco, conquered Ghana, and forced Islam on many Ghanians. Shortly thereafter the Almoravids fragmented, but Ghana never fully recovered its past power. By the early thirteenth century it had disintegrated. Hegemony over the markets of the western Sudan briefly passed to the kingdom of Soso and then to the state of Mali, which reached its greatest territorial extent under Mansa Musa (r. 1312–1327), whom we saw in Chapter 8 (source 66).

QUESTIONS FOR ANALYSIS

1. To whom did a monarch pass his royal power? What does this tradition of royal succession suggest about Ghanian society?
2. Describe the city of Ghana. What does its physical environment, especially its two centers, suggest about eleventh-century Ghanian culture?
3. How do we know that the empire of Ghana was not the only state in the western Sudan?
4. How would you characterize the authority and sources of power of the rulers of Ghana?
5. What role did Islam play in Ghanian society? What does your answer suggest about the way in which Islam entered the western Sudan?
6. What does the story of the conversion of the king of Malal suggest about the process of Islamization in the western Sudan?

Ghana is a title given to their kings; the name of the region is Awkar, and their king today, namely in the year 460 (1067–8),[1] is Tunka Manin. He ascended the throne in 455 (1063). The name of his predecessor was Basi and he became their ruler at the age of 85. He led a praiseworthy life on account of his love of justice and friendship for the Muslims. At the end of his life he became blind, but he concealed this from his subjects and pretended that he could see. When something was put before him he said: "This is good" or "This is bad." His ministers deceived the people by indicating to the king in cryptic words what he should say, so that the commoners could not understand. Basi was a maternal uncle of Tunka Manin. This is their custom and their habit, that the kingship is inherited only by the son of the king's sister. He has no doubt that his successor is a son of his sister, while he is not certain that his son is in fact his own, and he is not convinced of the genuineness of his relationship to him.

This Tunka Manin is powerful, rules an enormous kingdom, and possesses great authority.

The city of Ghana consists of two towns situated on a plain.[2] One of these towns, which is inhabited by Muslims, is large and possesses twelve mosques, in one of which they assemble for the Friday prayer. There are salaried imams and muezzins,[3] as well as jurists and scholars. In the environs are wells with sweet water, from which they drink and with which they grow vegetables. The king's town is six miles distant from this one and bears the name of Al-Ghaba.[4] Between these two towns there are continuous habitations. The houses of the inhabitants are of stone and acacia wood. The king has a palace and a number of domed dwellings all surrounded with an enclosure like a city wall. In the king's town, and not far from his court of justice, is a mosque where the Muslims who arrive at his court pray. Around the king's town are domed buildings and groves and thickets where the sorcerers of these people, men in

---

[1]The four hundred and sixtieth lunar year from Muhammad's *hijra* from Mecca to Medina of 16 July 622 — the beginning of the Muslim calendar. The Western equivalent is A.D. 1067/1068.

[2]Imagine a city consisting of two separate walled towns connected by a long, unwalled strip of private dwellings. This was probably the city of Koumbi-Saleh, whose ruins are located in the southern region of the modern

nation of Mauritania. At its eleventh-century height, this double city probably held some twenty thousand people.

[3]Imams are religious teachers, and muezzins are the chanters who ascend the minarets, or towers, of the mosques and call the faithful to prayer five times daily.

[4]The term means "the forest," and refers to the sacred grove mentioned below.

charge of the religious cult, live. In them too are their idols and the tombs of their kings. These woods are guarded and none may enter them and know what is there. In them also are the king's prisons. If somebody is imprisoned there no news of him is ever heard. The king's interpreters, the official in charge of his treasury and the majority of his ministers are Muslims. Among the people who follow the king's religion[5] only he and his heir apparent (who is the son of his sister) may wear sewn clothes. All other people wear robes of cotton, silk, or brocade, according to their means. All of them shave their beards, and women shave their heads. The king adorns himself like a woman, wearing necklaces round his neck and bracelets on his forearms, and he puts on a high cap decorated with gold and wrapped in a turban of fine cotton. He sits in audience or to hear grievances against officials in a domed pavilion around which stand ten horses covered with gold-embroidered materials. Behind the king stand ten pages holding shields and swords decorated with gold, and on his right are the sons of the vassal kings of his country wearing splendid garments and their hair plaited with gold. The governor of the city sits on the ground before the king and around him are ministers seated likewise. . . . When people who profess the same religion as the king approach him they fall on their knees and sprinkle dust on their heads, for this is their way of greeting him. As for the Muslims, they greet him only by clapping their hands.

Their religion is paganism and the worship of idols. When their king dies they construct over the place where his tomb will be an enormous dome of wood. Then they bring him on a bed covered with a few carpets and cushions and place him beside the dome. At his side they place his ornaments, his weapons, and the vessels from which he used to eat and drink, filled with various kinds of food and beverages. They place there too the men who used to serve his meals. They close the door of the dome and cover it with mats and furnishings. Then the people assemble, who heap earth upon it until it becomes like a big hillock and dig a ditch around it until the mound can be reached at only one place.

They make sacrifices to their dead and make offerings of intoxicating drinks.

On every donkey-load of salt when it is brought into the country their king levies one golden dinar,[6] and two dinars when it is sent out. From a load of copper the king's due is five mithqals,[7] and from a load of other goods ten mithqals. The best gold found in his land comes from the town of Ghiyaru, which is eighteen days' traveling distant from the king's town over a country inhabited by tribes of the Sudan whose dwellings are continuous.

The nuggets found in all the mines of his country are reserved for the king, only this gold dust being left for the people. But for this the people would accumulate gold until it lost its value. The nuggets may weigh from an ounce to a pound. It is related that the king owns a nugget as large as a big stone. . . .

The king of Ghana, when he calls up his army, can put 200,000 men[8] into the field, more than 40,000 of them archers. . . .

On the opposite bank of the Nil[9] is another great kingdom, stretching a distance of more than eight days' marching, the king of which has the title of Daw. The inhabitants of this region use arrows when fighting. Beyond this country lies another called Malal,[10] the king of which is known as *al-musulmani*.[11] He is thus called because his country became afflicted with

---

[5] The king was not a Muslim. He followed the ancient religious ways of the Soninke people.
[6] A standard gold coin in the Islamic world that weighed about 4.72 grams.
[7] A standard of weight equaling 4.72 grams; a dinar weighs one mithqal.

[8] An apparent exaggeration.
[9] Muslim geographers of this era mistakenly believed that the Niger River was the western source of the Nile.
[10] A Mandike kingdom that probably was the nucleus of the later empire of Mali.
[11] "The Muslim."

drought one year following another; the inhabitants prayed for rain, sacrificing cattle till they had exterminated almost all of them, but the drought and the misery only increased. The king had as his guest a Muslim who used to read the Qur'an and was acquainted with the Sunna.[12] To this man the king complained of the calamities that assailed him and his people. The man said: "O King, if you believed in God (who is exalted) and testified that He is One, and testified as to the prophetic mission of Muhammad (God bless him and give him peace) and if you accepted all the religious laws of Islam, I would pray for your deliverance from your plight and that God's mercy would envelop all the people of your country and that your enemies and adversaries might envy you on that account." Thus he continued to press the king until the latter accepted Islam and became a sincere Muslim. The man made him recite from the Qur'an some easy passages and

taught him religious obligations and practices which no one may be excused from knowing. Then the Muslim made him wait till the eve of the following Friday,[13] when he ordered him to purify himself by a complete ablution, and clothed him in a cotton garment which he had. The two of them came out towards a mound of earth, and there the Muslim stood praying while the king, standing at his right side, imitated him. Thus they prayed for a part of the night, the Muslim reciting invocations and the king saying "Amen." The dawn had just started to break when God caused abundant rain to descend upon them. So the king ordered the idols to be broken and expelled the sorcerers from his country. He and his descendants after him as well as his nobles were sincerely attached to Islam, while the common people of his kingdom remained polytheists. Since then their rulers have been given the title of *al-musulmani.*

Fourteenth-Century Ethiopia
▼▼▼

86 ▾ *THE GLORIOUS VICTORIES OF 'AMDA SEYON*

Ethiopia, a kingdom to the southeast of Kush (Chapter 1, source 10) in Africa's northeast highlands, looks out across the Red Sea to Yemen, the southern portion of the Arabian Peninsula. Settlers from Yemen crossed these waters perhaps as early as the seventh century B.C. and mixed with the indigenous inhabitants to produce a hybrid civilization, whose language, Ge'ez, was essentially Semitic but contained significant Kushitic elements. Because of its strategic location astride a trade route that linked Egypt and the Mediterranean world with the markets of East Africa, Arabia, and India, Ethiopia flourished. Greco-Roman records from the first century A.D. tell of the wealth and power of Axum, Ethiopia's cosmopolitan capital city.

According to Ethiopian chronicles, in A.D. 333 King 'Ezana converted to Christianity, and in turn the Ethiopian people gradually adopted the new faith.

---

[12]The traditions of Sunni, or mainstream, Islam.

[13]The beginning of the Muslim day of rest and community worship.

Like the Egyptians and Nubians to their north, the Ethiopians eventually subscribed to a type of Christianity known as *Monophysitism* (from the Greek words for "one nature"), which arose in the fifth century and centered on a doctrinal view of Jesus that deemphasized his human nature to the point of maintaining that Jesus had a single, divine nature. When the Churches of Constantinople and Rome condemned Monophysite teachings as heresy in 451, the Ethiopian Church was doctrinally separated from these centers of Christianity. The Arab-Muslim conquest of Egypt in the 640s further cut Ethiopia off from its Christian coreligionists in Byzantium and the West. In time, most of previously Christian Egypt converted to Islam, although its native Christians, known as Coptic Christians, remained an important minority, as they are even today. Nubia (the ancient land of Kush and the modern nation of Sudan) and Ethiopia vigorously fought to maintain their political autonomy and Christian identity in the face of Muslim pressure from the north. After the mid-thirteenth century, however, Nubian resistance to Egyptian-Muslim attacks weakened. By the mid-fourteenth century Nubia no longer had an independent Christian monarchy, and the Christian faith itself was fast losing out to Islam. By the sixteenth century, Nubia was essentially a Muslim land.

Farther the south, mountainous Ethiopia still held out. The following document, composed by an eyewitness to the events, tells the story of how in 1329 King 'Amda Seyon I (r. 1314–1344), whose throne name was Gabra Masqal, "servant of the Cross," resisted an invasion by Sabr ad-Din, the ruler of Ifat, a nearby Muslim principality. More than simply a monarch on the defensive, 'Amda Seyon was a militant expansionist who in his thirty-year reign undertook a series of offensive operations against neighboring Muslim states and achieved significant success at their expense. As the chronicle points out, Sabr ad-Din was actually a tributary prince who revolted against 'Amda Seyon's authority.

QUESTIONS FOR ANALYSIS

1. What picture emerges of Muslim-Christian relations in fourteenth-century Ethiopia?
2. The Ethiopian-Christian attitude toward Jews and Judaism has been characterized as ambivalent (containing conflicting attitudes). Do you find in this source any evidence to support such a judgment?
3. Reread Usamah's memoirs (Chapter 9, source 77) and the *Song of Roland* (Chapter 10, source 78). Do you see any parallels in the tones and messages of those two sources and this document? What are they? What conclusions do you draw?

Let us write, with the help of our Lord Jesus Christ, of the power and the victory which God wrought by the hands of 'Amda Seyon king of Ethiopia, whose throne-name is Gabra Masqal. . . . Now the king of Ethiopia . . . heard that the king of the Rebels[1] had revolted,

---

[1]The word *'elwan* can also be translated as "infidels."

and in his arrogance was unfaithful to him, making himself great, like the Devil who set himself above his creator and exalted himself like the Most High. The king of the Rebels, whose name was Sabradin, was full of arrogance towards his lord 'Amda Seyon, and said; "I will be king over all the land of Ethiopia; I will rule the Christians according to my law, and I will destroy their churches." And having said this, he arose and set out and came to the land of the Christians, and killed some of them; and those who survived, both men and women, he took prisoner and converted them to his religion.

And after this he said, "I will nominate governors over the provinces of Ethiopia." . . . And he appointed governors over all the provinces of Ethiopia, even those which he had not been able to reach.

But the feet cannot become the head, nor the earth the sky, nor the servant the master. That perverse one, the son of a viper, of the seed of a serpent, the son of a stranger from the race of Satan, thought covetously of the throne of David[2] and said, "I will rule in Seyon,"[3] for pride entered into his heart, as into the Devil his father. He said, "I will make the Christian churches into mosques for the Muslims, and I will convert to my religion the king of the Christians together with his people, and I will nominate him governor of one province, and if he refuses to be converted to my religion I will deliver him to the herdsmen . . . that they make him a herder of camels. As for the queen Zan Mangesa, the wife of the king, I will make her work at the mill.". . .

Saying this, he collected all the troops of the Muslims, and chose from among them the ablest and most intelligent. These in truth were not able and intelligent, but fools, men full of error, impostors who foretell the future by means of sand and take omens from the sun and moon and stars of heaven, who say, "We observe the stars," but they have knowledge only of evil, they have no knowledge of God, their knowledge is of men which fades and perishes, for as Saint Paul says, "God hath made foolish the wisdom of this world."[4]

Let us return to the original subject. This evil man then questioned the diviners, saying, "Now tell me, I pray you, shall we conquer when we fight with the king of the Christians?" And one of them rose, a prophet of darkness. . . .

When Sabradin the king of the Rebels examined him, this diviner answered him persuasively, saying, "Behold, the kingdom of the Christians is finished; it shall be given to us, and you shall reign in Seyon. Rise, make war on the king of the Christians, and conquering you shall rule him and his people." And all the diviners said likewise. So the Rebel king sent into all the lands of the Muslims and called together his troops, and formed them into three divisions: one division set out for the land of Amhara, another set out for the land of Angot, and he himself prepared for war and set out to invade Shoa where the king was, — the slave of slaves against the prince of princes, the tail of the dog against the head of the lion, trusting in the false prediction that the Christian kingdom was come to an end.

As for us, we have heard and we know from the Holy Scriptures that the kingdom of the Muslims, established for but seven hundred years, shall cease to be at the proper time. But the kingdom of the Christians shall continue till the second coming of the Son of God, according to the words of Holy Scripture; and

[2]The Ethiopian royal family, known as the Solomonic Dynasty (1270–1974), claimed descent from the union of the Queen of Sheba and King Solomon of Israel, son of King David (ca 1000 B.C.). According to this tradition, Menelik, son of the Queen of Sheba and Solomon, and first king of Ethiopia, brought the Ark of the Covenant to Ethiopia, where it is still revered as the kingdom's most sacred relic.

[3]The Ge'ez transliteration of *Zion,* one of Jerusalem's hills and a common symbolic term for Jerusalem and even the entire Holy Land. Here *Seyon* refers to Ethiopia, since the Ethiopians claim Hebraic descent (note 2). *'Amda Seyon* means "pillar of Zion."
[4]I Corinthians 1:20.

above all we know that the kingdom of Ethiopia shall endure till the coming of Christ, of which David prophesied saying "Ethiopia shall stretch her hands unto God."[5]

The messengers whom the king had sent to that Rebel returned to him the whole answer of the renegade, that rebel against righteousness. Hearing the insults of the evil man, the king called together his commanders. . . . He sent them forth to war against the evil Sabradin on the 24th day of Yakatit,[6] saying to them, "May God give you strength and victory, and may He help you." . . . And they fought with him and forced him out of his residence; and he fled before them. And they defeated him through the power of God. . . . And they pursued him till sunset; but he escaped them, going by a different road. God threw him down from his glory. . . .

Then the army of the king set forth and attacked the camp of the Rebel. They looted the rebel king's treasure houses and took gold and silver and fine clothes and jewels without number. They killed men and women, old men and children; the corpses of the slain filled a large space. And those who survived were made prisoners, and there were left none but those who had escaped with that evil man. But the soldiers could not find a place to camp because of the foul smell of the corpses; and they went to another place and made their camp there. . . .

The king, hearing that the Rebel had escaped, went into the tabernacle[7] and approached the altar; seizing the horns of the altar[8] he implored mercy of Jesus Christ saying, "Hear the petition of my heart and reject not the prayer of my lips, and shut not the gates of Thy mercy because of my sins, but send me Thy good angel to guide me on my road to pursue

mine enemy who has set himself above Thy sheep and above Thy holy name." And having said this, he gave an offering to the church of colored hangings for the altar, and went out. Then he sent other troops, . . . cavalry and foot-soldiers, strong and skilled in war, powerful without comparison in warfare and battle; he sent their commander . . . to make war in the land of the renegades who are like Jews, the crucifiers,[9] . . . Because like the Jews, the crucifiers, they denied Christ, he sent troops to destroy and devastate them and subject them to the rule of Christ. . . .

The Rebel was filled with fear, and not knowing where to turn, for fear had taken possession of him, he sent to the queen[10] saying, "I have done wrong to my lord the king, I have wrought injustice against him, and it is better that I fall into his hands than into the hands of a stranger. I will come myself and surrender to him, that he may do what he will to me." Thereupon the queen went to tell the king the whole of the message from that Rebel Sabradin, whose acts, like his name 'broken judgment,'[11] consist of insults, mad rage, errors, contentions, and arrogance. When the king heard this message which the Rebel had sent to the queen, he was exceedingly angry, and said to the queen, "Do you send him a message and say: 'If you come, or if you do not come, it will not trouble me; but if you go to a distant country I will pursue you through the power of God. And if you go into a cave, or if you just run away, I will not leave you alone nor will I return to my capital till I have taken you.'"

Now when he received this message, Sabradin set out and came to the king, and stood before him. And the king asked him, saying, "Why have you behaved thus to me? The gifts

[5]Psalms 68:31.
[6]18 February 1329.
[7]A tent used as a chapel in the king's camp.
[8]As was the fashion in ancient Israel, Ethiopian altars had horns on all four corners. Suppliants would grasp one while praying.
[9]The Falashas, or Ethiopian Jews, Kushitic people whose ancestors had intermarried with Jewish immigrants from

Yemen. They are termed "crucifiers" here because of the notion that the Jews were responsible for Jesus' crucifixion.
[10]Queen Mangesa, wife of King 'Amda Seyon.
[11]A pun. In Ge'ez *sabara* means "break" and *dayn* means "judgment." Actually, the Arabic name Sabr ad-Din means "constant in the faith."

which you formerly sent to me you have given to your servants; and the multitude of goods of silver and gold which I gave to the poor you have taken away. Those who traded with me you have bound in chains; and what is worse, you have aspired to the throne of my kingdom, in imitation of the Devil your father who wished to be the equal of his creator." When that Rebel heard these words of the king he was at a loss for an answer in the greatness of his fear, for he was afraid of the king's presence; and he answered, "Do with me according to your will." And immediately the soldiers who were on the left and right of the king stood forth in anger and said, "This man is not worthy of life, for he has burnt the churches of God, he has slain Christians, and those whom he did not kill he has compelled to accept his religion. Moreover he desired to ascend the high mountain of the kingdom." And some said, "Let us slay him with the edge of the sword"; others said, "Let us stone him to death"; and others again, "Let us burn him with fire that he may disappear from the earth." And they said to the king, "Think not, O king, that he comes to you honestly and freely, for he trusts in his magic art." And so saying, they lifted from his bosom and arm a talisman and revealed the form of his magic. Then said the king, "Can your talismans deliver you from my hands in which God has imprisoned you?" And he gave orders for his two hands to be bound with iron chains; he did not wish him to be killed, for he is merciful and forbearing. Thus was taken the Rebel in the net which he himself had woven, and in the snare which he himself had set. . . . After this the king sent news to the capital of his kingdom. . . . , "There is good news for you: with the help of your prayers I have defeated my enemy who is also the enemy of Christ."

A Yoruba Woman of Authority?
▼▼▼

87 ▼ SEATED FEMALE FIGURE

Like the Ethiopians, the Yoruba-speaking peoples of West Africa trace their ancestry back to Southwest Asia, specifically Mecca. Such oral traditions are suspect as historical evidence, since they may simply have arisen from a desire on the part of people converted to Islam well after A.D. 1200 to create for themselves an Arabic lineage. Whatever their origins, by the late fourteenth century the Yoruba had established a number of independent kingdoms in a region encompassed today by the nations of Nigeria and Benin. One of the most important of these was Oyo. Although it reached its apogee as a regional power in the period 1600–1830, Oyo's foundations as a city-state go back much earlier. Its first capital city, Old Oyo, located near the Niger River, was founded sometime between A.D. 800 and 1000.

The Yoruba of Oyo and elsewhere were great artists as well as state-builders. The town of Esie in Nigeria is the site of a collection of over a thousand soapstone carvings of human figures that have lain for centuries in a grove. The sculptures date to somewhere between 1100 and 1500 and seem to have come from either Old Oyo or the equally powerful Yoruba city-state of Ife.

A Yoruba Woman of Authority?

The sculpture pictured here is twenty-six inches high and represents a seated woman holding a cutlass that rests against her right shoulder. Note her elaborate hairstyle, which equals her face in height, the three-stringed necklace, and the scarification of her face. This arrangement of scars is found equally on male and female effigies within the collection. The figure probably represents an *iyalode* (literally, "mother in charge of external affairs"), an important officer among the Yoruba. Although the specific functions of the iyalode differed from kingdom to kingdom and from time to time, one can safely state that they enjoyed wide-ranging political, social, economic, and even military powers. Simply stated, the iyalode was a chief in her own right and one of the monarch's main lieutenants.

QUESTIONS FOR ANALYSIS

1. List and comment on all the clues that lead us to infer that this figurine represents a woman of authority. What do you think each symbol of authority represents?
2. Compare this statue with that of Caesar Augustus (Chapter 5, source 42). What do they have in common, and what do those common characteristics suggest about the way in which authority is perceived across cultures and time?

▼▼▼

The Americas

The date of the arrival of the first humans in the Americas is a matter of dispute. Based on fragmentary and controversial evidence, some scholars believe that migrants from Asia crossed into North America as early as 37,000 years ago and at least no later than 20,000 years ago. Others reject these dates as too early. All agree, however, that incontrovertible evidence shows the presence of hunters in the Americas by 10,000 B.C.

The original peopling of the Americas was an epochal event (or series of events, since it may have been achieved in successive waves of migration from northeast Asia), rivaled only in magnitude by the demographic shifts that took place following the arrival in force of Europeans and later Africans after 1492. With the advent of European and African peoples and their diseases, the whole population structure of the Americas underwent massive changes.

During the many years that separated these two periods, the Americas witnessed a variety of other, only slightly less monumental, developments. One of the most consequential was the indigenous development of agriculture based on the cultivation of more than one hundred different crops unknown to the peoples of Africa and Eurasia. Chief among these were maize ("corn" in American English), potatoes, tomatoes, peanuts, manioc, and various types of peppers and squashes. By the time the Europeans arrived, agriculture was practiced from the woodlands of eastern North America to the rain forests of the Amazon tropics. As elsewhere, agriculture imposed restrictions on the behavior and social patterns of the cultivators and also produced enough food in a sufficiently regular manner to allow for the growth of dense populations. One result was the rise of civilizations, first in Mexico and farther south in Meso- and South America and later in regions that are today part of the United States.

The civilizations of North America included: the Mississippian Mound Culture that between A.D. 1050 and 1200 created the city of Cahokia, which supported a population of over thirty thousand at a site that today is in East St. Louis, Illinois; the so-called Hohokam of the Sonoran Desert in the region of modern Phoenix, Arizona, who produced a complex urban society based upon their ability to construct and maintain some three hundred miles of irrigation canals; and the Anasazi of the Four Corners region of the American Southwest, whose thirteenth-century cities in Chaco Canyon, New Mexico, and at Mesa Verde in Colorado stand as silent testimony of the engineering skills of these people. All three civilizations participated in widespread trade networks and were influenced by the earlier civilizations of Mexico. All three also disappeared as urban cultures before the arrival of Europeans, who could only marvel at the ruins they left behind.

Because they left no written records behind and abandoned their urban centers so long ago, these North American civilizations remain still largely mysterious, despite the work of archeologists, whose work over the past half century has shed considerable new light on "those who have vanished," as the term *Hohokam* means in the language of their modern Pima descendants. The Maya, Aztec, and Inca peoples of farther south, however, still had identifiable cultures when European conquerors and missionaries arrived on the scene. Despite the best attempts of many of these Europeans to efface totally the "devilish" cultures that they had discovered, the Maya, Aztec, and Inca civilizations could not be forgotten. The three sources that follow, the products of Amerindian and European authors, combine to shed light on three important American civilizations that flourished between A.D. 500 and 1500.

Quiché Mayan Gods and Monarchs
▼▼▼

88 ▼ *THE BOOK OF THE COMMUNITY*

Among all the peoples of ancient America, only the Meso-Americans created systems of writing, although the Quechua-speaking people of the Andes, who carved out the Inca Empire, devised a system of record keeping by means of knotted strings that served almost as well (source 90). Of all the forms of writing used in Central America, the Maya had the most sophisticated, an exceedingly complex system based on a wide range of picture-symbols, technically known as *glyphs*, that variously represented objects, concepts, and sounds. Unfortunately, Spanish missionaries, zealous to destroy all remnants of indigenous paganism, burned most of the books of the Maya. Only three preconquest Mayan books, and fragments of a fourth, survived the fires of the Spanish Inquisition. Nevertheless, three factors allow us to know more about the preconquest Maya than virtually any other Amerindian civilization: their ancient written language has been partially deciphered; the classical Maya left behind a rich archeological heritage; and the Maya, as a people and culture, survive, and even flourish, today in Guatemala, Belize, and Mexico's Yucatan peninsula.

This document dates from shortly after the early sixteenth-century Spanish conquest of the Quiché Maya of Guatemala, the most powerful of the then-existing Mayan states of Central America. The Maya, who had a shared culture but were never organized under a single central authority, had reached their classical heights between about A.D. 300 and 800 but by 900 had abandoned many of their cities and ceremonial centers. Yet even with the collapse of many of their states and urban centers, the Maya persisted as a culture and even built a few new cities. When the army of Pedro de Alvardo invaded the territory of the Quiché in 1524, it found a vigorous society that initially offered spirited resistance. Eventually, however, the Spaniards prevailed.

Faced with the threat of losing all memory of the Mayan way of life, an anonymous Quiché Indian, who was at least nominally a convert to Catholicism, undertook to compile, in his native tongue, a collection of Mayan beliefs, traditions, and history down to 1550, because, as he noted: "The original book, written long ago, existed, but its sight is hidden to the searcher." The result was the *Popul Vuh*, or *Book of the Community*. The *Popul Vuh* remained hidden for about 150 years until it was discovered by a sympathetic Spanish priest, who was also a scholar of the Quiché culture. He transcribed the text from its manuscript, thereby preserving the original Quiché version, and translated it into Spanish in order "to bring to light what had been among the Indians in the olden days [and] . . . to give information on the errors which they had in their paganism and which they still adhere to among themselves."

The following selection tells about Tohil, chief god of the Quiché Maya, and his relationship with the *Ahpop*, or Quiché monarch, in the era preceding the coming of the Spaniards.

QUESTIONS FOR ANALYSIS

1. How do we know that this book was an attempt to recreate an ancient, lost book of Mayan traditions and priestcraft?
2. What special functions did the ancient Quiché monarchs have? Why did the monarchs fast?
3. What were the mutual responsibilities of monarch and subjects? What do they suggest about this society?
4. How was the Quiché state ruled? What does its having three royal houses suggest?
5. What did the people owe Tohil? What was expected in return?
6. How do we know that Tohil was a syncretic deity, whose manifestations and functions were drawn from a variety of sources? What does this suggest about the make-up of the Quiché state?
7. What evidence is there that the Quiché saw themselves as belonging to a single culture, despite their tribal divisions?
8. What allows us to infer that postclassical Quiché civilization was still vibrant?

We shall now tell of the House of the God. The house was also given the same name as the god. The Great Edifice of Tohil was the name of the Temple of Tohil, of those of Cavec.[1] . . .

Tzutuhá, which is seen in Cahbahá,[2] is the name of a large edifice in which there was a stone which all the lords of Quiché worshiped and which was also worshiped by all the tribes.

The people first offered their sacrifices before Tohil, and afterward went to pay their respects to the Ahpop and the Ahpop-Camhá.[3] Then they went to present their gorgeous feathers and their tribute before the king. And the kings whom they maintained were the Ahpop and the Ahpop-Camhá, who had conquered their towns.

Great lords and wonderful men were the marvelous kings Gucumatz and Cotuhá, the marvelous kings Quicab and Cavizimah.[4] They knew if there would be war, and everything was clear before their eyes; they saw if there would be death and hunger, if there would be strife. They well know that there was a place where it could be seen, that there was a book which they called the *Popol Vuh*.

But not only in this way was the estate of the lords great, great also were their fasts. And this was in recognition of their having been created, and in recognition of their having been given their kingdoms. They fasted a long time and made sacrifices to their gods. Here is how they fasted: Nine men fasted and another nine made sacrifices[5] and burned incense. Thirteen more men fasted, and another thirteen more made offerings and burned incense before Tohil. And while before their god, they nourished themselves only with fruits, with *zapotes, matasanos,* and *jocotes.* And they did not eat any *tortillas.* Now if there were seventeen men who made sacrifice, or ten who fasted, the truth is they

did not eat. They fulfilled their great precepts, and thus showed their position as lords.

Neither had they women to sleep with, but they remained alone, fasting. They were in the House of God, all day they prayed, burning incense and making sacrifices. Thus they remained from dusk until dawn, grieving in their hearts and in their breasts, and begging for happiness and life for their sons and vassals as well as for their kingdom, and raising their faces to the sky.

Here are their petitions to their god, when they prayed; and this was the supplication of their hearts:

"Oh, Thou, beauty of the day! Thou, Huracán[6]; Thou, Heart of Heaven and of Earth! Thou, giver of richness, and giver of the daughters and the sons! Turn toward us your power and your riches; grant life and growth unto my sons and vassals; let those who must maintain and nourish Thee multiply and increase; those who invoke Thee on the roads, in the fields, on the banks of the rivers, in the ravines, under the trees, under the vines.

"Give them daughters and sons. Let them not meet disgrace, nor misfortune, let not the deceiver come behind or before them. Let them not fall, let them not be wounded, let them not fornicate, nor be condemned by justice. Let them not fall on the descent or on the ascent of the road. Let them not encounter obstacles back of them or before them, nor anything which strikes them. Grant them good roads, beautiful, level roads. Let them not have misfortune, nor disgrace, through Thy fault, through Thy sorceries.

"Grant a good life to those who must give Thee sustenance and place food in Thy mouth, in Thy presence, to Thee, Heart of Heaven, Heart of Earth, Bundle of Majesty. And Thou,

---

[1] The principal branch of the Quiché people.
[2] The name of the ceremonial center where the temple called *Tzutuha* was located.
[3] The Ahpop-Camhá was a coreigning subking. Both the Ahpop and Ahpop-Camhá came from the chief royal family of the Quiché people, the Cavec.
[4] Gucumatz and Cotuhá were Ahpop and Ahpop-Camhá

during the fifth generation of the twelve generations of Cavec monarchs who ruled the Quiché before the Spanish conquest. They were the first of a line of sorcerer-kings. Quicab and Cavizimah were seventh generation Cavec monarchs.
[5] Possibly human sacrifices.
[6] One of Tohil's names.

Tohil; Thou, Avilix[7]; Thou, Hacavitz,[8] Arch of the Sky, Surface of the Earth, the Four Corners, the Four Cardinal Points. Let there be but peace and tranquility in Thy mouth, in Thy presence, oh, God!"

Thus [spoke] the lords, while within, the nine men fasted, the thirteen men, and the seventeen men. During the day they fasted and their hearts grieved for their sons and vassals and for all their wives and their children when each of the lords made his offering.

This was the price of a happy life, the price of power, the price of the authority of the Ahpop, of the Ahpop-Camhá, of the Galel and of the Ahtzic-Vinac.[9] Two by two they ruled, each pair succeeding the other in order to bear the burden of the people of all the Quiché nation.

One only was the origin of their tradition and [one only] the origin of the manner of maintaining and sustaining, and one only, too, was the origin of the tradition and the customs of those of Tamub and Ilocab and the people of Rabinal and the Cakchiquel, those of Tziquinahá, of Tuhalahá and Uchabahá.[10] And there was but one trunk [a single family] when they heard there in Quiché what all of them were to do.

But it was not only thus that they reigned. They did not squander the gifts of those whom they sustained and nourished, but they ate and drank them. Neither did they buy them; they had won and seized their empire, their power, and their sovereignty.

And it was not at small cost, that they conquered the fields and the towns; the small towns and the large towns paid high ransoms; they brought precious stones and metals, they brought honey of the bees, bracelets, bracelets of emeralds and other stones, and brought garlands made of blue feathers, the tribute of all the towns. They came into the presence of the marvelous kings Gucumatz and Cotuhá, and before Quicab and Cavizimah,[11] the Ahpop, the Ahpop-Camhá, the Galel, and the Ahtzic-Vinac.

It was not little what they did, neither were few, the tribes which they conquered. Many branches of the tribes came to pay tribute to the Quiché; full of sorrow they came to give it over. Nevertheless, the [Quiché] power did not grow quickly. Gucumatz it was, who began the aggrandizement of the kingdom. Thus was the beginning of his aggrandizement and that of the Quiché nation.

The Wonders of Tenochtitlán: City of the Aztecs

▼▼▼

89 ▼ THE SECOND LETTER OF HERNÁN CORTÉS

One of the greatest of the postclassical Meso-American civilizations was that of the Aztecs, who variously called themselves *Tenocha* and *Mexica*. Originally a migrant people from an unknown place of origin called *Aztlan* (hence, Aztecs), the Mexica entered the central valley of what is now known as Mexico following

---

[7]The god of Balam-Acab, one of the founders of the Quiché state.

[8]The god of the Ahau-Quiché, one of the three royal houses of the Quiché. See note 9.

[9]The Quiché had three royal houses. The Cavec supplied its two chief rulers (note 3). The Galel was a court official who was also king of the House of Nihaib; the Ahtzic-Vinac was head of the House of Ahau Quiché.

[10]Various Quiché tribes and regions.

[11]See note 4.

the collapse of the Toltec Empire (ca 1000–1200). According to Aztec tradition, their ancestral legends foretold that they would end their wanderings when they saw an eagle perched on a cactus with a snake in its beak. They saw such a scene on a marshy island in Lake Texcoco, the site of modern Mexico City, and settled down on the island in the early fourteenth century. Here, in the midst of the lake, they established their city of Tenochtitlán, expanding the island as the city grew by adding fill to create reclaimed land.

When they initially settled down in the lake, the Aztecs were a minor "barbarian" people who served as vassal-mercenaries of more powerful neighbors. A century later, in 1428, the Aztecs turned on their former masters and began the process of carving out their own empire. By the reign of Moctezuma II (r. 1502–1520), the last Aztec monarch, this still expanding empire dominated some 28 million people in central Mexico from the Pacific to the Gulf of Mexico. Tenochtitlán, the nerve center of this empire, had grown to a metropolis of about 250,000 inhabitants, with perhaps three times that number residing in the mainland suburbs.

Moctezuma II's reign witnessed the high point and sudden end of Aztec power because of the arrival of Spanish *conquistadores* under the command of Hernán Cortés (Chapter 13, source 101). In the following document, a portion of one of five letters that Cortés wrote to the king of Spain describing his conquest and subjugation of Mexico between 1519 and 1526, the conqueror of Mexico describes the Aztec capital.

QUESTIONS FOR ANALYSIS

1. What does this document tell us about the Aztec economy?
2. What can we infer from it about Aztec religious beliefs and practices?
3. What does this allow us to infer about the qualities of Aztec engineering?
4. Compare Tenochtitlán with Hangzhou (Chapter 9, source 72). What conclusions do you draw?

The great city of Tenochtitlán is built in the midst of this salt lake, and it is two leagues from the heart of the city to any point on the mainland. Four causeways lead to it, all made by hand and some twelve feet wide. The city itself is as large as Seville or Córdova. The principal streets are very broad and straight, the majority of them being of beaten earth, but a few and at least half the smaller thoroughfares are waterways along which they pass in their canoes. Moreover, even the principal streets have openings at regular distances so that the water can freely pass from one to another, and these openings which are very broad are spanned by great bridges of huge beams, very stoutly put together, so firm indeed that over many of them ten horsemen can ride at once. . . .

The city has many open squares in which markets are continuously held and the general business of buying and selling proceeds. One square in particular is twice as big as that of Salamanca[1] and completely surrounded by arcades where there are daily more than sixty

---

[1]A Spanish university town.

thousand folk buying and selling. Every kind of merchandise such as may be met within every land is for sale there, whether of food and victuals, or ornaments of gold and silver, or lead, brass, copper, tin, precious stones, bones, shells, snails and feathers; limestone for building is likewise sold there, stone both rough and polished, bricks burnt and unburnt, wood of all kinds and in all stages of preparation. There is a street of game where they sell all manner of birds that are to be found in their country, including hens, partridges, quails, wild duck, fly-catchers, widgeon, turtle doves, pigeons, little birds in round nests made of grass, parrots, owls, eagles, vulcans, sparrow-hawks and kestrels; and of some of these birds of prey they sell the skins complete with feathers, head, bill, and claws. They also sell rabbits, hares, deer, and small dogs which they breed especially for eating. There is a street of herb-sellers where there are all manner of roots and medicinal plants that are found in the land. There are houses as it were of apothecaries where they sell medicines made from these herbs, both for drinking and for use as ointments and salves. There are barbers' shops where you may have your hair washed and cut. There are other shops where you may obtain food and drink. There are street porters such as we have in Spain to carry packages. There is a great quantity of wood, charcoal, braziers made of clay and mats of all sorts, some for beds and others more finely woven for seats, still others for furnishing halls and private apartments. All kinds of vegetables may be found there, in particular onions, leeks, garlic, cresses, watercress, borage, sorrel, artichokes, and golden thistles. There are many different sorts of fruits including cherries and plums very similar to those found in Spain. They sell honey obtained from bees, as also the honeycomb and that obtained from maize

plants which are as sweet as sugar canes; they also obtain honey from plants which are known both here and in other parts as *maguey*,[2] which is preferable to grape juice; from *maguey* in addition they make both sugar and a kind of wine, which are sold in their markets. All kinds of cotton thread in various colors may be bought in skeins, very much in the same way as in the great silk exchange of Granada,[3] except that the quantities are far less. They have colors for painting of as good quality as any in Spain, and of as pure shades as may be found anywhere. There are leathers of deer both skinned and in their natural state, and either bleached or dyed in various colors. A great deal of chinaware is sold of very good quality and including earthen jars of all sizes for holding liquids, pitchers, pots, tiles, and an infinite variety of earthenware all made of very special clay and almost all decorated and painted in some way. Maize is sold both as grain and in the form of bread and is vastly superior both in the size of the ear and in taste to that of all the other islands or the mainland. Pasties made from game and fish pies may be seen on sale, and there are large quantities of fresh and salt water fish both in their natural state and cooked ready for eating. Eggs from fowls, geese, and all the other birds I have described may be had, and likewise omelettes ready made. There is nothing to be found in all the land which is not sold in these markets, for over and above what I have mentioned there are so many and such various other things that on account of their very number and the fact that I do not know their names, I cannot now detail them. Each kind of merchandise is sold in its own particular street and no other kind may be sold there: this rule is very well enforced. All is sold by number and measure, but up till now no weighing by balance has been observed. A very fine building in

[2]A Mexican aloe, the juice of which is fermented to create an alcoholic beverage.

[3]The capital city of the kingdom of Granada, the final Muslim bastion in the Iberian Peninsula which Ferdinand of Aragon and Isabella of Castile, the Catholic monarchs of Spain, captured in 1492, thereby effectively ending almost 800 years of Islamic presence in Iberia.

the great square serves as a kind of audience chamber where ten or a dozen persons are always seated, as judges, who deliberate on all cases arising in the market and pass sentence on evildoers. In the square itself there are officials who continually walk amongst the people inspecting goods exposed for sale and the measures by which they are sold, and on certain occasions I have seen them destroy measures which were false.

There are a very large number of . . . dwelling places for their idols throughout the various districts of this great city, all fine buildings, in the chief of which their priests live continuously, so that in addition to the actual temples containing idols there are sumptuous lodgings. These pagan priests are all dressed in black and go habitually with their hair uncut; they do not even comb it from the day they enter the order to that on which they leave. Chief men's sons, both nobles and distinguished citizens, enter these orders at the age of six or seven and only leave when they are of an age to marry, and this occurs more frequently to the first-born who will inherit their father's estates than to others. They are denied all access to women, and no woman is ever allowed to enter one of the religious houses. Certain foods they abstain from and more so at certain periods of the year than at others. Among these temples there is one chief one in particular whose size and magnificence no human tongue could describe. For it is so big that within the lofty wall which entirely circles it one could set a town of fifteen thousand inhabitants.

Immediately inside this wall and throughout its entire length are some admirable buildings containing large halls and corridors where the priests who live in this temple are housed. There are forty towers at the least, all of stout construction and very lofty, the largest of which has fifty steps leading up to its base: this chief one is indeed higher than the great church of Seville. The workmanship both in wood and stone could not be bettered anywhere, for all the stonework within the actual temples where

they keep their idols is cut into ornamental borders of flowers, birds, fishes, and the like, or trellis-work, and the woodwork is likewise all in relief highly decorated with monsters of very various device. The towers all serve as burying places for their nobles, and the little temples which they contain are all dedicated to a different idol to whom they pay their devotions. . . .

The images of the idols in which these people believed are many times greater than the body of a large man. They are made from pulp of all the cereals and greenstuffs which they eat, mixed and pounded together. This mass they moisten with blood from the hearts of human beings which they tear from their breasts while still alive, and thus make sufficient quantity of the pulp to mold into their huge statues: and after the idols have been set up still they offer them more living hearts which they sacrifice in like manner and anoint their faces with the blood. Each department of human affairs has its particular idol after the manner of the ancients who thus honored their gods: so that there is one idol from whom they beg success in war, another for crops, and so on for all their needs.

The city contains many large and fine houses, and for this reason. All the nobles of the land owing allegiance to Moctezuma have their houses in the city and reside there for a certain portion of the year; and in addition there are a large number of rich citizens who likewise have very fine houses. All possess in addition to large and elegant apartments very delightful flower gardens of every kind, both on the ground level as on the upper stories.

Along one of the causeways connecting this great city with the mainland two pipes are constructed of masonry, each two paces broad and about as high as a man, one of which conveys a stream of water very clear and fresh and about the thickness of a man's body right to the center of the city, which all can use for drinking and other purposes. The other pipe which is empty is used when it is desired to clean the former. Moreover, on coming to the breaks in the causeway spanned by bridges under which the salt water flows through, the fresh water flows into a kind of trough as thick as an ox which occupies the whole width of the bridge, and thus the whole city is served. The water is sold from canoes in all the streets, the manner of their taking it from the pipes being in this wise: the canoes place themselves under the bridges where the troughs are to be found, and from above the canoes are filled by men who are especially paid for this work.

At all the entrances to the city and at those parts where canoes are unloaded, which is where the greatest amount of provisions enters the city, certain huts have been built, where there are official guards to exact so much on everything that enters. I know not whether this goes to the lord or to the city itself, and have not yet been able to ascertain, but I think that it is to the ruler, since in the markets of several other towns we have seen such a tax exacted on behalf of the ruler. Every day in all the markets and public places of the city there are a number of workmen and masters of all manner of crafts waiting to be hired by the day. The people of this city are nicer in their dress and manners than those of any other city or province, for since Moctezuma always holds his residence here and his vassals visit the city for lengthy periods, greater culture and politeness of manners in all things has been encouraged.

Governing the Inca Empire
▼▼▼

90 ▼ Pedro de Cieza de Léon, CHRONICLES

Because no society of South America developed a system of writing, there are no written records of South America's civilizations before the arrival of the Spaniards. Our best sources for their preconquest history are, therefore, archeological artifacts and accounts composed by sixteenth- and early seventeenth-century Amerindian and Spanish writers who labored to preserve the memory of a past that was in imminent danger of being lost forever. One such ethnohistorian was Pedro de Cieza de León (1520–1554), who in 1535 arrived in the Americas as a teenage soldier-adventurer and spent the next seventeen years trekking throughout South America, falling increasingly under the spell of the continent and its native peoples. As he traveled and fought, he constantly took detailed notes of all he had observed and experienced. Believing, as he noted, "we and the Indians have the same origin," Cieza wrote with great sympathy for the many different Amerindian cultures that he encountered, even though he seems never to have doubted the righteousness of the Spanish conquest and conversion of these peoples. Indeed, one of his primary reasons for recording his observations was that he considered it "right that the world know how so great a multitude of these Indians were brought into the sanctity of the Church."

Although Cieza's *Chronicles* describe many different native South American cultures, their greatest value to modern historians is the wealth of detail they provide of the Inca Empire and the Quechua Amerindians who had created it. Like the Aztecs of Mexico, the Quechuas were recent arrivals on the scene who fashioned an imperial civilization that borrowed heavily from a variety of preceding cultures. Also like the Aztec Empire, the Inca Empire was quite young, having taken shape during the reigns of Pachacuti (r. 1438–1471) and his son Topac Yupanqui (r. 1471–1493). As was also true in Mexico, its life was cut short by *conquistadores.*

In the following selection Cieza deals with the manner in which the Inca monarchs governed an empire that covered about a half million square miles, stretched some 2,500 miles from end to end, and included anywhere from six to thirteen million people of various ethnic origins and languages.

QUESTIONS FOR ANALYSIS

1. What devices did the Incas use to govern their vast empire?
2. How did the Inca Empire manage to function without a system of writing?
3. From Cieza's perspective, what were the most admirable qualities of this empire?
4. What appear to have been the strengths of this empire? Can you perceive any weaknesses? Were the Incas aware of these shortcomings, and, if so, how did they attempt to counter them?
5. Compare the Inca Empire with the Roman Empire under Caesar Augustus (Chapter 5, source 33). Which strike you as more significant, the differences or similarities? What do you conclude from your answer?

It is told for a fact of the rulers of this kingdom that in the days of their rule they had their representatives in the capitals of all the provinces, . . . for in all these places there were larger and finer lodgings than in most of the other cities of this great kingdom, and many storehouses. They served as the head of the provinces or regions, and from every so many leagues[1] around the tributes were brought to one of these capitals, and from so many others, to another. This was so well organized that there was not a village that did not know where it was to send its tribute. In all these capitals the Incas had temples of the sun, mints, and many silversmiths who did nothing but work rich pieces of gold or fair vessels of silver; large garrisons were stationed there, and, as I have said, a steward or representative who was in command of them all, to whom an accounting of everything that was brought in was made, and who, in turn, had to give one of all that was issued. And these governors could in no way interfere with the jurisdiction of another who held a similar post, but within his own, if there were any disorder or disturbance, he had authority to punish it[s perpetrators], especially if it were in the nature of a conspiracy or a rebellion, or failure to obey the Inca,[2] for full power resided in these governors. And if the Incas had not had the foresight to appoint them and to establish the *mitimaes,*[3] the natives would have often revolted and shaken off the royal rule; but with the

---

[1]A league is three miles.

[2]*Inca* means "sovereign lord" and in its strictest sense should be used only to refer to this civilization's god-kings. Today, however, historians customarily use the term loosely to refer to the civilization, its empire, and the Quechua people who created them.

[3]Literally, "those moved from one land to another." This was the systematic practice of resettling groups from one area of the empire to another. These resettled people would serve as a check on the loyalties of the natives of the region to which they had been transferred and would, in turn, be kept in check by their new neighbors. This not only helped keep down rebellions and broke down regional and ethnic differences within the empire, it also was a means of cultivating land that needed settlers.

many troops and the abundance of provisions, they could not effect this unless they had all plotted such treason or rebellion together. This happened rarely, for these governors who were named were of complete trust, all of them *Orejones,*[4] and most of them had their holdings, or *chacaras,* in the neighborhood of Cuzco,[5] and their homes and kinfolk. If one of them did not show sufficient capacity for his duties, he was removed and another put in his place.

When one of them came to Cuzco on private business or to see the Inca, he left a lieutenant in his place, not one who aspired to the post, but one he knew would faithfully carry out what he was ordered to do and what was best for the service of the Inca. And if one of these governors or delegates died while in office, the natives at once sent word to the Inca how and of what he had died, and even transported the body by the post road if this seemed to them advisable. The tribute paid by each of these districts where the capital was situated and that turned over by the natives, whether gold, silver, clothing, arms, and all else they gave, was entered in the accounts of . . . [those] who kept the *quipus*[6] and did everything ordered by the governor in the matter of finding the soldiers or supplying whomever the Inca ordered, or making delivery to Cuzco; but when they came from the city of Cuzco to go over the accounts, or they were ordered to go to Cuzco to give an accounting, the accountants themselves gave it by the quipus, or went to give it where there could be no fraud, but everything had to come out right. Few years went by in which an accounting of all these things was not made. . . .

Realizing how difficult it would be to travel the great distances of their land where every league and at every turn a different language was spoken, and how bothersome it would be to have to employ interpreters to understand them, these rulers, as the best measure, ordered and decreed, with severe punishment for failure

to obey, that all the natives of their empire should know and understand the language of Cuzco, both they and their women. This was so strictly enforced that an infant had not yet left its mother's breast before they began to teach it the language it had to know. And although at the beginning this was difficult and many stubbornly refused to learn any language but their own, the Incas were so forceful that they accomplished what they had proposed, and all had to do their bidding. This was carried out so faithfully that in the space of a few years a single tongue was known and used in an extension of more than 1,200 leagues, yet, even though this language was employed, they all spoke their own [languages], which were so numerous that if I were to list them it would not be credited. . . .

As the city of Cuzco was the most important in all Peru, and the Incas lived there most of the time, they had with them in the city many of the leading men of the country, the most intelligent and informed of all, as their advisers. For all agree that before they undertook anything of importance, they discussed it with these counselors, and submitted their opinion to that of the majority. And for the administration of the city, and that the highways should be safe and nowhere should offenses or thefts be committed, from among the most highly esteemed of them he [the Inca] appointed those whose duty it was to punish wrongdoers, and to this end they were always traveling about the country. The Incas took such care to see that justice was meted out that nobody ventured to commit a felony or theft. This was to deal with thieves, ravishers of women, or conspirators against the Inca; however, there were many provinces that warred on one another, and the Incas were not wholly able to prevent this.

By the river that runs through Cuzco justice was executed on those who were caught or brought in as prisoners from some other place.

---

[4]Literally in Spanish, "big-ears." These were members of the ruling class, often of royal blood, who were distinguished by the large ear plugs they wore.

[5]The capital city of the empire.
[6]The Quechua system of record keeping by means of knotted strings that León describes later in this excerpt.

There they had their heads cut off, or were put to death in some other manner which they chose. Mutiny and conspiracy were severely punished, and, above all, those who were thieves and known as such; even their wives and children were despised and considered to be tarred with the same brush. . . .

We have written how it was ordered by the Incas that the statues be brought out at their feasts, and how they selected from the wisest among their men those who should tell what the life of their kings had been and how they had conducted themselves in the rule of their kingdoms, for the purpose I have stated. It should also be known that, aside from this, it was the custom among them, and a rule carefully observed, for each of them to choose during his reign three or four old men of their nation, skilled and gifted for that purpose, whom they ordered to recall all that had happened in the province during the time of their reign, whether prosperous or adverse, and to make and arrange songs so that thereby it might be known in the future what had taken place in the past. Such songs could not be sung or proclaimed outside the presence of the Inca, and those who were to carry out this behest were ordered to say nothing referring to the Inca during his lifetime, but after he was dead, they said to his successor almost in these words: "Oh, mighty and powerful Inca, may the Sun and Moon, the Earth, the hills and trees, the stones and your forefathers guard you from misfortune and make you prosperous, happy, and blessed among all who have been born. Know that the things that happened to your predecessor were these." And saying this, with their eyes on the ground and heads hanging, with great humility they gave an account and report of all they knew, which they could do very well, for there were many among them of great memory, subtle wit, and lively intelligence, and abounding in knowledge, as those of us who are here and hear them can bear witness. After they said this, when the Inca had heard them, he sent for other of his old Indians whom he or-

dered to learn the songs the others bore in their memory, and to prepare new ones of what took place during the time of his reign, what was spent, what the provinces contributed, and put all this down in the quipus, so that after his death, when his successor reigned, what had been given and contributed would be known. And except on days of great celebration, or on the occasion of mourning and lament for the death of a brother or son of the Inca, for on such days it was permitted to relate their grandeur and their origin and birth, at no other time was it permitted to deal with this, for it had been forbidden by their lords, and if they did so, they were severely punished.

[The Indians] had a method of knowing how the tributes of food supplies should be levied on the provinces when the Lord-Inca came through with his army, or was visiting the kingdom; or, when nothing of this sort was taking place, what came into the storehouses and what was issued to the subjects, so nobody could be unduly burdened. . . . This involved the quipus, which are long strands of knotted strings, and those who were the accountants and understood the meaning of these knots could reckon by them expenditures or other things that had taken place many years before. By these knots they counted from one to ten and from ten to a hundred, and from a hundred to a thousand. On one of these strands there is the account of one thing, and on the other of another, in such a way that what to us is a strange, meaningless account is clear to them. In the capital of each province there were accountants whom they called *quipu-camayocs,* and by these knots they kept the account of the tribute to be paid by the natives of that district in silver, gold, clothing, flocks, down to wood and other more insigificant things, and by these same quipus at the end of a year, or ten, or twenty years, they gave a report to the one whose duty it was to check the account so exact that not even a pair of sandals was missing. . . .

The *Orejones* of Cuzco who supplied me with information are in agreement that in olden times, in the days of the Lord-Incas, all the villages and provinces of Peru were notified that a report should be given to the rulers and their representatives each year of the men and women who had died, and all who had been born, for this was necessary for the levying of the tributes as well as to know how many were available for war and those who could assume the defense of the villages. This was an easy matter, for each province at the end of the year had a list by the knots of the quipus of all the people who had died there during the year, as well as of those who had been born. At the beginning of the new year they came to Cuzco, bringing their quipus, which told how many births there had been during the year, and how many deaths. This was reported with all truth and accuracy, without any fraud or deceit. In this way the Inca and the governors knew which of the Indians were poor, the women who had been widowed, whether they were able to pay their taxes, and how many men they could count on in the event of war, and many other things they considered highly important.

As this kingdom was so vast, as I have repeatedly mentioned, in each of the many provinces there were many storehouses filled with supplies and other needful things; thus, in times of war, wherever the armies went they draw upon the contents of these storehouses, without ever touching the supplies of their confederates or laying a finger on what they had in their settlements. And when there was no war, all this stock of supplies and food was divided up among the poor and the widows. These poor were the aged, or the lame, crippled, or paralyzed, or those afflicted with some other diseases; if they were in good health, they received nothing. Then the storehouses were filled up once more with the tributes paid the Inca. If there came a lean year, the storehouses were opened and the provinces were lent what they needed in the way of supplies; then, in a year of abundance, they paid back all they had received. Even though the tributes paid to the Inca were used only for the aforesaid purposes, they were employed to advantage, for in this way their kingdom was opulent and well supplied.

No one who was lazy or tried to live by the work of others was tolerated; everyone had to work. Thus on certain days each lord went to his lands and took the plow in hand and cultivated the earth, and did other things. Even the Incas themselves did this to set an example, for everybody was to know that there should be nobody so rich that, on this account, he might disdain or affront the poor. And under their system there was none such in all the kingdom, for, if he had his health, he worked and lacked for nothing; and if he was ill, he received what he needed from the storehouses. And no rich man could deck himself out in more finery than the poor, or wear different clothing, except the rulers and headmen, who, to maintain their dignity, were allowed great freedom and privilege, as well as the *Orejones,* who held a place apart among all the peoples.

Chapter 12

▼▼▼

Migrants, Merchants, and Missionaries: The Exchange and Clash of Cultures

Although Europe's late fifteenth-century transoceanic explorations inaugurated a new stage of global interconnectedness by virtue of Columbus's discovery of the Americas, in many respects the events of 1492 and following were a continuation of a process of long-range cultural exchange that had been gaining momentum throughout Eurasia and Africa since around A.D. 1000. This was due in part to the impetus provided by such peoples as the Turks, Vikings, and Mongols. Many of their travels and conquests were filled with wholesale destruction, yet these adventurers and empire builders created new pathways for the transmission of cultures between approximately 1000 and 1500.

Turkish converts to Islam spread their Muslim faith and culture into India, Anatolia (modern Turkey), the Balkan region of southeast Europe, and deeper into Central Asia as they carved out and expanded a variety of states. In less dramatic fashion, Scandinavian (also called Norse and Viking) seafarers established colonies in Iceland, Greenland, and even faraway "Vinland," in North America. Norse who had settled in France in the tenth century and become Norman French expanded the boundaries of European Christendom in the Mediterranean. During the last half of the eleventh century, Norman adventurers conquered southern Italy from the Byzantine Empire and took Sicily from its Muslim overlords. These same Normans assaulted the Balkan possessions of the emperor at Constantinople and also became part of medieval Western Europe's most energetic and protracted overseas colonial adventure — the crusades in the Levant. Of all these catalysts of cultural exchange, the most explosive and impressive were the Mongols. In the course of the thirteenth century, they created a Eurasian land empire that reached from the Pacific to Ukraine. After the initial shock of their conquests, they established a *Pax Mongolica* (Mongol Peace) that opened up lines of direct communication between East Asia and Western Europe. For about a century, people, goods, ideas, and diseases traveled fairly quickly from one end of the Eurasian land mass to the other.

As important as the conquerors and state builders were, it was the largely anonymous men and women traveling as merchants, pilgrims, missionaries, and curiosity seekers who played the most significant roles in this half millennium of long-distance travel and cultural interchange. Indian and Chinese merchants traveled into Southeast Asia, where they influenced the evolution of a hybrid culture that has been termed *Indo-Chinese*. Arabs in camel caravans trekked south across the Sahara to trade salt and manufactured goods for gold, slaves, and ivory. Italian merchants established bases in the Black Sea on the western edge of Central Asia. Pilgrims of many different faiths often traveled great distances to worship at their holy sites. Muslim and Christian missionaries, motivated by devotion and love, labored among foreign people who they believed would be damned to hell without spiritual guidance. African, Arab, Indian, Southeast Asian, Chinese, and even a few European sailors shared the waters of the Indian Ocean. Long before Columbus and da Gama, the globe was on its way toward becoming the home of an interconnected human community.

▼▼▼

Travel in the Age of the *Pax Mongolica*

Temujin (1167–1227), the Mongol lord who assumed the title Chinggis (Ghengis) Khan, or "universal lord," in 1206, believed he had a destiny to rule the world. He and his immediate successors, particularly his grandson Kubilai (1214–1294), actually came close to controlling all of Eurasia. Although the Mongols

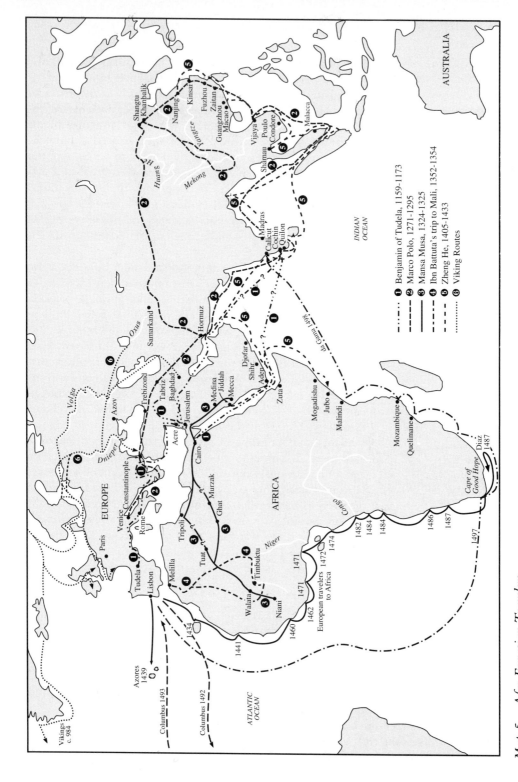

Map 5 *Afro-Eurasian Travelers,
1000–1500*

Benjamin of Tudela, 1159-1173
Marco Polo, 1271-1295
Mansa Musa, 1324-1325
Ibn Battuta's trip to Mali, 1352-1354
Zheng He, 1405-1433
Viking Routes

were stopped in Syria, in Southeast Asia, at the borders of India and Arabia, in Eastern Europe, and in the waters off Japan, by 1279 they had still managed to create the largest land empire in history.

Beginning about the time of the rule of Kubilai Khan (r. 1260–1294) and extending for more than half a century after his death, the Mongols ruled their enormous empire in relative peace and good order. Mongol discipline and organization made it possible to travel between Europe and China with a fair degree of safety and speed. Rabban Sauma (ca 1230–1294), for example, born in the Mongol capital of Khanbalik (modern Beijing) into a Nestorian Christian family of Onguts, a Turkic people from the steppes that lie west of China, set out sometime around 1278 for Jerusalem. Because of troubles in the Holy Land, he was forced to abandon his pilgrimage in Baghdad. In 1287 he accepted a commission from Arghun, Mongol il-khan (subordinate khan) of Persia, to travel to the Christian rulers of the West, bearing letters for the pope, the kings of France and England, and the emperor of Constantinople, in which the Mongol prince offered to become a Christian in return for an alliance against the Muslim Mamluk Sultans of Egypt. Arghun died before the proposed alliance could become a reality; nevertheless, the journey of this Turkish Christian monk from northern China to Constantinople, Rome, and France is but one example of the way in which the roads of Eurasia opened up in the age of Mongol dominance. Indeed, large numbers of merchants, ambassadors, fortune seekers, missionaries, and other travelers journeyed in all directions across the Mongol Empire. This steppe land-bridge between East Asia and Western Europe was severed after 1350, however, as the Mongol Empire broke up, and the opportunity for normal direct contact between the eastern and western extremities of Eurasia was lost for a century and a half.

A Summons from Chinggis Khan
▼▼▼

91 ▼ *Chinggis Khan, LETTER TO CHANGCHUN*

In 1210 the armies of Chinggis Khan captured the north Chinese city of Beijing, then the capital of the Jin Empire, which a Manchu steppe-people known as the *Jurchen* had established in northern China a century earlier. Nine years later Chinggis Khan commissioned a letter to be sent to the Daoist monk Changchun (1148–1227), bidding him to travel north to the court of the Great Khan in order to instruct him in the Way. Evidence clearly shows that Chinggis Khan desired instruction not in the Dao of saintly wisdom but in the way of achieving physical immortality. Changchun was the early thirteenth century's most famous master of the "Golden Lotus" sect of Daoism, whose members devoted themselves to searching in the spiritual world for the *dan*, a magical entity that contained the secret to everlasting life.

Despite his advanced age, Changchun traveled to Beijing in 1220, accompanied by nineteen disciples. When he arrived at the northern capital (the literal meaning of *Beijing*), Changchun learned that the Great Khan had left, in order to campaign in the West. Changchun and his disciples then set out to catch up with Chinggis Khan, finally reaching him in Afghanistan in May 1222. After instructing the Great Khan in "the ways of preserving life," Changchun received leave to return to China in April 1223, arriving back in Beijing in January 1224. There he settled down in a monastery provided for him by the Mongol khan and died on 23 July 1227, ironically the same month and year in which Chinggis Khan died.

The letter that initiated this series of adventures for Changchun was not actually written by Chinggis Khan, since he was illiterate. In all likelihood, one of the khan's Chinese advisers composed it, using traditional Chinese modes of expression and thought to communicate the Mongol leader's general ideas.

QUESTIONS FOR ANALYSIS

1. What traditional Chinese idioms and ways of thought do you find in this letter? In addressing this question, refer to source 6 of Chapter 1, and sources 24 and 25 of Chapter 4.
2. Notwithstanding these Chinese adornments, can you find any elements that appear to be distinctly "Mongol"?
3. On the basis of your answer to question 2, what would you say was the Mongol self-image?
4. What does the Great Khan's vision seem to be?
5. How does he propose to achieve it?
6. Can you find any evidence in this document that allows you to infer that Chinggis Khan saw himself as more than just a successful warlord of the steppes?

Heaven has abandoned China owing to its arrogance and extravagant luxury. But I, living in the northern wilderness, do not have inordinate passions. I have only one coat and one food. I eat the same food and am dressed in the same rags as my humble herdsmen. I consider the people my children and take an interest in talented men as though they were my brothers. We always agree in our principles, and we are always united by mutual affection. At military exercises I am always in the forefront, and in battle I am never in the rear. In the space of seven years I have accomplished a great work, uniting the whole world in one empire. I do not myself possess extraordinary qualities. However, the regime of the Jin is inconstant, and therefore Heaven assists me in obtaining the Jin throne. The Song to the south,[1] . . .

---

[1]See Chapter 9, source 72.

the Xi-Xia to the east,[2] and the barbarians in the west, have all acknowledged my supremacy.[3] It seems to me that such a vast empire has not been seen since the remote time of our ancestral khans.

But insofar as my calling is high, the obligations incumbent upon me are also heavy, and I fear that in my governance there might be something lacking. To cross a river we construct boats and rudders. Likewise we invite sage men, and choose assistants, to keep an empire in good order. Ever since I came to the throne, I have constantly taken to heart the ruling of my people, but I could not find worthy individuals to occupy the offices of the three and nine.[4] With respect to these circumstances, I inquired and heard that you, Master, have penetrated the truth, and that you walk in the way of right. Deeply learned and well experienced, you have greatly explored the laws. Your holiness is evident. You have conserved the rigorous rules of the ancient sages. You are endowed with the eminent talents of celebrated men. For a long time you have lived in rocky caverns and have retired from the world. Yet people who have themselves acquired sanctity flock to you in innumerable multitudes, like

clouds on the paths of the immortals. I knew that after the war[5] you had continued to live in Shandong,[6] at the same place, and I constantly thought of you. I know the stories of returning from the Wei River in the same cart and of the thrice-repeated invitations in the reed hut.[7] But what shall I do? We are separated by mountains and plains of great extent, and I cannot meet you. I can only descend from the throne and stand to the side.[8] I have fasted and washed.[9] I have ordered my adjutant, Liu Zhonglu,[10] to prepare an escort and cart for you.[11] Do not be afraid of the thousand *li*.[12] I implore you to move your sainted steps. Do not think of the extent of the sandy desert. Show pity for the people in the present state of affairs, or have pity on me, and communicate to me the means of preserving life. I shall personally serve you. I hope that you will at least leave me a trifle of your wisdom. Say but a single word to me and I will be happy.

In this letter I have briefly expressed my thoughts, and hope also that you, having penetrated the principles of the Great Dao, are in sympathy with all that is right and will not resist the wishes of the people. Dated: the first day of the fifth month (15 May 1219).

---

[2]A Tangut, or proto-Tibetan, people. See Chapter 5, source 35.

[3]Although the Southern Song at first allied with the Mongols in attacking their common enemy, the Jin, they in turn were attacked by the Mongols following the total collapse of the Jin in 1234. Song resistance was so spirited that the Mongols did not totally conquer southern China until 1279.

[4]The emperor's three chief councillors, known as the *gong*, and the heads of the nine different imperial ministries.

[5]In which the Mongols conquered the northern regions of the Jin Empire.

[6]A peninsula and province in northeast China, it had been part of the Jin Empire.

[7]These are allusions to two celebrated examples in Chinese history of sages who had been summoned to high office. The twelfth-century B.C. Zhou prince Wenwang found an old man fishing in the Wei River. His conversation proved so wise that the prince entreated him to enter his service as a minister and took him back to court in his own cart. The other story involves Zhu

Geliang, whom Liu Bei, founder of the Shu-Han Dynasty that ruled western China during the Age of the Three Kingdoms (221–265), sought out in A.D. 207 and found inhabiting a reed hut. Only after repeated entreaties did Zhu Geliang consent to leave his hermitage.

[8]A hyperbolic suggestion that he, Chinggis Khan, could step aside and allow Changchun to govern.

[9]A Chinese metaphor of politeness, meaning that the host has properly prepared himself to receive an honored guest.

[10]A deserter from the Jin army who entered Chinggis Khan's service.

[11]Traditionally, Chinese kings and emperors sent carts for the sages whom they invited to serve them.

[12]A *li* is a bit more than a third of a mile.

Mongol Culture
▼▼▼

92 ▼ William of Rubruck, *JOURNEY TO THE LAND OF THE TARTARS*

Between 1236 and 1241, Mongol forces under the command of Batu, grandson of Chinggis Khan, overran a number of Christian states in East Europe and even briefly reached the Adriatic Sea. As word of the devastations wrought by the Mongols reached Western Europe, the West's level of anxiety rose appreciably. Although the Mongol westward advance was stopped in 1241 by the sudden death of Ogodei (r. 1229–1241), Chinggis Khan's son and successor as Great Khan, there was no guarantee that the Mongols would not soon resume their assault on European Christendom.

It was in that context that, beginning in 1245, the Roman papacy initiated a series of embassies to various Mongol khans in order to discover their designs regarding Western Europe and to convert them to Catholic Christianity. The hope was that if the Mongols became Christians, they would join the West in crushing Islam in a final, glorious crusade. This double dream of conversion and crusade never became a reality, but it did initiate a century of Roman Catholic relations with the Mongols and involvement by a number of extraordinary Franciscan and Dominican friars in the mission fields of Central and East Asia. One such missionary, John of Monte Corvino (1247–ca 1328), arrived in Beijing in 1295, where he set up a Catholic church that lasted until 1369 when the Ming Dynasty (1368–1644) expelled Christians from the northern capital in a fit of xenophobia (fear of foreigners).

One of John of Monte Corvino's more illustrious predecessors to East Asia was Brother William of Rubruck, a Franciscan missionary to the Great Khan. Between May 1253 and June 1255, Friar William traveled from Constantinople to the court of Mongke Khan (r. 1251–1259) at Karakorum in Mongolia and then returned to the eastern Mediterranean. William's mission failed to convert the Great Khan but did result in a report that he submitted to King Louis IX of France of his adventures and observations while among the Mongols. An exceptionally observant individual, Brother William provides us with one of the most detailed accounts of thirteenth-century Mongol society.

QUESTIONS FOR ANALYSIS

1. Mongol religion is generally categorized as *shamanistic*. Based on what Rubruck tells us about their religious practices, what do you think this term means?
2. Many people think of nomads as wanderers who aimlessly travel about with their herds. What evidence does Rubruck provide to refute this misconception?

3. Consider the Mongols' attitude toward thunder. Why do you think these people of the steppes so feared it?
4. How would you characterize the status of women relative to men? In addressing this issue, consider the respective tasks of women and men and Mongol marriage customs.
5. On the basis of this account, how would you characterize Mongol society in the mid-thirteenth century?
6. In his letter to Changchun, Chinggis Khan contrasted Chinese ways of life with those of the Mongols. What was his point, and does William of Rubruck's account support that position?

THE TARTARS[1] AND THEIR DWELLINGS

The Tartars have no abiding city. . . . Each captain, according to whether he has more or fewer men under him, knows the limits of his pasturage and where to feed his flocks in winter, summer, spring, and autumn, for in winter they come down to the warmer districts in the south, in summer they go up to the cooler ones in the north. They drive their cattle to graze on the pasture lands without water in winter when there is snow there, for the snow provides them with water.

The dwelling in which they sleep has as its base a circle of interlaced sticks, and it is made of the same material; these sticks converge into a little circle at the top and from this a neck juts up like a chimney; they cover it with white felt and quite often they also coat the felt with lime or white clay and powdered bone to make it a more gleaming white, and sometimes they make it black. The felt round the neck at the top they decorate with lovely and varied paintings. Before the doorway they also hang felt worked in multicolored designs; they sew colored felt onto the other, making vines and trees, birds, and animals. They make these

houses so large that sometimes they are thirty feet across. . . .

In addition they make squares to the size of a large coffer out of slender split twigs; then over it, from one end to the other, they build up a rounded roof out of similar twigs and they make a little entrance at the front end; after that they cover this box or little house with black felt soaked in tallow or ewes' milk so that it is rain-proof, and this they decorate in the same way with multicolored handwork. Into these chests they put all their bedding and valuables; they bind them onto high carts which are drawn by camels so that they can cross rivers. These chests are never removed from the carts. When they take down their dwelling houses, they always put the door facing the south. . . .

The married women make for themselves really beautiful carts which I would not know how to describe for you except by a picture; in fact I would have done you paintings of everything if I only knew how to paint. A wealthy Mongol or Tartar may well have a hundred or two hundred such carts with chests. Baatu[2] has twenty-six wives and each of these has a large house, not counting the other small ones which are placed behind the large one and which are, as it were, chambers in which their attendants

---

[1]Westerners mistakenly called the Mongols *Tartars,* a corruption of *Tatars,* the name of a tribe of steppe nomads who dwelled near the Mongols. Tartar seems to have been a deliberate pun. The classical Latin name for hell was *Tartarus*; hence, the Mongols were the "devil's horsemen."

[2]Baatu or Batu (d. 1255/1256), grandson of Chinggis Khan and founder of the Golden Horde, the group of Mongols that conquered and ruled Russia.

live; belonging to each of these houses are a good two hundred carts. When they pitch their houses the chief wife places her dwelling at the extreme west end and after her the others according to their rank, so that the last wife will be at the far east end, and there will be the space of a stone's throw between the establishment of one wife and that of another. And so the orda[3] of a rich Mongol will look like a large town and yet there will be very few men in it.

One woman will drive twenty or thirty carts, for the country is flat. They tie together the carts, which are drawn by oxen or camels, one after the other, and the woman will sit on the front one driving the ox while all the others follow in step. If they happen to come on a bad bit of track they loose them and lead them across it one by one. They go at a very slow pace, as a sheep or an ox might walk.

When they have pitched their houses with the door facing south, they arrange the master's couch at the northern end. The women's place is always on the east side, that is, on the left of the master of the house when he is sitting on his couch looking toward the south; the men's place is on the west side, that is, to his right.

On entering a house the men would by no means hang up their quiver in the women's section. Over the head of the master there is always an idol like a doll or little image of felt which they call the master's brother, and a similar one over the head of the mistress, and this they call the mistress's brother; they are fastened on to the wall. Higher up between these two is a thin little one which is, as it were, the guardian of the whole house. The mistress of the house places on her right side, at the foot of the couch, in a prominent position, a goatskin stuffed with wool or other material, and next to it a tiny image turned toward her attendants and the women. By the entrance on the women's side is still another idol with a cow's udder for the women who milk the cows, for this is the women's job. On the other side of the door toward the men is another image with a mare's udder for the men who milk the mares.

When they have foregathered for a drink they first sprinkle with the drink the idol over the master's head, then all the other idols in turn; after this an attendant goes out of the house with a cup and some drinks; he sprinkles thrice toward the south, genuflecting each time; this is in honor of fire; next toward the east in honor of the air, and after that to the west in honor of water; they cast it to the north for the dead. When the master is holding his cup in his hand and is about to drink, before he does so he first pours some out on the earth as its share. If he drinks while seated on a horse, before he drinks he pours some over the neck or mane of the horse. And so when the attendant has sprinkled toward the four quarters of the earth he returns into the house; two servants with two cups and as many plates are ready to carry the drink to the master and the wife sitting beside him upon his couch. If he has several wives, she with whom he sleeps at night sits next to him during the day, and on that day all the others have to come to her dwelling to drink, and the court is held there, and the gifts which are presented to the master are placed in the treasury of that wife. Standing in the entrance is a bench with a skin of milk or some other drink and some cups.

In the winter they make an excellent drink from rice, millet, wheat, and honey, which is clear like wine. Wine, too, is conveyed to them from distant regions. In the summer they do not bother about anything except cosmos.[4] Cosmos is always to be found inside the house before the entrance door, and near it stands a musician with his instrument. Our lutes and viols I did not see there but many other instruments such as are not known among us. When the master begins to drink, then one of the attendants cries out in a loud voice "Ha!" and the

---

[3]Orda is a Turkic word meaning "camp," from which we derive the word "horde."

[4]More correctly qumiz, the Mongols' favorite alcoholic drink that they fermented from mares' milk.

musician strikes his instrument. And when it is a big feast they are holding, they all clap their hands and also dance to the sound of the instrument, the men before the master and the women before the mistress. After the master has drunk, then the attendant cries out as before and the instrument-player breaks off. Then they drink all round, the men and the women, and sometimes vie with each other in drinking in a really disgusting and gluttonous manner. . . .

THE FOOD OF THE TARTARS

As for their food and victuals I must tell you they eat all dead animals indiscriminately and with so many flocks and herds you can be sure a great many animals do die. However, in the summer as long as they have any cosmos, that is mare's milk, they do not care about any other food. If during that time an ox or a horse happens to die, they dry the flesh by cutting it into thin strips and hanging it in the sun and the wind, and it dries immediately without salt and without any unpleasant smell. Out of the intestines of horses they make sausages which are better than pork sausages and they eat these fresh; the rest of the meat they keep for the winter. From the hide of oxen they make large jars which they dry in a wonderful way in the smoke. From the hind part of horses' hide they make very nice shoes.

They feed fifty or a hundred men with the flesh of a single sheep, for they cut it up in little bits in a dish with salt and water, making no other sauce; then with the point of a knife or a fork especially made for this purpose — like those with which we are accustomed to eat pears and apples cooked in wine — they offer to each of those standing round one or two mouthfuls, according to the number of guests. Before the flesh of the sheep is served, the master first takes what pleases him; and also if he gives anyone a special portion then the one re-

ceiving it has to eat it himself and may give it to no one else. But if he cannot eat it all he may take it away with him or give it to his servant, if he is there, to keep for him; otherwise he may put it away in his *captargac,* that is, a square bag which they carry to put all such things in: in this they also keep bones when they have not the time to give them a good gnaw, so that later they may gnaw them and no food be wasted.

THE DUTIES OF THE WOMEN AND THEIR WORK

It is the duty of the women to drive the carts, to load the houses onto them and to unload them, to milk the cows, to make the butter and *grut,*[5] to dress the skins and to sew them, which they do with thread made out of tendons. They split the tendons into very thin threads and then twist these into one long thread. They also sew shoes and socks and other garments. They never wash their clothes, for they say that that makes God angry and that it would thunder if they hung them out to dry; they even beat those who do wash them and take them away from them. They are extraordinarily afraid of thunder. At such a time they turn all strangers out of their dwellings and wrap themselves in black felt in which they hide until it has passed over. They never wash their dishes, but when the meat is cooked, they wash out the bowl in which they are going to put it with some boiling broth from the cauldron which they afterwards pour back. The women also make the felt and cover the houses.

The men make bows and arrows, manufacture stirrups and bits and make saddles; they build the houses and carts, they look after the horses and milk the mares, churn the cosmos, that is the mares' milk, and make the skins in which it is kept, and they also look after the camels and load them. Both sexes look after the sheep and goats, and sometimes the men, sometimes the women, milk them. They dress

---

[5]A sour curd cheese.

skins with the sour milk of ewes, thickened and salted.

When they want to wash their hands or their head, they fill their mouth with water and, pouring this little by little from their mouth into their hands, with it they wet their hair and wash their head.

As for their marriages, you must know that no one there has a wife unless he buys her, which means that sometimes girls are quite grown up before they marry, for their parents always keep them until they sell them. They observe the first and second degrees of consanguinity,[6] but observe no degrees of affinity; they have two sisters at the same time or one after the other. No widow among them marries, the reason being that they believe that all those who serve them in this life will serve them in the next, and so of a widow they believe that she will always return after death to her first husband. This gives rise to a shameful custom among them whereby a son sometimes takes to wife all his father's wives, except his own mother; for the orda of a father and mother always falls to the youngest son[7] and so he himself has to provide for all his father's wives who come to him with his father's effects; and then, if he so wishes, he uses them as wives, for he does not consider an injury has been done to him if they return to his father after death.

And so when anyone has made an agreement with another to take his daughter, the father of the girl arranges a feast and she takes flight to relations where she lies hid. Then the father declares: "Now my daughter is yours; take her wherever you find her." Then he searches for her with his friends until he finds her; then he has to take her by force and bring her, as though by violence, to his house.

Another View of Mongol Society
▼▼▼

93 ▼ Marco Polo, DESCRIPTION OF THE WORLD

No chapter on trans-Eurasian travel in the Mongol Age would be complete without a selection from Marco Polo (ca 1253–1324), a Venetian who spent twenty years in East Asia, most of it in the service of Kubilai Khan. Around 1260 Marco's father and uncle, Niccoló and Maffeo, both merchants from Venice, set sail for the Black Sea and from there made an overland trek to Khanbalik and the court of Kubilai. When they were preparing to return home, the Great Khan requested that they visit the pope and ask him to send one hundred missionary-scholars to Cathay. The Polos arrived at the crusader port of Acre (in modern Israel) in 1269 and in 1271 received a commission from Pope Gregory X (r. 1271–1276) to return to China with two Dominican friars. The two friars quickly abandoned the expedition, afraid of the dangers that awaited them, but

---

[6]Siblings and first cousins are prohibited from marrying one another.
[7]The youngest son of his chief wife.

Niccoló's seventeen-year-old son, Marco, was made of sterner stuff. The brothers Polo, now accompanied by young Marco, returned to Khanbalik. Here Marco entered the khan's service and for close to two decades traveled extensively over much of Kubilai's empire as one of the many foreign officials serving the Mongol, or Yuan, Dynasty (1264–1368).

In 1292 the three men set sail for the West by way of the Indian Ocean and arrived home in Venice in 1295. In 1298 Marco was captured in a war with Genoa and, while in prison, related his adventures to a writer of romances known as Rustichello of Pisa. Together they produced a rambling, often disjointed account of the sites, peoples, personalities, and events Marco had encountered in Asia.

Despite its literary flaws, the book was widely translated and distributed throughout late medieval Europe. Its popularity was due in part to Marco's eye for ethnographic detail, as the book abounds with stories of customs that Westerners found fascinatingly different. In the following selections Polo, like Rubruck, tells his audience about Mongol culture.

Historical research generally consists of sifting through large amounts of textual evidence and comparing partial, and often conflicting, accounts of an event in the hope of arriving at a reasonably true reconstruction of the past. No single source ever gives us a complete and unbiased view of what we are studying. Polo's and Rubruck's descriptions of Mongol society, when studied together, allow us to test each other's worth. They also provide evidence of some of the continuities and changes in Mongol society over the last half of the thirteenth century.

QUESTIONS FOR ANALYSIS

1. Draw two columns. In one, list all the significant details regarding Mongol culture provided by Rubruck. In the other, list those provided by Polo. Where are they in agreement? Are there any significant disagreements? What details are provided by only one witnesss?
2. Consider the points on which they seem to differ. Assuming each is an honest and observant reporter, how do you explain those differences?
3. Based on the exercise you have just done, what can you say with confidence about thirteenth-century Mongol culture?
4. Based on your reading of all three sources (Chinggis Khan, Rubruck, and Polo), what would you conclude were the factors that contributed to the Mongols' success in forging and governing their empire?
5. Toward the end of his account, Polo provides a hint of one of the factors that would lead to the breakup of the Mongol Empire. What is it?
6. Do the Mongols seem to have changed significantly over the course of the latter half of the thirteenth century?

It is their custom that the bodies of all deceased grand khans and other great lords from the family of Chinggis Khan are carried for internment to a great mountain called Altai.[1] No matter where they might die, even if it is a hundred days' journey away, they nevertheless are brought here for burial. It is also their custom that, in the process of conveying the bodies of these princes, the escort party sacrifices whatever persons they happen to meet along the route, saying to them: "Depart for the next world and there serve your deceased master." They believe that all whom they kill in this manner will become his servants in the next life. They do the same with horses, killing all the best, so that the dead lord might use them in the next world. When the corpse of Mongke Khan[2] was transported to this mountain, the horsemen who accompanied it slew upward of 20,000 people along the way.

Now that I have begun speaking about the Tartars, I will tell you more about them. They never remain fixed in one location. As winter approaches they move to the plains of a warmer region in order to find sufficient pasturage for their animals. In summer they inhabit cool regions in the mountains where there is water and grass and their animals are free of the annoyance of gad-flies and other biting insects. They spend two or three months progressively climbing higher and grazing as they ascend, because the grass is not sufficient in any one spot to feed their extensive herds.

Their huts, or tents, are circular and formed by covering a wooden frame with felt. These they transport on four-wheeled carts wherever they travel, since the framework is so well put together that it is light to carry. Whenever they set their huts up, the entrance always faces south. They also have excellent two-wheeled vehicles so well covered with black felt that, no matter how long it rains, rain never penetrates.

These are drawn by oxen and camels and serve to carry their wives, children, and all necessary utensils and provisions.

It is the women who tend to their commercial concerns, buying and selling, and who tend to all the needs of their husbands and households. The men devote their time totally to hunting, hawking, and warfare. They have the best falcons in the world, as well as the best dogs. They subsist totally on meat and milk, eating the produce of their hunting, especially a certain small animal, somewhat like a hare, which our people call Pharaoh's rats,[3] which are abundant on the steppes in summer. They likewise eat every manner of animal: horses, camels, even dogs, provided they are fat. They drink mare's milk, which they prepare in such a way that it has the qualities and taste of white wine. In their language they call it *kemurs*.[4]

Their women are unexcelled in the world so far as their chastity and decency of conduct are concerned, and also in regard to their love and devotion toward their husbands. They regard marital infidelity as a vice which is not simply dishonorable but odious by its very nature. Even if there are ten or twenty women in a household, they live in harmony and highly praiseworthy concord, so that no offensive word is ever spoken. They devote full attention to their tasks and domestic duties, such as preparing the family's food, managing the servants, and caring for the children, whom they raise in common. The wives' virtues of modesty and chastity are all the more praiseworthy because the men are allowed to wed as many women as they please. The expense to the husband for his wives is not that great, but the benefit he derives from their trading and from the work in which they are constantly employed is considerable. For this reason, when he marries he pays a dowry to his wife's parents. The first wife holds the primary place in the household and is

---

[1]The Altai Mountain range is in eastern Mongolia.
[2]Mongke, or Mangu, ruled as Great Khan from 1251 to 1259.

[3]The brown marmot, a burrowing rodent of the steppes.
[4]*Qumiz*. See note 4 for source 92.

reckoned to be the husband's most legitimate wife, and this status extends to her children. Because of their unlimited number of wives, their offspring is more numerous than that of any other people. When a father dies, his son may take all of his deceased father's wives, with the exception of his own mother. They also cannot marry their sisters, but upon a brother's death they may marry their sisters-in-law. Every marriage is solemnized with great ceremony.

This is what they believe. They believe in an exalted god of heaven, to whom they burn incense and offer up prayers for sound mind and body. They also worship a god called Natigay, whose image, covered with felt or other cloth, is kept in everyone's house. They associate a wife and children with this god, placing the wife on his left side and the children before him. . . . They consider Natigay as the god who presides over their earthly concerns, protecting their children, their cattle, and their grain. They show him great respect. Before eating they always take a fat portion of meat and smear the idol's mouth with it, as well as the mouths of his wife and children. Then they take some of the broth in which the meat has been cooked and pour it outside, as an offering. When this has been done they believe that their god and his family have had their proper share. The Tartars then proceed to eat and drink without further ceremony.

The rich among these people dress in gold cloth and silks and the furs of sable, ermine, and other animals. All their accouterments are expensive.

Their weapons are bows, iron maces, and in some instances, spears. The bow, however, is the weapon at which they are the most expert, being accustomed to use it in their sports from childhood. They wear armor made from the hides of buffalo and other beasts, fire-dried and thus hard and strong.

They are brave warriors, almost to the point of desperation, placing little value on their lives, and exposing themselves without hesita-

tion to every sort of danger. They are cruel by nature. They are capable of undergoing every manner of privation, and when it is necessary, they can live for a month on the milk of their mares and the wild animals they catch. Their horses feed on grass alone and do not require barley or other grain. The men are trained to remain on horseback for two days and two nights without dismounting, sleeping in the saddle while the horse grazes. No people on the earth can surpass them in their ability to endure hardships, and no other people shows greater patience in the face of every sort of deprivation. They are most obedient to their chiefs, and are maintained at small expense. These qualities, which are so essential to a soldier's formation, make them fit to subdue the world, which in fact they have largely done.

When one of the great Tartar chiefs goes to war, he puts himself at the head of an army of 100,000 horsemen and organizes them in the following manner. He appoints an officer to command every ten men and others to command groups of 100, 1,000, and 10,000 men respectively. Thus ten of the officers who command ten men take their orders from an officer who commands 100; ten of these captains of a 100 take their orders from an officer in charge of a 1,000; and ten of these officers take orders from one who commands 10,000. By this arrangement, each officer has to manage only ten men or ten bodies of men. . . . When the army goes into the field, a body of 200 men is sent two days' march in advance, and parties are stationed on each flank and in the rear, to prevent surprise attack.

When they are setting out on a long expedition, they carry little with them. . . . They subsist for the most part on mare's milk, as has been said. . . . Should circumstances require speed, they can ride for ten days without lighting a fire or taking a hot meal. During this time they subsist on the blood drawn from their horses, each man opening a vein and drinking the blood. They also have dried milk. . . . When setting off on an expedition, each man takes about ten pounds. Every morning they put about half a pound of this into a leather flask, with as much water as necessary. As they ride, the motion violently shakes the contents, producing a thin porridge which they take as dinner. . . .

All that I have told you here concerns the original customs of the Tartar lords. Today, however, they are corrupted. Those who live in China have adopted the customs of the idol worshippers,[5] and those who inhabit the eastern provinces have adopted the ways of the Muslims.

Khmer Society in Chinese Eyes
▼▼▼

94 ▼ Zhou Daguan, *RECOLLECTIONS OF THE CUSTOMS OF CAMBODIA*

The Yuan emperors of China used foreign-born officials, such as Marco Polo, because of the high degree of mutual distrust and antipathy that existed between the old Confucian governing class and their new Mongol lords, but many Chinese did serve the Mongols faithfully. Among them was Zhou Daguan (d. after 1346), who spent nearly a year in the Khmer kingdom of Cambodia as a high-ranking member of an embassy sent by Kubilai Khan to secure the Cambodians' recognition of his overlordship.

When the successful legation returned home in 1297, Zhou Daguan set down his impressions of this land and its people. Although he modestly noted that, "It goes without saying that the customs and the activities of the country cannot be completely known in so short a time," he was able to provide posterity with the single best contemporary account of Khmer society at the height of its cultural brilliance. In the following selections Zhou describes the land's cultural divisions, its economic activities, and the ceremony that attended the Khmer king.

QUESTIONS FOR ANALYSIS

1. According to Zhou, what kinds of hill people inhabited the regions outside of Cambodia's centers of civilization, and what was their relationship with town and village dwellers?

---

[5]Buddhists.

2. What other divisions existed within Khmer society?
3. What sort of market economy did Cambodia have? What were its major items of export and import? How would you characterize its trade with China?
4. From Zhou's perspective, why did Cambodia seem so "barbarous and strange"?
5. What does the evidence allow you to infer about Cambodia's overall relations with China?
6. Based on Zhou's description of royal ceremony, how would you characterize Khmer kingship?
7. Overall, what picture emerges of late thirteenth-century Cambodia from these selections?

THE SAVAGES

There are two kinds of savages: those who know the language and are sold as slaves; the other are those who do not understand the language and could not adapt themselves to civilization. The latter have no permanent dwelling places, but, followed by their families, wander in the mountains carrying their few provisions in clay jars on their heads. If they find a wild animal, they will kill it with spears or bows and arrows, make a fire by striking stones together, cook the animal, eat it in common, and continue their wandering. Ferocious by nature, they use deadly poisons. Within their own band, they often kill one another. In recent times a few have started cultivating cardamom and cotton and weaving a cloth that is coarse and irregularly patterned.

SLAVES

Savages are brought to do the work of servants. When they are young and strong, they fetch a hundred pieces of cloth; old and weak, from thiry to forty. Wealthy families may have more than a hundred; even those of modest means have ten or twenty; only the poor have none at

all. The savages inhabit the wild mountains and belong to a different race; they are called *zhuangs*, thieves. If, in a quarrel, a man calls another a *zhuang*, it is a deadly insult, so despised are the savages, who are considered to be subhuman. Brought to the city, they never dare appear on the street. They are forced to live in the space under the houses which are built on stilts and when they come up into the house to do their work, they must first kneel and make the proper obeisance, prostrating themselves before they can advance. They call their owners "father" and "mother." If they make a mistake, they are beaten. They take their punishment with bent head and without making the slightest movement.

THE LANGUAGE

This country has its own language. Even though the sounds are fairly similar, the people of Champa[1] and of Siam[2] do not understand it. . . . The officials have an official style for their deliberations; the scholars[3] speak in a literary manner; the Buddhist monks and Daoist priests[4] have their own language; and different villages speak differently. It is absolutely the same as in China.

---

[1]Central Vietnam.
[2]Thailand.
[3]These so-called scholars were probably brahmin priests.
[4]Probably priests of Shiva and not Daoists.

PRODUCTS

Many strange trees are found in the mountains and in the clearings, herds of rhinoceros and elephants live, rare birds and many unusual animals are to be found. The most precious articles are the feathers of the kingfisher (valued in Canton to ornament gold jewelry), ivory, rhinoceros horn, and beeswax; cardamom and other forest products are more common.

The kingfisher is quite difficult to catch. In the thick woods are ponds and in the ponds are fish. The kingfisher leaves the forest to catch fish. Hidden under the leaves, by the side of the water, the Cambodian crouches. In a cage he has a female bird to attract the male and in his hand a small net. He waits until the bird comes and then catches him in his net. Some days he can catch as many as five; other days he waits vainly for a kingfisher.

Ivory is collected by the hill people. From a dead elephant one secures two tusks. Formerly it was thought that the elephant shed his tusks every year; this is not true. The ivory taken from an animal killed by a spear is the best. Then comes that which is found shortly after the animal has died a natural death; the least valued is that which is found in the mountains years after the death of the elephant.

Beeswax is found in rotted trees standing in the villages. It is produced by winged insects that have thin antlike waists. The Cambodians take it away from the insects; a boatload can carry from two to three thousand honeycombs.

Rhinoceros horn that is white and veined is the most valued; the black variety is of inferior quality.

Cardamom is cultivated in the mountains by the savages. Pepper is also found occasionally. It climbs up bushes and entwines itself like a common weed. The green-blue variety is the most bitter.

TRADE

In Cambodia, women attend to trade. Even a Chinese who arrives there and takes a woman will profit greatly from her trading abilities. They do not have permanent stores, but simply spread a piece of mat on the ground. Everyone has her own spot. I have heard that they pay an official for the right to a location. In small transactions, one pays in rice, grain, Chinese goods, and, lastly, fabrics; in large transactions they use gold and silver.

In a general way, the country people are very naïve. When they see a Chinese, they address him timidly, respectfully, calling him Fo — Buddha. As soon as they catch sight of him, they throw themselves on the ground and prostrate themselves. Lately some of them have cheated the Chinese and harmed them. This has happened to numbers of those who have gone into the villages.

CHINESE MERCHANDISE DESIRED IN CAMBODIA

I do not think that Cambodia produces either gold or silver; and what the Cambodians value most is Chinese silver and gold, then silks, lightly patterned in two-toned threads. After these items comes the pewter of Zhenzhou, lacquerware from Wenzhou, the blue porcelain of Quanzhou, mercury, vermilion, paper, sulphur, saltpeter, sandalwood, irisroot, musk, hemp cloth, umbrellas, iron pots, copper platters, sieves, wood combs, and needles. That which they desire most of all is beans and wheat — but their exportation is forbidden.

THE ARMY

The troops go naked and barefoot. They hold a lance in their right hand and a shield in their left. The Cambodians have neither bows nor arrows, war machines nor bullets, helmets nor armor. It is said that in the war against the Siamese everyone was obliged to fight, but they had no knowledge of tactics or strategy.

THE PRINCE'S APPEARANCES IN PUBLIC

When the king leaves the palace, first comes the cavalry, leading his escort, followed by an array of standards, banners, and music. Next comes a troupe of palace girls, anywhere from three to five hundred, dressed in flowered material, their heads garlanded with flowers and holding large candles lighted even in broad daylight. After them come more palace girls bearing the royal utensils of gold and silver and an assortment of all kinds of ornaments whose usage I don't understand. Then come the palace girls who, armed with lance and shield, form the king's private bodyguard; they, too, form a troupe. They are followed by carriages ornamented in gold and drawn by goats and horses. Ministers and nobles mounted on elephants look straight ahead, while clustered around them are their many, many red parasols of rank. After them in palanquins, carriages, and on elephants come the king's wives and concubines; they have more than a hundred parasols decorated in gold. Behind them comes the king. Holding the precious sword, he stands on the royal elephant, whose tusks are encased in gold. More than twenty white parasols, gold-trimmed and with golden handles, surround him. A great many elephants form a cordon around the king and the cavalry guards him. . . .

Twice each day the king holds an audience to conduct the affairs of government. There is no set procedure. Whoever desires to see the king — either officials or any private person — sits on the ground and awaits him. After a little while, one hears, far off in the palace, distant music; outside they blow on conchs to announce his approach. I have heard that he uses only a gold palanquin and does not come from very far away. An instant later, two palace girls lift the curtain on the Golden Window and the king, sword in his hand, appears. All those present — ministers and people — clasp their hands together and beat their foreheads on the ground. As the sound of the conchs ceases, they can raise their heads. At the king's pleasure, they may approach and sit down on a lion skin, which is considered a royal object. When all matters are disposed of, the king retires, the two palace girls let the curtain fall; everyone rises. Thus one sees that, though this country is barbarous and strange, they do not fail to know what it is to be a king.

Advice for Merchants Traveling to Cathay
▼▼▼

95 ▼ *Francesco Pegolotti,* THE BOOK OF DESCRIPTIONS OF COUNTRIES

Around 1340 Francesco Balducci Pegolotti, an otherwise unknown agent of the Florentine banking house of the Bardi, composed a handbook of practical advice for merchants. Pegolotti, who had served the Bardi family's interests from London to Cyprus, drew upon his years of mercantile experience to produce a work filled with lists of facts and figures on such items as local business customs, the taxes and tariffs of various localities, and the relative values of different standards of weights, measures, and coinage. In other words, the book contained just about everything a prudent merchant would want to know before entering a new market. In addition to these catalogues of useful data, Pegolotti included a short essay of advice for merchants bound for China.

QUESTIONS FOR ANALYSIS

1. What evidence is there that Pegolotti himself had not traveled the steppe route to Cathay? Considering that his advice is not based on firsthand experience, how knowledgeable does he appear to be on the subject, and what does this suggest?
2. Consider Pegolotti's advice regarding the types of interpreters the merchant will need. What language skills suffice to carry on this trans-Eurasian business enterprise? What does this suggest about the markets of northern China?
3. When and where could the trip be especially hazardous? What does this suggest about the *Pax Mongolica*?
4. What overall impression does Pegolotti give us of this journey and its rewards?

THINGS NEEDFUL FOR MERCHANTS WHO DESIRE TO MAKE THE JOURNEY TO CATHAY[1]

In the first place, you must let your beard grow long and not shave. And at Tana[2] you should furnish yourself with a dragoman.[3] And you must not try to save money in the matter of dragomen by taking a bad one instead of a good one. For the additional wages of the good one will not cost you so much as you will save by having him. And besides the dragoman it will be well to take at least two good menser-vants, who are acquainted with the Cumanian[4] tongue. And if the merchant likes to take a woman with him from Tana, he can do so; if he does not like to take one there is no obligation, only if he does take one he will be kept much more comfortably than if he does not take one. Howbeit, if he does take one, it will be well that she be acquainted with the Cumanian tongue as well as the men.

And from Tana traveling to Gittarchan[5] you should take with you twenty-five days' provisions, that is to say, flour and salt fish, for as to meat you will find enough of it at all the places

---

[1]China under the Yuan emperors. The name *Cathay* is derived from the Khitan Tatars, whose state of Liao in northwest China flourished from 946 to 1125. They were the first power to transform Beijing into a capital city.
[2]The modern city of Azov on the northeast coast of the Sea of Azov, which itself is an extension of the Black Sea. Tana was the easternmost point to which a person could sail from the Mediterranean.

[3]An interpreter fluent in Arabic, Persian, or Turkish.
[4]A Turkic people inhabiting the middle Volga.
[5]Modern Astrakhan, a city in the Volga delta, just north of the Caspian Sea.

along the road. And so also at all the chief stations noted in going from one country to another in the route, according to the number of days set down above, you should furnish yourself with flour and salt fish; other things you will find in sufficiency, and especially meat.

The road you travel from Tana to Cathay is perfectly safe, whether by day or by night, according to what the merchants say who have used it. Only if the merchant, in going or coming, should die upon the road, everything belonging to him will become the perquisite of the lord of the country in which he dies, and the officers of the lord will take possession of all. And in like manner if he die in Cathay. But if his brother be with him, or an intimate friend and comrade calling himself his brother, then to such a one they will surrender the property of the deceased, and so it will be rescued.

And there is another danger: this is when the lord of the country dies, and before the new lord who is to have the lordship is proclaimed; during such intervals there have sometimes been irregularities practiced on the Franks, and other foreigners. (They call "Franks" all the Christians of these parts from Romania[6] westward.) And neither will the roads be safe to travel until the other lord be proclaimed who is to reign in place of him who is deceased.

Cathay is a province which contains a multitude of cities and towns. Among others there is one in particular, that is to say the capital city, to which is great resort of merchants, and in which there is a vast amount of trade; and this city is called Cambalec.[7] And the said city has a circuit of one hundred miles, and is all full of people and houses and of dwellers in the said city. . . .

You may reckon also that from Tana to Sara[8] the road is less safe than on any other part of the journey; and yet even when this part of the road is at its worst, if you are some sixty men in the company you will go as safely as if you were in your own house.

Anyone from Genoa or from Venice, wishing to go to the places above-named, and to make the journey to Cathay, should carry linens with him, and if he visit Organci[9] he will dispose of these well. In Organci he should purchase sommi of silver,[10] and with these he should proceed without making any further investment, unless it be some bales of the very finest stuffs which go in small bulk, and cost no more for carriage than coarser stuffs would do.

Merchants who travel this road can ride on horseback or on asses, or mounted in any way that they choose to be mounted.

Whatever silver the merchants may carry with them as far as Cathay the lord of Cathay will take from them and put into his treasury. And to merchants who thus bring silver they give that paper money of theirs in exchange. This is of yellow paper, stamped with the seal of the lord aforesaid. And this money is called balishi; and with this money you can readily buy silk and all other merchandise that you have a desire to buy. And all the people of the country are bound to receive it. And yet you shall not pay a higher price for your goods because your money is of paper. And of the said paper money there are three kinds, one being worth more than another, according to the value which has been established for each by that lord.

---

[6]The European term for the Byzantine Empire.
[7]Khanbalik (City of the Khan), modern Beijing.
[8]Sarai on the Volga, the capital of the il-khans of Kipchak (also known as the Golden Horde), who ruled Russia and Kazakhstan.
[9]Urgench on the Oxus River in Central Asia.

[10]Sommi were weights of silver. Each sommo was equivalent to 5 golden florins, the standard coin of Florence. Pegolotti calculated that the average merchant would carry merchandise worth about 25,000 florins, and the expenses for the merchant, interpreter, and two personal servants would amount to a combined 60 to 80 sommi, or 300 to 400 florins.

Travel Beyond the Mongol Ecumene

Important as the Mongol Peace was in facilitating movement and trade across Eurasia, it was not the sole contributing factor to the upsurge of long-distance travel and cultural exchange after 1000. As the travels of Ibn Battuta demonstrate, the very nature of the community of Islam encouraged travel. Educated Muslims, no matter what their ethnic origins or native tongues, shared a sacred language — Arabic — and could communicate with one another. They also shared an obligation to make a pilgrimage at least once in a lifetime to Mecca. The pilgrimage routes that enabled African, Indian, and East Asian Muslims to travel to these holy sites were also important avenues of cultural and material exchange. Moreover, merchants spread Islam to such faraway regions as sub-Saharan Africa and the coastal lands of Southeast Asia. Once the faith had taken root, there was even more reason to maintain contact with these societies, many of which were so distant from Islam's Southwest Asian birthplace.

The breakup of the Mongol Empire around the middle of the fourteenth century did not end long-distance travel for the non-Muslim peoples of Eurasia. China and Europe had taken to the seas long before the rise of the Mongols and continued their interests in seafaring and naval technology throughout the thirteenth and fourteenth centuries and beyond. Early in the fifteenth century, Ming China sent seven massive naval expeditions into the Indian Ocean, and portions of several of those fleets reached the shores of East Africa. Also in the fifteenth century, Western Europe, finding the overland roads to Cathay mostly blocked by a resurgent Islam, began to seek alternate sea routes to the Indies. The consequences of those explorations were astounding. Before the century was over Europeans had sailed to East Africa, India, and the Americas.

A Moroccan Visitor in Sub-Saharan Africa
▼▼▼

96 ▼ Ibn Battuta,
A DONATION TO THOSE INTERESTED IN CURIOSITIES

The life and world travels of Abu 'Abdallah Muhammad ibn Battuta (1304–1369) provide eloquent testimony to the international cosmopolitanism of fourteenth-century Islam. Ibn Battuta was born into the religious upper class of Tangier, Morocco, where he received an education in Muslim law and Arabic literature. In 1325 he left home to make the first of what would be several pilgrimages to Mecca. In the course of the next three decades he visited Constantinople, Mesopotamia, Persia, India, where he resided and worked for seven years, Burma, Sumatra, Spain, Mali, and probably southern China. In all, his travels covered about 75,000 miles, and most of his stops along the way were within the cultural confines of *Dar-al-Islam* (the Abode of Islam), where the sacred law of the Qur'an prevailed. In 1354 he returned to Morocco to stay and almost immediately began to narrate his experiences and observations to Ibn Juzayy, a professional scribe who fashioned these stories into one of the most popular forms of literature in the Muslim world — a *rihla*, or book of travels.

Before settling down and recording his adventures for posterity, Ibn Battuta embarked in early 1352 on his last great adventure, a trip by camel caravan to the West African kingdom of Mali in the Niger River region. Almost two years later he arrived back home with marvelous tales to tell of this Malinke-speaking people of the land of gold, whose leaders had converted to Islam in the early thirteenth century.

QUESTIONS FOR ANALYSIS

1. What did Ibn Battuta admire most about these people? What did he find hardest to accept? Why?
2. Did Ibn Battuta understand fully all he encountered? Can you find any evidence of cultural or racial tension?
3. In what ways were the cultures of the people whom Ibn Battuta encountered a mixture of native African and Muslim elements?
4. Compare Ibn Battuta's cultural biases with those of Zhou Daguan. Are you struck more by the similarities or dissimilarities? Why?
5. How organized and controlled does the state of Mali appear to be?
6. Compare fourteenth-century Mali with eleventh-century Ghana (Chapter 11, source 85). What are their similarities and differences? Which seem more significant? What do you conclude from that answer?
7. Based on a careful study of sources 85 and 87 of Chapter 11, as well as of this document, what inferences do you draw about the social status of women in sub-Saharan West Africa?

Then we reached the town of Iwalatan . . . after a journey . . . of two whole months. It is the first district of the Sudan and the sultan's[1] deputy there is Farba Husayn. *Farba* means "deputy." When we arrived there the merchants[2] placed their belongings in an open space, where the Sudan[3] took over the guard of them while they went to the *farba*. He was sitting on a car-

---

[1]The sultan, or king, of Mali, for whom this was an outlying province.
[2]North Africans and Arab merchants.

[3]Local blacks.

pet under a *saqif*[4] with his assistants in front of him with lances and bows in their hands and the chief men of the Masufa[5] behind him. The merchants stood before him while he addressed them, in spite of their proximity to him, through an interpreter, out of contempt for them. At this I repented at having come to their country because of their ill manners and their contempt for white men.[6] I made for the house of Ibn Badda', a respectable man of Sala to whom I had written to rent a house for me. He had done so. Then the *mushrif*[7] (of Iwalatan), who is called the *manshaju,* invited those who had come with the caravan to receive his reception-gift (*diyafa*). I declined to go but my companions entreated me urgently, so I went with those who went. Then the *diyafa* was brought. It was *anili*[8] meal mixed with a little honey and yogurt which they had placed in half a gourd made into a kind of bowl. Those present drank and went away. I said to them: "Was it to this that the black man invited us?" They said; "Yes, for them this is a great banquet." Then I knew for certain that no good was to be expected from them and I wished to depart with the pilgrims of Iwalatan. But then I thought it better to go to see the seat of their king.

My stay in Iwalatan lasted about 50 days. Its inhabitants did me honor and made me their guest. Among them was the qadi[9] of the place Muhammad b. 'Abd Allah b. Yanumur and his brother the faqih[10] and teacher Yahya. The town of Iwalatan is extremely hot. There are a few little palm trees there in the shade of which they sow watermelons. . . . Mutton is abundant there and the people's clothes are of Egyptian cloth of good quality. Most of the inhabitants there belong to the Masufa, whose women are of surpassing beauty and have a higher status than the men.

THE MASUFA LIVING IN IWALATAN

These people have remarkable and strange ways. As for their men, they feel no jealousy. None of them traces his descent through his father, but from his maternal uncle, and a man's heirs are the sons of his sister only, to the exclusion of his own sons. This is something that I have seen nowhere in the world except among the Indian infidels in the land of Mulaybar, whereas these are Muslims who observe the prayer and study fiqh[11] and memorize the Qur'an. As for their women, they have no modesty in the presence of men and do not veil themselves in spite of their assiduity in prayer. If anybody wishes to marry one of them he may do so, but they do not travel with the husband, and if one of them wished to do so her family would prevent her.

The women there have friends and companions among the foreign men, just as the men have companions from among the foreign women. One of them may enter his house and find his wife with her man friend without making any objection. . . .

One day I went into the presence of Abu Muhammad Yandakan al-Masufi in whose company we had come and found him sitting on a carpet. In the courtyard of his house there was a canopied couch with a woman on it conversing with a man seated. I said to him: "Who is this woman?" He said: "She is my wife." I said: "What connection has the man with her?" He replied: "He is her friend." I said to him: "Do you acquiesce in this when you have lived in our country and become acquainted with the precepts of the Shar?"[12] He replied: "The association of women with men is agreeable to us and a part of good conduct, to which no suspicion attaches. They are not like the women of your country." I was astonished at

---

[4]A colonnade.
[5]A Berber people of the western Sahara.
[6]North Africans and Arabs.
[7]The sultan's overseer of the town's markets.
[8]Millet.

[9]A religious judge.
[10]A teacher of religion.
[11]Religion.
[12]*Shari'a,* or Muslim Sacred Law.

his laxity. I left him, and did not return thereafter. He invited me several times but I did not accept.

When I resolved to travel to Mali . . . I hired a guide from the Masufa, since there is no need to travel in company because of the security of that road, and set off with three of my companions. . . .

Then we . . . arrived at the River Sansara, which is about ten miles from the capital of Mali. It is their custom to prevent people from entering it except by authorization. I had written before this to the white community . . .to ask them to rent a house for me. When I reached the afore-mentioned river I crossed it by the ferry without anybody preventing me. I arrived at the town of Mali, the seat of the king of the Sudan. . . .

THE SULTAN OF MALI

He is the sultan Mansa Sulayman.[13] *Mansa* means "sultan" and Sulayman is his name. He is a miserly king from whom no great donation is to be expected. It happened that I remained for this period without seeing him on account of my illness. Then he gave a memorial feast for our Lord Abu 'l-Hasan[14] (may God be content with him) and invited the emirs and faqihs and the qadi and khatib,[15] and I went with them. They brought copies of the Qur'an and the Qur'an was recited in full. They prayed for our lord Abu 'l-Hasan (may God have mercy on him) and prayed for Mansa Sulayman. When this was finished I advanced and greeted Mansa Sulayman and the qadi and the khatib and Ibn al-Faqih told him who I was. He answered them in their language and they said to me: "The sultan says to you: 'I thank God.'" I replied: "Praise and thanks be to God in every circumstance."

THEIR TRIVIAL RECEPTION GIFT AND THEIR RESPECT FOR IT

When I departed the reception gift was sent to me and dispatched to the qadi's house. The qadi sent it with his men to the house of Ibn al-Faqih. Ibn al-Faqih hastened out of his house barefooted and came in to me saying: "Come! The cloth and gift of the sultan have come to you!" I got up, thinking that it would be robes of honor and money, but behold! it was three loaves of bread and a piece of beef fried in *gharti*[16] and a gourd containing yogurt. When I saw it I laughed, and was long astonished at their feeble intellect and their respect for mean things.

MY SPEAKING TO THE SULTAN AFTER THIS AND HIS KINDNESS TOWARDS ME

After this reception gift I remained for two months during which nothing was sent to me by the sultan and the month of Ramadan came in. Meanwhile I frequented the *mashwar* [council-place] and used to greet him and sit with the qadi and the khatib. I spoke with Dugha the interpreter, who said: "Speak with him, and I will express what you want to say in the proper fashion." So when he held a session at the beginning of Ramadan and I stood before him and said: "I have journeyed to the countries of the world and met their kings. I have been four months in your country without your giving me a reception gift or anything else. What shall I say of you in the presence of other sultans?" He replied: "I have not seen you nor known about you." The qadi and Ibn al-Faqih rose and replied to him saying: "He greeted you and you sent to him some food." Thereupon he ordered that a house be provided for me to stay

---

[13]The brother of Mansa Musa (Chapter 8, source 66), Mansa Sulayman ruled Mali from 1341 to 1360.
[14]The late sultan of Morocco (1331–1351).

[15]A public preacher at Friday mosque services.
[16]A vegetable oil.

in and an allowance to be allotted to me. Then, on the night of 27 Ramadan, he distributed among the qadi and the khatib and the faqihs a sum of money which they call *zakah*[17] and gave to me with them 33 1/3 mithqals.[18] When I departed he bestowed on me 100 mithqals of gold. . . .

THE SELF-DEBASEMENT OF THE SUDAN BEFORE THEIR KING AND THEIR SCATTERING OF DUST ON THEMSELVES BEFORE HIM AND OTHER PECULIARITIES

The Sudan are the humblest of people before their king and the most submissive towards him. They swear by his name, saying: *"Mansa Sulayman ki."* When he calls to one of them at his sessions in the pavilion which we have mentioned the person called takes off his clothes and puts on ragged clothes, and removes his turban and puts on a dirty *shashiyya*[19] and goes in holding up his garments and trousers half-way up his leg, and advances with submissiveness and humility. He then beats the ground vigorously with his two elbows, and stands like one performing a *rak'a*[20] to listen to his words.

If one of them addresses the sultan and the latter replies he uncovers the clothes from his back and sprinkles dust on his head and back, like one washing himself with water. I used to marvel how their eyes did not become blinded. . . .

WHAT I APPROVED OF AND WHAT I DISAPPROVED OF AMONG THE ACTS OF THE SUDAN

One of their good features is their lack of oppression. They are the farthest removed of people from it and their sultan does not permit anyone to practice it. Another is the security embracing the whole country, so that neither traveler there nor dweller has anything to fear from thief or usurper. Another is that they do not interfere with the wealth of any white man who dies among them, even though it be *qintar* upon *qintar*.[21] They simply leave it in the hands of a trustworthy white man until the one to whom it is due takes it. Another is their assiduity in prayer and their persistence in performing it in congregation and beating their children to make them perform it. If it is a Friday and a man does not go early to the mosque he will not find anywhere to pray because of the press of the people. It is their habit that every man sends his servant with his prayer-mat to spread it for him in a place which he thereby has a right to until he goes to the mosque. Their prayer-carpets are made from the fronds of the tree resembling the palm which has no fruit. Another of their good features is their dressing in fine white clothes on Friday. If any one of them possesses nothing but a ragged shirt he washes it and cleanses it and attends the Friday prayer in it. Another is their eagerness to memorize the great Qur'an. They place fetters on their children if there appears on their part a failure to memorize it and they are not undone until they memorize it.

I went into the house of the qadi on the day of the festival and his children were fettered so I said to him: "Aren't you going to let them go?" He replied: "I shan't do so until they've got the Qur'an by heart!" One day I passed by a youth of theirs, of good appearance and dressed in fine clothes, with a heavy fetter on his leg. I said to those who were with me: "What has this boy done? Has he killed somebody?" The lad understood what I had said and laughed, and they said to me: "He's only been fettered so that he'll learn the Qur'an!"

---

[17]Alms distributed at the end of Ramadan, the month devoted to fasting.
[18]A standard weight of gold (about 4.72 grams).
[19]A skull cap.

[20]A set sequence of utterances and gestures that form the *salah,* or obligatory ritual prayer, that Muslims must engage in five times daily.
[21]"Weight upon weight" (i.e., a large amount of wealth).

One of their disapproved acts is that their female servants and slave girls and little girls appear before men naked, with their privy parts uncovered. During Ramadan I saw many of them in this state, for it is the custom of the *farariyya*[22] to break their fast[23] in the house of the sultan, and each one brings his food carried by twenty or more of his slave girls, they all being naked. Another is that their women go into the sultan's presence naked and uncovered, and that his daughters go naked. On the night of 25 Ramadan I saw about 200 slave girls bringing out food from his palace naked, having with them two of his daughters with rounded breasts having no covering upon them. Another is their sprinkling dust and ashes on their heads out of good manners. . . . Another is that many of them eat carrion, and dogs, and donkeys.[24]

A European View of the World
▼▼▼

97 ▼ *John Mandeville, TRAVELS*

If Ibn Battuta's *rihla* illustrates a cosmopolitan Muslim's vision of the world, a curious work ascribed to a largely unknown person named Sir John Mandeville illustrates the Western European view of that same globe. First appearing in Europe between 1356 and 1366, Mandeville's *Travels* purported to be the first-hand account of an English knight's trans-Eurasian adventures between 1322 and 1356 in which the author claimed to have served both the sultan of Egypt and the Mongol khan of China. There is every good reason to believe this work is largely a fictional tour de force by a gifted author whose travels were largely imaginative. In fact, much of the work is plagiarized from a wide variety of sources, some of them genuine travel accounts. No matter the book's lack of authenticity, Mandeville's *Travels*, written originally in French, was widely circulated and translated into virtually every European language by 1400. Indeed, it became late medieval Europe's most popular travelogue in an age noted for its fascination with world travel and, in many ways, shaped Western Europeans' vision of the outside world (see Columbus's letter in the Prologue). Even though Sir John (if that was his name), did not travel to all the regions he claimed to have visited, his work is historically important because it illustrates the manner in which Europeans of the fourteenth and fifteenth centuries viewed the lands and peoples beyond their frontiers.

In the first selection Sir John deals with the shape and size of the earth. Most people today are unaware that the notion that medieval European scholars believed the world was flat is a modern myth created by the American writer Washington Irving in the nineteenth century. In the second selection Mandeville

---

[22]Emirs, or chief men.
[23]The daily fast of the month of Ramadan ends at sunset.
[24]Unclean meat, according to qur'anic law.

shares his putative firsthand knowledge of the wondrous land of Prester John, descendant of the Magi, or the three wise kings from the East who had visited the Christ Child. Prester John (John the priest) was a mythic emperor and priest of some "lost" Christian peoples whose existence was firmly accepted in the West from the mid-twelfth century onward. The Prester John myth was born partly out of rumors of actual distant Christian cultures, such as the Ethiopians of Africa, the Nestorians of Central and East Asia, and the "St. Thomas" Christians of India's west coast, and partly out of a crusading zeal to discover Christian allies in the war against Islam. As a consequence, European adventurers as late as the sixteenth century sought Prester John in Asia and Africa (source 100).

QUESTIONS FOR ANALYSIS

1. Can you find in this source any roots of the Western notion of the noble savage?
2. What was John Mandeville's vision of the world?
3. What do these stories suggest about his attitudes toward "alien" customs and the world beyond Europe?
4. Many societies cherish a myth of a promised redeemer, or hero-to-come. How had the Christian West created in the mythic Prester John a person who represented the fulfillment of some of their deepest wishes?
5. Reread the tale of Sindbad the Sailor (Chapter 9, source 76). Leaving details aside, can you discover any common themes between that tale and Mandeville's stories? What do these common motifs suggest to you?
6. Reread Columbus's letter of 1493 (Prologue). How had Mandeville prepared him to find in the Caribbean "evidence" that he had landed on an island off the coast of Asia? Conversely, does his letter in any way shape the evidence to fit Mandeville's portrait of the world?

From India people go by the ocean sea by way of many islands and different countries, which it would be tedious for me to relate. Fifty-two days' journey from that land there is another large country called Lamary [Sumatra]. That land is extremely hot, so that the custom there is for men and women to walk about totally naked, and they scorn foreigners who wear clothes. They say that God created Adam and Eve naked, and no person, therefore, should be ashamed to appear as God made him, because nothing that comes from nature's bounty is foul. They also say that people who wear clothes are from another world, or else they are people who do not believe in God. They say that they believe in God who created the world and made Adam and Eve and everything else. Here they do not marry wives, since all the women are common to all men, and no woman forsakes any man. They say that it is sinful to refuse any man, for God so commanded it of Adam and Eve and all who followed when he said: "Increase and multiply and fill the earth."[1] There-fore, no man in that country may say: "This is my wife." No woman may say: "This is my hus-band." When they bear children, the women present them to whatever man they wish of those with whom they have had sexual rela-tions. So also all land is held in common. What one man holds one year, another has another year, and everyone takes that portion which he desires. Also all the produce of the soil is held in common. This is true for grains and other goods as well. Nothing is held in private; noth-ing is locked up, and every person there takes what he wants without anyone saying "no." Each is as rich as the other.

There is, however, in that country an evil custom. They eat human flesh more happily than any other meat, this despite the fact that the land abounds in meats, fish, grains, gold, silver, and every other commodity. Merchants go there, bringing with them children to sell to the people of that country, and they purchase the children. If they are plump, they eat them immediately. If they are lean, they feed them until they fatten up, and then they eat them. They say this is the best and sweetest flesh in all the world.

In that land, and in many others beyond it, no one can see the Transmontane Star, known as the Star of the Sea, which is immoveable and stands in the north and is called the Lode Star.[2] They see, rather, another star, its opposite, which stands in the south and is called the Ant-arctic Star. Just as sailors here get their bearings and steer by the Lode Star, so sailors beyond those parts steer by the southern star, which we cannot see. So our northern star, which we call the Lode Star, cannot be seen there. This is proof that the earth and sea are round in shape

and form. For portions of the heavens that are seen in one country do not appear in another. . . . I can prove that point by what I have ob-served, for I have been in parts of Brabant[3] and seen, by means of an astrolabe, that the Trans-montane Star is 53 degrees in elevation. In Ger-many and Bohemia it is 58 degrees; and farther north it is 62 degrees and some minutes high. I personally have measured it with an astrolabe. Understand that opposite the Transmontane Star is the other known as the Antarctic Star, as I have said. These two stars never move, and around them all the heavens revolve, just like a wheel about an axle. So those two stars divide the heavens into two equal parts, with as much above [the equator] as below. . . .

I say with certainty that people can encircle the entire world, below the equator as well as above,[4] and return to their homelands, pro-vided they have good company, a ship, and health. And all along the way one would find people, lands, and islands. . . . For you know well that those people who live right under the Antarctic Star are directly underneath, feet against feet, of those who dwell directly under the Transmontane Star,[5] just as we and those who dwell under us[6] are feet to feet. For every part of the sea and the land has its opposite, which balances it, and it is both habitable and traversable. . . . So people who travel to India and the foreign isles girdle the roundness of the earth and the seas, passing under our countries in this hemisphere.

Something I heard as a youth has occurred to me often. A worthy man from our country de-parted some time ago to see the world. And so he passed through India and the islands beyond India, which number more than 5,000.[7] He traveled so far by sea and land and had so gir-

---

[1]Bible, Genesis 1:22.
[2]Polaris, or the North Star, which guides mariners.
[3]A region between modern Belgium and the Neth-erlands.
[4]Here Mandeville was refuting a notion, accepted by classical Greco-Roman geographers, that the antipodes,

or lands south of the equator, were uninhabitable be-cause of their extreme heat.
[5]In other words, the South Pole is 180 degrees south of (or under) the North Pole.
[6]The place directly opposite on the globe.
[7]The islands of Southeast Asia.

dled the globe over the period of so many seasons that he found an island where he heard his own language being spoken. . . . He marveled at this, not knowing what to make of it. I conclude he had traveled so far by land and sea that he had encircled the entire globe, circumnavigating to the very frontier of his homeland. Had he traveled only a bit farther, he would have come to his own home. But he turned back, returning along the route by which he had come. And so he spent a great deal of painful labor, as he acknowledged, when he returned home much later. For afterwards he went to Norway, where a storm carried him to an island. While on that island he discovered it was the island where earlier he had heard his own language spoken. . . .[8]

That could well be true, even though it might seem to simple-minded persons of no learning that people cannot travel on the underside of the world without falling off toward the heavens. That, however, is not possible, unless it is true that we also are liable to fall toward heaven from where we are on the earth. For whatever part of the earth people inhabit, above or below [the equator], it always seems to them that they are in a more proper position than any other folk. And so it is right that just as it seems to us that they are under us, so it seems to them that we are beneath them. For if a person could fall from the earth into the heavens, it is more reasonable to assume that the earth and sea, which are more vast and of greater weight, should fall into the heavens. But that is impossible. . . .

Although it is possible for a person to circumnavigate the world, nonetheless, out of a 1,000 persons, one might possibly return home. For, given the magnitude of the earth

and the sea, a 1,000 people could venture forth and follow a 1,000 different routes. This being so, no person could plot a perfect route toward the place from where he left. He could only reach it by accident or the grace of God. For the earth is very large and is some 20,425 miles in circumference, according to the opinion of wise astronomers from the past, whose words I am not going to contradict, even though it seems to me, with my limited understanding and with all due respect, that it is larger.[9]

.   .   .

This emperor, Prester John, commands a very large region and has many noble cities and fair towns in his realm, as well as many islands large and broad. For this land of India is divided into islands due to the great rivers that flow out of Paradise, dividing the land into many parts.[10] He also has many islands in the sea. . . . This Prester John has many kings and islands and many different peoples of various cultures subject to him. And this land is fertile and wealthy, but not as wealthy as the land of the Great Khan. For merchants do not as commonly travel there to purchase merchandise as they do to the land of the Great Khan, for it is too far to travel to. Moreover, people can find in that other region, the Island of Cathay, every manner of commodity that people need — gold cloth, silk, spices, and every sort of precious item. Consequently, even though commodities are less expensive in Prester John's island, nonetheless people dread the long voyage and the great sea-perils in that region. . . . Although one must travel by sea and land eleven or twelve months from Genoa or Venice before arriving in Cathay, the land of Prester John lies many more days of dreadful journey away. . . .

[8]This story, especially in light of the passage that follows, seems to claim that the Englishman traveled south to India and the islands of Southeast Asia and then continued south across the South Pole and up the far side of the globe across the North Pole to Scandinavia, and then he returned home by retracing his steps.
[9]Actually, it is closer to 25,000 miles.

[10]According to John, four rivers flow out of the Terrestrial Paradise from which Adam and Eve had been expelled, which lies far to the east of Prester John's country. These rivers, the Ganges, Nile, Tigris, and Euphrates, divide the major lands of the earth.

The Emperor Prester John always marries the daughter of the Great Khan, and the Great Khan likewise marries Prester John's daughter.[11] For they are the two greatest lords under heaven.

In Prester John's land there are many different things and many precious gems of such magnitude that people make vessels, such as platters, dishes, and cups, out of them. There are many other marvels there, so many, in fact, that it would be tiresome and too lengthy to put them down in a book . . . but I shall tell you some part.

This Emperor Prester John is Christian, as is a great part of his country as well. Yet they do not share all the articles of our faith. They believe fully in God, in the Son, and in the Holy Spirit. They are quite devout and faithful to one another, and they do not quarrel or practice fraud and deceit.

He has subject to him 72 provinces, and in every province there is a king. And these kings have kings under them, and all are tributaries to Prester John. And he has in his lordships many marvels. In his country is a sea that people call the Gravelly Sea.[12] It is all gravel and sand, without a drop of water, and it ebbs and flows in great waves, as other seas do, and never rests at any time. No one can cross that sea by ship or any other craft and, therefore, no one knows what land lies beyond that sea. Although it has no water, people find in it and on its banks plenty of good fish of a shape and size such as are found nowhere else, but they are tasty and delicious to eat. Three days journey from that sea are great mountains, out of which

flows a great river that originates in Paradise. And it is full of precious stones, without a drop of water. . . . Beyond that river, rising toward the deserts, is a great gravel plain set between the mountains. On that plain everyday at sunrise small trees begin to grow, and they grow until mid-day, bearing fruit. No one dares, however, to eat the fruit, for it is like a deceptive phantom. After mid-day the trees decrease and reenter the earth, so that by sunset they are no longer to be seen. And they do this every day. And that is a great marvel. In that desert are many wild people who are hideous to look at, for they are horned and do not speak but only grunt like pigs. . . .

When Emperor Prester John goes into battle against any other lord, he has no banners borne before him. Rather, he has three crosses of fine gold, which are massive and very tall and encrusted with precious stones. Each cross is set in a richly adorned chariot. To guard each cross, there is a detail of 10,000 mounted men at arms and 100,000 men on foot . . . , and this number is in addition to the main body of troops. . . . When he rides out in peace time with a private entourage, he has borne before him only one wooden cross, unpainted and lacking gold, silver, or gems, as a remembrance that Jesus Christ suffered death on a wooden cross.[13] He also has borne before him a golden platter filled with earth, in token of the fact that his nobility, might, and flesh will all turn to earth. He also has borne before him a silver vessel full of great nuggets of gold and precious gems, as a token of his lordship, nobility, and might.

---

[11]This particular version of the Prester John myth seems to reflect the reality of the Turkish Nestorian Christians, since many Mongol khans did have Nestorian wives.

[12]Apparently a garbled reference to the Gobi (Gravel) Desert of Central Asia.

[13]Keep in mind that *crusade* means "to bear a cross."

Zheng He's Western Voyages
▼▼▼

98 ▼ *Ma Huan,*
THE OVERALL SURVEY OF THE
OCEAN'S SHORES

Vigorous expansionism characterized the early Ming Dynasty (1368–1644), particularly during the reign of Yong Lo (r. 1402–1424). Between 1405 and 1421 this emperor sent out a series of six great fleets under the command of China's most famous admiral, a Muslim eunuch of Mongolian ancestry named Zheng He (1371–1435). If we can believe the records, several fleets carried in excess of 27,000 sailors, soldiers, and officials. The first expedition of 1405–1407 reportedly consisted of 317 vessels, including 62 massive "treasure ships," some of which were 300 feet long, 150 feet wide (imagine a ship the size of a football field), and weighed about 3,100 tons. These armadas, as well as a seventh that went out in 1431 and returned in 1433, sailed through the waters of Southeast Asia and the Indian Ocean, visiting numerous ports of call in such places as India, East Africa, and the Arabian Peninsula.

The main reason behind these voyages appears to have been the reassertion of Chinese prestige to the south and west. Like the expedition that Zhou Daguan joined a century earlier, these fleets were commissioned to accept the submission and tribute of the various "barbarian" rulers they encountered. A secondary purpose seems to have been to stimulate China's economy and strengthen its commercial position in South Asia, particularly in light of the fact that the armies of Timur the Lame had severed the old Silk Route.

Despite the psychological impact the fleets' show of strength had upon the people they visited (in one area of Thailand Zheng He was remembered as a god), China would never dominate the Indian Ocean. After Yong Lo's death, the imperial court did not follow through on what had begun so well for several reasons. The cost of mounting these expeditions was prohibitively high. Moreover, the Confucian literarchy, with its traditional contempt for commerce and foreign cultures, was on the ascendance after Yong Lo's death. Although Zheng He was allowed to lead a seventh expedition westward, it proved to be China's last moment of transoceanic greatness. The court called a halt to further overseas adventures; the fleet was allowed to decay; and China effectively forgot much of the naval technology that had made it the world's greatest maritime power in the ages of Song and early Ming.

The following account describes various sites visited in the course of three of Zheng He's expeditions in western waters. Its author, Ma Huan (ca 1380–after 1451), a Chinese Muslim, joined the fourth voyage (1413–1415) as an Arabic translator and upon his return transcribed his notes into book form. He later sailed on the sixth (1421–1422) and seventh (1431–1433) expeditions and amended his account accordingly, eventually publishing it in 1451.

QUESTIONS FOR ANALYSIS

1. What evidence is there that the emperor saw these expeditions as a way of extending Chinese influence abroad?
2. How did Zheng He use both diplomacy and military force to achieve this objective?
3. What evidence is there that these expeditions also served commercial purposes?
4. What evidence is there that there was a high level of international commerce in the Indian Ocean well before the coming of Zheng He's fleets?

THE COUNTRY OF MANLAJIA[1] (MALACCA)

From Zhan City[2] you go due south, and after traveling for eight days with a fair wind the ship comes to Longya strait,[3] after entering the strait you travel west; and you can reach this place in two days.

Formerly this place was not designated a "country"; and because the sea hereabouts was named "Five Islands," the place was in consequence named "Five Islands." There was no king of the country; and it was controlled only by a chief. This territory was subordinate to the jurisdiction of Xian Luo,[4] it paid an annual tribute of forty *liang*[5] of gold; and if it were not paid, then Xian Luo would send men to attack it.

In the seventh year of the Yong-Lo period,[6] the Emperor ordered the principal envoy, the grand eunuch Zheng He, and others to assume command (of the treasure-ships), and to take the imperial edicts and to bestow upon this chief two silver seals, a hat, a belt and a robe. Zheng He set up a stone tablet and raised the place to a city; and it was subsequently called the "country of Manlajia." Thereafter Xian Luo did not dare to invade it.

The chief, having received the favor of being made king, conducted his wife and son, and went to the court at the capital[7] to return thanks and to present tribute of local products. The court also granted him a sea-going ship, so that he might return to his country and protect his land. . . .

Whenever the treasure-ships of the Central Country[8] arrived there, they at once erected a line of stockading, like a city-wall, and set up towers for the watchdrums at four gates; at night they had patrols of police carrying bells; inside, again, they erected a second stockade, like a small city-wall, within which they constructed warehouses and granaries; and all the money and provisions were stored in them. The ships which had gone to various countries[9] returned to this place and assembled; they marshaled the foreign goods and loaded them in the ships; then waited till the south wind was perfectly favorable. In the middle decade of the fifth moon they put to sea and returned home.[10]

Moreover, the king of the country made a selection of local products, conducted his wife and son, brought his chiefs, boarded a ship and followed the treasure-ships; and he attended at court and presented tribute. . . .

---

[1]Malacca, a port on the west coast of the Malay Peninsula.
[2]In Champa (central Vietnam).
[3]Singapore Strait.
[4]Thailand.
[5]About 48 ounces.
[6]1409. This would be the third expedition of 1409–1411.

[7]Nanjing (the southern capital). The Ming court moved from the seaport capital of Nanjing to inland Beijing (the northern capital) in 1421, indicating a shift in China's focus.
[8]China, the Middle Kingdom.
[9]This is evidence that elements were detached from the main fleet and sent off on special missions.
[10]1433, the last expedition.

THE COUNTRY OF SUMENDALA[11] (SEMUDERA, LHO SEUMAWE)

The country of Sumendala is exactly the same country as that formerly named Xuwendana. This place is indeed the principal center of the Western Ocean. . . .

The king of the country of Sumendala had previously been raided by the "tattooed-face king" of Naguer; and in the fighting he received a poisoned arrow in the body and died. He had one son, who was young and unable to avenge his father's death. The king's wife made a vow before the people, saying "If there is anyone who can avenge my husband's death and recover his land, I am willing to marry him and to share with him the management of the country's affairs." When she finished speaking, a fisherman belonging to the place was fired with determination, and said "I can avenge him."

Thereupon he took command of an army and at once put the "tattooed-face king" to flight in battle; and later he avenged the former king's death when the "tattooed-face king" was killed. The people of the latter submitted and did not dare to carry on hostilities.

Whereupon the wife of the former king, failing not to carry out her previous vow, forthwith married the fisherman. He was styled "the old king," and in such things as the affairs of the royal household and the taxation of the land, everybody accepted the old king's decisions. In the seventh year of the Yong Lo period[12] the old king, in fulfillment of his duty, brought tribute of local products,[13] and was enriched by the kindness of Heaven;[14] and in the tenth year of the Yong Lo period[15] he returned to his country.

When the son of the former king had grown up, he secretly plotted with the chiefs, murdered his adoptive father the fisherman, usurped his position, and ruled the kingdom.

The fisherman had a son by his principal wife; his name was Suganla; he took command of his people, and they fled away, taking their families; and, after erecting a stockade in the neighboring mountains, from time to time he led his men in incursions to take revenge on his father's enemies. In the thirteenth year of the Yong-Lo period[16] the principal envoy, the grand eunuch Zheng He, and others, commanding a large fleet of treasure-ships, arrived there; they dispatched soldiers who captured Suganla; and he went to the capital;[17] and was publicly executed. The king's son was grateful for the imperial kindness, and constantly presented tribute of local products to the court. . . .

At this place there are foreign[18] ships going and coming in large numbers, hence all kinds of foreign goods are sold in great quantities in the country.

In this country they use gold coins and tin coins. The foreign name for the gold coin is *dinaer*;[19] they use pale gold, seventy percent pure, for casting it. . . . The foreign name for the tin coin is *jiashi*,[20] and in all their trading they regularly use tin coins. . . .

THE COUNTRY OF GULI[21] (CALICUT)

This is the great country of the Western Ocean. . . .

In the fifth year of the Yong-Lo period the court ordered the principal envoy, the grand eu-

---

[11]Semudera on the north coast of the island of Sumatra and across the Strait of Malacca from Malaysia.
[12]1409.
[13]To the Ming court at Nanjing.
[14]The emperor.
[15]1412.
[16]1415.
[17]Presumably Nanjing.

[18]Non-Chinese.
[19]From the Arabic *dinar*.
[20]The English would later transliterate this local word as *cash*.
[21]Calicut on India's southwest coast (not to be confused with Calcutta in the northeast).

nuch Zheng He, and others to deliver an imperial mandate to the king[22] of this country and to bestow on him a patent conferring a title of honor, and the grant of a silver seal, also to promote all the chiefs and award them hats and belts of various grades.

So Zheng He went there in command of a large fleet of treasure-ships, and he erected a tablet with a pavilion over it and set up a stone which said, "Though the journey from this country to the Central Country is more than a hundred thousand *li*,[23] yet the people are very similar, happy and prosperous, with identical customs. We have here engraved a stone, a perpetual declaration for ten thousand ages."

The king of the country is a Nankun[24] man; he is a firm believer in the Buddhist religion[25] and he venerates the elephant and the ox.

The population of the country includes five classes, the Muslim people, the Nankun people, the Zhedi people, the Geling people, and the Mugua[26] people. . . .

The king has two great chiefs who administer the affairs of the country; both are Muslims. . . .

The people are very honest and trustworthy. Their appearance is smart, fine, and distinguished.

Their two great chiefs received promotion and awards from the court of the Central Country.

If a treasure-ship goes there, it is left entirely to the two men to superintend the buying and selling; the king sends a chief and a Zhedi Weinuoji[27] to examine the account books in the official bureau; a broker comes and joins them; and a high officer who commands the ships discusses the choice of a certain date for fixing prices. When the day arrives, they first of all take the silk embroideries and the open-work silks, and other such goods which have been brought there, and discuss the price of them one by one; and when the price has been fixed, they write out an agreement stating the amount of the price; this agreement is retained by these persons. . . .

THE COUNTRY OF HULUMOSI[28] (HORMUZ)

Setting sail from the country of Guli, you go towards the north-west; and you can reach this place after traveling with a fair wind for twenty-five days. The capital lies beside the sea and up against the mountains.

Foreign ships from every place and foreign merchants traveling by land all come to this country to attend the market and trade; hence the people of the country are all rich. . . .

The king of this country, too, took a ship and loaded it with lions, *qilin*,[29] horses, pearls, precious stones, and other things, also a memorial to the throne written on a golden leaf; and he sent his chiefs and other men, who accompanied the treasure-ships dispatched by the Emperor, which were returning from the Western Ocean; and they went to the capital and presented tribute.[30]

---

[22]1407. This was the second expedition (1407–1409). While Zheng He was its nominal commander, he did not accompany it.

[23]A *li* is a bit more than a third of a mile.

[24]Upper class. He probably means a member of the kshatriya, or warrior-ruler, caste.

[25]Incorrect; he was Hindu.

[26]These would be the four castes.

[27]Probably an accountant.

[28]Hormuz, an island off the coast of Iran and at the mouth of the Persian Gulf.

[29]A giraffe.

[30]This probably took place at the end of the seventh expedition.

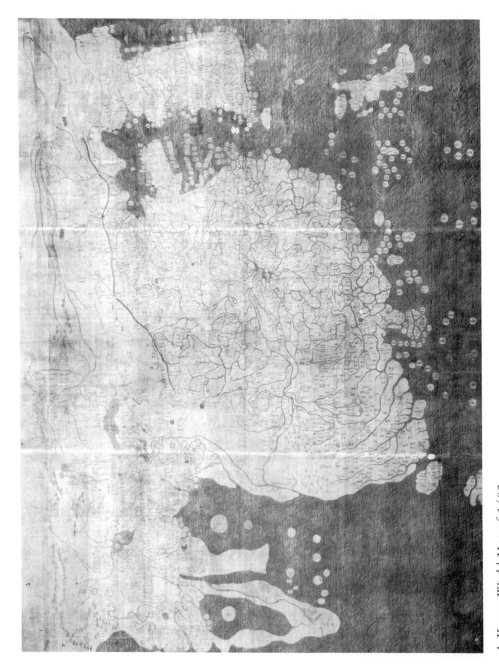

A Korean World Map of 1402

A Korean World Map of 1402
▼▼▼

99 ▼ *THE KANGNIDO*

The most noteworthy world map from the period immediately preceding the Europeans' arrival in the Americas comes from Korea. Titled *Map of Integrated Regions and Terrains and of Historical Countries and Capitals* but known more popularly as the *Kangnido*, the map was produced in 1402, early in the era of the Chonson Dynasty (1392–1910), an age of vigorous cultural renewal. The cartographers who created this masterpiece borrowed freely from Chinese, Islamic, and Japanese maps to fashion an integrated map that included almost every known area of the world. Once one becomes accustomed to the map's eccentricities, the modern viewer is astounded by its high degree of accuracy. To be sure, Japan is located directly south of Korea and farther away than it actually is. This may well represent a statement of supremacy over an age-old enemy by the Chonson court. Also the image of Europe leaves much to be desired, but the fact remains that Europe is on the map!

The *Kangnido* was copied many times, so prominent was it to the Chonson self-image and program of reform and regeneration. Although the original map is now lost, later fifteenth-century copies are extant. The map that appears here dates from about 1470.

QUESTIONS FOR ANALYSIS

1. Locate Korea. What does its relative size suggest?
2. Where does the center of the map lie? What does that suggest to you?
3. What have the mapmakers done with China, India, and mainland Southeast Asia? What do you infer from this?
4. Locate the Arabian Peninsula and Africa. What strikes you as particularly significant about these two features? In answering this question address their relative sizes and also the shape of Africa.
5. Locate Europe. Which areas are most recognizable? Which are most vague? What do your answers to these two questions suggest about the sources the Korean cartographers used for the far west?

The Origins of Portugal's Overseas Empire
▼▼▼

100 ▼ Gomes Eannes de Azurara, *CHRONICLE OF GUINEA*

At the same time that Zheng He's fleets were sailing majestically through the western seas and Muslim sailors dominated the coastal traffic of virtually every inhabited land washed by the Indian Ocean (except Australia), the Portuguese were tentatively inching down the west coast of Africa. From 1419 onward, Prince Henry (1394–1460), third son of King John I (r. 1385–1433), almost annually sent out a ship or two in an attempt to push farther toward the sub-Saharan land the Portuguese called *Guinea*, but only in 1434 did one of his caravels manage to round the feared Cape Bojador, along the western Sahara coast. Once this psychological barrier had been broken, the pace of exploration quickened. By 1460 Portuguese sailors had ventured as far south as modern Sierra Leone, an advance of about fifteen hundred miles in twenty-six years. Finally Bartolomeu Dias rounded the southern tip of Africa in early 1488, and Vasco da Gama, seeking, in his words, "Christians and spices," dropped anchor off Calicut on 20 May 1498. Although da Gama lost two of his four ships and many of his crew in this enterprise, Portugal was now in the Indian Ocean to stay.

Portugal's commercial empire was still more than a half-century in the future when Gomes Eannes de Azurara (ca 1400–after 1472) in 1452 began to compose a history of the life and work of Prince Henry "the Navigator," in so many ways the parent of an empire-to-be. Azurara's history details Portuguese explorations along the west African coast up to 1448. He promised a sequel because Henry was still alive and actively promoting voyages to West Africa when Azurara completed *The Chronicle of Guinea* in 1453. Azurara's other duties apparently intervened, and he never returned to the topic. Still, the chronicle he has given us is a revealing picture of the spirit behind Portugal's first generation of oceanic exploration and colonialism.

In the following excerpts Azurara explains why Prince Henry sponsored these expeditions and defends the consequent enslavement of black West Africans. Trade in Guinean slaves, which became an integral part of Portugal's commercial imperialism, began in 1441 with the capture of ten Africans, and Azurara estimated that 927 West African slaves had come into Portugal by 1448. This humane man, who was disturbed by many aspects of this exploitation, could not foresee that between 1450 and 1500 roughly 150,000 more Africans would enter Portugal and its colonies as slaves, and over the next four centuries untold millions of "heathens" would be transported out of Africa by European and Euro-American slavers.

QUESTIONS FOR ANALYSIS

1. What were Henry's motives? What seems to have been foremost in his mind — commercial, political, or religious gain or simple curiosity?
2. How does the author justify the enslavement of Africans?
3. It has been said that Henry was a fifteenth-century crusader. From the evidence, does this seem to be a fair judgment?
4. Compare this document with Christopher Columbus's letter of 1493 (the Prologue). Do they seem to share a common spirit? If so, what is it?
5. Compare the purposes behind the Portuguese and Spanish explorations with those of Zheng He's expeditions. In what ways do they differ, and to what do you ascribe those differences?

We imagine that we know a matter when we are acquainted with the doer of it and the end for which he did it. And since in former chapters we have set forth the Lord Infant[1] as the chief actor in these things, giving as clear an understanding of him as we could, it is meet that in this present chapter we should know his purpose in doing them. And you should note well that the noble spirit of this Prince, by a sort of natural constraint, was ever urging him both to begin and to carry out very great deeds. For which reason, after the taking of Ceuta[2] he always kept ships well armed against the Infidel, both for war, and because he had also a wish to know the land that lay beyond the isles of Canary and that Cape called Bojador, for that up to his time, neither by writings, nor by the memory of man, was known with any certainty the nature of the land beyond that Cape. Some said indeed that Saint Brendan[3] had passed that way; and there was another tale of two galleys rounding the Cape, which never returned. But this does not appear at all likely to be true, for it is not to be presumed that if the said galleys went there, some other ships would not have endeavored to learn what voyage they had made. And because the said Lord Infant wished to know the truth of this — since it seemed to

him that if he or some other lord did not endeavor to gain that knowledge, no mariners or merchants would ever dare to attempt it — (for it is clear that none of them ever trouble themselves to sail to a place where there is not a sure and certain hope of profit) — and seeing also that no other prince took any pains in this matter, he sent out his own ships against those parts, to have manifest certainty of them all. And to this he was stirred up by his zeal for the service of God and of the King Edward his Lord and brother,[4] who then reigned. And this was the first reason of his action.

The second reason was that if there chanced to be in those lands some population of Christians, or some havens, into which it would be possible to sail without peril, many kinds of merchandise might be brought to this realm, which would find a ready market, and reasonably so, because no other people of these parts traded with them, nor yet people of any other that were known; and also the products of this realm might be taken there, which traffic would bring great profit to our countrymen.

The third reason was that, as it was said that the power of the Moors in that land of Africa was very much greater than was commonly supposed, and that there were no Christians among

---

[1]Prince Henry. An *infante* (feminine: *infanta*) was any son of a Portuguese or Spanish monarch who was not an heir to the crown.

[2]A Muslim naval base in Morocco that Portugal captured in 1415.
[3]A wandering Irish monk of the sixth century.
[4]King Duarte (r. 1433–1438).

them, nor any other race of men; and because every wise man is obliged by natural prudence to wish for a knowledge of the power of his enemy; therefore the said Lord Infant exerted himself to cause this to be fully discovered, and to make it known determinately how far the power of those infidels extended.

The fourth reason was because during the one and thirty years that he had warred against the Moors, he had never found a Christian king, nor a lord outside this land, who for the love of our Lord Jesus Christ would aid him in the said war. Therefore he sought to know if there were in those parts any Christian princes, in whom the charity and the love of Christ was so ingrained that they would aid him against those enemies of the faith.

The fifth reason was his great desire to make increase in the faith of our Lord Jesus Christ and to bring to him all the souls that should be saved, — understanding that all the mystery of the Incarnation, Death, and Passion of our Lord Jesus Christ was for this sole end — namely the salvation of lost souls — whom the said Lord Infant by his travail and spending would fain bring into the true path. For he perceived that no better offering could be made unto the Lord than this; for if God promised to return one hundred goods for one, we may justly believe that for such great benefits, that is to say for so many souls as were saved by the efforts of this Lord, he will have so many hundreds of guerdons[5] in the kingdom of God, by which his spirit may be glorified after this life in the celestial realm. For I who wrote this history saw so many men and women of those parts turned to the holy faith, that even if the Infant had been a heathen, their prayers would have been enough to have obtained his salvation. And not only did I see the first captives,[6] but their children and grandchildren as true Christians as if the Divine grace breathed in them and imparted to them a clear knowledge of itself.

---

[5]Rewards.

[6]West African slaves who had been captured and transported to Portugal by licensed slave hunters.

Part Four

▾▾▾

A World of Change, 1500–1700

For many of the world's societies, the period from 1500 to 1700 was a time of significant change. In Japan, a century of civil war ended around 1600, when a new regime under the leadership of the Tokugawa clan brought an end to disorder and established a political system that maintained internal harmony for almost three centuries. In China, the Ming Dynasty, which had ruled the Middle Kingdom since 1368, was toppled and replaced by invading Manchus in 1644, who established the Qing Dynasty (1644–1912). For the first century and a half of their rule, the Qing gave China good government and strong leadership. The Russians, having ended their subservience to the "Tatar Yoke" of the Mongols in the late 1400s, struggled to establish a stable political order and initiated a campaign of eastward expansion that brought Russian settlers all the way to the shores of the Pacific. The Ottoman Turks consolidated and expanded an empire that included Anatolia, the Arabian Peninsula, the lands of Syria-Palestine, North Africa, southeastern Europe, and parts of Ukraine. To their east, Ismail Safavi, through a series of lightning conquests, in 1502 established the Safavid Empire in the region of modern Iran and Iraq. The last important upheaval took place in northern India, where the conquests of Babur laid the foundations of the Mughal Empire, the third great Islamic empire of West and South Asia.

As important as these events and movements were, none matched the eventual historical significance of Europe's transoceanic expansion. In the fifteenth century, ships flying the flag of the small kingdom of Portugal began to probe the waters of Africa's west coast in the hope of reaching the source of Muslim North Africa's sub-Saharan trade and of contacting Prester John, the legendary Christian king believed by some to live in Africa. Although the Portuguese finally made contact with the ancient Christian civilization of Ethiopia, they failed to convert it to Catholicism, and their missionaries were expelled in 1633. Portuguese commercial ventures in Africa and beyond proved to be enormously lucrative, however. Having reached India in 1498, the Malay coast in 1511, and China in 1513, the Portuguese were soon bringing back to Europe spices, silks, dyes, and other exotic items and reaping huge profits. Because of fierce competition among the European states, other European nations sought to rival the Portuguese by seeking new ocean routes to Asia. Columbus's voyage of 1492 was only the first of dozens of Spanish enterprises that established Spain as the dominant power, not in Asia, as hoped, but in the Americas. The nations of northern Europe also joined in. The French, Dutch, English, Danes, and Swedes claimed lands in the western hemisphere, and the French, Dutch, and English challenged the early Portuguese monopoly in African and Asian trade. By 1600, the European presence was beginning to be felt around the globe.

This initial burst of European expansion had little effect on the ancient centers of civilization in South and East Asia, the rulers of which tolerated a limited amount of trade but were strong enough to prevent the Europeans from undermining the political power or the cultural traditions of their subjects. In contrast, the Amerindian civilizations of Central and South America were all but obliterated by Spanish military conquests, economic exploitation, and the introduction of deadly new diseases. The story north of the Rio Grande was somewhat different. Some North American cultures were obliterated soon after the first arrival of Europeans. Apparently this was true for the Mississippian Mound Culture, which seems to have essentially disappeared in the mid-sixteenth century as a result of European diseases that travelled to its population centers along native trade routes. Most of the Amerindians of North America, however, faced similar threats of extinction only after 1600, when the French and English arrived in substantial numbers. Here the Native Americans' loss of territory and identity was generally not so sudden, but the process was no less painful and, in the end, the results were largely the same. In Africa, Europeans were unable to topple native rulers or impose their language and religion on most indigenous communities. They largely remained on the coast, relying on Africans to bring them commodities for trade. Tragically, in addition to gold and ivory, these commodities included human slaves, who at first were shipped to Europe and then, in ever greater numbers, to the plantations of the New World. Before it ended in the nineteenth century, the European slave trade robbed millions of human beings of their freedom, dignity, and lives.

Meanwhile, European society continued to transform itself in the sixteenth and seventeenth centuries. New wealth from overseas trade, mines, and plantations fueled further economic development, facilitated the consolidation of nation-states, and strengthened the position of the business class at the expense of the traditional landed aristocracy. Knowledge of new lands and cultures added to the intellectual ferment already initiated by the Renaissance, the Protestant Reformation, and the early Scientific Revolution. Europe by the end of the seventeenth century was far different from the Europe of 1500, and its continuing capacity for change made it the leading revolutionary element among the world's civilizations.

Chapter 13

▼▼▼

Europe's Expansion: Consequences and Counterattacks

Western Europe had begun to expand its frontiers as early as the eighth century, when Charlemagne campaigned against the pagan Saxons of northeast Germany, and its first great age of overseas colonialism began with the establishment of crusader states in the eastern Mediterranean in the late eleventh and twelfth centuries. Earlier, Scandinavians had advanced into the North Atlantic, setting up colonies in Iceland, Greenland, and, for a short while, North America by A.D. 1000.

Although aggressive expansion had already been part of the dynamics of European civilization for over 700 years, its transoceanic explorations from the late fifteenth century onward mark a turning point in the history not only of the West but of the entire world. Europe's push across wide expanses of ocean eventually became the single most important factor in the breakdown of regional isolation around the world and the creation of a true global community in the years after 1500.

The story is not simple. By 1700 Europeans had culturally and demographically altered forever vast areas of the Americas, but they had yet to visit other parts of those two great continents. The major civilizations of East Asia were still successfully resisting most unwanted European influences, and European penetration of India's interior had hardly begun. At the end of the seventeenth century, Western exploration and direct exploitation of the regions of Africa beyond the coasts were even less advanced. Moreover, although it is easy from a twentieth-century perspective to see in its early transoceanic ventures the origins of Europe's eventual dominance of the world, this would not have been apparent to most people living during these two centuries. For every area into which Europeans were expanding their influence, there was another in which they were retreating or being rebuffed. For example, sixteenth- and seventeenth-century Europeans fearfully witnessed the advancing menace of the Ottoman Turks into Europe itself.

Under Sultan Suleiman II (r. 1520–1566), the Ottoman Empire became a major force to be reckoned with so far as Europe was concerned. In 1522 Suleiman's armies established control over the eastern Mediterranean by seizing the island of Rhodes. In 1526 the Turks destroyed a Hungarian army and within two decades controlled most of that Christian kingdom. By the autumn of 1529 Ottoman forces besieged Vienna but were forced to withdraw. The Ottoman Turks remained Europe's greatest challenger for the next two centuries, and many believed that the next time Ottoman soldiers advanced on Vienna they would not be stopped. Indeed, the siege of 1683 failed only by the slightest margin.

Equally impressive was the expansion of Chinese borders, especially during the reign of Emperor Kangxi (r. 1661–1722), when China took control of the island of Formosa (modern Taiwan), incorporated Tibet into its empire, finally turned the nomads of Mongolia into quiescent vassals, and entered into a border treaty with imperial Russia that inaugurated a long period of Sino-Russian peace. On its part, Russia carved out the largest land empire of its day through a steady process of exploration and colonization across Eurasia's eastern forests and steppes. In 1637 Russian pioneers reached the Pacific, and colonists were not far behind. Given this state of affairs, Western Europeans did not see expansion as a one-way street, nor did they see themselves as aggressors and the rest of the world as their victim.

▼▼▼

Europeans in the Americas

The first contacts between Europeans and Native Americans posed immediate problems for each group. The Amerindians had to decide whether to cooperate with the new arrivals or to resist them. The Europeans needed to balance the often conflicting religious, commercial, and imperialist aspirations that inspired colonization of the Americas. Should they treat Native Americans as "savages," to be worked as slaves, deprived of their lands, ruled with an iron hand, and even killed? Or should they respect their customs and make honest efforts to "civilize" and protect them from exploitation?

As the following documents illustrate, neither the Amerindians nor the newcomers easily resolved these problems during the first two centuries of European presence in the "New World." In the end, however, European greed won out over altruism, and Old World diseases and firepower broke the back of Amerindian resistance. Native Americans lost their lands, self-determination, and much of their culture. Indeed, their numbers dramatically plummeted. By the early seventeenth century, the Native American populations of the Caribbean and Central and South America had been reduced by as much as 80 to 90 percent from preconquest levels.

Cortés in Mexico
▼▼▼

101 ▼ Bernardino de Sahagun,
GENERAL HISTORY OF THE THINGS
OF NEW SPAIN

Bernardino de Sahagun (ca 1499–1590) was one of the earliest Franciscan missionaries in Mexico, arriving from Spain in 1529. In addition to piety, he possessed a thorough knowledge of the Aztec language, a love of the Mexican people among whom he worked, and a scientific curiosity. Around 1545 he began a systematic collection of oral and pictorial sources for the culture of the Mexican people, which became the basis for his *General History of the Things of New Spain*. This history is rightly regarded as the first significant ethnographic work on an Amerindian society and remains today a principal source for the study of Mexican culture at the time of the Spanish conquest.

In his own day, many Spaniards opposed Sahagun's work, because they saw his efforts to preserve native culture as a threat to their policy of exploiting the land and its people. Sahagun consequently suffered the indignity of seeing his studies and notes confiscated by royal decree in 1578, and anthropologists and historians only rediscovered them in the nineteenth century.

The following selection comes from the twelfth and last book of the *General History*. Relying on the memories of people who had experienced the conquest less than three decades earlier and on Aztec picture narratives that elderly storytellers interpeted for him, Sahagun vividly portrays initial native reactions to Hernán Cortés's arrival in Mexico in 1519 (Chapter 11, source 89). The excerpt begins with the Aztec ruler Moctezuma (Montezuma) nervously awaiting news of the arrival from the sea of what he believes may be Topiltzin-Quetzalcoatl, a legendary, fair-skinned, bearded god-king prophesied to reappear after five centuries in 1519.

QUESTIONS FOR ANALYSIS

1. What did the Aztecs find most frightening about the Spaniards?
2. Why did they believe the Spaniards were gods?
3. What steps did Moctezuma take to deal with the Spaniards?
4. What led the Spaniards to think the natives of Mexico were "savages"?
5. What do we learn about Aztec religious beliefs and practices from this source?
6. The Spanish expeditionary force was quite small, yet many factors favored it. How many can you discover in this excerpt? From what you have read elsewhere, do you know of any factors that are not mentioned or even hinted at?

Meanwhile Moctezuma had been unable to rest, to sleep, to eat. He would speak to no one. He seemed to be in great torment. He sighed. He felt weak. He could enjoy nothing. . . .

Then the five emissaries arrived. "Even if he is asleep," they told the guards, "wake him. Tell him that those he sent to the sea have returned."

But Moctezuma said, "I shall not hear them in this place. Have them go to the Coacalli building." Further he commanded, "Have two captives covered with chalk."[1]

So the messengers went to the Coacalli, the house of snakes.[2]

Moctezuma came later. In front of the messengers, the captives were killed — their hearts torn out, their blood sprinkled over the messengers; for they had gone into great danger; they had looked into the very faces of the gods; they had even spoken to them.

After this they reported to Moctezuma all the wonders they had seen, and they showed him samples of the food the Spaniards ate.

Moctezuma was shocked, terrified by what he heard. He was much puzzled by their food, but what made him almost faint away was the telling of how the great lombard gun,[3] at the Spaniards' command, expelled the shot which thundered as it went off. The noise weakened one, dizzied one. Something like a stone came out of it in a shower of fire and sparks. The smoke was foul; it had a sickening, fetid smell. And the shot, which struck a mountain, knocked it to bits — dissolved it. It reduced a tree to sawdust — the tree disappeared as if they had blown it away.

And as to their war gear, it was all iron. They were iron. Their head pieces were of iron. Their swords, their crossbows, their shields, their lances, were of iron.[4]

The animals they rode — they looked like deer — were as high as roof tops.

They covered their bodies completely, all except their faces.

They were very white. Their eyes were like chalk. Their hair — on some it was yellow, on some it was black. They wore long beards; they were yellow, too. And there were some black-skinned ones with kinky hair.

What they ate was like what Aztecs ate during periods of fasting: it was large, it was white, it was lighter than tortillas; it was spongy like the inside of corn stalks; it tasted as if it had been made of a flour of corn stalks; it was sweetish.

Their dogs were huge. Their ears were folded over; their jowls dragged; their eyes blazed yellow, fiery yellow. They were thin — their ribs

[1]Slaves and captives were covered with chalk and feathers before sacrifice.
[2]A reception hall for visiting dignitaries.
[3]A ship deck gun, or cannon.
[4]The Native Americans effectively had no metals. Aztec weapons were made of stone, and their minimal body armor and shields were made of fibers.

showed. They were big. They were restless, moving about panting, tongues hanging. They were spotted or varicolored like jaguars.[5]

When Moctezuma was told all this, he was terror-struck. He felt faint. His heart failed him.

Nevertheless, Moctezuma then again sent emissaries, this time all the doers of evil he could gather — magicians, wizards, sorcerers, soothsayers. With them he sent the old men and the warriors necessary to requisition all the food the Spaniards would need, the turkeys, the eggs, the best white tortillas, everything necessary. The elders and fighting men were to care well for them.

Likewise he sent a contingent of captives, so that his men might be prepared in case the supposed gods required human blood to drink. And the emissaries indeed so thought, themselves. But the sacrifice nauseated the Spaniards. They shut their eyes tight; they shook their heads. For Moctezuma's men had soaked the food in blood before offering it to them; it revolted them, sickened them, so much did it reek of blood.

But Moctezuma had provided for this because, as he assumed them to be gods, he was worshiping them as gods. So were the Mexicans.[6] They called these Spaniards "gods come from the heavens"; the Mexicans thought they were all gods, including the black ones, whom they called the dusky gods. . . .

As for the magicians, wizards, sorcerers, and soothsayers, Moctezuma had sent them just in case they might size up the Spaniards differently and be able to use their arts against them — cast a spell over them, blow them away, enchant them, throw stones at them, with wizards' words say an incantation over them — anything that might sicken them, kill them, or turn them back. They fulfilled their charge; they tried their skill on the Spaniards;

but what they did had no effect whatsoever. They were powerless.

These men then returned to report to Moctezuma. "We are not as strong as they," was what they said as they described the Spaniards to him. "We are nothing compared to them.". . .

Moctezuma could only wait for the Spaniards, could only show resolution. He quieted, he controlled himself; he made himself submit to whatever was in store for him. So he left his proper dwelling, the great palace, so that the gods — the Spaniards — could occupy it, and moved to the palace he had originally occupied as a prince.

The Spaniards, pressing inland meanwhile to go through the city of Cempoalla, had with them a previously captured man known to have been a high warrior. He was now interpreting for them and guiding them, since he knew the roads and could keep them on the right ones.

Thus they came to reach a place called Tecoac, held by people of the Otomí tribe subject to the city of Tlaxcalla.[7] Here the men of Tecoac resisted; they came out with their weapons. But the Spaniards completely routed them. They trampled them down; they shot them down with their guns; they riddled them with the bolts of their crossbows. They annihilated them, not just a few but a great many.

When Tecoac perished, the news made the Tlaxcallans beside themselves with fear. They lost courage; they gave way to wonder, to terror, until they gathered themselves together and, at a meeting of the rulers, took counsel, weighed the news among themselves, and discussed what to do.

"How shall we act?" some asked. "Shall we meet with them?"

Others said, "The Otomís are great warriors, great fighters, yet the Spaniards thought nothing of them. They were as nothing. In no time,

[5]These were specially bred war dogs, which were used as attack animals.
[6]That is, the Aztecs, who called themselves the *Mexica*.

[7]Tlaxcalla was an independent state in the mountains east of the Aztec capital of Tenochtitlán.

with but the batting of an eyelash, they annihilated our vassals."

"The only thing to do," advised still others, "is to submit to these men, to befriend them, to reconcile ourselves to them. Otherwise, sad would be the fate of the common folk."

This argument prevailed. The rulers of Tlaxcalla went to meet the Spaniards with food offerings of turkey, eggs, fine white tortillas — the tortillas of lords.

"You have tired yourselves, O our lords," they said.

The Spaniards asked, "Where is your home? Where are you from?"

"We are Tlaxcallans," they answered. "You have tired yourselves. You have come to your poor home, Quauhtlaxcalla.". . .

The Tlaxcallans led the Spaniards to the city, to their palace. They made much of them, gave them whatever they needed, waited upon them, and comforted them with their daughters.

The Spaniards, however, kept asking them "Where is Mexico? What is it like? Is it far?"

"From here it is not far," was the answer; "it is a matter of perhaps only three days' march. It is a very splendid place; the Mexicans are strong, brave, conquering people. You find them everywhere."

Now the Tlaxcallans had long been enemies of the people of Cholula.[8] They disliked, hated, detested them; they would have nothing to do with them. Hoping to do them harm, they inflamed the Spaniards against them, saying, "They are very evil, these enemies of ours. Cholula is as powerful as Mexico. Cholula is friendly to Mexico."

Therefore the Spaniards at once went to Cholula, taking the Tlaxcallans and the Cempoallans with them all in war array. They arrived; they entered Cholula. Then there arose from the Spaniards a cry summoning all the noblemen, lords, war leaders, warriors, and common folk; and when they had crowded into the temple courtyard, then the Spaniards and their allies blocked the entrances and every exit.

There followed a butchery of stabbing, beating, killing of the unsuspecting Cholulans armed with no bows and arrows, protected by no shields, unable to contend against the Spaniards. So with no warning they were treacherously, deceitfully slain. The Tlaxcallans had induced the Spaniards to do this.

What had happened was reported quickly to Moctezuma: his messengers, who had just arrived, departed fleeing back to him. They did not remain long to learn all the details. The effect upon the people of Mexico, however, was immediate; they often rose in tumults, alarmed as by an earthquake, as if there were a constant reeling of the face of the earth. They were terrified.

After death came to Cholula, the Spaniards resumed their marching order to advance upon Mexico. They assembled in their accustomed groups, a multitude, raising a great dust. The iron of their lances and their halberds glistened from afar; the shimmer of their swords was as of a sinuous water course. Their iron breast and back pieces, their helmets clanked. Some came completely encased in iron — as if turned to iron, gleaming, resounding from afar. And ahead of them, preceding them, ran their dogs, panting, with foam continually dripping from their muzzles.

All this stunned the people, terrified them, filled them with fear, with dread.

---

[8]A city allied with the Aztecs, some fifty miles east of Tenochtitlán.

The "Mountain of Silver" and the Mita System
▼▼▼

102 ▼ *Antonio Vazquez de Espinosa,* COMPENDIUM AND DESCRIPTION OF THE WEST INDIES

Many of Columbus's dreams and promises for the lands he explored were never realized, but his vision that the inhabitants could be exploited proved all too correct. Queen Isabella was, by most accounts, disquieted by the idea of enslaving Amerindians, but forced labor came to the new Spanish colonies nevertheless, largely because it proved economically advantageous for the colonizers, especially on their plantations and in their mines.

In 1545 an Indian herder lost his footing on a mountain in Peru while chasing his llama, and to keep from falling he grabbed a bush, which he pulled from the ground to reveal a rich vein of silver. This is the most widely told story about how the Spaniards learned of the world's richest silver mine, at Potosí. Located two miles above sea level in a cold, desolate region of modern Bolivia, Potosí became the site of the western hemisphere's first and greatest silver rush. Within four decades, Potosí had a racially mixed population of 160,000, making it the largest, wildest, gaudiest, and richest city in the New World. With one fifth of all the silver extracted going directly to the Spanish crown, Potosí was also a major reason why the kings of Spain were able to launch a huge naval armada against England in 1588, carry on a crusade against the Ottoman Empire in the eastern Mediterranean, and send off armies to campaigns in France, the Low Countries, and central Europe. The silver of Potosí also contributed significantly to massive inflation in Spain and, as the wealth filtered out of the Iberian peninsula, throughout Western Europe.

The backbone of the Potosí operation was the *mita* system of labor, described in the following document by Antonio Vazquez de Espinosa (d. 1630), a Spanish Carmelite friar who abandoned an academic career to do missionary work in the Americas. He returned to Spain in 1622 where he wrote a half-dozen books on the Americas and topics relating to priestly work. His best-known book is his *Compendium and Description of the West Indies*, an extensive summary of observations made during his travels through Mexico and Spanish South America.

In the first part of the selection that follows Espinosa describes the mine and facilities at Huancavelica for extracting and processing mercury, a necessary element in the refining of silver. The second portion provides a wealth of details on the mining of silver ore at Potosí. Throughout the document, Espinosa presents insights into the functioning of the mita system of labor, which had its roots in the Inca Empire when villages had been required to provide an annual quota of laborers for public works projects. The Spaniards continued the practice of enforced labor quotas, at first for public works and later for work in mines, factories, and fields owned by private individuals.

QUESTIONS FOR ANALYSIS

1. What was the range of annual wages for each laborer at Huancavelica? How did this amount of money compare with the annual salary of the royal hospital chaplain? How did the annual sum of their wages compare with the cost of tallow candles at Potosí? Compare the wages of the mita workers at Potosí with the wages paid those Amerindians who freely hired themselves out. What do you conclude from all these figures?
2. What were the major hazards of the work connected with the extraction and production of mercury and silver?
3. What evidence does Espinosa provide of Spanish concern for the welfare of the Amerindian workers? What evidence is there of unconcern? Where does the weight of the evidence seem to lie?
4. Wherever huge profits justify the risks, there will be people who function beyond the constraints of the law. What evidence does Espinosa provide of such a phenomenon in Spanish South America?
5. How did the mita system work?
6. What appears to have been the impact of the mita system on native Peruvian society?

And so at the rumor of the rich deposits of mercury in the days of Don Francisco de Toledo, in the years 1570 and 1571, they started the construction of the town of Huancavelica de Oropesa in a pleasant valley at the foot of the range. It contains 400 Spanish residents, as well as many temporary shops of dealers in merchandise and groceries, heads of trading houses, and transients, for the town has a lively commerce. It has a parish church with vicar and curate,[1] a Dominican convent, and a Royal Hospital under the Brethren of San Juan de Diós for the care of the sick, especially Indians on the range; it has a chaplain with a salary of 800 assay pesos contributed by His Majesty; he is curate of the parish of San Sebastián de Indios, for the Indians who have come to work in the mines and who have settled down there. There is another parish on the other side of the town, known as Santa Ana, and administered by Dominican friars.

Every two months His Majesty sends by the regular courier from Lima[2] 60,000 pesos to pay for the mita of the Indians, for the crews are changed every two months, so that merely for the Indian mita payment {in my understanding of it} 360,000 pesos are sent from Lima every year, not to speak of much besides, which all crosses at his risk that cold and desolate mountain country which is the puna[3] and has nothing on it but llama ranches.

Up on the range there are 3,000 or 4,000 Indians working in the mine; it is colder up there than in the town, since it is higher. The mine where the mercury is located, is a large layer which they keep following downward. When I was in that town (which was in the year 1616) I went up on the range and down into the mine, which at that time was considerably more than 130 stades[4] deep. The ore was very rich black flint, and the excavation so extensive that it held more than 3,000 Indians working

---

[1] A parish priest and his assistant priest.
[2] Lima was the capital city of the viceroyalty of Peru, one of the two major administrative units of Spanish America, covering all of Spanish South America, except for part of the Caribbean coast.
[3] A high, cold plateau.
[4] A stade was a measure of length, approximately an eighth of a mile.

away hard with picks and hammers, breaking up that flint ore: and when they have filled their little sacks, the poor fellows, loaded down with ore, climb up those ladders or rigging, some like masts and others like cables, and so trying and distressing that a man empty-handed can hardly get up them. That is the way they work in this mine, with many lights and the loud noise of the pounding and great confusion. Nor is that the greatest evil and difficulty; that is due to thievish and undisciplined superintendents. As that great vein of ore keeps going down deeper and they follow its rich trail, in order to make sure that no section of that ore shall drop on top of them, they keep leaving supports or pillars of the ore itself, even if of the richest quality, and they necessarily help to sustain and insure each section with less risk. This being so, there are men so heartless that for the sake of stealing a little rich ore, they go down out of hours and deprive the innocent Indians of this protection by hollowing into these pillars to steal the rich ore in them, and then a great section is apt to fall in and kill all the Indians, and sometimes the unscrupulous and grasping superintendents themselves, as happened when I was in that locality; and much of this is kept quiet so that it shall not come to the notice of the manager and cause the punishment of the accomplices. . . .

This is how they extract the mercury. On the other side of the town there are structures where they grind up the mercury ore and then put it in jars with molds like sugar loaves on top of them, with many little holes, and others on top of them, flaring and plastered with mud, and a channel for it to drip into and pass into the jar or place where it is to fall. Then they roast the ore with a straw fire from the plant growing on the puna, like esparto grass, which they call ichu; that is the best sort of fire for the treatment of this ore. Under the onset of this fire it melts and the mercury goes up in vapor or exhalation until, passing through the holes in the

first mold, it hits the body of the second, and there it coagulates, rests, and comes to stop where they have provided lodging for it; [but] if it does not strike any solid body while it is hot, it rises as vapor until it cools and coagulates and starts falling downward again. Those who carry out the reduction of this ore have to be very careful and test cautiously; they must wait till the jars are cold before uncovering them for otherwise they may easily get mercury poisoning and if they do, they are of no further use; their teeth fall out, and some die. After melting and extracting the mercury by fire, they put it in dressed sheepskins to keep it in His Majesty's storehouses, and from there they usually transport it on llamaback to the port of Chincha . . . , where there is a vault and an agent appointed by the Royal Council, and he has charge of it there; then they freight it on shipboard to the port of San Marcos de Arica, from which it is carried by herds of llamas and mules to Potosí. In the treatment of the silver they use up every year more than 6,000 quintas,[5] plus 2,000 more derived from the ore dust, i.e., the silver and mercury which was lost and escaped from the first washing of the ore, made in vats.

• • •

The famous Potosí range, so celebrated all over the world for the great wealth which God has created unique in its bowels and veins, lies in the Province of the Charcas, 18 leagues from the city of Chuquisaca, which was later called La Plata, on account of the great richness of this range. It is in the midst of the Cordillera, and since that is high-altitude country, that region is usually colder than Germany, so much so that it was uninhabitable for the native tribes. . . . On account of the cold, not a fly, mosquito, or [any] other unpleasant creature can live there; there was no living thing on that waste but guanacos, vicuñas, ostriches, and vizcachas, which are characteristic of that cold country.

• • •

---

[5]A measure of weight equaling anywhere from 100 to 130 pounds.

According to His Majesty's warrant, the mine owners on this massive range have a right to the mita of 13,300 Indians in the working and exploitation of the mines, both those which have been discovered, those now discovered, and those which shall be discovered. It is the duty of the Corregidor of Potosí[6] to have them rounded up and to see that they come in from all the provinces between Cuzco over the whole of El Collao and as far as the frontiers of Tarija and Tomina;[7] this Potosí Corregidor has power and authority over all the Corregidors in those provinces mentioned; for if they do not fill the Indian mita allotment assigned each one of them in accordance with the capacity of their provinces as indicated to them, he can send them, and does, salaried inspectors to report upon it, and when the remissness is great or remarkable, he can suspend them, notifying the Viceroy[8] of the fact.

These Indians are sent out every year under a captain whom they choose in each village or tribe, for him to take them and oversee them for the year each has to serve; every year they have a new election, for as some go out, others come in. This works out very badly, with great losses and gaps in the quotas of Indians, the villages being depopulated; and this gives rise to great extortions and abuses on the part of the inspectors toward the poor Indians, ruining them and thus depriving the . . . chief Indians of their property and carrying them off in chains because they do not fill out the mita assignment, which they cannot do, for the reasons given and for others which I do not bring forward.

These 13,300 are divided up every 4 months into 3 mitas, each consisting of 4,433 Indians, to work in the mines on the range and in the 120 smelters in the Potosí and Tarapaya areas;

it is a good league[9] between the two. These mita Indians earn each day, or there is paid each one for his labor, 4 reals.[10] Besides these there are others not under obligation, who are mingados or hire themselves out voluntarily: these each get from 12 to 16 reals, and some up to 24, according to their reputation of wielding the pick and knowing how to get the ore out. These mingados will be over 4,000 in number. They and the mita Indians go up every Monday morning to the locality of Guayna Potosí which is at the foot of the range; the Corregidor arrives with all the provincial captains or chiefs who have charge of the Indians assigned them, and he there checks off and reports to each mine and smelter owner the number of Indians assigned him for his mine or smelter; that keeps him busy till 1 p.m., by which time the Indians are already turned over to these mine and smelter owners.

After each has eaten his ration, they climb up the hill, each to his mine, and go in, staying there from that hour until Saturday evening without coming out of the mine; their wives bring them food, but they stay constantly underground, excavating and carrying out the ore from which they get the silver. They all have tallow candles, lighted day and night; that is the light they work with, for as they are underground, they have need of it all the time. The mere cost of these candles used in the mines on this range will amount every year to more than 300,000 pesos, even though tallow is cheap in that country, being abundant; but this is a very great expense, and it is almost incredible, how much is spent for candles in the operation of breaking down and getting out the ore.

These Indians have different functions in the handling of silver ore; some break it up with bar or pick, and dig down in, following the

---

[6]A district military leader.
[7]This region consisted of approximately 139 Indian villages.
[8]Literally, "the royal deputy," he was appointed by the crown to serve as chief military and civil administrator over a vast region.

[9]A league is three miles.
[10]A Spanish silver coin.

vein in the mine; others bring it up; others up above keep separating the good and the poor in piles; others are occupied in taking it down from the range to the mills on herds of llamas; every day they bring up more than 8,000 of these native beasts of burden for this task. These teamsters who carry the metal do not belong to the mita, but are mingados — hired.

So huge is the wealth which has been taken out of this range since the year 1545, when it was discovered, up to the present year of 1628, which makes 83 years that they have been working and reducing its ores, that merely from the registered mines, as appears from an examination of most of the accounts in the royal records, 326,000,000 assay pesos have been taken out. At the beginning when the ore was richer and easier to get out, for then there were no mita Indians and no mercury process, in the 40 years between 1545 and 1585, they took out 111,000,000 of assay silver. From the year 1585 up to 1628, 43 years, although the mines are harder to work, for they are deeper down, with the assistance of 13,300 Indians whom His Majesty has granted to the mine owners on

that range, and of other hired Indians, who come there freely and voluntarily to work at day's wages, and with the great advantage of the mercury process, in which none of the ore or the silver is wasted, and with the better knowledge of the technique which the miners now have, they have taken out 215,000,000 assay pesos. That, plus the 111 extracted in the 40 years previous to 1585, makes 326,000,000 assay pesos, not counting the great amount of silver secretly taken from these mines . . . to Spain, paying no 20 percent or registry fee,[11] and to other countries outside Spain; and to the Philippines and China, which is beyond all reckoning; but I should venture to imagine and even assert that what has been taken from the Potosí range must be as much again as what paid the 20 percent royal impost.

Over and above that, such great treasure and riches have come from the Indies in gold and silver from all the other mines in New Spain and Peru, Honduras, the New Kingdom of Granada, Chile, New Galicia, New Bizcaya, and other quarters since the discovery of the Indies, that they exceed 1,800 millions.

▼▼▼

European Perspectives on the New World

As much as Europeans were surprised and intrigued by what their explorers and merchants encountered in Africa and Asia, nothing prepared them for the shocking implications of Columbus's discoveries across the Atlantic. Few knew what to make of two vast continents populated by people who were ignorant of Christianity and, by European standards, technologically backward, but who showed signs of sophisticated government and great wealth. Were the Indians, as Columbus called them, true human beings? Did they have souls and the gift of reason? If so, how should Europeans treat them? These questions became urgent when it became apparent that the Europeans' diseases, weaponry, horses, and war dogs made it impossible for the Indians to mount anything resembling effective resistance. Did the Amerindians' very weakness and "heathenism" jus-

---

[11]The 20 percent registry fee was the royal tax on all New World silver.

tify their exploitation and enslavement? Or did the Europeans have an obligation to convert the Americans to Christianity, to protect them from exploitation, and to make honest efforts to teach them the ways of Western civilization? Going further, did Europeans have the obligation to respect native cultures?

Of all the peoples of Europe, the Spaniards agonized over these issues with the greatest and most genuine concern. Churchmen, soldiers, royal officials, colonists, queens, and kings searched their souls and exercised their minds to find a policy that satisfied their quest for gain while expressing their religious principles. The controversy in Spain reached a climax in 1550, when at the command of King Charles I, two leading intellectuals, Juan Ginés de Sepúlveda and Bartolomé de Las Casas, debated the issue of Spain's Amerindian policy before a panel of judges at Valladolid for an entire week. The judges never came to a decision, and both Las Casas, who defended the Amerindians' rights, and Sepúlveda, who justified the Indians' enslavement, claimed victory.

Sadly, any objective observer would be forced to conclude that the history of Spanish colonialism confirmed Sepúlveda the winner. Although Spanish officials and churchmen continued to limit and regulate the exploitation of Native Americans, unquestionably, exploitation remained the Amerindians' lot.

The Uncivilized Have Been Justly Conquered
▼▼▼

103 ▼ Juan Ginés de Sepúlveda,
THE JUST CAUSES OF WAR AGAINST THE INDIANS

Juan Ginés de Sepúlveda (1490–1573) was born into a Spanish aristocratic family and studied classical languages and literature at the University of Alcala in Spain. With ambitions for a scholarly career, he moved to Italy, where he studied and taught for twenty years. He later served as the court chaplain and official historian for both Charles I and Philip II of Spain. Although best known for his translations of and commentaries on the various works of Aristotle, a fourth-century B.C. Greek philosopher and scientist, he also wrote a number of original philosophical and theological treatises. His theory that superior peoples had the right to enslave inferiors was an elaboration of an argument he found in Aristotle. Sepúlveda first expressed his views in 1547 in his *Democrates Secundus, or the Treatise on the Just Causes of War Against the Indians*, a fictitious dialogue between Democrates, who expresses the author's views, and Leopoldo, who serves as his foil. The arguments he advanced in 1550 against Las Casas were based on this work. He died in 1573, embittered by the controversies that had clouded his old age.

QUESTIONS FOR ANALYSIS

1. What proof does Sepúlveda offer to defend his argument that superior people have the right to enslave their inferiors?
2. According to Sepúlveda, what qualities of the Spaniards make them superior?
3. What qualities of the Amerindians make them worthy of enslavement in Sepúlveda's view?
4. What is there about the fate of the Aztecs that reinforces Sepúlveda's general views of the Amerindians?
5. If, for the sake of argument, one were to accept Sepúlveda's premises, do his conclusions necessarily follow?
6. What might the judges at Valladolid have found convincing in Sepúlveda's arguments? What weaknesses might they have discerned?

It is established then, in accordance with the authority of the most eminent thinkers, that the dominion of prudent, good, and humane men over those of contrary disposition is just and natural. Nothing else justified the legitimate empire of the Romans over other peoples, according to the testimony of St. Thomas in his work on the rule of the Prince. St. Thomas here followed St. Augustine, who, in referring to the empire of the Romans in the fifth book of *The City of God,* wrote: "God conceded to the Romans a very extensive and glorious empire in order to keep grave evils from spreading among many peoples who, in search of glory, coveted riches and many other vices."[1] In other words God gave the Romans their empire so that, with the good legislation that they instituted and the virtue in which they excelled, they might change the customs and suppress and correct the vices of many barbarian peoples. . . .

Turning then to our topic, whether it is proper and just that those who are superior and who excel in nature, customs, and laws rule over their inferiors, you can easily understand . . . if you are familiar with the character and moral code of the two peoples, that it is with perfect right that the Spaniards exercise their dominion over those barbarians of the New World and its adjacent islands. For in prudence, talent, and every kind of virtue and human sentiment they are as inferior to the Spaniards as children are to adults, or women to men, or the cruel and inhumane to the very gentle, or the excessively intemperate to the continent and moderate.

But I do not think that you expect me to speak of the prudence and talent of the Spaniards, for you have, I think, read Lucan, Silius Italicus, the two Senecas, and among later figures St. Isidore, who is inferior to none in theology, and Averroes and Avempace, who are ex-

---

[1]St. Thomas Aquinas (1225–1274), a member of the Dominican religious order, was a leading theologian in his day; during the sixteenth century the Catholic Church accepted his theological views as authoritative. St. Augustine of Hippo (354–430) was the dominant Christian thinker of the late Roman Empire whose writings on sal- vation, the Church, human nature, and the sacraments have exerted profound influence on Christian thought for the past 1,500 years. *The City of God,* one of his most original works, places all of human history into a theological perspective.

cellent in philosophy, and in astronomy King Alfonso,[2] not to mention others whom it would take too long to enumerate. And who is ignorant of the Spaniards' other virtues: courage, humanity, justice, and religion? I refer simply to the princes and to those whose aid and skill they utilize to govern the state, to those, in short, who have received a liberal education. . . . And what shall I say of their moderation in rejecting gluttony and lasciviousness, inasmuch as no nation or very few nations of Europe can compare with the frugality and sobriety of the Spaniards? I admit that I have observed in these most recent times that through contact with foreigners luxury has invaded the tables of our nobles. Still, since this is reproved by good men among the people, it is to be hoped that in a short while they may return to the traditional and innate sobriety of our native custom. . . .

As for the Christian religion, I have witnessed many clear proofs of the firm roots it has in the hearts of Spaniards, even those dedicated to the military. The best proof of all has seemed to me to be the fact that in the great plague that followed the sack of Rome, in the Pontificate of Clement VII, not a single Spaniard among those who died in the epidemic failed to request in his will that all the goods stolen from the citizens be restored to them.[3] And though there were many more Italians and Germans, no non-Spaniard, to my knowledge, fulfilled this obligation of the Christian religion. And I, who was following the army and was in the city observing it all diligently, was a witness to it. I recall that we have mentioned this in that Vatican meeting. What shall I say of the Spanish soldiers' gentleness and humanitarian sentiments? Their only and great solicitude and care in the battles, after the winning of the victory, is to save the greatest possible number of vanquished and free them from the cruelty of their allies. Now compare these qualities of prudence, skill, magnanimity, moderation, humanity, and religion with those of those little men [of America] in whom one can scarcely find any remnants of humanity. They not only lack culture but do not even use or know about writing or preserve records of their history — save for some obscure memory of certain deeds contained in painting.[4] They lack written laws and their institutions and customs are barbaric. And as for their virtues, if you wish to be informed of their moderation and mildness, what can be expected of men committed to all kinds of passion and nefarious lewdness and of whom not a few are given to the eating of human flesh. Do not believe that their life before the coming of the Spaniards was one of Saturnine peace,[5] of the kind that poets sang about. On the contrary, they made war with each other almost continuously, and with such fury that they considered a victory to be empty if they could not satisfy their prodigious hunger with the flesh of their enemies. This form of cruelty is especially prodigious among these people, remote as they are from the invincible ferocity of the Scythians,[6] who also ate human bodies. But in other respects they are so cowardly and timid that they can scarcely offer any resistance to the hos-

[2]All eight of these men were born in Spain: Lucan (65–39 B.C.) was a Latin poet; Silius Italicus (ca A.D. 25–100) was a Latin epic poet and Roman politician; Seneca the Elder (55 B.C.–A.D. 39) wrote a book on Roman rhetoricians; Seneca the Younger (4 B.C.–A.D. 65) was a statesman, philosopher, and tragedian; Isadore of Seville (560–636) was an historian and theologian; Averroes (1126–1198) and Avempace (d. 1138) were Spanish Arab philosophers; King Alfonso X of Castile and Leon (r. 1252–1284) was a famous patron of learning and literature.

[3]The Sack of Rome took place in 1527 during the Italian Wars (1494–1559) when troops loyal to Emperor Charles V (also, as king of Spain, known as Charles I), frustrated over unpaid back wages, went on a protracted rampage of looting, murder, rape, and vandalism. The pope at the time was Clement VII (r. 1523–1534).
[4]A reference to Aztec "picture writing." See source 101.
[5]The age of the Etruscan-Roman god Saturn was, in Roman mythology, a golden age of harmony.
[6]Originally from Central Asia, the Scythians moved into southern Russia in the eighth and seventh centuries B.C. They were known for their ferocity and cruelty, but the charge of cannibalism was probably unfounded.

tile presence of our side, and many times thousands and thousands of them have been dispersed and have fled like women, on being defeated by a small Spanish force scarcely amounting to one hundred.

So as not to detain you longer in this matter, consider the nature of those people in one single instance and example, that of the Mexicans, who are regarded as the most prudent and courageous. Their king was Montezuma, whose empire extended the length and breadth of those regions and who inhabited the city of Mexico, a city situated in a vast lake, and a very well defended city both on account of the nature of its location and on account of its fortifications. It was similar to Venice, they say, but nearly three times as large both in extent and in population.[7] Informed of the arrival of Cortés and of his victories and his intention to go to Mexico under pretext of a conference, Montezuma sought all possible means to divert him from his plan.[8] Failing in this, terrorized and filled with fear, he received him in the city with about three hundred Spaniards. Cortés for his part, after taking possession of the city, held the people's cowardliness, ineptitude, and rudeness in such contempt that he not only compelled the king and his principal subjects, through terror, to receive the yoke and rule of the king of Spain, but also imprisoned King Montezuma himself, because of his suspicion that a plot was on foot to kill some Spaniards in a certain province. This he could do because of the stupor and inertia of the people, who were indifferent to the situation and preoccupied with other things than the taking up of arms to liberate their king. And thus Cortés, though aided by so small a number of Spaniards and so few natives, was able to hold them, oppressed and fearful at the beginning, for many days. They were so immense a multitude that he seemed lacking not only in discretion and prudence but even in common sense. Could

there be a better or clearer testimony of the superiority that some men have over others in talent, skill, strength of spirit, and virtue? Is it not proof that they are slaves by nature? For the fact that some of them appear to have a talent for certain manual tasks is no argument for their greater human prudence. We see that certain insects, such as the bees and the spiders, produce works that no human skill can imitate. And as for the civil life of the inhabitants of New Spain and the province of Mexico, I have already said that the people are considered to be the most civilized of all. They themselves boast of their public institutions as if it were not a sufficient proof of their industry and civilization that they have rationally constructed cities, and kings appointed by popular suffrage rather than by hereditary right and age, and a commerce like that of civilized people. But see how they deceive themselves and how different is my opinion from theirs, since for me the foremost proof of the rudeness and barbarism and innate servitude of those people lies precisely in their public institutions, nearly all of which are servile and barbarous. They do have houses, and some rational mode of common life, and such commerce as natural necessity demands, but what does this prove other than that they are not bears or monkeys completely lacking in reason?

I have made reference to the customs and character of the barbarians. What shall I say now of the impious religion and wicked sacrifices of such people, who, in venerating the devil as if he were God, believed that the best sacrifice that they could placate him with was to offer him human hearts? . . . Opening up the human breasts they pulled out the hearts and offered them on their heinous altars. And believing that they had made a ritual sacrifice with which to placate their gods, they themselves ate the flesh of the victims. These are crimes that are considered by the philosophers

---

[7]See Chapter 11, source 89.
[8]See source 101.

to be among the most ferocious and abominable perversions, exceeding all human iniquity. . . .

How can we doubt that these people — so uncivilized, so barbaric, contaminated with so many impieties and obscenities — have been justly conquered by . . . a nation excellent in every kind of virtue, with the best law and best benefit for the barbarians? Prior to the arrival of the Christians they had the nature, customs, religion, and practice of evil sacrifice as we have explained. Now, on receiving with our rule our writing, laws, and morality, imbued with the Christian religion, having shown themselves to be docile to the missionaries that we have sent them, as many have done, they are as different from their primitive condition as civilized people are from barbarians, or as those with sight from the blind, as the inhuman from the meek, as the pious from the impious, or to put it in a single phrase, in effect, as men from beasts.

"They Are Our Brothers"
▼▼▼

104 ▼ Bartolomé de Las Casas,
IN DEFENSE OF THE INDIANS

Bartolomé de Las Casas (1474–1566), Spain's defender of Amerindian rights, was born into a family of small merchants. After abandoning his studies for a stint of soldiering, he embarked for Hispaniola in 1502 in the entourage of the new governor of the island, Nicolas de Ovando. Las Casas received grants of land and Indian labor from the governor and participated in the conquest of Cuba between 1511 and 1515. In 1515 he renounced all property and rights in the Americas and returned to Spain where he began to lobby the Spanish government on behalf of the Native Americans. In 1519, with royal approval, he sought to establish a cooperative Spanish-Amerindian farming community in Venezuela, but it generated little enthusiasm and the experiment failed. He then joined the Dominican order and continued to write and work on behalf of the Amerindians while living in Spanish America and traveling regularly back to Spain. His denunciations of Spanish policy and alleged cruelties so struck the conscience of Charles I that the king arranged for the debate between Las Casas and Sepúlveda in 1550. After the debate, Las Casas remained in Spain to live in a Dominican convent in Madrid. The following selection comes from Las Casas's actual response to Sepúlveda at Valladolid, which he read over a five-day period and later published as a treatise. Although the work, usually referred to as *In Defense of the Indians*, existed in several Latin manuscript versions, it was not published until the twentieth century.

QUESTIONS FOR ANALYSIS

1. Why, according to Las Casas, is it significant that the Indians have established effective governments?
2. How does Las Casas's definition of a *barbarian* seem to differ from that of Sepúlveda?
3. How do their respective views of the Spaniards differ?
4. How do Las Casas's historical arguments differ from those of Sepúlveda?
5. What positive qualities does Las Casas see in the Indians?
6. What, according to Las Casas, are the implications of Sepúlveda's arguments for international relations?
7. The judges could not decide a winner. What may explain this?
8. Put yourself in the place of one of the Valladolid judges, and write an explanation of why you have chosen Las Casas or Sepúlveda as the winner.

However, he admits, and proves, that the barbarians he deals with . . . have a lawful, just, and natural government. Even though they lack the art and use of writing, they are not wanting in the capacity and skill to rule and govern themselves, both publicly and privately. Thus they have kingdoms, communities, and cities that they govern wisely according to their laws and customs. Thus their government is legitimate and natural, even though it has some resemblance to tyranny. From these statements we have no choice but to conclude that the rulers of such nations enjoy the use of reason and that their people and the inhabitants of their provinces do not lack peace and justice. Otherwise they could not be established or preserved as political entities for long. . . . Therefore not all barbarians are irrational or natural slaves or unfit for government. Some barbarians, then, in accord with justice and nature, have kingdoms, royal dignities, jurisdiction, and good laws, and there is among them lawful government.

Now if we shall have shown that among our Indians of the western and southern shores (granting that we call them barbarians and that they are barbarians) there are important kingdoms, large numbers of people who live settled lives in a society, great cities, kings, judges and laws, persons who engage in commerce, buying, selling, lending, and the other contracts of the law of nations, will it not stand proved that the Reverend Doctor Sepúlveda has spoken wrongly and viciously against peoples like these, either out of malice or ignorance of Aristotle's teaching, and, therefore, has falsely and perhaps irreparably slandered them before the entire world? From the fact that the Indians are barbarians it does not necessarily follow that they are incapable of government and have to be ruled by others, except to be taught about the Catholic faith and to be admitted to the holy sacraments. They are not ignorant, inhuman, or bestial. Rather, long before they had heard the word Spaniard they had properly organized states, wisely ordered by excellent laws, religion, and custom. They cultivated friendship and, bound together in common fellowship, lived in populous cities in which they wisely administered the affairs of both peace and war justly and equitably, truly governed by laws that at very many points surpass ours, and could have won the admiration of the sages of Athens, as I will show in the second part of this *Defense*.

Now if they are to be subjugated by war because they are ignorant of polished literature, let Sepúlveda hear Trogus Pompey.[1]

Nor could the Spaniards submit to the yoke of a conquered province until Caesar Augustus, after he had conquered the world, turned his victorious armies against them and organized that barbaric and wild people as a province, once he had led them by law to a more civilized way of life.

Now see how he called the Spanish people barbaric and wild. I would like to hear Sepúlveda, in his cleverness, answer this question: Does he think that the war of the Romans against the Spanish was justified in order to free them from barbarism? And this question also: Did the Spanish wage an unjust war when they vigorously defended themselves against them?

Next, I call the Spaniards who plunder that unhappy people torturers. Do you think that the Romans, once they had subjugated the wild and barbaric peoples of Spain, could with secure right divide all of you among themselves, handing over so many head of both males and females as allotments to individuals? And do you then conclude that the Romans could have stripped your rulers of their authority and consigned all of you, after you had been deprived of your liberty, to wretched labors, especially in searching for gold and silver lodes and mining and refining the metals? And if the Romans finally did that, as is evident from Diodorus,[2] [would you not judge] that you also have the right to defend your freedom, indeed your very life, by war? Sepúlveda, would you have per-

mitted Saint James[3] to evangelize your own people of Córdoba in that way? For God's sake and man's faith in him, is this the way to impose the yoke of Christ on Christian men? Is this the way to remove wild barbarism from the minds of barbarians? Is it not, rather, to act like thieves, cut-throats, and cruel plunderers and to drive the gentlest of people headlong into despair? The Indian race is not that barbaric, nor are they dull witted or stupid, but they are easy to teach and very talented in learning all the liberal arts, and very ready to accept, honor, and observe the Christian religion and correct their sins (as experience has taught) once priests have introduced them to the sacred mysteries and taught them the word of God. They have been endowed with excellent conduct, and before the coming of the Spaniards, as we have said, they had political states that were well founded on beneficial laws.

Furthermore, they are so skilled in every mechanical art that with every right they should be set ahead of all the nations of the known world on this score, so very beautiful in their skill and artistry are the things this people produces in the grace of its architecture, its painting, and its needlework. . . .

In the liberal arts that they have been taught up to now, such as grammar and logic, they are remarkably adept. With every kind of music they charm the ears of their audience with wonderful sweetness. They write skillfully and quite elegantly, so that most often we are at a loss to know whether the characters are handwritten or printed. . . .

From this it is clear that the basis for Sepúlveda's teaching that these people are uncivilized and ignorant is worse than false. Yet even if we

---

[1] A Roman historian of the first century B.C.; only fragments survive of his ambitious history of Assyria, Persia, Greece, Rome, Gaul, and Spain.

[2] A Greco-Roman historian of the late first century B.C.

[3] According to legend, the body of St. James, one of the original twelve apostles, or closest friends of Jesus, was carried to Spain where, as St. James "the Moor-Slayer," he became the patron saint of the Christian Reconquest of the Iberian peninsula from Islam. The church of Santiago de Compostela in northwest Spain, believed to be the site of his relics, became one of the most popular pilgrimage destinations in all of Europe from the late ninth century onward.

were to grant that this race has no keenness of mind or artistic ability, certainly they are not, in consequence, obliged to submit themselves to those who are more intelligent and to adopt their ways, so that, if they refuse, they may be subdued by having war waged against them and be enslaved, as happens today. For men are obliged by the natural law to do many things they cannot be forced to do against their will. We are bound by the natural law to embrace virtue and imitate the uprightness of good men. No one, however, is punished for being bad unless he is guilty of rebellion. Where the Catholic faith has been preached in a Christian manner and as it ought to be, all men are bound by the natural law to accept it, yet no one is forced to accept the faith of Christ. . . .

Therefore, not even a truly wise man may force an ignorant barbarian to submit to him, especially by yielding his liberty, without doing him an injustice. This the poor Indians suffer, with extreme injustice, against all the laws of God and of men and against the law of nature itself. For evil must not be done that good may come of it, for example, if someone were to castrate another against his will. For although eunuchs are freed from the lust that drives human minds forward in its mad rush, yet he who castrates another is most severely punished. . . .

Now, if on the basis of this utterly absurd argument, war against the Indians were lawful, one nation might rise up against another and one man against another man, and on the pretext of superior wisdom, might strive to bring the other into subjection. On this basis the Turks, and the Moors — the truly barbaric

scum of the nations — with complete right and in accord with the law of nature could carry on war, which, as it seems to some, is permitted to us by a lawful decree of the state. If we admit this, will not everything high and low, divine and human, be thrown into confusion? What can be proposed more contrary to the eternal law than what Sepúlveda often declares? What plague deserves more to be loathed? . . .

Hence every nation, no matter how barbaric, has the right to defend itself against a more civilized one that wants to conquer it and take away its freedom. And, moreover, it can lawfully punish with death the more civilized as a savage and cruel aggressor against the law of nature. And this war is certainly more just than the one that, under pretext of wisdom, is waged against them. . . .

Again, if we want to be sons of Christ and followers of the truth of the gospel, we should consider that, even though these peoples may be completely barbaric, they are nevertheless created in God's image. They are not so forsaken by divine providence that they are incapable of attaining Christ's kingdom. They are our brothers, redeemed by Christ's most precious blood, no less than the wisest and most learned men in the whole world. Finally, we must consider it possible that some of them are predestined to become renowned and glorious in Christ's kingdom. Consequently, to these men who are wild and ignorant in their barbarism we owe the right which is theirs, that is, brotherly kindness and Christian love. . . . Christ wanted love to be called his single commandment. This we owe to all men. Nobody is excepted. . . .

▼▼▼

African Reactions to the European Presence

Due mainly to the catastrophic decline of the Amerindian population, Spanish and Portuguese colonists increasingly turned to African slaves for labor in the sixteenth century. Portugal, which had begun to explore the west coast of Africa in 1418, was initially in an especially advantageous position to supply this human chattel. During the 1480s the Portuguese established fortified posts along West Africa's Gold Coast, where it traded with such coastal kingdoms as Benin for gold, slaves, and ivory. By 1500 some seven hundred kilos of gold and approximately 10,000 slaves were arriving annually in Lisbon from West Africa. While engaging in this trade, the Portuguese were also pushing down the coast. Finally, in 1487–1488 Bartolomeu Dias rounded the Cape of Good Hope, opening the east coast of Africa to direct Portuguese contact. Under the leadership of Francisco de Almeida (ca 1450–1510), the Portuguese set up fortified trading posts along Africa's east coast, thereby successfully challenging Arab hegemony over East African trade.

The Portuguese led the way, but other European maritime powers were not far behind in establishing their presence in Africa. While the Spanish concentrated on North Africa, capturing Tunis in 1535 and holding it until 1574, the English under John Hawkins instituted their own slave trade from West Africa to the New World between 1562 and 1568. After 1713, when England won the right of *asiento*, by which it was granted license to transport African slaves to the Spanish Americas, the English came to dominate the African slave trade. In 1595 the Dutch began to trade on the Guinea coast, and in 1652 they founded Cape Town on the southern tip of the continent. The first French forts in Africa appeared in 1626 on the island of Madagascar, which France annexed in 1686, and by 1637 the French were building numerous forts on West Africa's Gold Coast and exploring Senegal. Even the Prussians had a minor presence in West Africa by 1683.

Slaves and gold were the two major attractions for all these European powers on the African coasts, and many Africans were quite willing to deal in these commodities with the outside world. Although the Europeans were becoming a major presence along the coasts, their penetration of the interior would have to wait for a later age. The general social and political strength of most African regional kingdoms, the wide variety of debilitating and often deadly African diseases, against which the Europeans had no immunities, and the absence of safe and fast inland transportation combined to block significant European thrust into the interior until the nineteenth century. The Europeans were thus forced to come largely as traders and not colonizers, and they had to negotiate with local African leaders for goods and slaves.

An African Voice of Protest
▼▼▼

105 ▾ *Nzinga Mbemba (Afonso I),* *LETTERS TO THE KING OF PORTUGAL*

The largest state in central West Africa by 1500 was the kingdom of Kongo, stretching along the estuary of the Congo River in territory that today lies within the nations of Angola and Zaire. In 1483 the Portuguese navigator Diogo Cão made contact with Kongo and several years later visited its inland capital. When he sailed home he brought with him Kongo emissaries, whom King Nzinga a Kuwu dispatched to Lisbon to learn European ways. They returned in 1491, accompanied by Portuguese priests, artisans, and soldiers, who brought with them a wide variety of European goods, including a printing press. In the same year, the king and his son, Nzinga Mbemba, were baptized into the Catholic faith.

Around 1506 Nzinga Mbemba, whose Christian name was Afonso, succeeded his father and ruled until about 1543. Afonso promoted the introduction of European culture into his kingdom by adopting Christianity as the state religion (although most of his subjects, especially those in the hinterlands, remained followers of the ancient ways), imitating the etiquette of the Portuguese royal court, and using Portuguese as the language of state business. His son Henrique was educated in Portugal and returned to serve as West Africa's first black Roman Catholic bishop. European firearms, horses, and cattle, as well as new foods from the Americas, became common in Kongo, and Afonso dreamed of achieving a powerful and prosperous state through cooperation with the Europeans. By the time of his death, however, his kingdom was on the verge of disintegration, in no small measure because of the Portuguese. As many later African rulers were to discover, the introduction of European products and customs unsettled the people and caused widespread dissension. Worse, the unceasing Portuguese pursuit of slaves undermined Afonso's authority and made his subjects restive.

In 1526 King Afonso wrote the following three letters to King João III of Portugal. The three documents are part of a collection of twenty-four letters that Afonso and his Portuguese-educated native secretaries dispatched to two successive kings of Portugal on a variety of issues. This collection is our earliest extant source of African commentary on the European impact.

QUESTIONS FOR ANALYSIS

1. According to King Afonso, how have the availability of Portuguese goods and the presence of slave traders affected Kongo society?
2. Does King Afonso see the Portuguese presence in his kingdom as a right or a privilege?
3. How has King Afonso attempted to control Portuguese activity?
4. How does King Afonso distinguish between legitimate and illegitimate trade in slaves?
5. What elements of Portuguese culture does he welcome? Why?
6. How would you characterize the general tone of these letters? What do they suggest about King Afonso's relations with the Portuguese?

Sir, Your Highness should know how our Kingdom is being lost in so many ways that it is convenient to provide for the necessary remedy, since this is caused by the excessive freedom given by your agents and officials to the men and merchants who are allowed to come to this Kingdom to set up shops with goods and many things which have been prohibited by us, and which they spread throughout our Kingdoms and Domains in such an abundance that many of our vassals, whom we had in obedience, do not comply because they have the things in greater abundance than we ourselves; and it was with these things that we had them content and subjected under our vassalage and jurisdiction, so it is doing a great harm not only to the service of God, but the security and peace of our Kingdoms and State as well.

And we cannot reckon on how great the damage is, since the mentioned merchants are taking every day our natives, sons of the land and the sons of our noblemen and vassals and our relatives, because the thieves and men of bad conscience grab them wishing to have the things and wares of this Kingdom which they are ambitious of; they grab them and get them to be sold; and so great, Sir, is the corruption of licentiousness that our country is being completely depopulated, and Your Highness should not agree with this nor accept it as in your ser-

vice. And to avoid it we need from those (your) Kingdoms no more than some priests and a few people to teach in schools, and no other goods, except wine and flour for the holy sacrament. That is why we beg of Your Highness to help and assist us in this matter, commanding your agents that they should not send here either merchants or wares, because it is *our will that in these Kingdoms there should not be any trade of slaves nor outlet for them.*[1] Concerning what is referred above, again we beg of Your Highness to agree with it, since otherwise we cannot remedy such an obvious damage. Pray Our Lord in His mercy to have Your Highness under His guard and let you do for ever the things of His service.

The King. Dom Afonso.

•   •   •

Moreover, Sir, in our Kingdoms there is another great inconvenience which is of little service to God, and this is that many of our people, keenly desirous as they are of the wares and things of your Kingdoms, which are brought here by your people, and in order to satisfy their voracious appetite, seize many of our people, freed and exempt men; and very often it happens that they kidnap even noblemen and the sons of noblemen, and our relatives, and take them to be sold to the white men who are in our Kingdoms; and for this purpose they have

---

[1]Emphasis appears in the original letter.

concealed them; and others are brought during the night so that they might not be recognized.

And as soon as they are taken by the white men they are immediately ironed and branded with fire, and when they are carried to be embarked, if they are caught by our guards' men the whites allege that they have bought them but they cannot say from whom, so that it is our duty to do justice and to restore to the freemen their freedom, but it cannot be done if your subjects feel offended, as they claim to be.

And to avoid such a great evil we passed a law so that any white man living in our Kingdoms and wanting to purchase goods in any way should first inform three of our noblemen and officials of our court whom we rely upon in this matter, and these are Dom Pedro Manipanza and Dom Manuel Manissaba, our chief usher, and Gonçalo Pires our chief freighter, who should investigate if the mentioned goods[2] are captives or free men, and if cleared by them there will be no further doubt nor embargo for them to be taken and embarked. But if the white men do not comply with it they will lose the aforementioned goods. And if we do them this favor and concession it is for the part Your Highness has in it, since we know that it is in your service too that these goods are taken from our Kingdom, otherwise we should not consent to this.

· · ·

Sir, Your Highness has been kind enough to write to us saying that we should ask in our letters for anything we need, and that we shall be provided with everything, and as the peace and the health of our Kingdom depend on us, and as there are among us old folks and people who have lived for many days, it happens that we have continuously many and different diseases which put us very often in such a weakness that we reach almost the last extreme; and the same happens to our children, relatives and natives owing to the lack in this country of physicians and surgeons who might know how to cure properly such diseases. And as we have got neither dispensaries nor drugs which might help us in this forlornness, many of those who had been already confirmed and instructed in the holy faith of Our Lord Jesus Christ perish and die; and the rest of the people in their majority cure themselves with herbs and breads and other ancient methods, so that they put all their faith in the mentioned herbs and ceremonies if they live, and believe that they are saved if they die; and this is not much in the service of God.

And to avoid such a great error and inconvenience, since it is from God in the first place and then from your Kingdoms and from Your Highness that all the good and drugs and medicines have come to save us, we beg of you to be agreeable and kind enough to send us two physicians and two apothecaries and one surgeon, so that they may come with their drugstores and all the necessary things to stay in our kingdoms, because we are in extreme need of them all and each of them. We shall do them all good and shall benefit them by all means, since they are sent by Your Highness, whom we thank for your work in their coming. We beg of Your Highness as a great favor to do this for us, because besides being good in itself it is in the service of God as we have said above.

---

[2]Slaves.

The West African Slave Trade
▼▼▼

106 ▼ *James Barbot,*
THE ABSTRACT OF A VOYAGE TO NEW CALABAR RIVER, OR RIO RIVER, IN THE YEAR 1699

The preceding document illustrates how an African king's attempt to control commerce between his subjects and the Portuguese was at least partially frustrated and how the slave trade had a number of tragic consequences for African society. This source offers another perspective. James Barbot, a member of a late seventeenth-century English slave-trading expedition to Ibani, describes trade negotiations with its king, William, in 1699. Ibani, or Bonny, as the English called it, was an island state in the Niger delta. By the late eighteenth century it was the principal slave market of the entire Guinea coast. One English captain, who sailed to Bonny between 1786 and 1800, estimated that at least twenty thousand slaves were bought and sold there annually. In this document we see how the trading system worked a century earlier.

QUESTIONS FOR ANALYSIS

1. How would you characterize trade at Bonny? Was it haphazard bartering? A well-developed system with specific currency? Something else?
2. How did the English benefit from the way in which trade was conducted?
3. What benefits did the king enjoy from this arrangement?
4. What was Barbot's attitude toward Ibani society?
5. How did the Ibani seem to regard the English?
6. What do the prices of the other commodities purchased by the English say about the relative value of one slave?
7. Who was the exploiter, and who was the exploited?
8. What does this account reveal about social structure in Ibani?

June 30, 1699, being ashore, had a new conference which produced nothing. Then Pepprell [Pepple] the king's brother delivered a message from the king.

He was sorry we would not accept his proposals. It was not his fault, since he had a great esteem and regard for the whites, who had greatly enriched him through trade. His insistence on thirteen bars[1] for male and ten for female slaves was due to the fact that the people of the country maintained a high price for slaves at their inland markets, seeing so many large ships coming to Bonny for them. However, to moderate matters and to encourage trade with us, he would be content with thirteen bars for males and nine bars and two brass rings for females, *etc.*

We offered thirteen bars for men and nine for women and proportionately for boys and girls, according to their ages. Following this we parted, without concluding anything further.

On July 1, the king sent for us to come ashore. We stayed there till four in the afternoon and concluded the trade on the terms offered them the day before. The king promised to come aboard the next day to regulate it and be paid his duties. . . .

The second [of July]. . . . At two o'clock we fetched the king from shore, attended by all his *Caboceiros*[2] and officers, in three large canoes. Entering the ship, he was saluted with seven guns. The king had on an old-fashioned scarlet coat, laced with gold and silver, very rusty, and a fine hat on his head, but bare-footed. All his attendants showed great respect to him and, since our arrival, none of the natives have dared to come aboard or sell the least thing, till the king adjusted trade matters.

We had again a long talk with the king and Pepprell, his brother, concerning the rates of our goods and his customs. This Pepprell was a sharp black and a mighty talking black, perpetually making objections against something or other and teasing us for this or that *dassy*[3] or present, as well as for drinks, etc. Would that such a one as he were out of the way, to facilitate trade. . . .

Thus, with much patience, all our affairs were settled equitably, after the fashion of a people who are not very scrupulous when it comes to finding excuses or objections for not keeping to the word of any verbal contract. For they do not have the art of reading and writing, and we therefore are forced to stand to their agreement, which often is no longer than they think fit to hold it themselves. The king ordered the public crier to proclaim permission to trade with us, with the noise of his trumpets . . . we paying sixteen brass rings to the fellow for his fee. The blacks objected against our wrought pewter and tankards, green beads and other goods, which they would not accept. . . .

We gave the usual presents to the king. . . . To Captain Forty, the king's general, Captain Pepprell, Captain Boileau, alderman Bougsby, my lord Willyby, duke of Monmouth, drunken Henry and some others[4] two firelocks, eight hats, nine narrow Guinea stuffs. We adjusted with them the reduction of our merchandise into bars of iron, as the standard coin, namely: one bunch of beads, one bar; four strings of rings, ten rings each, one ditto; four copper bars, one ditto. . . . And so on *pro rata* for every sort of goods. . . .

The price of provisions and wood was also regulated.

Sixty king's yams, one bar; one hundred and sixty slave's yams, one bar; for fifty thousand yams to be delivered to us. A butt[5] of water, two rings. For the length of wood, seven bars, which is dear, but they were to deliver it ready cut into our boat. For one goat, one bar. A cow, ten or eight bars, according to its size. A hog, two bars. A calf, eight bars. A jar of palm oil, one bar and a quarter.

We also paid the king's duty in goods; five hundred slaves, to be purchased at two copper rings a head.

---

[1]Bars of iron.
[2]A Portuguese term. Here it means "chiefs and elders."
[3]A trade term meaning "gift."

[4]The king's chiefs and elders.
[5]A large cask.

▼▼▼

Chinese and Japanese Reactions to the West

China and Japan were no exception to the rule that most societies in Africa and Eurasia were able to resist successfully European efforts during the sixteenth and seventeenth centuries to impose trade on Western terms and Christianity. Yet, although ultimately rebuffed by the Chinese and Japanese, European merchants and missionaries had good reason to believe during the sixteenth century that their labors in East Asia would be richly rewarded.

Portuguese traders reached south China in 1513, opened trade at Guangzhou (Canton) in 1514, and established a permanent trading base in Macao in 1557. In 1542, the first Portuguese merchants reached Japan and soon were reaping healthy profits by carrying goods between China and Japan. Later in the century, the Dutch and English successfully entered these East Asian markets. Roman Catholic Europeans, especially the Portuguese, energetically supported missionary efforts in China and Japan, usually in cooperation with the newly founded Society of Jesus, more popularly known as the Jesuits. Francis Xavier and other Jesuits began preaching in Japan in 1549, and by the early 1600s they had won approximately 300,000 converts to Christianity. Catholic missionary activities in China began later, in 1583, and followed a somewhat different strategy: the Jesuits did less preaching to the common people and instead sought the support of Chinese intellectuals, government officials, and members of the imperial court. The Jesuits were moderately successful because they impressed Confucian scholars with their erudition, especially in mathematics and science, and the Chinese appreciated the missionaries' willingness to understand and respect China's culture.

For all their efforts, the economic benefits and religious gains the Westerners obtained were meager. Although the Chinese tolerated learned Jesuit missionaries, they viewed European merchants as boorish, overly aggressive, and purveyors of shoddy goods. Preferring to deal with Arabs and other foreigners, they limited trade with Europeans to Guangzhou and Macao and placed it under numerous restrictions. Missionary activity resulted in a few converts, but feuding among Catholic religious orders, staunch opposition from many Chinese officials, and the unwillingness of most Chinese, even converts, to abandon such ancient rites as ancestor worship weakened the enterprise. When in 1742 Pope Benedict XIV decreed that Chinese Catholics must abandon Confucianism, Emperor Qianlong expelled the missionaries and Chinese Christianity withered.

Although European efforts to win souls and trade had a more promising start in Japan, by the mid-seventeenth century the Japanese had suppressed Christianity and restricted European trade to only one Dutch ship a year. This turn of events resulted from attempts by Japanese leaders to bring stability to Japan after a century of civil war and rebellion. Convinced that European merchants and missionaries had contributed to Japan's disorder, the government outlawed Christianity and essentially closed Japan to the outside world.

The Jesuits in China
▼▼▼

107 ▼ Matteo Ricci, JOURNALS

The most celebrated of the Jesuit scholar-missionaries to work in China was the Italian Matteo Ricci (1552–1610), who arrived in 1583. Father Ricci dazzled the Chinese literarchy with clocks, maps, and various types of scientific equipment, much of which he constructed himself. A gifted linguist, he composed over twenty-five works in Chinese on mathematics, literature, ethics, geography, astronomy, and, above all else, religion. He so impressed Confucian scholars that they accorded him the title Doctor from the Great West Ocean. In 1601 Emperor Wanli summoned Ricci to his court at Beijing and provided him with a subsidy to carry on his study of mathematics and astronomy. When Ricci died, the emperor donated a burial site outside the gates of the imperial city as a special token of honor.

During his twenty-seven years in China, Ricci kept a journal, with no thought of publishing it. Shortly after his death, however, a Jesuit colleague edited and published the journal, into which he incorporated a number of other, more official sources, and it became one of Europe's primary stores of information about China until the late eighteenth century, when accounts by European travelers to the Middle Kingdom became more common. In the following selection from that diary, Ricci tells of charges brought against certain Jesuits working at Nanchang. Here we can see some of the cultural barriers and attitudes that frustrated the Jesuits' efforts to accommodate Christianity to Chinese civilization.

QUESTIONS FOR ANALYSIS

1. What most offended the Confucians who brought charges against the Jesuits and their religion?
2. The Jesuits' association with Father Ricci seems to have favored them in the course of events. Why? What was there about Ricci that gave his Jesuit colleagues an aura of legitimacy?
3. Why did Ricci view the outcome as a Christian victory?

4. How do you think the Jesuits' Confucian opponents saw this confrontation and its resolution?
5. Imagine you are the Chief Justice, and you are preparing a report to the imperial court concerning your decision, the reasoning behind it, and what you believe will be its consequences. Compose that report.
6. Compare the charges brought against the Jesuits with Han Yu's *Memorial on Buddhism* (Chapter 6, source 51). Which are more striking, the differences or the similarities? What do you conclude from your answer?

During 1606 and the year following, the progress of Christianity in Nancian[1] was in no wise retarded. . . . The number of neophytes[2] increased by more than two hundred, all of whom manifested an extraordinary piety in their religious devotions. As a result, the reputation of the Christian religion became known throughout the length and breadth of this metropolitan city. . . .

Through the efforts of Father Emanuele Dias another and a larger house was purchased, in August of 1607, at a price of a thousand gold pieces. This change was necessary, because the house he had was too small for his needs and was situated in a flood area. Just as the community was about to change from one house to the other, a sudden uprising broke out against them. . . .

At the beginning of each month, the Magistrates hold a public assembly . . . in the temple of their great Philosopher.[3] When the rites of the new-moon were completed in the temple, and these are civil rather than religious rites,[4] one of those present took advantage of the occasion to speak on behalf of the others, and to address the highest Magistrate present. . . . "We wish to warn you," he said, "that there are certain foreign priests in this royal city, who are preaching a law, hitherto unheard of in this kingdom,[5] and who are holding large

gatherings of people in their house." Having said this, he referred them to their local Magistrate, . . . and he in turn ordered the plaintiffs to present their case in writing, assuring them that he would support it with all his authority, in an effort to have the foreign priests expelled. The complaint was written out that same day and signed with twenty-seven signatures. . . . The content of the document was somewhat as follows.

Matthew Ricci, Giovanni Soerio, Emanuele Dias, and certain other foreigners from western kingdoms, men who are guilty of high treason against the throne, are scattered amongst us, in five different provinces. They are continually communicating with each other and are here and there practicing brigandage on the rivers, collecting money, and then distributing it to the people, in order to curry favor with the multitudes. They are frequently visited by the Magistrates, by the high nobility and by the Military Prefects, with whom they have entered into a secret pact, binding unto death.

These men teach that we should pay no respect to the images of our ancestors, a doctrine which is destined to extinguish the love of future generations for their

---

[1]Nanchang, in the southern province of Kiangsi.
[2]Converts.
[3]Confucius.

[4]Ricci and his fellow Jesuits chose to regard all ceremonies of ancestor worship as purely "civil rites," thereby allowing their converts to continue to pay traditional devotion to deceased family members.
[5]Ricci refers to China throughout his journal as a "kingdom," even though it had an emperor, not a king.

forebears. Some of them break up the idols, leaving the temples empty and the gods to be pitied, without any patronage. In the beginning they lived in small houses, but by this time they have bought up large and magnificent residences. The doctrine they teach is something infernal. It attracts the ignorant into its fraudulent meshes, and great crowds of this class are continually assembled at their houses. Their doctrine gets beyond the city walls and spreads itself through the neighboring towns and villages and into the open country, and the people become so wrapt up in its falsity, that students are not following their course, laborers are neglecting their work, farmers are not cultivating their acres, and even the women have no interest in their housework. The whole city has become disturbed, and, whereas in the beginning there were only a hundred or so professing their faith, now there are more than twenty thousand. These priests distribute pictures of some Tartar or Saracen,[6] who they say is God, who came down from heaven to redeem and to instruct all of humanity, and who alone, according to their doctrine, can give wealth and happiness; a doctrine by which the simple people are very easily deceived. These men are an abomination on the face of the earth, and there is just ground for fear that once they have erected their own temples, they will start a rebellion. . . . Wherefore, moved by their interest in the maintenance of the public good, in the conservation of the realm, and in the preservation, whole and entire, of their ancient laws, the petitioners are presenting this complaint and demanding, in the name of the entire province, that a rescript of it be forwarded to the King, asking that these foreigners be sentenced to death, or

banished from the realm, to some deserted island in the sea. . . .

Each of the Magistrates to whom the indictment was presented asserted that the spread of Christianity should be prohibited, and that the foreign priests should be expelled from the city, if the Mayor saw fit, after hearing the case, and notifying the foreigners. . . . But the Fathers,[7] themselves, were not too greatly disturbed, placing their confidence in Divine Providence, which had always been present to assist them on other such dangerous occasions.

▷ Father Emanuele is summoned before the Chief Justice.

Father Emanuele, in his own defense, . . . gave a brief outline of the Christian doctrine. Then he showed that according to the divine law, the first be honored, after God, were a man's parents. But the judge had no mind to hear or to accept any of this and he made it known that he thought it was all false. After that repulse, with things going from bad to worse, it looked as if they were on the verge of desperation, so much so, indeed, that they increased their prayers, their sacrifices, and their bodily penances, in petition for a favorable solution of their difficulty. Their adversaries appeared to be triumphantly victorious. They were already wrangling about the division of the furniture of the Mission residences, and to make results doubly certain, they stirred up the flames anew with added accusations and indictments. . . .

The Mayor, who was somewhat friendly with the Fathers, realizing that there was much in the accusation that was patently false, asked the Magistrate Director of the Schools,[8] if he knew whether or not this man Emanuele was a com-

---

[6]The reference is to Jesus Christ.
[7]The Jesuits.

[8]The director of the local Confucian academy was one of the Jesuits' chief opponents.

panion of Matthew Ricci, who was so highly respected at the royal court, and who was granted a subsidy from the royal treasury, because of the gifts he had presented to the King. Did he realize that the Fathers had lived in Nankin[9] for twelve years, and that no true complaint had ever been entered against them for having violated the laws. Then he asked him if he had really given full consideration as to what was to be proven in the present indictment. To this the Director of the Schools replied that he wished the Mayor to make a detailed investigation of the case and then to confer with him. The Chief Justice then ordered the same thing to be done. Fortunately, it was this same Justice who was in charge of city affairs when Father Ricci first arrived in Nancian. It was he who first gave the Fathers permission, with the authority of the Viceroy, to open a house there. . . .

After the Mayor had examined the charges of the plaintiffs and the reply of the defendants, he subjected the quasi-literati[10] to an examination in open court, and taking the Fathers under his patronage, he took it upon himself to refute the calumnies of their accusers. He said he was fully convinced that these strangers were honest men, and that he knew that there were only two of them in their local residence and not twenty, as had been asserted. To this they replied that the Chinese were becoming their disciples. To which the Justice in turn replied: "What of it? Why should we be afraid of our own people? Perhaps you are unaware of the fact that Matthew Ricci's company is cultivated by everyone in Pekin, and that he is being subsidized by the royal treasury. How dare the Magistrates who are living outside of the royal city expel men who have permission to live at the royal court? These men here have lived peacefully in Nankin for twelve years. I command," he added, "that they buy no more large houses, and that the people are not to follow their law.". . .

A few days later, the court decision was pronounced and written out. . . . and was then posted at the city gates as a public edict. The following is a summary of their declaration. Having examined the cause of Father Emanuele and his companions, it was found that these men had come here from the West because they had heard so much about the fame of the great Chinese Empire, and that they had already been living in the realm for some years, without any display of ill-will. Father Emanuele should be permitted to practice his own religion, but it was not considered to be the right thing for the common people, who are attracted by novelties, to adore the God of Heaven. For them to go over to the religion of foreigners would indeed be most unbecoming. . . . It would therefore seem to be . . . [in] . . . the best interests of the Kingdom, to . . . [warn]. . .everyone in a public edict not to abandon the sacrifices of their ancient religion by accepting the cult of foreigners. Such a movement might, indeed, result in calling together certain gatherings, detrimental to the public welfare, and harmful also to the foreigner, himself. Wherefore, the Governor of this district, by order of the high Magistrates, admonishes the said Father Emanuele to refrain from perverting the people, by inducing them to accept a foreign religion. The man who sold him the larger house is to restore his money and Emanuele is to buy a smaller place, sufficient for his needs, and to live there peaceably, as he has done, up to the present. Emanuele, himself, has agreed to these terms and the Military Prefects of the district have been ordered to make a search of the houses

---

[9]Nanjing, the southern auxiliary capital.

[10]Ricci's term for the chief tormenters of the Jesuits in Nanchang. These were Confucian scholars who had passed the first and most basic of the three Confucian civil-service examinations and were thereby known popularly as "cultivated talents." By passing the first examination level, these men earned recognition simply as competent students (quasi-literati). They were subject to periodic reexamination at that level and could lose their status and privileges. Only those who passed the second, or provincial, level examination, and became "elevated men," attained a permanent rank and were eligible for appointment to one of the lower civil posts. Apparently these "cultivated talents" felt threatened by the Jesuits.

there and to confiscate the pictures of the God they speak of, wherever they find them. It is not permitted for any of the native people to go over to the religion of the foreigners, nor is it permitted to gather together for prayer meetings. Whoever does contrary to these prescriptions will be severely punished, and if the Military Prefects are remiss in enforcing them, they will be held to be guilty of the same crimes. To his part of the edict, the Director of the Schools added, that the common people were forbidden to accept the law of the foreigners, and that a sign should be posted above the door of the Father's residence, notifying the public that these men were forbidden to have frequent contact with the people.

The Fathers were not too disturbed by this pronouncement, because they were afraid that it was going to be much worse. In fact, everyone thought it was rather favorable, and that the injunction launched against the spread of the faith was a perfunctory order to make it appear that the literati were not wholly overlooked, since the Fathers were not banished from the city, as the literati had demanded. Moreover it was not considered a grave misdemeanor for the Chinese to change their religion, and it was not customary to inflict a serious punishment on those violating such an order. The neophytes, themselves, proved this when they continued, as formerly, to attend Mass.

The Seclusion of Japan
▼▼▼

108 ▼ *Tokugawa Iemitsu,*
"CLOSED COUNTRY EDICT OF 1635" AND "EXCLUSION OF THE PORTUGUESE, 1639"

When the first Europeans reached Japan, they encountered a land plagued by civil war and rebellion. The authority of the *shoguns*, military commanders who had ruled Japan on behalf of the emperor since the twelfth century, was in eclipse, as the *daimyo* (great lords) fought for power. Turbulence ended toward the close of the sixteenth century, when three military heroes, Oda Nobunaga (1534–1582), Toyotomi Hideyoshi (1536–1598), and Tokugawa Ieyasu (1543–1616), forced the daimyo to accept central authority. In 1603 the emperor recognized Tokugawa Ieyasu as shogun; the era of the Tokugawa Shogunate, which lasted to 1868, had begun.

Between 1624 and 1641, Iemitsu, grandson of Ieyasu and shogun from 1623 to 1651, issued edicts that closed Japan to virtually all foreigners. This was the culmination of policies begun under Toyotomi Hideyoshi, who had sought to limit contacts between Japanese and foreigners, especially Catholic missionaries. He and his successors viewed the missionaries' aggressive proselytizing as a potential source of social unrest and rebellion. The first document that follows, the most celebrated of Tokugawa Iemitsu's edicts, is directed to the two *bugyo*, or commissioners, of Nagasaki, a port city in southwest Japan and a center of Japanese Christianity; the second more specifically deals with the missionary activities of the Portuguese.

QUESTIONS FOR ANALYSIS

1. To what extent was the edict of 1635 directed against the activities of foreigners? To what extent was it directed against certain "antisocial" activities by Japanese?
2. Much of the 1635 edict dealt with trade issues. What do the various trade provisions suggest about the shogun's attitude toward commerce?
3. What was the major purpose behind the 1635 edict?
4. What can one infer about the reasons for promulgating the 1639 edict?

CLOSED COUNTRY EDICT OF 1635

1. Japanese ships are strictly forbidden to leave for foreign countries.
2. No Japanese is permitted to go abroad. If there is anyone who attempts to do so secretly, he must be executed. The ship so involved must be impounded and its owner arrested, and the matter must be reported to the higher authority.
3. If any Japanese returns from overseas after residing there, he must be put to death.
4. If there is any place where the teachings of padres[1] is practiced, the two of you must order a thorough investigation.
5. Any informer revealing the whereabouts of the followers of padres must be rewarded accordingly. If anyone reveals the whereabouts of a high ranking padre, he must be given one hundred pieces of silver. For those of lower ranks, depending on the deed, the reward must be set accordingly.
6. If a foreign ship has an objection [to the measures adopted] and it becomes necessary to report the matter to Edo,[2] you may ask the Ōmura[3] domain to provide ships to guard the foreign ship. . . .
7. If there are any Southern Barbarians[4] who propagate the teachings of padres, or otherwise commit crimes, they may be incarcerated in the prison. . . .
8. All incoming ships must be carefully searched for the followers of padres.

9. No single trading city shall be permitted to purchase all the merchandise brought by foreign ships.
10. Samurai are not permitted to purchase any goods originating from foreign ships directly from Chinese merchants in Nagasaki.
11. After a list of merchandise brought by foreign ships is sent to Edo, as before you may order that commercial dealings may take place without waiting for a reply from Edo.
12. After settling the price, all white yarns[5] brought by foreign ships shall be allocated to the five trading cities[6] and other quarters as stipulated.
13. After settling the price of white yarns, other merchandise [brought by foreign ships] may be traded freely between the [licensed] dealers. However, in view of the fact that Chinese ships are small and cannot bring large consignments, you may issue orders of sale at your discretion. Additionally, payment for goods purchased must be made within twenty days after the price is set.
14. The date of departure homeward of foreign ships shall not be later than the twentieth day of the ninth month. Any ships arriving in Japan later than usual shall depart within fifty days of their arrival. As to the departure of Chinese ships, you may use

---

[1]Fathers (Catholic priests).
[2]Modern Tokyo, the seat of the Tokugawa government.
[3]The area around Nagasaki.

[4]Westerners.
[5]Raw silk.
[6]The cities of Kyoto, Edo, Osaka, Sakai, and Nagasaki.

your discretion to order their departure after the departure of the Portuguese *galeota.*[7]

15. The goods brought by foreign ships which remained unsold may not be deposited or accepted for deposit.

16. The arrival in Nagasaki of representatives of the five trading cities shall not be later than the fifth day of the seventh month. Anyone arriving later than that date shall lose the quota assigned to his city.

17. Ships arriving in Hirado[8] must sell their raw silk at the price set in Nagasaki, and are not permitted to engage in business transactions until after the price is established in Nagasaki.

You are hereby required to act in accordance with the provisions set above. It is so ordered.

EXCLUSION OF THE PORTUGUESE, 1639

1. The matter relating to the proscription of Christianity is known [to the Portuguese]. However, heretofore they have secretly transported those who are going to propagate that religion.

2. If those who believe in that religion band together in an attempt to do evil things, they must be subjected to punishment.

3. While those who believe in the preaching of padres are in hiding, there are incidents in which that country [Portugal] has sent gifts to them for their sustenance.

In view of the above, hereafter entry by the Portuguese *galeota* is forbidden. If they insist on coming [to Japan], the ships must be destroyed and anyone aboard those ships must be beheaded. We have received the above order and are thus transmitting it to you accordingly.

The above concerns our disposition with regard to the *galeota.*

Memorandum

With regard to those who believe in Christianity, you are aware that there is a proscription, and thus knowing, you are not permitted to let padres and those who believe in their preaching to come aboard your ships. If there is any violation, all of you who are aboard will be considered culpable. If there is anyone who hides the fact that he is a Christian and boards your ship, you may report it to us. A substantial reward will be given to you for this information.

This memorandum is to be given to those who come on Chinese ships. [A similar note to the Dutch ships.]

▼▼▼

The Great Mughals and the West

Between 1526 and his death in 1530, the Turkish lord of Afghanistan, Babur, subdued north-central India with a small, well-equipped army that enjoyed the advantage of firearms received from the Ottoman Turks. This new Muslim lord of Hindustan, a direct descendant of the Mongol Chinggis Khan and the Turk Timur the Lame, initiated India's Mughal (the Persian word for Mongol) Age and laid the base for the reign of his grandson Jalal ad-Din Akbar (r. 1556–1605), known to history as simply Akbar (the Great).

---

[7]A galleon, an ocean-going Portuguese ship.
[8]A small island in the southwest, not far from Nagasaki.

Akbar's empire encompassed only the northern half of the Indian subcontinent. His great-grandson Aurangzeb (r. 1658–1707), the last effective Mughal emperor, reigned over twice that amount of land, holding all the subcontinent except its southern tip and the island of Ceylon (modern Sri Lanka). Nevertheless, Akbar fully deserved to be known as the "Great Mughal," a title awed European visitors to his court at Fatehpur-Sikri (the City of Victory) bestowed on him. From this court Akbar forged a centralized empire that during his reign of more than a half century enjoyed prosperity and a fair level of peace between Hindus and Muslims. Although the Portuguese had established three major bases along the west Indian coast by 1535, Akbar was secure enough in his power to keep them and other Europeans at arm's length throughout the last half of the sixteenth century.

The European presence, however, increased in the seventeenth century. In 1603 the English East India Company, chartered on 31 December 1600, the last day of the sixteenth century, sent its first envoy to Akbar's court. After defeating a Portuguese squadron in 1639, the English established their first trading station at Madras on India's east coast and in 1661 acquired Bombay on the west coast. As Portuguese influence in India declined, other European maritime powers secured trading privileges in the Mughal Empire. The Dutch acquired several important sites on both coasts between 1640 and 1663; in 1664 France founded an East India Company and several French trading bases followed. In time, the Dutch shifted their focus away from India to the islands of Southeast Asia, leaving the French and English to fight for control of the Indian markets.

Despite all these late seventeenth-century incursions along India's coasts, Emperor Aurangzeb was able to hold the West and its merchants at bay for the most part, even dealing the English a military setback in the 1680s. In 1700 the directors of the English East India Company rejected as unrealistic the notion of acquiring additional territory or establishing colonies in India. The decline of Mughal authority in the eighteenth century, however, changed the situation substantially, and toward mid-century the French and British were engaged in armed struggle for control of Indian territory.

Dealing with the *Faringis*
▼▼▼

109 ▼ *Abul Fazl, AKBARNAMA*

Assisting Akbar in formulating and carrying out his largely successful policies of state was Abul Fazl (1551–1602), the emperor's chief adviser and confidant from 1579 until Abul Fazl's assassination at the instigation of Prince Salim, the future Emperor Jahangir (r. 1605–1627). Abul Fazl's death cut short his composition of the *Akbarnama*, a gigantic, laudatory history of Akbar's distinguished ancestors and the emperor's own reign. Before he was murdered, Abul

Fazl carried his history to Akbar's forty-sixth year, creating a work universally regarded as one of the masterpieces of Mughal literature.

These thousands of pages of elegant Persian prose and poetry provide surprisingly few references to Akbar's or even India's relations with Europeans or *Faringis* (Franks), as they were called at the Mughal court. This silence speaks eloquently of the level of early Mughal concern with these foreigners. The following excerpts constitute the work's major references to Europeans in India.

QUESTIONS FOR ANALYSIS

1. What aspects of European culture most fascinated Akbar?
2. What did he and Abul Fazl believe they could gain from the *Faringis*?
3. What did they believe they could offer the Europeans?
4. How did Akbar and Abul Fazl regard the Portuguese coastal bases?
5. What does the discussion with Padre Radif (Father Rodolfo) tell us about Akbar and Abul Fazl's attitudes toward the teachings of Europe's Christian missionaries?
6. Jesuit missionaries to Akbar's court often believed they were on the verge of converting him to Roman Catholicism. Why do you suppose they believed this? What evidence strongly indicates there was never any chance Akbar would become a Christian?
7. Compare these accounts of Muslim-Christian relations with the memoirs of Usamah (Chapter 9, source 77). Which strike you as more significant, the similarities or the differences? What do you conclude from that answer?

One of the occurrences of the siege[1] was that a large number of Christians came from the port of Goa and its neighborhood to the foot of the sublime throne, and were rewarded by the bliss of an interview. Apparently they had come at the request of the besieged in order that the latter might make the fort over to them, and so convey themselves to the shore of safety. But when that crew saw the majesty of the imperial power, and had become cognizant of the largeness of the army, and of the extent of the siege-train they represented themselves as ambassadors and performed the *kornish*.[2] They produced many of the rarities of their country, and the appreciative Khedive[3] received each one of them with special favor and made inquiries about the wonders of Portugal and the manners and customs of Europe. It seemed as if he did this from a desire of knowledge, for his sacred heart is a storehouse of spiritual and physical sciences. But his . . . soul wished that these inquiries might be the means of civilizing this savage race.[4]

· · ·

---

[1]The siege of the west coast port of Surat in 1573 during Akbar's campaign in Gujarat (note 6). This successful expedition gave Akbar access to the sea. Through his conquests, Akbar more than tripled the empire he had inherited.

[2]The act of obeisance.
[3]Akbar.
[4]The Portuguese.

One of the occurrences was the dispatch of Haji Habibu-llah Kashi to Goa.[5] At the time when the country of Gujarat became included among the imperial dominions, and when many of the ports of the country came into possession, and the governors of the European ports became submissive,[6] many of the curiosities and rarities of the skilled craftsmen of that country became known to His Majesty. Accordingly the Haji,[7] who for his skill, right thinking and powers of observation was one of the good servants of the court, was appointed to take with him a large sum of money, and the choice articles of India to Goa, and to bring for His Majesty's delectation the wonderful things of that country. There were sent with him clever craftsmen, who to ability and skill added industry, in order that just as the wonderful productions of that country [Goa and Europe] were being brought away, so also might rare crafts be imported [into Akbar's dominions].

. . .

One of the occurrences was the arrival [at court] of Haji Habibullah. It has already been mentioned that he had been sent to the port of Goa with a large sum of money and skillful craftsmen in order that he might bring to his country the excellent arts and rarities of that place. On the 9th he came to do homage, attended by a large number of persons dressed up as Christians and playing European drums and clarions. He produced before His Majesty the choice articles of that territory. Craftsmen who had gone to acquire skill displayed the arts which they had learned and received praises in the critical place of testing. The musicians of that territory breathed fascination with the instruments of their country, especially with the organ. Ear and eye were delighted and so was the mind.

. . .

One night, the assembly in the 'Ibadatkhana[8] was increasing the light of truth. Padre Radif,[9] one of the Nazarene[10] sages, who was singular for his understanding and ability, was making points in that feast of intelligence. Some of the untruthful bigots[11] came forward in a blundering way to answer him. Owing to the calmness of the august assembly, and the increasing light of justice, it became clear that each of these was weaving a circle of old acquisitions, and was not following the highway of proof, and that the explanation of the riddle of truth was not present to their thoughts. The veil was nearly being stripped, once for all, from their procedure. They were ashamed, and abandoned such discourse, and applied themselves to perverting the words of the Gospels. But they could not silence their antagonist by such arguments. The Padre quietly and with an air of conviction said, "Alas, that such things should be thought to be true! In fact, if this faction have such an opinion of our Book, and regard the *Furqan* [the Qur'an] as the pure word of God, it is proper that a heaped fire be lighted. We shall take the Gospel in our hands, and the 'Ulama of that faith shall take their book, and then let us enter that testing-place of truth. The escape of any one will be a sign of his truthfulness." The liverless and black-hearted fellows wavered, and in reply to the challenge had recourse to bigotry and wrangling. This cowardice and effrontery displeased Akbar's equitable soul, and the banquet of enlightenment was made resplendent by acute observations. Continually, in those day-like nights, glorious subtleties and profound words dropped from his pearl-filled mouth.

---

[5]The chief Portuguese stronghold in India since 1510.
[6]In 1573 Akbar conquered the northwest coastal region of Gujarat, where the Portuguese held the ports of Diu and Bassein. In theory, but not fact, these Portuguese bases were now under imperial control.
[7]Haji Habibu-llah. He bore the title *Haji* because he had completed the hajj, or pilgrimage, to Mecca.

[8]The House of Worship, where Akbar held weekly Thursday-night discussions on theological issues with Muslim, Hindu, Zoroastrian, and Christian religious teachers.
[9]Father Rodolfo Acquaviva, a Jesuit missionary.
[10]Christian.
[11]Conservative Muslim *ulama,* or religious teachers.

Among them was this: "Most persons, from intimacy with those who adorn their outside, but are inwardly bad, think that outward semblance, and the letter of Islam, profit without internal conviction. Hence we by fear and force compelled many believers in the Brahman [i.e., Hindu] religion to adopt the faith of our ancestors. Now that the light of truth has taken possession of our soul, it has become clear that in this distressful place of contrarieties [the world], where darkness of comprehension and conceit are heaped up, fold upon fold, a single step cannot be taken without the torch of proof, and that that creed is profitable which is adopted with the approval of wisdom. To repeat the creed, to remove a piece of skin [i.e., to become circumcised] and to place the end of one's bones on the ground [i.e., the head in adoration]

from dread of the Sultan, is not seeking after God.

•   •   •

One of the occurrences was the appointing an army to capture the European ports.[12] Inasmuch as conquest is the great rule of princes, and by the observance of this glory-increasing practice, the distraction of plurality[13] places its foot in the peacefulness of unity, and the harassed world composes her countenance, the officers of the provinces of Gujarat and Malwa were appointed to this service under the leadership of Qutbu-d-din Khan on 18 Bahman, Divine month (February 1580). The rulers of the Deccan were also informed that the troops had been sent in that direction in order to remove the Faringis who were a stumbling-block in the way of the pilgrims to the Hijaz.[14]

Seventeenth-Century Commerce
▼▼▼

110 ▼ Jean-Baptiste Tavernier, TRAVELS IN INDIA

The increasing volume of French trade with seventeenth-century Mughal India attracted Jean-Baptiste Tavernier (1605–after 1689), a Parisian gem merchant, who arrived in India in 1640 on the first of five trips to the empire of the Great Mughal. Following his last voyage to India, which ended in 1668, Tavernier was able to live in wealthy semiretirement thanks to his profitable Eastern ventures. In 1670 he purchased the title of baron of Aubonne and settled down to write his memoirs, probably from notes he had made during his career in the East.

His *Travels* covers a pivotal period in Mughal-European relations. French and English merchants were becoming increasingly important in India, even as cracks were beginning to appear in the Mughal Empire under Shah Jahan (r. 1627–1658) and Aurangzeb (r. 1658–1707), whose respective building programs (Shah Jahan constructed the Taj Mahal) and military campaigns placed

---

[12]The ports of Diu and Bassein (note 6). This expedition was unsuccessful, and Abul Fazl tells us nothing else about it.

[13]That is, the distraction of multiple rulers.

[14]Pilgrims to Mecca. Many Muslims complained that, when embarking at Portuguese ports, they were forced to accept letters of passage imprinted with images of Jesus and Mary. Orthodox Muslims consider such images blasphemous, and some Muslim teachers went so far as to argue that it was better to forgo the pilgrimage than to submit to such sacrilege.

severe strains on the economy and general well-being of Indian society. In the following selection, Tavernier details the manner in which the Mughal government attempted to control and profit from the Western merchants and the tactics some Europeans employed to circumvent these controls and raise their profit margins.

QUESTIONS FOR ANALYSIS

1. Why do you think the English and Dutch East India companies paid a lower tariff on their imported goods and gold? What added to their costs of doing business in India, and why do you think they paid these extra expenses?
2. Did the European merchants take advantage of the Indian officials with whom they dealt? Did the Indian officials seem to resent or not want this business with the Europeans? What do your answers suggest?
3. Why do you think the officers of the Dutch and English East India companies were treated as described? Why did they refuse to engage in smuggling? What do your answers suggest about relations between the Mughal government and these trading companies?
4. What does the story of the roast pig suggest?
5. Do you perceive any significant differences in Indian-European relations between the era of Akbar and the period described by Tavernier? If so, what are they? What do these changes suggest to you?

As soon as merchandise is landed at Surat[1] it has to be taken to the custom-house, which adjoins the fort. The officers are very strict and search persons with great care. Private individuals pay as much as 4 and 5 percent duty on all their goods; but as for the English and Dutch Companies, they pay less. But, on the other hand, I believe that, taking into account what it costs them in . . . presents, which they are obliged to make every year at court, the goods cost them nearly the same as they do private persons.

Gold and silver are charged 2 percent,[2] and as soon as they have been counted at the custom-house the Mintmaster removes them, and coins them into money of the country, which he hands over to the owner, in proportion to the amount and standard of the bullion. You settle with him, according to the nature of the amount, a day when he is to deliver the new coins, and for as many days as he delays to do so beyond the term agreed upon, he pays interest in proportion to the sum which he has received. The Indians are cunning and exacting in reference to coin and payments; for when money has been coined for three or four years it has to lose $\frac{1}{2}$ percent,[3] and it continues in the same proportion according to age, not being able, as they say, to pass through many hands without some diminution. . . .

---

[1] A city on the west coast that served as India's main port of entry for Dutch, English, and French merchants and their goods at this time.

[2] For the Dutch and English East India companies.
[3] The Indians discounted these gold coins by $\frac{1}{2}$ of 1 percent because of the metal that had been rubbed off.

As regards gold, the merchants who import it use so much cunning in order to conceal it, that but little of it comes to the knowledge of the customs' officers. The former do all they can to evade paying the customs, especially as they do not run so much risk as in the custom-houses of Europe. For in those of India, when anyone is detected in fraud, he is let off by paying double, 10 percent instead of 5, the Emperor comparing the venture of the merchant to a game of hazard, where one plays double or quits.[4] However, for some time back this has been somewhat changed, and it is today difficult to compound with the customs' officers upon that condition. The Emperor has conceded to the English Captains that they shall not be searched when they leave their vessels to go on shore; but one day an English Captain, when going to Tatta,[5] one of the largest towns of India, a little above Sindi,[6] which is at the mouth of the river Indus, as he was about to pass, was arrested by the customs' guards, from whom he could not defend himself, and they searched him in spite of anything he could say. They found gold upon him; he had in fact already conveyed some in sundry journeys which he had made between his vessel and the town; he was, however, let off on payment of the ordinary duty. The Englishman, vexed by this affront, resolved to have his revenge for it, and he took it in a funny manner. He ordered a suckling-pig to be roasted, and to be placed with the grease in a china plate, covered with a napkin, and gave it to a slave to carry with him to the town, anticipating exactly what would happen. As he passed in front of the custom-house, where the Governor of the town, the Shah-bandar,[7] and the Master of the Mint were seated in a divan, they did not fail to stop him, but the slave still advancing with his covered plate,

they told his master that he must needs go to the custom-house, and that they must see what he carried. The more the Englishman protested that the slave carried nothing liable to duty, the less was he believed; and after a long discussion he himself took the plate from the hands of the slave, and proceeded to carry it to the custom-house. The Governor and the Shah-bandar thereupon asked him, in a sharp tone, why he refused to obey orders, and the Englishman, on his part, replied in a rage that what he carried was not liable to duty, and rudely threw the plate in front of them, so that the suckling-pig and the grease soiled the whole place, and splashed up on their garments. As the pig is an abomination to the Muslims, and by their Law they regard as defiled whatever is touched by it, they were compelled to change their garments, to remove the carpet from the divan, and to have the structure rebuilt, without daring to say anything to the Englishman, because the Shah-bandar and the Master of the Mint have to be careful with the Company,[8] from which the country derives so much profit. As for the Chiefs of the Companies, both English and Dutch, and their deputies, they are treated with so much respect that they are never searched when they come from their vessels; but they, on their part, do not attempt to convey gold in secret as the private merchants do, considering it beneath their dignity to do so. . . .

The English, seeing that the custom of searching them had been adopted, had recourse to little stratagems in order to pass the gold, and the fashion of wearing wigs having reached them from Europe, they bethought themselves of concealing . . . [gold coins] . . . in the nets of their wigs every time they left their vessels to go on shore.

---

[4]Tavernier writes elsewhere that another reason the Mughals had such a lenient policy in regard to smuggling was because Qur'anic law forbids charging interest and tariffs, and they were troubled by the practice.
[5]A city in modern Pakistan.
[6]Better known as Sind, this harbor at the mouth of the Indus River gave its name to the whole northwest corner of India (today Pakistan).
[7]The Mughal commissioner in charge of merchants.
[8]The English East India Company.

Chapter 14

▼▼▼

Religious and Intellectual Ferment

Historically, most societies have feared change and resisted innovation, especially when their basic religious beliefs and intellectual values are involved. This fact alone makes the period 1500–1700 so interesting to historians. Despite the weight of tradition, these two centuries witnessed great change in the ways certain people perceived their place in the cosmos.

The most striking changes took place in Europe and the Americas. In Europe a renaissance in art, literature, and the study and practice of statecraft produced new modes of expression and new aspirations. In the religious sphere, the Protestant Reformation, and the Catholic Counter Reformation it engendered, restructured and redefined Christianity for Protestants and Catholics alike. Most significantly, Europe's Scientific Revolution redefined the physical world.

The European impact on the thought processes and beliefs of Native Americans was even more profound than any changes taking place in Europe. Massive Amerindian depopulation from new diseases, which seemed to have little or no effect on the European invaders, likely played a major role in convincing many natives of Central and South America that the god of the Spaniards and the Portuguese was stronger than their own ancestral deities. This belief, combined with the missionary zeal of Catholic clerics, resulted in large numbers of conversions among the dispirited survivors.

India and Japan also experienced significant new directions in belief and thought. In India a new monotheistic faith called *Sikhism* arose. In Japan the Tokugawa shoguns adopted Chinese Neo-Confucianism, and *bushido*, "the way of the warrior," became a fully articulated code of behavior for the samurai class.

China, most of the Muslim world, and inland sub-Saharan Africa basically resisted change and continued to produce brilliant cultures along mainly traditional lines. None of these societies had reason to alter substantially or even challenge what had worked so well for centuries and even millennia. Yet these societies did not stagnate. Rather, they had reached such levels of cultural stability that they were able to absorb internal modifications and even moderate amounts of stimuli from outside without undergoing transformation.

▼▼▼

Europe

Sixteenth-century Europe saw the climax of the Renaissance, the explosion of the Protestant Reformation, and the beginnings of the Scientific Revolution. During the fourteenth and fifteenth centuries, a movement historians term *Renaissance humanism* emerged in Italy, and by the early 1500s it had spread to northern Europe. Because the roots of this movement lay firmly in the soil of the Middle Ages, the accuracy of the term *Renaissance* (rebirth) is questionable. There is no denying, however, that a spirit of self-conscious rediscovery and renewed cultural vitality united the people we call Renaissance artists and humanists. On their part, the Protestant Reformers rejected traditional Catholic doctrine concerning salvation, religious authority, and much else. By the mid-sixteenth century, at least 50 percent of all Europeans no longer considered themselves Roman Catholics and Europe's religious unity was shattered. Finally, during this century certain thinkers began to challenge the principles of ancient Greek science, a body of assumptions about nature and the universe that had served, with the Bible, as one of the two main foundations for most medieval philosophy and theology. By 1687, when Isaac Newton published his *Mathematical Principles of Natural Philosophy*, a new world view had seized Europe's intellectuals. Together, these three movements — humanism, religious change, and scientific discovery — illustrate one of the most striking features of Western European civilization: its willingness to challenge, debate, and, at times, discard values inherited from the past.

Meanwhile, in Europe's most eastern region, Russia, Western ideas were beginning to challenge established beliefs and ways of life by the mid-seventeenth century. The immediate result was a schism in the Russian Orthodox Church between imperially supported Westernizers and conservative Old Believers, thereby prefiguring the violent upheaval that would result from the radical reforms of Tsar Peter I (r. 1682–1725).

A Survival Manual for Princes
▼▼▼

111 ▼ *Niccolò Machiavelli, THE PRINCE*

Niccolò Machiavelli (1469–1527), a contemporary of Botticelli, Leonardo da Vinci, and Michelangelo, lived at a time when the artistic and intellectual creativity of the Italian Renaissance was at its peak. With his deep love and thorough knowledge of ancient history and literature, Machiavelli was a product of that Renaissance and became one of its most celebrated representatives. He also lived at a time when the states of Italy were engulfed in political turmoil and gradually succumbed to the control of France and Spain. The immediate cause of Italy's political troubles was its invasion by King Charles VIII of France in 1494. As a diplomat in the service of the Florentine republic, Machiavelli was an active participant in the wars that followed — and their victim. The Florentine republic was overthrown in 1512, and Machiavelli's political career was over. He retreated to his small country estate, read further in ancient history, and thought deeply about the reasons for Italy's political humiliation.

The most celebrated product of his rural exile was *The Prince*, a short, forceful, and controversial work. Essentially finished in 1514, *The Prince* was the result of Machiavelli's attempt to analyze, "from the wide experience of recent events and a constant reading of classical authors," the factors behind political success and failure and to reduce his findings to a series of general principles. This little handbook on the art of successful government expressed views about the realities of political life which had never before been so unambiguously articulated by a Western commentator. In the following selection, Machiavelli discusses several of the qualities a prince needs in order to succeed in the brutal world of power politics.

QUESTIONS FOR ANALYSIS

1. How does Machiavelli define "political virtue"?
2. According to Machiavelli, how does morality in politics differ from morality in one's private life?
3. In his view, what defines good government?
4. How does he characterize a good prince?
5. How does Machiavelli's view of human nature affect his political views?
6. What role does Christian ethical doctrine play in *The Prince*?
7. Most contemporaries were shocked when they read *The Prince*. Why do you think they found it unsettling?

XV. THE THINGS FOR WHICH MEN, AND ESPECIALLY PRINCES, ARE PRAISED OR BLAMED

It now remains for us to see how a prince must govern his conduct towards his subjects or his friends. I know that this has often been written about before, and so I hope it will not be thought presumptuous for me to do so, as, especially in discussing this subject, I draw up an original set of rules. But since my intention is to say something that will prove of practical use to the inquirer, I have thought it proper to represent things as they are in real truth, rather than as they are imagined. Many have dreamed up republics and principalities which have never in truth been known to exist; the gulf between how one should live and how one does live is so wide that a man who neglects what is actually done for what should be done learns the way to self-destruction rather than self-preservation. The fact is that a man who wants to act virtuously in every way necessarily comes to grief among so many who are not virtuous. Therefore if a prince wants to maintain his rule he must learn how not to be virtuous, and to make use of this or not according to need.

So leaving aside imaginary things, and referring only to those which truly exist, I say that whenever men are discussed (and especially princes, who are more exposed to view), they are noted for various qualities which earn them either praise or condemnation. Some, for example, are held to be generous, and others miserly. . . . Some are held to be benefactors, others are called grasping; some cruel, some compassionate; one man faithless, another faithful; one man effeminate and cowardly, another fierce and courageous; one man courteous, another proud; one man lascivious, another pure; one guileless, another crafty; one stubborn, another flexible; one grave, another frivolous; one religious, another sceptical; and so forth. I know everyone will agree that it would be most laudable if a prince possessed all the qualities deemed to be good among those I have enumerated. But, because of conditions in the world, princes cannot have those qualities, or observe them completely. So a prince has of necessity to be so prudent that he knows how to escape the evil reputation attached to those vices which could lose him his state, and how to avoid those vices which are not so dangerous if he possibly can; but, if he cannot, he need not worry so much about the latter. And then, he must not flinch from being blamed for vices which are necessary for safeguarding the state. This is because, taking everything into account, he will find that some of the things that appear to be virtues will, if he practices them, ruin him, and some of the things that appear to be vices will bring him security and prosperity. . . .

XVII. CRUELTY AND COMPASSION; AND WHETHER IT IS BETTER TO BE LOVED THAN FEARED, OR THE REVERSE

I say that a prince must want to have a reputation for compassion rather than for cruelty: nonetheless, he must be careful that he does not make bad use of compassion. Cesare Borgia was accounted cruel;[1] nevertheless, this cruelty of his reformed the Romagna, brought it unity, and restored order and obedience. On reflection, it will be seen that there was more compassion in Cesare than in the Florentine people, who, to escape being called cruel, allowed Pistoia to be devastated.[2] So a prince must not worry if he incurs reproach for his cruelty so

---

[1]Cesare Borgia (1475–1507), the son of Pope Alexander VI, had been duke of the Romagna, a region in central Italy; earlier in *The Prince,* **Machiavelli praises Borgia for his boldness and vision.**

[2]In 1501 Florence failed to act decisively in suppressing internal feuding in Pistoia, one of its subject cities.

long as he keeps his subjects united and loyal. By making an example or two he will prove more compassionate than those who, being too compassionate, allow disorders which lead to murder and rapine. These nearly always harm the whole community, whereas executions ordered by a prince only affect individuals. . . .

From this arises the following question: whether it is better to be loved than feared, or the reverse. The answer is that one would like to be both the one and the other; but because it is difficult to combine them, it is far better to be feared than loved if you cannot be both. One can make this generalization about men: they are ungrateful, fickle, liars, and deceivers, they shun danger and are greedy for profit; while you treat them well, they are yours. They would shed their blood for you, risk their property, their lives, their children, so long, as I said above, as danger is remote; but when you are in danger they turn against you. Any prince who has come to depend entirely on promises and has taken no other precautions ensures his own ruin; friendship which is bought with money and not with greatness and nobility of mind is paid for, but it does not last and it yields nothing. Men worry less about doing an injury to one who makes himself loved than to one who makes himself feared. The bond of love is one which men, wretched creatures that they are, break when it is to their advantage to do so; but fear is strengthened by a dread of punishment which is always effective.

The prince must nonetheless make himself feared in such a way that, if he is not loved, at least he escapes being hated. For fear is quite compatible with an absence of hatred; and the prince can always avoid hatred if he abstains from the property of his subjects and citizens and from their women. If, even so, it proves necessary to execute someone, this is to be done only when there is proper justification and manifest reason for it. But above all a prince must abstain from the property of others; because men sooner forget the death of their father than the loss of their patrimony.

XVIII. HOW PRINCES SHOULD HONOR THEIR WORD

Everyone realizes how praiseworthy it is for a prince to honor his word and to be straightforward rather than crafty in his dealings; nonetheless contemporary experience shows that princes who have achieved great things have been those who have given their word lightly, who have known how to trick men with their cunning, and who, in the end, have overcome those abiding by honest principles.

You must understand, therefore, that there are two ways of fighting: by law or by force. The first way is natural to men, and the second to beasts. But as the first way often proves inadequate one must needs have recourse to the second. . . .

So, as a prince is forced to know how to act like a beast, he must learn from the fox and the lion; because the lion is defenseless against traps and a fox is defenseless against wolves. Therefore one must be a fox in order to recognize traps, and a lion to frighten off wolves. Those who simply act like lions are stupid. So it follows that a prudent ruler cannot, and must not, honor his word when it places him at a disadvantage and when the reasons for which he made his promise no longer exist. If all men were good, this precept would not be good; but because men are wretched creatures who would not keep their word to you, you need not keep your word to them. And no prince ever lacked good excuses to color his bad faith.

A prince, therefore, need not necessarily have all the good qualities I mentioned above, but he should certainly appear to have them. I would even go so far as to say that if he has these qualities and always behaves accordingly he will find them harmful; if he only appears to have them they will render him service. He should appear to be compassionate, faithful to his word, kind, guileless, and devout. And indeed he should be so. But his disposition should be such that, if he needs to be the opposite, he knows how. You must realize this:

that a prince, and especially a new prince, cannot observe all those things which give men a reputation for virtue, because in order to maintain his state he is often forced to act in defiance of good faith, of charity, of kindness, of religion. And so he should have a flexible disposition, varying as fortune and circumstances dictate. As I said above, he should not deviate from what is good, if that is possible, but he should know how to do evil, if that is necessary.

Art as Religious Propaganda
▼▼▼

112 ▼ *Lucas Cranach the Younger,* TWO KINDS OF PREACHING: EVANGELICAL AND PAPAL

The Protestant Reformation was Europe's first major historical movement in which the printing press played a central role. Martin Luther's *Ninety-Five Theses* of 1517, in which he attacked papal authority and the theological basis for indulgences, might well have remained solely the subject of academic debate within the University of Wittenberg had they not been translated from Latin into German and disseminated throughout the Holy Roman Empire. Subsequently, Luther and his followers effectively used the printed page to advance their ideas in Latin treatises for learned audiences and, more tellingly, in numerous German books, pamphlets, and broadsheets for the general literate population. Many of these works contained woodcuts and engravings to illustrate their points and to make their ideas accessible even to the illiterate. Luther's Catholic opponents were slower to use the new technology, thus placing themselves at a disadvantage in the competition for the public's religious allegiance.

Two Kinds of Preaching: Evangelical and Papal by Lucas Cranach the Younger (1515–1586) is a rich, comparatively sophisticated example of a Lutheran popular woodcut. Its creator, who lived his whole life in Wittenberg where he enjoyed Luther's friendship, was the son of the Saxon court painter Lucas Cranach the Elder (1472–1553). *Two Kinds of Preaching*, executed in 1547, was distributed not as a book illustration but, in order to attract as wide an audience as possible, as a broadsheet — a single large printed page sold individually for a few small coins.

For the purpose of clarity, we have reproduced the woodcut on two pages, but in its original form it is undivided. A two-sided pulpit dominates the center of the sheet. The preacher facing left is Luther, who addresses an attentive crowd. Before him rests an open Bible, and on his side of the pulpit are the words: "All prophets attest to this, that there is no other name in heaven than that of Christ," which come from the New Testament's Book of Acts. Above Luther is a dove, representing the Holy Spirit, the third person of the Holy Trinity whose major divine functions are illumination, solace, and sanctification.

Two Kinds of Preaching: Evangelical

Two Kinds of Preaching: Papal

Luther's finger points to three heavenly apparitions: the Paschal Lamb (a symbol of the risen Christ), the crucified Christ, and God the Father, who holds an orb symbolizing his dominion over creation. The most important text consists of the words the crucified Christ directs toward God the Father: "Holy Father, save them. I have sacrificed myself for them with my wounds." Directly below is written: "If we sin, we have an advocate before God, so let us turn in consolation to this means of grace." In the center and lower left corner are illustrated the two Lutheran sacraments, baptism and the eucharist. It is noteworthy that in celebrating the eucharist both elements, the bread and wine, are offered to the laity, as opposed to the Catholic practice of restricting the drinking of the wine to the priest.

The right side of the woodcut is a Lutheran version of the shortcomings and abuses of Roman Catholicism. The preaching Franciscan friar receives his inspiration from the empty air blown into his ear by an implike demon. The message above his head summarizes the point of his message: The practices going on about him are not heretical and they offer an easy path to salvation. His audience consists largely of clergy, with only a handful of laypeople crowded in. In the upper right corner an angry God the Father rains down thunderbolts while St. Francis of Assisi (ca 1180–1226), the founder of the Franciscan order and a saint admired equally by Protestants and Catholics, attempts in vain to intercede on behalf of wayward humanity. The rest of the scene represents in an exaggerated way various Catholic religious practices rejected by the Lutherans. They include the sale of indulgences by the pope (in the lower right corner), who holds a sign reading: "Because the coin rings, the soul to heaven springs." The sign on the money bag reads: "This is shame and vice, squeezed from your donations." Directly behind the pope is a priest celebrating a private mass and an altar being consecrated by a birdlike demon. Still deeper in the background is a dying man having his hair clipped in the style of a monastic tonsure and having a monk's cowl, or hood, placed on his head — steps which supposedly would ensure his salvation. The attending nun sprinkles the man with holy water and holds a banner reading: "The cowl, the tonsure, and the water aid you." To the right of this scene a bishop consecrates a church bell. In the far background stands a small chapel toward which stride two pilgrims and around which marches a procession in honor of the saint depicted on the banner. To Lutherans all these practices represented Catholic superstition and misguided ritualism that replaced faith with meaningless "works."

QUESTIONS FOR ANALYSIS

1. What differences in the make-up of the crowds surrounding the pulpit do you see in the two sides of the picture? What is significant about those differences?

2. Note the figures in the Roman Catholic side of the picture who are members of religious orders (identifiable by their tonsures, or shaved crowns). How do their garb and general appearance support the Lutheran charge that monasticism was not a true Christian calling?

3. Compare the two preachers. What message is Cranach trying to communicate in their gestures and in his depiction of the pulpits from which they are preaching?

4. Consider the two Franciscans: St. Francis of Assisi and the Franciscan friar who is preaching. What is Cranach's message regarding the history of the Catholic Church?

5. In both scenes the eucharist, or holy communion, is being celebrated. What differences do you see, and what is their significance?

6. Cranach's woodcut is attempting to depict the Catholic Church as full of abuses. What are some of these abuses, and how does Cranach illustrate them? Which of these "abuses" would be clear even to someone who could not read the words on the broadsheet?

7. On the other hand, Cranach is attempting to depict Lutheranism as an expression of true Christianity. With what specific details does he attempt to communicate this Lutheran self-image? Again, how does Cranach make it possible for even the illiterate and the theologically unsophisticated to get his message?

8. What clues does this broadsheet provide concerning the *theological* differences between Luther and the Roman Catholic Church? In addressing this question, pay particular attention to the representations of Jesus Christ.

Science and the Claims of Religion
▼▼▼

113 ▼ *Galileo Galilei,*
LETTER TO THE GRAND DUCHESS CHRISTINA

The greatest European scientist of the early seventeenth century was the Italian physicist and astronomer Galileo Galilei (1564–1642), whose most important work was in mechanics, where he described the theory of inertia and developed a mathematical explanation for the movement of falling bodies. In astronomy, he pioneered the use of the telescope and strongly defended the theory of a sun-centered universe, as advanced by the Polish astronomer Nicholas Copernicus in 1543. His defense of Copernicus's ideas angered some powerful Roman Catholic clergymen and theologians, who believed the notion of a sun-centered universe threatened orthodox belief and the authority of the Church. In a similar manner, Martin Luther had rejected Copernican theory because it contradicted the literal word of the Bible.

In 1615, Galileo, a devout Catholic, defended his approach to science in a published letter addressed to Grand Duchess Christina of Tuscany. In the short run, Galileo lost his case. The Church officially condemned Copernicanism in 1616, and in 1632 a church court forced Galileo to renounce many of his ideas. His works continued to be read, however, and in the long run, his writings contributed significantly to the acceptance of not just Copernican theory but the new model of scientific inquiry.

QUESTIONS FOR ANALYSIS

1. How does Galileo perceive the motives of his enemies?
2. Why, in his view, do they raise religious arguments against him?
3. According to Galileo, why is it dangerous to apply scriptural passages to science?
4. To Galileo, how does nature differ from the Bible as a source of truth?
5. In Galileo's view, what is the proper relationship between science and religion?

Some years ago, as Your Serene Highness well knows, I discovered in the heavens many things that had not been seen before our own age. The novelty of these things, as well as some consequences which followed from them in contradiction to the physical notions commonly held among academic philosophers, stirred up against me no small number of professors — as if I had placed these things in the sky with my own hands in order to upset nature and overturn the sciences. They seemed to forget that the increase of known truths stimulates the investigation, establishment, and growth of the arts; not their diminution or destruction.

Showing a greater fondness for their own opinions than for truth, they sought to deny and disprove the new things which, if they had cared to look for themselves, their own senses would have demonstrated to them. To this end they hurled various charges and published numerous writings filled with vain arguments, and they made the grave mistake of sprinkling these with passages taken from places in the Bible which they had failed to understand properly, and which were ill suited to their purposes.

Persisting in their original resolve to destroy me and everything mine by any means they can think of, these men are aware of my views in astronomy and philosophy. They know that as to the arrangement of the parts of the universe, I hold the sun to be situated motionless in the center of the revolution of the celestial orbs while the earth rotates on its axis and revolves around the sun. They know also that I support this position not only by refuting the arguments of Ptolemy and Aristotle,[1] but by producing many counterarguments; in particular, some which relate to physical effects whose causes can perhaps be assigned in no other way. In addition there are astronomical arguments derived from many things in my new celestial discoveries that plainly confute the Ptolemaic system while admirably agreeing with and confirming the contrary hypothesis. Possibly because they are disturbed by the known truth of other propositions of mine which differ from those commonly held, and therefore mistrusting their defense so long as they confine themselves to the field of philosophy,[2] these men have resolved to fabricate a shield for their fallacies out of the mantle of pretended religion and the authority of the Bible. These they apply, with little judgment, to the refutation of arguments that they do not understand and have not even listened to.

First they have endeavored to spread the opinion that such propositions in general are contrary to the Bible and are consequently damnable and heretical. . . . Next, becoming bolder, and hoping (though vainly) that this seed which first took root in their hypocritical minds would send out branches and ascend to heaven, they began scattering rumors among the people that before long this doctrine would be condemned by the supreme authority.[3] They know, too, that official condemnation would not only suppress the two propositions which I have mentioned, but would render damnable all other astronomical and physical statements and observations that have any necessary relation or connection with these. . . .

Now as to the false aspersions which they so unjustly seek to cast upon me, I have thought it necessary to justify myself in the eyes of all men, whose judgment in matters of religion and of reputation I must hold in great esteem.

I shall therefore discourse of the particulars which these men produce to make this opinion detested and to have it condemned not merely as false but as heretical. To this end they make a shield of their hypocritical zeal for religion. They go about invoking the Bible, which they would have minister to their deceitful purposes. Contrary to the sense of the Bible and the intention of the holy Fathers, if I am not mistaken, they would extend such authorities until even in purely physical matters — where faith is not involved — they would have us altogether abandon reason and the evidence of our senses in favor of some biblical passage, though under the surface meaning of its words this passage may contain a different sense.

I hope to show that I proceed with much greater piety than they do, when I argue not against condemning this book,[4] but against condemning it in the way they suggest — that is, without understanding it, weighing it, or so much as reading it. . . .

The reason produced for condemning the opinion that the earth moves and the sun stands still is that in many places in the Bible one may read that the sun moves and the earth stands still. Since the Bible cannot err, it follows as a necessary consequence that anyone takes an erroneous and heretical position who maintains that the sun is inherently motionless and the earth movable.

With regard to this argument, I think in the first place that it is very pious to say and prudent to affirm that the holy Bible can never speak untruth — whenever its true meaning is understood. But I believe nobody will deny that it is often very abstruse, and may say things which are quite different from what its bare words signify. Hence in expounding the Bible if one were always to confine oneself to the unadorned grammatical meaning, one

---

[1]The traditional view of the universe blended the physics of Aristotle (384–322 B.C.), the astronomy of Claudius Ptolemy (second century A.D.), and the philosophy of Plato (429–347 B.C.) to create a cosmos centered on a stationary earth.

[2]"Philosophy" in this context means natural philosophy, or science.
[3]The pope.
[4]The Bible.

might fall into error. Not only contradictions and propositions far from true might thus be made to appear in the Bible, but even grave heresies and follies. Thus it would be necessary to assign to God feet, hands, and eyes, as well as corporeal and human affections, such as anger, repentance, hatred, and sometimes even the forgetting of things past and ignorance of those to come.[5] These propositions uttered by the Holy Spirit were set down in that manner by the sacred scribes[6] in order to accommodate them to the capacities of the common people, who are rude and unlearned. . . .

This being granted, I think that in discussions of physical problems we ought to begin not from the authority of scriptural passages, but from sense-experiences and necessary demonstrations; for the holy Bible and the phenomena of nature proceed alike from the divine Word[7] the former as the dictate of the Holy Spirit and the latter as the observant executrix

of God's commands. It is necessary for the Bible, in order to be accommodated to the understanding of every man, to speak many things which appear to differ from the absolute truth so far as the bare meaning of the words is concerned. But Nature, on the other hand, is inexorable and immutable; she never transgresses the laws imposed upon her, or cares a whit whether her abstruse reasons and methods of operation are understandable to men. For that reason it appears that nothing physical which sense-experience sets before our eyes, or which necessary demonstrations prove to us, ought to be called in question (much less condemned) upon the testimony of biblical passages which may have some different meaning beneath their words. For the Bible is not chained in every expression to conditions as strict as those which govern all physical effects; nor is God any less excellently revealed in Nature's actions than in the sacred statements of the Bible.

Religious Controversy in Seventeenth-Century Russia
▼▼▼

114 ▼ Avvakum, AUTOBIOGRAPHY AND LETTERS

Much of Russian history has been influenced by the fact that when the Russian people abandoned paganism for Christianity in the late tenth century and following, they embraced the faith and traditions of Constantinople, not Rome (Chapter 7, source 57). Russia's commitment to Eastern Orthodox religious culture substantially affected its art and learning, helped cut it off from Western Europe, and eventually enhanced the authority of the Russian *tsar* (Caesar), or emperor, who became, in keeping with the tradition of Byzantine civilization,

---

[5]Such arguments had been commonplace among Catholic theologians of the twelfth and thirteenth centuries, who argued against an absolutely literal reading of every biblical passage, even though they believed in the Bible's essential infallibility.

[6]The Holy Spirit is the third divine person of the Trinity (God the Father, God the Son, and God the Holy Spirit), who sanctifies and inspires humanity. Christians believe all the sacred authors of the Bible's Old and New Testaments wrote under the infallible inspiration of God the Holy Spirit.
[7]A Neo-Platonic term for God, the origin of all reality and truth.

the living image of God on earth and the absolute ruler of the community of God's people. Shortly after the fall of Constantinople in 1453, Ivan III (r. 1462–1505), prince of Moscow, adopted the titles of tsar and "autocrat by the grace of God" because he and his Muscovite subjects saw themselves as the only legitimate surviving heirs of the imperial Christian system that Constantine had established in the early fourth century. The theory was that the empires of Rome and Constantinople, the Second Rome, had fallen because they had deviated from the Orthodox faith, but Moscow, the Third Rome, would persist to the end of time because of its orthodoxy.

This essentially conservative vision did not preclude change and, therefore, conflict within the Russian Church, as Tsar Aleksei I (r. 1645–1676) discovered. In 1652, he appointed a reforming priest named Nikon as patriarch of the Russian Church. One of Nikon's first actions was to propose changes in certain religious manuals and rituals, in order to bring them closer to their original Greek models. Although the proposed changes, such as amending the spelling of Jesus' name and making the sign of the cross with three fingers instead of two, may seem minor today, they raised a storm of protest from clergy and laity alike, who were convinced the patriarch was defiling the Russian Orthodox way of life. Although Patriarch Nikon was eventually deposed, his proposed reforms were adopted, thus setting the stage for a major schism in the Russian Orthodox Church.

The opponents of reform came to be known as Old Believers. For the rest of the century they were associated with rebellions of every sort against tsarist authority and, in the face of government persecution, offered themselves up for martyrdom. More than 20,000 burned themselves to death in communal conflagrations rather than accept change. In the end, the Old Believers were outnumbered and lost their battle against religious innovation, even though large pockets of them persisted, and millions can be found even today in Russia.

Archpriest Avvakum (ca 1620–1682) was the most eloquent and celebrated critic of Nikon's reforms. He, his wife Anastasia, and their children suffered greatly for their zeal. After more than ten years of Siberian exile, Avvakum and his family were allowed to return to Moscow, but his and Anastasia's refusal to bend to the new order, or to be silent in their refusal, soon earned them additional persecution. The archpriest was incarcerated for fifteen years in a monastic dungeon, where he was allowed, however, to write his life story and inspirational letters to his many followers. Because Avvakum was generally regarded as a living saint and enjoyed the protection of Tsar Aleksei, his life was spared until 1682. With his imperial protector dead, Avvakum was burned at the stake as a heretic. The following excerpts come from works written in captivity. The first two are from his autobiography, the rest from his letters.

QUESTIONS FOR ANALYSIS

1. How does Avvakum view all Christian churches other than the Russian?
2. Why is he especially hostile toward the Church of Constantinople, which had introduced Christianity to Russia?
3. Why is it so important to him that the Russian Church retain its traditional ritual practices?
4. What were the core issues involved in this struggle, and what were the Old Believers ultimately resisting?

When they took me . . . to the Chudov monastery . . . in Moscow, they brought me before the ecumenical patriarchs[1] and all our Nikonian churchmen sat there like so many foxes. I spoke of many things in Holy Scripture with the patriarchs. God opened my sinful mouth and Christ put them to shame. The last word they spoke to me was this: "Why," said they, "do you remain stubborn? All our Christian lands, the Serbs and Albanians and Wallachians and Romans[2] and Poles, all cross themselves with three fingers; you alone remain obstinate and cross yourself with five fingers;[3] it is not seemly." And I answered them for Christ this way: "O you teachers of Christendom! Rome fell long ago and lies prostrate, and the Poles perished with it,[4] being enemies of Christians to the end. And your own Orthodoxy has been tainted by the violence of the Turkish sultan Mohammed;[5] and no wonder, for you have become impotent. And from now on it is you who should come to us to learn; for by the grace of God we are an autocratic [independent] realm. Before the time of Nikon, the apostate, in our Russia under our pious princes and tsars the Orthodox faith was pure and undefiled, and the church was free from turmoil. Nikon the wolf, together with the Devil, ordained that men should cross themselves with three fingers, but our first shepherds made the sign of the cross and blessed men with five fingers, according to the tradition of our holy fathers."

⋅   ⋅   ⋅

God will bless you: suffer tortures for the way you place your fingers, do not reason too much! And I am ready to die with you for this and for Christ. Even if I am a foolish man and without learning, yet this I know, that all the traditions of the church, handed down to us by the holy fathers, are holy and incorrupt, I will maintain them even unto death, as I received them. I will not alter the eternal rules that were laid down before our time; may they remain so unto ages of ages.

⋅   ⋅   ⋅

I know all your evil cunning, dogs, whores, metropolitans, archbishops,[6] Nikonians, thieves, renegades, foreigners in Russian garb. You have changed the images of the saints and all the

---

[1] "The ruling fathers of the entire Church." The clerical leaders of all the various Orthodox Churches that followed the religious traditions of Constantinople.

[2] *Romans* here means the subjects of the former Byzantine Empire, which was centered on Constantinople, the "New, or Second, Rome."

[3] Actually with two fingers, but because of their position it appeared that all five digits were being used.

[4] The Poles are Roman Catholics and follow the practices of "Old Rome." Avvakum is claiming here that Poles have fallen into the errors of the Roman Catholics of the West who long ago fell away from the true faith.

[5] To Avvakum's mind, Constantinople has also fallen away from the Orthodox faith due to its conquest in 1453 by Mehmed (Mohammed) II, sultan of the Ottoman Empire.

[6] *Metropolitan* and *archbishop* are synonyms. Each presides over a provincial church centered on a major city (a metropolis) and, thereby, has authority over a number of subordinate bishops, each of whom has his own church in a smaller city within the province.

church canons and rituals: and a bitter thing it is for good Christians!

. . .

Alas and alack! These apostates have now extinguished the last great light, the great Russian church of old, which worked for the enlightenment of souls, shining throughout the world.

Oh you dogs! What do you have against the olden ways? Impious ones, thieves, sons of whores. . . . It does not befit us, the faithful, to speak much to you pagans. . . . And that you curse us with your devil: we laugh at that. Even a child would burst into laughter at your madness. If you curse us for (maintaining) the holy olden ways: then also should you curse your fathers and mothers, who died in our faith.

. . .

(Addressed by Avvakum to Tsar Aleksei Mikhailovich:) Take a good, old-fashioned breath, as in Stefan's[7] time and say in the Russian tongue: "Lord, forgive me, a sinner!" And be done with *Kyrie eleison*,[8] this is what the Hellenes[9] say: spit on them! For you are a Russian, Mikhailovich,[10] not a Greek. Speak in your native tongue; do not degrade it in church, or at home, or in sayings. It befits us to talk as Christ taught us. God loves us no less than the Greeks; he taught us to read and write in our tongue, through the holy Cyril and his brother.[11] What better can we want? . . . Stop tormenting us! Seize those heretics who destroy your soul, and burn them all, the filthy dogs, Latins and Jews; but release us, your countrymen. Truly, it will be good.

. . .

We, the true believers, follow the Sacred Scriptures and hold steadfastly to what the old printed books teach us about the Deity and about other dogmas; we seek integrity of mind in the old books printed in Moscow in the reign of former pious tsars.

. . .

And thenceforth for twenty-three years . . . to this day they burn and hang the confessors of Christ without ceasing. The Russians . . . poor dears — one may think them stupid, but they rejoice that the tormentor has come at last — brave the fire in hosts, for the love of Christ, the Son of God's Light. The Greeks, those sons of whores, are cunning; their patriarchs eat delicate viands from the same dish with the Turkish barbarians. Not so our dear Russians — they throw themselves into the fire, rather than betray the true faith! In Kazan the Nikonians burned thirty men, in Siberia the same number, in Vladimir six, in Borovsk fourteen men; while in Nizhnii[12] a most glorious thing took place: some were being burned by the heretics, while others, consumed with love and weeping for the true faith, did not wait to be condemned by the heretics, but themselves braved the fire, so that they might keep the true faith intact and pure; and having burned their bodies and committed their souls into God's hands, they rejoice with Christ unto ages of ages, martyrs by choice, slaves of Christ. May their memory live forever unto ages of ages! Theirs was a noble deed.

---

[7]Stefan Vonifatievich, spiritual adviser and chaplain to Tsar Alexsei, who was later exiled for his opposition to Nikon.

[8]Greek for "Lord, have mercy."

[9]Greeks, or Byzantines.

[10]Tsar Alexsei. Mikhailovich means "son of Mikhail (Michael)," Mikhail being Tsar Mikhail Romanov (r. 1613–1645), Alexsei's predecessor. Avvakum's use of Tsar Alexsei's patronymic implies simultaneously respect and familiarity.

[11]Saints Cyril (or Constantine) and Methodius were two ninth-century Greek missionaries who worked among the Slavs of Moravia. These "Apostles to the Slavs" are credited with inventing the Cyrillic alphabet for their converts.

[12]Today the city of Gorky.

▼▼▼

America and Asia

Western European ways of belief and thought were transforming a number of Amerindian cultures, particularly the major civilizations of Central and South America. Massive depopulation of the native people, combined with generally sincere attempts to "save the souls" of the survivors by converting them to Christianity, resulted in wide-scale acculturation. Yet, in spite of this European intrusion, Native Americans managed to resist total cultural absorption.

Elsewhere in the world conflicts between traditional and new ideas were either largely nonexistent or substantially less dramatic and far-reaching. Tradition and authority provided the framework for scholarship and artistic creativity throughout most of Islam. Even the Ottoman Empire, which spanned portions of three continents, and Mughal India, which had the example of the inquisitive eclecticism of Akbar's court, ultimately resisted intellectual and religious challenges to Muslim orthodoxy. India, however, witnessed the rise of the religious vision of Sikhism, a noble but ultimately doomed attempt to end the bitter hostilities between Muslims and Hindus. China under the Ming (1368–1644) and Qing (1644–1912) dynasties remained anchored in the values of Confucian classicism, yet in Japan Chinese Neo-Confucianism provided intellectual support for the political and social changes of the Tokugawa Shogunate. The eminently practical educational program the shoguns patronized emphasized social order and stability, but because of its focus on the utilitarian arts and technology, Japan's form of Neo-Confucianism created an atmosphere for potential rapid change within the context of traditional values.

New Ways and Old Gods in Peru
▼▼▼

115 ▼ Christoval de Molina,
AN ACCOUNT OF THE FABLES AND RITES OF THE INCAS

One often wonders about the depth of sixteenth-century Amerindian conversions to Christianity. In the following selection, Padre Christoval de Molina, a Spanish priest of Cuzco, Peru, who served in that city's hospital for natives, tells of certain conflicts between the old and new ways that occurred during the 1560s. The most serious was a millenarian movement known as the *taqui uncu* (the ritual song of the festival dress), which flared up in 1565. Inca belief held that life consists of thousand-year cycles, and the present Inca Age had begun in a year that computed to the Christian year 565. This meant that the arrival of the Spaniards was the last act in the passing away of the Old Inca Age. Toward 1565 a number of Peruvian natives expectantly awaited a new age, which would begin with the overthrow of the Spaniards and their god.

Molina, a master of Quechua, the language of the Incas, interviewed large numbers of older natives in order to compile, sometime around 1575, his account of the folklore and religious practices of the Quechua people and their Inca lords. His avowed reason was "to root out these idolatries and follies." Despite the purpose of his research, without his work we would know far less about preconquest Inca culture and its resilient vitality under Spanish domination.

QUESTIONS FOR ANALYSIS

1. Can you find in this account any Amerindian attempt to explain why they suffered from Spanish diseases while the Spaniards remained largely immune?
2. How do the Quechua people explain their conquest by the Spaniards?
3. What must the people of the old gods do in order to win back their favor and usher in the new age?
4. How would the new age differ from the previous millennium?
5. How widespread was this movement? How and when was it finally suppressed?
6. Why do you think some natives committed suicide?
7. Molina claims that only a few Quechua wizards were still functioning around 1575. Are there any reasons why we should suspect his testimony on this issue?
8. Compare Molina with Sahagun (Chapter 13, source 101). What are their respective strengths and weaknesses as reporters of Amerindian culture? Do you think one is less biased or more accurate in some respect than the other? Why?

About ten years ago there was a joke among the Indians. They had a kind of song called *taqui uncu*. . . .

In the . . . diocese of Cuzco, . . . most of the Indians had fallen into the greatest apostasy,[1] departing from the Catholic Faith, which

they had received, and returning to the idolatries which they practiced in the time of their infidelity. It was not understood how this had come to pass; but it was suspected that the wizards,[2] whom the Incas[3] kept in Uiscacabamba,[4] were at the bottom of it. For in the year 1560,

---

[1] Abandonment of one's faith.
[2] Priests of the old faith.

[3] Technically, only those Quechua people who were of royal blood and thereby descended from the gods were Incas.
[4] An Inca stronghold that only fell in 1572.

and not before, it was held and believed by the Indians, that an ointment from the bodies of the Indians had been sent for from Spain to cure a disease for which there was no medicine there. Hence it was that the Indians, at that time, were very shy of the Spaniards, and they would not bring fuel or grass or anything else to the house of a Spaniard, lest they should be taken in and killed, in order to extract this ointment. All this had originated from that villainy, with the object of causing enmity between the Indians and Spaniards. The Indians of the land had much respect for the things of the Inca, until the Lord Viceroy, Don Francisco de Toledo,[5] abolished and put an end to them, in which he greatly served God our Lord. The deception by which the Devil deceived these poor people was the belief that all the huacas[6] which the Christians had burnt and destroyed had been brought to life again; and that they had been divided into two parts, one of which was united with the huaca *Pachacama*,[7] and the other with the huaca *Titicaca*.[8] The story went on that they had formed in the air, in order of battle against God, and that they had conquered Him. But when the Marquis[9] entered this land, it was held that God had conquered the huacas, as the Spaniards had overcome the Indians. Now, however, it was believed that things were changed, that God and the Spaniards were conquered, all the Spaniards killed, and their cities destroyed, and that the sea would rise to drink them up, that they might be remembered no more. In this apostasy they believed that God our Lord had made the Spaniards, and Castille, and the animals and provisions of Castille; but that the huacas had made the Indians, and this land, and all the things they possessed before the Spaniards came. Thus they stripped our Lord of his omnipotence. Many preachers went forth from among the Indians, who preached as

well in the desert places as in the villages, declaring the resurrection of the huacas, and saying that they now wandered in the air, thirsty and dying of hunger, because the Indians no longer sacrificed. . . . The huacas, it was announced, were enraged with all those who had been baptized, and it was declared that they would all be killed unless they returned to the old belief and renounced the Christian faith. Those who sought the friendship and grace of the huacas would, it was urged, pass a life of prosperity and health. Those who would return to the love of the huacas and live, were to fast for some days, not eating salt . . . nor colored maize, nor any Spanish thing, nor entering churches, nor obeying the call of the priests, nor using their Christian names. Henceforth the times of the Incas would be restored, and the huacas would not enter into stones or fountains to speak, but would be incorporated in men whom they would cause to speak: therefore the people were to have their houses prepared and ready, in case any huaca should desire to lodge in one of them. Thus it was that many Indians trembled and fell to the ground, and others tore themselves as if they were possessed, making faces; and when they presently became quiet, they said, when they were asked what they had felt, that such and such a huaca had entered into their bodies. Then the people took such a one in their arms, and carried him to a chosen spot, and there they made a lodging with straw and cloaks; and began to worship the huaca, offering sheep . . . and other things. Then they made a festival for two or three days, dancing and drinking, and invoking the huaca that was represented by the possessed man. Such persons, from time to time, preached to the people, threatening them, and telling them not to serve God, but the huacas; and to renounce all Christianity, with all Christian

---

[5]The king's deputy (viceroy) from 1568 to 1581.
[6]This word means anything sacred and often was used to refer to the gods and spirits, and images of them.
[7]The sun god and creator, the supreme deity in the Inca pantheon.

[8]The sacred lake where the first Incas came to earth.
[9]Francisco Pizarro (1470–1541).

names, and the shirts, hats, and shoes of Christians. . . .

This evil was so widely credited that not only the Indians on the *Repartimientos*[10] but those who lived in the cities, among Spaniards, believed and performed the prescribed fasts. . . .

As they believed that God and the Spaniards were conquered, the Indians began to rise, as happened in the year 1565. . . .

There were several forms of apostasy in the different provinces. Some danced and gave out that they had the huaca in their bodies. Others trembled for the same reason. Others shut themselves up in their houses and shouted. Others flung themselves from rocks and were killed. Others jumped into the rivers, thus offering themselves to the huacas. At last our Lord, in his mercy, was pleased to enlighten these miserable people; and those who were left were led to see the nonsense that they had believed, that the Inca was dead[11] . . . and that nothing of what had been predicted had taken place, but the very opposite.

By reason of this devilish teaching, there are still some Indian sorcerers and witches, though their number is small. When any Indian is sick, these witches are called in to cure him, and to say whether he will live or die. . . . They . . . make him breathe on a little coca, and offer it to the Sun, praying for health; and the same to the Moon and Stars. Then, with a little gold and silver of little value in his hand, the sick man offers sacrifice to the Creator. Then the wizard commands him to give food to the dead, placing it on their tombs. . . . For the wizard gives the patient to understand that he is visited with this sickness because the dead are starving. If he is able to go on foot to some junction of two rivers, the wizard makes him go there and wash his body with water and flour of white maize, saying that he will there leave his illness. At the end of this ceremony the wizard tells him that, if he would free himself from his sickness, he must confess all his sins, without concealing any. They call this *hichoco*. These Indians are so simple that some of them readily, and with little persuasion, fall into this apostasy and error, though some afterwards repent and confess their sins.

There are also a very great number of Indian men and women who, understanding the offense against our Lord that they commit in doing this, will not permit any such acts, but rather accuse those who do them . . . , that they may be punished. If some exemplary punishment was inflicted on the wizards, I believe that this great evil would soon disappear, although, as I have said, there are now few wizards.

The Sikh Vision
▼▼▼

116 ▼ *Nanak, ADI-GRANTH*

Sikhism is one of the world's newest monotheistic faiths, having grown out of Hinduism and Islam essentially between 1500 and 1700. Sikhs (the word means disciples) believe that their first *guru*, or teacher, Nanak (1469–1539), received

[10]Estates given to Spanish colonists who enjoyed the right to enlist the virtual slave labor of resident natives.

[11]As a result of this rebellion, the Inca Tupac Amaru was publicly beheaded in Cuzco in 1571.

a revelation from God and was charged with the mission of bringing the divided world to the worship of "the True Name," the Supreme Being whose names and attributes are limitless. Nanak wandered through all India seeking disciples who would accept his message of love, reconciliation, and total devotion to God. He taught that such externals of religion as pilgrimages to Mecca (which he had done, disguised as a Muslim), bathing in the sacred Ganges River, and asceticism, or rejection of all pleasure and comfort, are worthless before God unless accompanied by inward sincerity and true morality. As a strict and uncompromising monotheist, he declared that love of God alone suffices to free anyone of any caste from the law of karma, bringing an end to reincarnation and resulting in absorption into the One.

Nanak's sect began as a pacifistic religious movement that preached love and peace among all humans, regardless of caste, religion, or race. The Sikhs, however, became increasingly militant, in reaction to later Mughal persecution, and turned their holiest shrine, the Golden Temple at Amritsar, into an armed camp. Under their tenth and last guru, Govind Singh (1675–1708), the practice began of conferring the surname Singh (Lion) on all male members and charging them to bear a dagger ever after. Sikhism's call to people of all castes to be baptized by the sword was especially attractive to Hindus in the lowest castes. By 1700 the Sikhs were a military power to be reckoned with in the Punjab, and their subsequent history has been characterized by a tradition of military prowess and their often frustrated desire to carve out an independent Sikh state governed according to the democratic principle that all Sikhs are fully equal and the only ultimate authority is the *Adi-Granth*, their sacred book.

Compiled by Arjan (1563–1606), the fifth guru, the *Adi-Granth* (also known as the *Granth Sahid*) consists mainly of hymns composed by Nanak and the other early gurus. It attained its final form in 1705–1706, when Govind Singh added a number of hymns and declared that, from then onward, the *Adi-Granth* itself, not any individual, was Sikhism's one true guru. The following poems are attributed to Nanak. In them the poet describes the qualities of the True Name.

QUESTIONS FOR ANALYSIS

1. What relationship do the various Hindu deities have to the True Name?
2. What relationship does the True Name have to Brahman (Chapter 3, source 17)?
3. One of the most important influences on Sikhism was the bhakti movement (Chapter 6, sources 46 and 47). What evidence is there of bhakti influence in the hymns?
4. According to Nanak, what makes a person a true Muslim?
5. How has Sikhism borrowed from Islam and Hinduism, and in what ways does it claim to transcend, correct, or perfect each?

6. Which religion, Hinduism or Islam, seems to have had the stronger impact on Nanak's religious vision?
7. Why would the religion of the Sikhs constitute such a serious challenge to both Muslim and Hindu societies?

By his order are made the forms of all things, his order, however, cannot be told.
By his order are made the living beings, by his order greatness is obtained.
By his order are the high and the low, by his order pain and pleasure are set down.
By his order some are pardoned, some are by his order always caused to wander about in transmigration.
Every one is under his order, exempt from his order is no one.
O Nanak! if one understands his order, he will not speak in self-conceit. . . .

True is the Lord, . . . his love is infinite.
If they speak and ask, he gives, he gives, the Liberal bestows gifts.
What shall again be placed before him, by means of which his court may be seen?
What speech shall be uttered by the mouth, which having heard he may bestow love?
Reflect at early dawn on the greatness of the True Name! . . .
He cannot be established, he is not made. He himself is the Supreme Being. . . .

From the mouth of the Guru[1] is the sound, from the mouth of the Guru is the Veda,[2] in the mouth of the Guru it is contained.
The Guru is Isar,[3] the Guru is Gorakh,[4] Brahma, the Guru is the mother Parbati.[5]
If I would know, would I not tell? The story cannot be told.

O Guru! let me know the One! That the one liberal patron of all living beings may not be forgotten by me! . . .
If hand, foot, body, and trunk become defiled. By washing with water the dust will be removed.
If the cloth be polluted by urine. By applying soap it will be washed.
If the intellect be defiled with sins. It is washed in the dye of The Name.

. . .

That Supreme Being is Hari,[6] Hari is the Supreme Being, unattainable, unattainable, infinite.
All meditate, all meditate on you, O Hari, O true creator!
All creatures are yours, you are the provider of the creatures.
O saints! meditate on Hari, who causes to forget all pains!
Hari himself is the Lord, he himself is the worshipper, what is, O Nanak! the helpless being?
You, O Hari! the one Supreme Being, are unintermittingly contained in every body.
Some are donors, some are beggars, all are your wonderful shows.
You yourself are the donor, you yourself the enjoyer, without you I do not know another, Sir!
You are the Supreme Brahman, endless, endless, what can I tell and explain your qualities?
Who serve, who serve you, Sir, their sacrifice is humble Nanak.

[1] Here the Guru is God — the Ultimate Teacher.
[2] Chapter 2, source 12.
[3] Another name for Shiva (Chapter 6, source 47).
[4] Another name for Vishnu (Chapter 6, source 46).
[5] Shiva's consort and Mother Goddess.
[6] One of Vishnu's names.

Who meditate on you, O Hari! who
meditate on you, O Hari! those people
live comfortably in the world.
Those have become liberated, those have
become liberated, by whom Hari has
been meditated upon, the noose of
Yama[7] has broken away from them.

. . .

You are the creator, true, my Lord.
What is pleasing to you, that will be done;
what you give, that I obtain.
All is yours, you are meditated upon by
all.
On whom you bestow mercy, he obtains
the gem of your Name.
By the disciple of the Guru it is obtained,
by the self-willed it is lost.
By yourself one is separated from you, by
yourself one is united with you.
You are the ocean, all is in you.

. . .

O my mind! taste the juice of Hari and
your thirst will cease.
The disciples, by whom it has been tasted,
remain easily absorbed.
By whom the true Guru has been served,
they have obtained the treasure of the
Name.
In their heart the love of Hari dwells, in
their mind conceit has ceased.
The lotus of the heart has opened,
meditation is easily brought about.
The pure heart is delighted with Hari and
at the threshold honor is obtained.
Those who serve their own true Guru are
rare in the world.
By whom egotism and selfishness are
destroyed and Hari is kept in the breast.
Who have love to the Name, for them I
sacrifice myself.

Those are happy . . . in whom the
inexhaustible, endless Name is.
By meeting with the Guru the Name is
obtained, spiritual blindness and worldly
thirst cease.
With Hari their heart is delighted, in their
house they are solitary.
I shall sacrifice myself for those, who have
obtained the taste of Hari.
O Nanak! by his merciful look the True
Name is obtained, the vessel of virtues.

. . .

By means of the instruction of the Guru
death does not come near, as Yama is the
servant of the servants of Hari.
In whose heart is the true word of the
Guru and the True One, he is in his own
house living solitary.
Nanak says: who serve their own true
Guru, they are free from desires.

. . .

Make kindness the mosque,[8] sincerity the
prayer-carpet, rectitude the lawful food
according to the Qur'an.
Modesty, circumcision, good conduct,
fasting, thus you become a Muslim.
Good works the Ka'abah,[9] the true Pir[10]
the Kalimah,[11] kindness the prayer.
Make that the rosary,[12] which will please
him; Nanak says: he preserves your
honor.

. . .

Without the name there is no other wealth,
all the other objects are ashes.
Nanak says: he himself causes to be done
and does everything, he himself by his
order is arranging everything.

. . .

To be called a Muslim is difficult, when
one becomes it, then he may be called a
Muslim.

---

[7]The Hindu god of death and tormentor of the wicked.
[8]The Muslim place of communal worship.
[9]A Shrine in Mecca that serves as the focal point of the
Muslim pilgrimage, or hajj.
[10]A Sufi leader, or saint (Chapter 8, source 66).
[11]The Muslim creed of faith: "There is no God but God;
Muhammad is the Prophet of God."

[12]An aid to prayer consisting of beads linked together on
a string. The rosary began as an early Hindu device, was
adopted by Buddhists, and spread to Christianity and
Islam. The Muslim rosary, which is the reference here,
consists of ninety-nine beads for the ninety-nine names
of God.

Before all, having approved of religion, he
gives away his property to the saints.
Having become firm in the way of religion
he puts a stop to the gyration of death
and life.[13]
He obeys the will of the Lord on his head,

he minds the creator, he parts with his
own self.
Then, says Nanak, having become kindly
affected toward all living creatures he is
indeed called a Muslim.

Neo-Confucianism in Tokugawa Japan
▼▼▼

117 ▼ *Narushima Motonao and Yamazaki Ansai,* TWO SEVENTEENTH-CENTURY NEO-CONFUCIAN TEXTS

The early years of the Tokugawa Shogunate (1603–1867) marked a period of vigorous reorganization of Japanese society and laid the basis for that country's active role in world affairs by the end of the nineteenth century. An integral element in that reorientation was education. Ieyasu, the first Tokugawa shogun (r. 1603–1605), established a system of centralized feudalism which he reinforced by patronizing Neo-Confucian studies.

Neo-Confucianism had been formulated in China during the age of the Song Dynasty, and its greatest teacher had been Zhu Xi (1130–1200), whose voluminous writings were now avidly studied in Japan. The Neo-Confucians' essential message was that the world is real, not illusory as the Buddhists maintained, and that humans attain fulfillment by participating fully in society, not by remaining aloof as the Daoists believed. Neo-Confucians rejected all notions of immortality and spiritual salvation and concentrated instead on social and political reform. They believed that by applying reason to the study of natural and social phenomena, one could understand their underlying laws and, thereby, could act on the basis of sure knowledge. The single most important pathway to understanding government was the study of history.

The first source comes from an official chronicle account of Ieyasu's rule by Narushima Motonao that notes the shogun's promotion of learning through the medium of printing. Printing by block had been known in Japan for centuries, having been introduced from China. The technique of printing by means of moveable type had arrived around 1600 from Korea and the West. The second document is from the writings of Yamazaki Ansai (1618–1682), one of the mid-century's most prominent Neo-Confucian teachers. Here he comments on the

---

[13]The cycle of birth, death, and rebirth.

regulations of Zhu Xi's White Deer Cave School, where a generation of twelfth-century Chinese students had been instructed in the social maxims of Neo-Confucianism.

QUESTIONS FOR ANALYSIS

1. Despite his reputation as a person with a taste for elegant literature, Tokugawa Ieyasu actually preferred other types of books. What sort of books did he read, and what does his choice of reading matter tell us about his educational program and its objectives?
2. What elements of Japan's Neo-Confucian program were aimed at preserving order and stability in society?
3. What elements potentially prepared Japan for playing, at a later date, a major role in world affairs?
4. How do Ieyasu's concerns parallel those of Machiavelli (source 111) ?

IEYASU'S RULE

Having lived from boyhood to manhood in military encampments, and having suffered hardship after hardship in countless battles, large and small, His Lordship [Ieyasu] had little time to read or study. Although he had conquered the country on horseback, being a man of innate intelligence and wisdom, he fully appreciated the impossibility of governing the country on horseback. According to his judgment there could be no other way to govern the country than by a constant and deep faith in the sages and the scholars, and as a human being interested in the welfare of his fellow human beings, he patronized scholarship from the very

beginning of his rule. Thus, he soon gained a reputation as a great devotee of letters and as one with a taste for elegant prose and poetry. On one occasion, Shimazu Yoshihisa, whose Buddhist name was Ryūhaku, took the trouble to arrange a poetry composition party in Ieyasu's honor, only to learn that His Lordship did not care at all for such a vain pastime. He listened again and again to discourses on the *Four Books,*[1] the *Records of the Historian* by Sima Qian,[2] the *History of the Former Han Dynasty,*[3] and the *Precepts and Policies of Tang Taizong*[4] as well as the *Six Tactics* and the *Three Strategies.*[5] Among Japanese works he gave special attention to the *Institutes of Engi,* the *Mirror of the East,* and the *Kemmu Regulations.*[6] . . .

---

[1]The Four Books of the Neo-Confucians were Confucius' *Analects,* the *Book of Mencius, The Great Learning,* and *The Doctrine of the Mean.* The last two books were short works dating from the age of China's Han Dynasty (202 B.C.–A.D. 220).

[2]Sima Qian is generally regarded as China's greatest historian (Chapter 4, source 27, and Chapter 5, sources 35 and 36).

[3]The work of Ban Gu (A.D. 32–92) and his sister Ban Zhao (A.D. 45–114?). As historians, they rank only slightly behind Sima Qian in influence and reputation. Ban Zhao was the preeminent female intellectual of the Han Period (Chapter 5, source 39).

[4]The Tang Dynasty's first great emperor (r. 626–649), who was noted for his military expansion of the empire, his capable administration, and his patronage of education. He was especially tolerant in religious and philosophical matters. Ieyasu admired Tang Taizong and claimed him as a model.

[5]Chinese works on the art of war.

[6]The *Institutes of Engi* was a tenth-century compilation of governmental regulations; the *Mirror of the East* chronicled the Kamakura Shogunate from 1180 to 1266; the *Kemmu Regulations* was a fourteenth-century compilation of governmental regulations.

Whatever the subject, he was interested, not in the turn of a phrase or in literary embellishments, but only in discovering the key to government — how to govern oneself, the people, and the country. Ieyasu declared, "If we cannot clarify the principles of human relations, society and government will of itself become unstable and disorders will never cease. Books are the only means whereby these principles can be set forth and understood. Thus, the printing of books and their transmission to the public is the first concern of a benevolent government." For this reason steps were taken for the printing of various books.

PREFACE TO THE COLLECTED COMMENTARIES ON ZHU XI'S REGULATIONS FOR THE WHITE DEER CAVE SCHOOL

The philosopher Zhu styled Huian,[7] was conspicuously endowed with intellectual leadership. Following in the line of (the Song philosophers) Zhou Dunyi and the Cheng brothers, he advanced the cause of Confucianism in both elementary education and higher education. For the guidance of his students he established these regulations, but they failed to gain wide acceptance in his own time because of opposition from vile quarters. . . .

It would seem to me that the aim of education, elementary and advanced, is to clarify human relationships. In the elementary program of education the various human relationships are made clear, the essence of this education in human relationships being devotion to (or respect for) persons. The "investigation of things" in advanced studies (as set forth in *The Great Learning*)[8] simply carries to its ultimate conclusion what has already been learned from elementary instruction. . . .

Zhu Xi's school regulations list the Five Human Relationships as the curriculum, following an order of presentation which complements the curriculum of advanced education (as found in *The Great Learning*). Studying, questioning, deliberating, and analyzing — these four correspond to the "investigation of things" and "extension of knowledge" in advanced education. The article dealing with conscientious action goes with the "cultivation of one's person." From the emperor to the common people, the cultivation of one's person is essential, including both "making the thoughts sincere" and "rectifying the mind." The "managing of affairs" and "social intercourse" (in Zhu's Regulations) refer to "regulating the family," "governing the state" and "establishing peace" (in *The Great Learning*). These Regulations thus contain everything, and they should be used for instruction together with the *Book of Elementary Instruction* and the *Book of Advanced Education* (Great Learning). But so far they have gone almost unnoticed among the items in Zhu's collected works, scarcely attracting any attention from scholars. I have taken the liberty, however, of bringing them out into the light of day by mounting and hanging them in my studio for constant reference and reflection. More recently I have found a detailed discussion of these regulations in *Some Reflections of Mine* by the Korean scholar Yi T'oege. It convinced me more than anything else that these Regulations are the true guide to education. . . .

(*Signed*) Yamazaki Ansai
Keian 3 (1650): Twelfth Month, 9th Day

Regulations for the School of the White Deer Cave
(*The Five Regulations*)

Between parent and child there is intimacy.

Between lord and minister there is duty.

Between husband and wife there is differentiation.

Between elder and junior there is precedence.

Between friend and friend there is fidelity.

---

[7]Zhu Xi.
[8]Note 1.

These five articles of teaching are what the sage-kings Yao and Shun[9] commanded Qi, the Minister of Education, solemnly to promulgate as the five subjects of teaching. All that the student should study is contained in these five regulations, but in studying them he should follow five steps, as given below:

Study wisely.

Question thoroughly.

Deliberate carefully.

Analyze clearly.

Act conscientiously. . . .

In speech be loyal and true; in action be conscientious and reverent. Subdue ire and stifle passion. Change yourself for the better; do not hesitate to correct your errors. These things are essential to personal culture.

Do not do to others what you do not care for yourself. When action fails to get results, seek the reason for failure in yourself. These are important in social intercourse.

The aim of teaching and guidance given by ancient sages and scholars, it seems to me, is nothing more than to set forth moral principles, in order, first, to cultivate them in one's own person, and then to extend them to others. Simply to accumulate knowledge and learn to write well in order to gain fame and a well-paid position is far from being the true function of education. Nevertheless that is what most men pursue learning for today.

A Critique of Neo-Confucianism
▼▼▼

118 ▼ Gu Yanwu,
A LETTER TO A FRIEND DISCUSSING THE PURSUIT OF LEARNING

Although Neo-Confucianism dominated Chinese intellectual life in the sixteenth and seventeenth centuries, it did not lack critics, especially those who sought to strip away the philosophical overlays of Song- and Ming-era interpreters of the Confucian classics, whose work they perceived as obscurantist and "unclassical." The most damning charge brought against the Neo-Confucians was that, by expending so much energy in discussing abstract philosophical principles, they had neglected practical ethical issues relating to effective government. The result of this divergence from traditional Confucian concerns was poor government, internal weakness, and eventual conquest by foreign "barbarians." Song China eventually succumbed to the Mongols in the thirteenth century, and the Ming Dynasty gave way to the Qing Dynasty (1644–1912) of the Manchus, a Mongoloid people from Manchuria.

---

[9]Two of China's five mythical predynastic "Sage Emperors," who were believed to have collectively laid down the basis of Chinese civilization.

The most important early critic of Neo-Confucian thought was Gu Yanwu (1613–1682), who had served as a minor official during the late Ming years but refused to serve the new Qing Dynasty, holding himself aloof as a patriot who would not collaborate with foreign conquerors. The story is told that his refusal to serve was at least partly motivated by a promise to his dying mother, who had starved herself to death rather than live under Manchu domination. After her death, Gu Yanwu wandered about northern China, observing conditions and writing on such diverse topics as politics, literature, philology, and historical geography.

His extensive writings established Gu Yanwu as a founder of the School of Han Learning, a movement that sought to rediscover the pure teachings of the early masters of Confucian thought, before it had been tainted by the abstract metaphysics of Buddhism. Seeking to free Confucian philosophy from such "foreign" influences, the advocates of this school looked to the Han era (202 B.C.– A.D. 220) as the golden age of Confucian learning. Thanks to their patient scholarship, a number of ancient Confucian texts that had been forgotten or severely reworked or cut were republished and rescued from oblivion. In the following letter, written toward the end of his life, Gu Yanwu expresses his thoughts on the defects of Confucian scholarship in his own day.

QUESTIONS FOR ANALYSIS

1. How "traditional" does Gu Yanwu perceive contemporary Confucian philosophy to be?
2. What specific flaws does he see in the concerns, ideas, and methods of contemporary Confucian intellectuals?
3. With what kind of matters should intellectuals be concerned?
4. Reread Confucius's *Analects* (Chapter 4, source 25). Does Gu Yanwu's vision of the thrust of Confucius's philosophy seem valid? Why or why not?
5. How would you characterize Gu Yanwu's critique of contemporary philosophy? Was he a radical revolutionary or a conservative? What are the wider implications of your answer?
6. Compare Gu Yanwu's program of Confucian reform with such European movements as the Reformation (source 112) and the revolt of the Old Believers in Russia (source 114). Do you perceive any meaningful parallels? What do you conclude from your answer?

It is a matter of great regret to me that for the past hundred odd years, scholars have devoted so much discussion to the mind and human nature, all of it vague and quite incomprehensible. We know from the *Analects*[1] that "fate and humanity were things which Confucius seldom

---

[1]Chapter 4, source 25.

spoke of" and that Zigong[2] "had never heard him speak on man's nature and the way of Heaven." Though he[3] mentioned the principle of human nature and fate in the appendices to the *Book of Changes,*[4] he never discussed them with others. When asked about the qualities of a gentleman, Confucius said: "In his conduct he must have a sense of shame," while with regard to learning he spoke of a "love of antiquity" and "diligent seeking," discussing and praising Yao and Shun[5] and transmitting their tales to his disciples. But he never said so much as a word about the so-called theory of "the precariousness and the subtlety and of the refined and undivided,"[6] but only said "sincerely hold fast to the Mean — if within the four seas[7] there be distress and poverty, your Heaven-conferred revenues will come to a perpetual end." Ah, this is the reason for the learning of the sage. How simple, how easy to follow! . . . But gentlemen of today are not like this. They gather a hundred or so followers and disciples about them in their studies, and though as individuals they may be as different as grass and trees, they discourse with all of them on mind and nature. They set aside broad knowledge and concentrate upon the search for a single, all-inclusive method; they say not a word about the distress and poverty of the world within the four seas, but spend all their days lecturing on theories of "the weak and subtle," "the refined and the undivided.". . .

What then do I consider to be the way of the sage? I would say "extensively studying all learning" and "in your conduct having a sense of shame." Everything from your own body up to the whole nation should be a matter of study. In everything from your personal position as a son, a subject, a brother, and a friend to all your comings and goings, your giving and taking, you should have things of which you would be ashamed. This sense of shame before others is a vital matter. It does not mean being ashamed of your clothing or the food you eat, but ashamed that there should be a single humble man or woman who does not enjoy the blessings that are his due. This is why Mencius[8] said that "all things are complete in me" if I "examine myself and find sincerity." Alas, if a scholar does not first define this sense of shame, he will have no basis as a person, and if he does not love antiquity and acquire broad knowledge, his learning will be in vain and hollow. These baseless men with their hollow learning day after day pursue the affairs of the sage, and yet I perceive that with each day they only depart further from them.

---

[2]An early disciple of Confucius who contributed to *The Analects.*

[3]Confucius, who was incorrectly believed to be the compiler of the five core Confucian classics (Chapter 1, sources 6 and 7).

[4]The *Yi Jing* (*I Ching*), one of the core Confucian classics. It was a book of divination, with an appendix that included some philosophical speculation.

[5]Two of the five mythical Sage Emperors of China's predynastic past, they were models of enlightened rule.

[6]Four qualities of the mind frequently discussed by Ming Neo-Confucians.

[7]"Within the four seas" means "throughout the world." To the Chinese, the world was essentially China.

[8]The Latinized form of *Mengzi* (371–289 B.C.). His book *Mengzi* (*The Book of Mencius*) was accorded the status of a Confucian classic in the eleventh century and became one of the foundation blocks of Confucian orthodoxy.

Sources

Prologue

Christopher Columbus: R. H. Major, trans., *Select Letters of Christopher Columbus* (London, 1847), pp. 1–17, passim.

Part I   The Ancient World

Chapter 1

Source 1: Nancy K. Sandars, trans., *The Epic of Gilgamesh* (Penguin Classics, 1960, 2nd rev. ed., 1972), copyright © N. K. Sandars, 1960, 1964, 1972, pp. 91–93, 102, 106–114, 117–119. Reproduced by permission of Penguin Books Ltd.; **source 2:** Chilperic Edwards, *The Hammurabi Code* (1904), pp. 23–80, passim. Reprinted without copyright by Kennikut Press, 1971; **source 3:** E. A. Wallis Budge, trans., *The Chapters of Coming Forth by Day* (London: Kegan, Paul, 1898), pp. 190–192; **source 4:** James B. Pritchard, ed., *Ancient Near East in Pictures Relating to the Old Testament,* 2nd ed., with supplement, p. 365. Copyright © 1954, renewed 1969 by Princeton University Press. Reprinted by permission of Princeton University Press; **source 5:** James B. Pritchard, ed., *Ancient Near East in Pictures Relating to the Old Testament,* 2nd ed., with supplement, pp. 432–434. Copyright © 1954, renewed 1969 by Princeton University Press. Reprinted by permission of Princeton University Press; **source 6:** James Legge, trans., *The Sacred Books of China: The Texts of Confucianism,* in F. Max Mueller, ed., *The Sacred Books of the East,* 50 vols. (Oxford: Clarendon Press, 1879–1910, vol. 3, pp. 92–95; **source 7:** James Legge, trans., *The Book of Poetry* (New York: Paragon Book Reprint, 1967), pp. 16, 48, 99, 101–102, 300–301; **source 8:** Musée de l'Homme, Paris. Photo copyright © 1966 Eric Lessing, Art Resource, New York; **source 9:** *Seals 1–6:* Walter A. Fairservis, Jr., *The Roots of Ancient India: The Archaeology of Early Indian Civilization,* illustrated with drawings by Jan Fairservis (New York: Macmillan, 1971), pp. 276, 276, 279, 278, 274, 276. Copyright © 1971 by Walter A. Fairservis. Reprinted with the permission of Macmillan Publishing Company. *seal 7:* Musée du Louvre, Paris; *seals 8–9:* Copyright British Museum; *seal 10:* Ashmolean Museum, Oxford University; **source 10:** Courtesy, Hamlyn Publishing, London; Werner Forman Archive; **source 11:** Metropolitan Museum of Art, New York. Gift of Nathan Cummings, 1964 (64.228.63).

Chapter 2

Source 12: Ralph T. H. Griffith, trans., *The Hymns of the Rig Veda,* 4 vols. (Benares: E. J. Lazarus, 1889–1892), vol. 1, pp. 56–59; vol. 4, pp. 289–293; **source 13:** A. J. Andrea, trans., *The Odyssey of Homer;* **sources 14, 15, and 16:** *Revised Standard Version of the Bible.* Copyright © 1946, 1952, 1971 by the Division of Christian Education of the National Council of Churches of Christ in the USA. Used by permission. All rights reserved.

Chapter 3

Source 17: F. Max Mueller, trans., *The Upanishads,* in Mueller, *The Sacred Books of the East,* vol. 1, pp. 92, 104–105; vol. 15, pp. 173, 175–177, 168–169, passim; **source 18:** Tashinath Trmibak Telang, trans., *The Bhagavad Gita,* in Mueller, *The Sacred Books of the East,* vol. 8, pp. 43–46, 48–49, 51–52, 126–128, passim; **source 19:** Hermann Jacobi, trans., *Gaina Sutras,* in Mueller, *The Sacred Books of the East,* vol. 22, pp. 36, 81–87, 202–208, passim; **source 20:** T. W. Rhys Davids and Hermann Oldenberg, trans., *Vinaya Texts,* in Mueller, *The Sacred Books of the East,* vol. 13, pp. 94–97, 100–102, passim; **source 21:** Mueller, *The Sacred Books of the East,* vol. 20, pp. 320–326; **source 22:** James Hope Moulton, Yasnas 43, 44, 45, in *Early Zoroastrianism* (London: Williams and Norgate, 1913), pp. 364–370, passim; **source 23:** *Revised Standard Version of the Bible.* Copyright © 1946, 1952, 1971 by the Division of Christian Education of the National Council of Churches of Christ in the USA. Used by permission. All rights reserved.

Chapter 4

Source 24: Mueller, *The Sacred Books of the East,* vol. 39, passim; **source 25:** James Legge, trans., *Confucian Analects, the Great Learning, and the Doctrine of the Mean,* in *Chinese Classics Series of the Clarendon Press,* vol. 1 (Oxford: Clarendon Press, 1893). Reprinted without copyright by Dover in 1971; **source 26:** W. L. Liano, trans., *The Complete Works of Han Fei Tzu*

(London: Arthur Probsthain, 1939), vol. 1, pp. 40, 45–47. Copyright © 1939. Used by permission of Arthur Probstain; **source 27:** Yang Hsien-yi and Gladys Yang, *Records of the Historian* (Hong Kong: Commercial Press, 1974), pp. 170–172, 177–178. Copyright © 1974. Used by permission of Commercial Press (Hong Kong) Ltd.; **source 28:** A. J. Andrea, trans.; **source 29:** B. Jowett, trans., *Thucydides Translated into English* (Oxford: Clarendon Pres, 1881), vol. 1, pp. 115–129; **source 30:** Euripides, *Medea,* ed. by Paul MacKendrick and Herbert M. Howe (Madison: University of Wisconsin Press, 1952). Copyright 1952, Used by permission of the publisher; **source 31:** F. J. Church, trans., *The Trial and Death of Socrates* (London: MacMillan, 1880).

Chapter 5

Source 32: Horace L. Jones, trans., *The Geography of Strabo,* 8 vols. (New York: G. P. Putnam's Sons, 1917), vol. 1, pp. 451–455, 501–503, 277–385, passim; **source 33:** A. J. Andrea, trans., from Hans Volkmann, ed., *Res Gestae Divi Augusti* (Berlin, 1964); **source 34:** A. J. Andrea, trans., from M. Winterbottom and R. M. Ogilvie, eds., *Cornelii Taciti Opera Minora* (Oxford: Oxford University Press, 1975), pp. 21–23; **source 35:** Burton Watson, trans., *Records of the Grand Historian of China,* 2 vols. (New York: Columbia University Press, 1961), vol. 2, pp. 264–270, passim. Copyright © 1961 Columbia University Press. Reprinted with permission of the publisher (Wade-Giles transliterations changed to pinyin); **source 36:** Burton Watson, trans., *Records of the Grand Historian of China,* 2 vols. (New York: Columbia University Press, 1961), vol. 2, pp. 395–401, passim. Copyright © 1961 Columbia University Press. Reprinted with permission of the publisher (Wade-Giles transliterations changed to pinyin); **source 37:** N. A. Nikam and Richard McKeon, trans. and ed., *The Edicts of Asoka* (Chicago: University of Chicago Press, 1958), pp. 27–30, 33–36, 40–41, 46–47, 51, 60–61, passim; **source 38:** James Legge, trans., *A Record of Buddhistic Kingdoms* (Oxford: Clarendon Press, 1886), pp. 42–45, 77–79; **source 39:** Nancy Lee Swann, trans., *Pan Chao: Foremost Woman Scholar of China* (New York: Century Co., 1932), pp. 82–90; **source 40:** G. Buehler, trans., *The Laws of Manu,* in Mueller, *Sacred Books of the East,* vol. 25, pp. 24, 69, 84–85, 195–197, 260–326, 329–330, 343–344, 370–371, 402–404, 413–416, 420, 423, passim; **source 41:** A. J. Andrea, trans., from Lucius Apuleius, *Metamorphoses,* Book 11; **source 42:** Museo delle terme, Rome. Alinari/Art Resource, New York; **source 43:** Courtesy, Iraq Museum, Baghdad; **sources 44 and 45:** The University Museum, University of Pennsylvania (negs. S4.138081, S8.1267).

Part II Faith, Devotion, and Salvation: Great World Religions to A.D. 1500

Chapter 6

Source 46: H. H. Wilson, trans., *The Vishnu Purana,* 3rd ed. (Calcutta: Punthi Pustak, 1961), pp. 516–520, passim. Copyright © 1961. Used by permission of the publisher; **source 47:** National Museum, Madras. Lauros-Giraudon/Art Resource, New York; **source 48:** Benjamin Ben Jonah, *The Itinerary of Benjamin of Tudela,* Marcus N. Adler, trans. (London: H. Frowde, 1907), pp. 35–42, passim; **source 49:** Jacob S. Minkin, *The World of Moses Maimonides with Selections from His Writings* (New York: Thomas Yoseloff, 1957), pp. 371–373, 375–380, 398–399, 401. Copyright © 1957. Used by permission of Associated University Presses; **source 50:** William Theodore de Bary et al., eds. and trans., *Sources of Indian Tradition* (New York: Columbia University Press, 1958), pp. 163–165. Copyright © 1958 Columbia University Press. Reprinted with permission of the publisher; **source 51:** Edwin O. Reischauer, *Ennin's Travels in T'ang China* (New York: Ronald Press, 1955), pp. 221–224. Copyright © 1955 by the Ronald Press Company. Reprinted by permission of John Wiley & Sons; **source 52:** Lucian Stryk, *World of the Buddha: A Reader* (Garden City, N.Y.: Doubleday, 1968), pp. 364–365. Copyright © 1968 by Lucian Stryk. Used by permission of Grove Press, a division of Wheatland Corporation.

Chapter 7

Sources 53 and 54: *Revised Standard Version of the Bible.* Copyright © 1946, 1952, 1971 by the Division of Christian Education of the National Council of Churches of Christ in the USA. Used by permission. All rights reserved. **source 55:** P. R. Coleman-Norton, ed. and trans., *Roman State and Christian Church* (Reading, Eng.: S.P.C.K., 1966), vol. 1, pp. 74, 76, 219, 254, 342, 354; vol. 2, pp. 387–388, 392–393, 436–437, 438, 452, 459, 510, 559–560. Copyright © 1966. Used by permission of the Society for Promoting Christian Knowledge; **source 56:** A. J. Andrea, trans., from *Vitae Patrum;* **source 57:** Samuel Hazard Cross and Olgerd P. Sherbowitz-Wetzor, trans., *The Russian Primary Chronicle* (Cambridge, Mass.: Mediaeval Academy of America), pp. 110–113. Reprinted by permission; **source 58:** Elizabeth A. S. Dawes, trans., *The Alexiad of the Princess Anna Comnena* (New York: Barnes & Noble, 1967), pp. 33–34, 248–250, passim. Used by permission of Routledge and Kegan Paul; **source 59:** From *Unam Sanctam,* A. J. Andrea, trans.; **source 60:** "Death of the Virgin," Strasbourg Cathedral, France; Marburg/Art Resource, New York; "Dormition of the Virgin," wall painting, church of St. Clement (formerly St. Mary

Peribleptos), Ohrid, Yugoslavia, in Christa Schug-Wille, *Art of the Byzantine World* (New York: Harry N. Abrams, 1975), p. 217. Reproduced with permission.

Chapter 8

Source 61: Arthur J. Arberry, trans., *The Koran Interpreted* (George Allen and Unwin, 1955), pp. 41–46, 50–55, 65, 69, 71–72, passim. Copyright © 1955 by George Allen and Unwin. Used by permission of HarperCollins Publishers; **source 62:** Imam Nawawi, *Gardens of the Righteous,* trans. by Muhammad Zafrulla Khan (London: Curzon Press, 1975), pp. 60–63, 65–66, 68–69, 220–224, 226–228, passim. Copyright © 1975. Reprinted July 1989. Used by permission of the publisher; **source 63:** Hasan ibn Yusuf, "Creed Concerning the Imams," in A. A. A. Fyzec, ed. and rans., *A Shi'ite Creed* (New Delhi: Oxford, 1942). Copyright © 1942. Used by permission of Oxford University Press, New Delhi; **source 64:** Bernard Lewis, ed. and trans., *Islam from the Prophet Muhammad to the Capture of Constantinople,* 2 vols. (New York: Harper & Row, 1974), vol. 1, pp. 171–179, passim. Copyright © 1974 by Bernard Lewis. Reprinted by permission of Oxford University; **source 65:** Abu Hamid Muhammad al-Ghazali, *The Alchemy of Happiness,* trans. by Henry A. Homes (Albany, N.Y.: J. Munsell, 1873), pp. 104–105, 113; **source 66:** Bernard Lewis, ed., *Islam from the Prophet Mohammed to the Capture of Constantinople,* vol. 2. Copyright © 1974 by Bernard Lewis. Reprinted by permission of Oxford University Press.

Part III   Continuity, Change, and Interchange, 500–1500

Chapter 9

Source 67: W. G. Aston, trans., *Nihongi: Chronicles of Japan from the Earliest Times to A.D. 697,* 2 vols. in 1 (London: Kegan, Paul, Trench, Truebner and Co., 1896), vol. 2, pp. 128–133; **source 68:** Annie Shepley Omori and Kochi Doi, trans., *Diaries of Court Ladies of Old Japan* (Boston: Houghton Mifflin, 1920), pp. 71–73, 86–87, 89–90, 130–134; **source 69:** Helen Craig McCullough, trans., *The Taiheiki: A Chronicle of Medieval Japan* (New York: Columbia University Press, 1959), pp. 85–91. Copyright © 1959 by Columbia University Press. Reprinted with the permission of the publisher; **source 70:** Tu Fu, *Selected Poems,* trans. by Rewi Alley (Beijing: Foreign Languages Press, 1964), pp. 12–13, 131–132, 163; **source 71:** Chen Pu, "On Farming," trans. by Clara Yu, in Patricia Buckley Ebrey, ed., *Chinese Civilization and Society: A Sourcebook* (New York: Macmillan, 1981), pp. 109–112. Copyright © 1981 by The Free Press. Reprinted with permission of The Free Press, a divi-

sion of Macmillan, Inc.; **source 72:** "The Attractions of the Capital," trans. by Clara Yu, in Buckley, *Chinese Civilization and Society: A Sourcebook,* pp. 100–102, 104–105, passim; **source 73:** Arthur L. Basham, *The Wonder That Was India* (New York: Grove Press, 1954), pp. 444–446. Reprinted by permission of Sidgwick & Jackson, a division of Pan Macmillan Ltd.; **source 74:** Franklin Edgerton, ed. and trans., *Vikrama's Adventures,* 2 vols. (Cambridge, Mass.: Harvard University Press, 1926), vol. 1, pp. 228–230. Copyright © 1926 by Harvard University Press. Reprinted by permission; **source 75:** H. M. Elliot and John Dowson, eds. and trans., *The History of India as Told by Its Own Historians,* 8 vols. (London: Truebner, 1867–1877), vol. 3, pp. 374–388, passim; **source 76:** *The Arabian Nights' Entertainments* (London: George Routledge, 1890), pp. 113–116; **source 77:** Philip K. Hitti, trans., *Memoirs of an Arab-Syrian Gentleman* (Beirut: Khayats, 1964), pp. 161, 163–164, 167–170. Copyright © 1929 by Philip K. Hitti.

Chapter 10

Source 78: A. J. Andrea, trans., *The Song of Roland;* **source 79:** E. P. Cheyney, trans. "Magna Carta," in *University of Pennsylvania Translations and Reprints* (Philadelphia: University of Pennsylvania, 1897), vol. 1, no. 6, pp. 6–15, passim; **source 80:** John of Viterbo, *Book on the Government of Cities,* trans. by A. J. Andrea, in A. Gandenzi, ed., *Bibliotheca Juridica Medii Aevi,* 3 vols. (Bologna, 1888–1901), vol. 3, pp. 218–219, 228–229, 260; **source 81:** From John of Paris, "Tractatus de Potestate Regie et Papali," in Brian Tierney, *The Crisis of Church and State, 1050–1300,* with selected documents, copyright © 1964 (Englewood Cliffs, N.J.: Prentice-Hall, Inc., Englewood Cliffs, New Jersey. **source 82:** Daniel D. McGarry, trans., *The Metalogicon of John of Salisbury* (Berkeley: University of California Press, 1955), pp. 32–33, 36–37, 74–75, 266–268, 272–273, passim. Reprinted by permission of the author; **source 83:** Jean Birdsall, trans., and Richard A. Newhall, ed., *The Chronicle of Jean de Venette* (New York: Columbia University Press, 1953), pp. 31–32, 48–52, passim. Copyright © 1953. Used by permission of Jane Lyons; **source 84:** Johann Nider, *Formicarius* (Douaii, 1602), p. 385, trans. by A. J. Andrea.

Chapter 11

Source 85: J. F. P. Hopkins, trans., and N. Levtzion and J. F. P. Hopkins, eds., *Corpus of Early Arabic Sources for West African History* (Cambridge: Cambridge University Press, 1981), pp. 79–83, passim. Copyright © University of Ghana, International Academic Union, Cambridge University Press, 1981. Reprinted with permission of Cambridge University Press; **source 86:** G. W. B. Huntingford, *The Glorious Victories of 'Amda*

Seyon, King of Ethiopia (Oxford: Oxford University Press, 1965), pp. 53–65, passim. Copyright © 1965 Oxford University Press. Reprinted by permission of Oxford University Press; **source 87:** Phillips Stevens, *The Stone Images of Esie, Nigeria* (New York: Africana Publishing Co., a division of Holmes and Meier, 1978), p. 205, photo 383. Copyright © 1978 Ibadan University Press and the Nigerian Federal Department of Antiquities; **source 88:** Adrian Recinos, trans., *Popol Vuh: The Sacred Book of the Ancient Quiché Maya* (Norman, Okla.: University of Oklahoma Press, 1950; **source 89:** J. Bayard Morris, trans., *Five Letters of Hernando Cortes, 1519–1526* (New York: W. W. Norton Co., [n.d.]), pp. 86–90, 92–93. Reprinted by permission of W. W. Norton & Co., Inc. all rights reserved. Norton Paperback Edition published 1969, reissued 1991; **source 90:** Harriet de Onis, trans., and Victor W. Von Hagen, ed., *The Incas of Pedro de Cieza de Leon* (Norman, Okla.: University of Oklahoma Press, 1959), pp. 165–167, 169–174, 177–178, passim. Copyright © 1959 by the University of Oklahoma Press.

Chapter 12

Source 91: Adapted by A. J. Andrea, from E. Bretschneider, *Mediaeval Researches from Eastern Asiatic Sources* (London, 1875), vol. 1, pp. 37–39; **source 92:** Christopher Dawson, ed., *The Mongol Mission* (New York: Sheed and Ward, 1955), pp. 93–98, 103–104, passim; **source 93:** W. Marsden, trans., *The Travels of Marco Polo* (1818); rendered into modern English by A. J. Andrea; **source 94:** Jeannette Mirsky, ed., *The Great Chinese Travelers* (New York: Pantheon Books, 1964), pp. 214–216, 222–224, 231–233, passim; **source 95:** Henry Yule, ed. and trans., *Cathay and the Way Thither,* 4 vols. (2nd ed. rev. by H. Cordier) (London: Hakluyt Society, 1913–1916), vol. 3, pp. 151–155. Copyright © 1913–1916. Used by permission of the publisher; **source 96:** J. F. P. Hopkins and N. Levtzion, eds. and trans., *Corpus of Early Arabic Sources for West African History* (Cambridge: Cambridge University Press, 1981), pp. 284–286, 288–291, 296–297, passim. Copyright © University of Ghana, International Academic Union, Cambridge University Press, 1981. Reprinted with the permission of Cambridge University Press; **source 97:** Adapted into Modern English by A. J. Andrea, from the Cotton Manuscript of the British Museum, printed 1725, chs. 20, 30; **source 98:** Ma Huan, *The Overall Survey of the Ocean's Shores* (London: Hakluyt, 1970), pp. 108–109, 113–117, 120, 137–140, 165, 172. Copyright © 1970. Used by permission of the publisher; **source 99:** owned by Ryukoku University, Kyoto, Japan; **source 100:** Gomes Eannes de Azurara, *The Chronicle of the Discovery and Conquest of Guinea,* trans. by Charles Raymond Beazely and Edgar Prestage, 2 vols. (London: Hakluyt Society, 1896), vol. 1, pp. 27–29, 83–85.

Part IV   A World of Change, 1500–1700

Chapter 13

Source 101: Bernardino de Sahagun, *The War of Conquest: How It Was Waged Here in Mexico,* trans. by Arthur O. Anderson and Charles E. Dibble (Salt Lake City: Utah, 1978), pp. 16–17. 19–23. Copyright © 1976. Used by permission of the publisher; **source 102:** Antonio Vazquez de Espinosa, *Compendium and Description of the West Indies* (Washington, D.C.: Smithsonian Institution, 1942), pp. 621–625, 629, 631–634; **source 103:** Charles Gobson, ed., *The Spanish Tradition in America* (New York: Harper & Row, 1968), pp. 113–120. Copyright © 1968 by Charles Gibson. Reprinted by permission of HarperCollins Publishers. **source 104:** Bartolome de las Casas, *In Defense of the Indians,* ed. and trans. by Stafford Poole (DeKalb, Ill.: Northern Illinois Press, 1992). Copyright © 1974 by Northern Illinois University Press. Used with permission of the publisher. **source 105:** Basil Davidson, trans., *The African Past* (London: Curtis Brown Ltd.), pp. 191–194. Copyright © Basil Davidson, 1964. Reproduced by permission of Curtis Brown Ltd.; **source 106:** Awnsham Churchill and John Churchill, eds., *Collections of Voyages and Travels,* 3rd ed., 8 vols. (London: H. Lintot, 1744–1747) vol. 5, p. 459. Modernized by A. J. Andrea; **source 107:** Louis J. Gallagher, S.J., trans., *China in the Sixteenth Century: The Journals of Matthew Ricci: 1583–1610.* Copyright © 1953 by Louis J. Gallagher, S.J. Reprinted by permission of Random House, Inc.; **source 108:** David John Lu, ed. and trans., *Sources of Japanese History* (New York: McGraw-Hill, 1974), vol. 1, pp. 207–209. Copyright © 1974. Used by permission of McGraw-Hill Publishing Co.; **source 109:** Henry Beveridge, trans., *The Akbar Nama of Abu-l-Fazl,* 3 vols. (New Delhi: Ess Ess Publications, 1902–1939), vol. 1, pp. 37, 207, 322–323, 368–370, 410–411; **source 110:** Jean-Baptiste Tavernier, *Travels in India,* 2nd ed., ed. by William Ball, trans. by V. Ball (Oxford: Oxford University Press, 1925), pp. 7–11. Used by permission of the publisher.

Chapter 14

Source 111: Niccolo Machiavelli, *The Prince,* trans. by George Bull (London: Penguin Classics, 1961), pp. 61–66, 90–102. Copyright © George Bull, 1961, 1975, 1981 (rev. ed.). Reproduced by permission of Penguin Books Ltd.; **source 112:** Staatliche Museen zu Berlin, Preu-Bischer Kulturbesitz-Kupferstichkabinett-Sammlung der Zeichnungen Druckgraphik; **source 113:** Galileo Galilei, *Discoveries and Opinions of*

Galileo, ed. and trans. by Stillman Drake (New York: Doubleday, 1957), pp. 172–175. Copyright © 1957 by Stillman Drake. Used by permission of Doubleday, a division of Bantam Doubleday Dell Publishing Group, Inc.; **source 114:** George Verdansky, *A Source Book for Russian History from Early Times to 1917* (New Haven: Yale University Press, 1972), vol. 1, pp. 260–261. Copyright © 1961. Used by permission of the publisher; **source 115:** Christoval de Molina, "The Fables and Rites of the Yncas," in Clements R. Markham, ed. and trans., *Narratives of the Rites and Laws of the Yncas* (London: Hakluyt, 1873), pp. 59–64. Used by permission of the publisher; **source 116:** Ernest Trump, trans., *The Adi Granth, or the Holy Scriptures of the Sikhs* (1877), pp. 2–3, 7, 16, 17, 40–41, 194–195, passim; **source 117:** Ryusaku Tsunoda, William Theodore de Bary, and Donald Keene, eds., *Sources of the Japanese Tradition,* pp. 340–342, 364–366. Copyright © 1927 and 1958, Columbia University Press. Used by permission. **source 118:** William Theodore de Bary, *Sources of Chinese Tradition,* p. 608. Copyright © Columbia University Press, 1966. Used by permission.